Communications in Computer and Information Science   1759

More information about this series at https://link.springer.com/bookseries/7899

Sridaran Rajagopal · Parvez Faruki ·
Kalpesh Popat (Eds.)

Advancements in Smart Computing and Information Security

First International Conference, ASCIS 2022
Rajkot, India, November 24–26, 2022
Revised Selected Papers, Part I

 Springer

Editors
Sridaran Rajagopal 🆔
Marwadi University
Rajkot, India

Parvez Faruki 🆔
AVPTI
Rajkot, India

Kalpesh Popat 🆔
Marwadi University
Rajkot, India

ISSN 1865-0929   ISSN 1865-0937 (electronic)
Communications in Computer and Information Science
ISBN 978-3-031-23091-2   ISBN 978-3-031-23092-9 (eBook)
https://doi.org/10.1007/978-3-031-23092-9

This Springer imprint is published by the registered company Springer Nature Switzerland AG
The registered company address is: Gewerbestrasse 11, 6330 Cham, Switzerland

Preface

"The number one benefit of Information Technology is that it empowers people to do what they want to do…" - Steve Balmer.

Considering the immense potential of Information Technology (IT) in developing pragmatic solutions to every other field, our initiative with respect to the 1st International Conference on Advancements in Smart Computing and Information Security (ASCIS 2022) started approximately a year ago. Based on the various survey results, the steering committee decided to focus on the following four tracks: Artificial Intelligence, Smart Computing, Information Security, and Industry 4.0 (aka Industry).

In a futuristic list of 10 applications, it is very much evident that the technologies listed above have a major role. Based on this fact, a call for papers was floated to attract original, unpublished papers highlighting some of the innovative research areas in each of the four tracks. We are very much thankful to the editorial board of Springer CCIS who came forward to support us with the proceedings, even though it was our maiden conference.

All of the 200+ papers received were included in the Open Peer Review process and, in the end, 55 papers were shortlisted for the Springer CCIS proceedings (an acceptance rate of approximately 27%). Each submission was reviewed by at least 3 members of the Program Committee. The selected papers either made a contribution in terms of complete and classified surveys or solutions in the form of implemented models or algorithms. The papers belonging to this volume have considered AI and its allied fields and smart computing as the base technologies to govern the solutions of other fields. Research problems in the fields of healthcare, engineering, astronomy, sociology, agriculture, and education were explored and novel solutions were presented by the authors.

The conference, which was held during November 24–26, 2022, started off with a pre-conference workshop on the first day wherein eminent academicians and industry experts were invited to share the future research scope in their respective fields of specialization. On the second day after the inaugural ceremony, papers were presented by the authors under the four parallel tracks in the presence of committee members, research students, and other participants.

This two-volume set titled "Artificial Intelligence-based Smart and Secured Applications" consolidates the papers presented at ASCIS 2022, which describe solutions employing AI and smart computing in different fields and seek to address both theoretical and real-world research problems, including those which demand security solutions.

We believe that this collection will be highly useful for researchers and practitioners of AI and machine learning as well as smart computing.

November 2022

Sridaran Rajagopal
Parvez Faruki
Kalpesh Popat

Organization

Steering Committee

Manoj Singh Gaur	Indian Institute of Technology, Jammu, India
Lalit Kumar Awasthi (Director)	Computer Science & Engineering, NIT Hamirpur, India
Sudeep Tanwar	Computer Science and Engineering Department, Nirma University, India
Parvez Faruki (Head of Department)	A.V. Parekh Technical Institute, India
Sachin Shetty (Executive Director)	Old Dominion University, USA
Mohamed Mosbah (Director)	University of Bordeaux, France
Vijay Laxmi	Malaviya National Institute of Technology, India
Akka Zemmari	University of Bordeaux, France
Vincenzo Piuri	University of Milan, Italy
Ankur Dumka	Women Institute of Technology, Dehradun, India
Sandeep Sancheti (Provost, Vice Chancellor)	Marwadi University, India
Sridaran Rajagopal (Principal Investigator and Dean)	Faculty of Computer Applications, Marwadi University, India
R. B. Jadeja (Dean-Research)	Faculty of Engineering, Marwadi University, India
Shree Naresh Jadeja (Registrar)	Marwadi University, India
Divyakant Meva (Head)	Marwadi University, India

Program Chairs

Sridaran Rajagopal	Marwadi University, India
Parvez Faruki (Head of Department)	A.V. Parekh Technical Institute, India
Kalpesh Popat	Marwadi University, India

Program Committee

A. P. Nirmala	New Horizon College of Engineering, India
Ajay Parikh	Gujarat Vidhyapith, India
Ajay Patel	Ganpat University, India
Ajmery Sultana	Algoma University, Canada
Akka Zemmari	University of Bordeaux, France
Akash Dutt Dubey	Jaipuria Institute of Management, India

Akshara Dave	Indus University, India
Amit Ganatra	CHARUSAT, India
Amit Lathigara	RK University, India
Amit Vadera	Sunshine College, India
Anjali Jivani	MS University, India
Ankit Bhavsar	GLS University, India
Ankit Faldu	CHARUSAT, India
Ankit Subhash Didwania	Gujarat Technological University, India
Anand Sharma	Mody University of Science and Technology, India
Anwar Basha H.	Reva University, India
Apurva Shah	MS University, India
Ashish Rastogi	Indian Institute of Technology, Delhi, India
Ashwin Dobariya	Marwadi University, India
Ashwin Makwana	CHARUSAT, India
Ashwin Raiyani	Nirma University, India
Atul Gonsai	Saurashtra University, India
Balasubramanian Raman	IIT, Roorkee, India
B. Lakhsma Reddy	SJES College of Management Studies, India
B. Muruganantham	SRMIST, India
C. K. Kumbharana	Saurashtra University, India
C. Mahesh	Vel Tech Rangarajan Dr. Sagunthala R&D Institute of Science and Technology, India
C. P. Chandran	Ayya Nadar Janaki Ammal College, India
Chhagan Lal	TU Delft, Netherlands
Chintan M. Bhatt	Pandit Deendayal Energy University, India
Chintan Patel	University of Sheffield, UK
Chintan Thacker	Parul University, India
Chirag Thakar	LD College of Engineering, India
D. Swamydoss	Adhiyamaan College of Engineering, India
Darshita Pathak	A. V. Parekh Technical Institute, India
Daxa Vekariya	Parul University, India
Debabrata Swain	Pandit Deendayal Energy University, India
Deepak Verma	Dr. Rammanohar Lohia Avadh University, India
Dhiren Patel	Gujarat Vidyapith, India
Digvijaysinh Rathod	National Forensics Science University, India
Dimple Thakar	Marwadi University, India
Dinesh Kumar	Marwadi University, India
Dineshkumar Vaghela	Shantilal Shah Engineering College, India
Dipak Ramoliya	CHARUSAT, India
Dippal Prabhudas Israni	R. C. Technical Institute, India
Disha Jigar Shah	GLS University, India

Durgesh Mishra	Sri Aurobindo Institute of Technology, India
Durgesh Srivastava	Chitkara University, India
Dushyantsinh Rathod	Gujarat Technological University, India
Gaurav Singal	Netaji Subhash University, India
Galiveeti Poornima	Presidency University, India
Hardik Joshi	Gujarat University, India
Hardik Molia	GEC, Rajkot, India
Hardik M. Patel	Kadi Sarva Vishwavidyalaya, India
Hetal Thaker	GLS University, India
Himali Ruparelia	Gujarat Technological University, India
Irfan Ahmead	Thassim Beevi Abdul Kader College for Women, India
Ipseeta Nanda	Gopal Narayan Singh University, India
Iyyappan. M.	Adani University, India
J. Lenin	University of Technology and Applied Sciences, India
Jagruti	PM Patel College, India
Jaimin N. Undavia	CHARUSAT, India
Jasminder Kaur Sandhu	Chandigarh University, India
Jatinderkumar R. Saini	Symbiosis Institute of Computer Studies and Research, India
Jay Teraiya	Marwadi University, India
Jaydeep Ramniklal Ramani	Atmiya University, India
Jaykumar Dave	Silver Oak University, India
Jaypalsinh Gohil	Marwadi University, India
Jayshree Nair	AIMS Institutes, India
Jignesh Doshi	LJ University, India
Jinal Tailor	S. S. Agrawal Institute of Management and Technology, India
Jotindra Dharwa	Ganpat University, India
Jitendra Kumar Rout	NIT Raipur, India
Jitendra Kumar Samriya	National Institute of Technology, Jalandhar, India
Jyoti Batra	Banasthali University, India
Kamal Kishorbhai Sutaria	Parul University, India
K. Priya	Marudhar Kesari Jain College for Women, India
K. K. Goyal	R.B.S. Management Technical Campus, India
Kajal Patel	GEC, Chandkheda, India
Kalpesh Gundigara	Swaminarayan College, India
Kedir Lemma Arega	Ambo University, Ethiopia
Karthikeyan E.	Government Arts College, India
Keshav K. Singh	University of Alabama at Birmingham, UK
Krunal Vaghela	Marwadi University, India

Krupa Mehta	GLS University, India
Kumar Chandar S.	CHRIST University, India
Kushagra Kulshreshtha	GLA University, India
Lilly Florence M.	Adhiyamaan College of Engineering, India
Lokesh Gagnani	KSV University, India
Madhu Shukla	Marwadi University, India
Mahesh Podar	Pune University, India
Mallika Ravi Bhatt	S. S. Agrawal Group of Colleges, India
Mamta Chawla	Amity University, India
Mamta Padole	Maharaja Sayajirao University of Baroda, India
Manisha Rawat	Marwadi University, India
Manishankar S.	Amrita Vishwavidyapeeth, India
Manojkumar Bohra	Manipal University, India
Manojkumar Deka	Bodoland University, India
Manohar N.	Amrita Vishwavidyapeeth, India
Mastan Vali Shaik	Malla Reddy Engineering College, India
Maulika Patel	G. H. Patel College of Engineering, India
Mauro Conti	University of Padua, Italy
Mehul Rawal	Ahmedabad University, India
Mladen Konecki	University of Zagreb, Croatia
Mohamed Mosbah	University of Bordeaux, France
Mohammad Wazid	Graphic Era University, India
Mohdshafi Pathan	MIT ADT University, India
Mohit Kumar	Dr. B. R. Ambedkar National Institute of Technology, India
Monika Arora	Amity University, India
Nagaraju Kilari	New Horizon College, India
Nagappan Govindarajan	Saveetha Engineering College, India
Narayan Joshi	Dharmsinh Desai University, India
Navin Chaudhari	National Forensics Science University, India
Neelam Padhy	GITU, India
Neha Soni	SVIT, India
Nidhi Patel	SAL College of Engineering, India
Nilesh Modi	Dr. Babasaheb Ambedkar Open University, India
Nisha Khurana	Gandhinagar University, India
Nour El Madhoun	EPITA, France
N. Noor Alleema	SRMIST, India
P. Naga Srinivasu	Prasad V Potluri Siddhartha Institute of Technology, India
P. V. Virparia	Sardar Patel University, India
Pallavi Kaliyar	NTNU, Norway
Parag Rughani	National Forensics Science University, India

Parag Shukla	National Forensics Science University, India
Paresh Tanna	RK University, India
Paras Kothari	Rajasthan Technical University, India
Pradip M. Jawandhiya	Pankaj Laddhad Institute of Technology and Management Studies, India
Prashant M. Dolia	Bhavnagar University, India
Prashant Pittalia	Sardar Patel University, India
Priya R. Swaminarayan	Parul University, India
Priyank Nahar	Gujarat Technological University, India
Priyanka Sharma	Rashtriya Raksha University, India
Puspanjali Mohapatra	IIT Bhuvneshwar, India
R. A. Thakur	King Khalid University, Saudi Arabia
Rajasekaran Selvaraju	University of Technology and Applied Sciences-Ibri, Oman
Ramesh Prajapati	Shri Swaminarayan Institute of Technology, India
Ravirajsinh Vaghela	Marwadi University, India
Ripal Ranpara	R.K. University, India
Riti Kushwaha	Bennett University, India
Roshan Anant Gangurde	K. K. Wagh Institute of Engineering Education & Research, India
Rutvi Shah	Chimanbhai Patel Institute, India
Sabiyath Fatima	B.S. Abdur Rahman Crescent Institute of Science & Technology, India
S. D. Panchal	Gujarat Technological University, India
Sachin Shetty	Old Dominion University, USA
Safvan Vora	Government Engineering College, Modasa, India
Sailesh Iyer	Rai University, India
Samir B. Patel	Pandit Dindayal Energy University, India
Sanjay Chaudhari	Ahmedabad University, India
Sanskruti Patel	CHARUSAT, India
Satyen Parikh	Ganpat University, India
Satvik Khara	Silver Oak University, India
Savita Gandhi	GLS University, India
Senthil Kumar	Saveetha Engineering College, India
Shikha Maheshwari	Manipal University, India
Suneet Gupta	Mody University of Science and Technology, India
Sunil Bajeja	Marwadi University, India
T. Amudha	Bharathiar University, India
T. Devi	Bharathiar University
Umang Rasiklal Thakkar	Ganpat University, India
V. Asha	New Horizon College of Engineering, India

V. Rashmi	Amrita University, India
V. Bhuvaneswari	Bharathiar University, India
V. Ilango	CMR Institute of Technology, India
V. Vinothina	Kristu Jayanti College, India
Vaibhav Gandhi	B H Gardi College, India
Vijay Katkar	Marwadi University, India
Vimal Parmar	Dr. Subhash University, India
Vinay Kukreja	Chitkara University, India
Vinod Desai	Gujarat Vidyapith, India
Vincenzo Piuri	University of Milan, Italy
Vipin Tyagi	Jaypee University, India
Vipul Vekariya	Parul University, India
Vishal R. Dahiya	Indus University, India
Wafa ben Jaballah	Thales, France
Yogesh Ghodasara	Anand Agriculture University, India
Yogesh Kumar	Pandit Deendayal Energy University, India

Sponsors

CSI

Department of Science and Technology

GUJCOST

ICT Academy

MIT Square

Qtonz Infosoft Pvt. Ltd.

Raj Square

Abstracts of Keynotes

Post-pandemic Applications of AI and Machine Learning

Priti Srinivas Sajja

Sardar Patel University, India

The history of mankind has witnessed many pandemics since its inception. Fortunately, the collective knowledge of mankind has helped us a lot to fight the pandemic and better immune and well-evolved society. The recent pandemic of SARS-Covid-19 pandemic has taught us many things too. Fields such as healthcare, education, production, sales and marketing, and education have suffered a lot during the lockdown and pandemic period. The needs such as working in an independent & isolated way, increased automation in many businesses, quick and secure solutions, and effective control and monitoring became inevitable.

The ubiquitous nature of Artificial Intelligence and Machine Learning (AIML) offers a way to meet the above-mentioned need. Healthcare is the first domain where AIML can help. Starting from tracking patients, finding medical resources such as hospital beds, oxygen, and other drugs, diagnosing diseases to inventing novel drugs & vaccines for the disease, AIML can help. The scarce resources are difficult to manage quickly and efficiently without the techniques such as genetic algorithms, neural networks, and other machine learning methods such as generative networks, decision trees and clustering; to name a few. AIML can also be used in managing big data from health informatics.

Another important domain is training and education. Using many online platforms, education can be continued in a non-traditional manner. However, it cannot distinguish and handle different levels of students and hence customization is needed. Similar challenges arise in monitoring people in work-from-home scenarios. Domains such as production, sales & marketing, planning & designing, military and defense, eCommerce, egovernance, etc. also required the support of AIML techniques to increase degree automation, security, and intelligence. While lockdown, entertainment, web surfing, awareness, and morale-boosting types of applications are also highly needed which are intelligent, learn from data, and offer a significant amount of customization.

The problems and needs within the aforementioned domains are discussed here with the challenges & requirements. The possible solutions through the AIML techniques are discussed with brief solution outlines. Possible research applications in each domain are also enlisted using techniques such as deep learning, generative neural networks, hybrid neuro-fuzzy systems, etc. It is to be noted that, in absence of generalized logic AIML based system can learn from data to provide quick as well as better quality solutions.

Smart and Soft Computing Methods for Prioritizing Software Requirements in Large-Scale Software Projects

Vassilis C. Gerogiannis

University of Thessaly, Greece

Large-scale software projects often have numerous candidate functional requirements/software features needed to be prioritized, under multiple prioritization criteria by various stakeholders, who need to decide which requirements/features will be implemented in the next software releases. Most existing requirements prioritization approaches perform well on small sets of candidate requirements, but suffer from scalability for large number of requirements. Furthermore, all involved stakeholders may do not have enough knowledge to accurately and objectively prioritize all candidate requirements. Particularly in distributed software projects, stakeholders can be geographically dispersed and they often do not have the ability to negotiate and reach a consensus on the final list of requirements' priorities. To support these challenges, we propose the use from smart and soft computing methods (e.g., Intuitionistic Fuzzy Sets, Clustering Analysis and Recommender Systems) to handle stakeholders' uncertainty, minimize stakeholders' information overload, as well as to identify patterns that summarize the stakeholders' preferences on the candidate software features. The suggested methods have been applied to requirements datasets of existing large-scale software projects and to illustrative artificial datasets as well. The results are promising since they indicate that the suggested methods can effectively support multiple stakeholders in order to prioritize sufficiently a large number of requirements, under multiple criteria, while combining scalability and flexibility.

Your Readiness for Industry 4.0

Nitin Bawsay

VP Operations, India at Cin7 Americas

As the world witnesses development, from the wheels to steam engines, to electricity and mass production to digitization - we are NOW at the cusp of adopting the 4th leap into industrialization. We will now witness more and more of the Artificial Intelligence (AI), Robotics, Internet of Things (IoT), Mixed Reality (MR) and much more of volume-based technology aspects in our day-to-day life. The overall industry impact of this will be the single, most obvious thing - Development.

As the world gets ready to embrace this new tech termed Industry 4.0 (or X.0?), it is important that everyone of us gets ready to adapt and adopt to the new. Multiple areas that mark the Industry 4.0 are fascinating and do include:

- Automations
- Cost-saving
- Lower labor
- Unlearning and Relearning
- Capital sensitivity

All this holds value today and will continue to do so. However, adoption to the new tools and technics will be the key to this and this Change will be inevitable. The key to Your Readiness to this Change will make the difference.

We will dig into some instances of change in the Industry 4.0 with the right kind of tools and technology for today and tomorrow.

Securing NexGen Automotives - Threats and Trends

Ramkumar G.

Cyber Security and Risk Leader, Nissan Digital, Nissan Motor Corporation, India

In today's connected world, it is no surprise that new age connected car technologies are targeted by Cyber criminals. There are many instances where hackers specifically target automotive sector – computer networks, applications, factories, Cars exploiting technology and people vulnerabilities. This leads to hundreds of millions to billions of USD in litigation, brand damage, loss of business, and market share decline and damage reputation for automotive original equipment manufacturers (OEMs).

In order to ensure connected cards are safe for people from cyber-attacks, governments' world over are introducing more strict regulations and penalties on automotive OEMs. The business impact of a large cyber-security incident/data Breach at an OEM is significant and could run into Billions of USD including through:

Regulatory penalties, mass recall on multiple vehicle lines, factory refit, decline in sales, etc and Reputation Risk. Given the prevailing scenario, it is imperative for automotive OEMs to have critical focus on our end-to-end cyber security program and have the right tools, processes and people to drive this effectively. The keynote address covers the following aspects related to connected cars cyber security.

1. More Connected Cars = Higher Risks
2. Potential attacks on connected vehicles
3. Top Industry sectors targeted by Hacker groups
4. Key cyber security incidents in automotive sector
5. Affected Automotive Segments
6. Automotive Threats in the Deep & Dark Web
7. Standards & Regulations
8. What OEMs need to do?
9. What Suppliers need to do?
10. What CISOs need to do?

Cyber Attacks Classification and Attack Handling Methods Using Machine Learning Methods

Padmavathi Ganapathi

Avinashilingam Institute for Home Science and Higher Education for Women, Coimbatore, India

Cyber-attacks are predominantly increasing day by day due to the tremendous growth of latest technologies and innovations. There are different kinds of cyber-attacks are evolving in every day to day life. Some of the trending cyber-attacks between 2021 and 2022 include Ransomware attacks, Internet of Things (IoT) attacks, Cloud attacks, Phishing attacks, Malwares, cyber extortion and many more. The goal of the attacker or cyber criminals is to steal the user personal credentials without the knowledge of the user in an illegitimate way. Once, the user access control of the network devices are hacked by the criminals they take over the system control and monitor all the legitimate user activities. To detect the unavoidable illegal intrusions by the attackers through cyber-attacks in various forms are handled by vigilant intrusion detection system. Through, Intrusion Detection System (IDS) mechanism, it must be able to detect and protect the unlawful intrusions through various attacks handling methods. Some of the robust intrusion detection techniques such as signature based, anomaly based and protocol based methods. By incorporating appropriate intrusion detection and prevention system (IDPS) method in an organization will help to detect and mitigate the cyber-attacks effectively. An IDPS is a robust mechanism followed by the worldwide cyber security professionals and network administrators to safeguard the network connected devices. However, IDPS mechanism provides a stout framework to handle cyber intrusions. Similarly, Artificial Intelligence (AI) based attack detection methods using the machine learning (ML) and deep learning (DL) algorithms provides a user friendly automation model to detect the attacks evidently without any human interface.

The Internet of Things (IoT) Ecosystem Revolution in the World of Global Sports

Shamala Subramaniam

Universiti Putra Malaysia

Industrial Revolution 4.0 (IR 4.0) has changed the demographics of multiple significant areas such as robotics, simulation, travel, healthcare, and sports. The emergence and extensive development and deployment of IR 4.0 completely altered the methodologies of sports performance monitoring distinctly. IR 4.0 has seen the birth of multiple new computing.

Paradigms, and tools computer scientists use in the sports sector. This keynote will address the eco-systems in sports and the leverage the Internet of Things (IoT) has in this exponentially growing domain. A detailed discussion on focused on methodologies of sports performance analysis, sport-specific analysis and other technology revolving around sports performance analysis will be done. The talk encompasses detailed analyses on the correlation between the athlete, the sports aspect of their life, the non-sport aspect and the methodologies of sports performance analysis. The development and deployment of an off-field sports performance analysis system developed will be used as a core element in the address the harnessing of IoT in sports. The further integration and enhancements with a comprehensive eco-system encompassing a developed Games Management System will conclude the talk with the discussions on a wide spectrum of open issues.

Orchestration of Containers: Role of Artificial Intelligence

Ramkumar Lakshminarayanan

Assistant Dean for Academic and Scientific Research, University of Technology and Applied Sciences-Sur, Sultanate of Oman

The container is a novel technology that revolutionizes the development of cloud computing in creating and controlling the platforms by bundling the codes of applications with libraries and configuration files. Containers are easily deployable, isolated, have data sharing and are portable. The challenges to be addressed in the orchestration of containerized cloud computing are application portability, performance, and the new architecture development. Machine Learning and Deep Learning-the subset of AI makes it possible to solve the problems in selecting, deploying, monitoring, and dynamically controlling the containerized application. This research presents the difficulties of autonomous container orchestration, along with modern AI solutions and unresolved issues.

Enterprise Cybersecurity Strategies in the Cloud

Andrew Hodges

Senior Security Advisor, Asia Pacific and Japan
Amazon Web Services (AWS)

This session shared numerous insights about the threats that public and private sector organizations face and the cybersecurity strategies that can mitigate them.

During this session the various cybersecurity strategies are examined that have ultimately failed over the past 20 years, along with a few that have actually worked. It gave a very good insight to executives and security and compliance professionals to understand how cloud computing is a game changer for them.

By the end of the session, some examples were shown for how to effectively measure the effectiveness of organizations cybersecurity strategy, the ingredients for a successful cybersecurity strategy, cybersecurity investment roadmaps and efficacy, and how you can help employ and protect your organizations and yourself.

Contents – Part I

Contents – Part II

Industry

Artificial Intelligence

Galaxy Classification Using Deep Learning

Premanand Ghadekar, Kunal Chanda, Sakshi Manmode$^{(\boxtimes)}$, Sanika Rawate, Shivam Chaudhary, and Resham Suryawanshi

Department of Information Technology, Vishwakarma Institute of Technology, Pune, India
sakshi.manmode19@vit.edu

Abstract. In this paper, the framework of Deep CNN (Deep Convolutional Neural Network) is basically used for classifying the galaxies. It is shown that galaxies can basically be classified with the help of distinct features into the different categories namely Disturbed galaxies, merging galaxies, Round Smooth galaxies, In-between Round Smooth galaxies, Cigar Shaped Spiral galaxies, Barred Tight Spiral galaxies, Unbarred Loose Spiral galaxies, Edge-on galaxies without bulge and Edge-on galaxy with the bulge. The model that we are proposing is a ConvNet galaxy architecture consists of one input layer having 16 filters, followed by 4 hidden layers, 1 penultimate dense layer, along with an Output Softmax layer. we also included data augmentation such as shear, zoom, rotation, rescaling, and flip. we used the activation function.

The dataset which is used in the proposed research is Galaxy 10 DECals, which has taken its images from DESI Legacy Imaging Surveys and got labeled by Galaxy Zoo. The dataset used contains 256 × 256 pixel-colored Galaxy images (g, r, and z band). The proposed model and framework is training over 17736 images and accomplished above 84.04% in testing accuracy. When a comparison is made between the results and the testing accuracy was compared with other existing models.

Keywords: Galaxy Classification · Deep convolutional neural networks · Feature extraction

1 Introduction

Galaxy is a spiral combination of stars, dark matter, dust, and glasses. Galaxies are of several types and kinds with different features. There are innumerable galaxies in the universe. The study of these galaxies, their types as well as their properties is really crucial [1]. The reason behind this is that galaxies are an important indication of the origin of the universe and its development [2]. Galaxy Classification plays an important role in evaluating the universe in order to understand galaxy formation [3]. Basically, Galaxy Classification is nothing but the system which dissects the galaxies morphologically on the basis of their appearance and impression. There are some strategies that are used to classify the galaxies morphologically in order to get accurate results. The challenges faced by astrophysicists are solved by these classification strategies. Operations are performed on large databases containing information about galaxies so that astrophysicists could test the propositions and get new solutions [4]. Using this, they can elaborate on the formation of stars, the evolution of this universe, and the science behind the processes which administer the galaxies.

So, classifying galaxies is studying, operating, and graphically inspecting galaxy images in 2-D (two-dimensional) form and then differentiating them as per their look [5]. This process is becoming time-consuming day by day because of the evolution of cameras with charged coupled devices and the increasing size of telescopes which is resulting in an increase in the size of databases containing astronomical data, for example, the dataset which is used by the proposed model [6]. The size of the database makes it impossible to analyze the data manually. This model training and testing are most important based on the images to be classified. Classification of galaxies has become more challenging because galaxies are complicated in nature and image quality [7].

The most helpful part of galaxy classification is it will help the astronomers in differentiating the galaxies accurately. In recent years, the evolution of computational tools and training algorithms have advanced the research and analysis of galaxies and their appearance [8].

In the field of Visual Detection as well as Recognition, deep learning plays an important role as it has brought a great scope for improvement. Unprocessed data is fed as an input to Deep Learning Techniques for optimizing the segmentation parameters or feature designs which do not need any prior expertise in the field.

2   Literature Review

1. In recent years, data on galaxies is generated in a large amount due to some sky-surveys like Sloan Digital Sky Survey i.e., SDSS. That's why an efficient classification was a need in this speedy Deep Learning Era. So, Algorithms were intended to differentiate the galaxies into multiple classes. Earlier galaxies were classified into six classes. But the proposed model is classifying the galaxies into eight classes [1]. The proposed model is having a framework that extracts the important features making it reliable. The model got 84.73 percent of testing accuracy after considering important features.
2. As the neural network algorithms are broadly focusing on the survey information, the Radio Galaxy Classification has become a researcher's need. Whether the trained algorithms are having the cross-survey identification potential or not was the main query before researchers. The authors thought of building a Transfer Learning Model to solve this problem. It was used in different radio surveys. The model was also trained for Random Initialization and got good accuracy. First pre-trained images with inherited model weights were trained in such a way that they became performance boosters. The model was trained with NVSS data [10].
3. The paper presented the model with Deep Convolutional Network in order to classify Galaxies. According to features observed morphologically, classification was

done with three main classes namely Elliptical, Spiral and Regular. The framework which was proposed in the research had broadly 8 layers, along with one main layer consisting of 96 filters for extracting main features. The model was training near about 1356 images which give a good testing accuracy. The proposed model was performing well with the classification queries efficiently [12].

4. Morphological Classification of Galaxy is becoming trending in recent years. As far as we are discovering the universe in a broader vision, there is a need to build a robust and reliable model to classify the galaxies from their images. Researchers proposed two fundamental approaches, one was based upon traditional machine learning techniques with non-parametric morphology and the other was based on Deep Learning. Researchers built a system called CyMorph with a non-parametric approach. The dataset used was Sloan Digital Sky Survey i.e., SDSS with release 7 (DR7). In this work, three classes were considered. Overall Accuracy obtained was great because Decision Tree Models were used to approach the quality of the classification morphologically [13].

3   Methodology

3.1   Dataset Collection

The dataset which is used in our proposed research is the Galaxy10 DECals Dataset which is basically an improved version of the Galaxy10 Dataset. The dataset of Galaxy10 was

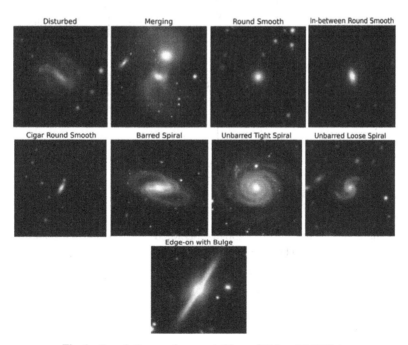

Fig. 1. Sample Images from each Class of Galaxy10 DECals

originally created by Galaxy Zoo (GZ) Data Release 2 where they were classifying 270 thousand SDSS galaxy images among which 22 thousand of those images were selected in the grouping of 10 broader classes. It was done on the basis of votes given to every image. Later, the images from DECals is DESI Legacy Imaging Surveys were utilized by Galaxy Zoo in order to get images perfectly resoluted and greater image quality. The Galaxy10 DECals which merged all the three (GZ i.e., Galaxy Zoo DR2 with DECals images rather than SDSS images and DECals campaign ab, c) which then results in 441 thousand unique galaxies covered by DECals. After that 18 thousand of those images were selected in 10 broader classes. This was obtained after the continuous filtering with the votes obtained for each image. There was one more class named Edge-on Disk with Boxy Bulge which was later abandoned due to less number of images which was just 17 images. This was done to make the dataset of Galaxy10 DECals more distinct and precise in the formed 10 broader classes (Figs. 1, 2 and 3).

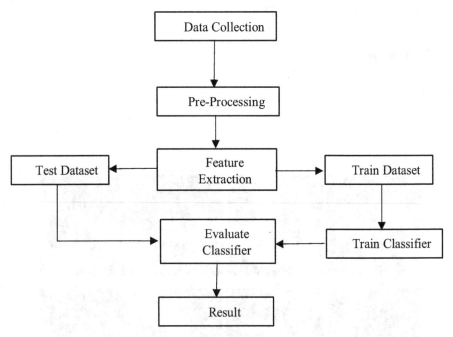

Fig. 2. Flow diagram of the proposed model

The dataset used contains 256×256 pixel-colored Galaxy images (g, r, and z band). It contains 17736 images which are broadly classified into 10 major classes. Images of the dataset come from DESI Legacy Imaging Surveys and labeling was done by Galaxy Zoo.

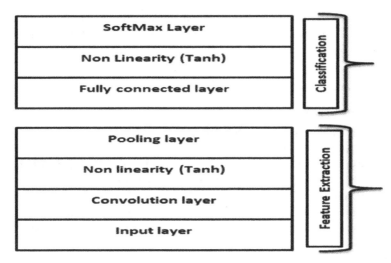

Fig. 3. Proposed model architecture

Table 1. Type of galaxies with the number of images

Name of class	Type of galaxy	Total pictures
Class-0	Disturbed Galaxies	1081
Class-1	Merging Galaxies	1853
Class-2	Round Smooth Galaxies	2645
Class-3	In-between Round Smooth Galaxies	2027
Class-4	Cigar Shaped Smooth Galaxies	334
Class-5	Barred Spiral Galaxies	2043
Class-6	Unbarred Tight Spiral Galaxies	1829
Class-7	Unbarred Loose Spiral Galaxies	2628
Class-8	Edge-on Galaxies without Bulge	1423
Class-9	Edge-on Galaxies with Bulge	1873

3.2 Proposed Deep Galaxies CNN Model

This project is based on morphological classification using Deep Convolution Neural Network. It shows how computational cosmology could help to make hard classification easy. The galaxy can be classified in various ways, they can be in three classes namely - Elliptical, Spiral, Irregular or they could be classified deeper as Disturbed, Merging, round smooth, barred spiral, bulge, etc.

This project uses astroNN dataset, this dataset is generated from [DESI Legacy Imaging Survey], and images got themselves labeled by [Galaxy Zoo].

The important advantage of the proposed model will be classifying the results into more classes (class 0 to class 9, as explained in Table 1). This is obligating to Astrophysicist and Astronomers.

3.3 Overview of Algorithms

3.3.1 Machine Learning

That works on building software applications being accurate in predicting the results and outcomes which will not need any external programming help. Machine Learning can help industries and companies to understand as well as examine their customers and consumers subordinately [4]. In addition to this, this predictive learning method can help in the formation of operating systems (OS) of self-driving cars, for example, Tesla. Data of the consumers is collected and correlated with their behaviors all the time. Machine Learning is used as an important as well as the primary driver for the business models of the companies such as Uber.

3.3.2 Deep Learning

In Deep Learning, a machine that imitates the neuron network in a human's brain can be created. The basis of it is on Deep Networks in which a task is divided and then distributed to machine learning algorithms. The algorithm includes many connected layers. A set of hidden layers is in between the input layer (1st layer) and the output layer (last layer), which gives the word Deep, meaning that the networks that join neurons are in more than 2 layers [8]. The interconnected neurons propagate the input signal and after that, it goes through the process [14].

3.3.3 Convolutional Neural Network

Convolutinnal Neural Networks or CNNs are types of artificial neural network that is ANN, which is broadly used for image classification and object recognition. They are types of discriminative models that are initially developed to work on images that are not pre-processed. Now, these models can also work with text and sound recognition and classification. CNN architecture was framed and designed for recognition models which can read the zip codes and digits, which was constructed in the era of the 90s (1990) which initiated the deep artificial neural networks or ANNs [6].

3.3.4 Dropout Layer

Dropout layer in CNN architecture acts as a filtering layer that nullifies the efforts of some neurons when passing to the next layer. A dropout layer is added to the input vector which normalizes some features. These layers play an important role in preventing the overfitting problem while training the data.

3.3.5 Optimizers

Optimizers are techniques or algorithms that are used to change the features of neural networks which includes learning rate and weights. These are used to minimize losses and errors. Also, as the functions are minimized, optimizers are used in the Optimization Problems wherever needed. The following update equation is used to initialize some policies with renovated Epoch.

$$W_{New} = W_{old} - \text{lr} * (\nabla\text{WL})W_{old} \tag{1}$$

Equation 1 is used to Renovate Epoch.

3.3.6 Pooling Layer

Pooling Layer is used to minimize the size of the image which is obtained from the reduction of dimensions of the feature maps. The number of learning parameters is reduced as well as computational efforts are minimized by using this Pooling Technique [11]. It basically recollects all the important features present in the convolution layer. There are two types of Pooling which are as follows:

a. Max Pooling: Selection of the maximum values from the matrix of specified size (basically, the default size is 2 X 2) takes place. Due to this Feature Extraction of more important parameters takes place.
b. Average Pooling: The average of all the pixel values of the matrix (basically, the default size is 2 X 2) takes place in the pooling layer.

3.3.7 Dense Layer

After the Pooling procedure, the output is then passed on to the Dense Layer. The constraint of the Dense layer is that the input should be in a One-Dimensional or 1-D shape (the array should be 1-D) [14]. The image classification takes place in this layer on the basis of the output of previous convolutional layers. The input received is known as Dense.

3.3.8 Flatten Method

Flatten method is used in the conversion of a multi-dimensional matrix to a single-dimensional matrix. This method avoids the overfitting problem thus data is easier to interpret. It includes Preprocessing of Data and Data Augmentation (Table 2).

4 Comparative Results

Table 2. Comparative analysis of existing and proposed model

Related work	Year	Paper title	Total accuracy
1	2022	Galaxy classification: a deep learning approach for classifying Sloan Digital Sky Survey images	84.73%
2	2019	Machine and Deep Learning applied to galaxy morphology—A comparative study	82%
3	2020	Optimizing automatic classification of galaxies with ML and DL using Dark Energy Survey imaging	92.2%
Proposed model	2022	Galaxy Classification using Deep Learning	84.04%

4.1 Model Accuracy

A validation method used in the classification problems in the Machine Learning Model is known as Accuracy. The overall accuracy of the proposed model is 84.04% (Figs. 4, 5, 6 and 7).

(1)	Actual: Edge-on Galaxies without bul	Predicted: Disturbed
(2)	Actual: Merging	Predicted: Merging
(3)	Actual: Cigar Shaped Smooth	Predicted: Cigar Shaped smooth
(4)	Actual: Round Smooth	Predicted: Round smooth
(5)	Actual: Disturbed	Predicted: Edge-on Galaxies with bulge
(6)	Actual: Unbarred loose spiral	Predicted: Edge-on Galaxies without bulge
(7)	Actual: Merging	Predicted: Merging
(8)	Actual: Distributed	Predicted: Merging
(9)	Actual: Distributed	Predicted: Unbarred
(10)	Actual: Unbarred loose	Predicted: Edge-on Galaxies
(11)	Actual: Cigar Shaped Smooth	Predicted: Cigar Shaped
(12)	Actual: Unbarred tight spiral	Predicted: Unbarred tight spiral
(13)	Actual: Merging	Predicted: Merging
(14)	Actual: Merging	Predicted: Merging
(15)	Actual: Round Smooth	Predicted: Round Smooth
(16)	Actual: Distributed	Predicted: Distributed
(17)	Actual: In-between Round Smooth	Predicted: In-between Round Smooth
(18)	Actual: Round Smooth	Predicted: Round Smooth
(19)	Actual: Merging	Predicted: Merging
(20)	Actual: Distributed	Predicted: Distributed
(21)	Actual: Merging	Predicted: Merging

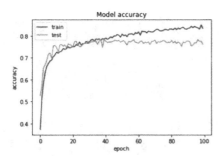

Fig. 4. Graph of model accuracy

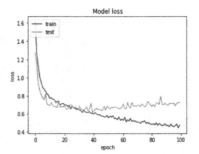

Fig. 5. Graph of model loss

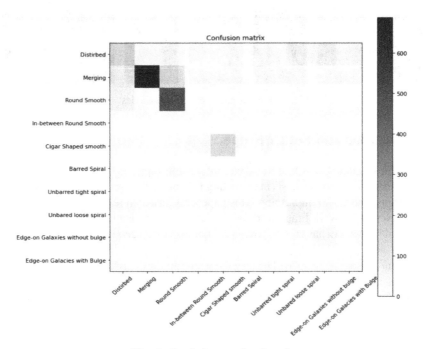

Fig. 6. Confusion matrix of result

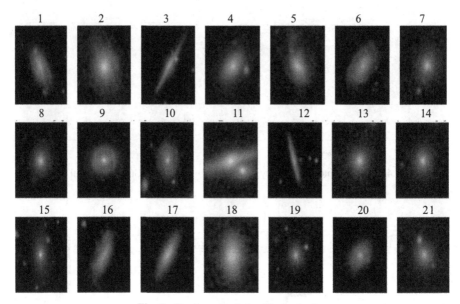

Fig. 7. Final result of classified galaxies

5   Conclusion and Future Scope

Galaxy Classification is a traditional yet interesting topic. It has helped researchers, astronomers, and astrophysicists in dissecting the galaxies morphologically on the basis of their appearance and impression. This paper was based on research on Deep Convolutional Neural Network Framework on the Galaxy Classification issue. The proposed model and framework have trained over 17736 images and accomplished 84.04% testing accuracy.

In future work, the focus will be on galaxy morphology classification should be done to a greater extent with more accuracy. The next step of the research will be training the model with larger and higher quality databases and the dataset. Advancement of the Algorithms for Galaxy Morphological Classification will be taken to a greater extent with the help of advanced Deep Learning Techniques.

References

1. Gharat, S., Dandawate, Y.: Galaxy classification: A deep learning approach for classifying Sloan Digital Sky Survey images. Month. Notic. R. Astrono. Soc. **511**(4), 5120–5124 (2022)
2. Abd Elfattah, M., Elbendary, N., Elminir, H.K., Abu El-Soud, M.A., Hassanien, A.E.: Galaxies image classification using empirical mode decomposition and machine learning techniques. In: 2014 International Conference on Engineering and Technology (ICET), p. 15 (2014)
3. Nadolny, J., Bongiovanni, Á., Cepa, J., Cerviño, M., María Pérez García, A., Pović, M., Pérez Martínez, R., Sánchez-Portal, M., de Diego, J.A., Pintos-Castro, I., Alfaro, E., Castañeda, H.O., Gallego, J., Jesús González, J., Ignacio González-Serrano, J., Lara-López, M.A., Padilla Torres, C.P.: The OTELO survey is a morphological probe. Last ten Gyr of galaxy evolution. Astron. Astrophys. **647**, A89 (2021)

4. Dominguez, A.: A history of the convolution operation. IEEE Pulse **6**(1), 3849 (2015)
5. Kim, E.J., Brunner, R.J.: Star–galaxy classification using deep convolutional neural networks. Month. Notic. R. Astrono. Soc. **464**(4), 4463–4475 (2017)
6. Srinivas, S., Sarvadevabhatla, R.K., Mopuri, K.R., Prabhu, N., Kruthiventi, S.S.S., Babu, R.V.: A Taxonomy of deep convolutional neural nets for computer vision. Front. Robot. AI **2**, 36 (2016)
7. Jiang, H., Learned-Miller, E.: Face detection with the faster R-CNN. In: 2017 12th IEEE International Conference on Automatic Face & Gesture Recognition (FG 2017), p. 650657 (2017)
8. Barchi, P.H., et al.: Machine and deep learning applied to galaxy morphology: a comparative study. Astron. Comput. **30**, 100334 (2020)
9. Marin, M., Sucar, L.E., Gonzalez, J.A., Diaz, R.: A hierarchical model for morphological galaxy classification. In: Proceedings of the Twenty-Sixth International Florida Artificial Intelligence Research Society Conference, 438443 (2013)
10. Tang, H., Scaife, A.M.M., Wong, O.I., Shabala, S.S.: Radio galaxy zoo: Giant radio galaxy classification using multidomain deep learning. Month. Notic. R. Astrono. Soc. **510**(3), 4504–4524 (2022)
11. Selim, I.M., Abd El Aziz, M.: Automated morphological classification of galaxies based on a projection gradient nonnegative matrix factorization algorithm. Exp. Astron. **43**(2), 131144 (2017)
12. Cheng, T.-Y., et al.: Optimizing automatic morphological classification of galaxies with machine learning and deep learning using Dark Energy Survey imaging. Month. Notic. R. Astrono. Soc. **493**(3), 4209–4228 (2020)
13. Tang, H., Scaife, A.M.M., Leahy, J.P.: Transfer learning for radio galaxy classification. Month. Notic. R. Astrono. Soc. **488**(3), 3358–3375 (2019)
14. Mohan, D., Anna, M., Scaife, M., Porter, F., Walmsley, M., Bowles, M.: Quantifying uncertainty in deep learning approaches to radio galaxy classification. Month. Notic. R. Astrono. Soc. **511**(3), 3722–3740 (2022)

Word Sense Disambiguation for Hindi Language Using Neural Network

Binod Kumar Mishra[(✉)] and Suresh Jain

Computer Science and Engineering Department, Medi-Caps University, Indore, India
bkmishra21@gmail.com, suresh.jain@rediffmail.com

Abstract. One of the major hurdles in the development of Natural language Processing applications is ambiguity and the process to solve is known as Word Sense Disambiguation. It is useful to determine the appropriate meaning of polysemy words in each context using computational methods. In every language, ambiguity exists, and to resolve this Knowledge, Supervised, and Unsupervised based approaches are used. Over the past ten years, the Indian government has launched a large number of digital services for its citizens. To better serve Indian citizens, these services are primarily based on Hindi or other Indian languages. For it to be easily accessed by web portals or any electronic device, natural language processing is required. Since English and other languages such as Chinese, Japanese, and Korean have abundant resources for natural language processing application development. Due to the limited resources available for disambiguating polysemous words in Hindi and other Indian languages, building applications based on these languages becomes challenging. This paper provides a very gentle introduction to the simplest version of neural network techniques for solving ambiguity problems who are not familiar with integration with IndoWordNet. The outcomes demonstrate that the suggested technique performs consistently and significantly better than the alternatives.

Keywords: Word Sense Disambiguation · RNN · LSTM · IndoWordNet · LESK · Naïve bayes

1 Introduction

Language technologies are the basic tools used by millions of people in their everyday life. These technologies are based on Natural Language Processing (NLP) having various applications such as Machine Translation, Web Search Engine, Information Extraction, Sentiment Analysis and many more. Since, it relies on linguistic knowledge and it is not being easily available in his own language, this development did not make a high impact on most of the people. Ambiguity is also one of the most fundamental and important hurdles found in every NLP application. It is also considered an AIcomplete problem (Navigli 2009).

Word Sense Disambiguation (WSD) is a tool that assists NLP application for better understanding language and performing effectively. Words can have various meanings depending on the context they are used such type of words known as polysemous word.

© The Author(s), under exclusive license to Springer Nature Switzerland AG 2022
S. Rajagopal et al. (Eds.): ASCIS 2022, CCIS 1759, pp. 14–25, 2022.
https://doi.org/10.1007/978-3-031-23092-9_2

The task of WSD is to find out correct sense of polysemous word according to context of the sentence. Consider the word "tie" having various sense such as a necktie, cord used for fastening, a bond of kinship or affection, equality in a contest etc. Sometimes, part-of-speech (POS) tags can help resolve ambiguity to some extent, but even for the same part-of-speech words with the same POS tags, the word senses are still very unclear (Taghipour and Ng 2015). As a person, it appears to be quite simple to determine the appropriate sense of the given context, but for a machine, it is highly challenging task to find out exact sense. In order to determine the appropriate meaning using WSD, it is necessary to process an extremely large amount of data and appropriate algorithms (Ng and Lee 1996; Nguyen et al. 2018; Sarika and Sharma 2015).

Over the past decade, the government of India has initiated a wide variety of digital services in Hindi and other Indian languages to better serve Indian citizens. All these digital services must apply WSD solutions to find the correct sense of polysemous words. Since English and other languages like Chinese, Japanese, and Korean have plenty of resources available to perform this task but very limited resources are available in Hindi and other Indic languages. To solve ambiguity problems various methods are used such as knowledge-based, Supervised, and Unsupervised based approaches. Also, it required resources like IndoWordNet and Corpus.

In Summary, we make the following contribution to this work:

- We propose a Word Embedding technique to convert words into vectors for Hindi text.
- Through extensive evaluation, we demonstrate the effectiveness of LSTM over stateof-art work.

The following sections of the paper are arranged as follows: The resources, variants and existing work related to WSD are explained in Sect. 2. The proposed work and result discussion are in Sects. 3 and 4 respectively. The conclusion and future directions are discussed in Sect. 5.

2 Related Work

2.1 Background

To disambiguate Hindi text various resources such as IndoWordNet and Corpus are required. IndoWordNet is a collection of words for many Indian language. It was created by IIT Bombay's Centre for Indian Language Technology (CFILT) (Jha et al. 2001) for Hindi and other Indian languages known as IndoWordNet. It contains synset, hypernymy, hyponymy, holonomy, meronymy, antonymy, and many more relationship between words for 19 Indian languages.

Corpus is a collection of texts for a single language or multiple languages used to build language models. There are two types of corpora required i.e., sense annotated and raw corpus, for supervised and unsupervised word sense disambiguation. A sense annotated corpus is created by person who is expert in this language. The linguistic experts create sense annotation corpus using manual approach. The raw corpus contains

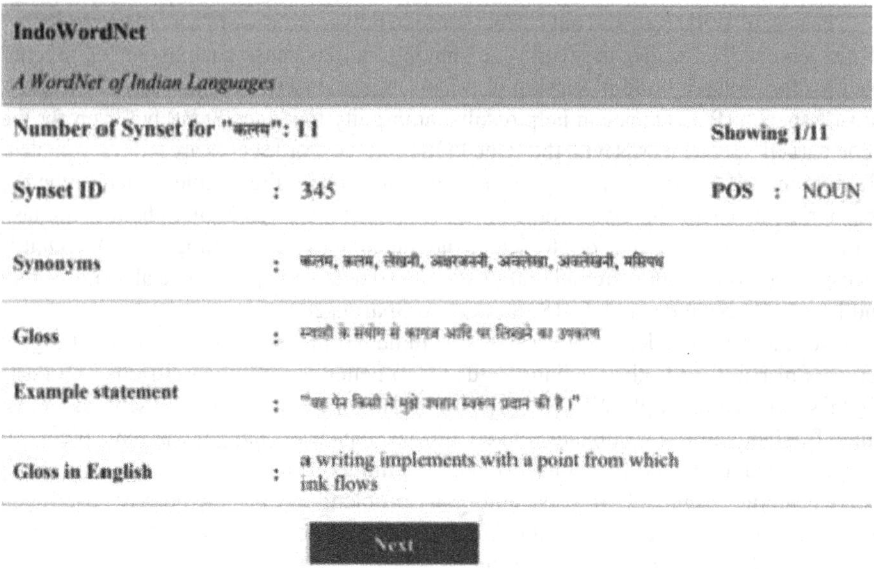

IndoWordNet		
A WordNet of Indian Languages		
Number of Synset for "कलम": 11		Showing 1/11
Synset ID	: 345	POS : NOUN
Synonyms	: कलम, क़लम, लेखनी, अक्षरजननी, अक्षलेखा, अक्षलेखनी, मसिपथ	
Gloss	: स्याही के संयोग से कागज़ आदि पर लिखने का उपकरण	
Example statement	: "वह पेन किसी ने मुझे उपहार स्वरूप प्रदान की है ।"	
Gloss in English	: a writing implements with a point from which ink flows	

Next

Fig. 1. IndoWordNet (Bhattacharyya 2010; Jha et al. 2001)

plain text taken from different domains including tourism, health, news, sports, stories, literature, history, etc. (Choudhary et al. 2019; Singh and Siddiqui 2016).

A snapshot of IndoWordNet is shown in Fig. 1 taken from (Jha et al. 2001; Narayan et al. 2002) for the word "कलम". It gives 11 different meanings,all meaning is decided according to the context they used. These senses can be used to disambiguate polysemous words. Out of 11, five sense are as follow:

- स्याही के संयोग से कागज़ आदि पर लिखने का उपकरण

Here meaning is "an item used to write with that has an ink-flowing tip".

- पेड़ की वह टहनी जो दूसरी जगह बैठाने या दूसरे पेड़ में पैबंद लगाने के लिए काटी जाए

Here meaning is related to "a portion of a plant that is occasionally removed in order to root or graft a new plant".

- सिर के वे बाल जो कनपटी के पास होते हैं

Here meaning is "beard that has grown in front of a man's ears down the side of his face, especially when the rest of the beard has been shaven".

- चित्रकार के रंग भरने की कलम

Here meaning is related to "a brush used as an applicator (to apply paint)".

• बही-खाते आदि में लिखा जाने वाला कोई मद

Here meaning is "a line of numbers stacked one on top of the other".

2.2 Variants of Word Sense Disambiguation Work

THERE are two major categories of Word Sense Disambiguation work, Lexical sample or Target word and All-word WSD (Bhingardive and Bhattacharyya 2017) Lexical sample would apply when the system is required to disambiguate a single word in a particular sentence. In this case a machine learning approach are used for this dedicated word, to trained the model by using corpus. With the help of this it can determine the correct meaning for the target word in the given context.

In case All-Word WSD, it can predict more ambiguous word in the given sentence. In the provided context, it identifies every word that falls within the open-class category, including Nouns, Adjectives, Verbs, and Adverbs. Since Machine learning specially in supervised approach it required a large amount of tagged corpus also it cannot easily scale up. So, in this case knowledge-based or Graph based are most suitable methods for all-word WSD tasks.

2.3 Existing Approaches for Disambiguation

WorD Sense Disambiguation techniques used different resources, generally, knowledge-based approach used IndoWordNet whereas supervised and unsupervised based approach used sense annotated and raw corpus respectively.

In knowledge-based approach generally we extract information from wordnet. Since lexical resources like WordNet playing important role to find out glosses of target word. Initially this approach developed by (Lesk 1986) which used overlap function between glosses of target word and context word. In this method it selects the word that most overlaps with words in context. Later this work is modified by Banerjee & Pedersen (Banerjee and Pedersen 2003; Banerjee et al. 2002) by using semantic relation of word with the help of WordNet. Basile et al. (Basile et al. 2014) extend the LESK's work using distribution semantic model. The Distributional Semantics Models (DSM) realize the architectural metaphor of meanings, which have been represented as points in a space, where proximity is estimated by semantic similarity.

Most of the research on word sense disambiguation that has been published in the literature focuses on English as well as a number of other languages, including Arabic, Chinese, Japanese, and Korean. The first attempt to address the WSD problem in Hindi was made by (Sinha et al. 2004).

The supervised approach and Unsupervised technique require sense annotated corpus and raw corpus respectively (Bhingardive and Bhattacharyya 2017; Bhingardive et al. 2015). A sense annotated corpus was manually constructed by a language expert,as a result, it took a lot of time and labor and was occasionally improperly annotated. This method uses a word-specific classifier to determine the correct meaning of each word. It involves two steps. In the first step training the model is required and for this thing sense tagged corpus is used and this classifier capture the syntactic and semantic classifiers.

The second step entails using classifiers to identify the meaning of an ambiguous word that better represents the surrounding context (Vaishnav and Sajja 2019).

Unsupervised approaches do not require sense-annotated corpora, saving a lot of time on corpus formation. With the help of context clustering, it discriminates different senses. Context and sense vectors are amalgamated to create clusters. By mapping the ambiguous word to a context vector in word space, the word is disambiguated in the given context. The closest sense vector receives the meaning reference. By mapping an ambiguous word to a context vector in Word Space, the context of the word is revealed. The sense with the closest sense vector is given the context. Another method is commonly used for disambiguation is known as Co-occurrences graphs. A graph for the target word is constructed with the use of corpora. In one paragraph, there are edges connecting two words that occur together. Each edge is given a weight in order to determine the relative frequency of the co-occurring words. Any nodes that represent a word's senses are connected to the target word when they are chosen. The distance is calculated by using Minimum Spanning Tree and result obtained from this is stored. All word WSD operations are performed using this spanning tree. Since supervised WSD approaches gives very good result in terms of accuracy, hence it overlap other approaches of Word Sense Disambiguation (Zhong and Ng 2010). Neural network technique also used corpus as well as it considers local context of the target word.

Through extensive literature review, it is observed that several shortcomings are associated with Hindi WSD. For this, we should not only depend upon WordNet but also Corpus. It is also noted down that word embedding technique is required for Hindi Text. To increase the accuracy for Hindi WSD, it is important to develop new techniques which will combine both senses and corpus to train the model.

The majority of the Indian language does not have rich resources like English who helps to solve the problem of WSD, so it requires more resources and efficient algorithms for better accuracy. (Sinha et al. 2004) developed a first-time statistical technique for Hindi WSD with the help of Indo-WordNet. Later many researchers developed models to solve Word Sense Disambiguation in Hindi and other Indian languages. Details of each approach are given in Table 1.

Table 1. Comparison of various word sense disambiguation approaches

Approach	Type			
	Method used	Resources	Language	Accuracy
Knowledge based	LESK (Lesk 1986)	Machine readable dictionary	English	31.2%
	Extended LESK (Banerjee et al., 2002; Banerjee and Pedersen 2003)	WordNet	English	41.1%

(continued)

Table 1. (*continued*)

Approach	Type			
	Method used	Resources	Language	Accuracy
	Extended LESK with TF-IDF (Basile et al., 2014)	BabelNet	English	71%
	LESK with Bigram and Trigram (Gautam and Sharma 2016)	Indo WordNet	Hindi	52.98%
	Map-Reduce function on Ha-doop (Nair et al. 2019)	WordNet	English	51.68%
	Overlap based with Semantic relation (Sinha et al. 2004)	Indo WordNet	Hindi	40–70%
Graph based	Score based LESK (Tripathi et al. 2020)	Indo WordNet	Hindi	61.2%
	Using Global and Local measure (Sheth et al. 2016)	Indo WordNet	Hindi	66.67%
Supervised based	SVM (Zhong and Ng 2010)	SemCor annotated corpus	English	65.5%
	Naïve Bayes (Singh et al. 2014)	Indo WordNet	Hindi	80.0%
	Cosine similarity (Sharma 2016)	Indo WordNet	Hindi	48.9%
	SVM with Embedding (Iacobacci et al. 2016)	WordNet	English	75.2%
	Random forest with Embedding (Agre et al. 2018)	SemCor	English	75.80%
	IMS with Massive Contest (Liu and Wei 2019)	SemCor	English	67.7%
	Embedding like Doc2Vec (Li et al. 2021)	WordNet	English	63.9%

(*continued*)

Table 1. (*continued*)

Approach	Type			
	Method used	Resources	Language	Accuracy
Unsupervised	Expectation Maximization (Bhingardive and Bhattacharyya 2017; Khapra et al. 2011)	Indo WordNet	Hindi	54.98%
	Word2Vec Kumari and Lobiyal, 2020; 2021)	Indo WordNet	Hindi	52%
	Word2Vec with Cosine distance (Soni et al. 2021)	Indo WordNet	Hindi	57.21%
	ShotgunWSD 2.0 (Butnaru and Ionescu 2019)	WordNet	English	63.84%
	Train-O-Matric (Pasini and Navigl 2020)	WordNet	English	67.3%

3 Proposed Approach for WSD

OVErview of the proposed WSD model explained in this section. It contains architecture, implementation details and evaluation.

3.1 Architecture of the Proposed WSD Model

Figure 2 depicts the suggested WSD model's general architecture, taken some ideas from (Kumari and Lobiyal 2020) There are three modules in it:

Distributed Word Representation: In this sub-module, numerical representation in terms vectors is generated. It requires corpus for Hindi text. After creating corpus, preprocessing is required which will remove punctuation, special symbols and stop words. Morphology is also required so that root words can be found and size of the corpus is reduced. After preprocessing, each word or tokens is converted into vector representation using Bag of words, TF-IDF and Word2Vec approach.

Create Context and Sense Module: With the aid of the preceding phase, this submodule generates vector representations of the input sentence. In each sentence at least one word represents as an ambiguous word or target word and remaining words represent as a context words. The context vector is a single representation of the context words and sense vector is a generated for each sense of target word. These senses are defined at Indo WordNet developed by (Jha et al. 2001).

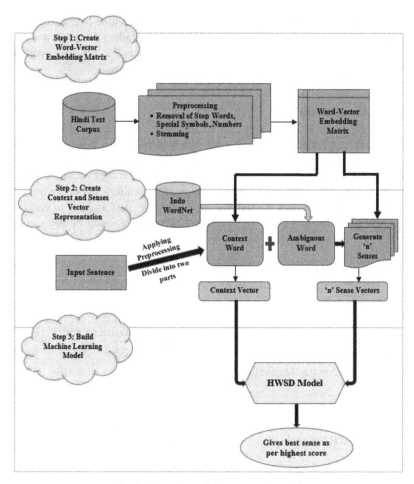

Fig. 2. Overview of the proposed model

Build Machine Learning WSD Model: Two inputs are necessary for creating a machine learning model: the context vector C and sense vectors for the ambiguous word those senses are defined WordNet. The sense vectors may be two or more, it depends upon the senses defined on Indo WordNet. In this model, memory module is also introduced, which will update memory to refine the sense.

3.2 Implementation Details

HWSD model build by using rule based, machine learning and neural network model was setup. Each model having own setup and keep dataset same for each model. To train model sense annotated corpus built, as well as to validate separate setup was built, it also includes same number of senses. For rule based WSD model using overlap based LESK approach used to find out maximum score. For classical machine leaning naïve bayes classifier is used. It contains groups of characteristics surrounding the target word within a specified timeframe, such as co-location and co-occurrence. For Neural network, RNN and LSTM model is used to maintain the sequences of the words.

4 Result Discussion

IN this section, comparison of each model which include rule based also known as overlap based, classical machine learning naïve based and two neural network RNN and LSTM model used. All approaches used same datasets for training and for validation same datasets are used so that results can be comparable. Evaluation for each model, five different ambiguous sentences is used. Table 2 shown the performance of each model which is discussed above. The performance shown for each model in terms of recall, accuracy, precision, and F1-score with our own dataset.

Table 2. Result with respect to Accuracy, Precision, Recall and F1-Score

HWSD Models	Results			
	Accuracy	Precision	Recall	F1-Score
Rule based (Jha et al. 2001)	31.2%	25.2%	50.1%	33.53%
Classical Machine Learning (Ng and Lee 1996) (Naïve Bayes)	33.67%	35.6%	38.71%	37.08%
RNN based Neural Network	**41.61%**	**55.9%**	**35.71%**	**43.58%**
LSTM based Neural Network	**43.21%**	**56.39%**	**36.29%**	**44.16%**

On observing Table 2, it shows that RNN based neural network gives 43.58% and LSTM based neural network model gives 44.16% F1-Score, which are highest performance over others approach. This score has been found by applying concatenation of all ambiguous words. Figure 3 show compare scores of each model.

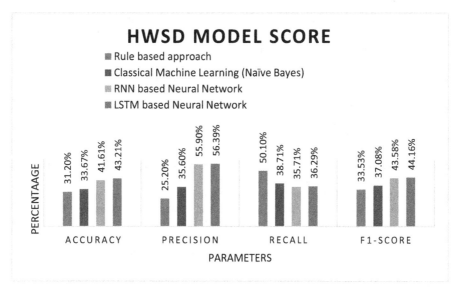

Fig. 3. Compare performance over existing approach

5 Conclusion and Future Directions

WorD Sense Disambiguation is essential for any application of natural language processing. This work incorporates the IndoWordNet-defined concept of meaning into neural network algorithms. This article compares rule-based, statistical machine learning, and neural network-based RNN models on four very ambiguous terms, as well as the remaining seven ambiguous words combined. The results of the suggested model demonstrate that it outperforms the current techniques.

There remains one remaining challenge for future development. Since the knowledge-based technique does not include local context, it relies on WordNet, whereas the word-specific classifier employed in the supervised and neural-based approaches takes local context into account but disregards lexical information. For greater precision, disambiguation of every term requires both local context and lexical information. Combining knowledge-based and machine-learning methodologies in future work yields a superior outcome. Additionally, constructing a model utilizing the LSTM model may yield a superior outcome.

References

Agre, G., Petrov, D., Keskinova, S.: A new approach to the supervised word sense disambiguation. In: International Conference on Artificial Intelligence: Methodology, Systems, and Applications, pp. 3–15 (2018)

Banerjee, S., Pedersen, T.: Extended gloss overlaps as a measure of semantic relatedness. Ijcai **3**, 805–810 (2003)

Banerjee, S., Pedersen, T., Gelbukh, A.: An Adapted Lesk Algorithm for Word Sense Disambiguation Using WordNet, pp. 136–145 (2002)

Basile, P., Caputo, A., Semeraro, G.: An enhanced lesk word sense disambiguation algorithm through a distributional semantic model. In: Proceedings of COLING 2014, the 25th International Conference on Computational Linguistics: Technical Papers, pp. 1591–1600 (2014)

Bhattacharyya, P.: Indowordnet. In: Lexical Resources Engineering Conference 2010 (lrec2010), Malta, May (2010)

Bhingardive, S., Bhattacharyya, P.: Word sense disambiguation using IndoWordNet. In The WordNet in Indian Languages, pp. 243–260. Springer (2017)

Bhingardive, S., Singh, D., Murthy, R., Redkar, H., Bhattacharyya, P.: Unsupervised most frequent sense detection using word embeddings. DENVER (2015)

Butnaru, A. M., Ionescu, R.T.J.I.A.: ShotgunWSD 2.0: An improved algorithm for global word sense disambiguation. 7, 120961–120975 (2019)

Gautam, C.B.S., Sharma, D.K.: Hindi word sense disambiguation using Lesk approach on bigram and trigram words. In: Proceedings of the International Conference on Advances in Information Communication Technology Computing, pp. 1–5 (2016)

Iacobacci, I., Pilehvar, M.T., Navigli, R.: Embeddings for word sense disambiguation: An evaluation study. In: Proceedings of the 54th Annual Meeting of the Association for Computational Linguistics, Vol. 1: Long Papers, pp. 897–907 (2016)

Jha, S., Narayan, D., Pande, P., Bhattacharyya, P.: A wordnet for hindi. In: International Workshop on Lexical Resources in Natural Language Processing, Hyderabad, India (2001)

Khapra, M.M., Joshi, S., Bhattacharyya, P.: It takes two to tango: A bilingual unsupervised approach for estimating sense distributions using expectation maximization. In: Proceedings of 5th International Joint Conference on Natural Language Processing, pp. 695–704 (2011)

Kumari, A., Lobiyal, D.K.: Word2vec's distributed word representation for hindi word sense disambiguation. In: International Conference on Distributed Computing and Internet Technology, 325–335 (2020)

Kumari, A., Lobiyal, D.K.: Efficient estimation of Hindi WSD with distributed word representation in vector space. J. King Saud Univ. Comput. Inf. Sci (2021)

Lesk, M.: Automatic sense disambiguation using machine readable dictionaries: how to tell a pine cone from an ice cream cone. In: Proceedings of the 5th Annual International Conference on Systems Documentation, pp. 24–26 (1986)

Li, X., You, S., Chen, W.J.I.A.: Enhancing accuracy of semantic relatedness measurement by word single-meaning embeddings. 9, 117424–117433 (2021)

Liu, Y., Wei, J.: Word sense disambiguation with massive contextual texts. In: International Conference on Database Systems for Advanced Applications, pp. 430–433 (2019)

Miller, G.A.: WordNet: a lexical database for English. Commun. ACM 38(11), 39–41 (1995)

Nair, A., Kyada, K., Zadafiya, N.: Implementation of word sense disambiguation on hadoop using map-reduce. In: Information and Communication Technology for Intelligent Systems, pp. 573–580. Springer (2019)

Narayan, D., Chakrabarti, D., Pande, P., Bhattacharyya, P.: An experience in building the indo wordnet-a wordnet for hindi. In: First International Conference on Global WordNet, Mysore, India, 24 (2002)

Navigli, R.: Word sense disambiguation: A survey. ACM Comput. Surv. 41(2), 1–69 (2009)

Ng, H.T., Lee, H.B.: Integrating multiple knowledge sources to disambiguate word sense: an exemplar-based Approach. In: 34th Annual Meeting of the Association for Computational Linguistics, pp. 40–47 (1996). https://www.aclweb.org/anthology/P96-1006

Nguyen, Q.-P., Vo, A.-D., Shin, J.-C., Ock, C.-Y. J.I.A.: Effect of word sense disambiguation on neural machine translation: A case study in Korean. 6, 38512–38523 (2018)

Pasini, T., Navigli, R.: Train-O-Matic: Supervised word sense disambiguation withno (manual) effort. Artif. Intell. 279, 103215 (2020). https://doi.org/10.1016/j.artint.2019.103215

Narayan Choudhary, R., et al.: A Gold Standard Hindi Raw Text Corpus. Central Institute of Indian Languages, Mysore (2019)

Sarika, S.D.K.: A comparative analysis of Hindi word sense disambiguation and its approaches. In: International Conference on Computing, Communication Automation, pp. 314–321 (2015). https://doi.org/10.1109/CCAA.2015.7148396

Sharma, D.K.: Hindi word sense disambiguation using cosine similarity. In: Proceedings of International Conference on ICT for Sustainable Development, pp. 801–808 (2016)

Sheth, M., Popat, S., Vyas, T.: Word sense disambiguation for Indian languages. In: International Conference on Emerging Research in Computing, Information, Communication and Applications, pp. 583–593 (2016)

Singh, S., Siddiqui, T.J.: Sense Annotated Hindi Corpus. In: 2016 International Conference on Asian Language Processing (IALP), pp. 22–25 (2016)

Singh, S., Siddiqui, T.J., Sharma, S.K.: Naïve Bayes classifier for Hindi word sense disambiguation. In: Proceedings of the 7th ACM India Computing Conference, pp. 1–8. (2014)

Sinha, M., Kumar, M., Pande, P., Kashyap, L., Bhattacharyya, P.: Hindi word sense disambiguation. In: International Symposium on Machine Translation, Natural Language Processing and Translation Support Systems, Delhi, India

Soni, V.K., Gopalaniî, D., Govil, M.C.: An adaptive approach for word sense disambiguation for the Hindi language. IOP Conf. Ser. Mater. Sci. Eng. **1131**(1), 12022 (2021)

Taghipour, K., Ng, H. T.: Semi-supervised word sense disambiguation using word embeddings in general and specific domains. In: Proceedings of the 2015 Conference of the North American Chapter of the Association for Computational Linguistics: Human Language Technologies, pp. 314–323 (2015)

Tripathi, P., Mukherjee, P., Hendre, M., Godse, M., Chakraborty, B.: Word Sense Disambiguation in Hindi Language Using Score-Based Modified Lesk Algorithm. International Journal of Computing and Digital Systems **10**, 2–20 (2020)

Vaishnav, Z.B., Sajja, P.S.: Knowledge-based approach for word sense disambiguation using genetic algorithm for Gujarati. In: Information and Communication Technology for Intelligent Systems, pp. 485–494. Springer (2019)

Wilks, Y., Slator, B.M., Guthrie, L.M.: Electric Words: Dictionaries, Computers, and Meanings. MIT Press, Cambridge, MA (1996)

Zhong, Z., Ng, H.T.: It makes sense: A wide-coverage word sense disambiguation system for free text. In: Proceedings of the ACL 2010 System Demonstrations, pp. 78–83 (2010)

Social Media Addiction: Analysis on Impact of Self-esteem and Recommending Methods to Reduce Addiction

Zarana Ramani[(✉)] and Hiteishi Diwanji

L.D. College of Engineering, Ahmedabad, India
zaranaramani@gmail.com, hiteishi@ldce.ac.in

Abstract. In today's world, everything moves towards virtual from the real world especially business, meetings, shopping, and connections to people. As technology makes life easier, everyone is slowly moving towards it. A platform that allows people to connect with other people all over the world is known as social media. Social media has a wide variety of features that make people stay on that platform. The use of social media has many benefits but excessive use of social media can degrade mental health, and physical health and can affect daily-functional life. Also, human mental health is closely connected to self-esteem. In this research, we have identified the impact of social media addiction on self-esteem and the impact of different variables such as notification response, age, gender, etc. on self-esteem and social media addiction. After analyzing the impact, we have suggested methods to reduce social media addiction based on all groups of people and based on similar social media addiction level groups of people using a collaborative filtering algorithm. As a result, we have found that there is a significant difference in self-esteem based on notification response, and a significant difference in social media addiction based on social media daily usage but there is no significant difference in social media addiction and self-esteem based on gender. Recommending methods to reduce social media addiction based on a similar group of people perform a bit better than all groups of people.

Keywords: Social media addiction · Self-esteem · Recommendation system · reduce social media addiction

1 Introduction

Over the last decade, there is numerous changes happening in smart technology. As technology innovates and updates, online platforms are becoming smarter day by day which leads to making people slaves to these platforms. Social media is a web and mobile based platform where individuals build a personal and professional network with other users, and communities and share their opinions, interests, and explore new things. As these platforms are easily accessible from everywhere, more people are started using them. According to global social media statistics research [1], up to July 2022, 63.1% people of the total population uses the internet, among them 59% of the total population

S. Rajagopal et al. (Eds.): ASCIS 2022, CCIS 1759, pp. 26–34, 2022.
https://doi.org/10.1007/978-3-031-23092-9_3

of the world actively used social media and the daily time spent on social media is on an average 2 h and 29 min. Total users of social media and time spent on social media are still increasing.

Nowadays, multiple social media platforms are available to use based on different use cases that all have some common features such as attractive designs, interactive, creating and sharing own content, indefinite scrolling, smart recommendation, and building a network with other users. Although online platforms open a large number of opportunities for business, career, and day-to-day life activities in a very convenient and easy way, there is more chance to depend on these technologies. Social media provides individuals with continuous rewards that they're not receiving in real life, so they end up engaging in the activity more and more. This continuous use eventually leads to engaging more in social networking. When social network users repeat this cyclical pattern of relieving undesirable moods with social media use, the level of psychological dependency on social media increases [2].

Social media addiction is a behavioral addiction that is characterized as being overly concerned about social media, driven by an uncontrollable urge to log on to or use social media, and devoting so much time and effort to social media that it impairs other important life areas. In the non-virtual world, it's estimated that people talk about themselves around 30 to 40% of the time, in the virtual world people talk about themselves a staggering 80% of the time [2].

Being more active on social media can lead to physical diseases such as headaches, back, and joints pain due to unusual sitting positions, and eye strain. Unintentionally, staying in the same positions and focusing on screens for a long time without any fruitful work would also create mental health problems, that can affect behaviour, mood, concentration power, perception, self-esteem, life satisfaction, and more [3]. So, this study explores the impact of social media usage, and notification response on self-esteem and social media addiction based on different age groups and identifying relationship between social media addiction and self-esteem. Also, this study represents the recommendation of remedies to reduce or prevent social media addiction according to the social media addiction level of a particular user using a machine learning algorithm.

2 Related Work

Addiction is mainly related to using drugs and alcohol. In this digital era, as the number of smartphone users increases, it also increases the risk of addiction to technology especially addiction to social media [4]. As we all know that things are moving from offline to online, and excessive use of online tools can impact physical health as well as mental health that is proven by different studies.

One study is shown that social media addiction has a negative impact on self-esteem and social-avoidance and distress [5]. Some researchers in their study [6–9] pointed out that social media addiction has a positive correlation with depression, anxiety, and stress and a negative correlation with mental health. In the last decade, research conducted to find the effect of social media addiction on academic performance in different fields of students. The results from these studies concluded that academic performance is negatively impacted by social media addiction [6, 10, 11]. Another study [12], showed that based on the type of use of social media has a different impact on social media addiction levels. Their research proved that entertainment use has more chance to lead to addiction and social use can reduce the impact of social media addiction.

The previous studies showed the direct and indirect impact of social media addiction on different variables and the effect of some mediators too by different analysis techniques yet very few research towards the reduction or prevention the effect of social media addiction. For that purpose, we created a recommendation logic that can help to reduce the effect of social media addiction based on addiction level and that helps to make an individual's life healthier at the physical and mental level.

3 Measures

3.1 Bergen Social Media Addiction Scale (BSMAS) [5]

The BSMAS consists of six items that are measured using 5 standard responses—1: very rarely, 2: rarely, 3: sometimes, 4: often, and 5: very often. The BSMAS score range is from 6 to 30. According to the score, it is interpreted as follows: 1: Low Addiction (score less than 12), 2: Moderate Addiction (score between 12 to 19), 3: High risk of being addicted (score more than 19) [13], 4: High addiction (More than 3 items scored more than 3 out of 6 items).

3.2 Rosenberg Self-esteem Scale (RSES) [5]

RSES has 10 questions of which 5 are positive and 5 are negative. The RSES items are measured using 4 standard responses – 0: strongly disagree, 1: disagree, 2: agree, 3: strongly disagree for positive questions, and 3: strongly disagree, 2: disagree, 1: agree, 0: strongly disagree for negative questions. The RSES score range is from 0 to 30. The score is interpreted as follows: 1: Low self-esteem (score less than 15), 2: Moderate self-esteem (score between 15 to 25), and 3: High self-esteem (More than 25).

3.3 Recommendation Methods [14, 15]

We have collected ratings for 17 methods which are taken from the internet and have ratings range 1 to 5 based on feasibility, effectiveness, and implementation complexity to reduce social media usage according to users' opinions. This rating is interpreted as 0: No preference, 1: ineffective/complex to 5: most effective/feasible/easy. The methods used for recommendation are defined in tips_data.csv [16].

3.4 Dataset Collection 1

We have collected data through google Forms which includes Bergen social media addiction scale (to calculate social media addiction score), Rosenberg self-esteem scale (to calculate self-esteem score), and users' information like age, gender, social media usage, etc. For the collection of data, we shared google form among students, faculties, and friends who are daily using social media. In total, we have collected 216 samples, of which 122 were male (56.49%) and 94 were female (43.51%). The collected data have a raw value which is converted to standard value according to likert scale mapping to use in this research.

Cronbach's alpha is used to check the internal consistency of a survey. The survey used in our study has Cronbach's alpha is 0.699 which is acceptable for BSMAS and for RSES Cronbach's alpha value is 0.711 which is good. Descriptive statistics for social media addiction (SMA) and self-esteem (SE) are displayed in Table 1. Skewness and kurtosis values suggested that data were normally distributed, thus we applied linear regression for identifying the relationship between these two. Detailed questionaries, collected data, and preprocessed data are available on Kaggle [16].

Table 1. Descriptive Statistics of SMA and SE from dataset collection 1

Variable	n	M	SD	Skewness	Kurtosis
SMA	216	14.53	4.32	0.272	0.168
SE	216	19.03	4.14	0.047	0.622

3.5 Dataset Collection 2

We have collected the data through an online survey for user characteristics (age, gender, and daily social media usage), questionaries of BSMAS (to calculate social media addiction score), and ratings of recommended methods. In this dataset, we have collected 55 users' data for 17 methods which are mentioned in Sect. 3.3 that can reduce social media addiction. So, a total of 877 ratings are there after preprocessing collected dataset. The Questionaries used for this dataset collection, collected data, and preprocessed datasets which include users, ratings, and tips datasets that are used in current research are available on Kaggle [16].

4 Proposed Methodology

Our proposed system mainly focuses on two points:

1. Analyze the relationship between social media addiction and self-esteem using regression algorithms.
2. Suggesting methods that can reduce social media addiction using user-based collaborative filtering (user-based CF) and user-based CF with similar levels of addiction.

4.1 Statistical Analysis

1. Dataset collection 1 is used to analyze and find the relationship between self-esteem and social media addiction.

2. Next step, that we performed is data preprocessing which includes calculating the social media addiction score and self-esteem score based on Likert scale values. Also, assigned labels to the level of social media addiction and self-esteem based on social media addiction score and self-esteem score according to mentioned in Sects. 3.1 and 3.2.
3. After that, we applied different statistical tests to check the significance of different variables. We have applied a t-test to check the significance of the variable that is divided into two groups. For the variable that has more than two groups, applied the rank based the Krushkal-Wallis test to check the significance.
4. In step 4, we have done the multiple linear regression analysis between social media addiction and self-esteem. In this regression analysis, we used independent variables social media addiction, age, social media usage, notification response, and dependent variable self-esteem.
5. The last step is to evaluate the regression model using an R-squared value.

4.2 Recommendation System

1. Dataset collection 2 is used to create a recommendation engine model.
2. Using this data, calculated social media addiction scores and addiction labels of users for the collected dataset. Then, Split the dataset into user-item ratings and user personal information to use in the next steps. Also, the Rating dataset is split into train and test datasets.
3. The next step is to apply the recommendation logic and the steps are as follows:

   a. Find the social media addiction level of the particular user.
   b. Get a set of users (similar users) with the same social media addiction level. (skip this step for user-based CF)
   c. Find cosine similarity of a current user with all similar user Cosine similarity between users X and Y

   $$sim(X, Y) = \frac{\sum_{i=1}^{n} Xi * Yi}{\sqrt{\sum_{i=1}^{n} Xi^2} \sqrt{\sum_{i=1}^{n} Yi^2}} \tag{1}$$

   where Xi is the rating score for item X by user i and Yi is the rating score for item Y by user i

4. Find the Rating score of similar users for a particular item
5. Remove the Rating score which has 0 value (Ratings not given) and cosine similarity values according to the removed rating score
6. Predict the user rating for a particular item using the sum of rating methods. Calculate the rating score of user u for item X using

   $$R_{u,X} = \frac{\sum_{i=1}^{n} sim(u, i) * R_{i,x}}{\sum_{i=1}^{n} sim(u, i)} \tag{2}$$

   where i represents the user from the filtered user and Ri,x represents the rating for item X by user i.

7. Evaluate the model using the Root Mean Squared Error (RMSE) score

$$RMSE = \sqrt{\frac{\sum_{i=1}^{n}(P_i - O_i)^2}{n}} \qquad (3)$$

where Pi is the predicted value of i and Oi is the actual value of i.

8. And the last step is to recommend 2 methods with the highest ratings that can reduce social media addiction.

NOTE: If the user is new and doesn't have any ratings then find the average ratings for each time and recommend 2 methods with the highest average ratings.

5 Results and Discussion

5.1 Statistical Analysis

We have collected a total of 216 samples which have 122 male (56.49%) and 94 female (43.51%) samples. After calculating the social media addiction score and self-esteem score, we have given labels to samples for the same. we have identified the relationship between social media addiction and self-esteem and the results show that a weak negative correlation exists between social media addiction and self-esteem. The R-squared score for this regression analysis is 0.214. Results from the statistical significance t-test and Krushkal-Wallis test are shown in the table (Table 2, 3, and 4).

Table 2. Statistical significance in SMA and SE by gender.

Variable	Category	N	M	SD	t-value
Gender					
SMA	Male	122	14.17	4.30	−1.398
	Female	94	15.0	4.33	
SE	Male	122	18.97	4.28	−0.229
	Female	94	19.10	3.97	

Table 3. Statistical significance in SMA and SE by age, social media usage time, notification response

Variable	Category	h-value
Age		
SMA	13–18, 19–25, 26–35, > 35	4.517
SE		6.143

(continued)

Table 3. (*continued*)

Variable	Category	h-value
Social media daily usage		
SMA	Less than an hour, 1–2 h, 2–3 h, 3–4 h, >4 h	37.764*
SE		5.098
Notification response		
SMA SE	Immediately, Immediately only if it's important, I don't respond if it's not important, As soon as possi-ble, Whenever took a phone, I put off the notification	7.436 12.153*

Table 4. Performance measurement for collaborative filtering algorithms.

Algorithm	RMSE
User based CF	1.355
User based CF with similar level of addiction	1.334

Results of the t-test showed that there is no significate difference in social media addiction and self-esteem by gender. And, in Krushkal-Wallis test results show that there is a significant difference in self-esteem according to a group of people based on notification response and a significant difference in social media addiction according to a group of people based on social media daily usage.

5.2 Recommendation System

We have applied two algorithms to predict ratings of tips and recommend the top 2 tips to the users. In the first algorithm, we predicted the ratings based on finding similarities between all users, and in another algorithm, we filtered the users based on addiction level and then recommended tips by finding similarities between groups of people with the same level of addiction. The performance is measured by calculating RMSE according to Eq. 3.

The results are shown that recommended tips for reducing social media addiction based on a similar group of people have a bit fewer error than simple user-based recommendations.

6   Conclusion

Even though many works have been done on the impact of social media addiction on various mental health factors such as stress, anxiety, depression, etc., day-to-day life activities such as job/studies, etc., and on physical health but there is very few research available that can allow users to reduce or prevent from addiction. We have applied multiple linear regression to find out the relationship between social media addiction and self-esteem and found that they have a weakly negative correlation with each other. Also, responding to notifications has a significant difference in people's self-esteem and daily usage of social media has a significant difference in social media addiction levels. To reduce social media addiction levels or to prevent being addicted to social media, we have created a recommendation engine model that will suggest methods based on social media addiction levels. And the results have shown that the recommendation model with a group of a similar level of addiction users (RMSE 1.334) is slightly better than the recommendation model with all users (RMSE 1.355). In the future, these results can be verified by the defining group based on notification responses or daily social media usage. The recommended methods can also be collected from professional psychiatrists for more effective results. Even this study can be conducted as longitudinal research to find the reliability and effectiveness of different methods.

References

1. Global Social Media Statistics Research Summary (2022). https://www.smartinsights.com/social-media-marketing/social-media-strategy/new-global-social-media-research/
2. Social Media Addiction—Addiction Center. https://www.addictioncenter.com/drugs/social-media-addiction/
3. Ramani Hiteishi Diwanji, Z.: A review on impact of social media addiction. Multidiscip. Int. Res. J. Gujarat Technol. Univ. **4**, 34 (2022)
4. Abbasi, G.A., Jagaveeran, M., Goh, Y.N., Tariq, B.: The impact of type of content use on smartphone addiction and academic performance: Physical activity as moderator. Technol. Soc. **64**, 101521 (2020). https://doi.org/10.1016/j.techsoc.2020.101521
5. Ahmed, O., Nayeem Siddiqua, S.J., Alam, N., Griffiths, M.D.: The mediating role of problematic social media use in the relationship between social avoidance/distress and selfesteem. Technol. Soc., **64**, 101485 (2020). https://doi.org/10.1016/j.techsoc.2020.101485
6. Hou, Y., Xiong, D., Jiang, T., Song, L., Wang, Q.: Social media addiction: Its impact, mediation, and intervention. Cyberpsychology **13**(1) (2019 https://doi.org/10.5817/CP2 019-1-4
7. Malak, M.Z., Shuhaiber, A.H., Al-amer, R.M., Abuadas, M.H., Aburoomi, R.J.: Correlation between psychological factors, academic performance and social media addiction: model-based testing. Behav. Inf. Technol. **41**(8), 1583–1595 (2021)
8. Sujarwoto, Saputri, R.A.M., Yumarni, T.: Social media addiction and mental health among university students during the COVID-19 pandemic in Indonesia. Int. J. Ment. Health Addict. (2021). https://doi.org/10.1007/s11469-021-00582-3
9. Haand, R., Shuwang, Z.: The relationship between social media addiction and depression: a quantitative study among university students in Khost, Afghanistan". Int. J. Adolesc. Youth **25**(1), 780–786 (2020). https://doi.org/10.1080/02673843.2020.1741407
10. Bhandarkar, A.M., Pandey, A.K., Nayak, R., Pujary, K., Kumar, A.: Impact of social media on the academic performance of undergraduate medical students. Med. J. Armed Forces India **77**, S37–S41 (2021). https://doi.org/10.1016/j.mjafi.2020.10.021
11. Wan Pa, W.A.M., Mahmud, M.S., Zainal, M.S.: Implications of social media addiction on academic performance among generation z student-athletes during COVID-19 lockdown. Int. J. Learn. Teach. Educ. Res. **20**(8), 194–209 (2021). https://doi.org/10.26803/IJLTER.20.8.12

12. Zhao, L.: The impact of social media use types and social media addiction on subjective well-being of college students: A comparative analysis of addicted and non-addicted students. Comput. Hum. Behav. Rep. **4**, 100122 (2021). https://doi.org/10.1016/j.chbr.2021.100122

13. Lin, C.-Y., Broström, A., Griffiths, M.D., Pakpour, A.H.: Psychometric validation of the Persian Bergen social media addiction scale using classic test theory and Rasch models. (2017). https://doi.org/10.1556/2006.6.2017.071

14. How can you recover from social media addiction?|Digital|Bridging Science And Life: https://bridgingscienceandlife.com/social-media-addiction-recovery/

15. How to reduce social media use—12 simple proven steps: https://unscreen.org/how-toreduce-social-media-use/

16. SMA22: Analysis and reducing social media addiction|Kaggle: https://www.kaggle.com/datasets/ad09f5f9fc2f57421926a9295da5ae6e35e1ea697297969f26c8df4b7bffe89c

A Combined Method for Document Image Enhancement Using Image Smoothing, Gray-Level Reduction and Thresholding

Prashant Paikrao[✉], Dharmpal Doye, Milind Bhalerao, and Madhav Vaidya

Shri Guru Gobind Singhaji Institute of Engineering and Technology, Nanded, India
{2019pec201,dddoye}@sggs.ac.in

Abstract. Document digitization is becoming popular with its enhanced portability, efficient storage, processability and easy retrieval. Document images acquired using the scanning process are filled with additional noise. These noises in document images are associated with document paper quality, the typing machine or printer, or the scanner during the scanning process. Aging, folded corners, stains, shadow-through, and bleed-through noises are also present in this process. During digitization, these noises may get amplified and make the digital representation further noisy. Noise removal methods, techniques, or algorithms refer to the process of removing noises from digital images utilizing image processing, image analysis, or filtering approaches. The transmission, scanning, and aging processes individually or in combination could lead to introducing noise in images. So, here speckle noise is considered for modeling the noise during transmission, Gaussian noise during scanning procedures considering the thermal radiations of the scanning mechanism, and the salt and pepper noise (impulse valued noise) for representing the aging phenomenon. To eliminate a certain kind of noise, a particular noise removal technique uses a special kind of filter. Based on the aforementioned noises, a combined method for noise reduction from scanned document images is proposed. The result of the proposed method is presented considering the resultant image quality. The metrics like Mean Square Error, Signal-to-Noise Ratio, Peak Signal to Noise Ratio, and Structural Similarity Index Metrics are used to evaluate the quality of resultant image.

Keywords: Document images · Noise removal · Image enhancement · Conserve smoothing · Gray level reduction · Otsu's thresholding algorithm

1 Introduction

Nowadays, with the increase in use of e-resources, it has become essential to transform paper documents into usable digital versions. Paper document can be converted to digital format by scanning them. Digital documents are present almost everywhere, to further enhance advantages of digitization are images needed to be compressed using suitable compression technique. The presence of noise in image will become significance after any digital process like compression. This resultant noise amount decides whether any

© The Author(s), under exclusive license to Springer Nature Switzerland AG 2022
S. Rajagopal et al. (Eds.): ASCIS 2022, CCIS 1759, pp. 35–48, 2022.
https://doi.org/10.1007/978-3-031-23092-9_4

enhancement or reconstruction technique will be effective or otherwise [1]. Partial of almost entire information in image may be lost if the noise is noise paid sufficient attention prior to applying any image processing operation. Noise is also the most vital factors to consider when processing digital images; it is crucial to remove or minimize noise or degradation that will be carried through transmission, storage, and retrieval. The undesirable part(s) of the document image known as noise is likely to increase the cost of transmission and storage because they take up valuable resources. The scanned document images frequently suffer from degradations including uneven contrast, show through, interfering strokes, background spots, humidity absorbed by paper in various locations, and uneven backgrounds. These days digital images of documents are acquired using image acquisition tools like digital cameras, mobile phone cameras or scanners. While capturing or acquiring images, these image acquisition devices may introduce undesired elements into the images [8]. In such a scenario, noise reduction is necessary to accomplish the image compression and subsequent objectives of useful portability, storage and retrieval of the document images.

2 Types of Noises

Digitization of documents involves its scanning using digital scanners and cameras. Some of the documents to be digitized are of poor quality, and the illumination conditions or scanning process may also be responsible for introduction of noise during digitization. The possible reasons for the introduction of noise are poor paper and ink quality used, ageing in case of old documents, an older printing process or mechanism, or the scanning equipment itself. The presence of noise affects image quality, noise removal is an important low-level operation in digital image preprocessing [10]. It can appear in the foreground or background of an image, the noises generated before or during digitization process are discussed here. Some noises considered in scanned document images are as follows.

2.1 Speckle Noise

The pixels in grayscale images are affected by this multiplicative noise, which is most evident in low level luminance images [3]. Image enhancement is an essential lowlevel task in image processing to reduce speckle noise before performing subsequent higher-level task like edge detection, image segmentation, object detection, etc. Let I(m, n) represent the noiseless image and O(m, n) is its corresponding distorted image. According to the multiplicative noise model the relation is shown using Eq. 1.

$$O(m, n) = I(m, n) \times N(m, n) \tag{1}$$

where N (m, n) represents the speckle noise and the multiplication here is point multiplication.

The grey levels statistics of an image is affected by the speckle noise. This influence of speckle noise on the grey values increases with speckle noise variation, making it more difficult to recover the original image with less or no noise. To show the effect of speckle noise with variances of 0.1 and 0.9 on the text image, the respective histograms are shown in Fig. 1. The variations in histogram and the effect of noise addition are evident here. The noise is closely linked with the high-frequency content of image, i.e. its detail features. As a result, maintaining a balance between minimizing noise as much as possible while maintaining the image information intact becomes difficult.

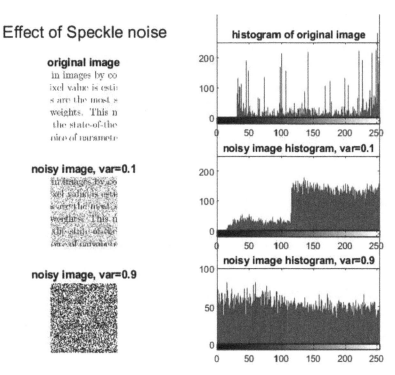

Fig. 1. Effect of Speckle Noise on image Histogram

2.2 Gaussian Noise

Gaussian noise is also referred to as electronic noise since it is originated in amplifiers or detectors. The discrete nature of warm object radiation and the thermal vibration of atoms are considered as parameters to study its mechanisms that cause Gaussian noise. Gaussian noise typically distorts grey levels in digital images. As a result, the histogram of the image or the probability density function (PDF) of Gaussian noise gives its basic nature and characteristics. This statistical noise, also known as the Gaussian distribution, is present in an image with a PDF equal to the normal distribution. The noise is referred to as white Gaussian noise when the values at any pair of times are statistically independent and uncorrelated. The formula of Gaussian noise may be given as below

$$p_{G(Z)} = \frac{1}{\sigma\sqrt{2\pi}} e^{\frac{(z-\mu)^2}{2\sigma^2}} \tag{2}$$

In the above Eq. 2, 'p' is the rate of Gaussian noise. It depends on the standard deviation and mean value. The statistical noise with its PDF termed as the Gaussian distribution. Gaussian noise was not considered in digital image processing earlier, although it is there most of the time when looking at the intensity of the images and the amount of error. But here the mechanism used for digitization is prone to this kind of noise. To better explain the influence of Gaussian noise with variances of 0.01 and 0.5 on the text image is shown in Fig. 2, by means of variations in the histogram.

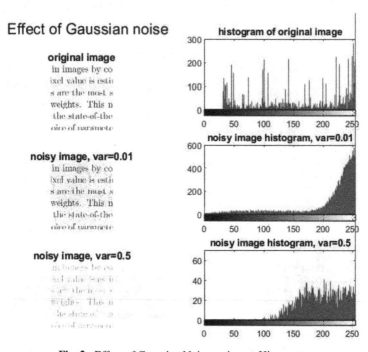

Fig. 2. Effect of Gaussian Noise on image Histogram

2.3 Salt and Pepper Noise

Salt and pepper noise, which may be caused by dirt and stains on the document paper, might appear in a document image during the conversion process. While one or more pixels may be contaminated by this noise, it is considered that they are very tiny and smaller than the size of the textual elements. Generally, to eliminate this noise, simple filters like median are effective and used, but if the noise is more widespread, techniques like k-fill or other morphological operators should be used [11]. Printed documents can be found in a wide variety of writing inks. While the pepper noise results in spurious representations of textual characters in the document images, the salt noise appears to be a lack of ink. Because noisy pixels are alternately adjusted to the minimum or maximum intensity values, images distorted by impulse noises, such as salt and pepper noise, appear "salt and pepper" [12]. Unaffected pixels, however, always maintain their original state. One can formulate it using the following mathematical expression, as mentioned in Eq. 3.

$$I(m, n) \xrightarrow{yields} S_{\min} \text{ with probability q, } S_{\max} \text{ with probability q, } u(m, n) \text{ with probability } 1 - (p + q)$$
(3)

where, respectively, The noisy image and the noise-free image are denoted by I(m,n) and O(m,n), respectively. The range [Smin, Smax] indicates u(m,n). The image intensity value ranges between [0,1], making Smin = 0 denote pepper noise and Smax = 1 represent salt noise, can be used; the probability p+q indicates the quantity of salt and pepper noise. Using modifications to the histogram, Fig. 3 shows the impact of Salt and Pepper noise on the text picture with variances of 0.01 and 0.5.

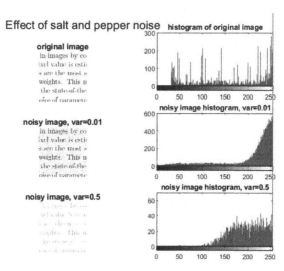

Fig. 3. Effect of Salt and Pepper Noise on image Histogram

3 Proposed Work for Document Image Enhancement

Image enhancement is the initial pre-processing step in image processing. Real-time document images may include one or all common distortions like contrast variation, blur, salt and pepper noise, and others. Image enhancement tasks are commonly used to improve the perception of the image quality through spatial or frequency domain. Direct pixel level manipulations are carried over in spatial domain methods, whereas in the frequency domain, changes occur indirectly through transformations. Process of enhancing the low-level blur in an image is a difficult task. Enhancement of lowlevel distortion in an images using existing image smoothing techniques, as the mean filter, median filter, conservative smoothing, and proposed modified conservative smoothing is studied here. The techniques of thresholding and grey level reduction are then used to further improve the readability of the textual contents in the image.

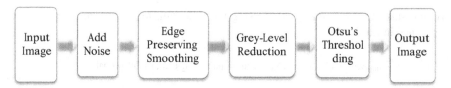

Fig. 4. Flow of proposed scheme for document image enhancement

As shown in Fig. 4. The process of adding noise individually or combinedly is performed. Then as a part of proposed methodology to reduce the noise added the first step of image smoothing is carried out using Edge Preserving Smoothing method like Conserve Smoothing (CS) first, and second time using Modifies Conserve Smoothing (MCS). This smoothened image is fed for Grey-level reduction process, which is developed based on the color level reduction algorithm proposed in [21]. Finally, the Otsu's thresholding algorithm is applied, and the output image is produced. This resultant image and input image are compared by various image quality metrics and the performance of the CS and MCS are recorded.

3.1 Edge Preserving Image Smoothing

Noise in the digital image can be minimized or suppressed by smoothing. The smoothing techniques rely on low-pass filters, which traverse an image and modify the central pixel value with the mean or median of the surrounding pixels [2]. Point processing and neighbourhood processing are the two spatial domain techniques that are more effective for real-time image processing [6]. The point processing method directly modifies each pixel to enhance the image. Each pixel in an image is modified with a mathematical function in neighbourhood processing or spatial filtering to improve the image [4]. Correlation and convolution are two crucial concepts in spatial filtering. Correlation measures the degree of similarity between two images by moving the kernel over entire pixels in an image and performing the predetermined transformation in each pixel position. Image convolution is like correlation except that the spatial mask is rotated by 180° before processing. Image convolution is frequently used to recovering from effects (such as blurring, edge sharpening, etc.) in an image. Combining a mathematical function with a convolution mask is the fundamental idea behind spatial filtering. It is mostly used to remove extraneous or superfluous information from images. In case of spatial domain filtering, the filters used can be linear or nonlinear. Linear filters modify the value of the targeted pixel by using precise linear combinations of surrounding pixels, on the other hand the non-linear filters, uses arbitrary non-linear combinations of surrounding pixels. The most fundamental linear spatial filter, mean filtering is used to smooth images for noise reduction by minimizing the variability in pixel values. The idea of spatial convolution is used in this method. The filtering kernel, which has dimensions of 3×3, 5×5, and so forth, slides over the entire image. The central pixel value of the current cell of image pixels is changed to a new value that represents the mean of its eight adjacent pixels and centre pixel values. This technique is very effective at reducing noise, but at the same time high frequency information in the image is lost at greater extents. If a smaller size kernel is used, undesirable local features may get added and when big size kernel is applied, some important features may get lost. The mathematical computations used to replace this centre value of the kernel might vary, and changes to the replacement criterion should be made while keeping in mind the loss of image information and energy compaction, etc.

3.1.1   Conserve Smoothing

The noise is reduced by the smoothing process, but the sensitive details are also lost, and the object boundaries are also un-sharped. A solution to this challenge, particularly for document images, is to use an edge-preserving smoothing technique (adaptive mean filter), where the degree of blurring for each pixel is determined after acquiring local information in its 3×3 neighbourhood (Harwood et al., 1987; Perona and Malik, 1990). Here, a fast and effective Edge Preserving Spatial Filtering (EPSF) algorithm is applied to complete the work.

3.1.2   Modified Conserve Smoothing

Here, the centre pixel replacement policy in conserve smoothing is changed slightly, the results obtained shows good edge preserving ability. Following Fig. 5., shows the outcome of using various smoothing algorithm on a test image (a textual portion of a document image). It is evident that the output of the modified conserve smoothing algorithm is more readable than other outputs. The saturation of noise is less than the conservative smoothing method and the granularity of the text symbols is more than that of the median filter, because of edge preserving nature of this algorithm.

Fig. 5. Result of various smoothing algorithms

3.2 Gray Level Reduction

Reducing the number of grey levels in an image is crucial for implementing image compression, segmentation, presentation, and transmission on it. A common technique for reducing the number of grey levels in a digital image is multi-thresholding. Multi-thresholding establishes the proper threshold values that set the boundaries of the grey-level classes of images, by using the data from the image histogram. Multithresholding techniques can be classified into three categories. They are zerocrossing in second order derivatives, histogram based, and entropy based. Other processes depend on grey-level error diffusion or nearest-grey-level merging. Each pixel in the image changes its value to the grey level in a palette that matches some typical neighbouring pixel the closest in the nearest-grey-level procedures. Dithering procedures serve as the foundation for error diffusion strategies. The difference between actual pixel values and true values is referred to as the "error". All the low pass filtering-based techniques presented here are based on thresholding the pixel intensities of the surrounding grey levels. This leads to a procedure that is like averaging, which reduces important edge features of image. The colour level quantization method is used to colour spaces in colour images; it decreases the number of distinct colours in an image, typically with the goal of making the new image as visually as the original image as possible. Most of the conventional approaches consider colour quantization as a problem of point clustering in three dimensions, where the points correspond to colours present in the original image and the three axes to the three colour channels. This view is considered by the proposed approach for grey level image. It uses neighbouring grey-level values of the pixel and apply clustering on it considering the new centroid as average of neighbouring values. All the pixels should be in one cluster if the 8-neighbours are considered, and they should follow the intra-class and inter-class similarity criteria.

The proposed document grey-level reduction technique consists of the following steps:

Step 1. Application of Edge preserving smoothing filter

Step 2. Edge detection of image regions

Step 3. Gray level subsampling

Step 4. Tentative grey-level reduction

Step 5. Mean-shift procedure

Step 6. Final grey-level reduction

Figure 6, shows the output of the grey-level reduction scheme for a representative test image, the same algorithm is applied on the ten other text images and the grey-levels reduced by the said algorithm without introducing perceptual difference are listed in Table 1.

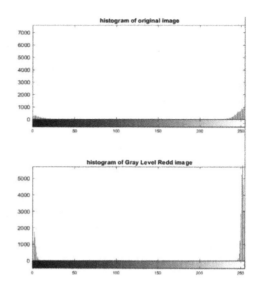

original image

This is a test text file
used for testing the
RLE and BWT
combination over a
sample text image.

- P L Paikrao
Research Scholar
SGGSIE&T, Nanded

Gray Level Redd image

This is a test text file
used for testing the
RLE and BWT
combination over a
sample text image.

- P L Paikrao
Research Scholar
SGGSIE&T, Nanded

Fig. 6. Effect of image grey-level reduction

Table 1. Effect of Grey-level reduction algorithm

Sr. No.	Name of the image [256, 256]	Original gray levels	Reduced gray levels
1	TextDocument1.png	256	128
2	TextDocument2.jpg	256	126
3	TextDocument3.jpg	256	127
4	TextDocument4.jpg	256	127
5	TextDocument5.jpg	229	113
6	TextDocument6.jpg	256	127
7	TextDocument7.png	152	71
8	TextDocument8.jpg	256	125
9	TextDocument9.jpg	256	127
10	TextDocument10.jpg	256	127

3.3   Image Thresholding Using Otsu's Method

Using a intensity threshold value, every pixel in the image is assigned to image object or the image background, called as image thresholding. As a result, each image pixel is either classified as a background point or an object point [5]. In many image processing applications, the grey levels of the pixels that belong to the object and the background substantially differ from each other. Thresholding then turns into a simple technique for separating objects from the background. Map processing, where lines, legends, and characters can be found; document image analysis, where the goal is to extract printed characters, logos, graphic content, or musical scores, etc. [9]. By continually running through all the plausible threshold values, Otsu's thresholding method determines the spread for the pixel levels on either side in the foreground and background [7]. Finding the value below which the sum of the foreground pixels and background pixels is at its minimum is the objective of this exercise [13]. As a result, thresholding is frequently used to distinguish between light and dark areas. This greyscale image is converted into a binary image by setting all of the pixels below threshold to ZERO and all of the pixels above the threshold value to ONE. The thresholding of images, which can be thought of as a more extreme form of grey-level quantization, is its most straightforward example. Assume that a grey-level image 'I' has 'K' existing grey levels, including 0, 1, 2,... ,K 1. Let us define an integer threshold, 'Th', that has value between 0, 1, 2, . . . , K 1. Each image pixel value in 'I' is compared with the threshold, 'Th', during this process. A binary value is selected, that represent the value of the pixel under consideration, in the output binary image 'O', based on this comparison.

If O(m, n) is result of thresholding of I(m, n) at selected global threshold 'Th'. Generalized Algorithm:

1. Process the input image using smoothing and grey level reduction algorithms
2. Obtain image histogram
3. Compute the threshold value 'Th'

    (i)   calculate the histogram-based intensity level probabilities
    (ii)   initialize probabilities and means
    (iii) iterate over possible thresholds
    (iv)   update the values of probabilities and means
    (v)   calculate within-class variance
    (vi)   calculate between-class varience

4. Replace image pixels to '1', where pixel value is greater than 'Th' and to '0' in the rest of the cases (Fig. 7).

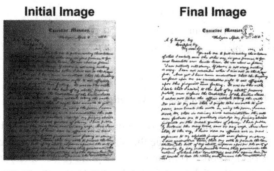

Fig. 7. Outcome of Otsu's image thresholding algorithm

4   Experimentation and Results

This set of steps mentioned in method of document image enhancement is implemented using MATLAB programming. Hundred document images, ten each of ten different classes were used for the experimentation. The results with respect to the considered image quality metric are presented in this section. All the three types of noises including speckle noise (var=0.1 to 0.9), gaussian noise (var=0.01 to 0.5), and salt and pepper noise (var=0.01 to 0.5) noise were added to the set of images individually and a combination of all these noises was also applied. The various groupings considering noise variance levels also made to create such 10 classes of noisy images. Then, the combination scheme consisting of edge preserving smoothing, color level reduction based grey-level reduction and the Otsu's thresholding are performed one after other. The result of proposed method is presented considering the resultant image quality metrics like Mean Square Error (MSE), Signal to Noise Ratio (SNR), Peak Signal to Noise Ratio (PSNR) and Structural Similarity Index Metrics (SSIM). Tables 2, 3, and 4 shows the performance of proposed method considering one noise at a time with varied variance/saturation, for Gaussian Noise, Speckle Noise, and Salt-and-Pepper Noise respectively. Whereas Table 5 shows the performance of algorithm on the combinational noise. The 7th row in each of the table almost shows the promising values of metrics and Fig. 8. Shows the overall result of the method, which signifies the perceptual improvement.

Table 2. Gaussian noise: (Smoothing + GrayLevelReduction + Thresholding)

SN	Operation	MSE	SNR	PSNR	SSIM
1	Noisy Image	337.04	22.0828	22.9339	0.5557
2	Conserve Smoothing (CS)	808.93	18.3208	19.1039	0.6078
3	CS + Gray Level Reduction (GLR)	757.21	18.6573	19.4285	0.8103
4	CS + GLR + Thresholding (Th)	797.34	18.7433	19.6996	0.9166
5	Modified CS (MCS)	263.84	23.1648	23.9750	0.6105
6	MCS + GLR	121.86	26.5385	27.3339	0.8205
7	MCS + GLR + Th	30.88	32.7452	33.2347	0.9823

Table 3. Salt and pepper noise: (Smoothing + GrayLevelReduction + Thresholding)

SN	Operation	MSE	SNR	PSNR	SSIM
1	Noisy Image	16147	15.4212	16.0499	0.5107
2	CS	13019	16.5057	16.9850	0.7968
3	CS + GLR	12384	16.6676	17.2024	0.8003
4	CS + GLR + Th	12051	16.7863	17.3207	0.8119
5	MCS	641.64	19.5467	20.0579	0.8521
6	MCS + GLR	627.53	19.5999	20.1544	0.8540
7	MCS + GLR + Th	621.52	19.6444	20.1962	0.8625

Table 4. Spekle noise: (Smoothing + GrayLevelReduction + Thresholding)

SN	Operation	MSE	SNR	PSNR	SSIM
1	Noisy Image	14381	15.2452	16.5529	0.4059
2	CS	14387	15.4172	16.5512	0.4098
3	CS + GLR	11229	16.5577	17.6275	0.5314
4	CS + GLR + Th	10315	16.4735	15.2718	0.7490
5	MCS	12304	15.9787	17.2305	0.4216
6	MCS + GLR	862	17.5630	18.7733	0.4714
7	MCS + GLR + Th	11477	17.4051	17.8205	0.5930

Table 5. Combination of all noises: (Smoothing + GrayLevelReduction + Thresholding)

SN	Operation	MSE	SNR	PSNR	SSIM
1	Noisy Image	12530	16.64	17.14	0.4322
2	CS	13342	15.31	16.68	0.4753
3	CS + GLR	11720	16.82	17.15	0.6412
4	CS + GLR + Th	11680	17.97	18.23	0.8737
5	MCS	778	18.01	19.12	0.4891
6	MCS + GLR	521	19.46	20.83	0.6217
7	MCS + GLR + Th	183	24.85	25.16	0.9415

Fig. 8. The result of combining smoothing, grey level reduction and thresholding

5   Conclusions and Future Work

The process of noise removal is indeed lossy and may lose some important attribute in the image, keeping this loss minimal and enhancing the perceptual quality (readability in our case) of the image is a challenge. The quality of resultant image is evaluated using quality metrics like MSE, SNR, PSNR and SSIM. It is evident from the results that the proposed method had succeeded up to significant extends. The results of document pre-processing shows that the Edge Preserving Image Smoothing gives better results than the traditional averaging and mean filtering approach. The grey-level reduction based on color level quantization is a better alternative to the other grey-level quantization approaches. The Otsu's method also works fine, it involves fast and simple calculations that are seldomly affected by the brightness and contrast of input image and lead to satisfactory image thresholding. Especially the text part of the document images is very well processed and made more readable. The proposed combinational algorithm gives satisfactory results over the images affected with noises like Speckle noise, Gaussian noise, salt-and-pepper noise, and its mixture. For the natural noise that gets added through various unmodelled processes, an advance algorithm may be required.

References

1. Hu, L., Hu, Z., Bauer, P., Harris, T.J., Allebach, J.P.: Document image quality assessment with relaying reference to determine minimum readable resolution for compression. In Electronic Imaging, pp. 323–331 (2020)
2. Yamaguchi, Y., Ichiro, Y., Kondo, Y.: Proposal of edge-preserving, image noise reduction filter for using l2-norm. Eng. Proc. **11**(1), 27 (2021)
3. Arulpandy, P., Pricilla, M.T.: Speckle noise reduction and image segmentation based on a modified mean filter. Comput. Assis. Methods Eng. **27**(4), 221–239 (2020)
4. Chen, L.: Fu, G: Structure-preserving image smoothing with semantic cues. Vis. Comput. **36**(10), 2017–2027 (2020)
5. Mustafa, W.A., Mydin, M., Abdul Kader, M.: Binarization of document image using optimum threshold modification. J. Phys.: Conf. Ser. **1019**(1), 12022 (2018)
6. Prabha, D.S., Satheesh Kumar, J.: Performance analysis of image smoothing methods for low level of distortion. In: 2016 IEEE International Conference on Advances in Computer Applications (ICACA), pp. 372–376. IEEE (2016)
7. Ruishuai, C.: Otsu's image segmentation algorithm with memorybased fruit fly optimization algorithm. In: Complexity, Hindawi, pp. 1–11 (2021)
8. Ganchimeg, G.: History document image background noise and removal methods. Int. J. Know. Content Develop. Technol. **5**(2), 11–24 (2015)
9. Ranota, H.K., Kaur, P.: Review and analysis of image enhancement techniques. Int. J. Inf. Comput. Technol. **4**(6), 583–590 (2014)
10. Farahmand, A., Sarrafzadeh, H., Shanbehzadeh, J.: Document image noises and removal methods (2013)
11. Nath, A.: Image denoising algorithms: A comparative study of different filtration approaches used in image restoration. In: International Conference on Communication Systems and Network Technologies, pp. 157–163. IEEE Computer Society (2013)
12. Farahmand, A., Sarrafzadeh, H., Shanbehzadeh, J.: Document image noises and removal methods. In: IMECS (2013)
13. Liu, X., Pedersen, M., Wang, R.: Survey of natural image enhancement techniques: Classification, evaluation, challenges, and perspectives. Digit. Sig. Process. **127** (2022)
14. Nikolaou, N., Papamarkos, N.: Color reduction for complex document images. Int. J. Imag. Syst. Technol. **19**(1), 14–26 (2009)
15. Kumar Panigrahi, S., Gupta, S., Vamsee Krishna, S.: Quantitative evaluation of different thresholding methods using automatic reference image creation via PCA. Int. J. Comput. Appl. **43**(7), 653–662 (2021)

16. Sharma, M.K.: A survey of thresholding techniques over images. INROADS-An International Journal of Jaipur National University **3**(2), 461–478 (2014)
17. Nezamabadi-pour, H., Saryazdi, S.: An efficient method for document image enhancement. In: Proceedings of International Symposium on Telecommunications, pp. 175–180 (2005)
18. Acuna, R.G.G., Tao, J., Klette, R.: Generalization of Otsu's binarization into recursive colour image segmentation. In: 2015 International Conference on Image and Vision Computing New Zealand (IVCNZ), pp. 1–6. IEEE (2015)
19. Fan, K.-C., Wang, Y.-K., Lay, T.-R.: Marginal noise removal of document images. Pattern Recogn. **35**(11), 2593–2611 (2002)
20. Fuguo, D., Hui, F., Da, Y.: A Novel Image Median Filtering Algorithm based on Incomplete Quick Sort Algorithm. Int. J. Digit. Content Technol. Appl. **4**(6) (2010)
21. Lopes, D.: Anisotropic Diffusion (Perona & Malik) (2022). https://www.mathworks.com/matlabcentral/fileexchange/14995-anisotropic-diffusion-perona-malik, MATLAB Central File Exchange

A Comparative Assessment of Deep Learning Approaches for Opinion Mining

Nidhi N. Solanki[1]([⊠]) [iD] and Dipti B. Shah[2] [iD]

[1] M.K. Institute of Computer Studies, Bharuch, Gujarat, India
nidhi17.solanki@gmail.com
[2] Department of Computer ScienceandTechnology, Sardar Patel University, V.V. Nagar, Gujarat, India

Abstract. Opinion mining is a branch of artificial intelligence being used in a variety of applications that transforms human emotions into digital form and tries to better understand the customers. Good customer relationship is a key formula for business intelligence. Deep learning is a subset of machine learning and is comparatively more powerful. Opinion mining techniques illustrated in the last few years have shown that noble performance can be achieved by the use of neural networks. Automation performs good time utilization with the help of illustrated online and offline tools. This study emphasizes the reviews of research in opinion analysis using deep learning models with their advantages and disadvantage. It also investigated different neural networks, their architecture, dataset, and other techniques.

Keywords: Long Short Term Memory · Recurrent Neural Network · Convolutional Neural Network · Deep Belief Network · Hybrid Network

1 Introduction

Opinion mining uses natural language processing and better understands the viewers based on their remarks on a specific object [14, 15]. Opinion mining sometimes also refers as sentiment analysis converts public opinions into categories of negative, positive, or neutral tags [18].

Every domain treats their customer as the primary importance because customer satisfaction and consistency play a significant role in target achievement for a service provider. It increases the demand for opinion mining in knowing the service holders in almost all fields, like education, health care, government policies and activities, public actions, finance, all businesses, companies, entertainment, etc. This list is not limited here, application of opinion mining has no boundary. Therefore it is one of the striking areas of research.

Machine learning algorithms require extensive and sometimes manual work of pre-processing and feature extraction. The unavailability of perfect NLP tools results in accuracy compromise and affects the accuracy of the final model [1].

S. Rajagopal et al. (Eds.): ASCIS 2022, CCIS 1759, pp. 49–61, 2022.
https://doi.org/10.1007/978-3-031-23092-9_5

G. E. Hinton firstly proposed the deep learning model in 2006. Neural networks result in good accuracy of opinion mining.

Deep Learning is a sub-field of machine learning [2]. It supports learning with several levels of data representations such as a hierarchy of features. In it, lower-level concepts help in defining many higher-level concepts.

The study is performed using various good resources like IEEE, Springer, ACM, Google Scholar, Research Gate, Science Direct, etc.

2 Literature Review

A hybrid sentiment analysis model of Rim China achieved a good performance compared to the Bert model. A combination of deep learning and fuzzy logic techniques solved opinions with several aspects and opposing polarities. The work has AspectBased Opinion Mining (ABOM) and Sentence-Based Opinion Mining (SBOM) separately in the framework. The ABOM model has used Bi-LSTM and multi-channel convolution layers. SBOM has used an embedding layer, ANFIS model, and dense layer. The fuzzy-Neuro model results in a 90.20 F-score for the restaurant dataset and an 88.05 score for the laptop dataset. ABOM model results in an 87.16 F-score for the restaurant dataset and a 90.18 score for the laptop dataset [3].

Elmurod Kuriyozov [4] developed the first opinion mining model on the Uzbek language on reviews of Google play store applications, both machine learning, and deep learning techniques were used. Convolutional neural network (CNN) results in 88.89% accuracy for manual dataset and Logistic regression (LR) with word and character n-grams provided 89.56 % accuracy on a translated dataset. Reviews were automatically translated from English to Uzbek using MTRANSLATE, an unofficial Google translate API.

Colón-Ruiz [5] has experimentally compared deep learning techniques such as CNN, LSTM, and RNN for sentiment analysis of drug reviews. He proved that bidirectional encoder representations from transformers obtained the best result with very high training time whereas CNN obtained better results with less training time.

Yiwen Bian [6] has worked on the improvement of aspect-opinion pair identification performance for customer reviews in the hotel domain with the CNN model. The Author has used structured as well as unstructured features. The sentiment intensity value is found with the help of the refined fine-grained sentiment analysis method.

Angela Braoudaki [7] has developed an opinion mining model on annotated textual reviews gathered from online hotel reservation sources. The researcher has performed a hybrid data-driven approach and rule-based opinion mining on the Greek text. The team has projected four deep learning designs and worked on training input of review texts, annotated text, and its combination. Lower memory utilization and a requisite of a dense layer for classification leads to the usage of the dense tags model.

Priyadarshini [8] proposed an LSTM-CNN grid search-based model with hyperparameter optimization for sentiment analysis on multiple datasets. The author observed a result of accuracy greater than 96%.

Nandwani [9] performed an investigation of various levels of sentiment analysis and models for predicting sentiment's polarity for the text data. The various techniques for mining opinions are lexicon-based, dictionary-based, corpus-based, etc. The performance of deep learning depends on the pre-processing and dataset size. The coverage of long-term dependencies and feature extraction proved LSTM as one of the best models. Comparative and ironic sentences, resource shortage, web slang, and multiple aspects are some major common problems during opinion mining.

Our teamwork found that deep learning has many characteristics and power for opinion-mining tasks. It relies on conditions like large and clean dataset, high-performing algorithms, and their combinations. CNN-LSTM and transformers are more appropriate. Speeded and corrected results based on hardware, libraries, and optimization techniques.

3 Tools for Opinion Mining

Tools are programs that simplify opinion mining task and saves time and effort. Many authors searched and worked with varied tools, some of them are:

- Meaning Cloud: A multilingual textual data opinion mining tool available in 57 languages. It requires an API key, language, and text for its work. Only registered users can use it. Supports industries like banking, healthcare, insurance, and publishing. It mines emotions at a document as well as aspect level.
- SentiStrenght: It finds the strength of sentiments of textual data in formal as well as informal language. It allocates strength in the range of -1 to -5 for negative comments and 1 to 5 for positive comments. A researcher can download this free tool from http://sentistrength.wlv.ac.uk/.
- RSentiment: Only registered R users can use this package utility for finding opinions on textual input. It supports Positive, Negative, Very Positive, Very Negative, Neutral, and Sarcasm polarities and is dedicated to the English language only. It is accompanied by relevant functions for finding scores, sentiments, and sentences.
- Senti WordNet: A lexical resource available with pubic visibility mode that works with three polarities of positivity, negativity, and objectivity.
- AFINN: It ponders a wordlist for opinion mining in foreign languages. Finn Årup Nielsen developed this lexicon with more than 3300 words with their emotion polarities. It can be installed in jupyter, windows, or Linux. Python has an inbuilt library for the same.

This is not limited here, there are many tools readily available in open search for opinion mining. Some more tools are EMOTICONS, SenticNet,sentiment140, FRN, NRC, EWGA, Happiness Index, LIWC, Review Seer tool, Web Fountain, PANAS-t, etc. [47, 48].

4 Deep Learning Techniques

A study of many papers concluded that widely used approaches for opinion mining are RNN, LSTM, DNN, CNN, and hybrid approaches. The following Fig. 1 shows the various applied approaches. The model's effectiveness depends on the Datasets [21], deep learning algorithms, and a feature extraction technique [10].

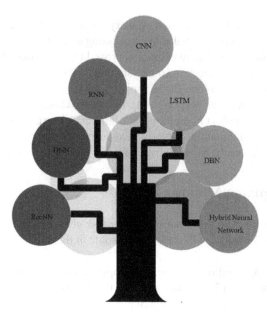

Fig. 1. Deep Learning Approaches for Opinion Mining

4.1 Convolutional Neural Network (CNN)

The main structural component of CNN is the convolutional layers and pooling [20, 25]. Convolutional layers with multiple filters train the different features. A pooling layer increases the data robustness [10]. Finally, fully connected layers provide an output vector and perform emotion classification. It is a mathematical operation to unite two sets of information [13]. CNN design allows the system to find hidden semantics from a huge unlabeled dataset and controlled coverage of lexical resources [6]. It provides good capturing of lexical and syntactic features [6] and also builds good stability between accuracy and CPU runtime [10]. Dynamic CNN uses dynamic pooling operations [11].

4.2 Recurrent Neural Network (RNN)

RNN is very useful for sequential inputs such as text. It doesn't represent a fixed-length context that contaminates all historical words [11, 13]. Vanilla RNN is complex due to exploding gradients. Gated recurrent units provide persistent memory and help learn long-term dependencies. In many cases, RNN proved to be best than CNN in terms of reliability but causes longer computational time [10]. Its combination with convolutional layers strengthens pixel neighborhoods. The hierarchical bidirectional recurrent neural network through network parameters with fine-tuning leads to improved performance [11].

4.3 Long Short Term Memory (LSTM)

LSTM is a Recurrent Neural network type proficient in learning long-period dependencies and takes flows in a single input direction [24]. LSTM is preferred when RNN fails. Its hidden layer is a gated unit. LSTM model has various methods like LSTM, TD-LSTM, and TC-LSTM. TD-LSTM uses two LSTM neural networks.TC-LSTM is an extension of TD-LSTM [8].

4.4 Deep Neural Networks (DNN)

A deep neural network comprises more than two layers, some of which are hidden layers. A neural network exhibits sophisticated mathematical modeling with several layers, an input layer of input data; hidden layers of processing nodes called neurons; and an output layer of one or several neurons [10, 22].

4.5 Deep Belief Networks (DBN)

DBN contains several hidden layers composed of restricted Boltzmann machines. There is a connection between each layer to the next one. The units within a layer are not connected [8]. It uses the unlabeled data and solves the labeled analysis issues. Weakly Shared Deep Neural Networks are effective for cross-lingual sentiment analysis. A deep belief network with feature selection conquers vocabulary troubles and results in better accuracy and lower training time.

4.6 Recursive Neural Network (RECNN)

RecNN belongs to supervised learning. It is a generalization of RNN, used to learn a directed acyclic graph structure from data [26]. Its hierarchical structure is settled before training and the nodes pertain to different matrices. RNN doesn't require any input reconstruction [11]. Some more models of this category are the Recursive Neural Deep Model, Recursive Neural Tensor Network, etc.

4.7 Hybrid Neural Network

Hybrid neural networks provide better accuracy in some opinion analysis research [27]. This approach combines two or more deep learning techniques for data classification [17] like CNN and LSTM or probabilistic neural network and a two-layered Restricted Boltzmann. Some more proven and quality models for emotion analysis are deep bidirectional long short-term memory neural network, radial basis function neural network, back propagation neural network, and dynamic artificial neural network [11] (Tables 1 and 2).

Table 1. Some well-known sample Deep learning Models of Opinion Mining

Model	Model Architecture	Study
Hybrid		[34]
RNN		[35]
CNN		[36]

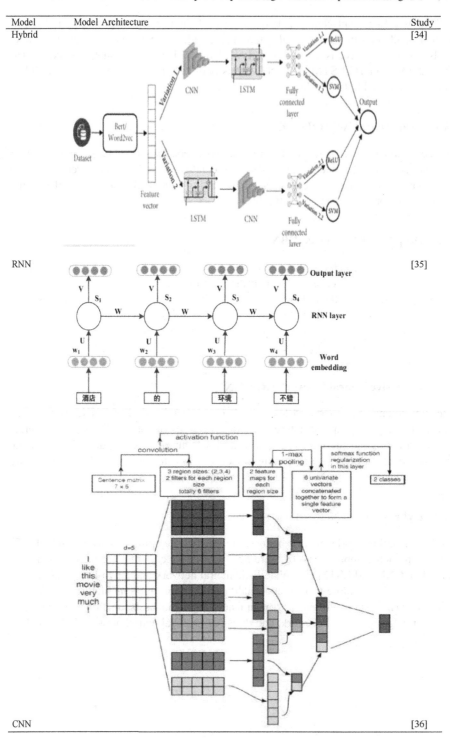

(*continued*)

Table 1. (*continued*)

Model	Model Architecture	Study
LSTM	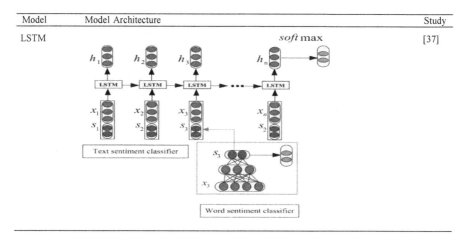	[37]

Table 2. Advantages - disadvantages of deep learning approaches [29–33]

Approach	Advantages	Disadvantages
CNN	• The automatic finding of features without any human care.	• Not spatially invariant to the input.
	• Computationally proficient and fast.	• Bulky training data is needed.
	• Weight sharing.	• Complex for lengthy text.
	• Effective for short text.	
RNN	• Useful in time series prediction.	• A Problem in processing long sequences.
	• Effective handling of sequence information.	• Difficult training.
	• Requires only one label for the whole sequence.	• Vanishing gradient and gradient exploding problems
	• Easy to implement and less error-prone.	• Call for a lot of resources and schedule to get trained.
LSTM	• Reduces vanishing gradient problem.	• Need high memory bandwidth.
	• Relative insensitivity to gap length.	• Prone to overfitting.
	• Good for long-term dependencies.	

(*continued*)

Table 2. (*continued*)

Approach	Advantages	Disadvantages
DNN	• Quality and accurate results.	• More computational cost and intricate architecture.
	• Reduced training time.	• Expansion of Parameter number
DBN	• Solves vanishing gradient problem.	• Costly.
	• Robust classification and feature learning.	• Runtime complexity.
	• Avoids data overfitting and underfitting.	
RecNN	• Can learn tree-like structure.	• Time-consuming to create data labeling.
	• Useful in classification job.	• In the training time, the tree diagram of each input sample is mandatory.
	• prospective capture of long-distance dependencies	• Hard training due to the change in a tree structure for each training sample.
Hybrid Neural Network	• Fast computation and searching.	• Convoluted structure.
	• Higher performance.	• A careful combination of varied methods is needed.
	• Effective input selection and data characterization.	

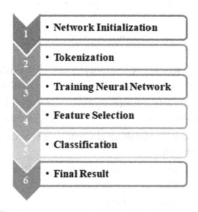

1 • **Network Initialization**

2 • **Tokenization**

3 • **Training Neural Network**

4 • **Feature Selection**

5 • **Classification**

6 • **Final Result**

Fig. 2. Architecture of Deep Learning Model

5 System Architecture

The following figure presents the system architecture of the deep learning model for emotion mining (Fig. 2).

Firstly the network is defined and initialized using the optimal initialization technique. The model building practically starts with the selection of the right and standard dataset for a particular domain. Datasets can be readily fetched from Application Programming interfaces, relevant organizations, online field-specific websites, or dataset sites like Google Dataset, Kaggel, Github, etc. A practitioner can create their dataset also. The network initialization steps greatly impact the performance of a model and sets arguments for the network. Resultant accuracy varies with changes in different initializations like Zeros initialization, random initialization, and He initialization, etc. He initialization is the most favorable type.

The input layer helps in token generation [5]. Pre-processed data (which is free from stopwords, HTML marks, punctuation marks, spelling mistakes, etc. that don't contribute to opinion mining tasks) is used for tokenization. It slices input statements into a single token of words for analyzing opinions. Scanning individual words and their relationship helps in identifying opinion categories whether they belong to positive, negative, or neutral. Deep learning algorithms process data with small factors called tokens. Spacy is the best and most widely used library for tokenization, NLTK library can also be used for it.

After getting the right form of data, train the model using deep learning techniques like CNN. So algorithm gets trained and learns what output is to be given on which input. The complete dataset is divided into train and test sets using the sklearn library. The model is trained on a train set. A test set is used for checking model performance by again using sklearn.

The feature selection technique identifies the most pertinent set of features [41, 42]. Features generally refer to the columns in the dataset. If basic features do not provide the desired result then advanced features are created based on statistical measures. Fuzzy features can also be used. Optimal feature selection depends on the creativity and logic of the programmer.

Finally, the output of the top layer and optimized feature set is concatenated and feed to a selected classifier. A suitable classifier can be imported from the sklearn library and implemented with the best-performing algorithm. It gives the final result on the screen [16]. The result can be more effectively depicted using graphical statistical diagrams like charts, graphs or bars, etc. If a reliable result is not obtained then optimization techniques like stacking, boosting, and bagging can be applied for performance enhancement.

6 Advantages of Deep Learning

Deep learning is an enhanced form of machine learning [19]. There are varied reasons for the researcher's choice of deep learning for the opinion mining job. It is a first-sight choice for researchers for the opinion mining job. Automatic feature engineering [1, 23] added charm to the work. Comparatively, the deep learning model results in a good performance with the hike in the amount of data [43–46].

Technological updates provide required and cheap hardware for the model [11] enhancement in terms of speed, reliability, and scalability. The transformation of the machine learning model into a deep learning model is possible but not vice versa [1]. Neural networks are language and domain-independent [5]. Therefore it opens the door to many research opportunities in varied domains and regional plus international languages.

Complex deep-learning networks accurately detect sentiment polarity [7]. It has the potential to represent the relations between targets and their context without losing the correlation between textual tokens [8]. Hidden layers strengthen the models to perform better than SVMs and smaller neural networks [11]. Neural models work for both supervised and unsupervised modes [11].

7 When to Use Deep Learning

A deep learning approach is preferable for the below conditions [39, 40] (Table 3):

Table 3. Conditions for deep learning selection

Conditions
A Large number of features
The highly complex or huge dataset
Automatic feature selection
Complex problem

8 Disadvantages of Deep Learning

As nothing is perfect in this world, so the Deep learning. Although it has many advantages over existing techniques, it has some pinpoints. A good neural model demands a requirement of a large dataset [11]. Firstly the model is to be trained on an enormous dataset because learning with more samples results in enhanced quality. The large size of the dataset is hard to manage and pre-process. It is time-consuming during training and result generation, and for speedy execution, expense increases due to additional and costly resources [38].

The over-fitting problem may come from a small dataset. Its overcome includes several ways. Data augmentation, hyper-parameter tuning, cross-validation, appropriate data pre-processing, regularization, ensembling, and dropout mechanisms are the ways to overcome the problem. The model's Complexity leads to an extensive schedule [11]. Principle architecture with multiple neurons, layers, parameters, features, connections, extensive labelling, and high-level mathematical logic makes a complex model. These features only provide actual strength to it. The Neural network is also unable to indirect handling of symbols [12].

9 Conclusion

Opinion mining computationally transforms the textual opinions into categories of negative, positive, or neutral tags. This paper enlightened varied techniques of opinion mining using deep learning. In many kinds of research, performance by CNN and LSTM is awe-inspiring. Many types of research on regional languages have been done using machine learning techniques. In the future, we would like to bridge the gap between opinion mining and regional language reviews using deep learning and will explore more of its challenges and solutions.

References

1. Singhal, P., Bhattacharyya, P.: Sentiment Analysis and Deep Learning: A Survey. Center for Indian Language Technology, Indian Institute of Technology, Bombay (2016)
2. Hinton, G., LeCun, Y., Bengio, Y.: Deep Learn. **521**(7553), 436–444 (2015)
3. Chiha, R., Ayed, M.B. and Pereira, C.D.C.: A complete framework for aspect-level and sentence-level sentiment analysis. Appl. Intell. pp. 1–19 (2022)
4. Kuriyozov, E., Matlatipov, S., Alonso, M.A. and Gómez-Rodriguez, C.: Deep learning vs. classic models on a new Uzbek sentiment analysis dataset. In: Human Language Technologies as a Challenge for Computer Science and Linguistics, pp.258–262 (2019)
5. Colón-Ruiz, C., Segura-Bedmar, I.: Comparing deep learning architectures for sentiment analysis on drug reviews. J. Biomed. Inf. **110**, 103539 (2020)
6. Bian, Y., Ye, R., Zhang, J., Yan, X.: Customer preference identification from hotel online reviews: A neural network based fine-grained sentiment analysis. Comput. Indus. Eng. **172**, 108648 (2022). https://doi.org/10.1016/j.cie.2022.108648
7. Braoudaki, A., Kanellou, E., Kozanitis, C., Fatuous, P.: Hybrid data driven and rule based sentiment analysis on Greek text. Proc. Comput. Sci. **178**, 234–243 (2020)
8. Priyadarshini, I., Cotton, C.: A novel LSTM–CNN–grid search-based deep neural network for sentiment analysis. J. Supercomput. **77**(12), 13911–13932 (2021). https://doi.org/10.1007/s11227-021-03838-w
9. Nandwani, P., Verma, R.: A review on sentiment analysis and emotion detection from text. Soc. Netw. Anal. Min. **11**(1), 1–19 (2021). https://doi.org/10.1007/s13278-021-00776-6
10. Dang, N.C., Moreno-García, M.N.D., De la Prieta, F.: Sentiment analysis based on deep learning: A comparative study. Electronics **9**(3), 483 (2020)
11. Ain, Q.T., et al.: Sentiment analysis using deep learning techniques: a review. Int. J. Adv. Comput. Sci. Appl. **8**(6), 424 (2017)
12. Li, H.: Deep learning for natural language processing: advantages and challenges. Nat. Sci. Rev. (2017)
13. Rani, S., Kumar, P.: A journey of Indian languages over sentiment analysis: a systematic review. Artif. Intell. Rev. **52**(2), 1415–1462 (2018). https://doi.org/10.1007/s10462-018-9670-y
14. Hussain, A., Cambria, E.: Semi-supervised learning for big social data analysis. Neurocomputing **275**, 1662–1673 (2018)
15. Torregrosa, J., D'Antonio-Maceiras, S., Villar-Rodríguez, G., et al.: A mixed approach for aggressive political discourse analysis on Twitter. Cogn. Comput. (2022). https://doi.org/10.1007/s12559-022-10048-w
16. Yuan, J., Chen, C., Yang, W., Liu, M., Xia, J., Liu, S.: A survey of visual analytics techniques for machine learning. Computational Visual Media **7**(1), 3–36 (2020). https://doi.org/10.1007/s41095-020-0191-7

17. Cambria, E., Das, D., Bandyopadhyay, S., Feraco, A.: Affective computing and sentiment analysis. In: Cambria, E., Das, D., Bandyopadhyay, S., Feraco, A. (eds) A Practical Guide to Sentiment Analysis: Socio-Affective Computing, vol. 5. Springer, Cham (2017). https://doi.org/10.1007/978-3-319-55394-8_1

18. Cambria, E., Xing, F., Thelwall, M., Welsch, R.: Sentiment analysis as a multidisciplinary research area. IEEE Trans. Artif. Intell. 3(2), 1–3 (2022)

19. Cambria, E., Schuller, B., Xia, Y., Havasi, C.: New avenues in opinion mining and sentiment analysis. IEEE Intell Syst. 28(2), 15–21 (2013)

20. Camacho, D., Luzón, M.V., Cambria, E.: New Research Methods and Algorithms in Social Network Analysis. Elsevier (2021)

21. Tessore, J.P., Esnaola, L.M., Lanzarini, L., Baldassarri, S.: Distant Supervised Construction and Evaluation of a Novel Dataset of Emotion-Tagged Social Media Comments in Spanish. Cogn. Comput. 14(1), 407–424 (2021). https://doi.org/10.1007/s12559-020-09800-x

22. Hajek, P., Barushka, A., Munk, M.: Opinion Mining of Consumer Reviews Using Deep Neural Networks with Word-Sentiment Associations. In: Maglogiannis, I., Iliadis, L., Pimenidis, E. (eds.) AIAI 2020. IAICT, vol. 583, pp. 419–429. Springer, Cham (2020). https://doi.org/10.1007/978-3-030-49161-1_35

23. Jin, Z., Tao, M., Zhao, X., et al.: Social media sentiment analysis based on dependency graph and co-occurrence graph. Cog. Comput. 14, 1039–1054 (2022). https://doi.org/10.1007/s12559-022-10004-8

24. Chen, Y., Yuan, J., You, Q., Luo, J.: Twitter sentiment analysis via bi-sense emoji embedding and attention-based LSTM. In: Proceedings of the 26th ACM international conference on Multimedia, Association for Computing Machinery, New York, pp. 117–25 (2018). https://doi.org/10.1145/3240508.3240533

25. Tao, Y., Zhang, X., Shi, L., Wei, L., Hai, Z., Wahid, J. A.: Joint embedding of emoticons and labels based on CNN for microblog sentiment analysis. In: Proceedings of the Fourth IEEE International Conference on Data Science in Cyberspace, pp. 168–175 (2019). https://doi.org/10.1109/DSC.2019.00033

26. Xu, G., Meng, Y., Qiu, X., Yu, Z., Wu, X.: Sentiment analysis of comment texts based on BiLSTM. IEEE Access. 7, 51522–51532 (2019). https://doi.org/10.1109/ACCESS.2019.2909919

27. Basiri, M.E., Nemati, S., Abdar, M., Cambria, C.: Acharya UR. ABCDM: an attention-based bidirectional CNN-RNN deep model for sentiment analysis. Fut. Genet. Comput. Syst. 115, 279–94 (2021)

28. Ligthart, A., Catal, C., Tekinerdogan, B.: Systematic reviews in sentiment analysis: a tertiary study. Artif. Intell. Rev. 54(7), 4997–5053 (2021). https://doi.org/10.1007/s10462-021-09973-3

29. Shofiqul, M.S.I., Ab, Ghani, N., Ahmed, M.M.: A review on recent advances in Deep learning for Sentiment Analysis: Performances, Challenges and Limitations (2020)

30. Lin, P. , Luo, X. , Fan, Y.: A survey of sentiment analysis based on deep learning. World Academy of Science, Engineering and Technology, Open Science Index 168. Int. J. Comput. Inf. Eng. 14(12), 473–485 (2020)

31. Prabha, M. I., Umarani Srikanth, G.: Survey of sentiment analysis using deep learning techniques. In: 2019 1st International Conference on Innovations in Information and Communication Technology (ICIICT), pp. 1–9 (2019). doi:https://doi.org/10.1109/ICIICT1.2019.8741438

32. Pang, G., Shen, C., Cao, L., Van Den Hengel, A.: Deep learning for anomaly detection: A review. ACM Comput. Surv. 54(2), 38 (2021). https://doi.org/10.1145/3439950

33. Alswaidan, N., Menai, M.E.B.: A survey of state-of-the-art approaches for emotion recognition in text. Knowl. Inf. Syst. 62(8), 2937–2987 (2020). https://doi.org/10.1007/s10115-020-01449-0

34. Dang, C.N., Moreno-García, M.N., De la Prieta, F.: Hybrid deep learning models for sentiment analysis. Complexity **16**, 9986920 (2021). https://doi.org/10.1155/2021/9986920

35. Xu, G., Meng, Y., Qiu, X., Yu, Z., Wu, X.: Sentiment analysis of comment texts based on BiLSTM. IEEE Access **7**, 51522–51532 (2019)

36. Bahdanau, D., Cho, K., Bengio, Y.: Neural machine translation by jointly learning to align and translate (2014)

37. Fu, X., Yang, J., Li, J., Fang, M., Wang, H.: Lexicon-enhanced LSTM with attention for general sentiment analysis. IEEE Access **6**, 71884–71891 (2018). https://doi.org/10.1109/ACCESS.2018.2878425

38. What Is Deep Learning?|How It Works, Techniques and Applications: https://www.mathwo rks.com/discovery/deep-learning.html

39. Hargravea, M.: How Deep Learning Can Help Prevent Financial Fraud. Investopedia. https://www.investopedia.com/terms/d/deeplearning.asp.

40. Habib, M. A.: Tweet Sentiment Analysis using Deep Learning Technique

41. Mikolov, T., Chen, K., Corrado, G.S., Dean, J.A.: Computing numeric representations of words in a highdimensional space. US9740680B1. https://patents.google.com/patent/US9 740680B1/en

42. Gensim: Topic Modelling for Humans: https://radimrehurek.com/gensim/#

43. R. Johnson, T. Zhang, Supervised and semi-supervised text categorization using lstm for region embeddings. In: Proceedings of the 33rd International Conference on International Conference on Machine Learning, vol. 48, ICML'16, pp. 526–534 (2016)

44. Howard, J., Ruder, S.: Universal language model fine-tuning for text classification. In: Proceedings of the 56th Annual Meeting of the Association for Computational Linguistics, Vol. 1: Long Papers, Association for Computational Linguistics, pp. 328–339 (2018)

45. B.N. Patro, V.K. Kurmi, S. Kumar, V. Namboodiri, Learning semantic sentence embeddings using sequential pair-wise discriminator. In: Proceedings of the 27th International Conference on Computational Linguistics, pp. 2715–2729 (2018)

46. Yang, Z., Dai, Z., Yang, Y., Carbonell, J., Salakhutdinov, R.R., Le, Q.V.: Xlnet: generalized autoregressive pretraining for language understanding. In: Advances in Neural Information Processing Systems, pp. 5754–5764 (2019)

47. Singh, L.G., Singh, S.R.: Empirical study of sentiment analysis tools and techniques on societal topics. Journal of Intelligent Information Systems **56**(2), 379–407 (2020). https://doi.org/10.1007/s10844-020-00616-7

48. Alessia, D., Ferri, F., Grifoni, P., Guzzo, T.: Approaches, tools and applications for sentiment analysis implementation. Int. J. Comput. Appl. **125**(3) (2015)

Performance Enhancement in WSN Through Fuzzy C-Means Based Hybrid Clustering (FCMHC)

Roma Saxena$^{(\boxtimes)}$ ⓘ and Akhtar Husain ⓘ

Department of CSIT, Faculty of Engineering and Technology, MJP Rohilkhand University, Bareilly, India
saxenaroma25@gmail.com

Abstract. The researches in Wireless Sensor Networks (WSNs) strive for the efficient data transmission with optimized lifetime of the system. Load Balanced Clustering contributes energy efficiency by ensuring the even load distribution restricting thereby the premature energy drain at the level of nodes. The authors of this research study propose a Fuzzy C-Means based Hybrid Clustering (FCMHC) approach that forms the clusters using Fuzzy C-Means algorithm and thereafter applies Fuzzy Logic for selection of Cluster Head (CH). A critical comparison of the proposed approach with the representative protocols in the domain of WSNs viz. LEACH and CHEF was accomplished on the basis of performance. The results reveal that FCMHC outperforms LEACH and CHEF on the parameters viz. Network throughput, energy utilization and network stability caused by improving the active nodes in the system.

Keywords: Clustering · Fuzzy C-Means · Wireless sensor network · Fuzzy logic · Routing

1 Introduction

Wireless Sensor Networks (WSNs) have got a lot of recognition in present times because of its significant applications in every sector ranging from medical, agriculture, smart building to environmental monitoring and real-time critical systems demanding high level of performance assurance thereby imposing a number of challenges due to its limited resources. The nodes in WSNs are randomly deployed in the dynamic environment which is vulnerable to noise, interference and link quality. These nodes are constrained with limited resources viz. Computational capability, transmission power, energy and storage [1, 2].

One of the major design aims of WSNs is to accomplish data communication with prolonged lifetime of the desired network while preventing connectivity degradation with aggressive energy management methods in routing. The design of routing protocol is highly influenced by lot of challenging reasons due to numerous sensor nodes and dynamics of the operating environment. In the emerging real-life WSN applications,

S. Rajagopal et al. (Eds.): ASCIS 2022, CCIS 1759, pp. 62–76, 2022.
https://doi.org/10.1007/978-3-031-23092-9_6

a routing scheme is desired that simultaneously optimize various performance metrics thereby demanding for the multi - objective optimization. Most of the real-world problems strive for multi-objective optimization to be exercised on the various parameters viz. Energy efficiency, delay, reliability, residual energy of nodes and the network lifetime in WSNs [3].

In this paper we propose the performance enhancement in WSN wherein Sect. 2 briefly focuses on the related work; further Sect. 3 explains the Network Model used for radio communication; moreover Sect. 4 depicts the Algorithm proposed by the authors, Sect. 5 focuses on Performance Evaluation and Analysis and finally Sect. 6 depicts the Conclusion.

2 Related Work

Low-Energy Adaptive Clustering Hierarchy (LEACH) [4], the pioneer hierarchical protocol for routing in WSN is based on clustered architecture, partitions network into clusters then selects one node as Cluster Head (CH) aiming for collection and aggregation of data from the member nodes and aggregated data transmission to the base station (BS). The mechanism for CH selection is based on the comparison of a generated random number with a threshold. LEACH balances the energy consumption to some extent by giving chance to all the nodes to be elected as CH but being a probabilistic approach while not considering other parameters such as location of CH with respect to the cluster and BS and residual energy of nodes, it causes uneven load distribution among the nodes. To calculate a node's likelihood of becoming the CH, Fuzzy based Distributed Clustering for Energy Efficiency [5], implemented the TSK fuzzy model. Node degrees, residual energy of both, the nodes as well as the neighbouring nodes, are the input parameters of a fuzzy system. The experimental findings demonstrate its superiority over comparable protocols as energy use, data transmission, and lifetime of a network.

The clusters in WSNs are built under Cluster Head Election Mechanism using fuzzy logic [6]. The three fuzzy variables i.e., concentration, energy and centrality are used to elect any node as a CH. It is found that the network' lifetime is extended and CHEF performs more efficiently than LEACH by 22.7%. The clustering protocol based on Fuzzy C-Means (FCM) [7] partitions the nodes into clusters using Fuzzy C- Means partitioning scheme. FCM outperformed K-Means, LEACH and MTE (Minimum Transmission Energy) protocol by decreasing the energy utilization and thus increasing the life span of the system. An improved version of LEACH wherein clusters are built by using FCM algorithm and CH is chosen based on minimization of objective function comprising of node's distance from the centroid position of that cluster and its residual energy was proposed in [8].

A decentralized routing protocol based on FCM that partitions the nodes into clusters by applying FCM followed by the competition of the candidate nodes with each other for assuming the role of CH in view of the residual energy, location within the cluster and location with reference to the BS was proposed in [9]. A clustering algorithm in WSNs based on fuzzy C- Means that builds clusters with FCM algorithm and optimizes the overall energy consumption by defining an energy related cost function to elect a node as CH was proposed in [10] for IoT applications which revealed 50% improvement in network lifetime.

A hybrid and adaptive clustering is proposed in [11] for minimizing the use of node energy through Fuzzy C - Means (FCM) using parameters Euclidean distance, position of BS, and nodes' residual energy. To economize on energy, it chooses the CH using an energy-efficient fitness function that adapts to the leftover energy of the nodes. It also suggested employing Direct and Central variants of Cluster Heads chosen based on various fitness functions to act as relays for few other CHs through a hierarchical packet routing method. Three-tier structure is the foundation of the protocol namely EHCR-FCM presented in [12]. The grid and cluster are formed dynamically with energy-efficient routing to ensure optimal energy utilisation using the relative Euclidean distances, centroid of the grids and clusters, and leftover energy of the nodes. To form load balanced clusters, [13] proposed a density based fuzzy c-means clustering method that lowers the energy consumption by the network which in turn increases the network lifetime and packet delivery ratio.

Residual Energy based Hybrid Routing (REHR) [14] proposed a method for packet routing comprising of two communication strategies viz. Single-hop and multi-hop between the direct nodes and clustering nodes in a hybrid manner for efficient packet transmission considering leftover energy of alive nodes and relative Euclidean distances. The author presented an algorithm to form high quality clusters with fuzzy logic based cluster head selection in [15]. It emphasizes on quality of clusters that leads to higher reliability, lower error rate and better scalability. EADCR [16] protocol emphasizes CH selection through newly introduced fitness function and extends the lifespan of WSN through FCM. It also uses relative Euclidean distances from the cluster centroid and the BS along with leftover energy of nodes.

In view of the aforesaid review of related work, it is realized that clustering, a process that partitions a given data set into groups called clusters based on some similar feature, has tremendous influence on the performance in WSNs. Further, the aforesaid review point to the fact that the minimization of communication costs and efficient load distribution among the nodes can be controlled by optimally distributing the nodes among clusters and effectively selecting the cluster head. This study proposes the use of FCM [7] to split WSN nodes into clusters for efficient load balancing, followed by the application of fuzzy algorithms to pick the CH based on remnant energy and the distance of the node from its cluster centre.

3 Network Model

3.1 Radio Model

The total transmission energy needed during one round is the sum of energy used for data transmission from cluster members to CH and CH to sink. The CH consumes energy in three aspects: data reception, data transmission and aggregation. The energy consumed for aforesaid aspects in WSN is denoted by data reception energy ERX, data transmission energy ETX and aggregation energy Eda respectively. The Eda is consumed by the CH only which remains fixed over time while ETX depends on the transmission distance and ERX depends on the length of the received data. Two different radio models were considered on the basis of the distance between sender and receiver. The energy dissipation model [17] is used to evaluate the consumption of energy made by the nodes in radio communication. The energy consumed by power amplifiers at the transmitter front end can be expressed as,

$$E_{amp} = \begin{cases} E_{fs}d^2 & d \le d_o \\ E_{mp}d^4 & d > d_o \end{cases} \tag{1}$$

E_{amp} is the energy consumed by the power amplifiers, E_{fs} is the power consumed for free space propagation, E_{mp} is the multi-path power consumption and d is Euclidian distance to be calculated between transmitter and receiver. 'd_o' is the threshold value for the distance and can be computed as

$$d_o = \sqrt{\frac{E_{fs}}{E_{mp}}} \tag{2}$$

To transmit l-bit packet from a cluster member to its CH over distance d can be given by following equation:

$$E_{TX}(1, d) = l\left(E_{elec} + E_{amp}\right) \tag{3}$$

where E_{elec} represents the energy consumed in order to transfer per bit.

E_{RX} is the reception energy, required to convert the received signal to data. To receive l bits, the energy required by the CH is given by

$$E_{RX} = lE_{elec} \tag{4}$$

After receiving the data, CH aggregates it and sent it to the sink. Hence total energy utilized by the CH for transmission of information can be given by:

$$E_{Ch\_RX} = l(E_{elec} + E_{amp} + E_{da}) \tag{5}$$

3.2 Assumptions

To simulate the operations of WSN, the assumptions are as follows:

- The sensor nodes are deployed randomly in the field. These nodes are homogeneous as far as initial energy, memory and computational power are concerned.
- BS has no limitations regarding energy, memory and processing capability and is placed outside the field.
- All the sensor nodes and BS remain stationary after the deployment.
- All the nodes have the capability to monitor and sense the environmental parameters and forward the information to BS. They can also operate as cluster head to gather data from its member nodes, further process it and forward to the BS.

4   Proposed Algorithm

We propose an algorithm for cluster formation that efficiently balances the load distribution among the nodes based on Fuzzy C-Means algorithm. Our algorithm operates in three phases:

4.1 Cluster Formation Phase

Initially all sensor nodes share the information of their location to the BS. The BS forms the cluster, finds cluster centre and assigns each node to the cluster based on their distance from the cluster centre using Fuzzy C-Means (FCM). FCM [7] is a centralized unsupervised learning that partitions the network into predefined number of clusters. It assigns a membership value between 0 and 1 to each node on the basis of proximity of the node from centre of the cluster. The summation of membership values of each node is 1. Initially, all the sensor nodes share their location to the BS where the cluster formation takes place and each node is assigned to the specific cluster based on maximum membership value evaluated on the basis of number and location of the nodes relative to the cluster centre. FCM involves the minimization of the following objective function:

$$J_m = \sum_{i=1}^{D} \sum_{j=1}^{N} \mu_{ij}^m d_{ij}^2 \tag{6}$$

where, 'D' – No. of data points, 'N' – No. of clusters, 'm' - Fuzziness parameter normally considered as 2, d_{ij} – Euclidean distance of node 'i' from the centroid of cluster 'j'.

The Algorithm starts by initializing the cluster membership values randomly. FCM is iterative algorithm where cluster centres and membership values are updated in each iteration. The centroid of each cluster is calculated by taking the mean value of all data points weighted with their membership value by using the following formula:

$$C_{jx} = \frac{\sum_{i=1}^{D} \mu_{ij}^m x_i}{\sum_{i=1}^{D} \mu_{ij}^m} \tag{7}$$

$$C_{jy} = \frac{\sum_{i=1}^{D} \mu_{ij}^m y_i}{\sum_{i=1}^{D} \mu_{ij}^m} \tag{8}$$

$$C_j = (C_{jx}, C_{jy}) \tag{9}$$

where (x_i, y_i) -Position of ith node and C_j- Coordinate of the centroid of jth cluster.

The membership value for each node is based on its Euclidean distance from all the cluster centroids, is updated during each iteration by using following formula

$$\mu_{ij} = \frac{1}{\sum_{k=1}^{C} \frac{d_{ij}^2}{d_{ik}^2}} \tag{10}$$

$$i = 1, 2, \ldots N, \quad j = 1, 2, \ldots, C$$

where, 'N'- the total count of nodes and 'C' – the count of clusters

The algorithm terminates when the difference between the values of objective function in successive iteration is lower than the set threshold value or a predefined maximum count of iterations is completed. In Algorithm-1, the FCM algorithm is given. After convergence reaches, the algorithm terminates and each node is designated as member of the specified cluster for which it attains the highest membership value.

Algorithm-1: Fuzzy C-Means (FCM) Clustering in WSN

Input:[X,Y]position of N number of participated nodes
C: number of clusters
Output: cluster centres with each node is assigned to a cluster
1. Randomly initialize the cluster membership values   .
 	
2.For C do
Compute location of cluster centroid C_j using equation 9.
end
3. For N do
   For C do
     Compute Euclidean distance between node and C_j as d_{ij}
   end
Update   according to equation 10.
end
4. Compute the objective function J_m using equation 6.
5 Repeat steps 2 to 4 until the values of J_m in successive iteration is lower than the set threshold value or a predefined maximum count of iterations is completed
6. For N do
      Node is assigned to a cluster as a member for which its   is maximum
   end

4.2 Cluster Head Selection Phase

An effective node that satisfies a number of conditions must be chosen as the cluster head for ensuring load balancing at the cluster level. Based on leftover energy and the proximity of a node from the cluster centre, the fuzzy system seeks to estimate the likelihood that a node will become the Cluster Head (CH) inside each cluster. A multi-valued logic called fuzzy logic [18] allows for the definition of linguistic values that fall anywhere in between sharp threshold values. The range of actual values across which a fuzzy set is mapped serves as its description. The domain is the range of real values.The membership function assigns a membership value between 0 and 1 to each point. By defining the dynamic behaviour of the system by a collection of linguistic fuzzy rules, fuzzy systems enable the use of fuzzy sets to draw conclusions and make judgements. The fuzzifier, fuzzy rule base, inference engine and defuzzifier are a fuzzy system's main components. The collection of fuzzy rules is presented as propositions. The inference engine translates fuzzy input to fuzzy output based on these propositions.

Fuzzy Input Variables: The node's remnant energy and the distance between the cluster centre and the node have been two key considerations when choosing a node to serve as a cluster head.

(i) **Residual Energy (ResE):** The main element important for the network's longevity is energy. Since a CH node must expend energy to gather data from its member nodes, aggregate it, and deliver it to base station, it consumes more energy than a cluster member node. Therefore, if a node has enough remaining energy, it will become the CH. As illustrated in Fig. 1, the fuzzy linguistic variables for residual energy are Low, Med, and High.

(ii) **Distance to Cluster Centre (DistCN):** The amount of energy used is dependent to the separation between sender and receiver. Therefore, it is necessary to reduce the distance between the CH and its members in order to preserve energy. This setting guarantees that we choose the CH close to its cluster members, reducing the transmission distance. As illustrated in Fig. 2, the fuzzy linguistic variables for distance to cluster centre are Near, Avg, and Far.

Fuzzy Output Variables: Fuzzy system has one output variable namely chance which assigns a value to each active node that describes the claim of a node to become the CH.

(i) **Chance:** The cluster's CH is chosen from all the nodes having the highest chance value. The probability is divided into six language categories: Very very high, Very high, High, Medium, Med low, Very low, and Very very low. Table 1 lists the language input and output variables for the fuzzy system. Figure 3 displays the membership function for the chance variable. While Med and Avg follow a triangle membership function, Low, High, Near, and Far follow a trapezoidal membership function.

The fuzzy Mamdani technique is used to map the input parameter to the output parameter. The crisp output values are then obtained using the Centroid technique. Table 2 contains a list of the fuzzy rule base.

Table 1. Fuzzy linguistic variables

Input	Linguistic variables	Output	Linguistic variables
Residual energy	Low, Med, High	Chance	Very very high, Very high, High, Medium, Med low, Very low, Very very low
Distance to cluster centre	Near, Avg, Far		

4.3 Communication Phase

After cluster formation and cluster head selection, the transmission of data will be initiated in communication phase. TDMA schedule will be broadcasted among its members by the newly elected CHs. Further, the member nodes will send their data to the respective CH as per the specified TDMA schedule. Finally, CH nodes collect the data from all its members, aggregate it into one packet and send it to the BS.

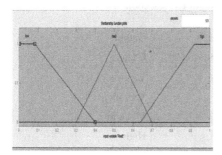 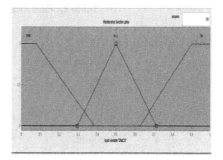

Fig. 1. The membership function plot for input variable 'ResE'

Fig. 2. The membership function plot for input variable 'DistCN'

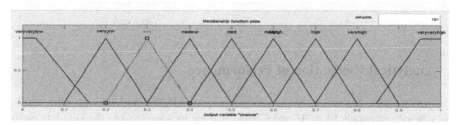

Fig. 3. The membership function plot for output variable 'Chance'

Algorithm 2: FCMHC (Fuzzy C-Means based Hybrid Clustering in WSN)

Initialization:
Deploy sensor nodes randomly with sink
Assign an ID to each sensor node
Nodes activated and sends its location to the sink
Main function :
For every round
    Execute FCM algorithm
    For every cluster
        For every cluster member
            Calculate Euclidean distance between cluster member and cluster centre
            Execute FLS to compute the chance for the member to become CH
        end
A member having highest chance value will be selected as CH
CH broadcasts the TDMA schedule to their respective members
Cluster members share the sensed data to the respective CH
    end
  Data aggregation is done by CH
  CH transmits the aggregated data to BS
end

Table 2. Fuzzy rule base for CH selection

S.No	Input		Output
	Residual Energy	Distance to CN	Chance
1	High	Near	Very very high
2	High	Avg	Very high
3	High	Far	Medium
4	Medium	Near	High
5	Medium	Avg	Medium
6	Medium	Far	Med Low
7	Low	Near	Med Low
8	Low	Avg	Very Low
9	Low	Far	Very very low

5 Analytical Evaluation of Performance

The performance evaluation of the scheme proposed by the authors with other existing scheme (protocols LEACH and CHEF) is done by carrying out the simulations in MATLAB 14.1a. The comparison is based on different performance metrics.

5.1 Performance Metrics

(i) **Alive Nodes per Round:** The count of alive nodes has directly affect the network lifetime which in turn responsible for the network performance.

(ii) **Average Energy Consumed:** Energy is the main constraint for the network performance because nodes consume energy for wireless communication.

(iii) **Network Throughput**: throughput refers to the successfully transmitted number of packets from CH to BS. **(iv) FND, QND, HND:** FND, QND, HND refers to the first node died, quarter of the nodes died and half of the nodes died respectively.

5.2 Simulation Parameters

To demonstrate the performance, the key parameters for simulation are depicted in Table 3. The sensor nodes are randomly deployed in the field of $100 \times 100 \, \text{m}^2$. The base station is situated at far off place from the target place at (50,150). The percentage of CH is kept 10% of active nodes in the network. To check the efficiency of the proposed scheme, the simulations are performed with two different scenarios. In first scenario, different performance metrics are tested against number of rounds while keeping number of nodes fixed. In the second scenario, the number of rounds is fixed and demonstrates the output with the variation of number of nodes from 100 to 300.

Table 3. Parameters for simulation

Parameters	Values
Network area	$100 \times 100 \text{ m}^2$
Number of sensor nodes	100–300
Multi-path fading model (E_{fs})	10 pJ/bit/m^4
The free space model (E_{mp})	0.0013 pJ/bit/m^2
The reception or transmission of energy consumption (E_{elec})	50 nJ/bit
Data fusion energy (EDA)	5 nJ/bit/signal
Nodes' initial energy	1 J
Size of data packet	4000 bits

5.3 Results and Discussion

Scenario 1: Simulation results when number of round varies

Alive Nodes Per Round

Number of alive nodes indicates the lifetime of the network. A comparison of number of active sensor nodes present in the network for the proposed protocol with LEACH and CHEF is shown in Fig. 4. It can be observed that almost no node left alive after 2600 rounds for LEACH and 3000 rounds with CHEF but FCMHC shows a fair improvement for alive nodes and nodes are alive till approximate 4800 rounds.

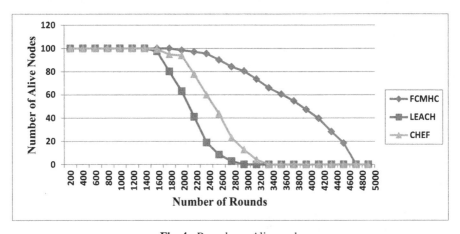

Fig. 4. Rounds vs. Alive node

Network's Average Remnant Energy

The network's remnant energy reduces as the number of rounds increases because a large amount of energy consumes in radio communication which causes the death of sensor nodes and it affects the connectivity and coverage of the network. Figure 5 shows that the average remnant energy of the network is always higher for FCMHC than other two protocols, LEACH and CHEF. Remnant energy of the network becomes too less after 2400 rounds with LEACH and 2800 rounds for CHEF but network has some residual energy till 4600 rounds with proposed scheme. Hence it is evident that the given protocol distributes the load among the nodes evenly which in turn contributes stability to the system.

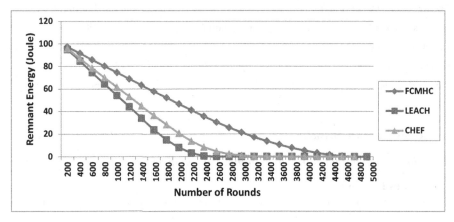

Fig. 5. Rounds vs. Remnant energy

Network Throughput
Network throughput can be measured as number of packets delivered from the CHs to the Base Station (BS). The proposed protocol gives higher network throughput as compared to other specified protocols because the cluster formation is done by using FCM which is a soft clustering technique that provides an efficient way to handle uncertainty in real world problems and give better results. Further cluster head selection is done using fuzzy logic system by calculating the chance of each cluster member to become CH based on different parameters that leads to an optimized cluster formation. Figure 6 reveals that the throughput for FCMHC is 42% higher than that of LEACH and 30% higher than that of CHEF.

Network Lifetime
Network lifetime can be estimated with various metrics. Here, FND tells the number of round when the first sensor node dies. QND and HND give the number of rounds when 25% and 50% of total nodes die respectively. These metrics are important to estimate the stability of network. The results of Fig. 7 reveal that FND for FCMHC is extended by 20%and 15% than LEACH and CHEF respectively. Similarly QND for is prolonged by 50% and 32% in comparison to LEACH and CHEF respectively. Finally HND for FCMHC is delayed by 47%% and 35% against LEACH and CHEF respectively.

Scenario 2: Simulation results when number of nodes varies
In this simulation, the numbers of nodes are varied from 100 to 300 while number of rounds is kept fixes as 2500 for all predefined parameters.

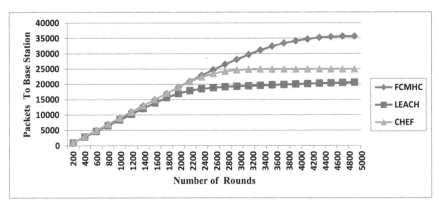

Fig. 6. Rounds vs. Packets to base station

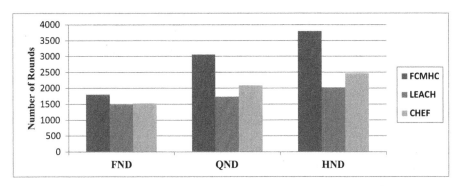

Fig. 7. FND, QND and HND for Scenario 1

Energy Consumption

Figure 8 reveals the comparative analysis of energy consumption for FCMHC with respect to LEACH and CHEF. It can be noticed that proposed scheme has better energy usage as compared to the other two considered protocols for any number of nodes.

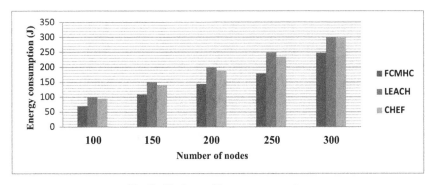

Fig. 8. Nodes vs. Energy consumption

Network Throughput

From Fig. 9, It can clearly be analyzed that FCMHC sends higher number of packets to the BS against LEACH and CHEF thereby our proposed protocol achieves higher throughput irrespective of the count of active nodes in the network because less energy is required for inter- cluster and intra-cluster communication.

Number of Dead Nodes

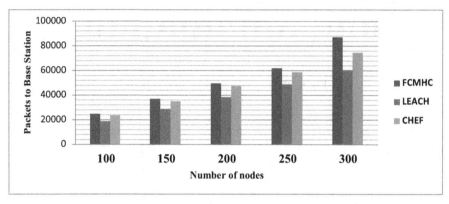

Fig. 9. Nodes vs. Packets to base station

Figure 10 presents a comparative study of all the considered schemes viz. FCMHC, LEACH, and CHEF in terms of the number of dead nodes with increasing number of sensor nodes. It is clear that in all the cases, the 90%–100% nodes for LEACH are dead while with CHEF approximate 45%–90% nodes run out of energy with increase in the number of nodes. With the proposed scheme, the number of dead nodes are too less in all the cases which is approximate 20%. FCMHC shows a fair improvement in the number of active nodes which leads to provide more stable network.

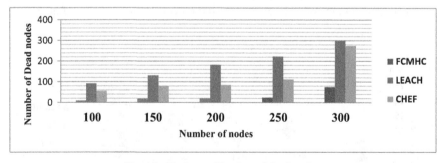

Fig. 10. Nodes vs. Number of dead nodes

6 Conclusion

In this paper we proposed a clustering protocol for routing in wireless sensor network wherein clusters are formed by using Fuzzy C-Means algorithm to achieve optimal partition of nodes in the network. Cluster Heads (CHs) within the cluster are selected with fuzzy logic based system based on the input parameters viz. Node's remnant energy and its distance from cluster centre so as to emphasize effective load balancing. The results of simulating the proposed approach i.e. FCMHC and its comparisons with the other two approaches viz. LEACH & CHEF reveal the following inferences:

- Network stability is increased as more nodes are active for longer period of time because of even load distribution across the nodes of WSN.
- The proposed approach forwards higher volume of information to the BS with less energy consumption than the other approaches under study.

The network lifetime increases due to the reduction in premature death of the nodes because CH is selected while keeping in view the proximity with its members so as to reduce the energy utilization in transmission as the required transmission power is exponential to the Euclidian distance. In future, the artificial intelligence can be supported with fuzzy logic to create more efficient clusters that can handle some quality of service (QoS) issues in WSN.

References

1. Jubair, A.M., et al.: Optimization of clustering in wireless sensor networks: techniques and protocols. Appl. Sci. **11**, 23 (2021). https://doi.org/10.3390/app112311448
2. Patel, N.R., Kumar, S.: Wireless sensor networks' challenges and future prospects. In: 2018 International Conference on System Modeling & Advancement in Research Trends (SMART), pp. 60–65 (2018). https://doi.org/10.1109/SYSMART.2018.8746937
3. Iqbal, M., Naeem, M., Anpalagan, A., Ahmed, A., Azam, M.: Wireless sensor network optimization: multi-objective paradigm. Sensors. **15**(7), 17572–17620 (2015)
4. Tyagi, S., Kumar, N.: A systematic review on clustering and routing techniques based upon LEACH protocol for wireless sensor networks. J. Net. Comput. Appl. **36**(2), 623–645 (2013). ISSN 1084–8045. https://doi.org/10.1016/j.jnca.2012.12.001
5. Zhang, Y., Wang, J., Han, D., Wu, H., Zhou, R.: Fuzzy-logic based distributed energy-efficient clustering algorithm for wireless sensor networks. Sensors **17**, 1554 (2017)
6. Kim, J., Park, S., Han, Y., Chung, T.: CHEF: cluster head election mechanism using Fuzzy logic in wireless sensor networks. In: 2008 10th International Conference on Advanced Communication Technology, Gangwon, Korea (South), pp. 654–659 (2008)
7. Hoang, D.C., Kumar, R., Panda, S.K.: Fuzzy C-Means clustering protocol for wireless sensor networks. In: 2010 IEEE International Symposium on Industrial Electronics, Bari, Italy, pp. 3477–3482 (2010)
8. Dasgupta, S., Dutta, P.: An improved leach approach for head election strategy in a Fuzzy-C means induced clustering of a wireless sensor network. In: Proceedings of the IEMCON Organized by IEM in Collaboration with IEEE, pp. 203–208 (2011)
9. Alia, O.M.: A decentralized Fuzzy C-Means-based energy-efficient routing protocol for wireless sensor networks. Sci. World J. (2014). https://doi.org/10.1155/2014/647281

10. Bensaid, R., Said, M.B., Boujemaa, H.: Fuzzy C-Means based clustering algorithm in WSNs for IoT applications. In: 2020 International Wireless Comm. and Mobile Computing (IWCMC), pp. 126–130 (2020)
11. Panchal, A., Singh, R.K.: EEHCHR: Energy Efficient Hybrid Clustering and Hierarchical Routing for Wireless Sensor Networks. Ad Hoc Networks (2021)
12. Panchal, A., Singh, R.K.: EHCR-FCM: energy efficient hierarchical clustering and routing using Fuzzy C-Means for wireless sensor networks. Telecommun. Syst. **76**(2), 251–263 (2021)
13. Kalaimani, D., Zah, Z., Vashist, S.: Energy-efficient density-based Fuzzy C-Means clustering in WSN for smart grids. Aust. J. Multi-Disciplin. Eng. **17**(1), 23–38 (2021). https://doi.org/10.1080/14488388.2020.1811454
14. Panchal, A., Singh, R.K.: REHR: residual energy based hybrid routing protocol for wireless sensor networks. In: International Conference on Information and Communication Technology, pp.1–5 (2019). https://doi.org/10.1109/CICT48419.2019.9066144
15. Baradaran, A.A., Navi, K.: HQCA-WSN: high-quality clustering algorithm and optimal cluster head selection using fuzzy logic in wireless sensor networks. Fuzzy Sets Syst. **389**, 114–144 (2020). ISSN 0165-0114. https://doi.org/10.1016/j.fss.2019.11.015
16. Panchal, A., Singh, R.K.: EADCR: energy aware distance based cluster head selection and routing protocol for wireless sensor networks. J. Circuits Syst. Comput. **30**(4) (2021)
17. Lee, J.G., Chim, S., Park, H.: Energy-efficient cluster-head selection for wireless sensor networks using sampling-based spider monkey optimization. Sensors **2019**(19), 2093–2109 (2019). https://doi.org/10.3390/s19235281
18. Mehra, P.S., Doja, M.N., Alam, B: Fuzzy based enhanced cluster head selection (FBECS) for WSN. J. King Saud Univ Sci. **32**(1), 390–401 (2020). ISSN 1018-3647. https://doi.org/10.1016/j.jksus.2018.04.031

A Review of Gait Analysis Based on Age and Gender Prediction

Charmy Vora[✉] and Vijay Katkar

Marwadi University, Rajkot, Gujarat, India
charmyvora07@gmail.com

Abstract. The tools for creating and analyzing gaits are improving all the time. Demand for a gait-based dataset that can be recognized and used to extract useful information is at an all-time high. Gait analysis has been around for a while, however, inertial sensor-based gait datasets are a relatively recent development. As a result, the majority of studies employing machine learning algorithms on the gait dataset rely on visual representations. Among the several analyses that may be performed on a person's gait to determine their identity, determining their gender and age proves particularly difficult. Recent studies on gait-based age and gender detection are summarized and compared in this study. This also reveals where researchers want to go in the future and what obstacles they'll have to overcome.

Keywords: Gait analysis · Gait energy image · Gait based gender detection · Gait based age prediction · Machine learning · Deep learning

1 Introduction

Over the last few years, commercial enterprises, governmental organizations, educational institutions, and the general public sectors have all shown attention to video surveillance. It does an excellent work of locating and identifying temporal and spatial abnormalities in videos [1, 2]. In comparison to just capturing data, the use of video analysis in security monitoring offers several advantages. It sees widespread use in the supervision of parking lots, the implementation of safety regulations, the protection of sensitive information, and the supervision of facility protection. However, to analyze surveillance footage, a variety of different approaches, such as automatic number plate identification, crowd detection, people tracking, image change/tamper detection, and people counting, are utilized. In addition, It supports the categorization of a wide variety of items into groups such as common and uncommon, as well as the recognition of faces, motion tracking, classification, tamper detection, and auto-tracking.

Systems for video surveillance may enhance situational awareness through the use of personalized real-time alerts when abnormal behavior is detected that may require a response. One issue with this method of video analysis is how to properly identify people's faces. When it comes to targeted surveillance, face detection is one of the most investigated topics. It has been successfully used in many commonplace scenarios,

S. Rajagopal et al. (Eds.): ASCIS 2022, CCIS 1759, pp. 77–89, 2022.
https://doi.org/10.1007/978-3-031-23092-9_7

including surveillance cameras, computer-human interaction, automated target recognition, safe driving, and medical diagnostics [3]. One of the most popular face recognition methods can identify facial characteristics in each frame, allowing for dynamic face tracking. The use of face detection has several advantages, including extreme security, confidentiality, and difficulty in hacking. Face identification is one of the most complicated natural structural targets, making face detection a challenging area of study. Individuals vary physiologically in a wide range of ways, including how their appearance, communication style, and complexion [4]. In Face detection, Low-resolution surveillance footage is quite challenging due to out-of-focus blur [5]. Therefore, Gait Analysis is the element of human detection that is most advantageous.

The use of biometric features for individual identification is a hotspot of study in the field of computer vision [6]. The term "Gait Recognition" is a way of identifying individuals according to measurements of the uniqueness, one-of-a-kind characteristics of their movement patterns (walking) and behavior [7]. This method is used to recognize persons. In open and public areas, the process of automatically capturing and extracting components of human motion and then using these characteristics to recognize the individual while they are moving can be extremely valuable. However, as compared to a more controlled situation with a fixed view angle, situations like these make Gait identification far more challenging. Because of this, a person's Gait may be altered by a broad variety of circumstances, including the clothes they are wearing, the objects they are carrying, the speed at which they are moving, the shoes they are wearing, and the direction from which they are approaching the ground. One of the most important problems with Gait recognition is presented by shifts in view angle since these shifts can rapidly affect the distinct features that are available for matching. Particular benefits come into play for the Gait biometric, which evaluates behavior, in situations in which the camera is located at a considerable distance and the visuals are of poor quality. Therefore, Gait recognition has been utilized in surveillance to assist in investigations. The Gait biometric, which monitors behavior, is particularly useful in circumstances when the camera is located at a remote location and the visuals are poor. As a result, the use of Gait recognition in surveillance for investigations has been adopted.

The majority of studies on Gait Analysis being conducted today are focused on authenticating and identifying individuals [8]. The human Gait is a major biometric feature that is used in a variety of circumstances, including the estimation of age and the classification of gender, the classification of a person based on their age and gender are two types of general features that have various applications along a wide range of situations [9, 10]. These uses include access control, which restricts the entrance of people who are over a certain age or gender; a commercial application that makes use based on age also monitoring services that provide age restriction functionality or healthcare based on gender and age grouping; Traffic and driving safety improvements in ageing societies; advertising recommendation systems. In all of these cases, the information is presented in a manner that is appropriate to the audience.

Computer vision is becoming increasingly popular for its use in image processing, feature extraction, object recognition, and classification; Gait Analysis is one of the subfields that belongs within computer vision [1]. The human posture may be captured more accurately, which is useful for Gait Analysis. It is common knowledge that computer vision relies on machine learning and deep learning algorithms to achieve greater accuracy. This is especially true when it comes to the process of extracting image features with requirements. Numerous machine learning and deep learning algorithms and methods, like Random Forest (RF), Support Vector Machine (SVM), K-Nearest Neighbor (KNN), Artificial Neural Network (ANN), Convolution Neural Network (CNN), and many more were utilized to classify the features gathered during Gait Analysis to estimate age and gender. The majority of research done in recent years has focused on wearable and visual sensor datasets in an attempt to achieve the highest level of accuracy possible when determining age and gender.

2 Gait Analysis and Feature Extraction

2.1 Gait and Gait Cycle

The term "Gait" describes the humans walking pattern [4]. And the time interval or sequence that occurs among one foot of a human hitting the floor and the next time that foot hits the floor is defined as the Gait Cycle [11]. When one foot touches the ground as a reference and then again when the same foot touches the ground, we say that a single sequence of function has been performed by that limb. Some of the most vital components of Gait are:

Stance phase: 60% of the limb is in touch with the floor during the stance phase, which consists of four phases: i) initial contact, ii) loading response, iii) mid stance, and iv) terminal stance.

Swing phase: Reference to swing at 40 % stages that are not in touch with the floor include following phase: i) the pre-swing, ii) the first swing, iii) the mid swing, and iv) the terminal swing.

Stride: The distance between two successive instances of heel contact made by the same foot is referred to as the stride [12].

2.2 Gait and Gait Cycle

Authentication of a person's identity based on their physiological characteristics. It is a pattern recognition system that compares a person's information to characteristics in order to determine their identity. For example, face detection, voice recognition, fingerprints, and handwritten signatures. The analysis of biometric Gait is known as the term "Biometric Gait Analysis" which refers to the process of determining a person's walking style [6, 8]. The process of authenticating a person based on the way they walk is referred to as Gait recognition.

We need Gait recognition because it is effective even when performed remotely, does not require high-quality footage, and can be performed with minimally invasive equipment. When other identifying features, such as a person's face or fingerprints, are hidden, Gait recognition can still, be effective, and also capturing a person's walk from a considerable distance is possible.

2.3 Gait and Gait Cycle

Silhouette Images

In order to enable more accurate object recognition, the procedure of feature extraction was applied to the video and resulted in the visual sequence being displayed as silhouettes. In order to recover the body silhouette, a straightforward removal of the background and thresholding were utilized. This was then followed by the application of a 3×3 median filter operator to suppress any isolated pixels [13].

Gait Image Energy (GEI)

The GEI is a representation of the Gait pattern of a cycle that uses a weighted average. Walking patterns that coordinate Gait Cycles are called binary silhouettes [14, 15]. It is possible to calculate the Gait energy picture in the following manner when the Gait Cycle image sequence is Bt(x, y):

$$G(x, y) = \frac{1}{N} \sum_{t=1}^{N} Bt(x, y) \tag{1}$$

Bt(x, y) in the context of a series at time t. x and y describe the coordinates of each frame B or image B, and N is the total number of images taken in a Gait Cycle.

Gait Energy Image Projection Model (GPM)

The GPM, is a model that evaluates many characteristics of Gait, such as body size and the movement of the arms and legs. The General Procedures Manual is separated into two major groups of mathematical processes and procedures. Both the GEI Longitudinal Projection (GEL) and GEI Transverse Projection (GTP) are projected in GLP [16, 17]. With the help of the GTP, information about body shape and stride length may be delivered more efficiently. According to the GLP, the slouched posture and head pitch of each GEI image are mathematically connected to the following Gait Cycle. This was discovered by analyzing the Gait Cycles of people walking.

For GLP,

$$GLPcycle = \frac{1}{K} \sum_{j=1}^{K} GLP_j \tag{2}$$

For GTP,

$$GTPcycle = \frac{1}{K} \sum_{j=1}^{K} GTP_j \tag{3}$$

where K elucidates count of frames, *GLPj* and *GTPj* generate *jth* frame-vector of GLP and GTP. GPM now incorporates GTP and GLP in addition to the concatenation approach.

For GPM,

$$GPM = \{GLP_{cycle} \ U \ GTP_{cycle}\} \tag{4}$$

Frame to Exemplar Distance (FED)
When figuring out a person's FED, the whole Gait Cycle is taken into consideration. The silhouette is evaluated by the feature to exemplar distance or FED. This is done by placing 60 points on the silhouette's contours and measuring the Euclidean distance between the centroid of the silhouette and the points. Every six degrees of rotation, up to a total of $360°$ in the opposite direction, contour points are determined.

$$FED_{cycle} = \frac{1}{N} \sum_{i=1}^{N} (FED_{image}) \tag{5}$$

where the N is Number of frames and i^{th} is iteration number.

GEINet
It is suggested that the GEI, be extracted from the ensuing Gait silhouette sequence and then transferred into GEINet. The ability to identify Gaits was achieved through the use of a CNN [10, 18, 19]. There are layers for convolution, pooling, and normalization in the two sequential triplets of the modified GEINet along with fully connected layers with normalization and activation function as softmax.

GaitSet
GaitSet can recognize sets of silhouette images, unlike standard Gait recognition networks that use GEI. Using a CNN, frame-level properties of each reconstructed Gait features are extracted [19]. The set pooling technique combines various frame-level features into a single set-level feature. The set-level feature is then merged with features from different spatial scales and locations using horizontal pyramid mapping to create a discriminative representation [10]. GaitSet used a fully connected layer and Softmax normalization to identify the characteristic.

2.4 Motivation and Application of GEI Motivation

The motivation for using gait analysis for person identification and recognition is given below:

- Gait recognition has numerous advantages over other biometrics. This allows gait to be monitored from a great distance. For some biometric approaches, the user must contact a biometric collector.
- Low-resolution gait analysis is possible. Face recognition may be less accurate with low-quality footage. For this purpose, gait recognition is the preferred method.
- Simple instruments can recognize gait. Human stride data can be collected using a camera, smartphone accelerometer, and floor sensor.
- Gait characteristics are challenging to reproduce. This is because gait recognition uses motions and silhouettes. This characteristic is vital for criminology.
- Gait recognition is possible without participant engagement. In contrast, fingerprints require a person to touch the sensor.

Application of GEI
The following are the application of GEI based Gait recognition and identification:

- Based on the GEI image, we are able to analyze the individual's stance and swing frequency to provide an accurate prediction as to their best possible stride frequency. In addition, we are able to determine the order of the angles and forecast the angles that will arrive. As a consequence of this, it will be beneficial to assume a more accurate pattern of human walking style from the motions of their physical existence, such as the motions of their head, arms, and legs.
- Additionally, it will provide age and gender prediction, which can be helpful in the process of designing applications based on age and gender queries. Some examples of such applications are college entrance purposes based on age, crime, hostels, and movies based on gender category.

3   Evolution Metric

Confusion Matrix: The confusion matrix is a common classifier. It works for binary and multiclass classification and provides True Positive (TP), False Positive (FP), True Negative (TN) and False Negative (FN) statistics based on classification models performance.

Precision: To calculate precision, divide the number of actual positive results by the total number of outcomes that were expected to be positive.

$$Precision = \frac{TP}{TP + FP} \tag{6}$$

Recall: To get the recall, also known as the true positive rate, divide the number of actual positive results by the total number of results that were expected to be positive.

$$Recall = \frac{TP}{TP + FN} \tag{7}$$

Correct Classification Rate (CCR): CCR is calculated by the total number of correct predictions that divided by the total number of data points in the dataset, the CCR is calculated. The highest possible accuracy rating is 1.0, while the lowest is 0.0.

$$CRR = \frac{TP + TN}{TP + TN + Fp + FN} \tag{8}$$

The Mean Squared Error (MSE): MSE measures the average squared difference between the estimated and actual values. It is a risk function whose value should be expected squared error loss. It can't take a negative value, thus closest to zero is ideal.

$$MSE = \frac{1}{N} \sum_{i=1}^{N} (Y_i - \hat{Y}_i) \tag{9}$$

where $\hat{Y}_i$ is predicted values and Y_i is observed values and N is the number of data points.

Root Mean Square Error (RMSE): It measures differences between expected and observed values.

$$RMSD = \sqrt{\frac{\sum_{i=1}^{N} (Y_i - \hat{Y}_i)^2}{N}} \tag{10}$$

where i_{th} is variable, N denotes the number of data points that are not missing, $\hat{Y}_i$ is the estimated series of time and Y_i actual observations series of time.

Mean Absolute Error (MAE): It calculates the difference in error between two observations of the same occurrence. Y versus X includes predicted versus observed, subsequent versus starting time, and one measuring technique versus another.

$$MAE = \frac{\sum_{i=1}^{N} |y_i - x_i|}{n} \tag{11}$$

where the n is t total number of data points x_i represents true value and y_i shows the prediction.

Correlation Coefficient (CC): It is also often known as Pearson's r, is a measurement for the linear correlation of two sets of data.

$$r = \frac{\sum (x_i - \bar{x})(y_i - \bar{y})}{\sqrt{\sum (x_i - \bar{x})^2 \sum (y_i - \bar{y})}} \tag{12}$$

where r is the CC, y_i shows the y variable's value in a sample and $\bar{y}$ is the mean of the y variable's value and x_i represents the x variable's value in a sample, $\bar{x}$ is the mean of the x variable's value.

R-squared (R^2) score: In a regression model, it indicates the proportion of a dependent variable's variance that is described by independent variables. Correlation displays the strength of an independent-dependent relationship, whereas R^2 indicates the proportion that one variable's variation described another's variance.

$$R^2 = 1 - \frac{\sum_{i=1}^{n} (y_i - f(x_i))^2}{\sum_{i=1}^{n} (y_i - \bar{y})^2} \tag{13}$$

4 Related Work

Hema M. and Pitta S. [16] used OU-ISIR dataset for the purpose of age classification, and the SVM is used as the classifier. For the purpose of age classification, a method known as the GPM is utilized. They compared GEI, SM, GPM, and FED (Silhouette Model), where GPM had 89.1% CCR which was 4.1% higher than GEI, 26.1% more than FED, and 14.63% higher than SM. Descriptor fusion for GPM, FED, and GEI gave a 91.8% CCR better outcomes than individual descriptors.

K. Khabir et al. [20] proposed a system for forecasting the age and gender from the Osaka University-ISIR Gait Database's inertial sensor-based Gait dataset [21]. The database had taken into consideration data from an accelerometer, a gyroscope, and a smartphone worn around the subject's waist. These components make up the three inertial measuring units. They used regression in order to estimate ages, and gender was used as the classification feature. They used KNN, SVM (RBF), and DT (Decision Tree) for age regression, where the DT had the maximum variance R^2 score is 0.64 and the Mean square error is 0.36. For gender classification, SVM had the highest accuracy at 84.76% compared to KNN, and RF.

Sun Bei et al. [22] examined an innovative visual camera sensor-based approach to gender detection. Instead of employing a single GEI, SubGEI from the Gait Cycle was used to extract optical flow as temporal body movement data for complex Gait Analysis [15]. Compared to CNN-based models, two-stream CNN produced better results since it made use of both temporal and spatial data [1, 2]. The following view angles, including 18°, 36°, 54°, 72°, 90°, 108°, 126°, 144°, and 172°, are used to establish the results. Additionally, they created custom CNNs with 4 layers and also used Inception-V3 and VGG16. Additionally, there were three sets of the SubGEI, designated as Tl-1, TL-2, and TL-3, with respect to 4, 6, and 8 numbers of frames. When contrasting CNN, CNN+SVM, and two stream networks using the following parameters as a normal situation, caring bags, wearing clothes, and mixed situation. Where the TL-2 set had 6 frames of the SubGEI in inception-v3 they achieved close to 95% accuracy on 90° angle utilizing two-stream networks in normal conditions.

Q. Riaz et al. [23] examined the method that based on 50 handcrafted [6D acceleration/angular velocity ratio-temporal characteristics] non-visual characteristics, this method did not require a highly computational model to estimate age. RFR (Random Forest Regressor) is best for age estimation among SVR (Support Vector Regressor), and MLP (Multi-Layer Perceptron). On hybrid data (phone-embedded and wearable Inertial Measurement Unit (IMU), used a complete dataset where RFR's 10-fold RMSE is 3.32 years and subject-wise is 8.22 years. Using only smartphone MPU-6500 data and the whole dataset, the RFR generated a 10-fold RMSE of 2.94 years and a subject-wise of 6.84 years giving good results as compared to hybrid data. RFR's average RMSE error for 10-fold cross-validation is 5.42 years and 11.35 years for subject-wise cross-validation.

S. Gillani et al. [24] used various machine learning methods to estimate ages and classify people's genders, and then they extracted features from those analyses. They used 3 IMUZ sensors where the inertial signals are captured by a triangle accelerometer and gyroscope. Three sensors were mounted to the waist: two on the sides and one in the middle. IMUZ can be replaced by a smartphone with accelerometer and gyroscope sensors. Signals were captured as subjects walked on a specified path when arriving (Sequence 0) and leaving (Sequence 1). Age estimation included CC, MAE, and RMSE. Where Liner Regression, MLP, SVM, and RF are used, SVM had good results such as 0.57 CC, 11.6 MAE, and 14.0 RMSE in sequence 0. And gender classification was based on True Positive rate, recall, and classification accuracy, and they used methods such as Logistic Regression, MLP, SVM, RF, and Naive Bayes (NB). The logistic regression method gave the best results with 72.2% male recall, 63.9% female recall, and 68.2% classification accuracy in sequence 0.

C. Xu et al. [19] focused on uncertainty age application that is age-dependent. An application that queries or groups by age. By adopting distribution of label, the learning framework can assist with uncertainty-based age estimation by adopting appearance-based Gait features and discrete label distribution instead of a single estimate age and reduced loss function. MAE was used to evaluate age estimation accuracy. By overlapping expected and ground truth statements, IOU is calculated. We received 95% IOU for predicting the age statistic, which is closer to the ground truth, and Gait Set's MSE is 4.91 years, which is better than GEINet's MSE of 5.41 years.

C. Xu at al. [10] used the Single Image, Instead of a sequence of Gait features. The Single Image of Gait set is utilized to estimate the probability distribution of integer age labels and gender recognition. That will improve in real-world applications in the future. The results were better at 75° to 90° degrees (side view). The results of age and gender on a single image were an MAE of 8.93 and a CS of 16.39 respectively. And the outcomes for gender classification results for a single image are 94.27% was determined using CCR.

B. Kwon and S. Lee [25] examined 3D gender classification using joint swing energy (JSE). JSE calculates the distance between model skeleton joints and anatomical planes when a person is striding. Anatomical planes are commonly extracted from fixed poses instend of the motion. They studied an innovative technique for gaining crosswise, median and frontal planes by utilizing sequence of 3D gait. They enable human-centered measurements to be used to represent the motion of each joint. They identified JSEs from 3D Gait sequences using the provided approaches. They examined 4 datasets and applied KNN, NB, DT, and SVM. They acquired the best accuracy (98.08%) using JSE-SVM in dataset B, which has 104 users (50 male, 54 female).

J. Upadhyay and T. Gonsalves [9] found out to make the system more lightweight and strong, and to avoid the perception of Pearson's moment based on angles, the best possible results may be obtained when classifying people according to their gender. Utilizing the discrete cosine transform (DCT) that was implemented on GEI in order to extract DCT) vectors that were applied on XGBoost to perform gender classification. Based on 14 view angles of Gait data, we calculated the mean CCR for gender classification, which was 95.33 %.

Y. Chen et al. [26] recorded 960 steps from 24 younger and older subjects applying a sole pressure mat and estimating the Centre of pressure trajectory. SVM was applied to 30 features, including initial contact, forefoot contact, foot flat, and forefoot pushoff. SVM-kernel RBF compared linear, sigmoid, and polynomial where the RBF-SVM kernel COP (Center of Pressure) features with 99.65% accuracy. Moreover, they used 13 different stages that were required for each participant and achieved 95% accuracy in age recognition. And 5 steps for each participant and achieved 97% accuracy in gender detection.

5   Comparison and Summary of Related Research Work

Comparison and summary of related research work carried out by various researchers is presented in Table 1. It can be easily observed from the comparison table that huge amount of scope is available for applying deep learning and transfer learning approaches to improve the performance of Gait recognition.

Table 1. Comparison and Summary of related research work

References	Gait features	Dataset	Machine learning model	Purpose of study (age/gender detection)	Evolution metric	Accuracy
[16]	GPM + GEI + FED	OU-ISIR	SVM	Age	CCR	91.8%
[20]	Accelerometer and Gyro scope used to Capture Gait Features	OU-ISIR	SVM	Gender	CCR	84.76%
			DT	Age	R^2	0.64
					MSE	0.36
[22]	Multiple Sub GEI for Temporal Events	CASIA B	Inception-V3	Gender	CCR	Near to 95%
[23]	Inertial data of human walk to compute the spatio spectral features from 6D acceleration and angular velocity	Using Chest–mounted inertial measurement Units	RF	Age	RMSE 10 fold Cross Validation	2.94 years
[24]	Accelerometer and Gyroscope used to Capture Gait Features	OU-ISIR	LR	Gender	CCR	68.2%
			SVM	Age	CC	0.57
					MAE	11.6
					RMSE	14.0
[19]	GaitSet, GEINet	OULP-Age from OU-ISIR	Age label distribution using KL divergences	Age	MAE	4.91 years
[10]	GaitSet, GEINet	OU-MLVP	SVM	Gender	CCR	96.04%
			Age label distribution using KL divergences	Age	MAE	6.63 years
[25]	JSE	4 custom datasets used	SVM	Gender	CCR	98.08%
[9]	GEI	OU-MVLP	XGBoost	Gender	CCR	95.33%
[26]	COP (960 steps of 24 young and participated)	Using in-sole pressure mats	SVM	Gender	CCR	94%

6   Future Work

Huge amount of work is done by the researchers in this field of research but still many things can be added to enrich this field. Some of the pointers for future research work are listed below:

1) Gait Analysis can be used to predict the height and weight of a person.
2) Focus on overcoming the issue of Gait obstruction and creating a robust system that can compete with partially accessible Gait.
3) Additional data should be obtained from a wider variety of groups, particularly those that differ in terms of their ethnicity and body shape, in order to make the model better resilient.
4) One possible direction for research in the future is to find ways to smooth out the predicted age and gender distribution. Sometimes there is a drastic shift in the odds between two consecutive age labels. As a result, a dataset that is both symmetrical and comprehensive is required.
5) Develop an age and gender predictor that is sensitive to the impact of many parameters, including carrying status and also walking speed.

7 Limitations and Challenges

Huge amount of work is done by the researchers to solve many problems but still some problems are there. These are listed below:

1) The performance of the system is negatively impacted whenever there is a change in the person's clothing condition or the camera view angle.
2) The pattern of gait is influenced by a variety of different elements, one of which is age, walking is dependent on the strength of one's muscles, which naturally decreases as a person gets older. Variations in muscular strength of persons of the same age have an effect on walking style.
3) It is understood that there are alterations in the Gait pattern that occur during pregnancy.
4) Because of the increased sample rate required for faster person movement, accuracy decreases.

8 Conclusion

High demand exists for a gait-based dataset that may be utilized to extract useful information. Gait analysis isn't new, but sensor-based gait datasets are. The majority of machine learning studies on the gait dataset rely on visual representations. Identifying a person's gender and age from their gait is challenging. In this study, gait-based age and gender detection studies are compared. It also shows where researchers wish to go and what challenges they face.

References

1. Zhao, Y.: Effective Gait Feature Extraction Using Temporal Fusion and Spatial Partial School of Computer Science, School of Artificial Intelligence, Optics and Electronics (iOPEN), Northwestern Polytechnical University, Xi' an 710072, Shaanxi, P. R. China, pp. 1244–1248 (2021)

2. Arai, K., Andrie, R.: Human gait gender classification in spatial and temporal reasoning. Int. J. Adv. Res. Artif. Intell. **1** (2012). https://doi.org/10.14569/ijarai.2012.010601

3. Zafaruddin,G.M., Fadewar, H.S.: Face Recognition Using Eigenfaces. Springer, Singapore (2018). https://doi.org/10.1007/978-981-13-1513-8_87

4. Wan, C., Wang, L., Phoha, V. V.: A survey on gait recognition. ACM Comput. Surv. **51** (2018). https://doi.org/10.1145/3230633

5. Singh, J.P., Jain, S., Arora, S., Singh, U.P.: Vision-based gait recognition: a survey. IEEE Access. **6**, 70497–70527 (2018). https://doi.org/10.1109/ACCESS.2018.2879896

6. Zhang, Z., Hu, M., Wang, Y.: A survey of advances in biometric gait recognition. Lect. Notes Comput. Sci. (including Subser. Lect. Notes Artif. Intell. Lect. Notes Bioinformatics). 7098 LNCS, 150–158 (2011). https://doi.org/10.1007/978-3-642-25449-9_19

7. Jawed, B., Khalifa, O.O., Newaj Bhuiyan, S.S.: Human gait recognition system. In: Proceedings 2018 7th International Conference on Computer and Communication Engineering (ICCCE 2018), pp. 89–92 (2018). https://doi.org/10.1109/ICCCE.2018.8539245

8. Kale, A., et al.: Identification of humans using gait. IEEE Trans. Image Process. **13**, 1163–1173 (2004). https://doi.org/10.1109/TIP.2004.832865

9. Upadhyay, J., Gonsalves, T.: Robust and lightweight system for gait-based gender classification toward viewing angle variations. Ai. **3**, 538–553 (2022). https://doi.org/10.3390/ai3 020031

10. Xu, C., et al.: Real-time gait-based age estimation and gender classification from a single image. In: Proceeding - 2021 IEEE Winter Conference on Applications of Computer Vision (WACV 2021), pp. 3459–3469 (2021). https://doi.org/10.1109/WACV48630.2021.00350

11. Babaee, M., Li, L., Rigoll, G.: Maryam Babaee Linwei Li Gerhard Rigoll. In: 2018 25th IEEE International Conference on Image Processing, pp. 768–772 (2018)

12. Yaacob, N.I., Tahir, N.M.: Feature selection for gait recognition. In: SHUSER 2012–2012 IEEE Symposium on Humanities, Science and Engineering Research, pp. 379–383 (2012). https://doi.org/10.1109/SHUSER.2012.6268871

13. Collins, R.T., Gross, R., Shi, J.: Silhouette-based human identification from body shape and gait. In: Proceedings of the Fifth IEEE International Conference on Automatic Face and Gesture Recognition (FGR 2002), pp. 366–371 (2002). https://doi.org/10.1109/AFGR.2002. 1004181

14. Luo, J., Zi, C., Zhang, J., Liu, Y.: Gait recognition using GEI and curvelet. Guangdian Gongcheng/Opto-Electronic Eng. **44**, 400–404 (2017). https://doi.org/10.3969/j.issn.1003-501X.2017.04.003

15. Liu, T., Sun, B., Chi, M., Zeng, X.: Gender recognition using dynamic gait energy image. Proceeding 2017 IEEE 2nd Information Technology, Networking, Electronic and Automation Control Conference (ITNEC 2017), 2018-Janua, pp. 1078–1081 (2018). https://doi.org/10. 1109/ITNEC.2017.8284905

16. Hema, M., Pitta, S.: Human age classification based on gait parameters using a gait energy image projection model. In: Proceedings International Conference on Trends in Electronics and Informatics (ICOEI 2019), pp. 1163–1168 (2019). https://doi.org/10.1109/ICOEI.2019. 8862788

17. Hema, M., Esther Rachel, K.: Gait energy image projections based on gender detection using support vector machines. In: Proceedings 5th International Conference on Electronics and Communication Systems (ICECS 2020), pp. 1315–1320 (2020). https://doi.org/10.1109/ICC ES48766.2020.09137900

18. Shiraga, K., Makihara, Y., Muramatsu, D., Echigo, T., Yagi, Y.: GEINet: View-invariant gait recognition using a convolutional neural network. In: 2016 International Biometric Conference (ICB 2016) (2016). https://doi.org/10.1109/ICB.2016.7550060

19. Xu, C., et al.: Uncertainty-aware gait-based age estimation and its applications. IEEE Trans. Biom. Behav. Identity Sci. **3**, 479–494 (2021). https://doi.org/10.1109/TBIOM.2021.3080300

20. Khabir, K.M., Siraj, M.S., Ahmed, M., Ahmed, M.U.: Prediction of gender and age from inertial sensor-based gait dataset. In: 2019 Joint 8th International Conference on Informatics, Electronics & Vision (ICIEV 2019) & 3rd International Conference on Imaging, Vision & Pattern Recognition (icIVPR 2019) with International Conference on Activity and Behavior Computing (ABC 2019), pp. 371–376 (2019). https://doi.org/10.1109/ICIEV.2019.8858521

21. Sprager, S., Juric, M.B.: Inertial sensor-based gait recognition: a reviewa. Sensors. **15**(9), 22089–22127 (2015). https://doi.org/10.3390/s150922089

22. Bei, S., Deng, J., Zhen, Z., Shaojing, S.: Gender recognition via fused silhouette features based on visual sensors. IEEE Sens. J. **19**, 9496–9503 (2019). https://doi.org/10.1109/JSEN.2019.2916018

23. Riaz, Q., Hashmi, M.Z.U.H., Hashmi, M.A., Shahzad, M., Errami, H., Weber, A.: Move your body: age estimation based on chest movement during normal walk. IEEE Access. **7**, 28510–28524 (2019). https://doi.org/10.1109/ACCESS.2019.2901959

24. Gillani, S.I., Azam, M.A., Ehatisham-Ul-Haq, M.: Age estimation and gender classification based on human gait analysis. In: 2020 International Conference on Emerging Trends in Smart Technologies (ICETST 2020), pp. 5–10 (2020). https://doi.org/10.1109/ICETST49965.2020.9080735

25. Kwon, B., Lee, S.: Joint swing energy for skeleton-based gender classification. IEEE Access. **9**, 28334–28348 (2021). https://doi.org/10.1109/ACCESS.2021.3058745

26. Chen, Y.J., Chen, L.X., Lee, Y.J.: Systematic evaluation of features from pressure sensors and step number in gait for age and gender recognition. IEEE Sens. J. **22**, 1956–1963 (2022). https://doi.org/10.1109/JSEN.2021.3136162

Handwritten Signature Verification Using Convolution Neural Network (CNN)

Dhruvi Gosai[✉], Shraddha Vyas, Sanjay Patel, Prasann Barot, and Krishna Suthar

CHARUSAT, Changa, India
{dhruvigosai.dce,shraddhavyas.ce,sanjaypatel.dce,
prasannbarot.dce}@charusat.ac.in

Abstract. Despite recent widespread research in the field, handwritten signature verification is still an unresolved research problem. A person's signature is an important biometric trait of a human that can be used to verify a person's identification. There are two primary biometric identification methods: (i) A method of identification based on vision and (ii) An identification method without the use of vision. Examples of vision-based identification include face reading, fingerprint identification, and retina scanning. The other examples for non-vision-based identification include speech recognition and signature verification. In financial, commercial, and legal activities, signatures are crucial. Two methods are widely studied and investigated for signature verification: the online method (dynamic method) and the offline method (Static approach). Offline systems are more practical and user-friendly than online systems, but because they lack dynamic information, offline verification is regarded to be more difficult. Systems for verifying signatures are designed to determine if a particular signature is authentic (made by the claimed individual) or a forgery (produced by an impostor). The data collection, feature extraction, feature selection, and classification model make up the bulk of the suggested model. A convolutional neural network is used to extract features, and machine learning algorithms are used to verify handwritten signatures. To train CNN models for feature extraction and data augmentation, raw images of signatures are employed. VGG16, Inception-v3, Res-Net50, and Xception CNN architectures are employed. The recovered attributes are classified as authentic or false using Euclidean distance, cosine similarity, and supervised learning techniques such as Logistic Regression, Random Forest, SVM, and its variants. Data from ICDAR 2011, including pairwise-organized Signature Datasets, was used for testing. The database comprises the signatures of 69 different people.

Keywords: Neural network · Signature recognition and verification · Verification system · Features extraction · Classification

1 Introduction

A person's signature is a crucial component of their authenticity. In the financial industry, both before biometrics and, unexpectedly, today. The most important way to authenticate an individual's identity is through a signature. The primary goal of this study is to create

S. Rajagopal et al. (Eds.): ASCIS 2022, CCIS 1759, pp. 90–106, 2022.
https://doi.org/10.1007/978-3-031-23092-9_8

a deep learning-based handwriting verification system. This system generates output as a Boolean value from a pair of two signatures in the portable network graphics pictures (PNG) format as its input parameter (1 or 0).

The signature serves as authorization for all legal dealings. People's handwritten signatures are distinctive and challenging to imitate [2]. It comes naturally and instinctively to verify signatures. It is simple to understand and have confidence in the innovation [1]. There are two methods available for verifying signatures: (i) An online strategy and (ii) An offline strategy. In the online approach, an electronic slate and pen tied to a computer are used to obtain features about a signature and capture dynamic data for verification purposes, such as pressure, velocity, and writing speed. Online signature verification systems analyze handwritten signatures properly using signal processing techniques like normalization, Fourier transforms, and correlation functions. The offline solution leverages signature images that have been taken by a scanner or camera and uses less electrical control [1]. The characteristics utilized for digital signature verification are far more basic. Only the pixel image should be evaluated in this [2]. Offline signature verification systems examine the accuracy of the signatures using image processing methods. This method can be helpful in a variety of applications, including bank checks, medical certifications, and prescriptions, among others. Here, we discuss an offline method of recognizing signatures. The outcome of this process is typically expressed as a fit ratio (1 for authenticity and 0 for fabrication) in terms of 0 or 1 [3], which are related to intra and interpersonal variability. Interpersonal variation is the difference between a person's signatures. Interpersonal Variation is the term used to describe the difference between originals and counterfeit [5].

In signature verification systems there are three types of forgeries signatures available:

1. Random forgeries: signatures that are executed without regard for the signer's name or signature style
2. Simple forgeries: a signature that just contains the signer's name and no other information.
3. Skilled forgeries: a signature that accurately mimics the original's shape and signatory name [4] (Fig. 1).

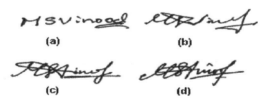

Fig. 1. Examples of forgery signature a) Random type b) Unskilled type c) Skilled type d) Original Signature

These methods are widely used for authentication purposes in the following fields:

- e-KYC
- Instant Document Verification
- Banking and Financial Services
- Government Official work
- Health
- Real Estate
- Insurance
- Telecom
- Commercial

Numerous strategies have been applied to Handwritten Signature Verification (HSV), especially offline HSV, and the field is continuously being researched [2]. Different features were extracted and classification algorithms were applied to the approaches.

The sections of this essay are as follows: Information regarding this field is provided in Section 0. The relevant work is provided in Sect. 1. Introduced in Sect. 2 is the suggested system. The experimental findings are presented in Sect. 3, and the conclusion and suggested future study are presented in Sect. 4.

1.1 About the Domain

Image processing: Image processing is the application of mathematical operations to an image, a sequence of pictures, or a video, such as photographs or video frames; the outcome of image processing might be an image or a set of features or parameters associated with an image. Most image processing systems allow for the picture to be treated as a two-dimensional array or signal and typical signal-processing methods to be applied to it [9].

Biometrics: Biometrics is the assessment or quantifiable analysis of a person's physical/behavioral characteristics. The approach is mostly used for identification, security, and access control, as well as for investigating persons who are being watched. The core concept of biometric validation is that each individual is distinct and may be identified by physical or behavioral characteristics [9].

Machine Learning: Machine learning is a branch of science that deals with programming computers such that they may learn on their own and improve over time. In machine learning, learning entails identifying and comprehending input data and proceeding with and making sound judgments based on that data. Taking particular care of all potential data inputs is exceedingly tough. To address this issue, researchers create algorithms that generate knowledge from explicit data and prior engagement in standards such as insights, reasoning, likelihood hypothesis, search, combinatorial advancement, support learning, and control hypothesis [9].

2 Related Work

[1] Pansare et al. suggested a "Handwritten signature verification using neural network," This is essentially a signature validation approach that combines image prepossessing,

geometric feature extraction, neural network training using wavelet transforms, and validation. Preprocessing is broken into four stages: (i) Image conversion to binary (ii) image scaling (iii)thinning (iv)signature bounding box to produce a noiseless and standard image in the following stage, several properties are obtained to build normalized vector for use as input to a neural network. These cycles are repeated throughout the testing procedure. In this publication, classification is accomplished using a neural network and the error backpropagation training technique.

[2] Hatkar et al. offered an "Offline Handwritten Signature Verification using Neural Network" that provided a signature verification method that may be broken into two stages: (A) the Stage of training and (B) The testing phase. A training stage consists of four basic steps: picture retrieval, image preprocessing, feature extraction, and neural network training. The image retrieval process is the initial phase. Images are collected from the database in this stage. Preprocessing is the second phase. Using resizing and thinning, we achieved great high-quality photos in this phase. The third phase is feature extraction, which comprises obtaining the center of mass, maximum horizontal and vertical histograms, aspect ratio, Tri surface, the six-fold surface, and Transition feature. These characteristics are combined to form a vector. All of these processes are performed for testing signatures during the Testing stage. Following that, a trained neural network is used to apply a normalized feature vector of a test signature to determine if a signature is real or counterfeit. In this study, neural networks achieved an accuracy of 86.25%.

[4] Al-Omari et al. proposed a "State-of-the-art in offline signature verification system" that focuses on knowledge-based signature verification and includes five key stages such as image acquisition and preprocessing where input signatures are preprocessed with two techniques: (i)enhancement process (ii)segmentation process to obtain standard and qualitative images. Personal (local and global) characteristics are retrieved and saved in the knowledge base during the Post Processing step. This research article conducts a comparison investigation on several classification approaches such as DWT, HMM, SVM, NN, Template matching technique, and statistical approach.

[6] Sisodia et al suggested an "Off-line handwritten signature verification using artificial neural network classifier" that focused on the static signature verification system (SSV) and included four stages: pre-processing, feature extraction, classification, and decision-making. The input signature samples are further processed by the preprocessor to make them suitable for feature extraction. In this study, classification is done using an Artificial Neural Network (ANN) with Error Back Propagation (EBP), which has a verification efficiency of 94.27%.

[7] Kancharla et al has developed "Handwritten signature recognition: a convolutional neural network method," which presents a Convolution Neural Network model for off-line signature detection using image preprocessing techniques on raw images: To reduce noisy backdrop, do (A) Grayscale Conversion & Finalization, (B) Morphological Transformation, and (C) Image Resizing.

[8] "Indian Number Handwriting Features Extraction and Classification Using Multi-Class SVM," suggested Jeiad et al. A Multi-Class SVM-based model for extracting and categorizing handwriting features is presented in this paper. The model is divided into four fundamental phases. The first process is image acquisition, in which the interested handwritten number is scanned and acquired at 300 dpi to ensure sufficient quality. The

preparation phase follows, which includes picture improvement and noise reduction by converting the image to grayscale and building a composite image thinning to show the skeleton of the target item. The third stage is the features extraction phase, in which a 16-element features vector is created by assessing four parameters such as one element's beginning locations, junction points, the average zone of four elements, and the normalized chain vector of 10 elements. In this research, the multi-class SVM (MSVM) model is employed to obtain around 97% of accurate recognition.

[9] "Handwritten Signature Verification Using Local Binary Pattern Features and KNN," suggested Tejas Jadhav. This paper describes the phases of pre-processing, LBP image conversion, feature extraction, and classification. Before building the system below, a total of 40 distinct signature recognition algorithms from various research articles were reviewed and studied. The system would assign a decision class to each of the testing photos, which we could then compare to their real classes to determine the system's correctness. The feature vector set has 16 features, including 8 normal and 8 texture features. The pre-processed picture is used to extract normal features, whereas the LBP image is used to extract texture features. Aspect Ratio, Center of Gravity - X, Center of Gravity - Y: The Y-Center of Gravity, Baseline Shift, Energy, Dissimilarity, Haralick, and Kurtosis are the pre-processed pictures. Contrast, Normalized Area, Homogeneity, Energy, Dissimilarity, Haralick, Skewness, and Kurtosis are the LBP texture-based characteristics retrieved from the LBP picture. The suggested system's accuracy is 85.66%, according to experimental findings.

[14] Muhammed Mutlu Yapc, Adem Tekerek, and Nurettin Topaloglu suggested a "Convolutional Neural Network Based Offline Signature Verification Application." To prevent hostile actors from forging signatures, this study proposes an offline signature verification technique based on Deep Learning (DL). The DL technique used in the paper is the Convolutional Neural Network (CNN). CNN was built and trained separately for two unique models, one Writer Dependent (WD) and one Writer Independent (WI) (WI). WI had a success rate of 62.5%, whereas WD had a success rate of 75%. The GPDS synthetic Signature database is used in this analysis.

[15] "Offline Handwritten Signature Verification - Literature Review" was proposed by Luiz G. Hafeman, Robert Sabourin, and Luiz S. Oliveira. Preprocessing, feature extraction, and categorization are all part of the planned effort. Signature verification relies heavily on preprocessing. Signature pictures might differ in terms of pen thickness, size, and rotation. Signature Extraction, Noise Removal, Size Normalization, and Signature Representation are all signature alignment processes used to treat the picture. A description that takes the signature's curvature into account is proposed. Fitting Benzier curves to the signature contour (particularly, the largest region of the signature) and utilizing the curve parameters as features enabled this.

[16] Subham Kedia, Ramesh Kumar Mohapatra, and Kumar Shaswat [16] offered "Offline Handwritten Signature Verification using CNN Inspired by the Inception V1 Architecture." Image capture, preprocessing, feature extraction, and classification are all part of the proposed study. The image acquisition method digitizes handwritten signatures. Even among legitimate signatures of a person, signature samples might vary in terms of pen thickness, size, pivot, and so on. The preprocessing stage removes noise from the image and converts it to the proper format. The signature traits are then extracted

and integrated into a feature set before training the model for a writer-independent classifier and testing it on the test set. In this work, the Convolutional Neural Network was employed to teach writer independent features for each user. Convolutional neural networks were used to take advantage of the fact that counterfeit and authentic signatures differ in numerous key areas. Experiment results indicate that the InceptionSVGNet Architecture is more efficient at identifying patterns in pictures by leveraging bigger networks.

3   Proposed Methodology

(See Fig. 2)

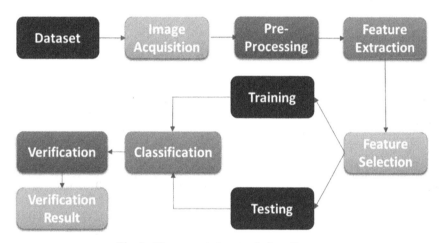

Fig. 2. The suggested system's flow diagram

1. Dataset:
The datasets utilized in this suggested system were authentic and faked by diverse writers. To train and validate the model for signature recognition, only utilize real signature samples.

We took data from ICDAR 2011, which comprises Signature Datasets, and structured it in paired form for testing. The database comprises the signatures of 69 individuals. The graphics are in Portable Network Graphics format (PNG).

Dataset Structure:

1. Authentic signatures: 30 genuine signatures, 5 samples each.
2. Forged: 5 samples of forged signatures from the same 30 persons as in the real folder.

File naming convention:	NFI-XXXYYZZZZ
Explanation:	XXX - The ID number of the individual who signed the document.
	YY denotes the image sample number.
	ZZZ - The ID number of the individual whose signature appears in the photo.

For example, NFI-00702024 is a picture of person number 024's signature done by person 007. This is a forgery of a signature.

NFI-02203022 is a picture of person number 022's signature done by person 022. This is an authentic signature (Fig. 3).

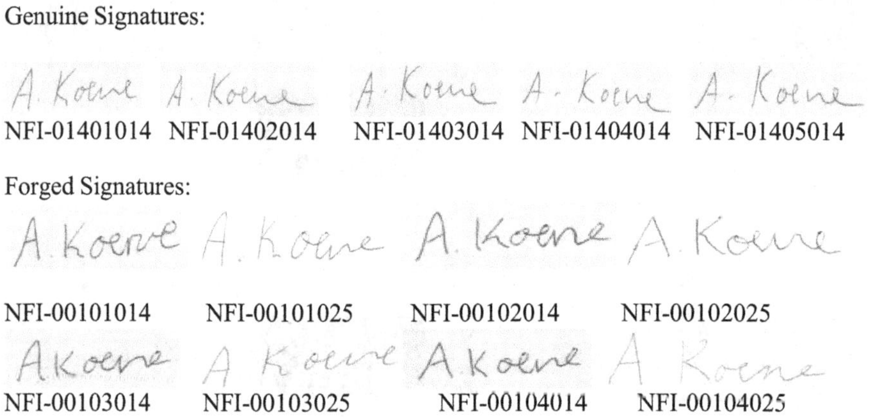

Genuine Signatures:

NFI-01401014   NFI-01402014   NFI-01403014   NFI-01404014   NFI-01405014

Forged Signatures:

NFI-00101014   NFI-00101025   NFI-00102014   NFI-00102025

NFI-00103014   NFI-00103025   NFI-00104014   NFI-00104025

Fig. 3. Dataset of signature images

2. Libraries for simulation

Matplotlib: Matplotlib is a Python package that enables you to produce static, animated, and interactive visualizations.

Pandas: Pandas is a free open-source library designed primarily for dealing with structured or labelled data in a straightforward and easy manner. It provides an assortment of data structures and methods for processing quantitative data and time series. This library is based on the NumPy library. Pandas is quick, with great efficiency and productivity for individuals.

Numpy: NumPy is a Python tool for multidimensional array manipulation. It contains a powerful multidimensional array object as well as utilities for manipulating these arrays. It is the essential Python library for numerical computation. It is free and open-source solution.

Seaborn: Seaborn is a phenomenal Python package for visual quantitative charting presentation. Seaborn has a variety of colour palette and aesthetic styles via design to make creating a variety of statistical visualizations in Python more appealing.

Sklearn: Scikit-learn (Sklearn) is the most efficient and powerful Python machine learning package. It provides a set of essential tools for statistical and machine learning modelling, including such classification, regression, clustering, and dimensionality reduction, through the use of a Python platform.

TensorFlow: Google developed and made available TensorFlow, a Python library for efficient numerical processing. It is an architecture package that can be used to build Deep Learning models directly and through wrapper libraries built on top of TensorFlow.

3. Preprocessing:

The signature verification technique relies heavily on preprocessing. Throughout the training and testing phases, the pre-processing step is employed. Signatures in grayscale are scanned. The goal of this stage is to develop signature standards so that feature extraction may begin. Pre-processing enhances picture quality and prepares it for feature extraction [1]. The preceding stage includes:

3.1 Converting Image to Binary

TO facilitate feature extraction, a grayscale signature picture is transformed into binary [1]. This stage involves RGB to Gray picture conversion, which converts the three-dimensional color signature images into a two-dimensional grey image with intensities ranging from 0 to 255. Finally, we trim the picture such that it contains only the signature object and no unnecessary white borders [9].

3.2 Noise Removal

NOISE is common in scanned signature pictures. Use a noise reduction filter, such as a median filter, to eliminate noise from the picture [10].

3.3 Image Enlargement

THE signatures acquired from signatories are of varied sizes; scaling is performed to get the signatures to the standard size of 256*256 [1].

4 Feature Extraction

IT is the most used method for extracting elements or characteristics from a picture. The retrieved characteristics are responsible for the accuracy of signature verification in the design system [4]. Extracted features are classified into two types: (i) Global characteristics and (ii) Local Characteristics

Global elements, such as the signature's height and breadth, describe the signature images as a whole. Local features, on the other hand, characterize areas of images by segmenting the image (using linked components, for example) or, more commonly, by dividing the image in a grid (of Cartesian or polar coordinates) and applying feature extractors to each region of the image [10].

Convolutional neural networks (CNN) are widely used neural network topologies for processing image collections. First, the CNN model is trained with the real and fake signatures as independent classes. On the dataset, we train the model with an 80–20 split (which may be modified based on requirements). To compare the accuracy, 16 models were trained. The four architectures used for feature extraction are VGG16, Inception-v3, ResNet-50, and Xception.

Optimizers used to compile the models are: -

- SGD stands for Stochastic gradient descent
- RMSProp stands for Root Mean Square Propagation
- Adagrad stands for Adaptive Gradient Algorithm
- Adam stands for Active Design and Analysis Modeling (Tables 1 and 2 and Fig. 4)

Table 1. Parameters

Architecture	VGG16	Inception-v3	ResNet-50	Xception
Parameters	138M	24M	23M	23M
Features	512	2048	2048	2048

Table 2. Feature extraction result

	Optimizers			
	SGD	RMSprop	Adagrad	Adam
VGG16	0.8648	0.9645	0.8821	0.9584
Inception-v3	0.8042	0.9827	0.9567	0.9922
ResNet50	0.9515	0.9991	0.9991	0.9974
Xception	0.7730	0.9835	0.8215	0.9939

Training Accuracy (3-Fold)

	Optimizers			
	SGD	RMSprop	Adagrad	Adam
VGG16	0.7091	0.9717	0.5111	0.9556
Inception-v3	0.5818	0.4202	0.6020	0.6323
ResNet50	0.4182	0.5879	0.5818	0.4182
Xception	0.5697	0.5818	0.5657	0.5899

Validation Accuracy (3-Fold)

	Optimizers			
	SGD	RMSprop	Adagrad	Adam
VGG16	0.4497	0.0918	0.3716	0.1069
Inception-v3	0.4485	0.0448	0.2218	0.0176
ResNet50	0.1561	0.0050	0.0324	0.0084
Xception	0.5424	0.0642	0.4889	0.0221

Training loss (3-Fold)

	Optimizers			
	SGD	RMSprop	Adagrad	Adam
VGG16	0.5971	0.0793	0.9206	0.1127
Inception-v3	0.7371	8.5688	0.7872	2.3959
ResNet50	1.2646	0.6738	1.4782	0.7494
Xception	0.7339	7.0186	0.7754	3.2455

Validation loss (3-Fold)

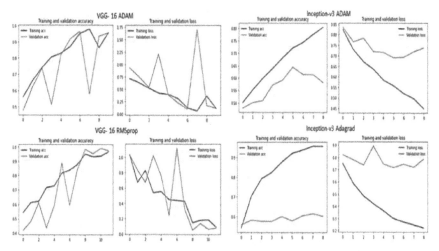

Fig. 4. Graphs of best performing models

5 Feature Selection

THE VGG16 design surpassed all alternative architectures and features from models that might be used for classification, with at least 95% training accuracy and 60% validation accuracy, according to the previous tables.

We chose four models to test our classification algorithms on: -

- VGG16 with Adam
- VGG16 with RMSprop
- Inception-v3 with Adam
- Inception-v3 with Adagrad (Fig. 5)

6 Classification

GeOMetRic characteristics are used to define features in this research. As a result, we classified using a Euclidean distance model [5].

Let A (a1, a2,...,an) and B (b1,b2,...,bn) be two vec-tors of size n each. Using equation, we can calculate the Euclidean distance(d)

$$distance(d) = \sqrt{\sum_{i=1}^{n} (a_i - b_i)^2} \qquad (i)$$

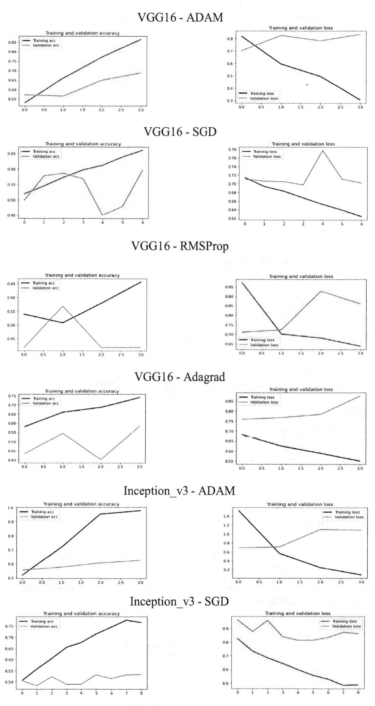

Fig. 5. Result analysis

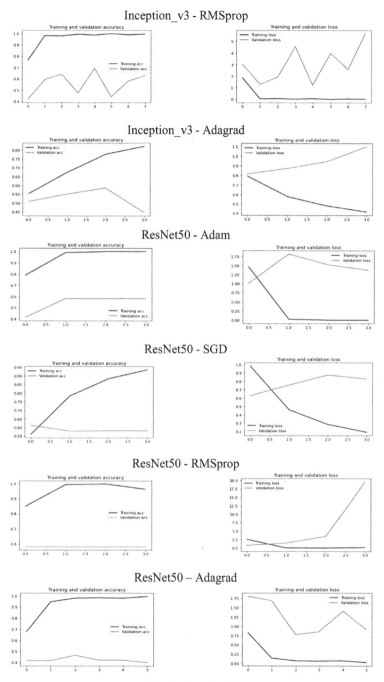

Fig. 5. (*continued*)

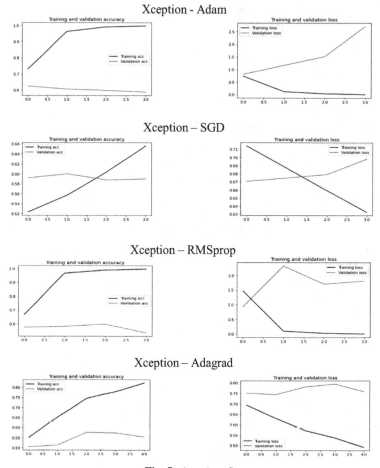

Fig. 5. (*continued*)

Models chosen for feature extraction are used in conjunction with supervised learning techniques to categories: -

- Logistic Regression
- Random Forest
- Linear-SVM
- RBF-SVM
- Sigmoid-SVM
- Poly-SVM (Tables 3, 4, 5, 6, and 7)

Table 3. Logistic regression test

Sr No	Model name	Accuracy	Precision	Recall	F1 score
1	VGG16 Adam	0.991	0.987	0.993	0.990
2	VGG16RMSprop	0.990	0.985	0.992	0.989
3	InceptionV3Adam	0.990	0.985	0.992	0.989
4	InceptionV3Adagrad	0.991	0.988	0.993	0.990

Table 4. Linear SVM test

Sr No	Model name	Accuracy	Precision	Recall	F1 score
1	VGG16 Adam	0.992	0.988	0.994	0.991
2	VGG16RMSprop	0.991	0.987	0.993	0.990
3	InceptionV3Adam	0.930	0.913	0.948	0.925
4	InceptionV3Adagrad	0.988	0.983	0.989	0.986

Table 5. RBF SVM test

Sr No	Model name	Accuracy	Precision	Recall	F1 score
1	VGG16 Adam	0.928	0.929	0.906	0.916
2	VGG16RMSprop	0.960	0.955	0.954	0.955
3	InceptionV3Adam	0.903	0.883	0.908	0.893
4	InceptionV3Adagrad	0.993	0.989	0.994	0.992

Table 6. Sigmoid SVM test

Sr No	Model name	Accuracy	Precision	Recall	F1 score
1	VGG16 Adam	0.485	0.417	0.416	0.417
2	VGG16RMSprop	0.555	0.499	0.499	0.499
3	InceptionV3Adam	0.666	0.618	0.615	0.617
4	InceptionV3Adagrad	0.918	0.906	0.910	0.908

Table 7. Poly SVM test

Sr No	Model name	Accuracy	Precision	Recall	F1 score
1	VGG16 Adam	0.861	0.904	0.793	0.822
2	VGG16RMSprop	0.863	0.900	0.809	0.835
3	InceptionV3Adam	0.902	0.886	0.897	0.891
4	InceptionV3Adagrad	0.992	0.989	0.994	0.991

Classification Best Performing Models

- Inception-v3-Adagrad architecture has a much shorter average training time than other architectures.
- Poly SVM is the best-performing model, with an accuracy of 99.28%.
- We categorized the scam signature with 99.999% correctness.
- We classified the authentic with a 99.00% accuracy (Fig. 6).

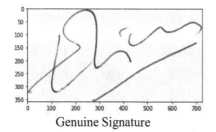
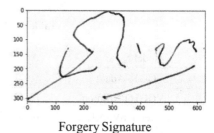

Genuine Signature   Forgery Signature

Fig. 6. Experimental result

7   Conclusion and Future Work

A technique based on neural networks for validating handwritten signatures. The app-roach derives characteristics from preprocessed signature photos. The characteristics that have been retrieved are utilized to train a neural network. All authentic and coun-terfeit signatures were successfully detected by the network [1]. And research has been conducted on the performance of a model based on five distinct datasets.

The approach typically fails due to poor image quality and a large difference between two signatures. More characteristics in the input data set might increase the system's recognition and verification skills. The study's purpose is to minimise business trans-action forgeries [3]. A substantial amount of study has been done on the subject of automated offline signature verification. While most research has concentrated on ran-dom forgery detection, additional work is needed to address the challenges of competent forgery detection [5].

References

1. Pansare, A., Bhatia, S.: Handwritten signature verification using neural network. Int. J. Appl. Inform. Syst. **1**(2), 44–49 (2012)
2. Hatkar, P.V., Salokhe, B.T., Malgave, A.A.: Offline handwritten signature verification using neural network. Methodology. **2**(1), 1–5 (2015)
3. Kumar, P., Singh, S., Garg, A., Prabhat, N.: Hand written signature recognition & verification using neural network. Int. J. Adv. Res. Comput. Sci. Soft. Eng. **3**(3) (2013)
4. Al-Omari, Y.M., Abdullah, S.N.H.S., Omar, K.: State-of-the-art in offline signature verification system. In: 2011 International Conference on Pattern Analysis and Intelligence Robotics, vol. 1, pp. 59–64. IEEE (2011)
5. Majhi, B., Santhosh Reddy, Y., Prasanna Babu, D.: Novel features for off-line signature verification. Int. J. Comput. Commun. Control. **1**(1), 17–24 (2006)
6. Sisodia, K., Mahesh Anand, S.: Off-line handwritten signature verification using artificial neural network classifier. Int. J. Recent Trends Eng. **2**(2), 205 (2009)
7. Kancharla, K., Kamble, V., Kapoor, M.: Handwritten signature recognition: a convolutional neural network approach. In: 2018 International Conference on Advanced Computation and Telecommunication (ICACAT), pp. 1–5. IEEE (2018)
8. Jeiad, H.A.: Indian number handwriting features extraction and classification using multi-class SVM. Eng. Technol. J. **36**(1A) (2018)
9. Jadhav, T.: Handwritten signature verification using local binary pattern features and KNN. Int. Res. J. Eng. Technol. (IRJET) **6**(4), 579–586 (2019)
10. Hafemann, L.G., Sabourin, R., Oliveira, L.S.: Offline handwritten signature verification—literature review. In: 2017 Seventh International Conference on Image Processing Theory, Tools and Applications (IPTA), pp. 1–8. IEEE (2017)
11. Sanmorino, A., Yazid, S.: A survey for handwritten signature verification. In: 2012 2nd International Conference on Uncertainty Reasoning and Knowledge Engineering, pp. 54–57. IEEE (2012)
12. Sam, S.M., Kamardin, K., Sjarif, N.N.A., Mohamed, N.: Offline signature verification using deep learning convolutional neural network (CNN) architectures GoogLeNet inception-v1 and inception-v3. Procedia Comput. Sci. **161**, 475–483 (2019)
13. Gideon, S.J., Kandulna, A., Abhishek Kujur, A., Diana, A., Raimond, K.: Handwritten signature forgery detection using convolutional neural networks. Procedia Comput. Sci. **143**, 978–987 (2018)
14. Yapici, M.M., Tekerek, A., Topaloglu, N.: Convolutional neural network based offline signature verification application. In: 2018 International Congress on Big Data, Deep Learning and Fighting Cyber Terrorism (IBIGDELFT), pp. 30–34. IEEE (2018)
15. Hafemann, L.G., Sabourin, R., Oliveira, L.S.: Writer-independent feature learning for offline signature verification using deep convolutional neural networks. In: 2016 International Joint Conference on Neural Networks (IJCNN), pp. 2576–2583. IEEE (2016)
16. Mohapatra, R.K., Shaswat, K., Kedia, S.: Offline handwritten signature verification using CNN inspired by inception V1 architecture. In: 2019 Fifth International Conference on Image Information Processing (ICIIP), pp. 263–267. IEEE (2019)
17. Rana, T.S., Usman, H.M., Naseer, S.: Static handwritten signature verification using convolution neural network. In: 2019 International Conference on Innovative Computing (ICIC), pp. 1–6. IEEE (2019)
18. Shethwala, R., Pathar, S., Patel, T., Barot, P.: Transfer learning aided classification of lung sounds-wheezes and crackles. In: 2021 5th International Conference on Computing Methodologies and Communication (ICCMC), pp. 1260–1266. IEEE (2021)

19. Sudharshan, D.P., Vismaya, R.N.: Handwritten signature verification system using deep learning. In: 2022 IEEE International Conference on Data Science and Information System (ICDSIS), pp. 1–5. IEEE (2022)

20. Tamrakar, P., Badholia, A.: Handwritten signature verification technology using deep learning–a review. In: 2022 3rd International Conference on Electronics and Sustainable Communication Systems (ICESC), pp. 813–817. IEEE (2022)

21. Mosaher, Q.S., Hasan, M.: Offline handwritten signature recognition using deep convolution neural network. Eur. J. Eng. Technol. Res. **7**(4), 44–77 (2022)

22. Xiao, W., Ding, Y.: A Two-Stage Siamese Network Model for Offline Handwritten Signature Verification. Symmetry **14**(6), 1216 (2022)

23. Tsourounis, D., Theodorakopoulos, I., Zois, E.N., Economou, G.: From text to signatures: knowledge transfer for efficient deep feature learning in offline signature verification. Expert Syst. Appl. **189**, 116136 (2022)

24. Thilakaraj, K., Uvaprasanth, S., Santha Perumal, T.: Signature verification using deep learning.

25. Hung, P.D., Bach, P.S., Vinh, B.T., Tien, N.H., Diep, V.T.: Offline handwritten signature forgery verification using deep learning methods. In: Zhang, Y.D., Senjyu, T., So-In, C., Joshi, A. (eds.) Smart Trends in Computing and Communications. Lecture Notes in Networks and Systems, vol. 396. Springer, Singapore (2023). https://doi.org/10.1007/978-981-16-9967-2_8

Comparative Analysis of Energy Consumption in Text Processing Models

Krishna Sriharsha Gundu[1] (ID), Lakshmi Padmaja Dhyaram[2](✉) (ID),
GNV Ramana Rao[3] (ID), and G Surya Deepak[2] (ID)

[1] Computer Science Department, Arizona State University, Tempe, USA
kgundu1@asu.edu
[2] School of Engineering, Anurag University, Hyderabad, India
lakshmipadmajait@anurag.edu.in
[3] Wipro Ltd, Hyderabad, India
ramana.rao@wipro.com
https://anurag.edu.in/faculties/dr-d-lakshmi-padmaja/

Abstract. In this paper, we examine different ways to analyze text from live feed. This analysis is mandatory for large organizations such as YouTube and Facebook to keep their platform user-friendly. The challenge in performing natural language processing to a live feed is the energy required to train a model which can perform the task. we have attempted to address the problem of performing sentiment analysis by taking an example, of live comments in Law and Crime Network's live feed of Amber Heard vs Johnny Depp that has taken place recently. The results from the experimentation are used to show the energy consumption patterns of different text processing models and choose the most efficient one.

Keywords: Natural language processing · Sentiment analysis · DistilBERT · Gaussian Naive Bayes · Inference · Energy efficient NLP

1 Introduction

Machine Learning and Deep Learning as a field are on the steep rise for a couple of years now [19]. The advantages of machine learning models are numerous and useful in understanding the data and patterns. They are especially helpful when the process is unknown with only a clear understanding of inputs and outputs. This useful of algorithms generally masks the need of additional compute hardware and power. Therefore in this paper, we explore the power required by various algorithms to perform a simple natural language processing task (Sentiment Analysis). The amount of power consumed by each model depends on its complexity, size and accuracy. The following is a list of the most common factors such as Model size, Performance, Training time, etc.

In addition to these factors, there are also environmental conditions that can affect how much energy your ML model uses—for example, if you're using a cloud platform like AWS Lambda or Google Cloud Functions instead of running locally on your own

S. Rajagopal et al. (Eds.): ASCIS 2022, CCIS 1759, pp. 107–116, 2022.
https://doi.org/10.1007/978-3-031-23092-9_9

servers then those services might charge more per hour than running locally itself would cost!

The training power consumption is usually much higher than the inference power consumption. In fact, we can say that the training power consumed in machine learning algorithms may be up to 10 times more than what you would use for inference.

If a small company is considering to build a model, budget and time is of top priority. Therefore the model should be developed according to such metric if it is at a reasonable trade-off with accuracy. The company should also have data on how many training runs your company has done so that you can compare the performance of different models with their corresponding power consumption.

Deep learning requires more computation power than traditional machine learning methods. It also uses a lot more memory for storing the processed information in its neural networks. In order to train a network with thousands of nodes on large datasets, the model should be stored in secondary storage device while getting prepared for training and in RAM while the actual training process.

The impact of power consumption for deep learning models compared to traditional machine learning models is that the neural networks have more neurons and thus use a lot of memory to store them, which requires extra electricity. This means that deep learning algorithms tend towards resource-intensive solutions for any given task.

In this paper, we explore various architectures to perform sentiment analysis on the given list of YouTube comments during the live telecast of Johnny Depp's court case. This paper specifically observes the power and inference of the model. We also look into the sustainability of the speed of inference of the model with the speed of comments being sent to the live feed.

2 Existing Approaches

Garcia Martin et al and Strubel et al [8, 10, 23]. Computer architecture has examined energy use. While energy is becoming a machine learning metric, most research focuses on accuracy. We think their disinterest stems from unfamiliarity with energy appraisal methodologies. We use energy estimation and machine learning to overcome this problem. Our goal is to teach machine learning how to build energy estimation algorithms. We also show energy estimation software and machine learning use cases.

Alessandro et al demonstrated in their work as Businesses need energy-efficient computers [16]. Energy-saving batteries. CPUs overheat supercomputers. Current and future hardware make energy forecasting difficult. A power forecast is needed. Power utilization may be a future performance and cost metric. Energy projections affect power-aware programming, compilation, and runtime monitoring. We monitor how nodes consume power. Stress CPU and memory commands. Each basic command has an energy micro-benchmark. Optimized hardware/software cuts energy costs. Linear extrapolation predicts algorithm energy. Three multimeter applications test our prediction algorithm.

In the recent works of Treviso stated that, the advancement of natural language processing (NLP) research and practice is enabled by making the most of the resources that are available while maintaining a frugal approach to resource management. These resources might include information, time, space, or even energy. Scaling has been used in recent work in natural language processing, which has shown interesting results. However, employing scale alone to improve results means that resource usage also scales. Because of this connection, there is a growing interest in researching more effective approaches that make use of fewer resources yet produce results that are comparable. This survey relates and synthesizes approaches and discoveries in those efficiencies in NLP. The goal of their survey is to guide new researchers entering the area and stimulate the creation of new methods.

In all the above methods the details experimentation and comparative study is not available which enthused me to attempt the same.

3 Exploration of the Data-Set

The dataset can be found on Kaggle website. The dataset contains the data about all 24 days except on the days 9, 11, 13, 14. There are 4 columns in the dataset: name of the author, content of the message, time stamp of the message and the amount of money donated with that message. Since the trial occured for a total of 24 days, the dataset directory contains messages sent on each day in a different file. This information is visualized in the following graphs according to the day number.

3.1 Average Word Length

It can be seen that on average the word length per comment is about 6–8. The variation is not significant between the first and last days of the trail. This could be because of the large number of comments received per day ($>10k$) that have neutralized the occasional outlier comment lengths.

3.2 Average Character Length

On close comparision of the graphs, we see that the distribution followed by the character and the word graphs is the same. This indicates that the presence of emojis and other symbols is present uniformly throughout the trail. In other words, the average number of special characters used per day per comment is proportional to the number of words used per comment. This has lead to the presence of similar distribution in both the bar graphs (Figs. 1 and 2).

Word length distribution across the trail

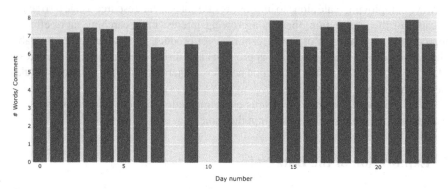

Fig. 1. Bar graph of day wise word length

Character length distribution acorss the trail

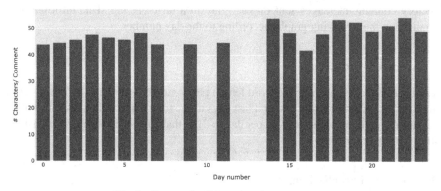

Fig. 2. Bar graph of day wise character count

3.3 Number of Comments

The graph shows that for the first 7 days of the trial, the interest of the audience (proportional to active participation) is relatively very less. Days 15–19 has witnessed a constant attention. This active participation has peaked on the judgement day which is on day 24.

4 Modelling

The data used for training the model is obtained from another dataset of youtube comments. These comments are not labeled and have other metrics related to them, such as contributed amount and the timestamp of comment. Using the nltk Sentiment Analyzer, we get the degree of sentiment in all of the comments. Such labeled dataset is used for training the model. This trained model is used for inferencing the live stream comments on the Amber heard's telecast. This is done to make the training samples representative of the testing samples (Fig. 3).

Number of unique accounts leaving comments

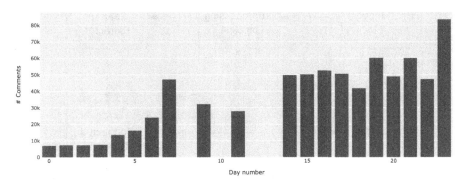

Fig. 3. Number of comments throughout the trial

The experiment is set up such that the same task is performed using different computational methods. Using this variety in computation methods, we can use the measures metrics to understand the trade-offs for selecting each model. TensorFlow 2.8 native environment is chosen for creating the models. A Linux desktop system (ASUS lambda) is used with 4 × 2080 Ti GPUs and 64 GB RAM with i9-7920X CPU (24 count) operating at 2.90 GHz. A specific setup for distributed training is not created therefore the following methods use the inherent and default parallelization in TensorFlow native environment.

The training process and network structure is replicated mutatis mutandis for all the models. They are trained for 5 epochs by the same Adam optimizer and the same CategoricalCrossentropy loss is minimized. Therefore it is easier for the comparison of these model's power and performance levels (Fig. 4).

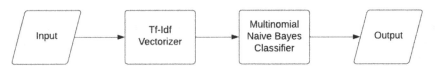

Fig. 4. Scikit-learn Pipeline

4.1 Simple Machine Learning Model

A simple machine learning solution is created using Scikit learn's pipeline feature. Using the Tf-Idf vectorizer with Multinomial Naive Bayes classifier, makes it a robust solution for simple sentiment analysis task. This solution can be used as a baseline to compare the rest of the neural network based architectures. Although this solution takes the least footprint for this task, it has its own short comings. This model cannot be used for more complex samples such as the sentences that have irony/sarcasm where the label tends to contradict the kind of words used in the sentence. Hence such a solution cannot be achieved natively through deep learning models but closer the better (Fig. 5).

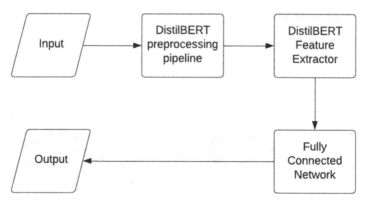

Fig. 5. DistilBERT training process

4.2   DistilBERT Model

BERT model is known for its large number of connections and large number of layers which is pre-trained on English data found on the internet. Each word is converted into BERT embeddings and is passed on to the neural network for training for various tasks, such as sentence generation, question and answering, etc. Based on this text, the model tunes the values of the embeddings and weights of the fully connected layers. This model is pretrained by Google. Such a model can be downloaded from the TensorFlow website https://www.tensorflow.org/ [1] and can be used to perform natural language processing tasks with the help of transfer learning. Natural language processing tasks such as hate speech detection, sentiment analysis, etc. Since the embeddings have meaning associated with them, the performance of this model is much higher than that of Tf-Idf vectorizer values.

The biggest disadvantage of this solution is the speed of execution. BERT model is very large therefore takes longer to compute the matrix multiplications. It has 110 million parameters which are used in the computation of the result, while the DistilBERT model only has 66 million parameters. Therefore this model is 60% faster than BERT model. The most important factor in analyzing the social media live feed is the speed of execution. A model can be trained on a particular values of recall/precision metric to overcome the reduction of accuracy. The cost of misclassification is set by the business team based on the importance of type 1 and type 2 errors.

The current model performs with an average speed of processing one comment in 85 ms with a variation of 1.56 ms (Fig. 6).

4.3   Conv1D Model

This solution operates on Convolution and Pooling operations. A 1-Dimensional convolution is performed across the embeddings of the input text. The embeddings are created with uniform distribution using the Text Vectorizer inputs. Features will be learned from the convolution and will be used for classification of the input text. This model is connected to dense network for sentiment classification.

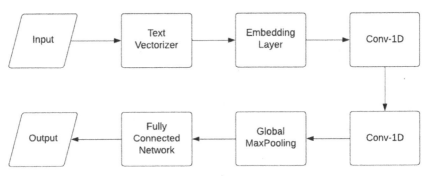

Fig. 6. Convolution network

4.4 Gated Recurrence Unit - GRU Model

Gated Recurrence Unit is a special form of Recurrent Neural Network that has gates to forget/selectively learn the information from previous layers. This special structure of GRU cell implies that there will be less number of trainable parameters when compared to the LSTM solution (Fig. 7).

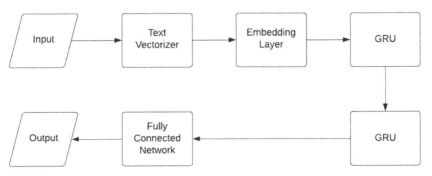

Fig. 7. GRU training network

5 Results

The results of the experimentation are mentioned in Table 2 and Table 3. The power values are obtained from a package called PyJoules which measures the power of internal components of the computer. The duration of execution is also provided by the same library.

The most interesting point that can be noted is that the GRU model consumed the most energy of all the models in the experimentation yet still scoring less accurate than the Bi-directional LSTM model. When observing the performance per watt metric, we can see that 1 dimensional convolution is the best model that can be used for performing sentiment analysis task (Table 1).

Table 1. Accuracy per epoch

# Epoch	GRU (%)	Bi-LSTM (%)	Conv-1D (%)	DistilBERT* (%)
1	90.65	90.81	90.22	77.36
2	93.43	93.45	93.15	80.03
3	94.94	95.04	94.77	81.13
4	95.99	96.23	96.05	81.83
5	96.77	97.11	96.87	82.37

* The weights of the DistilBERT are frozen, and only the fully connected network at the end is trained.

Based on the epoch-wise accuracy score in Table 5, we can observe that the models on average have improved by 6 % irrespective of the model architecture. The dataset contains 21k samples of youtube comments for training the models. This indicates that the model's first epoch accuracy can be one of the quick ways to approximate the final accuracy of the model after completing the training process.

Table 2. Training statistics

Model	Time (seconds)	Measured energy - CPU	Measured energy - GPU	Accuracy
GRU	1167.14	201,879.35 J	114.88 J	96.77%
Bi-LSTM	1701.42	72,656.79 J	166.67 J	97.11%
MNB	7.29	395.55 J	0.65 J	77.41%
Conv-1D	880.39	47,319.45 J	86.05 J	96.87%
Distil-BERT	13545.57	68,206.60 J	2916.87 J	82.37%

Table 3. Inference statistics

Model	Inference time (seconds)	Measured energy - CPU	Measured energy – GPU
GRU	8.96	271.87 J	0.85 J
Bi-LSTM	13.06	395.55 J	1.25 J
ML	0.25	13.36 J	0.02 J
Conv-1D	6.26	189.34 J	0.60 J
Distil-BERT	161.49	7051.78 J	36.52 J

6 Conclusion

In this paper, we explored the energy footprint of various deep learning natural language processing models. Although the inference is performed on the tensorflow native model, it is a very good representative of the final model that would be optimized for the hardware. The text models such as multinomial naive bayes use a small fraction of Distil-BERT and takes less time but cannot model difficult tasks. This model is used only for a fixed dictionary of words that is used in training. Therefore this solution can only be used in applications where the universal set of words is less such as a chat bot application. Advanced tasks such as stance detection would definitely require a deep learning solution. Models such as GRU and Bi directional LSTM can be used for processing different streams of data. Once the embeddings are processed, it can be merged into a single representation vector. In this way, we can use the above information to merge multiple streams of text data for a single model. There are libraries such as Nvidia©TensorRT™and TensorFlow Lite enable the model acceleration by performing necessary changes to the data types and other characteristics of the model such that there is large improvement in speed for a negligible compromise in accuracy. These libraries will be explored in the future scope of experimentation to visualize the power vs accuracy trade-off that will be made in edge computing inference cases.

References

1. Abadi, M., et al.: TensorFlow: large-scale machine learning on heterogeneous systems (2015). https://www.tensorflow.org/, software available from tensorflow.org
2. Ahmad, R.W., Gani, A., Hamid, S.H.A., Xia, F., Shiraz, M.: A review on mobile application energy profiling: taxonomy, state-of-the-art, and open research issues. J. Netw. Comput. Appl. **58**, 42–59 (2015)
3. Bridges, R.A., Imam, N., Mintz, T.M.: Understanding GPU power: a survey of profiling, modeling, and simulation methods. ACM Comput. Surv. **49**(3), 1–27 (2016)
4. Cai, E., Juan, D.C., Stamoulis, D., Marculescu, D.: Neuralpower: predict and deploy energy-efficient convolutional neural networks. In: Asian Conference on Machine Learning, pp. 622–637. PMLR (2017)
5. Chen, Y.H., Krishna, T., Emer, J.S., Sze, V.: Eyeriss: an energy-efficient reconfigurable accelerator for deep convolutional neural networks. IEEE J. Solid-State Circuits **52**(1), 127–138 (2016)
6. Dernoncourt, F., Lee, J.Y.: Pubmed 200k RCT: a dataset for sequential sentence classification in medical abstracts (2017). https://doi.org/10.48550/ARXIV.1710.06071, https://arxiv.org/abs/1710.06071
7. Desrochers, S., Paradis, C., Weaver, V.M.: A validation of dram rapl power measurements. In: Proceedings of the Second International Symposium on Memory Systems, pp. 455–470 (2016)
8. Garcia-Martin, E., Lavesson, N., Grahn, H.: Identification of energy hotspots: a case study of the very fast decision tree. In: International Conference on Green, Pervasive, and Cloud Computing, pp. 267–281. Springer (2017)
9. García-Martín, E., Lavesson, N., Grahn, H., Casalicchio, E., Boeva, V.: How to measure energy consumption in machine learning algorithms. In: Joint European Conference on Machine Learning and Knowledge Discovery in Databases, pp. 243–255. Springer (2018)
10. García-Martín, E., Rodrigues, C.F., Riley, G., Grahn, H.: Estimation of energy consumption in machine learning. J. Parallel Distrib. Comput. **134**, 75–88 (2019). https://doi.org/10.1016/j.jpdc.2019.07.007, https://www.sciencedirect.com/science/article/pii/S0743731518308773
11. Gauen, K., Rangan, R., Mohan, A., Lu, Y.H., Liu, W., Berg, A.C.: Low-power image recognition challenge. In: 2017 22nd Asia and South Pacific Design Automation Conference (ASP-DAC), pp. 99–104. IEEE (2017)

12. Goel, B., McKee, S.A.: A methodology for modeling dynamic and static power consumption for multicore processors. In: 2016 IEEE International Parallel and Distributed Processing Symposium (IPDPS), pp. 273–282. IEEE (2016)

13. Goel, B., McKee, S.A., Själander, M.: Techniques to measure, model, and manage power. In: Advances in Computers, vol. 87, pp. 7–54. Elsevier (2012)

14. Hoque, M.A., Siekkinen, M., Khan, K.N., Xiao, Y., Tarkoma, S.: Modeling, profiling, and debugging the energy consumption of mobile devices. ACM Comput. Surv. **48**(3), 1–40 (2015)

15. Lane, N.D., Bhattacharya, S., Georgiev, P., Forlivesi, C., Kawsar, F.: An early resource characterization of deep learning on wearables, smartphones and internet-of-things devices. In: Proceedings of the 2015 International Workshop on Internet of Things Towards Applications, pp. 7–12 (2015)

16. Leite, A., Tadonki, C., Eisenbeis, C., de Melo, A.: A fine-grained approach for power consumption analysis and prediction. Procedia Comput. Sci. **29**, 2260–2271 (2014). https://doi.org/10.1016/j.procs.2014.05.211, https://www.sciencedirect.com/science/article/pii/S1877050914003883, 2014 International Conference on Computational Science

17. Mazouz, A., Wong, D.C., Kuck, D., Jalby, W.: An incremental methodology for energy measurement and modeling. In: Proceedings of the 8th ACM/SPEC on International Conference on Performance Engineering, pp. 15–26 (2017)

18. O'Brien, K., Pietri, I., Reddy, R., Lastovetsky, A., Sakellariou, R.: A survey of power and energy predictive models in hpc systems and applications. ACM Comput. Surv. **50**(3), 1–38 (2017)

19. Qiu, J., Wu, Q., Ding, G., Xu, Y., Feng, S.: A survey of machine learning for big data processing. EURASIP J. Adv. Signal Process. **2016**(1), 1–16 (2016)

20. Rethinagiri, S.K., Palomar, O., Ben Atitallah, R., Niar, S., Unsal, O., Kestelman, A.C.: System-level power estimation tool for embedded processor based platforms. In: Proceedings of the 6th Workshop on Rapid Simulation and Performance Evaluation: Methods and Tools, pp. 1–8 (2014)

21. Rouhani, B.D., Mirhoseini, A., Koushanfar, F.: Delight: adding energy dimension to deep neural networks. In: Proceedings of the 2016 International Symposium on Low Power Electronics and Design, pp. 112–117 (2016)

22. Shao, Y.S., Brooks, D.: Energy characterization and instruction-level energy model of intel's xeon phi processor. In: International Symposium on Low Power Electronics and Design (ISLPED), pp. 389–394. IEEE (2013)

23. Strubell, E., Ganesh, A., McCallum, A.: Energy and policy considerations for deep learning in NLP. arXiv preprint arXiv:1906.02243 (2019)

24. Treviso, M., et al.: Efficient methods for natural language processing: a survey. arXiv preprint arXiv:2209.00099 (2022)

25. Yang, T.J., Chen, Y.H., Sze, V.: Designing energy-efficient convolutional neural networks using energy-aware pruning. In: Proceedings of the IEEE Conference on Computer Vision and Pattern Recognition, pp. 5687–5695 (2017)

Evolution Towards 6G Wireless Networks: A Resource Allocation Perspective with Deep Learning Approach - A Review

Pradnya Kamble[1,2]([⊠]) and Alam N. Shaikh[3]

[1] Thadomal Shahani Engineering College, Mumbai, Maharashtra, India
[2] Electronics and Telecommunication Engineering K J Somaiya Institute of Engineering and Information, Mumbai, Maharashtra, India
pkamble@somaiya.edu
[3] Vasantdada Patil Pratishthan's College of Engineering and Visual Art, Mumbai, Maharashtra, India
dralamshaikh99@gmail.com

Abstract. Currently, the number of mobile devices is growing exponentially. To cope with the demand, a highly efficient network is required. This rising need for high-speed mobile data rates of up to 1 Tbps might well be satisfied by the sixth generation of mobile networks. It is anticipated that the 6G network would feature a sub-terahertz band and be able to achieve speeds of at least 100 Gbps. A significant amount of resources are required due to the rapid expansion of IoT and other applications. 6G wireless networks can give worldwide coverage from the air to the sea, ground to space. Included in the new model is artificial intelligence with capable security. Dynamic resource allocation is essential to support the exponential growth of data traffic caused by holographic movies, AR/VR, and online gaming. This paper focuses on various resource allocation methodologies and algorithms using deep learning techniques like CNN, DNN, Q learning, deep Q learning, reinforcement learning, actor critic, etc. briefly. Optimal allocation of resources dynamically in real time can improve overall system performance. Consideration is given to computing, radio, power, network, and communication resources. To establish a solid theoretical foundation for the resource allocation in 6G wireless networks, several deep learning techniques and approaches have been examined. The key performance indicators such as efficiency, latency, resource hit rate, decision delay, channel capacity, throughput are discussed.

Keywords: Artificial intelligence · Deep learning · 6G wireless networks · Resource · Allocation

1 Introduction

End-to-end latency, data throughput, energy efficiency, dependability, spectrum utilization, and coverage have changed from 1G to 5G networks. ITU defines 5G networks as improved mobile broadband (eMBB), massive machine type communication (mMTC),

© The Author(s), under exclusive license to Springer Nature Switzerland AG 2022
S. Rajagopal et al. (Eds.): ASCIS 2022, CCIS 1759, pp. 117–132, 2022.
https://doi.org/10.1007/978-3-031-23092-9_10

and ultra-reliable and low latency communication (URLLC) [1–3] 5G won't match the demands of the 2030 technologies. 6G wireless networks will deliver worldwide coverage, intelligence, security, and increased spectrum/energy/cost efficiency [7, 8]. 5G may have trouble supporting large-scale heterogeneous devices. Most 5G networks save offline calculations on a server. 6G can meet real-time resource acquisition during job execution to improve network performance [13]. Storage and computational resources can be placed at the mobile edge for delay-sensitive and battery-limited devices. For uncertain situations, online CNN-based algorithms have been suggested [17]. DRL solves continuous and discrete actions. For discrete offloading choices, new actor-critic models were created [23]. DQN model [29] optimizes resource allocation and offline offloading (Table 1; Fig. 1).

Table 1. Abbreviations of key components of 5G and 6G

5G	6G
eMBB- Enhanced Mobile Broadband	feMBB-Further Enhanced Mobile Broadband
mMTC- Massive Machine type Communication	umMTC-Ultra Massive Machine Type Communication
uRLLC- Ultra Reliable Low Latency	euRLLC- Extremely Ultra Reliable Low Latency

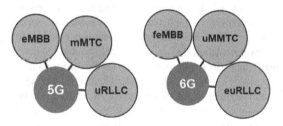

Fig. 1. Key components of 5G and 6G

Organization of Paper

This paper discusses the vision and technical objectives of 6G wireless networks. Authors have emphasized on how optimally and dynamically various resources like computing, communication, networking, storage, bandwidth can be allocated to the requesting users/devices using various deep learning algorithms. Discussion on various measuring parameters is done like throughput efficiency system capacity decision delay, which defines the system performance. Appendix gives the summary of algorithms with resources used, type of devises used, cost and complexity analysis. Also, future research directions are listed.

1.1 6G Vision

6G will provide terrestrial as well as non-terrestrial communication. 6G wireless networks cover all frequencies like Sub-6 GHz, Tera Hz and optical spectrum which will support increase in the data rates as well as it can support dense environment of devices [1]. 6G wireless networks intended to tremendously diverse, dynamic with high quality of service (QoS), with complex architecture. Unique and basic solution to this is artificial intelligence, specifically machine learning and deep learning, is upcoming solution to form a compete intelligent framework emerging as a fundamental solution to realize fully intelligent network management and organization [4–6].

6G will be powerful force for and rugged need for the forthcoming IoT enabled applications to overcome the 5G constraints, 6G, as growing generation, will be based on 5G. 6G will revolve human life and society which transforms human life as well as society. Figure 2. Shows the vision of 6G wireless networks and technical objectives for 6G [1, 15, 18, 26]

1.2 Technical Objectives of 6G

Detailed technical objectives are listed below (Fig. 2; Table 2).

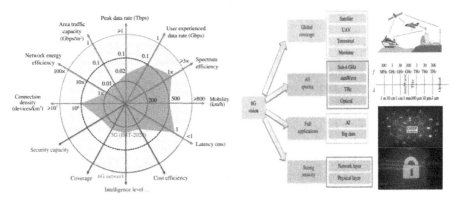

Fig. 2. Vision of 6G wireless networks and technical objectives for 6G [1, 18]

Table 2. Technical objectives of 6G are listed below [18, 27]

6G parameters	Specification
Peak data rate	At least 1 Tb/s to 10 Tb/s peak data rate (for THz backhaul and fronthaul), 100 times greater than 5G
User experienced data rate	1 Gb/s and10 Gb/s for some cases like indoor hotspots. Which is 10 times greater than 5G
Latency	10–100 μs in the air, high mobility ($> = 1,000$ km/h)
Connectivity density	up to 10^7 devices/km, ten times greater than 5G
Traffic capacity for hotspots scenarios	up to 1 / Gb/s m^2
Energy efficiency	10–100 times more those of 5G
Spectrum efficiency	5–10 more those of 5G

2 Resource Allocation for 6G Wireless Networks

As applications diversify, dynamic real-time resource allocation is needed. Variety of algorithms and methodologies have been devised and assessed based on the need for networking and computational resources, research gaps, and to provide a backbone for resource allocation challenges in 6G wireless networks [16].

3C resources include physical (computing, wireless access, storage) and logical (subset of physical) resources [12]. Real-time resource allocation in dynamic tasks.

Using 6G wireless network features like low latency and high speed, fair resource allocation may enhance network performance by assigning resources dynamically in real time using deep learning algorithms. Dynamic resource assignments will improve usage. So, it's overworked. AI is 6G and beyond [7–9, 12]. Some common AI techniques will be used for the Resource Allocation for 6G Wireless Networks are listed below [2, 10, 11] (Table 3).

Table 3. Summary of AI techniques used for the resource allocation for 6G wireless networks

AI approach, Ref	Techniques	Specifications	Performance metrics
Supervised Learning [11, 14]	K-nearest neighbours (KNN), Gaussian process regression (DPR), Support vector regression (SVR), support vector machines (SVM), decision trees (DT)	Labeled data, uses classification and regression	Less complex
Unsupervised Learning [10, 11, 18]	K-means clustering and hierarchical clustering, Isometric mapping (ISOMAP). Reinforcement Learning (RL), Principal component analysis (PCA)	Extract features from Unlabeled data	Computationally complex, real time data analysis
Deep Learning [11, 28]	Deep neural network (DNN),), long short-term memory (LSTM), Convolutional neural network (CNN), recurrent neural network (RNN)	Has several layers of neurons, generates patterns using artificial neural networks	Requires large amount of data Computationally expensive

(continued)

Table 3. (*continued*)

AI approach, Ref	Techniques	Specifications	Performance metrics
Reinforcement Learning [11, 18]	Q-learning, policy learning, Markov decision process (MDP), actor critic (AC), multi-armed bandit	Learns to map states to actions	Make appropriate decisions

3 Summary of Deep Learning Algorithms Used for 6G Wireless Networks Resource Allocation

Yang, Helin, et al. [11] demonstrate AI-powered 6G network location and management. Handover, spectrum, mobility, and edge computing were considered. Offline training, residual networks, and feature matching graphics processing were also investigated. CPU/storage. Parallel plans are made. Lin, Mengting, and Youping Zhao [12] address AI resource management strategies. Authors discussed about radio resources as well as computing and cashing resources. They reviewed 6G wireless network issues and prospects. Deep Q-learning, deep double Q-learning, and their types are studied for resource management.

Lin, Kai, et al [17] proposed a resource-allocating algorithm for 6G-enabled massive IoT. Examining task change's impact. Authors employed a backtracking dynamic nested neural network. Stable system with faster decision-making. They cited Hu, Shisheng, et al. [19] suggested Deep Reinforcement Learning using block chain for dynamic resource sharing. Authors reduced blockchain overheads and simplified AI data gathering. Further studies are needed to reduce computational complexity while using private and public block chains.

Mukherjee, Amrit, et al. [20] proposed algorithm based on convolutional neural network (CCN) with back propagation. They analysed the allocation of resources to the discrete nodes in cluster. Wastage of resources due to redundant data reduced, improvement in the overall efficiency of network shown in the simulation. Networking and computational resources are used.

Guan, Wanqing, et al. [21] derived a deep reinforcement learning (DRL) technique that enabled service-oriented resource allocation employing several logical networks in network infrastructure that offered AI-customized slicing. Authors employed computational resources to evaluate service quality for resource allocation. Fast E2E slicing based on real-time user demand prediction was a future goal.

Kibria, Mirza Golam, et al. [22] discussed about efficient operation, optimization and control using AI and ML. Authors mentioned system can be made smart, systematic and intelligent by using big data analytics, resources mentioned were networking. They also discussed advantages and difficulties of using big data analytics. They mentioned that the processing, managing and leveraging massive amount of data is difficult and it is complex.

Liu, Kai-Hsiang, and Wanjiun Liao [23] DRL was used to deal with time-varying user requests. Energy consumption and enduring delay in multi user system is focused. Which ensured good service for tasks uploads. They did optimization jointly of computational and radio resources.

Yongshuai, Jiaxin, Xin Liu. [24] Computing, storage, and network resources were allocated using limited MDP and reinforcement learning. The authors introduced instantaneous and cumulative network slicing limits using reinforcement learning. Their strategy reduces constraint costs, they said.

Sami, Hani, et al. [25] introduced Deep Reinforcement Learning (DRL) and Markov Decision Process for allocating computing resources in dynamically changing service demands. IScaler is a revolutionary IoE resource scaling and service placement solution. It used DRL and MDP to estimate resource placement and intelligent scaling. Google Cluster traces datasets to provide simulation resources.

Bhattacharya, Pronaya, et al. [29] proposed dynamic resource allocation to solve spectrum allocation difficulties. Block chain is used to model 6G DQN-based dynamic spectrum allocation. Q learning and DQN algorithms are used to simulate system performance. Block chain improves spectrum allocation fairness by 13.57% compared to non-DQN solutions.

Li, Meng, et al. [30] propose using blockchain technology to overcome restricted computing resources and non-intelligent resource management. Authors suggest novel reinforcement learning to improve resource allocation and reduce waste. Markov decision procedure forms cloud edge collaborative resource allocation.

Waqar, Noor, et al. [31] built network access and infrastructure. The author presents a time-varying dynamic system model for HAPs with MEC servers. Decentralizing reinforcement learning-based value iteration reduces computation and communication overhead. I vehicles as intelligent agents are assessed using Q learning, deep Q learning, and double deep Q learning in terms of competency, complexity, cost, and size.

Ganewattha, Chanaka et al. [32] used deep learning to allocate wireless resources in shared spectrum bands for reliable channel forecasting. Encoder-decoder-based Bayesian models are used to model wireless channel uncertainty. University of Oulu provided channel usage and fake data. The RA technique reaches Nash equilibrium under 2N access points. The channel allocation process converges quickly, enhancing network Sam rates.

Alwarafy et al. [33] discussed the 6G network scalability and heterogeneity problems in paper. Deep reinforcement learning technique is used to solve resource allocation problem. Dynamic power allocation and multi-RAT assignment in 6G HET Nets are addressed by the suggested solution.

Gong, Yongkang, et al. [9] presented deep reinforcement learning for industrial IoT systems to allocate resources and schedule tasks. Author emphasized energy use and delay. Loading is distinguished by a new isotone action generating technique and an adaptive action updating strategy. Convex optimization solves time-varying resource allocation problems. Gain rate, batch size, RHC intervals, and training steps measure system performance.

Kasgari, Ali Taleb Zadeh, et al. [34] presented free resource allocation for the downlink wireless network (uR LLC) 6G. Under specified data limitations, achieve end-to-end high reliability and low latency. A GAN-based model enables deep reinforcement learning. To capture network conditions and run reliable systems. Proposed resource allocation model leverages multi-user OFDM (OFDMA). Deep reinforcement learning network is fed rate constraints and latency to minimize power while maintaining reliability. The proposed model reduces transition training time, according to simulations.

Sanghvi, Jainam, et al. [35] proposed edge intelligent model uses micro base station units, which are used for resource allocation MBS guarantees increased channel gain and decreased energy loss. Deep reinforcement enabled edge AI scheme supports responsive edge cache and better learning. Proposed scheme is compared with 5Gfor throughput and latency.

Xiao, Da, et al. [36] author proposed deep Q network, DQN to maximize acceptance ratio and high priority placement for uRLLC request first, that was slicing as MDP characterized. Reward function based on service prioritization defined. MDP selected for easy action in DQN, once trained DQN approximate ideal solution.

Authors have proposed in previous research work [37] a deep learning network to optimize resource allocation to base stations in a 6G communications network. The 6G network was simulated using standard 6G parameter values. On the MATLAB software, a neural network called Base Station Optimization Network (BSOnet) was created, and a dataset with varying parameter values was fed to it for training. When this network was deployed in the simulated 6G network, it consumed less power. This network is a step toward optimizing the developing 6G networks, and authors have hoped that this study will provide the scientific community with a path to further research in this area. Table 4. Shows Summary of Deep Learning Algorithms used for Resource Allocation for 6G Wireless Networks (Fig. 3).

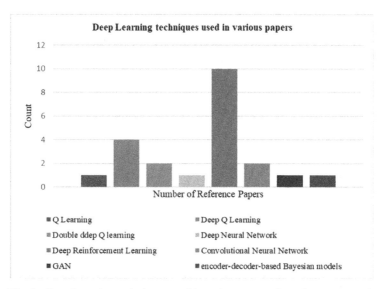

Fig. 3. Deep Learning techniques used in various papers from the survey made

4 Conclusion and Future Scope

This study discusses vision, trends, and the convergence of artificial intelligence for the 6G wireless networks. The authors have informed of numerous AI algorithms that will be employed for resource allocation. A summary of several deep learning-based algorithms for resource optimization in support of varied services, emphasising certain research paths and possible solutions for 6G wireless networks. Other topics to be studied include choosing between several deep learning algorithms for different application scenarios and designing techniques to lower computing costs. Deep learning algorithms' powerful learning and reasoning abilities can improve network performance. Deep learning techniques are being designed to improve accuracy and computing efficiency. 6G networks will require effective resource allocation to provide diversified services and huge connections. Collaborations between hardware and deep learning algorithms may be possible.

Appendix

Table 4. Summary of deep learning algorithms used for resource allocation for 6G wireless networks

Ref	Algorithm	Resources used/devices	Findings	Measuring parameters	Research gap/future scope	Cost/complexity analysis
[11]	Machine Learning, Deep Learning	Computing	Addressed smart spectrum, intelligent mobility, handover management	Computational efficiency, accuracy, robustness	Require high computational speed, Complex system	–
[12]	deep Q- learning, deep double Q- learning, and its variations	Radio, Computing	Discussed various resource Management schemes	Latency, throughput, Quality of service, reliability	Include AI/ML/DL model Lack of uniform test cases and standardized interfaces	–
[17]	Dynamic neural network	Computational and storage/ IoT devices	Influence of task change is examined	Decision delay, resource hit rate	Mutual influence in parallel task execution	8% less nested resource hits resource hits
[19]	Deep Reinforcement Learning	Network	Maximize the profit of users, reduces user heads of block chain	Average profit and throughput per licenced time slot with training epoch	Private and public blockchains can lower computational costs for different applications	Profit ratio vs. training epoch moving average
[20]	Backpropagation NN(BPNN) and CNN	Computing and network/Cellular users	Node positioning guidelines for cell-less designs in various huge IoT applications are optimised	Improved channel capacity Higher reliability and better network performance	Requires more computational time	Service quality is measured by resource allocation and power consumption per node

(continued)

Table 4. (*continued*)

Ref	Algorithm	Resources used/devices	Findings	Measuring parameters	Research gap/future scope	Cost/complexity analysis
[21]	Deep Reinforcement Learning	Computing/Massive machine type, URLLC users	Enables logical networks, slicing, service quality evaluation, and real-time prediction	eMBB, mMTC, uRLLC execution time reduction, increased RAR and efficiency	Complex	Cost is the sum of network node capacity and link bandwidth
[23]	Deep Reinforcement Learning,	Radio resource and Computing/IoT devices	Enhances upload Multi-user system latency Delay and energy consumption per training episode are used to calculate costs./ and energy usage are targeted	Reduced energy utilisation and user delay		Delay and energy consumption per training episode are used to calculate costs
[24]	Constrained reinforcement Learning	Compute Storage and network/video, voice,URLLC users	Decision constraints Markov process for RL network slicing methods	Efficiency, throughput, dissatisfaction, latency, convergence	High complexity	Throughput and iterations are used to calculate costs
[25]	IScaler, Deep Reinforcement Learning	Computing/IoT devices	Server resource prediction, horizontal/vertical scaling, and service placement	Cost/iterations	Complex	Remaining load and iterations are used to analyse complexity

(*continued*)

Table 4. (*continued*)

Ref	Algorithm	Resources used/devices	Findings	Measuring parameters	Research gap/future scope	Cost/complexity analysis
[29]	Deep-Q Learning	Bandwidth/IoT Devices	Channel allocation, blockchain, resource blocks, costs	Energy utilisation, resource blocks, cost reduction, channel allocation	Complex Markov decision model can improve system accuracy and learning rate in less epoch	rewards per50 episodes for 500 episodes are higher
[30]	Collective Reinforcement Learning	Computing/IoT devices	Cloud edge collaborative resource allocation, Markov decision process, CRL algorithm swiftly converge	total reward increases with increase in training episodes stop	Impact of increased number of base stations on latency can be considered	Total rewards versus episodes are used to calculate time cost
[31]	Q, deep Q, Double deep Q learning	Computation, Communication/Mobiles, vehicles, UAV	6G network supports different services, enormous connectivity	Accuracy and computational efficiency	Hardware and deep learning algorithms may collaborate	Total cost is based on sub bands, task size/megabits, and computational capacity
[32]	Deep Learning, encoder-decoder-based Bayesian models	Spectrum/Wireless users	RA technique reaches Nash equilibrium under 2N access points	Sam rates in the network	Channel allocation converges fast, boosting network sum rates	Average sum rates vs step number determine time complexity

(*continued*)

Table 4. (*continued*)

Ref	Algorithm	Resources used/devices	Findings	Measuring parameters	Research gap/future scope	Cost/complexity analysis
[33]	Deep Reinforcement Learning	Radio/Mobile edge devices	6G HET Nets dynamic resource, power, and multi-RAT assignment	Scalability, heterogeneity		InP's average leasing reward
[9]	Deep reinforcement learning	Computing/IoT edge devices	IIoT planning convex optimization decreases RA rate-limiting and delay transition training time	Gain rate, batch size, RHC intervals, and training steps		Cost function defined by network sum rate and Energy- and spectral-efficiency
[34]	GAN, Deep Reinforcement Learning	Spectrum/AR/VR, UAV	Network monitoring, dependable systems, multi-user OFDM(OFDMA)	Latency, Transition training time		Service quality satisfaction vs. time determines total cost. 500 s at 0.8 sqs
[35]	Deep Reinforcement learning	Spectrum/IoT	MBS improves growth and loss. Responsive edge cache	Throughput and latency	MDP accelerate s learning in fewer iterations	System cost in terms of delay weight factor

(*continued*)

Table 4. (*continued*)

Ref	Algorithm	Resources used/devices	Findings	Measuring parameters	Research gap/future scope	Cost/complexity analysis
[36]	DQN	H/W, VNF/aerial and terrestrial users	uRLLC, MDP slicing. Reward priorities. DQN optimizes MDP once taught	Acceptance ratio		FeMBB users' total data rate vs.Mobility
[37]	CNN	Base Station	Deep learning network for 6G base station resource allocation	Power consumed/no. of users		Time complexity isn't proportional to user or resource block count

References

1. You, X., et al.: Towards 6G wireless communication networks: vision, enabling technologies, and new paradigm shifts. Sci. China Inform. Sci. **64**(1), 1–74 (2021)
2. Dogra, A., Jha. R.K., Jain, S.: A survey on beyond 5G network with the advent of 6G: architecture and emerging technologies. IEEE Access 9, 67512–67547 (2020)
3. Guo, W.: Explainable artificial intelligence for 6G: improving trust between human and machine. IEEE Commun. Mag. **58**(6), 39–45 (2020)
4. Shafin, R., Liu, L., Chandrasekhar, V., Chen, H., Reed, J., Zhang, J.C.: Artificial intelligence-enabled cellular networks: a critical path to beyond-5G and 6G. IEEE Wirel. Commun. **27**(2), 212–217 (2020)
5. Kato, N., Mao, B., Tang, F., Kawamoto, Y., Liu, J.: Ten challenges inadvancing machine learning technologies toward 6G. IEEE Wirel. Commun. **27**(3), 96–103 (2020)
6. Sheth, K., Patel, K., Shah, H., Tanwar, S., Gupta, R., Kumar, N.: A taxonomy of AI techniques for 6G communication networks. Comput. Commun. **161**, 279–303 (2020)
7. Jiang, W., Han, B., Habibi, M.A., Schotten, H.D.: The road towards 6G: a comprehensive survey. IEEE Open J. Commun. Soc. **2**, 334–366 (2021)
8. Matinmikko-Blue, M., Yrjölä, S., Ahokangas, P.: Spectrum management in the 6G era: the role of regulation and spectrum sharing. In: 2020 2nd 6G Wireless Summit (6G SUMMIT), pp. 1–5. IEEE (2020)
9. Gong, Y., Yao, H., Wang, J., Li, M., Guo, S.: Edge intelligence-driven joint offloading and resource allocation for future 6G industrial internet of things. IEEE Trans. Netw. Sci. Eng. (2022)
10. Zafar, S., Jangsher, S., Al-Dweik, A.: Resource allocation using deep learning in mobile small cell networks. IEEE Trans. Green Commun. Netw. (2022)
11. Yang, H., Alphones, A., Xiong, Z., Niyato, D., Zhao, J., Kaishun, W.: Artificial-intelligence-enabled intelligent 6G networks. IEEE Netw. **34**(6), 272–280 (2020)
12. Lin, M., Zhao, Y.: Artificial intelligence-empowered resource management for future wireless communications: a survey. China Commun. **17**(3), 58–77 (2020)
13. Du, J., Jiang, C., Wang, J., Ren, Y., Debbah, M.: Machine learning for 6G wireless networks: carrying forward enhanced bandwidth, massive access, and ultrareliable/low-latency service. IEEE Veh. Technol. Mag. **15**(4), 122–134 (2020)
14. Tang, F., Mao, B., Kawamoto, Y., Kato, N.: Survey on machine learning for intelligent end-to-end communication toward 6G: from network access, routing to traffic control and streaming adaption. IEEE Commun. Surv. Tutor. **23**(3), 1578–1598 (2021)
15. Guo, F., Yu, F.R., Zhang, H., Li, X., Ji, H., Leung, V.C.M.: Enabling massive IoT toward 6G: a comprehensive survey. IEEE Internet Things J. **8**(15), 11891–11915 (2021)
16. Jayakumar, S., S, N.: A review on resource allocation techniques in D2D communication for 5G and B5G technology. Peer-to-Peer Netw. Appl. **14**(1), 243–269 (2020). https://doi.org/10.1007/s12083-020-00962-x
17. Lin, K., Li, Y., Zhang, Q., Fortino, G.: AI-driven collaborative resource allocation for task execution in 6G-enabled massive IoT. IEEE Internet Things J. **8**(7), 5264–5273 (2021)
18. Xu, X., et al.: Dynamic resource allocation for load balancing in fog environment. Wirel. Commun. Mob. Comput. **2018** (2018)

19. Hu, S., Liang, Y.-C., Xiong, Z., Niyato, D.: Blockchain and artificial intelligence for dynamic resource sharing in 6G and beyond. IEEE Wirel. Commun. **28**(4), 145–151 (2021)
20. Mukherjee, A., Goswami, P., Khan, M.A., Manman, L., Yang, L., Pillai, P.: Energy-efficient resource allocation strategy in massive IoT for industrial 6G applications. IEEE Internet Things J. **8**(7), 5194–5201 (2020)
21. Guan, W., Wen, X., Wang, L., Zhaoming, L., Shen, Y.: A service-oriented deployment policy of end-to-end network slicing based on complex network theory. IEEE Access **6**, 19691–19701 (2018)
22. Kibria, M.G., Nguyen, K., Villardi, G.P., Zhao, O., Ishizu, K., Kojima, F.: Big data analytics, machine learning, and artificial intelligence in next-generation wireless networks. IEEE Access. **6**, 32328–32338 (2018)
23. Liu, K.-H., Liao, W.: Intelligent offloading for multi-access edge computing: a new actor-critic approach. In: ICC 2020–2020 IEEE International Conference on Communications (ICC), pp. 1–6. IEEE (2020)
24. Liu, Y., Ding, J., Liu, X.: Resource allocation method for network slicing using constrained reinforcement learning. In: 2021 IFIP Networking Conference (IFIP Networking), pp. 1–3. IEEE (2021)
25. Sami, H., Otrok, H., Bentahar, J., Mourad, A.: AI-based resource provisioning of IoE services in 6G: a deep reinforcement learning approach. IEEE Trans. Netw. Serv. Manage. **18**(3), 3527–3540 (2021)
26. Alsharif, M.H., Kelechi, A.H., Albreem, M.A., Chaudhry, S.A., Zia, M.S., Kim, S.: Sixth generation (6G) wireless networks: vision, research activities, challenges and potential solutions. Symmetry. **12**(4), 676 (2020)
27. Bernardos, C.J., Uusitalo, M.A.: European vision for the 6G network ecosystem. In: Zenodo, Honolulu, HI, USA, Tech. Rep. (2021)
28. Zhang, S., Zhu, D.: Towards artificial intelligence enabled 6G: state of the art, challenges, and opportunities. Comput. Netw. **183**, 107556 (2020)
29. Bhattacharya, P., et al.: A deep-Q learning scheme for secure spectrum allocation and resource management in 6G environment. IEEE Trans. Netw. Serv. Manag. (2022). https://doi.org/10.1109/TNSM.2022.3186725
30. Li, M., et al.: Cloud-edge collaborative resource allocation for blockchain-enabled internet of things: a collective reinforcement learning approach. IEEE Internet Things J. **9**(22), 23115–23129 (2022)
31. Waqar, N., Hassan, S.A., Mahmood, A., Dev, K., Do, D.-T., Gidlund, M.: Computation offloading and resource allocation in MEC-enabled integrated aerial-terrestrial vehicular networks: a reinforcement learning approach. IEEE Trans. Intell. Trans. Syst. **23**(11), 21478–21491 (2022)
32. Ganewattha, C., Khan, Z., Latva-Aho, M., Lehtomäki, J.J.: Confidence aware deep learning driven wireless resource allocation in shared spectrum bands. IEEE Access **10**, 34945–34959 (2022)
33. Alwarafy, A., Albaseer, A., Ciftler, B.S., Abdallah, M., Al-Fuqaha, A.: AI-based radio resource allocation in support of the massive heterogeneity of 6G networks. In: 2021 IEEE 4th 5G World Forum (5GWF), pp. 464–469. IEEE (2021)
34. Kasgari, A.T.Z., Saad, W., Mozaffari, M., Vincent Poor, H.: Experienced deep reinforcement learning with generative adversarial networks (GANs) for model-free ultra-reliable low latency communication. IEEE Trans. Commun. **69**(2), 884–899 (2020)

35. Sanghvi, J., Bhattacharya, P., Tanwar, S., Gupta, R., Kumar, N., Guizani, M.: Res6Edge: an edge-AI enabled resource sharing scheme for C-V2X communications towards 6G. In: 2021 International Wireless Communications and Mobile Computing (IWCMC), pp. 149–154. IEEE (2021)
36. Xiao, D., Ni, W., Andrew Zhang, J., Liu, R., Chen, S., Qu, Y.: AI-enabled automated and closed-loop optimization algorithms for delay-aware network. In: 2022 IEEE Wireless Communications and Networking Conference (WCNC), pp. 806–811. IEEE (2022)
37. Kamble, P., Dr Shaikh.: Optimization of base station for 6G wireless networks for efficient resource allocation using deep learning. In: Optimization of Base Station for 6G Wireless Networks for Efficient Resource Allocation using Deep Learning (April 9, 2022) (2022)

Automation of Rice Leaf Diseases Prediction Using Deep Learning Hybrid Model VVIR

Sheikh Gouse[1（✉）] and Uma N. Dulhare[2]

[1] Computer Science and Engineering Department, Osmania University, Hyderabad, Telangana, India
sheikh.gouse@gmail.com
[2] Computer Science and Artificial Intelligence Department, Muffakham Jah College of Engineering and Technology, Hyderabad, Telangana, India

Abstract. The main cereal crop in the world is rice (Oryza sativa). As a primary source of energy, more than 50 percent of population of the worlds relies on its use. Several elements impact rice grain yield and quality, such as rainfall, soil fertility, diseases, pests, weeds, bacteria and viruses. To control the diseases, the farmers invest a great deal of time and money and they identify problems with their poor unqualified techniques, which results in poor yield growth with losses. Technology in agriculture makes it easier than ever before to detect pathogenic organisms in rice plant foliage automatically. Convolutional neural network (CNN) is a deep learning technique used to solve computer vision issues such as image classification, object segmentation, image analysis, etc. In the proposed five models achieved the VGG16 98.43%, VGG19 98.65%, InceptionV4 98.57, ResNet-50 98.57% model to identify diseases in rice leaf images with a transfer learning technique. Using these model parameters, the final proposed VVIR model accurately classified objects with a accuracy of 98.80%.

Keywords: Rice leafs diseases · Convolutional Neural Network (CNN) · Artificial Intelligence · Deep Learning · VGG16 · VGG19 · ResNetV2

1 Introduction

The global economy cannot function without agriculture. GVA (Gross Value Added) in 2020–21 is 96.54 lakh crore, with agriculture accounting for 20.19% of the country's GDP. Agriculture has a more significant contribution to the Indian economy than any other industry globally, at 6.4 percentage points. Besides China, Indonesia, Vietnam, Burma, the Philippines, Japan, Pakistan, Brazil, the USA, Nigeria, Egypt and South Korea have the second most significant rice output (Oryza Sativa) in the world after India. In India, Telangana is at the top in area and production. Nizamabad, Karimnagar, Kamareddy, Yadadri, Khammam, Siddipet, Jagityal and Warangal are the central rice-growing districts of Telangana.

Rice is a product of the paddy field. It is a yearly harvest. It is a staple meal for half of the world's population and it provides 40% of the daily protein needs. Rice research

© The Author(s), under exclusive license to Springer Nature Switzerland AG 2022
S. Rajagopal et al. (Eds.): ASCIS 2022, CCIS 1759, pp. 133–143, 2022.
https://doi.org/10.1007/978-3-031-23092-9_11

center in India, International Rice Research Institute (IRRI), ICAR(Indian Council of Agricultural Research) Hyderabad, NRRI (National Rice Research Institute) Hyderabad and ISRAC (International Rice Research Institute South Asia region).

Rice infections pose a severe danger to the world's food supply by reducing the crop's yield and quality. As a result, disease prevention is essential to the production of rice. Correct and prompt detection of diseases is critical to successful pesticide application. This ensures the timely application of pesticides. As the population grows, so does the need for rice, increasing consumption. By 2030, rice output must rise by more than 40% to fulfill the rising global demand for grain. Due to the devastating effects of diseases, the rice crop has lost between 60 and 100 percent of its production.

It is challenging to find enough competent workers in the region to do these responsibilities quickly. Researchers have employed a variety of Computer Vision (CV), Artificial Intelligence (AI), Machine Learning(ML) and Deep Learning (DL) technologies that help in hyper spectral detection and multispectral remote sensing pictures to diagnose crop diseases throughout the last few decades in Fig. 1 [1].

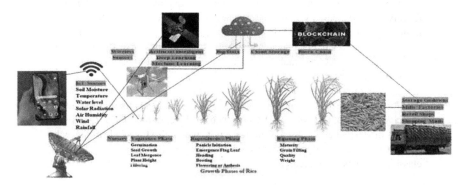

Fig. 1. Rice crop from growth to market is controlled by modern technologies

Even while some of the currently available technologies can diagnose agricultural diseases with a high degree of accuracy, most of them handle the manual due to a lack of resources. As a result, ideas are constrained, making it harder to extrapolate from the findings. Aside from that, specific techniques need specialized equipment that may not be readily available to the general public. Crop disease diagnosis is challenging because of these disadvantages. The disadvantages of crop disease diagnostic methods can be solved by using deep learning technology. In recent years, object recognition, picture categorization and content recommendation have significantly benefited from the widespread use of deep learning techniques. Researchers have used DL to identify diseases in various crops [2].

The dataset obtained is summarized in Sect. 2, as it gives a general introduction to the method. In this part, the procedures for identifying rice diseases and associated studies and the recommended approach are mostly presented. In Sect. 3, experiments are carried out to test the performance of the suggested approach and the findings are compared to those of other methods. Lastly, Sect. 4 wraps things up with a call for future research.

2 Literature Survey

Kamal et al. (2019) used Reduced MobileNet with a depth-wise separable convolution architecture. There have been a variety of assertions made about the accuracy of 98.65 percent of recognition [3]. Chen et al. (2020), for the categorization of rice diseases, employed VGGNet- Inception Model, they obtained an accuracy of 92 percent [4]. Rahman et al. (2020), with 1426 images, developed CNN architecture with two stages, were able to detect 93.30 percent of the rice diseases and pests correctly [5]. Feng Jiang et al. (2020), with the 10-fold cross-validation approach, was utilized to test CNN-SVM. Rice blast, rice blight, rice stripe blight and rice sheath blight were classified and predicted using CNN-SVM, which reached an accuracy of 98.6 percent [6]. Zhencun Jiang et al. (2021), with the Visual Geometry Group Network-16 (VGG16) model, was utilized to represent bacterial rice leaf blight, rice brown spot, rice leaf smut, wheat leaf rust, wheat powdery mildew [7].

Prabira Kumar Sethy et al. (2020), a CNN ResNet50-SVM model developed by four different formstungro, brownspot, blast and bacterial blight of diseases and produced an F1 score of 0.9838 [8]. Murat Koklu et al. (2021), ANN, DNN and CNN models applied to 75,000 grain images of five distinct types of rice to obtain 99.87 percent accuracy for ANN, 99.95 percent accuracy for DNN and 100 percent accuracy for CNN [9]. Radhakrishnan Sree vallabha dev (2020), used the CNN-SVM for predicting blast diseases and attained an accuracy rate of 96.8 percent [10].

Junde Chen et al. (2021), using the MobileNet-V2 model, studied 12 rice disease outbreaks and found an average accuracy of 98.48 percent [11].

Pitchayagan Temniranrat et al. (2021), used the YOLOv3 model to acquire an average True Positive Point of 95.6% for diseases including rice blast, rice blight, rice brown spot and rice narrow brown spot [12].

Yibin Wang et al. (2021), used an attention-based depth wise separable neural network (ADSNN-BO) model to classify brown spot, hispa and leaf blast in rice. The test accuracy is 94.65 percent [13].

If you're looking to identify diseases in crops, deep learning is an excellent option because it can reach high accuracy. Deep learning for rice disease research has been confined to a small number of disorders. In the field of rice disease categorization, there are just a few publicly available datasets. Our dataset on rice disease is used to train and evaluate a convolutional neural network- based disease classification model to fill this gap (CNN).

This research aimed to improve rice disease diagnostics in terms of accuracy, efficiency, price and convenience. A Deep Learning network model for identifying six distinct rice diseases was developed, evaluated and then used to execute the diagnosis process and put it through rigorous testing in a real-world setting.

3 Methodology

The methodological approach to any experiment serves as a road-map for conducting any experimental endeavor. Data collection, preparation, data separation into training, validation and finally, the use of a DL model to identify rice images dataset are the four stages of our technique. This is the first stage in every experiment is vital to remember that datasets are the foundation of any ML and DL model; therefore, we started by collecting real-time datasets from primary and secondary sources. As a backup plan, if the primary data sources fail or the preliminary data gathered is insufficient or does not meet the criteria, secondary data sources such as online repositories and data websites will be utilized to acquire the dataset. Rice leaf diseases were employed to collect dataset images, which are a must for the following phases in this process [14]. Pre-processing is the next phase in our technique, as it is highly usual for the dataset acquired after collection to be noisy in Fig. 2. This data may be used for additional experiments [15].

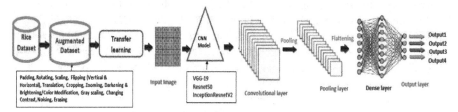

Fig. 2. CNN architecture for rice model

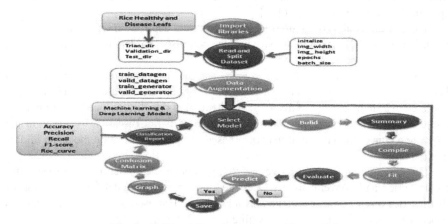

Fig. 3. CNN and Deep Learning working model

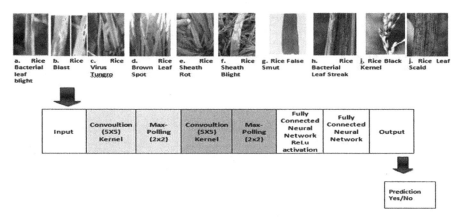

Fig. 4. Depicts a variety of rice diseases using CNN

To avoid the computational load in the model, the picture was scaled appropriately before reading. This was followed by applying random affine modification to the picture. Images must be filliped, scaled, rotated, translated and resized in any way it pleased at random [16]. The training algorithm needs resized final images by 224 × 224 pixels in Figs. 3 and 4 [17]. The primary goals of these operations were the model's over fitting on the initial dataset [18]. After that, the ImageNet dataset's mean and standard deviation were used to normalize the images, resulting in the most uniform distribution of color values possible [19]. In each training period, the number of images read by each model varied and the number of image samples available in the dataset increased as a result in VGG16, VGG19, Inception models in Fig. 5a, b, c).

CNN greatly influences final model performance. For rice disease, a comparison of network performance was essential. The five network models' performance evaluations were compared to choose the top models. Each network model's of rice leaf disease prediction findings were categorized into four groups as TPLD, TNLD, FPLD and FNLD in Fig. 6.

TPLD: A predicted rice leaf disease is same to the actual rice leaf disease. So both the actual and predicted leaf diseases are positive.

TNLD: A predicted rice leaf disease is not same to the actual rice leaf disease. So both the actual and predicted leaf diseases are negative.

FPLD: A predicted rice leaf disease is same to the actual rice leaf disease. So the actual leaf disease is negative and predicted leaf disease is positive.

FNLD: A predicted rice leaf disease is same to the actual rice leaf disease. So the actual leaf disease is positive and predicted leaf disease is negative.

$$\text{Precision}(P) : (TPLD)/(TPLD + FPLD) \tag{1}$$

$$\text{Recall}(R) : (TPLD)/(TPLD + FPLD) \tag{2}$$

$$\text{Accuracy}((A) : (TPLD + TNLD)/(TPLD + TNLD + FPLD + FNLD) \tag{3}$$

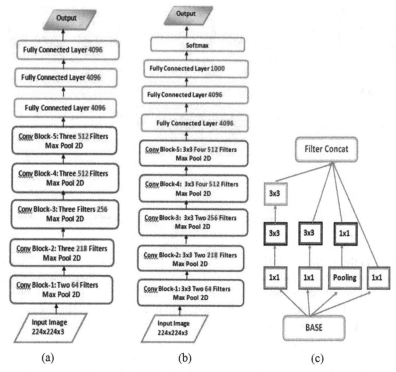

Fig. 5. 5(a) VGG16 Architecture, 5(b) VGG19 Architecture, 5(c) Inception Architecture

		Predicted Rice Leafs Disease	
		Positive	Negative
Actual Rice Leafs Disease	Positive	True Positive Leaf Disease (TPLD)	False Positive Leaf Disease (FPLD)
	Negative	False Negative Leaf Disease (FNLD)	True Negative Leaf Disease (TNLD)

Fig. 6. Confusion matrix for Rice leaf disease

$$F1 - SCORE : 2 * (P * R)/(P + R) \tag{4}$$

With the Eq. (1), Eq. (2), Eq. (3), Eq. (4) demonstrate how these results were utilized to calculate the following performance indicators: accuracy, precision, recall and F1 score. For each disease type, the accuracy was tested; for each disease type, the other indicators were analyzed. Another way to judge the models is by looking at their loss value. In contrast to the other metrics, loss measures how well the training set fits the test set. Loss changes during training can be used to evaluate the model's fit state, even though it cannot directly reflect model performance.

4   Results

Successful model testing took roughly a week because the entire dataset was run on varied batch sizes and epochs, which resulted in superior model performance of VVIR (Table 1).

Table 1. Rice model the accuracy obtained from the training and validation datasets

Epoch	Time	Loss	Accuracy	Val-loss	Val- accuracy
1/100	124 s	2.7649	0.1738	2.0936	0.23
2/100	123 s	2.1389	0.2476	2.0615	0.25
3/100	135 s	2.0554	0.3024	1.9620	0.30
4/100	139 s	1.9367	0.3214	1.9142	0.31
5/100	142 s	1.8987	0.3095	1.7976	0.40
6/100	150 s	1.8158	0.3452	1.8196	0.35
7/100	146 s	1.8078	0.3905	1.7557	0.34
8/100	145 s	1.7494	0.4000	1.7481	0.40
9/100	148 s	1.6657	0.4286	1.6914	0.42
10/100	150 s	1.6891	0.4167	1.6914	0.43
…					
100/100	1420 s	0.0598	0.9880	0.0418	0.98

IT is possible to achieve a best accuracy of 98.80% in training and 98% on the 100th epoch of the model's execution in the validation phase. The resulting performance measure is created based on how many epochs and the output accuracy the model is tested. Model performance for rice disease identification is visible from the correctness of validation data encountered. Because we only have a small quantity of data to train the model on, the number of epochs is higher in this situation, increasing the likelihood that the model will successfully detect images of rice diseases (Table 2).

Table 2. Accuracy of various Deep Learning different models with proposed models

SNo	Authors	Model	Accuracy
1	Kamal et al. (2019)	[3] MobileNet	98.65
2	Chen et al. (2020),	[4] VGGNet - Inception	92
3	Rahman et al. (2020),	[5] CNN two stages	93.3
4	Feng Jiang et al. (2020),	[6] CNN-SVM	98.6
5	Zhencun Jiang et al. (2021),	[7] VGG16	95.5

(continued)

Table 2. (*continued*)

SNo	Authors	Model	Accuracy
6	Prabira Kumar Sethy et al. (2020),	[8] ResNet50-SVM	98.38
7	Murat Koklu et al. (2021),	[9] ANN	99
8	Murat Koklu et al. (2021),	[9] DNN	95
9	Murat Koklu et al. (2021),	[9] CNN	100
10	RadhakrishnanSreevallabhadev (2020)	[10] CNN-SVM	96.8
11	Junde Chen et al. (2021),	[11] MobileNet-V2	98.48
12	PitchayaganTemniranrat et al. (2021),	[12] YOLOv3	95.6
13	Yibin Wang et al. (2021)	[13] ADSNN-BO	94.65
14	Proposed	VGG16	98.43
15	Proposed	VGG19	98.65
16	Proposed	ResNet150	98.55
17	Proposed	Inception-v3	98.57
18	Proposed Hybrid Model	VVRI	98.80

We've had to deal with a wide range of difficulties during the experiment and those difficulties appear at every stage.

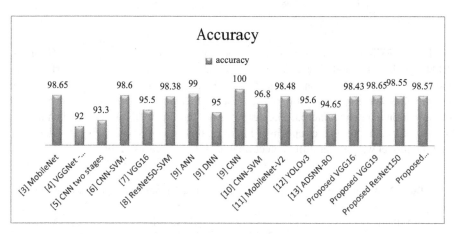

Fig. 7. Comparison of accuracy of various deep learning models

The following challenges are encountered in the process of collecting and executing a model on a dataset:

Because there are so few rice plants affected by rice diseases that there are no photographs of rice plants with rice diseases in the dataset, gathering many images of these plants is first problem. In the case of CNN implementation, a limited dataset causes underfitting and overfitting of the data, which reduces the final detection accuracy. The accuracy of the model may be increased by increasing the number of convolutional and dense layers used to train the data. Research into the severity of rice diseases has not yet been fully completed; therefore, this study's findings can be built upon in the future.

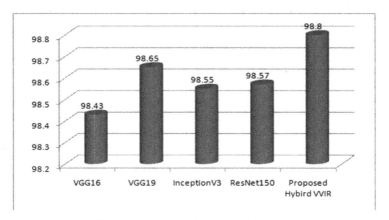

Fig. 8. Accuracy of proposed hybrid model

Applying the four models VGG16 VGG19 Inception ResNetV2 and taking outputs each model and gives the maximum of the models is VVIR in Fig. 7 and Fig. 8.

5   Discussion

Diseases are all frequent growth stages of the rice plant. Identification of these pathogens is critical for the discovery of new rice-related diseases. We divided the dataset into three parts training (70%), a validation (20%) and a test (10%). The model acquired the essential characteristics of each disease from the trained results. As a result of the trained set's high degree of resemblance to the test set, various disease images from diverse sources were gathered to create a separate test set. This study's network design is generalizable and used for practical purposes based on the independent test findings. A collection of 600 images of seven different rice diseases was created in this study. Five sub-models based on these images were trained and evaluated and achieved an accuracy of VGG16 is 98.43%, VGG19 is 98.65%, InceptionV4 is 98.57, ResNet-50 is 98.57% and final proposed Hybrid-VVIR is 98.80% were the top performers in this comparison. An examination of visual data validated the sub models' ability to learn about rice diseases Ensemble Model features many characteristics that might slow down the identification process. Efforts to minimize the number of parameters will be made in future investigations.

References

1. Dulhare, U.N., Gouse, S.: Automation of rice cultivation from ploughing–harvesting with diseases, pests and weeds to increase the yield using AI. In: Kumar, A., Mozar, S. (eds.) ICCCE 2021. Lecture Notes in Electrical Engineering, vol. 828. Springer, Singapore (2022). https://doi.org/10.1007/978-981-16-7985-8_51
2. Keceli, A.S., Kaya, A., Catal, C., Tekinerdogan, B.:Deep learning-based multi-task prediction system for plant disease and species detection. Ecol. Inform. **69**, 101679, ISSN 1574-9541 (2022). https://doi.org/10.1016/j.ecoinf.2022.101679
3. Kamal,K.C., Yin, Z., Wu, M., Wu, Z.: Depthwise separable convolution architectures for plant disease classification. Comput. Electron. Agric. **165**, 104948, ISSN 0168-1699 (2019). https://doi.org/10.1016/j.compag.2019.104948
4. Chen, J., Chen, J., Zhang, D., Sun, Y., Nanehkaran, Y.A.:Using deep transfer learning for image-based plant disease identification. Comput. Electron. Agric. **173**, 105393, ISSN 0168-1699 (2020). https://doi.org/10.1016/j.compag.2020.105393
5. Rahman, C.R., Arko, P.S., Ali, M.E., Khan, M.A.I., Apon, S.H., Nowrin, F., Wasif, A.: Identification and recognition of rice diseases and pests using convolutional neural networks. Biosyst. Eng. **194**, 112–120, ISSN 1537-5110 (2020). https://doi.org/10.1016/j.biosystemseng.2020.03.020
6. Jiang, F, Lu, Y, Chen, Y, Cai, D, Li, G.:Image recognition of four rice leaf diseases based on deep learning and support vector machine, Comput. Electron. Agric. **179**, 105824, ISSN 0168-1699 (2020). https://doi.org/10.1016/j.compag.2020.105824
7. Jiang, Z., Dong, Z., Jiang, W., Yang, Y.: Recognition of rice leaf diseases and wheat leaf diseases based on multi-task deep transfer learning. Comput. Electron. Agric. **186**, 106184, ISSN 0168-1699 (2021). https://doi.org/10.1016/j.compag.2021.106184
8. Sethy, P.K., Barpanda, N.K., Rath, A.K., Behera, S.K.: Deep feature based rice leaf disease identification using support vector machine. Comput. Electron. Agric. **175**, 105527, ISSN 0168-1699 (2020). https://doi.org/10.1016/j.compag.2020.105527
9. Koklu, M., Cinar, I. and Taspinar, Y.S.: Classification of rice varieties with deep learning methods. Comput. Electron. Agric. **187**, 106285, ISSN 0168-1699 (2021) https://doi.org/10.1016/j.compag.2021.106285
10. SreevallabhadevRadhakrishnan. An improved machine learning algorithm for predicting blast disease in paddy crop. Materials Today: Proceedings **33**, Part 1, 682–686, ISSN 2214-7853 (2020). https://doi.org/10.1016/j.matpr.2020.05.802
11. Chen, J., Zhang, D., Zeb, A., Nanehkaran, Y.A.: Identificationof rice plant diseases using lightweight attention networks. Expert. Syst. Appl. **169**, 114514, ISSN 0957-4174 (2021). https://doi.org/10.1016/j.eswa.2020.114514
12. Temniranrat, P., Kiratiratanapruk, K., Kitvimonrat, A., Sinthupinyo, W., Patarapuwadol, S.: A system for automatic rice disease detection from rice paddy images serviced via a Chatbot. Comput. Electron. Agric. **185**, 106156, ISSN 0168-1699 (2021). https://doi.org/10.1016/j.compag.2021.106156
13. Wang, Y., Wang, H., Peng, Z.: Rice diseases detection and classification using attention based neural network and bayesian optimization. Expert. Syst. Appl. **178**, 114770, ISSN 0957-4174 (2021). https://doi.org/10.1016/j.eswa.2021.114770
14. Dulhare, U.N., Gouse, S.: Hands on MAHOUT—Machine Learning Tool (2020). https://doi.org/10.1002/9781119654834.ch14
15. Dulhare, U., Khaled, A.M., Ali, M.H.: A Review on Diversified Mechanisms for Multi Focus Image Fusion (May 18, 2019). In: Proceedings of International Conference on Communication and Information Processing (ICCIP) 2019, https://ssrn.com/abstract=3424480 or http://dx.doi.org/10.2139/ssrn.3424480

16. Dulhare, U.N., Khaleed, A.M. (2020). Taj-Shanvi framework for image fusion using guided filters. In: Sharma, N., Chakrabarti, A., Balas, V. (eds.) Data Management, Analytics and Innovation. Advances in Intelligent Systems and Computing, vol. 1016. Springer, Singapore. https://doi.org/10.1007/978-981-13-9364-8_30

17. Dulhare, U.N., Ali, M.H.: Underwater human detection using faster R-CNN with data augmentation. Materials Today: Proceedings, ISSN 2214-7853 (2021). https://doi.org/10.1016/j.matpr.2021.05.653

18. Krishnamoorthy, N., Prasad, L.N., Kumar, C.P., Subedi, B., Abraha, H.B., Sathishkumar, V.E.: Rice leaf diseases prediction using deep neural networks with transfer learning. Environ. Res. **198**, 111275, ISSN 0013-9351 (2021). https://doi.org/10.1016/j.envres.2021.111275

19. Sobiyaa, P., Jayareka, K.S., Maheshkumar, K., Naveena, S., Rao, K.S.: Paddy disease classification using machine learning technique. Materials Today: Proceedings **64**, Part 1, 883–887, ISSN 2214-7853 (2022). https://doi.org/10.1016/j.matpr.2022.05.398

A Review Based on Machine Learning for Feature Selection and Feature Extraction

R. S. Preyanka Lakshme[✉] and S. Ganesh Kumar

Department of Data Science and Business Systems, SRM Institute of Science and Technology,
Kattankulathur Campus, Chennai, India
preyankalakshme14@gmail.com, ganeshk1@srmist.edu.in

Abstract. Feature selection (FS), which reduces data dimensionality and enriches the performance of any suggested framework, is one of the most crucial parts of machine learning (ML). In real-world applications, computational, large dimensionality and noisy or ambiguous nature, storage complexity, high performance, and other difficulties beset FS work. As a pre-processing phase, dimension reduction is used to improve the accuracy of learning features and reduce training time by removing irrelevant data, noise, and duplicated features. The feature selection (FS) and feature extraction (FE) methods were used to conduct dimensionality reduction (DR). Due to the increasing rate of data creation, FS is a practical method for addressing several serious dimensionality problems, like decreasing duplication, eradicating unneeded data, and enhancing comprehensibility in the outcomes. The efficiency of data processing and storage can be enriched by FE that handles the challenge of selecting the most distinct, instructive, and constrained collection of features. This research focuses on contemporary feature selection and feature extraction algorithms that aid in reducing data dimensionality.

Keywords: Feature selection · Machine learning · Feature extraction Dimensionality reduction · Data processing

1 Introduction

Human requirements for various types of employment have grown fast as a result of computer usage in the modern world. Every minute, billions, if not trillions, of bytes of data are produced for this purpose. In recent years, data has become a valuable asset due to its many applications. As a result, this information is now classified as big data, with a large dimensionality [1].The exponential rise of data presents a plethora of new issues for data management. The advancement of Artificial Intelligence (AI) and data mining strategies or ideas that automatically extract key information from gathered or stored data is therefore essential.

The Curse of Dimensionality (COD), a significant problem, develops when these massive datasets are subjected to machine learning (ML) or data mining techniques.

The COD [2] phenomenon occurs when high-dimensional data fails to organise, categorise, and analyse in a lower-dimensional environment; it occurs in practise as a result

S. Rajagopal et al. (Eds.): ASCIS 2022, CCIS 1759, pp. 144–157, 2022.
https://doi.org/10.1007/978-3-031-23092-9_12

of data closeness and sparsity. Because of the enormous amount of feature spaces in big data, the classification model tends to be over fitted, resulting in performance latency for data items that aren't visible. Highdimensional data adds to the classification model's computational difficulty as well as the storage needs' space complexity [3].Because not all characteristics are required, the performance of the classifier may be severely harmed by any irrelevant or redundant features. One type of technique that solves the concerns mentioned above is reducing the dimensionality [2]. Feature selection is subdivided into: feature extraction (FE) and FS. A new feature subset is extracted from an old one using the FS approach [4].As a result, the FS and FE approaches improve the performance of the classifier while lowering space, time, and storage needs. These strategies so demonstrate that they are effective dimensionality reduction techniques. The FS, which is a dimensionality reduction approach, was the only focus of this work. The field of FS is quite broad, and the FS problem has lately had a considerable influence on the various ML areas in terms of performance, time, and space complexity. We conducted a detailed survey in the different domains of ML for the FS job in this study. The importance of this survey and our contribution to this study are explored in the following subsections. This survey mainly focuses on two issues in feature selection one is reducing the dimensionality of the dataset and the next is to identify the already available feature selection methodologies and its area of use.

The following is an outline of the paper. The backdrop of feature selection techniques is described in Sect. 2. Section 3 provides a quick overview of the present feature selection and extraction algorithms for decreasing data dimensionality. Section 4 examines prior work and outlines a plan for future study. Section 5 brings the article to a close.

2 Preliminaries

2.1 Feature Selection

The most essential stages in the machine learning process for improving results are FS. In the case of a data set, a feature simply refers to a column. Machine Learning is based on basic rules: if we input trash values, we will only get garbage values as an output [25]. It is not required for every characteristic in a dataset to have a positive influence on the output variable. If we include these irrelevant features in the model, the model's performance will deteriorate. This has increased the need of integrating feature selection. If the proper subset of features is chosen, feature selection can also assist to reduce over fitting and improve model accuracy. To extract the ideal feature subset from the supplied feature space and increase the model's effectiveness and efficiency, several methods and techniques are available. Figure 1 illustrates the classification of the literature survey.

Following are the steps involved in feature selection approach.

- Feature set
- Obtain the feature subset
- Evaluate the obtained feature set
- Termination condition
- Validating the output for a specific feature subset.

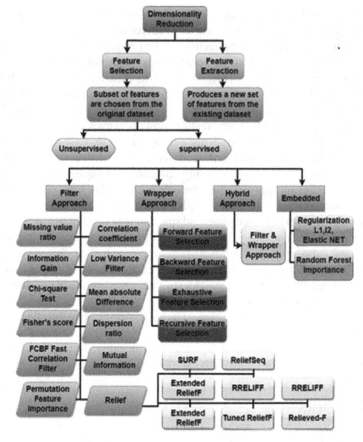

Fig. 1. Classification of the literature survey

Filter Approach. Filter approach, as the name implies, are those in which we filter and maintain only a subset of the significant information. As a preprocessing step, this model is frequently utilised. The relevant characteristics are chosen based on their results in several statistical tests demonstrating their association with the outcome variable. This feature selection is fully unaffected by Machine Learning methodologies [5]. Figure 2 describes the flow of the filter approach. Some of the common filter approaches are chi-square, Pearson's Correlation, and so on.

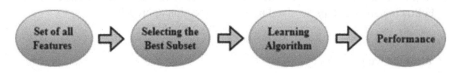

Fig. 2. Procedure for filter approach

Wrapper Approach. Feature selection in filter techniques is not dependent on any Machine Learning approaches, whereas wrapper techniques require one Machine Learning algorithm to work on and then use the model's performance as the evaluation criteria to choose the optimal feature subset. Wrapper approaches choose the optimal feature subset by treating it as a search problem in which several subsets of features are created, analysed, and compared to each other [5]. The predictive model then evaluates this selection of characteristics and assigns a score depending on model accuracy. Figure 3 describes the flow of the wrapper approach. Some of the common wrapper approaches are Backward Selection, Forward Selection, Recursive feature elimination, and so on.

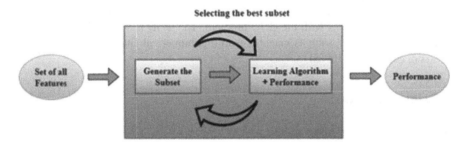

Fig. 3. Procedure for wrapper approach

Embedded Approach. Filter and wrapper techniques are combined in these approaches. Algorithms with their own built-in feature selection technique implement embedded methods [5]. They choose the aspects that help to the creation of the most accurate model when the model is being built. Embedded approaches are iterative in the sense that they carefully examine each iteration of the model's training process and then create a subset of the most essential features by examining their contribution to the model's training for certain iteration. Figure 3 describes the flow of the embedded approach. Random forest (tree feature importance), LASSO, and RIDGE regression are some examples of embedded approach (Fig. 4).

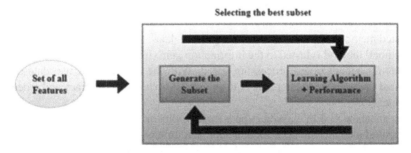

Fig. 4. Procedure for embedded approach

2.2 Reducing the Dimensionality

Reducing the dimensionality refers to converting the high dimensional information representation to low dimensional representation. All classification challenges or tasks are carried out depending on the quantity of features included in the datasets. The number of features in the datasets affects how well all machine learning techniques work. Only those characteristics are needed for the ML strategy challenge. To improve the effectiveness of the machine learning technique, dimensionality reduction [2] assists in reducing the number of features from the initial collection.

Dimensionality reduction has a number of ramifications, including: Dimensionality reduction reveals the most significant characteristics, increasing the accuracy of machine learning algorithms. As the dimension reduces the total temporal complexity of the ML method falls. It also deals with the COD problem. The COD is a phenomena in which some domain problems, such as machine learning, numerical analysis, combinatorics, and so on, can only be solved.

3 Related Works

3.1 Feature Selection Approaches

Niu et al. [6] suggested a strategy for dealing with multivariate financial time series nonlinearity in order to increase forecasting accuracy and the standard of financial judgements. The suggested approach was divided into three stages: feature selection, deep learning framework, and error correlation section. The duplicate feature was eliminated by combining the RReliefF technique, an improved version of the ReliefF algorithm, with a wrapper-based strategy. A gated recurrent unit (GRU), an LSTM, and an optimizer based on an adaptive moment estimate were also included in the deep learning component (Adam). A subset of the first half was created and used to train the deep leaning segment. Additionally, to increase the method's accuracy, the error correlation was used. The method was evaluated against 16 benchmarks and three datasets, and the findings showed that it was superior.

Churmonge and Jena [7] presented a strategy based on clustering and correlation filter subset selection to overcome the dimensionality issue. The K-means clustering technique revealed significant characteristics, while the correlation measure detected redundant features in clusters and deleted them. The Naive Bayes (NB) classifier used the suggested method to classify data from eight text datasets and four microarray datasets. The authors' method is tested to the information gain (IG) and ReliefF feature selection methods for accuracy and processing speed. With the exception of two datasets, the suggested strategy fared better than both approaches in terms of accuracy and processing performance.

For unbalanced data classification with high dimensionality, Hosseini and Moattar [8] proposed a feature subset selection approach. In this multiple subsets of the features are formed during each iteration of the algorithm, with the best subset being used in the following iteration. The candidate characteristics chosen by the Symmetric Uncertainty Algorithm (SUA) are discussed in greater depth initially. After using multivariate interaction data to evaluate the candidate feature subset, the ideal feature subset was selected based on the dominant relationship. In addition, classifiers such as KNN, Nave Bayes, and CART were utilised. The suggested method's effectiveness was tested using 13 datasets from various sources. The strategy performed better than 10 other feature selection techniques in terms of accuracy and the number of reduced features.

Hafiz et al. [9] explored power quality event feature selection concerns and developed a two-dimensional PSO feature selection approach. In order to properly steer the particle swarm's search space, they relied on the two-dimensional. The Gaussian investigated the noise measurement against the smaller subset. KNN and Nave Bayes were the induction algorithms employed in this investigation. Furthermore, the performance of the suggested technique was compared to that of the Ant Colony Optimization (ACO), Genetic Algorithm (GA), Binary PSO (BPSO), Chaotic BPSO (CHBPSO), and Catfish BPSO. The outcomes demonstrated that the suggested strategy could more accurately than the other techniques identify a meaningful and robust feature subset.

ReliefF and PCA methods were used in a hybrid feature selection technique developed by Jain and Singh [10]. First, the weights for each feature in the datasets were determined, and the first method provided a set of satisfied features. In the created set, the second algorithm was used. The suggested technique took into account two types of datasets (text and microarray), with 10 datasets used in the tests. The effectiveness of the method was examined in terms of the calculation time and a number of selected features. The findings showed that the proposed method outperformed current methods in both low-dimensional and high-dimensional datasets while excluding 50% of the redundant and unnecessary features.

Han et al. [11] proposed an unsupervised FS strategy with the limitations of the local linear embedding (LLE) approach. They used graph matrix learning and low-dimensional space learning. The trials made use of 15 datasets). Additionally, the decision tree (DT) and SVM were used as classifiers. The proposed technique was also compared to eight unsupervised feature selection methods. In comparison to the eight feature selection approaches, the suggested method achieved superior accuracy in the DT and SVM classifiers except in two datasets, and both classifiers had better stability.

In order to classify the quality of rice, Duong and Hoang [12] created a technique based on a feature selection approach and the HOG descriptor. They extracted the HOG features from the rice image and assigned a score to each feature based on the fisher score FS.The VNRICE dataset was employed in the suggested method's experimentation. In addition, the NN classifier was used. The findings showed that using the fisher score technique increased classification accuracy by 42% while reducing calculation time.

Using operational taxonomic units, Qu et al. [13] developed feature selection for colorectal cancer prediction. The suggested method included three additional feature selection strategies. The subset of the most significant operational taxonomic units generated by different dimension-reduction strategies is first shown. Then, in order to decrease dimensionality and boost efficiency, a combination of maximal relevance maximum distance (MRMD) and correlation-based feature selection (CFS) was used. Furthermore, the top characteristics were chosen based on the taxonomy file. Two datasets were used in the experiment, and three classifiers (DT, Nave Bayes, and RF) needed evaluation. The findings showed that the correlation-based feature selection technique reduced data more effectively, whereas the MRMD took more time and memory to compute.

For gene classification for dimensionality reduction, Arshak and Eesa [14] proposed a feature selection strategy that depend on cuttlefish algorithm(CFA). A subset of the ideal features was generated using the cuttlefish. The KNN was also employed as a classifier for the proposed method's assessment and classification. Eight distinct datasets from the ELVIRA biomedical dataset collection were used in the experiment. In terms of accuracy and computing time, the suggested technique was matched to SVM and DT, as well as the hidden Markov model. The results showed that the provided strategy outperformed the other methods in five datasets.

Farokhmanesh and Sadeghi [15] suggested a sparse feature selection and deep neural network feature selection approach. In the beginning, three sparse approaches were examined and compared: Sparse Group Lasso (SGL), Discriminative Least Squares Regression (DLSR), andCorrentropy-induced. The SGL and deep neural grid were then integrated, and the combined performance was assessed. In the meanwhile, the SGL technique grouped characteristics by the K- means strategy. For finding the effectiveness of the different strategies, the closest neighbour algorithm was utilised as a classifier. On the MNIST dataset, we tested and valued three sparse and combination approaches. The results showed that when the SGL was used in conjunction with a deep neural network, the accuracy was improved.

The Alharan et al. [16] strategy for classifying texture images is based on feature extraction and feature selection techniques. The group of characteristics were first extracted from the datasets using three different approaches. In the second stage, the obtained features were evaluated using five alternative approaches. The feature selection was then completed using the K-means clustering technique based on the findings of the prior research. Three datasets were utilised in the experiment using the suggested methodology, and SVM, NB, and KNN classifiers were employed for classification. The outcomes demonstrated that the first dataset's NB and KNN performed better than the second and third datasets' SVMs.

Color-based techniques for feature extraction and feature selection were proposed by Osman et al. [17] as a way for automatically recognising origin. The procedure was broken down into three phases. In the first stage, a skin colour detection method was used to retrieve the skin colour information from human faces. Then, redundant or superfluous features are removed using the GA approach and wrapper subset evaluator. Additionally, the scientists used 1550 face pictures from diverse locations and six classifiers for classification, including NB, RF, Bayes Net, KNN, Multilayer Perceptron (MLP), andSVM. The findings showed that individual colour characteristic accuracy was lower than combination colour feature accuracy. Furthermore, the NB, SVM, and Bayes Net could not be used for the recommended technique because to their poor accuracy.

Umbarkar and Shukla [18] proposed a way for improving the instruction detection system's performance. They used IG, gain ratio (GR), and CFS techniques to lessen the dataset's dimensionality. They partitioned the original collection into many sections to get the best-reduced set of characteristics, then applied each method to those portions and chose the most accurate. On the KDD-Cup 99 dataset, the developed system was evaluated using DT as the classifier. The outcomes showed that the correlation-based feature selection strategy performed more effectively than the alternative methods.

Manbari et al. [19] suggested a clustering-based binary ant system-based hybrid unsupervised feature selection approach. The method's technique is split into two parts: The features were clustered in the first step, and the best feature was determined from each cluster in the second stage using the Ant process iteration. In the meantime, the suggested method's second stage was performed multiple times until the dominating traits were gathered. The offered strategy was examined against seven other unsupervised feature selection methods using eight datasets from the UCI and Pablo de Olavide research groups. Based on feature selection and PSO, Kaur and Singh [21] suggested an image steganalysis approach. The dominating traits were first chosen based on mutual information. Furthermore, the authors employed adaptive PSO to choose prominent traits. For the experiment of the described approach, 10000 stego pictures were collected from the BOSSbase dataset. KNN, SVM, and DT classifiers, as well as three more PSO-based algorithms, were used to assess the techniques' classification accuracy. The proposed strategy outperformed existing methods, according to the findings.

3.2 Feature Extraction Approaches

Li et al. [22] focused on defect detection and designed a feature extraction approach using a discriminative graph regularised autoencoder (DGAE). They developed a complicated neural network structure to transfer process input to feature space, avoid issues with manually building features, and ensure that the learnt feature reflect accurately reflects the data attributes. For the purpose of preserving locality and learning internal representation, the neural network structural model and the graph are combined. Training samples for label information were also added to the graph to enhance classification performance. NN was used as a classifier. The proposed method beat earlier approaches to defect diagnostic feature extraction.

Berbar [23] used feature extraction to study malignant tumours in mammograms. TThe recommended method was based on the researcher's three hybrid approaches for extracting Gray Level Co-occurrence Matrix (GLCM) texture characteristics. Three hybrid strategies are ST-GLCM, Wavelet CT1, and Wavelet CT2. The intriguing area of the picture was divided into sub-images before feature extraction, and a contrast stretching step was used. Then, feature extraction methods were applied on the sub-image. The GLCM was then used to extract the seven-feature texture, which was then combined with seven statistical features. In addition, two picture datasets and an SVM classifier were employed in this study. In terms of the number of extracted features, the suggested approaches outperformed multi-resolution feature extraction methods.

Chen et al. [24] presented an experiment to determine bone age using X-ray pictures. To extract information from X-ray pictures, they employed a deep neural network. Local Binary Patterns (LBP) and Glutamate Cysteine Ligase Modifier Subunit (GCLM) features are two of the traits that were taken from the picture. More specifically, a convolution neural network was used to automatically determine the bone age, and deep learning was employed to automatically recover the components of the X-ray hand bone image. Additionally, the dimension of the retrieved features was decreased via the PCA method. SVM classifier was used to categorise the extracted characteristics. A taken photograph from multiple guys and girls of various ages served as the test data, training data, and verification data. The results showed that the provided study outperformed existing strategies in this sector.

Liu et al. [25] developed a feature extraction method by combining discriminant analysis with the low ranks representation of the original data samples. The recommended feature extraction method by the supervisor is discriminative low rank preserving projection. The effectiveness of the provided strategy was compared to that of seven other feature extraction methods on images from six different datasets (LPP, DPSR, LSDA, LSPP, LRRDP, FOLP, and LRPP). The DLRPP.

Zhang et al. [26] recommended a strategy for reducing the dimensionality of hyperspectral pictures.. As an integrated technique, they relied on the sparse graph and spatial. To partition hyperspectral pictures into superpixel patches, they used PCA and entropy rate. Furthermore, superpixel segmentation was used to create the graph's training data. On the basis of the gathered data, sparse and low-rank graphs were created, and they were able to recover spatial-spectral data. The graph embedding was then transferred to nonlinear space using the kernel technique once the input data had been translated into a high-dimensional space. Two datasets were used to evaluate the suggested approach, with the SVM algorithm serving as a classifier. The findings demonstrate that the recommended approach is more precise than other ones that are already in use.

Ma and Yuan [27] devised a deep CNN and PCA-based method for extracting features from photos. They employed a neural network to extract characteristics. They utilised simulated experiments to enhance and optimise the PCA approach using deep learning due to the enormous dimension of the recovered features. The PCA's performance was then compared before and after the changes. The memory use was above 6000 MB before the algorithms were optimised, but it was less than 1000 MB after they were optimised. The time used by the PCA method before and after optimization was also significantly different. Besides the increased PCA's efficiency, the classifier accuracy was also improved by using the SVM approach.

Alipourfard et al. [28] investigated the high dimensionality of hyperspectral images and presented a solution to minimise it. CNN and the subspace feature extraction approach were combined in the suggested system. The authors employed the subspace approach to decrease the dimensionality of the hyperspectral pictures in order to provide high-quality training data. Furthermore, the researchers tested the proposed approach on two well-known datasets (Pavia University scenes and the)Indiana Pines. Even with the restricted sets of training samples, the testing findings showed that the suggested technique accuracy was enhanced and received better marks.

The examination of the discriminative graph signal by Lin et al. [29] led to the recommendation of a feature extraction technique that might extract useful features for performing the necessary classification. Graph training samples that have been established. They also used eigenvector decomposition to determine the Fourier foundation of the graph. For high accuracy, a large number of discriminative signals were retrieved simultaneously, particularly in a situation with many classes. The suggested approach was tested on four datasets in four distinct tests. The results showed that the approaches offered might produce positive outcomes, and that supervised categorization was more successful. Table 1 gives the overall comparison of the algorithms that are reviewed in this manuscript.

Table 1. Overall comparison of the algorithms

References	Method	Technique used	Advantages	Limitations
[6]	Hybrid Approach	Wrapper-based method Extreme learning machine combined with multi-objective binary grey wolf optimizer using Cuckoo search Filter-based method RReliefF Approach	Provides better accuracy	Sensitive to optimizer and rate of learning. So poor generalization if optimizer and its learning rate are not selected correctly
[7]	Hybrid method	k-means clustering method and correlation measure to eradicate irrelevant features	Faster computation Diminishes relevant features and enrich COD	Lower similarity measure in selecting certain specific features
[9]	Wrapper-based method	NB and KNN	Produces reduced feature subsets	Poor Generalization Extra learning is required for enhancing the search
[10]	Hybrid method	ReliefF and Principal Component Analysis	Diminishes dimensionality issues Low computation time	Performance is based only on selected number of features Only 50% of redundant and irrelevent datas are removed
[11]	Unsupervised	Graph matrix learning and the low-dimensional space learning	Provided good accuracy And also improved stability	Does not suitable for all type of datasets
[13]	Hybrid method	Dimension reduction approaches correlation-based FS and maximum relevance–maximum distance	Reduce dimensionality and increase efficiency	Take more memory and also computation time

(*continued*)

Table 1. (*continued*)

References	Method	Technique used	Advantages	Limitations
[14]	Hybrid method	Cuttlefish Algorithm (CFA) and KNN	Provides better accuracy and computation time	Poor generalization
[15]	Embedded Approach	SparseGroup Lasso (SGL) algorithm	Provides good generalization Provide an effective precision	Poor dimensionality reduction
[16]	Filter Approach	Symmetric, oneR, Gain ratio, ReliefF, and info gain	On testing with different classifiers only SVM produces better performance	Poor generalization
[17]	Wrapper Approach	Viola-Jone face detection algorithm	Provide better performance only for selected dataset	Poor generalization and dimensionality reduction
[18]	Filter Approach	Correction based FS, Gain ratio (GR) and Information gain(IG) approaches	Provide superior performance in selecting features. Good Generalization	Can enhance dimensionality reduction for improving the performance
[19]	Hybrid filter Approach	Integrating clustering and modified Binary Ant System (BAS)	Enriches the performance of learning algorithm Takes low computation time Effective in high-dimensional data	Low sensitivity

4   Discussion

Different techniques/algorithms are employed in the suggested feature selection approaches to reduce the dataset's dimensionality, reduce computation time, and increase classification accuracy. Some of the techniques are based on the clustering methodology utilising K-means may be found in the related work. In [7], the authors utilised K-means to eliminate irrelevant features. In [20], they used the similarity value to divide features into various clusters, and in [30], they used the approach to separate features into the most noisy and relevant clusters. Text, microarray, and texture image classification are three examples of highdimensional datasets that were employed in the three methodologies outlined above. The computing time was reduced by more than half when the researchers in [7] compared the ReliefF and IG strategies. In addition, the authors compared the fulfilment of their techniques to the fulfilment of three other ant colony-based feature selection techniques in [19], demonstrating that the calculation time was 5–8 times faster than the other methods.

Traditional feature selection approaches like ReliefF were employed in [6, 10, 16], and Information Gain was used in [18] and [16]. ReliefF was used with LSTM in [16], the PCA algorithm in [10], and IG, symmetric, and K-means in [16]. Its main purpose in the employed methods was to choose significant features, and it was used with other approaches in the majority of studies. The IG approach was used with other methods including GR, correlation-based features, and symmetric techniques to minimise the dimensionality of the datasets.

The accuracy of the approaches under consideration varies from one approach to the next. The optimization-based feature selection methods outperformed more conventional approaches in terms of performance. The most often utilised classifiers in the techniques were KNN and SVM, both of which were employed in 8 approaches, and NB in 6 investigations. Several different classifiers were used in certain papers. Nonetheless, in papers that employed several classifiers, the SVM had superior accuracy than the others. Additionally, as computing times vary, it was essential to use clustering and optimization techniques to reduce computational complexity. When compared to IG and ReliefF approaches, the execution time in study [7] was roughly 50 percent to 70 percent faster. Furthermore, the CFA and GA lowered execution time by 40% and 50%, respectively, in the studies [17] and [31]. However, the best computational time was reached, which was 5–8 times quicker than the other three ACO approaches, when the Ant system and clustering algorithm were integrated in the research [19].

On analysing all the approaches the highest accuracy was obtained on those who relied on PCA algorithms; they refined the algorithm using deep learning. Additionally, in the study [27], the enhanced PCA by the CNN reduced the amount of computation time significantly, from 1300 without the CNN to 100 when the PCA technique was improved.

5 Conclusion

The learning technique, processing time, computer resources (memory), and model accuracy all suffer as a result of the large dimensionality of data. As a result, lowering dimensionality and overcoming its curse has become a hot issue in the search and development fields in order to give the most dependable, versatile, and accurate computerised tools and applications. As a result, various feature selection and feature extraction-based methodologies and procedures have been developed in the previous two decades. This paper reviews recent research in a number of areas, including medical disease analysis, ethnicity identification, emotion recognition, gene classification, text classification, image steganography, data visualisation, hyperspectral image classification, network malware detection, and a number of engineering tasks. The authors used certain methodologies, algorithms, datasets, and classifier approaches, and their findings on the precision and computational efficiency for each feature selection and feature extraction method are provided. According to the study, KNN and SVM classifiers are the two most popular classifiers, and the SVM approach has the best accuracy. In contrast, CNN and DNN algorithms play a significant part in feature extraction methods. While the PCA is still a popular feature extraction approach applied in various methodologies.

Acknowledgements. I confirm that all authors listed on the title page have contributed significantly to the work, have read the manuscript, attest to the validity and legitimacy of the data and its interpretation, and agree to its submission.

References

1. Sahu, B., Dehuri, S., Jagadev, A.: A study on the relevance of feature selection methods in microarray data. Open Bioinform. J. Bentham Open **11**, 117–139 (2018)
2. Li, J., Cheng, K., Wang, S., Morstatter, F., Trevino, R.P., Tang, J., LiuH.: Feature Selection: A Data Perspective. ACM Comput .Surv. **50** (2017)
3. Liu, H., Motoda, H.: Feature Selection for Knowledge Discovery and Data Mining. Kluwer Academic Publishers, New York (1998)
4. Agarwal, S., Dhyani, A., Ranjan, P.: Newton's second lawbased PSO for feature selection: Newtonian PSO. J Intell. Fuzzy Syst. **37**, 4923–4935 (2019)
5. Thakkar, A., Lohiya, R.: Attack classification using feature selection techniques: a comparative study. J. Ambient. Intell. Humaniz. Comput. **12**(1), 1249 1266 (2020) https://doi.org/10.1007/s12652-020-02167-9
6. Niu, T., Wang, J., Lu, H., Yang, W., Du, P.: Developing a deep learning framework with two-stage feature selection for multivariate financial time series forecasting. Expert. Syst. Appl. **148**, 113237 (2020)
7. Chormunge, S., Jena, S.: Correlation based feature selection with clustering for high dimensional data. J. Electr. Syst. Inf. Technol. **5**(3), 542–549 (2018)
8. Hosseini, E.S., Moattar, M.H.: Evolutionary feature subsets selection based on interaction information for high dimensional imbalanced data classification. Appl. Soft Comput. **82**, 105581 (2019)
9. Hafiz, F., Swain, A., Naik, C., Patel, N.: Efficient feature selection of power quality events using two dimensional (2D) particle swarms. Appl. Soft Comput. **81**, 105498 (2019)
10. Jain, D., Singh, V.: An efficient hybrid feature selection model for dimensionality reduction. Procedia Comput. Sci. **132**, 333–341 (2018)
11. Han, X., Liu, P., Wang, L., Li, D.: Unsupervised feature selection via graph matrix learning and the low-dimensional space learning for classification. Eng. Appl. Artif. Intell. **87**, 103283 (2020)
12. Duong, H.-T., Hoang, V.T.: Dimensionality reduction based on feature selection for rice varieties recognition. In: 2019 4th International Conference on Information Technology (InCIT), pp. 199–202. IEEE (2019)
13. Qu, K., Gao, F., Guo, F., Zou, Q.: Taxonomy dimension reduction for colorectal cancer prediction. Comput. Biol. Chem. **83**, 107160 (2019)
14. Arshak, Y., Eesa, A.: A new dimensional reduction based on cuttlefish algorithm for human cancer gene expression. In: 2018 International Conference on Advanced Science and Engineering (ICOASE), pp. 48–53. IEEE (2018)
15. Farokhmanesh, F., Sadeghi, M.T.: Deep feature selection using an enhanced sparse group lasso algorithm. In: 2019 27th Iranian Conference on Electrical Engineering (ICEE), pp. 1549–1552. IEEE (2019)

16. Alharan, A.F., Fatlawi, H.K., Ali, N.S.: A cluster-based feature selection method for image texture classification. Indones. J. Electr. Eng. Comput. Sci. **14**(3), 1433–1442 (2019)
17. Osman, M.Z., Maarof, M.A., Rohani, M.F., Moorthy, K., Awang, S.: Multi-scale skin sample approach for dynamic skin color detection: an analysis. Adv. Sci. Lett. **24**(10), 7662–7667 (2018)
18. Umbarkar, S., Shukla, S.: Analysis of heuristic based feature reduction method in intrusion detection system. In: 2018 5th International Conference on Signal Processing and Integrated Networks (SPIN), pp. 717–720: IEEE (2018)
19. Manbari, Z., AkhlaghianTab, F., Salavati, C.: Hybrid fast unsupervised feature selection for high-dimensional data. Expert. Syst. Appl. **124**, 97–118 (2019)
20. Tan, P., Wang, X., Wang, Y.: Dimensionality reduction in evolutionary algorithms-based feature selection for motor imagery brain-computer interface. Swarm Evol. Comput. **52**, 100597 (2020)
21. Kaur, J., Singh, S.: Feature selection using mutual information and adaptive particle swarm optimization for image steganalysis. In: 2018 7th International Conference on Reliability, Infocom Technologies and Optimization (Trends and Future Directions) (ICRITO), pp. 538–544. IEEE (2018)
22. Li, Y., Chai, Y., Zhou, H., Yin, H.: A novel feature extraction method based on discriminative graph regularized autoencoder for fault diagnosis, IFAC-PapersOnLine **52**(24), 272–277 (2019)
23. Berbar, M.A.: Hybrid methods for feature extraction for breast masses classification. Egypt. Inform. J. **19**(1), 63–73 (2018)
24. X. Chen., J. Li., Y. Zhang., Y. Lu., S. Liu.: Automatic feature extraction in X-ray image based on deep learning approach for determination of bone age, Future Generation Computer Systems, (2019)
25. Liu, Z., Wang, J., Liu, G., Zhang, L.: Discriminative low-rank preserving projection for dimensionality reduction. Appl. Soft Comput. **85**, 105768 (2019)
26. Lin, W., Huang, J., Suen, C.Y., Yang, L.: A feature extraction model based on discriminative graph signals. Expert. Syst. Appl. **139**, 112861 (2020)
27. Ma, J., Yuan, Y.: Dimension reduction of image deep feature using PCA. J. Vis. Commun. Image Represent. **63**, 102578 (2019)
28. Kasongo, S.M., Sun, Y.: A deep learning method with wrapper based feature extraction for wireless intrusion detection system. Comput. & Secur. **92**, 101752 (2020)
29. Balasaraswathi, V.: Enhanced Cuttle Fish Algorithm Using Membrane Computing for feature selection of intrusion detection, vol. 10, special issue (2018)
30. Eesa, A.S., Abdulazeez, A.M., Orman, Z.: A DIDS based on the combination of Cuttlefish Algorithm and decision tree. Science Journal of University of Zakho **5**(4), 313–318 (2017)
31. Fatima, A., Maurya, R., Dutta, M.K., Burget, R., Masek, J.: Android malware detection using genetic algorithm based optimized feature selection and machine learning. In: 2019 42nd International Conference on Telecommunications and Signal Processing (TSP), pp. 220–223 (2019)

Automating Scorecard and Commentary Based on Umpire Gesture Recognition

Medha Wyawahare[✉], Amol Dhanawade, Shreyas Dharyekar, Asavari Dhole, and Mugdha Dhopade

Department of Electronics and Telecommunication, Vishwakarma Institute of Technology, Pune 411038, India
medha.wyawahare@vit.edu

Abstract. Cricket is the most played sport in the Indian subcontinent. While the sport enjoys abundant financial and human resources at the highest levels, the lower levels lack these resources which creates a resource parity between players playing at various levels. This paper aims to develop a system capable of detecting the various umpire signals from images and then automating the scorecard accordingly. The system uses a camera to capture the image of the umpire then a processor-based system is used to identify the signal and update the scorecard. In the detection process, the image is pre-processed and SIFT descriptor is applied to extract image features. The dimensions of the features is reduced with k-means and PCA. Finally, the classification of signals is done using 3 classifiers that are KNN, Decision tree and Random Forest. The model is trained with 6000 images of 6 classes which include Six, Four, Out, No ball, wide ball and a no action class. The random forest classifier gives the best accuracy at 81 percent. A novel algorithm is used for updating the scorecard. Audio commentary is provided through predefined templates.

Keywords: Computer vision · Gesture recognition · SIFT · Scorecard automation

1 Introduction

Cricket is also a resource and equipment-heavy sport. For playing the sport at any level properly a full kit consisting of a bat, ball, pads, gloves, helmet, etc. is required. A scorecard visible to players and the audience is a necessity and audio commentary describing the developments on the field enhances the audience experience. While international fixtures and top-flight domestic leagues such as the Indian premier league enjoy an abundance of monitory and manpower resources such is not the case in lower divisions or student sports. Manual scorecard updating and commenting on the game require special personnel and hence becomes too expensive. Automating these tasks will reduce the cost of organizing the games and enhance the audience experience in such games.

Automatic gesture detection in the video has been an important research area in the field of computer vision because it is widely used in image/video indexing, robot

S. Rajagopal et al. (Eds.): ASCIS 2022, CCIS 1759, pp. 158–168, 2022.
https://doi.org/10.1007/978-3-031-23092-9_13

navigation, video surveillance, computer interfaces, and gaming. Throughout decades of research and numerous promising advancements, automating cricket scorecards and commentary based on umpire gesture identification remains a difficult problem, owing to the many different gesture categories and large intra-category variances. Differences in views and visual signals such as color, texture, and scale variance all contribute to the issue. Gestures in everyday life can be classified into a variety of categories based on their application domains, such as deaf sign languages, diving signals, and referee signals. Because of the variety of gestures, different visual information from films (e.g., finger and lip movements, body attitude) must be evaluated in gesture detection. In reality, static umpire movements (such as six, four, no ball, out) and dynamic motions (such as waving one's hand) provide the majority of the data needed for the audience to grasp complex gestures. Researchers have been inspired to employ these two types of data to depict complex actions.

In this paper, we propose a novel gesture recognition for the Automating Cricket Scorecard and Commentary based on Umpire Gesture Recognition.

2 Literature Survey

Gesture recognition is recognized by using Hidden Markov's Model, low pass filter to capture the moving entities while reducing the noise background elimination. A technique of binarization is used to identify the moving objects in order to generate blobs in paper [1]. In [2] The method is tested on the Chalearn IsoGD dataset and NATOPS dataset and it utilizes an enhanced depth Gesture Model and a Static Pose Map from depth videos to recognize gestures. In [3] a principal motion component for one-shot gesture recognition, the method was highly effective for dynamic gestures. The method can be used in combination with other approaches.

This research [4] proposes a deep learning approach for computer vision that is used for gesture recognition and converts hand pose estimate and targeting gesture recognition information to training objectives. A technique of hand gesture recognition is used by using YCbCR technique in [5].Convex hull algorithm is used to get hand gestures, and angles and distance between the fingers are used to calculate hand gestures. Adaptive color segmentation by using adaptive color by using the background color of the image, YCbCr is used for recognizing the skin tone in [6], Gaussian model to match every pixel as skin pixel for back Author Emails round. Along with the skin color the background is recognized to prevent any corner cases.

All the development in gesture recognition is then used for varied applications, one of them is umpire hand gesture recognition. A technique of subtracting a skin color threshold from every pixel is used to convert the skin color to white and the background to black [7]. Region of Interest is found by using Standard Deviation, variance, covariance, eigenvectors and the interpretation of gesture takes place. A technique of segmenting silhouettes from the background. In [8], the corresponding configurations in the same coordinate system are used to display silhouettes across time. In [9–11] the hand gestures are used to update the scoreboard to reduce the efforts and errors. The system is trained to find the recognition of gestures that are shown by the umpire. The [12] discusses the video shots good for detection of player's gestures and then categorizes the video shot on gesture recognition. Labelling system for sports using the gestures used by the umpire, HHMM model is used which is trained from the Markov model in [14].

Gestures of umpires from the video clips are recognized by using the 30 fps, long term RCNN model is used for recognition in [15]. In paper [16] a method using the frames of the Umpire in each scene is identified and Vertical and horizontal intensity projection profiles were used to analyze the data. Video is segmented to individual scenes and then is converted to grey level co-occurrence Matrix. In [17] multiple Inertial Measurement Unit (IMU) sensors, for gesture recognition of basketball referees. After applying FFT to the input signal it was separated into higher and lower frequency parts. A live commentary is given for every single update on the game in [18, 19]. This is done via two steps first a listener's belief model is created which takes into account what the listener already knows, this is an accumulation of past conveyed facts. This model was tested with normal and blind individuals. In [20] this proposed system a new HDNN-EPO technique was proposed to identify the theme of an extracted fascinating clip using audio features.

There is a lack of quality work done on cricket umpire gesture detection. The systems discussed earlier used deep learning models for detecting the gestures of the umpire which is computationally expensive as compared to machine learning modes. Some systems had wearable hardware models that could be worn by the umpire which are inconvenient and bulky. While camera-based systems have been trained on a small amount of data which affects the reliability of the system. The work done in this paper discusses detecting the gestures of umpires classifying them and updating the scoreboard and automating the commentary of the scoreboard.

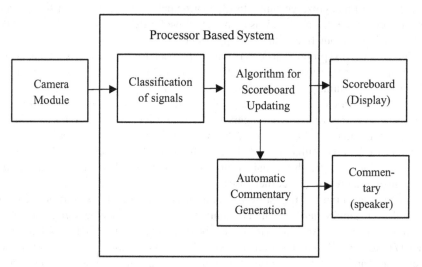

Fig. 1. System Block Diagram

3   Methodology

The proposed system detects the umpire signals such as Wide ball, Six, and Four. The block diagram of the system is shown in Fig. 1. This system comprises a camera, a processor-based system, a display, and a speaker. The camera captures the umpire image then the machine learning-based model detects the signal indicating the update needed in the scorecard. A novel algorithm is then used to update the scorecard accordingly and provide audio commentary.

3.1   Umpire Gestures

To indicate the results of the delivery umpire used different types of gestures. The gestures detected in this system are given below:

Out: The umpire has upheld the fielding side's appeal and the player has been dismissed with an Out judgment. The batsman is 'out' and must leave the field of play when the system recognizes the umpire's raised index finger in the air.

No Ball: When a bowler sends down an illegal delivery that is considered a No Ball under the rules, a No Ball signal is given. When the system recognizes that one of the umpire's arms has fully extended horizontally. As a result, the batting side's total is increased by one run (two runs in certain limited-overs forms of cricket). Also, no balls can happen for a variety of reasons, such as the bowler overstepping or pitching the ball off the wicket.

Wide Ball: When a batsman is standing in his typical posture, a wide ball passes him and is declared out of reach. Both arms of the umpire are extended horizontally when the system senses this. The batting side's total will be increased by one run, and the bowler will have to deliver that ball again. Wide's can also be assigned depending on a person's height.

Four Runs: When the ball passes the boundary after bouncing at least once, it is counted as four runs. The signal is made by sweeping the right hand of the umpire three or four times across the chest. The batting side's total will be increased by four runs. The umpire will make the appropriate signal before signaling four runs if the four runs are the result of byes, leg byes, no balls, or wide.

Six Runs: When a batsman hits the ball over the boundary without it bouncing, he scores six runs. The arms of umpire are raised high above their heads. The batting side's total is then increased by six runs.

3.2   Dataset

A total of 6000 images were used in the dataset. The dataset contained 6 classes. The distribution of images among classes is given in Table 2. A additional no action class is added as a negative class. The total dataset was compiled by combining the web scrapped images which were 30% of the total dataset images and the rest 70% images were compiled by the authors.

The images from the dataset were resized to 300 × 300 to bring uniformity to the dataset and converted to grayscale to aid feature extraction process.

Fig. 2. Dataset sample: six, four, out, no ball, wide ball signals

3.3 Feature Extraction

Scale-InvARiaNT feature transform (SIFT) was used to perform feature extraction. It is an algorithm that identifies key features and provides a feature vector of 128 values for each feature. SIFT was selected because it is invariant to scaling and rotation. Each image in the dataset was converted to grayscale before applying SIFT descriptor to it. The descriptors from each image are normalized to reduce variance before appending them to a total feature vector of all images and their features. The total size of the resulting feature vector was [17307067 × 128].

The large size of the feature vector was reduced for smooth performance of the system and a faster detection process. Dimensionality reduction was performed with the K-Means clustering algorithm. Initially, the large features vector was divided into 10 clusters by K-Means clustering. Then the individual image was predicated into 10 histogram bins by the trained K-Means. The cluster(10) value was determined by using the Elbow method. Standardization was performed on the resulting values. Principal component analysis was applied to reduce the dimensions further to Seven. In PCA, principal components that explain the variance are created. The first 7 components explain 98% of the variance in the dataset. The final feature vector after reducing dimensions was of size [6000 × 7].

3.4 Classification of Umpire Gestures

The reduced feature vector was provided to four classification algorithms. These were (i) Decision Tree classifier, (ii) Random Forest classifier (iii) K-Nearest Neighbor's (KNN).

A decision tree is a supervised learning classifier based on a tree-like structure with some structures called roots and leaves. One of the parameters used in the model is "entropy". Entropy helps to split the data according to entropy information. The advantage of a decision tree is that it considers all possible results.

Random forest is used for better comparison of classification. Instead of considering a single decision tree, the algorithm takes multiple decision trees and makes the final prediction based on the majority. One significant advantage of this algorithm is that it can handle large datasets and perform with relatively higher accuracy along with a fast execution time.

KNN is used as the next classifier. KNN uses K neighbor's to classify the given point into different classes. The model makes the use of K to be 5. With the help of KNN, we could classify the data point into one of the considered classes. The distance is calculated in KNN as of three types: Manhattan distance, Euclidean Distance and Minkowski. The Minkowski distance is calculated as,

$$Dist(x, y) = (\sum_{i=1}^{n} |x_i - y_i|^p)^{1/p} \tag{1}$$

Here the value of p decides the distance nature. For p = 2, it is Euclidian distance, p = 1 it is Manhattan distance and finally when the value of p is infinite, we get Chebyshev distance.

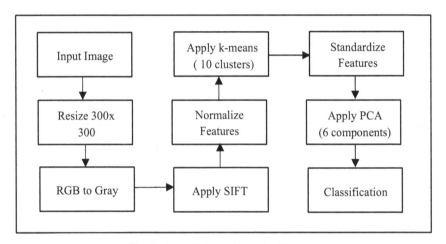

Fig. 3. Overall Flow Diagram of System

3.5 Scorecard Updating Feature

After detection, an algorithm is used to update the scorecard. The algorithm takes team names, player names as input. At the start, it initializes variables such as team runs, wickets, overs played, and personal scores such as runs scored and balls played as 0. After detecting a gesture, the related variables in the scorecard are either incremented or reset to 0. Algorithm 1 explains this in detail.

Input: Team and Player Names
Output: Updated scorecard

---

1. Take names via user input
2. Initialize scorecard variables to 0.
3. Run model to detect the umpire signal
4. If detected signal == 4
5.   Runs = Runs+4
6.   Overs = overs + 0.1
7. If detected signal == 6
8.   Runs = Runs+6
9.   Overs = overs + 0.1
10.   If detected signal == out
11.   Wickets = Wickets+ 1
12.   Overs = overs + 0.1
13.   Batsman
14.   If detected signal == Wide
15.   Runs = Runs+1
16.   If detected signal == No Ball
17.   Runs = Runs+1
18.   Free hit == True
19.   Play pre-decided sentence in commentary.
20.   Repeat from step 3.

For commentary generation predefined sentences are used mixed with the scorecard information at the end of each over. Python text to speech.

4   Results and Discussion

The model was trained on HP 14s laptop having a Ryzen 5 processor and 8GB RAM. More than 6000 images belonging to 6 classes were used in the training and testing phase. The 3 classifiers are (i) Decision Tree classifier, (ii) Random Forest classifier (iii) K-Nearest Neighbor's (KNN) 2, precision which is given in Table 1. The performance of the model was evaluated using accuracy as given in Eq. 2, precision which is given in Eq. 3, recall and f1 score parameters which are given in Eq. 4 and Eq. 5.

$$Accuracy = \frac{TP + TN}{TP + FP + TN + FN} \times 10 \tag{2}$$

$$precision = \frac{TP}{TP + FP} \tag{3}$$

$$Recall = \frac{TP}{TP + FN} \tag{4}$$

$$F1\ score = \frac{2}{\frac{1}{precision} + \frac{1}{recall}} = \frac{2 \times precision \times recall}{precision + recall} \tag{5}$$

From the above tables and graph is clear that the random forest classifier provides the best accuracy at 81%. Followed by KNN at 79.66% and Decision tree at 75.33%. The Four signal is best detected across various classifiers. The reason for this is that it

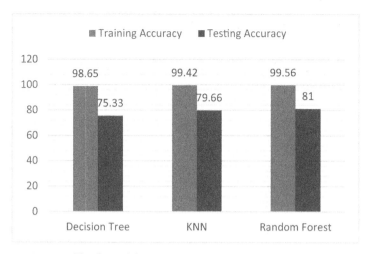

Fig. 4. Training and testing accuracies obtained

Table 1. Distribution of dataset among the classes

Sr. No	Class	Number of images
1	Out	1000
2	No Ball	1000
3	Wide Ball	1003
4	Four	987
5	Six	1008
6	No Action	1002

has a very distinct action. There are huge misclassifications in two signals that are Six and Out signal since both the gestures are very similar to each other. Random forest gives the best accuracy because it's a combination of decision trees and the final output is the maximum vote from all the decision trees.

The scorecard updating algorithm works successfully to keep the scorecard in-tandem with the game. Commentary generation works well and is beneficial to those who have less attention span or visually impaired to follow the game.

Table 2. Comparison of Classification Parameters

Class	Test parameter	Decision tree	KNN	Random forest
Four	Precision	0.82	0.82	0.84
	Recall	0.94	0.96	0.98
	F1-Score	0.87	0.88	0.90
Six	Precision	0.74	0.82	0.89
	Recall	0.84	0.80	0.82
	F1-Score	0.79	0.81	0.85
Out	Precision	0.77	0.82	0.76
	Recall	0.68	0.70	0.66
	F1-Score	0.72	0.76	0.71
No Ball	Precision	0.70	0.70	0.73
	Recall	0.73	0.76	0.80
	F1-Score	0.71	0.73	0.83
Wide Ball	Precision	0.75	0.84	0.85
	Recall	0.71	0.77	0.80
	F1-Score	0.73	0.80	0.83
No Action	Precision	0.84	0.76	0.78
	Recall	0.73	0.81	0.81
	F1-Score	0.78	0.79	0.79
Overall Accuracy		0.77	0.79	0.82

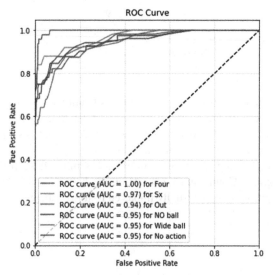

Fig. 5. ROC curve for Random Forest classifier

5   Conclusion

The paper proposes a system to aid Grade cricket with low resources. It uses a camerabased system for detection of the cricket umpire signal to automate the scorecard updating process and provides generic commentary to follow the game for viewers. Traditional machine learning and computer vision algorithms have been used so the system can be implemented on a low paper embedded device. As per the knowledge of the authors, this is the first system that performs the three aforementioned tests with only machine learning and computer vision algorithms. After experimenting with three classifiers the Random Forest classifier gives the maximum accuracy of 81%.

While the system can accurately detect the 5 mentioned umpire signals, it lacks application ability because it cannot detect some rare signals such as leg bye and a dead ball. Also, there are no special umpire signals for singles and doubles so the scorecard needs to be updated manually there. The system can be improved in the future by increasing the size and variety of the dataset. Adding additional pre-processing to focus on the region of interest can be helpful. And commentary can be made more engaging by using storytelling methods rather than a play-by-play module.

References

1. Mitra, S., Acharya, T.: Gesture recognition: a survey. IEEE Trans. Syst., Man Cybern., Part C (Appl. Rev.) **37**(3), 311–324 (2007)
2. Zhang, Z., Wei, S., Song, Y., Zhang, Y.: Gesture recognition using enhanced depth motion map and static pose map. In: 2017 12th IEEE International Conference on Automatic Face & Gesture Recognition (FG 2017), pp. 238–244. IEEE (2017)
3. Escalante, H.J., Guyon, I., Athitsos, V., Jangyodsuk, P., Wan, J.: Principal motion components for one-shot gesture recognition. Pattern Anal. Appl. **20**(1), 167–182 (2017)
4. Escalera, S., Athitsos, V., Guyon, I.: Challenges in multi-modal gesture recognition. Gesture Recogn., 1–60 (2017)
5. Lai, H.Y., Lai, H.J.: Real-time dynamic hand gesture recognition. In: 2014 International Symposium on Computer, Consumer and Control, pp. 658–661. IEEE (2014)
6. Wang, W., Pan, J.: Hand segmentation using skin color and background information. In: 2012 International Conference on Machine Learning and Cybernetics, vol. 4, pp. 1487–1492. IEEE (2012)
7. Nandyal, S., Kattimani, S.L.: Umpire gesture detection and recognition using HOG and non-linear support vector machine (NL-SVM) classification of deep features in cricket videos. J. Phys.: Conf. Ser. **2070**(1), 012148. IOP Publishing (2021)
8. Wang, L., Tan, T., Hu, W., Ning H.: Automatic gait recognition based on statistical shape analysis. IEEE Trans. Image Process. **12**(9), 1120–1131 (2003)
9. Nair, V.K., Jose, R.R., Anil, P.B., Tom, M., Lekshmy, P.L.: Automation of cricket scoreboard by recognizing umpire gestures
10. Balbudhea, P., Mulikb, A., Mulikb, V., Patilb, K., Sontakkeb, K., Gujarkarb, M.: Cricket umpiring wrist gadget for score updation. Int. Res. J. Eng. Technol. (IRJET) (June 2021)
11. John, D.T., Kumar, K.S., Nair, V.T., Visakh, P., Poorna, B.R.: Cricket scoreboard automation using umpire gestures. Int. J. Res. Eng. Sci. Manag. **2**
12. Sen, A., Deb, K., Dhar, P.K. and Koshiba, T.: Cricshotclassify: an approach to classifying batting shots from cricket videos using a convolutional neural network and gated recurrent unit. Sensors 21(8), 2846 (2021)

13. Chambers, G.S., Venkatesh, S., West, G.A.: Automatic labeling of sports video using umpire gesture recognition. In: Joint IAPR International Workshops on Statistical Techniques in Pattern Recognition (SPR) and Structural and Syntactic Pattern Recognition (SSPR), pp. 859–867. Springer, Berlin, Heidelberg (2004)
14. Kumar, R., Santhadevi, D., Barnabas, J.: Outcome classification in cricket using deep learning. In: 2019 IEEE International Conference on Cloud Computing in Emerging Markets (CCEM), pp. 55–58. IEEE (2019)
15. Choroś, K.: Highlights extraction in sports videos based on automatic posture and gesture recognition. In Asian Conference on Intelligent Information and Database Systems, pp. 619–628. Springer, Cham (2017)
16. Hari, R., Wilscy, M.: Event detection in cricket videos using intensity projection profile of Umpire gestures. In: 2014 Annual IEEE India Conference (INDICON), pp. 1–6. IEEE (2014)
17. Pan, T.Y., Chang, C.Y., Tsai, W.L. and Hu, M.C.: Multisensor-based 3D gesture recognition for a decision-making training system. IEEE Sensors J. **21**(1), 706–716 (2020)
18. Kumano, T., Ichiki, M., Kurihara, K., Kaneko, H., Komori, T., Shimizu, T., Seiyama, N., Imai, A., Sumiyoshi, H., Takagi, T.: Generation of automated sports commentary from live sports data. In: 2019 IEEE International Symposium on Broadband Multimedia Systems and Broadcasting (BMSB), pp. 1–4. IEEE (2019)
19. Shahjalal, M.A., Ahmad, Z., Rayan, R., Alam, L.: An approach to automate the scorecard in cricket with computer vision and machine learning. In: 2017 3rd International Conference on Electrical Information and Communication Technology (EICT), pp. 1–6. IEEE (2017)
20. Shingrakhia, H., Patel, H. Emperor penguin optimized event recognition and summarization for cricket highlight generation. Multimed. Syst. **26**(6), 745–759 (2020)

Rating YouTube Videos: An Improvised and Effective Approach

Abhishek Jha[1]([✉]), Arti Jha[2], Aditya Sindhavad[1], Ramavtar Yadav[1], Ashwini Dalvi[1], and Irfan Siddavatam[1]

[1] KJ Somaiya College of Engineering, Mumbai, India
{jha.as,a.sindhavad,ramavtar.y,ashwinidalvi,
irfansiddavatam}@somaiya.edu
[2] Atharva College of Engineering, Mumbai, India

Abstract. YouTube is one of the best sources of video information on the Internet. While it serves as the best media for creators to communicate to a broad audience, it has become less user-friendly over the past few years. Some official changes to the YouTube app have triggered many global audiences. One significant change that took place in the past year was the removal of the dislike count from every YouTube video. Without a dislike count, the current YouTube rating system has become ineffective. The proposed work recommends more user-friendly methods over the current inadequate rating system.

Some previous researchers like Alhujaili and Rawan Fahad (Alhujaili, R.F., Yafooz, W.M.: Sentiment analysis for youtube videos with user comments. In: 2021 International Conference on Artificial Intelligence and Smart Systems (ICAIS)) have already given insights on how sentiment analysis can be used on video comments to know the fairness of the video. So, the authors try to create a robust rating system that primarily uses sentiment analysis to provide fair ratings to every video depending on comment sentiment and would be easier to embed in the official YouTube app as a plugin. This rating system even helps to detect clickbait videos to a certain extent, making it much better than the previous systems.

Keywords: Youtube · Machine learning · Sentiment analysis · Comment analysis · Video rating

1 Introduction

With YouTube removing the dislike count, it has now become challenging for users to predict a video's fairness accurately. As a result, users are forced to watch the entire video without knowing whether it will be helpful to them. So authors try to tackle this challenge with a new lightweight rating system that can accurately predict a video's fairness. In doing so, the authors considered three main properties that define every YouTube video.

1. Video thumbnail: This is one of the most common ways creators try to falsify their content.

2. Video description: Creators try to spam their descriptions with all popular/unwanted tags to rank their videos and improve their search engine optimization (SEO) score.
3. User Comments: This is the essential feature used for the proposed research.

User comments contain users' sentiments about a particular video. It is one of the most actual data available for each video, as the video creators cannot tamper with this data. So these comments can give insights into the fairness of a video.

Since the goal of the proposed work is to design a rating system, the user comment becomes the essential feature for the proposed analysis.

2 Previous Work

Now that YouTube does not show the number of dislikes, every user has to scan through the comments to get a quick summary regarding the fairness of a video. The user comments can have any words ranging from positive to negative. Alhujaili and Rawan Fahad [1] have given some insights on different methods one can use to detect these comment sentiments. Even Chen and Yen-Liang [19] showed us how user opinions could be efficiently predicted using sentiment analysis on video comments. These comment sentiments have many practical applications, like detecting clickbait videos or identifying popular video trends.

While enough research has been done on how sentiment analysis helps to identify user opinions, there is very little to no information available on how a rating system can be developed with the help of comment analysis.

3 Implementation

The authors collected 1000 videos of all categories for proposed analysis and labeled them as Fair or False (clickbait videos). The proposed model predicts the required output for any video on YouTube. Due to the fact that there was no publicly accessible dataset for our application, we had to manually create our dataset, which is why it is modest in size.

3.1 Comment Collection and Preprocessing

In this section, the authors tried to collect all the comments associated with a selected YouTube video using Youtube data API. Youtube Data API is an official API provided by Youtube that gives access to all the public properties of a video, like Title, Description, and Comments. The Youtube data api limits queries to only 20,000 comments per day for non premium users and there is a high possibility that we may end up fetching 20,000 comments from just one video which also significantly reduced our ability to create larger datasets. Also, the extracted comments need to be preprocessed as they were heterogeneous regarding the users' use of different symbols and languages. Therefore, the authors carried out some data cleaning and preprocessing on these comments to make them more compatible with the proposed model.

The following preprocessing is applied to the comments:

- Eliminate any phrasing or punctuation marks like (".",",","-",",",",",";").
- Tokenization of comments.
- Apply PorterStemmer on each comment word to obtain the root word.

Another challenge is choosing the subset of comments that can represent the video in the best way possible. This subset is chosen so that it is not biased, and this subset of the comments can judge the video. Also, the size of this subset is kept small so that the proposed model performs faster. However, this challenge could be handled by accessing the number of likes associated with each user comment and sorting them in decreasing order, then choosing the first k comments such that the model performs the best depending on the value of k. From experiments the size of subset(k) was calculated to be

$$k = min(157, \; len(TotalCommentSet))$$

Sorting also ensures that spam comments get filtered from entering our model, as spam comments end up getting no to very low number of likes.

3.2 Sentiment Measure

In this section, the authors try to develop a model that can accurately determine the sentiment score of a word and thus can classify the complete sentence as Fair or False with their appropriate confidence levels. To do this Alhujaili and Rawan Fahad [1] has performed a survey on how different methods can be used to classify a video, based on comments rating. Authors make use of similar NLP techniques to develop the proposed model and tuned it to give the best results possible.

To perform the classification process, authors have used average word vector with TF-IDF to vectorize the comments and then tested the model using various algorithms like svm, logistic regression and xgboost. The analysis showed that the model achieved the best results when authors used Logistic Regression and unigrams with TF-IDF.

3.3 Word Cloud

With proper data cleaning and feature extraction techniques, authors came up with word clouds for both fair and falsified/clickbait videos which gave us some great insights on how frequently a word occurs depending upon its category.

As shown in Fig. 1, bad words like "fake", "shit", "fight", "kill", etc. occur more frequently in false contents, whereas fair videos generally have positive words like "love", "good", "amazing", "beautiful", etc. and make use of these words to rate the video and provide a Fairness label(Fair or Falsified/clickbait).

Fig. 1. Word cloud of Fair and False videos

3.4 Video Rating

In this section, the authors try to determine the quality of the video with the help of comments ratings. First, authors merge the k topmost comments into one large corpus and use this corpus to get the required predictions using NLP model. The predictions are such that it can classify the video as Fair or Falsified. However, a rating system can be created from these predictions by knowing the confidence levels of both classes (fair and falsified/clickbait).

Using these confidence score model provide every YouTube video with a rating that is fairly based on comments' sentiment. This rating system provides users with what other people are thinking of that video, unlike the existing rating system (as shown in Fig. 4) in which one can view only the number of likes associated with that video, and in such cases, users have no idea about the negative reviews at all.

Table 1 represents the ratings obtained depending on the different models like Support vector machines, Logistic regression and XgBoost.

Now to chose the best model we calculate the standard deviation(SD) of the predicted rating and the actual rating.

$$SD = \sqrt{\frac{\sum (x - y)^2}{N}}$$

where x, y are predicted and actual ratings respectively.

Table 1. A brief comparison between actual and predicted ratings

Video ID	Support Vector Machine	Logistic Regression	XG Boost	Actual Rating	Flagged as
2W-oMj8Ddo	90% (Fair)	77% (Fair)	25%(Clickbait)	81%	Fair
vJtISoZagb4	67% (Fair)	68% (Fair)	60% (Fair)	71%	Fair

(continued)

Table 1. (*continued*)

Video ID	Support Vector Machine	Logistic Regression	XG Boost	Actual Rating	Flagged as
zIB4c9rCn9k	87% (Fair)	71% (Fair)	83% (Fair)	76%	Fair
B0BROZCNRic	85% (Fair)	77% (Fair)	86% (Fair)	89%	Fair
6IU0ZXjdUVs	97% (Fair)	88% (Fair)	89% (Fair)	91%	Fair
ba08lxJx4kI	98% (Fair)	85% (Fair)	88% (Fair)	91%	Fair
n9oBKqpcZsc	98% (Fair)	86% (Fair)	60% (Fair)	90%	Fair
H0fr7AwqxnA	99% (Fair)	87% (Fair)	84% (Fair)	93%	Fair
ztpnM1XwCxw	69% (Fair)	53% (Clickbait)	77% (Fair)	60%	Clickbait
uy4mOlYwZbA	91% (Fair)	78% (Fair)	87% (Fair)	74%	Fair
Mquits0Ob2U	89% (Fair)	78% (Fair)	90% (Fair)	77%	Fair
aCHnFnBcRpc	85% (Fair)	78% (Fair)	76% (Fair)	78%	Fair

The standard deviation of 200 videos for different types of models were calculated to be

$$SD_{LR} = 7\%, \ SD_{SVM} = 13.8\%, \ SD_{XG} = 19.2\%$$

The model with a least SD of 7 comes out to be of logistic regression. It should be noted that YouTube doesn't publicly disclose the actual rating of a video; the dislikes count is not visible to the general audience but is still visible to the video creator. So with the help of a few authentic creators, authors collected the actual video rating by knowing

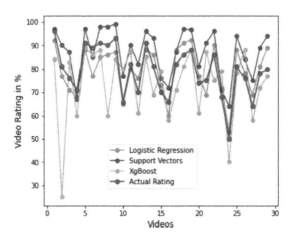

Fig. 2. Comment ratings predicted by different type of models

the count of likes and dislikes. Also, the labels like Fair and clickbait are discussed in Sect. 4.

As shown in Fig. 2, although logistic regression gives the best performance, it gets opposed once it reaches a rating of 90–93%. Even if the video is really good, the rating given by logistic regression will not surpass 93; however other models seem to rate even higher but with a trade-off for overall performance.

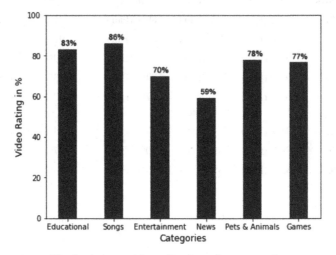

Fig. 3. Average video rating for various categories

Figure 3 depicts the average rating for different types of categories present on YouTube. It can be seen from the graph that categories like songs and educational videos are generally rated higher. In contrast, political videos are rated much lower because of variations in public opinion.

4 Performance Review of Proposed Approach

In this section, the authors discussed the benefits of the proposed rating system over the existing inadequate rating system.

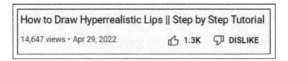

Fig. 4. Current Rating system employed by YouTube

Figure 4 represents the current rating system used by YouTube. Although the number of likes is visible, the dislike count is not publicly available. And in the absence of dislike count the like count becomes ineffective as well, since users don't have access to any negative reviews to compare with. Thus to solve this challenge, the authors created a rating system (as shown in Fig. 5) that uses publicly available data like user comments to calculate the video rating and is visible to everyone on YouTube.

Fig. 5. New rating system based on comments rating

4.1   Major Application: Detection of Clickbait Videos

Fig. 6. Depiction of Clickbait videos

Clickbait is a form of false content that creators purposely design to reach a large audience. The detection of these types of videos becomes so important because often the video content is completely different than what their Title, Thumbnail, and description try to convey. There is a great possibility of users getting misinformed by those types of content.

Authors use the rating model developed in the previous steps, and with the help of a threshold confidence score, authors can accurately classify videos as clickbait or fair.

Authors tested results on 1000 videos and came up with a threshold value that gave us the best precision score of 98.6% for clickbait labels and the best possible threshold value comes out to be 56% i.e. if the video rating is

- <56%: The video will be labelled as a clickbait.
- >=56%: The video will be labelled as fair.

5 Limitations and Loopholes

Authors have used publicly available data for the proposed system, but there are still some limitations:

- Like, YouTube lets the creators disable the comments.
- YouTube also has disabled comments on Videos that are made for kids per the coppa policy.

and in such cases proposed model may not able to fetch any comments at all and thus may not offer the required predictions.

6 Result

This section presents the experimental results of the proposed sentiment analysis approach. To evaluate the proposed model a total of 800 videos were considered for training and 200 for testing.

The actual video ratings were calculated with the help of a manual inspection done by 10 authentic YouTube creators, as these creators have the rights to view their own YouTube video parameters such as "like", "dislike" count and thus the actual rating. A total of 1000 videos were considered from these authentic channels so that the most generalized categories are covered. Among all videos, the highest variation of the developed rating system from the actual system (visible only to video creators and not publicly available) was not more than 15% while the average deviation was observed to be 7% as shown in the logistic regression model.

The authors also found that the proposed model gave the highest video rating at 92.6%, which was based on the educational category. The lowest rating of 33.3% was given to an entertainment video, and it was tagged as clickbait by the model as well as by many numbers of users on YouTube. Some categories in which the model did not perform really well were political, news, etc., as every individual has completely different views on these topics; the content may be exciting for some people but awful for others.

On the same set of 1000 videos, authors tried to analyze our system for clickbait content predictions, and we found that our model gave a precision score of 98.6% for clickbait labels. The clickbait comments are highly volatile and thus the model has high accuracy in predicting those types of content.

Since the model requires a considerable amount of text (comments) to predict required results, authors found that the proposed model worked best when videos with views of more than 1,00,000 were considered, as these videos have enough popular comments required by the model to predict results accurately. However, videos with views in the range of 0-100k have many comments ranging from 0–100, many of which can be noise, spam, etc., and thus these comments add very less value.

7 Conclusion

The proposed model discussed how sentiment analysis can be used to replace YouTube's current rating system (which doesn't consider any negative reviews at all) with better and more efficient ones. Proposed model ratings depict user sentiment for a particular video as these ratings are entirely based on sentiment analysis of comments and reviews. This model offered a robust rating system with a deviation of 7% from actual ratings and with a precision score of 98% in classifying clickbait labels.

8 Future Work

Although authors were successfully able to develop a rating system for YouTube videos there is still a great amount of work and research that needs to be done to make sure this rating system provides accurate and reliable results. Some major scope of improvements are:

- The dataset considered was manually created by authors and was limited as it only contained comments from 1000 videos. The accuracy scores can be increased and tested more efficiently by creating a larger dataset having comments from more than 10k videos flagged as fair or clickbait.
- The vectorizer used was frequency based, however, the precision for clickbait detection can be greatly increased by increasing priority for words like "clickbait", "fake", etc.
- With the help of larger datasets, one can even use neural networks to improve the model performance further
- Most of the YouTube comments have incomplete words or misspelled words, like fak or fek which corresponds to the word Fake, the current model considers these incomplete words as a completely different new word and thus this somewhat reduces the accuracy score. With the help of some libraries like Word complete, etc., these inconsistencies can be removed.

References

1. Alhujaili, R.F., Yafooz, W.M.: Sentiment analysis for youtube videos with user comments. In: 2021 International Conference on Artificial Intelligence and Smart Systems (ICAIS)
2. Bhuiyan, H., et al.: Retrieving YouTube video by sentiment analysis on user comment. In: 2017 IEEE International Conference on Signal and Image Processing Applications (ICSIPA)

3. Cunha, A.A.L., Costa, M.C., Pacheco, M.A.C.: Sentiment analysis of youtube video comments using deep neural networks. In: International Conference on Artificial Intelligence and Soft Computing. Springer, Cham, (2019)

4. Qu, J., et al.: Towards crowdsourcing clickbait labels for YouTube videos. HCOMP (WIPDemo) (2018)

5. Shang, L., et al.: Towards reliable online clickbait video detection: a contentagnostic approach. Knowl.-Based Syst. **182**, 104851 (2019)

6. Baravkar, A., et al.: Sentimental Analysis of YouTube Videos (2020)

7. Anitha, K. M., et al.: An approach to comment analysis in online social media. In: 2019 3rd International Conference on Computing and Communications Technologies (ICCCT). IEEE (2019)

8. Asghar, M.Z., et al.: Sentiment analysis on youtube: a brief survey. arXiv preprint arXiv: 1511.09142 (2015)

9. Obadimu, A., et al.: Identifying toxicity within youtube video comment. In: International Conference on Social Computing, Behavioral-cultural Modeling and Prediction and Behavior Representation in Modeling and Simulation. Springer, Cham (2019)

10. Poecze, F., Ebster, C., Strauss, C.: Social media metrics and sentiment analysis to evaluate the effectiveness of social media posts. Procedia Comput. Sci. **130**, 660–666 (2018)

11. Tanesab, F.I., Sembiring, I., Purnomo, H.D.: Sentiment analysis model based on Youtube comment using support vector machine. Int. J. Comput. Sci. Softw. Eng. **6**(8), 180 (2017)

12. Abdullah, A.O., et al.: A comparative analysis of common YouTube comment spam filtering techniques. In: 2018 6th International Symposium on Digital Forensic and Security (ISDFS). IEEE (2018)

13. Yue, L., Chen, W., Li, X., Zuo, W., Yin, M.: A survey of sentiment analysis in social media Knowl. Inf. Syst. **60**(2), 617–663 (2018). https://doi.org/10.1007/s10115-018-1236-4

14. Jindal, K., Aron R.: A systematic study of sentiment analysis for social media data. Mater. Today: Proc. (2021)

15. Muhammad, N., Bukhori, S., Pandunata, P.: Sentiment analysis of positive and negative of YouTube comments using naïve Bayes – Support Vector Machine (NBSVM) classifier. In: 2019 International Conference on Computer Science, Information Technology, and Electrical Engineering (ICOMITEE), pp. 199–205 (2019). https://doi.org/10.1109/ICOMITEE.2019. 8920923

16. Alhujaili, R.F., Yafooz, W.M.S.: Sentiment analysis for Youtube videos with user comments: review. In: 2021 International Conference on Artificial Intelligence and Smart Systems (ICAIS), pp. 814–820 (2021). https://doi.org/10.1109/ICAIS50930.2021.9396049

17. Mehta, R.P., et al.: Sentiment analysis of tweets using supervised learning algorithms. In: First International Conference on Sustainable Technologies for Computational Intelligence. Springer, Singapore (2020)

18. Savigny, J., Purwarianti, A.: Emotion classification on youtube comments using word embedding. IN: 2017 International Conference on Advanced Informatics, Concepts, Theory, and Applications (ICAICTA), pp. 1–5 (2017) https://doi.org/10.1109/ICAICTA.2017.8090986

19. Chen, Y.-L., Chang, C.-L., Yeh, C.-S.: Emotion classification of YouTube videos. Decis. Support Syst. **101**: 40–50 (2017)

20. Hemmatian, F., Sohrabi, M.K.: A survey on classification techniques for opinion mining and sentiment analysis. Artif. Intell. Rev. **52**(3), 1495–1545 (2019) https://doi.org/10.1007/s10 462-017-9599-6

21. Mulholland, E., et al.: Analysing emotional sentiment in people's YouTube channel comments. In: Interactivity, Game Creation, Design, Learning, and Innovation, pp.181–188. Springer, Cham (2016)

22. Nawaz, S., Rizwan, M., Rafiq, M.: Recommendation of effectiveness of Youtube video contents by qualitative sentiment analysis of its comments and replies. Pak. J. Sci. **71**(4), 91 (2019)
23. Chauhan, G.S., Meena, Y.K.: YouTube video ranking by aspect-based sentiment analysis on user feedback. In: Soft Computing and Signal Processing, pp. 63–71. Springer, Singapore (2019)
24. Abd El-Jawad, M.H., Hodhod, R., Omar, Y.M.K.: Sentiment analysis of social media networks using machine learning. IN: 2018 14th International Computer Engineering Conference (ICENCO), pp. 174–176 (2018). https://doi.org/10.1109/ICENCO.2018.8636124
25. Ramya, V.U., Thirupathi Rao, K.: Sentiment analysis of movie review using machine learning techniques. Int. J. Eng. Technol. **7**(2.7), 676–681 (2018)
26. Khan, A.U.R, Khan, M., Khan, M.B.: Naïve Multi-label classification of YouTube comments using comparative opinion mining. Procedia Comput. Sci. **82**, 57–64 (2016)

Classification of Tweet on Disaster Management Using Random Forest

T. Kanimozhi[✉] and S. Belina V J Sara

Department of Computer Science, SRM Institute of Science and Technology (Ramapuram Campus), Chennai, Tamilnadu, India
{kanimozt,belinavs}@srmist.edu.in, kanimozhimcaa@gmail.com

Abstract. The disaster management is highly responsible for managing the evacuation and deploying rescue teams to reduce the loss of lives and properties. However, it is considered challenging to obtain accurate information in timely fashion from various regions of the affected zones. With the advent of social media and networks, the information dissemination on such events can sense wide information from different zones but the information is in unstructured form. It is hence necessary to acquire correct or relevant information relating to that event. In this paper, we utilize random forest (RF) model to effectively classify the information from tweets (twitter.org) to find the location in case of a natural disaster. The proposed classification engine involves the collects of tweets, pre-processing of texts, RF classification and the extraction of location and determination. The classification is made effective using a pre-trained word vectors that includes the crisis words and global vectors for word representation (GLoVe). This pre-training captures the semantic meaning from the input tweets. Finally, extraction is performed to increase the accuracy of the model and in addition it determines the location of the disaster. The experiments are conducted on a real datasets from recent hurricanes. The results of simulation shows that the RF performs in a better way than other existing models in terms of accuracy, recall, precision and F1-score. It is seen that RF classifies effectively the tweets and analyses the accurate location.

Keywords: Machine learning · Classification · Tweet · Disaster management · Word

1 Introduction

The exponential growth of social media, such as Twitter and Facebook, is being massively adapted in several applications. Social media has extended its role to, but not limited to, the analysis and detection of health and disease [1], the quantification of controversial information [2] and the management of disasters [3, 4]. Natural disasters frequently disrupt regular communication due to damaged infrastructures [5], resulting in information outflow.

A Hurricane Sandy report [6] shows that more people communicate through social media. People sought help promptly and quickly, seeking information on transportation, shelter, and food, while trying to get better communication via family/friends in and

S. Rajagopal et al. (Eds.): ASCIS 2022, CCIS 1759, pp. 180–193, 2022.
https://doi.org/10.1007/978-3-031-23092-9_15

out of the disaster region. This makes it more beneficial to manage a natural disaster by means of the huge information flow across social media. Twitter demonstrated its utility during Hurricane Sandy, and it again played an important role in restoration, donations, and recovery following Hurricanes Harvey and Irma.

Social media allows individuals in the areas concerned to publish messages reflecting the exact situation, losses caused and healing status, people needs, status of the operations in rescue and relief, etc. Individuals or associations, on the other hand, can say how they can help or indicate exactly how they can help reduce the effect of the disaster. Although the use of social networks appears to be appealing [7], the majority of applications still lack features and are inoperable. Although social media has enormous potential for crisis response, much of it has yet to be realized. Only recently, work on the use of twitter in emergency situations has begun. Since tweets posted during disasters can include different types of information, the exact information that exists in a given tweet could be identified automatically. It will help to determine if various groups as well as different organizations have different insights into the disaster scenario.

The information in a tweet may be on damage to infrastructure, medical help, medical resources such as drugs, available medical tools, resources such as food, water, clothing, clothing, etc. We want to identify what kind of information the tweet contains when a tweet is posted. Different types of information, such as available resources, infrastructure damage, necessary medical resources etc., are seen in various categories. A single tweet may, in several cases, contain information about several categories of information.

The present study considers mainly the problem associated with automated classification from a tweet a problem of the classification of multiple classes and examine the applicability to this task of different algorithms. The major challenges to this task seem to be due to the informal writing manner and shorter tweet length. For this scenario, we define multiple big data feature sets and evaluate the performance of a variety of classifiers. Besides that, some of these tweets may not be visible because of the variety of aid request tweets. Therefore, an automated classification system is essential for understanding the Twitter context, classifying the specific rescue tweets, giving priority to context-based tweets, and then scheduling rescue missions and allocating appropriate resources.

In this paper, we utilize random forest (RF) model to effectively classify the information from tweets to find the location in case of a natural disaster. The proposed classification engine involves the collects of tweets, pre-processing of texts, RF classification and the extraction of location and determination. The classification is made effective using a pre-trained word vectors that includes the crisis words and global vectors for word representation (GLoVe). This pre-training captures the semantic meaning from the input tweets. Finally, extraction is performed to increase the accuracy of the model and in addition it determines the location of the disaster.

2 Related Works

This section reviews relevant studies on the classification of actionable social media tweets [15–19]. The analysis of actionable tweet content and feelings has gradually been applied in the development of machine learning. Ferrara et al. [8] have applied

Social Media text machine learning technology to detect extreme user interaction. The system has been experimented with a set of over 20,000 tweets generated by Twitter actionable tweet accounts.

To the same effect, [9] is proposed for the classification of actionable tweets as a machine-based training technique. With the classic feature set, the Naïve Bayes is applied. In order to identify which sentimental class is associated with actionable tweet communication, the system is based on the classification of user reviews into positive and negative classes.

Contrary to the work in [8], which mainly focuses on the classification of extremism in skewed data, the NB algorithm is used for balanced data with robust results. The total dependencies of the sentence are not, however, taken into account. This problem can be addressed through the application of machine learning models using word embedding. Researchers have also begun researching several ways to analyze actionable tweets in non-English languages automatically.

Hartung et al. [10] proposed, in this connection, a method of machine learning to detect extreme posts on German Twitter accounts. Various features, such as textual indices and linguistic patterns, are being experimented with. The system produced better results by utilizing cutting-edge technology.

Over 30,000 tweets related to marijuana have been collected by Nguyen et al. [11]. The technique of text mining offers some useful insights into the data obtained. The unsupervised sentiment classification techniques used in Lexicon rely primarily on certain sentimental lexicons and sentiment scoring modules. As with other areas of feeling analysis, Ryan et al. [12] investigated actionable tweet affiliations by proposing a new technique based on sentiment detection and part-of-speech by actionable tweet writers. The system can detect suspect activities online by actionable tweet users in a flexible way.

Chalothorn and Ellman [13] have suggested an analysis of sentiment to analyze radical posts using various lexical resources online. The intensity and class of feelings in the text are calculated. Following the completion of necessary pre-processing tasks, textual information was sent to web forums such as Montada and Qawem, and various feature-driven measures to manipulate and detect the actionable tweet content are used. Experimental results indicate that the forum Montada is better than the forum Qawem. It has been concluded that there are radical posts on the Qawem forum. Another noteworthy task is to collect a large data set of actionable tweet ideologies from [14]. The topics under discussion and categorized into positive and negative classes were studied using different sentiment analysis techniques. In addition, the opinions on tweets expressed by both men and women were also emphasized in terms of sex.

The studies mentioned before have been based on different approaches, like supervised machine training, an approach such as a lexicon and a clustering based and hybrid model for classification of actionable tweets. The applicability of sentiment-based profound learning models to the state of the art in classifying tweets must nevertheless be investigated.

3 Proposed Method

The proposed method involves the process of extracting and classification of actionable tweets using RF classifier. The process of which is illustrated in Fig. 1.

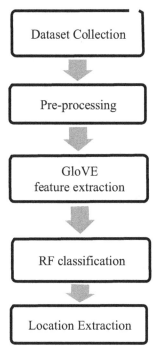

Fig. 1. Proposed framework

3.1 Preprocessing

We have applied various methods of preprocessing, such as tokenization, removal of words, conversion of cases and removal of a special symbol. It further involves acronym expansion [21], removal of non-ASCII characters and smiley [22], case folding, punctuation removal and stop word removal [23], special character removal [24] and phone number or URL handling. The tokenization gives a unique set of tokens (356,242) which contribute to the construction of the vocabulary used to encode the text from the training set.

3.2 Training, Validation and Testing

The dataset was divided into three components: train, test and validate. The training, validation and testing are displayed in Fig. 2.

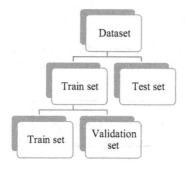

Fig. 2. Training/Testing/Validation set

Training Data: Data for training the model is used, where 80% of the data is used and can vary according to the experimental requirements.

Data Validation: This minimizes the problem of overfitting as often occurs because the accuracy of the training phase is high and the performance against test data is degraded. A total of 10% from the entire datasets is regarded as the validation set, which is thus used by applying parameter tuning to prevent performance mistakes. We used automated dataset monitoring, which ensures an uneven model assessment and minimizes overfitting, for this purpose.

Testing Data: 20% of the entire datasets checks the performance of the trained model with the data not seen. When fully trained, it is used for the model evaluation.

3.3 Feature Extraction

The study uses a pretrained Glove word vectors model for the generation of feature word vectors based on the statistical co-occurrences. The extraction using embedded Glove word vectors model is present in [25], where at the end of each extraction, the model is tested in terms of three different metrics as below:

$$Accuracy = \frac{TP + TN}{TP + TN + FP + FN}$$

$$Sensitivity = \frac{TP}{TP + FN}$$

$$Specificity = \frac{TN}{TN + FP}$$

The determination of all the three essential metrics helps in valid evaluation of the features extracted thereby eliminating the unwanted words present during the validation of classifier.

3.4 Random Forest Classification

A random forest is a set of decisions, each formed by a sub-sampling of data [20]. The forest is a collective approach. It also adds randomness to the feature selection as well as the training data. It considers the optimal function among the random subsets of features, instead of choosing the best function among all features split into a node. The RF is found by avoiding over fitting via an average model to achieve greater generalization performance. Prediction is done by selecting a class from the individual decision treaties with majority voting. The RF improves the predictability of decision-making trees.

The bagging technique is combined with the random functional selection method. As shown in Fig. 3, the RF algorithm works. The training dataset x is classified by y_i with a n dimension vector. The RF collects a random sample and recurrently builds divisions based on features selection in random manner until the size of the tree matches with the dataset (step 1–5). The rest of the data is removed from the tree in order to obtain the leaf classes. The process of forest construction is repeated several times (step 6–10).

Algorithm:

Step 1: for i : 1 to M //initialization

Step 2: $x \in x_i$

Step 3: forest = forest U Randomized Tree (x)

Step 4: end for

Step 5: Assign each instance to a final category based on a majority vote over forest

$$P(c \mid v) = \frac{1}{T} \sum_{t=1}^{T} P_t(c \mid v)$$

Step 6: Function Randomized Tree (x)

Step 7: While Tree.size<MaxTreesize

Step 8: f $\in$F$\wedge$f=max InformationGain(x)

Step 9: Tree.splitOn(f)

Step 10: Return tree

Fig. 3. Random forest algorithm

Training data will then be entered into the random forest model and a final category will be assigned to each instance, based on a forest majority vote. Here, the example that is fed into every decision tree is described. The *Pt* function defines the predicted class probability using the instance v obtained over each tree and the *P* function shows that the projected class is based on a random forest (step 5). A higher likelihood determines the final category. Due to the random choice of the selected features and sampled data from the data set, each tree is separate, resulting in a slight variance (Step 9).

3.5 Location Extraction

Most tweets do not contain the location information because of the Twitter privacy policy. In these cases, we extract the location using meta-information from the user's profile and location information from the Twitter text.

4 Results and Discussions

In this section, the study presents the validation of proposed RF model with conventional classifiers in terms of various metrics that includes the following:

Accuracy is defined as the total true predictions for optimal functioning of the system and that provides the ratio of correct actionable tweets classified and total true actionable tweets.

where:

$$Accuracy = \frac{TP + TN}{TP + TN + FP + FN} \tag{1}$$

TP - true positive actionable tweets
TN is the true negative actionable tweets
FP is the false positive actionable tweets
FN is the false negative actionable tweets
F-measure is the weighted harmonic mean of the recall and precision values, which ranges between zero and one. Higher the value of F-measure refers to higher classification performance.

F-measure is defined as the weighted mean of sensitivity and precision that defines the performance of a classifier and it is formulated as below.

$$F\text{-}measure = \frac{2TP}{2TP + FP + FN} \tag{2}$$

G-mean is an aggregation of specificity and sensitivity metrics that ensures an optimal balance between the variables in the datasets and it is defined as below:

$$G\text{-}mean = \sqrt{\frac{TP}{TP + FN} \times \frac{TN}{TN + FP}} \tag{3}$$

Mean Absolute Percentage error (MAPE) is the measure on actional tweet classification accuracy that finds total possible errors during the process of classification.

$$MAPE = \frac{100}{n} \sum_{t=1}^{n} \left| \frac{A_t - F_t}{A_t} \right| \tag{4}$$

where,
At - actual classes
Ft - predicted class
n - fitted points.
Sensitivity is the ability of the RF classifier to identify the true positive rate correctly.

$$Sensitivity = \frac{TP}{TP + FN} \tag{5}$$

The specificity defines the ability to correctly identify the true negative rate.

$$Specificity = \frac{TN}{TN + FP} \tag{6}$$

5   Datasets

The actionable tweets are classified from the input datasets namely Natural-Hazards-Twitter-Dataset. The dataset includes various hurricanes in United States that includes 2011 Tornado, Sandy (2012), Floods in 2013, Blizzard hurricane (2016), Matthew hurricane (2016), Hurricane (2017), Michael hurricane and Wildfires in 2018, Dorian hurricane in 2019. Further, the splitting of dataset undergoes training, testing and validation using RF classifier, where the results are given in Fig. 4 (Table 1).

Table 1. Datasets collected from various natural disasters

Dataset	Total Tweets
Tornado	3573
Sandy	2190
Floods	3597
Blizzard	3649
Matthew	5204
Hurricane	7823
Michael	4227
Wildfires	4596
Dorian	7140

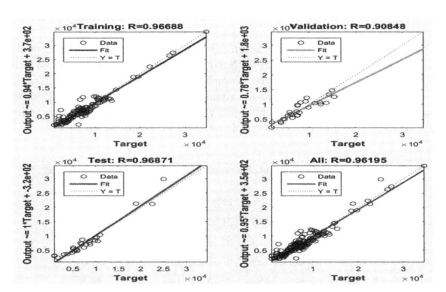

Fig. 4. Regression analysis on training/testing and validation

6 Experiment

The entire simulation is conducted in python environment and anaconda framework, where the classification of actionable tweets is carried out in a high end computing system that consists of CPU of AMD Threadripper 3970X 32-core, 120 GB SSD, 64 GB RAM on Windows 10, 64 bits.

7 Validation

Table 2. Comparison of accuracy between various models on different datasets

Dataset	KNN	NB	LR	SVM	ANN	RF
Tornado	55.87	56.17	58.26	58.52	59.88	**80.95**
Sandy	56.46	59.07	61.43	62.8	66.04	**82.89**
Floods	59.27	66.05	69.07	74.29	78.13	**85.17**
Blizzard	94.16	94.31	94.39	94.44	94.62	**94.96**
Matthew	96.1	96.12	96.13	96.22	96.24	**96.63**
Hurricane	96.65	97.37	97.4	97.48	97.49	**97.96**
Michael	97.56	97.56	97.64	97.64	97.66	**98.05**
Wildfires	97.63	97.63	97.71	97.71	97.73	**98.12**
Dorian	97.92	97.94	97.96	97.96	97.97	**98.31**

Table 2 shows the comparison of accuracy between various machine learning models including K-Nearest Neighbor (KNN), Naïve Bayes (NB), Support Vector Machine (SVM), Logistic Regression, Artificial Neural Network (ANN) and the proposed Glove-RF on different datasets. The results of simulation shows that the Glove-RF obtains improved accuracy on all datasets than other existing methods. The presence of Glove boost the RF to classify well the actionable instances than other methods.

Table 3. Comparison F-measure between various models on different datasets

Dataset	KNN	NB	LR	SVM	ANN	RF
Tornado	38.59	40.69	51.93	52.09	54.46	**62.93**
Sandy	52.57	60.24	60.58	61.04	62.57	**79.83**
Floods	58.45	66.99	67.88	69	74.04	**79.87**
Blizzard	66.94	69.92	70.25	70.49	75.05	**80.55**

(continued)

Table 3. (*continued*)

Dataset	KNN	NB	LR	SVM	ANN	RF
Matthew	69.88	70.14	70.31	73.13	76.36	**80.87**
Hurricane	77.58	77.71	78.23	79.31	79.99	**84.14**
Michael	86.08	86.2	88.14	88.17	89.53	**89.85**
Wildfires	86.14	86.26	88.2	88.23	89.59	**89.91**
Dorian	89.39	90.82	90.97	91.48	91.69	**92.65**

Table 3 shows the comparison of F-measure between various machine learning models including K-Nearest Neighbor (KNN), Naïve Bayes (NB), Support Vector Machine (SVM), Logistic Regression, Artificial Neural Network (ANN) and the proposed Glove-RF on different datasets. The results of simulation shows that the Glove-RF obtains increased F-measure on all datasets than other existing methods.

Table 4. Comparison G-mean between various models on different datasets

Dataset	KNN	NB	LR	SVM	ANN	RF
Tornado	43.71	56.63	59.66	44.91	74.92	**79.68**
Sandy	70.19	70.42	72.14	74.2	76.29	**81.93**
Floods	72.74	72.97	74.47	74.51	76.66	**82.46**
Blizzard	79.34	79.85	80.14	80.61	81.46	**86.07**
Matthew	79.63	79.87	80.38	81.14	81.72	**86.48**
Hurricane	82.08	82.93	84.55	86.11	91.15	**92.99**
Michael	93.46	94.22	94.59	94.66	94.99	**95.36**
Wildfires	94.22	94.29	94.66	94.73	95.06	**95.43**
Dorian	94.29	96.86	97.41	97.71	97.85	**98.19**

Table 4 shows the comparison of g-mean between various machine learning models including K-Nearest Neighbor (KNN), Naïve Bayes (NB), Support Vector Machine (SVM), Logistic Regression, Artificial Neural Network (ANN) and the proposed Glove-RF on different datasets. The results of simulation shows that the Glove-RF obtains increased g-mean on all datasets than other existing methods (Table 5).

Table 5 shows the comparison of MAPE between various machine learning models including K-Nearest Neighbor (KNN), Naïve Bayes (NB), Support Vector Machine (SVM), Logistic Regression, Artificial Neural Network (ANN) and the proposed Glove-RF on different datasets. The results of simulation shows that the Glove-RF obtains reduced MAPE on all datasets than other existing methods. This shows that the proposed method reduces the rate of classification errors than other methods.

Table 5. Comparison MAPE between various models on different datasets

Dataset	KNN	NB	LR	SVM	ANN	**RF**
Tornado	86.84	70.87	62.97	61.64	54.83	**15.62**
Sandy	71.05	70.82	62.92	61.59	54.28	**20.78**
Floods	71	64.67	57.95	39.83	54.24	**18.74**
Blizzard	68.31	30.99	30.47	28.86	36.97	**25.24**
Matthew	31.35	29.38	28.49	28.14	28.36	**18.14**
Hurricane	30.11	27.22	24.19	21.61	26.31	**25.58**
Michael	28.53	25.72	22.95	20.28	21.03	**21.28**
Wildfires	27.11	25.59	20.46	11.96	10.81	**16.38**
Dorian	19.58	16.91	16.82	9.48	10.63	**9.52**

Table 6. Comparison of sensitivity between various models on different datasets

Dataset	KNN	NB	LR	SVM	ANN	**RF**
Tornado	61.94	65.01	65.53	67.14	67.64	**68.2**
Sandy	64.65	65.45	67.51	67.87	69.69	**70.77**
Floods	65.89	66.62	72.07	73.84	74.04	**81.17**
Blizzard	68.89	70.29	73.06	75.74	85.19	**86.83**
Matthew	76.43	71.35	73.36	84.04	85.38	**89.1**
Hurricane	77.72	79.11	79.2	85.74	86.4	**92.79**
Michael	89.14	90.72	91.53	91.66	92.4	**92.86**
Wildfires	90.72	90.79	91.6	91.73	92.47	**96.78**
Dorian	90.79	95.77	96.87	97.45	97.73	**98.08**

Table 6 shows the comparison of sensitivity between various machine learning models including K-Nearest Neighbor (KNN), Naïve Bayes (NB), Support Vector Machine (SVM), Logistic Regression, Artificial Neural Network (ANN) and the proposed Glove-RF on different datasets. The results of simulation shows that the Glove-RF obtains increased sensitivity on all datasets than other existing methods. This shows that the Glove-RF identifies correctly the true positive rate than other methods.

Table 7 shows the comparison of specificity between various machine learning models including K-Nearest Neighbor (KNN), Naïve Bayes (NB), Support Vector Machine (SVM), Logistic Regression, Artificial Neural Network (ANN) and the proposed Glove-RF on different datasets. The results of simulation shows that the Glove-RF obtains increased specificity on all datasets than other existing methods. This shows that the Glove-RF identifies correctly the true negative rate than other methods.

Table 7. Comparison of specificity between various models on different datasets

Dataset	KNN	NB	LR	SVM	ANN	**RF**
Tornado	70.6	72.48	75.55	78.1	79.47	**80.58**
Sandy	73.59	74.57	77.41	80.57	82.09	**82.78**
Floods	74.38	76.47	78.08	80.78	82.57	**84.95**
Blizzard	94.91	94.97	95.01	95.66	95.7	**96.08**
Matthew	95.44	95.6	95.61	96.24	96.65	**97.34**
Hurricane	96.72	96.97	96.97	96.97	96.97	**97.95**
Michael	96.95	97.51	97.71	97.75	97.81	**98.18**
Wildfires	97.65	97.66	97.75	97.79	97.84	**98.21**
Dorian	97.72	97.73	97.82	97.82	97.91	**98.25**

The Glove-RF appears to indicate that the derived features generally do not boost the algorithms' performance with manual features (list of units, available related verbs, requirement related verbs, medical words, plural words and vocational words). This is something that is expected, because the addition of manual features is carried out to preserve the human expertise and intuition, and derived features depend heavily on data statistics. As a result, derived characteristics from a smaller dataset are likely to be noisy. However, the improvements in performance achieved in some 50% of cases indicate that the derived characteristics could be useful if there was a bigger dataset.

Despite its advantages, the study provides certain limitations that includes lacks of models on cleaning, crawling, storing the twitter data, consideration of social and visual features in acquiring robust classification after the application of machine learning hybrid model for classifying the multi- class labels.

8 Conclusions

In this study, RF effectively classifies the actionable tweets to accurately identify the disaster location and required help in disaster zone. The model involves collection of tweets, pre-processing, classification and the extraction the information including the determination of location. GLoVe word representation with pre-trained word vectors enables the RF classifiers to perform well in classifying the actionable tweets. This helps in the determination of location and enables optimal classification of actionable tweets. This model thus helps in classifying the tweets posted by the users on twitter.org. The classification of actionable and non-actionable classes via RF classifiers shows increased accuracy, sensitivity, specificity and reduced MAPE than conventional machine learning models. In future, the inclusion of features related to context can be utilized to increase the system performance.

References

1. Park, M., Sun, Y., McLaughlin, M.L.: Social media propagation of content promoting risky health behavior. Cyberpsychol. Behav. Soc. Netw. **20**(5), 278–285 (2017)
2. Garimella, K., Morales, G.D.F., Gionis, A., Mathioudakis, M.: Quantifying controversy on social media. ACM Trans. Soc. Comput. **1**(1), 1–27 (2018)
3. Alexander, D.E.: Social media in disaster risk reduction and crisis management. Sci. Eng. Ethics **20**(3), 717–733 (2014)
4. Yang, Z., Nguyen, L.H., Stuve, J., Cao, G., Jin, F.: Harvey flooding rescue in social media. In: 2017 IEEE International Conference on Big Data (Big Data), pp. 2177–2185. IEEE, December 2017
5. Shklovski, I., Burke, M., Kiesler, S., Kraut, R.: Technology adoption and use in the aftermath of Hurricane Katrina in New Orleans. Am. Behav. Sci. **53**(8), 1228–1246 (2010)
6. Baer, D.: As Sandy became# Sandy, emergency services got social. Fast Company, vol. 9 (2012)
7. Lindsay, B.R.: Social media and disasters: current uses, future options, and policy considerations (2011)
8. Ferrara, E., Wang, W.Q., Varol, O., Flammini, A., Galstyan, A.: Predicting Online Extremism, Content Adopters, and Interaction Reciprocity. International Conference on Social Informatics, pp. 22–39. Springer, New York (2016)
9. Azizan, S.A., Aziz, I.A.: Terrorism detection based on sentiment analysis using machine learning. J. Eng. Appl. Sci. **12**(3), 691–698 (2017)
10. Hartung, M., Klinger, R., Schmidtke, F., Vogel, L.: Identifying right-wing extremism in German Twitter profiles: a classification approach. In: Frasincar, F., Ittoo, A., Nguyen, L.M., Métais, E. (eds.) NLDB 2017. LNCS, vol. 10260, pp. 320–325. Springer, Cham (2017). https://doi.org/10.1007/978-3-319-59569-6_40
11. Nguyen, A., Hoang, Q., Nguyen, H., Nguyen, D., Tran, T.: Evaluating marijuana-related tweets on Twitter. In: IEEE 7th Annual Computing and Communication Workshop and Conference (CCWC), pp. 1–7. IEEE, New Jersey (2017)
12. Ryan, S., Garth, D., Richard, F.: Searching for signs of extremism on the web: an introduction to sentiment-based identification of radical authors. Behav. Sci. Terror. Polit. Aggres. **10**, 39–59 (2018)
13. Chalothorn, T., Ellman, J.: Using SentiWordNet and sentiment analysis for detecting radical content on web forums (2012)
14. Bermingham, A., Conway, M., McInerney, L., O'Hare, N., Smeaton, A.F.: Combining social network analysis and sentiment analysis to explore the potential for online radicalisation. In: IEEE International Conference on Advances in Social Network Analysis and Mining, ASONAM 2009. pp. 231–236 (2009)
15. Zahera, H.M., Jalota, R., Sherif, M.A., Ngomo, A.N.: I-AID: identifying actionable information from disaster-related tweets. arXiv preprint arXiv:2008.13544 (2020)
16. Garvey, W.T., Mechanick, J.I.: Medically actionable disease classification system for obesity. Obesity (Silver Spring, Md.) **28**(7), 1169 (2020)
17. Garvey, W.T., Mechanick, J.I.: Proposal for a scientifically correct and medically actionable disease classification system (ICD) for obesity. Obesity **28**(3), 484–492 (2020)
18. Tzacheva, A.A., Ranganathan, J., Bagavathi, A.: Action rules for sentiment analysis using Twitter. Int. J. Soc. Netw. Mining **3**(1), 35–51 (2020)
19. Kruspe, A., Kersten, J., Klan, F.: Detection of actionable tweets in crisis events. Nat. Hazard. **21**(6), 1825–1845 (2021)
20. Roy, S.S., Dey, S., Chatterjee, S.: Autocorrelation aided random forest classifier-based bearing fault detection framework. IEEE Sens. J. **20**(18), 10792–10800 (2020)

21. Adams, G., Ketenci, M., Bhave, S., Perotte, A., Elhadad, N.: Zero-shot clinical acronym expansion via latent meaning cells. In: Machine Learning for Health, pp. 12–40. PMLR, November 2020
22. Miller, M., Romine, W.L.: Anthrax event detection using Twitter: analysis of unigram and bigrams for relevant vs non-relevant tweets (2020)
23. HaCohen-Kerner, Y., Miller, D., Yigal, Y.: The influence of preprocessing on text classification using a bag-of-words representation. PLoS ONE 15(5), e0232525 (2020)
24. Duan, Z., et al.: Towards cleaner wastewater treatment for special removal of cationic organic dye pollutants: a case study on application of supramolecular inclusion technology with β-cyclodextrin derivatives. J. Clean. Prod. 256, 120308 (2020)
25. Pennington, J., Socher, R., Manning, C.D.: Glove: global vectors for word representation. In: Proceedings of the 2014 Conference on Empirical Methods in Natural Language Processing (EMNLP), pp. 1532–1543, October 2014

Numerical Investigation of Dynamic Stress Distribution in a Railway Embankment Reinforced by Geogrid Based Weak Soil Formation Using Hybrid RNN-EHO

M. A. Balasubramani[✉], R. Venkatakrishnaiah, and K. V. B. Raju

Department of Civil Engineering, Bharath Institute of Higher Education and Research, Chennai, India
mabalacivil@gmail.com, Venkatakrishnaiah.civil@bharathuniv.ac.in

Abstract. As the primary method of track support, traditional sloping embankments are typically used by railroad lines. Geosynthetically Reinforced Soil (GRS) systems, as an alternative to traditional embankments, have gained appeal, notably for high-speed lines in India. This system's reduced base area compared to traditional embankments means that less ground stabilisation, improvement, and land taking is necessary. The research's findings provide intriguing strategies that may be implemented into the way tracks are designed now to accommodate faster freight trains pulling greater loads. This research explains how to anticipate the bearing capacity of weak sand supported by a method of compacted granular fill over natural clay soil using a hybrid Recurrent Neural Network (RNN) and Elephant Herding Optimization (EHO) with Geogrid reinforced soil foundation. The exact prediction target for the proposed model was developed by using displacement amplitude as an output index. A number of elements influencing the foundation bed's properties, Geogrid reinforcement, and dynamic excitation have been taken into account as input variables. The RNN-anticipated EHO's accuracy was compared to that of three other popular approaches, including ANN, HHO, CFA, and MOA. Strict statistical criteria and a multi-criteria approach were principally used to assess the predictive power of the developed models. The model is also examined using fresh, independent data that wasn't part of the initial dataset. The hybrid RNN-EHO model performed better in predicting the displacement amplitude of footing laying on Geogrid-reinforced beds than the other benchmark models. Last but not least, the sensitivity analysis was used to highlight how input parameters might affect the estimate of displacement amplitude.

Keywords: Recurrent Neural Network (RNN) · Elephant Herding Optimization (EHO) · Geogrid · Settlement · Soil reinforcement · Weak Sand · Mayfly optimization algorithm · Jellyfish search algorithm · Cuttlefish algorithm and artificial neural network

S. Rajagopal et al. (Eds.): ASCIS 2022, CCIS 1759, pp. 194–207, 2022.
https://doi.org/10.1007/978-3-031-23092-9_16

1   Introduction

High-speed train track and ground responses are primarily influenced by the interplay of train loads and Rayleigh surface waves on the railway embankment and track bed [1–3]. One of the most crucial elements in explaining, forecasting, or predicting a track reaction and considering the proper remedial action is the bed's Rayleigh wave velocity. Studies have demonstrated the requirement for safety on soft ground railroads due to the high-speed trains' extensive range of vibration, particularly while operating at critical speed. The inherent vibrating characteristics of the rail systems define this speed. The important speed is the train speed that induces a pseudo-resonance event in the bed and is roughly equal to or larger than the Rayleigh wave speed of the bed [4, 5]. The critical speed also leads to significant track deviations, severe embankment vibration, and cone-shaped ground wave motion. The processes for bed soil augmentation are influenced by a number of variables, including train speed, soil type, embankment height, and the thickness of soft and loose sediments. Numerous methods, including geosynthetics (geogrid), vibro-replacement with stone columns, dry deep soil mixing (cement columns), concrete piles with or without integrated caps, removal replacement methods with suitable materials, and the installation of mechanical reinforcements like plate anchors and helical piles, can be used to improve the soils beneath railway embankments [6, 7].

While geogrid reinforcement has long been employed in other geotechnical applications, there hasn't been much research on how it may be applied in railway engineering. This could be the case since there isn't a design procedure especially for railway embankments and the industry is cautious [8]. Although it has been shown that the reinforcement improves performance under static and cyclic loads, little is known about where the geogrid works best and how it performs in difficult conditions like railway gravel. Additional knowledge of how ballast and geogrid behave in a railway application may aid in the advancement of useful design techniques. In terms of cost and the environment, such an application may have an effect on future train design and track restoration [9]. To sustain the repeated stress caused by train passes, ballast acts as a foundation to absorb energy, drain easily, and withstand pressures acting both vertically and laterally (Selig and Waters). However, significant technological issues [10] make it difficult to carry out these important duties. Train loading forces may cause ballast to be rearranged and degraded during several loading cycles, diminishing grain interlocking and allowing lateral particle migration. As ballast particles migrate laterally, track stability may suffer as a result of a reduction in frictional strength. Loss of track geometry results from vertical and lateral deformations brought on by spreading or foundation issues. Maintaining the ballasted foundation's shape is essential since track maintenance due to geotechnical issues is more costly than other track expenditures.

Numerous studies have focused at ways to improve the bearing capacity of shallow foundations as well as how to produce construction materials like concrete and geopolymer bricks from waste resources. Ziegler et al. [11].'s comparison of the reinforced case with the unreinforced one under the same load revealed an improvement in bearing capacity and a discernible reduction in indisplacements. These results were shown to be caused by the geogrid reinforcement's limiting effect and interlocking mechanism, which convert the reinforced case's more or less straight deviatoric stress route into an isotropic stress path. Ballasted railway track samples that had been exposed to mixed vertical-horizontal cyclic stresses experienced settlement at high relative train speeds, according to Yu *et al.* [12]. At the ballast-subballast contact, the subballast-subgrade interface, and the effect of subgrade stiffness on geogrid performance at the subballast-subgrade interface, we looked at the performance advantages of installing geogrid. Using laboratory testing and finite element modeling, Esmaeili *et al.* [13] have shown how geogrid affects the stability and settlement of high railway embankments. To achieve this, the crest of a loading chamber with dimensions of 240 x 235 x 220 cm was covered with five sets of 50 cm-high embankments created at a scale of 1:20. The original embankments weren't strengthened with geogrid layers. In order to lessen the persistence of train-induced deformation, Zhang *et al.* [14] developed a ground rehabilitation strategy that includes continual permeation grouting injections into the bearing strata of the group piles. The consequences of the suggested mitigation strategy were then investigated using numerical simulations based on complex constitutive models and soil-water linked finite element-finite difference (FE)-(FD) compound arithmetic. Recycled concrete aggregates and geosynthetics may improve the performance of ballasted railway tracks, according to study by Punetha *et al.* [15]. Employing two-dimensional finite element analysis, the value of using geogrids, geocells, and recycled concrete aggregates in the ballasted railway tracks is examined. Effectiveness is assessed using the track settlement. The results show that using recycled aggregates and geosynthetics significantly lowers track settlement and could enable greater train speeds at the same allowable settlement level. Understanding the operation of the geogrid material layers used to reinforce high railway embankments is the major goal of this investigation. The study focuses on two elements that impact the serviceability of railway embankments: reducing crest settling and preventing sliding in the embankment body. The results of all reinforced numerical models and preliminary numerical modeling were taken into account to determine the appropriate level for installing the geogrid layers. This was accomplished by adding one to four layers of geogrid to each of the second through fifth set of embankments to strengthen them. No additional geogrid reinforcement was used while building the original sequence of embankments.

2 Proposed Methodology

2.1 Model Clay Barrier's Compositional Characteristics

Sand and kaolin were combined in a 4:1 dry weight ratio, much as the soil in the current experiment, to imitate the clay barrier and attain the required hydraulic conductivity of 109 m/s. The model clay barrier material was determined to have a maximum dry unit weight of 15.9 kN/m^3, a liquid limit of 38%, a plastic limit of 16%, a coefficient of permeability of 0.4 109 m/s, and an ideal moisture content of 22% (standard Proctor compaction test). The Unified Soil Classification System (UCSC), which classifies the chosen combination as a CL type, was found to have qualities that are equivalent to those of the bulk of locally accessible organically generated clays in most of India. Additionally, it illustrates the clay barriers used in landfills' fine-grained soil bandwidth features [16]. When wet compacted at OMC + 5%, it was discovered that the clay barrier had a comparable dry unit weight and shear strength of between 30 and 40 kN/m^2.

2.2 Geogrid

Bi-directional geogrids are used throughout all series of experiments. Table 1 displays the geogrid's characteristics utilised in this investigation.

Table 1. Geogrid index characteristics

Parameter	Value
Thickness (mm)	1.8
Mass per unit area (Kg/m^2)	0.532
Ultimate tensile strength (kN/m)	7.6
Aperture size (mm)	23

2.3 Measuring Subgrade Stiffness

The stiffness and strength characteristics of the subgrade and formation were evaluated at various testing phases (the formation layer was replaced prior to each test). Unrestricted compression tests were used to measure strength, and a circular plate load test was used to measure stiffness under the Losenhausen piston. These figures were contrasted with studies utilizing pocket penetrometers, dynamic penetration tests, and light falling deflectometers [17]. The plate load test stiffness results were thought to be the most trustworthy, and the Young's modulus was calculated using:

$$S_{pit} = \frac{2P(1 - PR^2)}{\pi r \mu} \tag{1}$$

The plate applied load is P, Poisson's ratio is PR and μ plate deflection is all present and the plate's radius is r located. In order to prevent problems with early setup S_{pit}, the phrase is used to describe the tangent Young's modulus computed from the first half of the second load cycle curve (i.e. plate-surface contact errors).

Although a track settling analysis is provided, the approach used here employs the route restriction (t) given by:

$$t = \frac{S_{pit}}{P} = \frac{Sriff}{Press} \tag{2}$$

The relevant unreinforced ballast control tests in this research are designated as CT_1, CT_2, and CT_3, along with details regarding the testing. The consistency of the tests was shown by the fact that the predicted resilient modulus values at the breakpoint stress for each test often followed the same pattern as the measured plate load $S_{pit}(t)$ modulus values.

2.4 Multi Objective Function

The bad sand's stability is improved in this step using the optimization parameter of the hybrid RNN-EHO method, which is also employed to improve the appearance of the proposed Geogrid. The main goal of the suggested hybrid RNN-EHO approach in this case is to reduce the form characteristic, which is scientifically unique in Eq. (3),

$$OF = Min_E(\delta_P, \delta_{bc}, \delta_s)$$ (3)

where, δ_s are the pressure and bearing capacity error minimizations and the pressure and δ_P, δ_{bc} are bearing capacity error minimizations of the weak soil formation.

2.5 Improving Settlement-Based Geogrid using Hybrid RNN-EHO Technique

Use RNN to choose the most appropriate subset of dataset attributes in this case to discriminate between susceptible and regular data. RNN mimics the creation of goal functions and feature selection. According to the same theory, an RNN enhances the answer by progressively choosing the best options while removing the less desirable ones [18]. Figure 1 shows the RNN model's architectural layout. The input layer is made up of vectors that x, $y(t)$, $z(t)$ and, $w(t-1)$ respectively, correspond to the present user, item, response action, and hidden layer state. The user m is referenced in the model via $l * 1$ a vector, where m^{th} element is 1 and the remaining elements are 0. An $n * 1$ or $1 * 1$ vector refers to each item (or kind of feedback action) in the same manner. H and m stand for the user's and the item's respective hidden layers. The hidden layer's output w at the current period stage t is referenced by the vector $w(t)$. O is the layer of output.

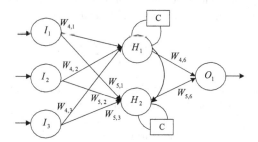

Fig. 1. The architecture of the RNN model

Through the weight matrix A the user vector x from the input layer is linked to the hidden layer H. This portion is non-recurring, and equation is used to compute the hidden layer's output (4),

$$H = f(Ax)$$ (4)

The dimension of the concealed layer H is represented by the vector $D * 1$ in this area. A is a $D * m$ matrix with a user's choice referred to in each column. The equation provides the sigma function f as the Eq. (5).

$$f(x) = \frac{1}{1 + e^{-x}}$$ (5)

The weight matrices M, N and L respectively, link the input layer's vectors and to the hidden layer's vectors x, $y(t)$, $z(t)$ and $w(t-1)$. The hidden layer records $s(t-1)$ prior user behaviour while this section of the model is repeated. To determine the hidden layer's output at the time stamp, t, $w(t)$ apply Eq. (6).

$$w(t) = f(Mx(t) + Ny(t) + Lw(t-1)) \tag{6}$$

where, $D*1$ a vector is $w(t)$. M, N and L are DXn, $DX1$ and DXD are the corresponding matrices M. The feature of an item is referenced in each column of the matrix N. Additionally, each column in the matrix denotes a certain kind of feedback activity. A vector $nX1$ is produced by the system at the period imprint and t, $O(t)$ is computed using Eq. (7),

$$O(t) = g(Ys(t) + Zh) \tag{7}$$

The weight matrices for the hidden layer and the output layer are Y and Z. The equation provides the softmax function as g.

$$g(x) = \frac{e^x}{\sum_{i=1}^{k} e^{xi}} \tag{8}$$

The assessment of the likelihood that the user m would approach the item j at the following timestamp provided by the historical feedback that is calculated using Eq. (9) $O_j(t+1)$ is the output element j^{th} after the network has been trained.

$$O_j(t+1) = P(v_j(t+1) = 1/x, y(t), z(t), w(t-1) \tag{9}$$

When a proposal is executed, the output at the model's final time stamp is determined for each user. Simply choose the P output's largest items, and it is advisable to use their indexes. The Geogrid controller is then given the RNN as input based on the weak soil development in the railway track.

2.6   The Procedure of the EHO in Realizing the Learning of RNN

The learning function of the RNN algorithm is implemented by the EHO algorithm. The programme was inspired by the herding behaviour of elephants. Due to the gregarious character of the elephant, there are several factions of female elephants in the group, each of which is carrying a calf [19]. Each group's movement is influenced by its matriarch or leader elephant. As seen in Fig. 2, the Female Elephant (FE) once lived with family gatherings while the Male Elephant (ME) grew up and lives alone while maintaining contact with his family group.

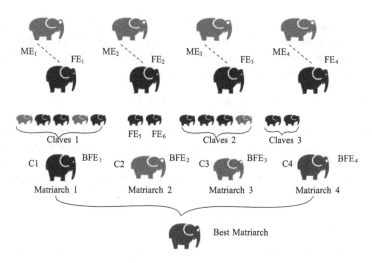

Fig. 2. EHO elephants' behaviours

The following assumptions about herding are taken into consideration in EHO:

- The total elephant population is divided into clans, with each clan containing a specified number of elephants.
- A established population of ME permits their clan and life to be left alone.
- A matriarch oversees the operations of each tribe.

One can infer that there are the same number of elephants in each clan. The matriarchal group in the elephant herd is organised in the greatest way possible, whereas the male elephant herd is positioned in the worst way possible. The EHO framework or initiatives were shown as follows [20].

Step 1: Initialization Process.

These procedures set the hidden layers, neurones, basis weights (which range from −10 to + 10), and reference values for the RNN using real learning function values. The EHO parameters are scaling factors and the optimisation model starts with random values.

Step 2: Process for Evaluating Fitness.

The weak soil formation and EHO settling are taken into consideration by this Geogrid model. Below is the equation that is produced when this value is derived utilising the best hidden layers and RNN structure neurones.

$$FF = \delta \tag{10}$$

Utilizing the hybrid algorithm, the fitness is attained.

Step 3: Current elephant location.

The best and worst options for each elephant in each family in this third stage, with the exception of the matriarch and a male elephant, are included in the status of each elephant P and each clan C_i has elephants. The elephant's $i = 1, 2, 3, \ldots \ldots P$ rank and j^{th} clan $i = 1, 2, 3, \ldots \ldots C$ are symbolised by $L_{c_{i,j}}$. The elephant's current location i^{th} is stated as,

$$L_{new,c_{i,j}} = L_{c_{i,j}} + \alpha \left(L_{best,c_{i,j}} - L_{c_{i,j}} \right) * r \tag{11}$$

Here $L_{new,c_{i,j}}$ is the updated position, $L_{c_{i,j}}$ is the old position, $L_{best,c_{i,j}}$ is the Position of best in the clan. α and $\beta = o \ to \ 1$.

By following the methods above, the optimum position that reflects the matriarch cannot be modified.

Step 4: Movement update for each clan's fittest elephant.

The position update for the clan member that fits in best is provided by,

$$L_{new,c_{i,j}} = \beta * L_{cemter,c_j} \ and \ L_{cemter,c_i} = \sum_{i=1}^{n} \frac{L_{c_{i,j}}}{n_l} \tag{12}$$

Here n_l the overall quantity of elephants in individually clan and $\beta \in \{0, 1\}$

Step 5: Separating the worst of the clan's elephants.

Male elephants or the worst elephants would be taken away from their family groupings. The lowest ranking changed to,

$$L_{worst,c_{i,j}} = L_{min} + (L_{max} - L_{min} + 1) * r \tag{13}$$

where $L_{worst,c_{i,j}}$ is the clan's worst male elephants, L_{max} and L_{min} are, as well as the elephants' permitted maximum and lowest range.

Step 6: Ending procedure.

It completes one iteration since the weakest elephant in the clan has been separated. The process is continued until the RNN's leaning function for settling weak soil formation is achieved, at which time it is deemed complete. Steps 2 through 6 are repeated until the convergence requirements are met if the criteria are not met. The process flow diagram for the hybrid RNN-EHO technique is shown in Fig. 3.

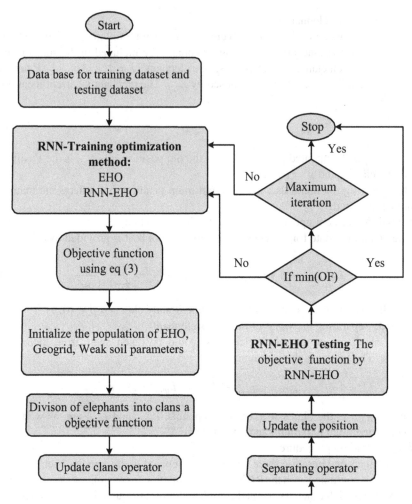

Fig. 3. Flowchart of proposed hybrid RNN-EHO method

3   Results and Discussion

Two reinforced and unreinforced examples with the test results are provided. It will be explained how bearing pressure compares to normalised settlement, how much of the load is supported by piles, and how axial stress is distributed throughout the length of the pile. The ideal cushion thickness and pile spacing were found in the unreinforced case, while in the reinforced case, the ideal placement of the first layer of the geogrid and the ideal length of geogrids were discovered. The Geogrid sand foundations are powered by Matlab 7.10.0 (R2021a) and an Intel (R) Core (TM) i5 CPU with 4GB RAM. In order to confirm its performance, the new system was put to the test and its processing parameters were compared to a number of techniques, including the Artificial Neural

Network (ANN), Harris Hawks Optimization (HHO), Cuttlefish algorithm (CFA), and Mayfly Optimization Algorithm (MOA) models.

3.1 Uncertainty Analysis

Wilmot's Index of Agreement (WI), Mean Absolute Percentage Error (MAPE), Mean Absolute Percentage Error (RMSE), Mean Absolute Percentage Error (MAPE), Mean Absolute Percentage Error (RMSE), coefficient of correlation (R^2), and mean absolute error (MAE) were all calculated to evaluate the performance of the final selected architecture for the proposed ANN-MGSA (i.e., testing information that the network hasn't encountered throughout the training process). Equations (14) to (18) are used to compute the values of MAE (mean absolute error), RMSE (root-mean-square error), and R for the training and testing portions.

Five indicators were used to assess how well the suggested machine learning models performed:

RMSE: The standard errors between predicted values and actual values can be represented using RMSE. The algorithm is defined as being given in Eq. (14) and is said to be more exact the smaller the RMSE.

$$RMSE = \sqrt{\frac{1}{n} \sum_{i=1}^{n} (O_s^i - P_s^i)^2} \tag{14}$$

Correlation Coefficient (R): R Measures how strongly the measured values and the variation in forecasted values are related. The R value varies from -1 to 1, where -1 denotes a completely inverse correlation and -1 denotes a completely inverse correlation. The definition of R is given in Eq. (15)

$$R\left(p^i, O^i\right) = \frac{cov\left(p^i, O^i\right)}{\sqrt{var\left[p^i\right] * var[O^i]}} \tag{15}$$

Mean Absolute Percentage Error (MAPE): A dimensionless measure called MAPE may be used to rate a model's ability to anticipate outcomes. The greater the model's derived predictive performance, the closer MAPE is to 0. Equation represents the MAPE definition (16).

$$MPA = \frac{100\%}{n} \sum_{i=1}^{n} \frac{|P_S^i - O_S^i|}{P_S^i} \tag{16}$$

Coefficient of Determination (R^2): R^2 measures how closely the anticipated value resembles the actual value. R^2 is between 0 and 1. The perfect match between the anticipated value and the actual value is shown by an R^2 of 1. Equation (17) displays R^2's definition.

$$R^2 = 1 - \frac{\sum_{i=1}^{n} |P_S^i - O_S^i|}{\sum_{i=1}^{n} |O_S^i - O_S|} \tag{17}$$

Wilmot's Index of Agreement (WI): WI, which ranges from 0 to 1, is a standardised index to measure the prediction efficacy of established models. A WI of 0 shows no match at all, whereas a WI of 1 shows complete agreement between predicted values and actual values. Equation (18) displays the WI definition.

$$WI = 1 - \frac{\sum_{i=1}^{n}|P_S^i - O_S^i|}{\sum_{i=1}^{n}|O_S^i - O_S|} \qquad (18)$$

where, O_S^i, P_S^i and n stands for i^{th} the observed value of settlement, i^{th} the anticipated value of settlement, and the quantity of data samples, respectively (Table 2) (Fig. 4).

Table 2. Analysis of suggested models and other approaches based on statistical indices for comparison

Statistical index	ANN	HHO	CFA	MOA	Proposed
RMSE	0.813	0.586	0.512	0.481	0.352
MAE	0.44	0.321	0.28	0.26	0.22
Efficiency	0.963	0.974	0.977	0.98	0.985
RWI	0.897	0.885	0.905	0.933	0.951

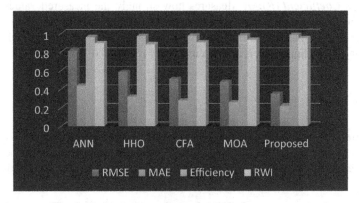

Fig. 4. Performance analysis of statistical measurement

Three different scenarios' pressure-settlement behaviours are compared in Fig. 5. The bearing capacity of the geogrid reinforced foundation bed increased with the height of the geogrid. Comparable observational methods that rely on numerical analysis. As the geocell's height increases, the footing load will be dispersed across a larger area. Figure 6 illustrates typical data on settlement variation for a 53 mm thick granular subbase layer with various geosynthetic reinforcement layer types. The results demonstrated that the initial modulus of the poor sand is relatively high; as settlement increased with the number of cycles, the modulus value decreased; and ultimately, near the conclusion of

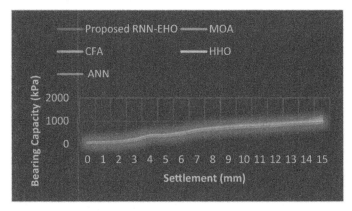

Fig. 5. Comparative analysis of Pressure–settlement performed on 150 mm thick granular subbase layer

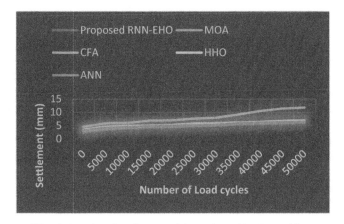

Fig. 6. Results of settlement with number of load repetitions

22000 cycles, the modulus value stabilised at a constant value. Figure 7 shows that with geogrid of an 80 mm height, the ultimate bearing capacity of lime stone aggregate bases reinforced with geogrid increases by 1.1 times over unreinforced bases. Additionally, a 76 percent increase in the total bearing capacity augmentation factor was made. The findings show a significant increase in the performance of the suggested RNN-EHO approach employing Geogrid compared to other techniques such as ANN, CFA, MOA, and HHO, respectively, when the proposed method course was correctly compacted.

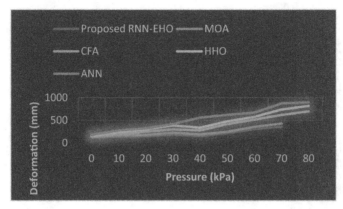

Fig. 7. Showing comparison of deformation of exiting methods and proposed method at the centre with 120 mm thick base

4   Conclusion

Analyses and pertinent conclusions were reached by applying the geogrid to the precise geometry of a ballasted railway track substructure utilizing a proven recommended hybrid RNN-EHO technique. It may be possible to analyze the system's performance on actual railroads using realistic geometry and applications. The assessments mimicked weaker track material, compressible subgrades, and the impacts of reinforcing material on overall performance by varying the stiffness of the foundation, the geogrid, and the ballast. In this report, a hybrid recurrent neural network (RNN)-elephant herding optimization (EHO) technique was introduced to investigate the geogrid-reinforced sand's improvement under static stress. The containment of the ballast using geogrid was particularly efficient in decreasing vertical deformations, even when low-quality material was utilized, according to numerical modeling of geogrid applied to a railway scenario.

- Although geogrid confinement was used, the reduction in vertical settlement was not as substantial as anticipated. This is promising since it could allow for longer maintenance cycles when the ballast loses shear strength or the use of weaker ballast materials, including recycled ballast or well-graded particles.
- The likely cause of this is because the subgrade is subject to significant forces whether or not there is a geogrid. The geogrid did help with the loads being distributed more uniformly, which may have prevented the development of significant shear stresses and collapse, particularly on softer subgrades. The geogrid reduces vertical settling on stronger foundations by lessening the lateral ballast pressure brought on by heavy loads.

References

1. Nguyen, V.D., et al.: Monitoring of an instrumented geosynthetic-reinforced piled embankment with a triangular pile configuration. Int. J. Rail Transp. 1–23 (2022)

2. Schary, Y.: Case studies on geocell-based reinforced roads, railways and ports. In: Sitharam, T.G., Hegde, A.M., Kolathayar, S. (eds.) Geocells. STCEE, pp. 387–411. Springer, Singapore (2020). https://doi.org/10.1007/978-981-15-6095-8_15

3. Deshpande, T.D., et al.: Analysis of railway embankment supported with geosynthetic-encased stone columns in soft clays: a case study. Int. J. Geosyn. Ground Eng. **7**(2), 1–16 (2021). https://doi.org/10.1007/s40891-021-00288-5

4. Lazorenko, G., et al.: Failure analysis of widened railway embankment with different reinforcing measures under heavy axle loads: A comparative FEM study. Transp. Eng. **2**, 100028 (2020)

5. Sweta, K., Hussaini, S.K.K.: Effect of geogrid on deformation response and resilient modulus of railroad ballast under cyclic loading. Constr. Build. Mater. **264**, 120690 (2020)

6. Hubballi, R.M.: Stabilization of railway tracks using geosynthetics—a review. In: Dey, A.K., Mandal, J.J., Manna, B. (eds.) Proceedings of the 7th Indian Young Geotechnical Engineers Conference. LNCE, vol. 195, pp. 387–396. Springer, Singapore (2022). https://doi.org/10.1007/978-981-16-6456-4_40

7. Banerjee, L., Chawla, S., Dash, S.K.: Application of geocell reinforced coal mine overburden waste as subballast in railway tracks on weak subgrade. Constr. Build. Mater. **265**, 120774 (2020)

8. Meena, N.K., et al.: Effects of soil arching on behavior of pile-supported railway embankment: 2D FEM approach. Comput. Geotechn. **123**, 103601 (2020)

9. Jain, S.K., Saleh Nusari, M., Acharya, I.P.: Use of geo-grid reinforcement and stone column for strengthening of mat foundation base. In: Proceedings of Materials Today (2020)

10. Mei, Y., et al.: Experimental study of the comprehensive technology of grouting and suspension under an operating railway in the cobble stratum. Transp. Geotechn. **30**, 100612 (2021)

11. Ziegler, M.: Application of geogrid reinforced constructions: history, recent and future developments. Procedia Eng. **172**, 42–51 (2017)

12. Yu, Z., et al.: True triaxial testing of geogrid for high speed railways. Transp. Geotechn. **20**, 100247 (2019)

13. Esmaeili, M., et al.: Investigating the effect of geogrid on stabilization of high railway embankments. Soils Found. **58**(2), 319–332 (2018)

14. Zhang, C., Su, L., Jiang, G.: Full-scale model tests of load transfer in geogrid-reinforced and floating pile-supported embankments. Geotext. Geomembr. **50**, 869–909 (2022)

15. Punetha, P., Nimbalkar, S.: Performance improvement of ballasted railway tracks for high-speed rail operations. In: Barla, M., Di Donna, A., Sterpi, D. (eds.) Challenges and Innovations in Geomechanics. LNCE, vol. 126, pp. 841–849. Springer, Cham (2021). https://doi.org/10.1007/978-3-030-64518-2_100

16. Esen, A.F., et al.: Stress distribution in reinforced railway structures. Transp. Geotechn. **32**, 100699 (2022)

17. Watanabe, K., et al.: Construction and field measurement of high-speed railway test embankment built on Indian expansive soil "Black Cotton Soil." Soils Found. **61**(1), 218–238 (2021). https://doi.org/10.1016/j.sandf.2020.08.008

18. Bonatti, C., Mohr, D.: On the importance of self-consistency in recurrent neural network models representing elasto-plastic solids. J. Mech. Phys. Solids **158**, 104697 (2022)

19. Li, W., Wang, G.-G.: Elephant herding optimization using dynamic topology and biogeography-based optimization based on learning for numerical optimization. Eng. Comput. **38**(2), 1585–1613 (2021). https://doi.org/10.1007/s00366-021-01293-y

20. Guptha, N.S., Balamurugan, V., Megharaj, G., Sattar, K.N.A., DhiviyaRose, J.: Cross lingual handwritten character recognition using long short term memory network with aid of elephant herding optimization algorithm. Pattern Recogn. Lett. **159**, 16–22 (2022). https://doi.org/10.1016/j.patrec.2022.04.038

Efficient Intrusion Detection and Classification Using Enhanced MLP Deep Learning Model

G. Gowthami[✉] and S. Silvia Priscila

Department of Computer Science, Bharath Institute of Higher Education and Research, Chennai, India
Gowthami.ramya@gmail.com,
Silviaprisila.cbcs.cs@bharathuniv.ac.in

Abstract. Everyone has entered a new stage of the digital world during this era. The digital world has created numerous opportunities and facilities, but it has also become a threat to the data that is kept there. Internet security is seen by many enterprises as a major challenge. Organizations use a variety of methods, including firewalls, virtual private networks (VPNs), authentication, and encryption, to protect credential data. The primary goals are to protect network infrastructure security and internet communication security. The arsenal of technologies for securing security has expanded. One of the most recent advancements in security technology is intrusion detection. In this study, EMLP (MLP + PSO) is used to identify and categorise paper incursions which is been compared over ANN and MLP (MLP + PSO) deep learning models. The dataset used for analysis is KDD CUP99 dataset. Among these models, Enhanced MLP (MLP + PSO) produces better outcomes in terms of accuracy of about 93%, precision of about 0.88, and recall of about 0.84 respectively. The tool used for analysis is python.

Keywords: Intrusion · Attacks · Anomaly · Accuracy · Networking · Hacker · Security · Digital services

1 Introduction

As more networked digital devices adopt various technologies on a daily basis, the risk of various forms of attacks by large numbers of attackers also rises. It becomes necessary to bridge the gap between the attack and the data's safety.

The network administrator may identify suspicious online activity with the use of IDS, and it also alerts the administrator to secure the data by launching the necessary defences against those threats. In networking, the phrase intrusion refers to any hostile application of information or unauthorised access of any type. Attackers or invaders are those who intend to obtain unauthorised access to guarded data. They cause damage to the information stored by their malicious activities [3].

The most important requirements for effective IDS have been identified by researchers as ML (Machine Learning) and DL approaches (Deep Learning). Both of the IDS methodologies are branches of AI (Artificial Intelligence), which tries to analyse the critical facts concealed within huge data. Due to the development of powerful GPUs over the past ten years, the aforementioned methodologies have gained popularity in the field of network security (Graphics Processor Units). With the help of robust technologies like ML and DL, it is possible to discover the best characteristics of network traffic. Additionally, it is employed to estimate the typical and exceptional works pertaining to the ingrained patterns. The ML-based IDS technique relies on feature engineering, which is used to study the useful information present in the network traffic whereas the IDS based on DL doesn't depend on feature engineering and automatically studies the complex attributes received from raw data because of its strong structure [7].

2 Literature Review

The intrusion detection system based on DL proposed by Akhil Krishna et al., 2020, effectively detects malicious attacks including Probe, DOS, U2R, and R2L coupled with attack prevention. The MLP, which is trained using high accuracy dataset, is used to detect intrusions using the DL model. A CSV file containing the relevant data is downloaded from the network and added to the used DL model in real-time intrusion detection, obtaining the detection as a result. The second stage involves running a script in the background to prevent the incursion. In the script, a precise choice is made to protect the data from numerous assaults during the prevention phase. The Multi-Layer Perceptron model is used to make judgments using the data that was gathered from the classification part. The proposed combination approach, which combines IDS and IPS, accomplishes the objective of intrusion prevention and detection rapidly and effectively [1].

The 2017 study by Jin Kim et al. focuses on the application of AI-based IDS with the DNN model to effectively detect attacks. The given data were extracted into samples for the investigation. The entire dataset, which contains around 4.9 million records, was used for the process of confirming the testing set, while the training data used for the study only includes 10% of the corrected data. The findings from the suggested model demonstrate an astonishingly high rate of 99% accuracy in detecting the attack. Additionally, the rate of false alarms was found to be roughly 0.08%, showing how infrequently routine data was mistaken for a danger. The investigations that have been done so far have only examined a single traffic data point. To combat Distributed Denial of Service (DDoS) assaults, time series data analysis using the recurrent neural network (RNN) model and the LSTM (Long Short Term Memory) model is required [2].

S. Santosh Kumar et al., 2021 organised a successful study to achieve the goal of detecting intrusion, different methods used for intrusion detection, a significant category of hacker attacks, a variety of tools and techniques used to protect, the area of research to improve the efficiency of identifying intrusion, challenges faced by the user, and finally the evolution of new IDS tools in terms of research. The instruments that were created have the ability to recognise and guard against incursion brought on by intruders. IDS has been integrated into many businesses that want to safeguard their digital data within the network perimeter since the introduction of firewall technology. IDS has been recognized as a competent technology to protect valuable information from internal attackers and external hackers where the traffic doesn't move ahead of the firewall itself [3].

The implementation of the DL technique using binary classification to separate the regular, legitimate message packets from the suspicious message packets has been the focus of Vipparthy Praneeth et al., 2021. The method begins with the creation of a training dataset made up of 1,20,223 network packets with 41 attributes that were taken from the open-source CICIDS 2018 and KDD 99 datasets. The chosen one-dimensional network dataset is first pre-processed by using an autoencoder to remove any extraneous data. Out of forty-one qualities, 23 were deemed deserving. The structured DNN is used to assess the suggested model. Additionally, it is combined with Softmax classifier and Relu activation algorithms. The proposed intrusion deterrent approach has been researched and tested using Google Colab, a non-proprietary tensor flow and an open forum for cloud services. Using a simulation dataset produced via network simulation, the recommended intrusion prevention classifier model was validated. The experimental findings show an accuracy of 99.57%, which is the highest level among the current CNN and RNN-based models. In a short time, the method can be studied with various datasets that result in the process of improving the precision and effectiveness of the suggested model [5].

Vijayakumar R et al., 2019, offer their opinion on how to choose the best method for effectively identifying upcoming cyberattacks. The use of existing DNNs and other traditional ML classifiers on a variety of benchmarked malware datasets that are publically accessible has been thoroughly evaluated. The network topologies specifically for DNNs and the most important network parameters were determined using the hyperparameter methods of selection in relation to the KDD Cup 99 dataset. The trials used DNNs with a training rate range of 0.01 to 0.5 over a period of 1000 epochs. To create a benchmark, the well-performing DNN model from the KDD Cup 99 dataset was applied to the UNSW-NB15, NSL-KDD, WSN-DS, CICIDS 2017, and Kyoto datasets. The recommended DNN model studies the high-dimensional attribute recognition of the IDS data by transferring them into various hidden layers. This method is recommended for real-time usage ineffective monitoring of the network traffic and it also assists the host-level events by sending early alerts of the cyberattacks that are possible [6].

M. Azhagiri et al., 2015 render an outlook of IDPS techniques. The research on IDPS summarizes all the key functions utilized in performing the IDPS techniques and it also evaluates the detection methodologies utilized by it. In addition, the technique embosses the significant properties of every chief class of the IDPS system. The paper has elaborated on the different kinds of IDPS security competencies, the challenges identified, and the limitations of the technique. Securing the sensitive information stored in a computer has become a legal concern by organizations because of the growing trust in electronic transactions and operations. Many methods are utilized to support the organizations intending to protect their information against attacks [8].

Now a day, the blending of methods has become very popular which leads to confusion in choosing the apt methodology that deploys to secure the system. David Mudzingwa et al., 2012 demonstrate and provide a clear clarification of every methodology along with the way to compare the performance and efficiency of each methodology. The research has considered four important methodologies which are used to detect and prevent systems from intrusion. Even though the anomaly-based methodology performs well than the other methods in the process of detecting new attacks without any updates in the software or without any change fed by the user, the current network world moves for IDPS makes a mixture of four chief methodologies. The research also concentrates on the comparison and estimation procedure of the IDPS methodologies which are utilized by the IDPS products in the market [9].

Due to the nature of the network, security has become a threat to utilizing a wireless network. With this concern, many researchers are thinking to find a suitable and reliable solution for the issue. Jafar Abo Nada et al., 2018 propose a novel IDPS, particularly for a wireless system. The study discusses the framing of a new system, especially for a wireless network, and named it WIDPAS. The framework is designed to perform three important tasks such as monitoring, analyzing, and defending. The system initially monitors the network for any type of false networks or service attacks, then it analyses the characteristics of the attack and finds out the intruder. Finally, the system safeguards the network users. The research paper demonstrates the method to improve the effectiveness of the prevailing system. The proposed system monitors all the attacks and it is equipped to defend against any type of attack from counterfeit networks. It cut the path of the attacker and safeguards the user from being scammed. The future of network systems is developed with AI and ANN. A large amount of data is involved in every transaction. Therefore, it is essential to monitor, analyze and study the data and secure it safely from intruder attack [10].

3 Proposed Methodology

IDS has become a highly propounded approach that aids in securing digital data. The major change occurs in the collected data set that includes different samples of intrusion algorithms similar to denial of service, brute force, or at least an infiltration taking place within a network. Figure 1 depicts a passive deployment of NIDS which is associated with a network switch that is configured with the technology of port mirroring.

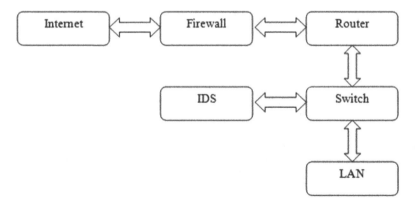

Fig. 1. Network-based IDS

Artificial Neural Network (ANN)

The single layer of ANN consists of multiple nodes that perform the actual computation. The computation process in ANN is designed in such a way that it reflects the actions of neurons present in the human neural network. The nodes in the neural network react to the stimulus at a particular degree or extensively. The magnitude of the reaction is related proportionally to the feed value multiplied by the node weight. The nodes commonly consist of weights achieved from multiple inputs. Different weights are extracted by modifying many inputs. Finally, each multiplied value was summed up and the added value is fed into the activation function. At last, its outcome is implemented into the regression or classification analysis. The application of the ANN approach has increased in recent times and it is used for various categories, reasoning, prediction, and demonstration of positive results for endorsement [2].

The familiar quality of the objective kind method contains two components, training type loss, and the regularization component.

$$obj(\theta) = L(\theta) + \Omega(\theta) \tag{1}$$

From the above formula (1) L describes the training loss mode and Ω represents the regularization component. The loss value computes the system's capability to project information. The common option of the value L is MSE, which is described by

$$L(\theta) = \sum_i \left(y_i - \hat{y}_i\right)^2 \tag{2}$$

Another type of common loss function is logistic kind loss. It is expressed as

$$L(\theta) = \sum_i \left[y_i \ln\left(1 + e^{-\hat{y}_i}\right) + (1 - y_i)\ln\left(1 + e^{\hat{y}_i}\right) \right] \tag{3}$$

ANN model is composed mathematically as portrayed below:

$$\hat{y}_i = \sum_{k=1}^{K} f_k(x_i), f_k \in \mathcal{F} \tag{4}$$

In formula (4) K denotes the total quantity of layers, function space represents the symbol, and a cluster of possible classifications is depicted by $\mathcal{F}$. Layer complexity of the value $\Omega(f)$, and the description of the layer f(x) is expressed by

$$f_t(x) = w_{q(x)}, w \in R^T, q : R^d \rightarrow \{1, 2, \ldots, T\} \tag{5}$$

Here T denotes the definite number of layers, and q portrays the method to assign each data point equivalent to the leaf information. The MLP model complexity level is usually described as

$$\Omega(f) = \gamma T + \frac{1}{2}\lambda \sum_{j=1}^{T} w_j^2 \tag{6}$$

Multi Layer Perceptron (MLP)

MLP is based on the concept of evaluating the values of neurons present in the current layer in the form of activated summation of the weighted outcomes of the neurons from the previous layer that is connected to each neuron. The term activation infers to the sum of weighted inputs that are used as inputs for the above-termed activation function for mapping the input to the output performed either directly by identity activation or with certain restrictions like tanh or sigmoid or mapping it during the removal of unwanted values. The process is illustrated with an example of ReLU that removes the negative values along with the direct mapping with positive ones. At the initial stage, the weights of the neuron links are random. Some adjustments are done using the backward propagation process where the error found for the forward propagation of the MLP outcomes receives back-propagated through, and the weights are altered proportionally according to the error.

Commonly MLP model is trained in a supervised manner, with a backpropagation technique to measure the weight derivatives. Here the error function E is illustrated as:

$$E = \sum_{k=1}^{n} d^{(k)} - y^{(k)} \tag{7}$$

In the above equation, d describes the target value and y denotes the MLP output-based vector. After measuring the error value E, the formulas are used to keep posted the bias value θ and the value of the weight w.

$$w_{new} = w_{prev} - \eta \frac{\partial E}{\partial w_{prev}} \tag{8}$$

$$\theta_{new} = \theta_{prev} - \eta \frac{\partial E}{\partial \theta_{prev}} \tag{9}$$

From the Eq. (8) and (9) η shows the learning value, and $d^{(k)}$ describes the position of the target vector. θ denotes the weight value used in the learning process, the identifier w manages the weight, and y indicates the output vector information.

Enhanced Multi Layer Perceptron (EMLP)

The main reason for the selection of MLP as the technique for utilizing in research was to ease the implementation process of such techniques. MLP technique, which is known for rendering high-quality models it keeps the time needed for training relatively lower than the other compared complex methods.

PSO (Particle Swarm Optimization)

In continuation to it, the position and velocity updates are done, as the values of every particle are as discrete numbers with the utilization of the sigmoid equation for updating the position concerning the necessary velocity based on the following Eq. 10.

$$v_n = w * v_n + c_1 \, rand_1 * (Pbest - x_n) + c_2 \, rand_2 * (Gbest - x_n) \tag{10}$$

From the Eq. 10 v_n indicates the nth particle velocity, w describes the inertial weight, $rand_1$ and $rand_2$ describes the random value between 1 and 0, and x_n indicates the present position.

$$sigmoid = \frac{1}{1 + e^{-v_n}} \qquad (11)$$

$$x_{i,j}(t+1) = \{x_{i,j}(t+1) = rand(B_i), rand(t) < sigmoid\left(v_{i,j}(t+1)\right)x_{i,j}(t+1)$$
$$= x_{i,j}(t+1), rand(t) < sigmoid\left(v_{i,j}(t+1)\right) \qquad (12)$$

To move the particle into a new position, a sigmoid equation is needed, when a velocity is added to the earlier position which is a discrete number that results in a continuous number that doesn't work in the prevailing case. Therefore, to search for a new position concerning the velocity, the positions are mapped into the sigmoid equation. After that, the outcomes are compared with random numbers ranging from zero to one.

It provides more extra weight values of the weak observation. The DS method can be illustrated using the following equation.

$$f(x) = s(x_k > c) \qquad (13)$$

$f(x)$ will create a forecasting value 1 when the component of K of the x vector is advanced the threshold value c and the value will be set as -1. The value of s is -1 or 1 which will create the two methods named $x_k > c$ and $x_k \leq c$. Then all the predicted values are integrated, and the higher votes are producing the final forecasting result. The iterative process consists of relating weighting value $t = 1 \ldots T$ for every learning sample in the Eqs. 14, 15, 16 and 17.

Given that: $(x_1, y_1), \ldots, (x_m, y_m)$ where $x_i \in X$, $y_i \in Y = \{-1, +1\}$.
Initialization of $D_1(i) = \frac{1}{n}$, here n denotes the quantity of data.

For $t = 1$ to T : train the base learner with D_t distribution

Find the week type hypothesis $h_t: X \rightarrow \{-1, +1\}$ with error

$$\epsilon_t = Pr_{i \sim D_t}\left[h_t(x_i) \neq y_i\right] \qquad (14)$$

$$a_t = \frac{1}{2}\lambda v\left(\frac{1 - \epsilon_t}{\epsilon_t}\right) \qquad (15)$$

Update:

$$D_{t+1}(i) = \frac{D_t(i)}{Z_t} \times \begin{cases} e^{-at}, jika\ h_t(x_i) = y_i \\ e^{at}, jika\ h_t(x_i) \neq y_i \end{cases}$$
$$= \frac{D_t(i)\exp(-a_t y_i h_t(x_i))}{Z_t} \qquad (16)$$

From the above equation Z_t method is called the normalization factor, so the outcome in the following equation:

$$H(x) = sign\left(\sum_{t=0}^{T} a_t h_t(x)\right) \qquad (17)$$

4 Results and Discussion

When the word IDS is mentioned, it indicates two concepts namely intrusion and detection system. The word intrusion has become familiar among many network hosts, as they are confronted with the problem of unauthorized access of attackers and hackers to the valuable information in a network or computer system compromising their confidentiality, availability, or integrity.

The performance of the model was evaluated by tabulating and calculating the features like accuracy, false alarms, and detection rate. TP represents true positive that means the data of real attacks which are segregated as attacks, FP represents false positives that provide the real attack data which are separated as normal from the dataset, FN means false negative which indicates the real attack data that are categorized as normal and TN stands for true negative which are the normal data that are assorted as normal.

The term accuracy infers to the rate at which data are classified rightly. In other words, the cases for which actual attack data are classified as attacks and normal data as normal. Accuracy can be mathematically represented as:

$$Accuracy = \frac{TP + TN}{TP + TN + FP + FN} \tag{18}$$

Recall and precision are additional measures that we take into account in this study and are defined as follows:

$$Precision = \frac{TP}{TP + FP} \tag{19}$$

$$Recall = \frac{TP}{TP + FN} \tag{20}$$

KDD CUP99 Dataset Analysis

For our research work we have downloaded cyber hacking dataset from a online database provider. It consists of 10244 Rows and 12 Columns. The attributes used in the dataset are Time, Date, Delivery ratio, Packet Length etc. We have measured output parameters such as Accuracy, Precision and Recall respectively.

Accuracy Analysis

Now we are going to apply our proposed EMLP algorithm along with existing algorithms such as ANN and MLP over KDDCUP99 Dataset. The following Table 1 and Fig. 2 represents Accuracy Analysis of proposed EMLP compared over ANN and MLP. From the results its proved that proposed EMLP produces Accuracy of about 93% which is higher than ANN Accuracy which is 84% and MLP Accuracy which is 89% respectively.

Table 1. Accuracy comparison of proposed EMLP with other existing algorithms

No of Iterations	ANN Accuracy (%)	MLP Accuracy (%)	EMLP Accuracy (%)
10	82.1	87.3	91.3
20	82.6	88.5	92.5
30	83.2	89.3	92.6
40	84.4	89.5	93.1
50	84.5	89.8	93.3

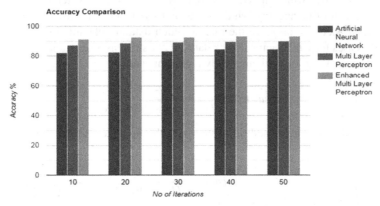

Fig. 2. Accuracy comparison of proposed EMLP with other existing algorithms graph

Precision Analysis

Now we are going to apply our proposed EMLP algorithm along with existing algorithms such as ANN and MLP over KDDCUP99 Dataset. The following Table 2 and Fig. 3 represents Precision Analysis of proposed EMLP compared over ANN and MLP. From the results its proved that proposed EMLP produces Precision of about 0.88 which is higher than ANN Precision which is 0.80 and MLP Precision which is 0.85 respectively.

Table 2. Precision comparison of proposed EMLP with other existing algorithms

No of Iterations	ANN Precision (%)	MLP Precision (%)	EMLP Precision (%)
10	80.3	84.6	87.6
20	80.4	85.2	88
30	80.7	85.3	88.2
40	81.1	85.5	88.6
50	81.2	85.7	88.8

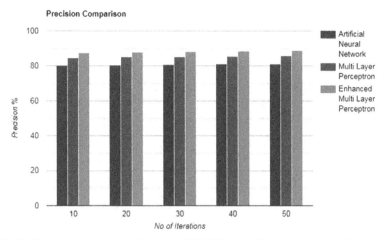

Fig. 3. Precision comparison of proposed EMLP with other existing algorithms graph

Recall Analysis

Now we are going to apply our proposed EMLP algorithm along with existing algorithms such as ANN and MLP over KDDCUP99 Dataset. The following Table 3 and Fig. 4 represents Recall Analysis of proposed EMLP compared over ANN and MLP. From the results its proved that proposed EMLP produces Recall of about 0.84 which is higher than ANN Recall which is 0.79 and MLP Recall which is 0.81 respectively.

Table 3. Recall comparison of proposed EMLP with other existing algorithms

No of Iterations	ANN Accuracy (%)	MLP Accuracy (%)	EMLP Accuracy (%)
10	78.5	81.4	82.1
20	78.1	81.5	83.3
30	79.3	81.7	83.6
40	79.5	81.9	84.2
50	79.7	82.4	84.7

In terms of Accuracy we have evaluated three algorithms with 50 iterations on KDD-CUP99 dataset. From the Accuracy Table and graph we can analyze that the average Accuracy of ANN is 84%, MLP is 89% and EMLP is 93%. From the results we can prove that EMLP outperforms other algorithms in terms of Accuracy.

In terms of Precision we have evaluated three algorithms with 50 iterations on KDD-CUP99 dataset. From the Precision Table and graph we can analyze that the average Precision of ANN is 0.80, MLP is 0.85 and EMLP is 0.88. From the results we can prove that EMLP outperforms other algorithms in terms of Precision.

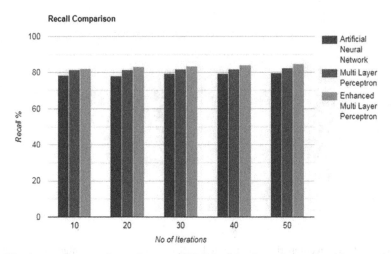

Fig. 4. Recall comparison of proposed EMLP with other existing algorithms graph

In terms of Recall we have evaluated three algorithms with 50 iterations on KDD-CUP99 dataset. From the Recall Table and graph we can analyze that the average Recall of ANN is 0.79, MLP is 0.81 and EMLP is 0.84. From the results we can prove that EMLP outperforms other algorithms in terms of Recall.

5 Conclusion

In today's world of the internet, data security has become a dare for many organizations. Protecting authorized data from the attack of intruders is very much essential. Intrusion detection plays a crucial role in achieving the best accuracy in securing data and filling the gaps of the existing techniques. IDS is the new evolution in the digital world that enhances network security by safely preserving the credential data of the organization. The IDS technology assists the network administrator and the host of the network in identity any type of malicious functions performed on the network. The system alerts the host to take appropriate corrective actions against the threat identified. The research proves that IDS is the best solution for conserving the critical data from intruders who are real-world entities with the help of deep learning techniques.

References

1. Krishna, A., Lal M.A., A., Mathewkutty, A.J., Jacob, D.S., Hari, M.: Intrusion detection and prevention system using deep learning. In: IEEE International Conference on Electronics and Sustainable Communication Systems (ICESC) (2020)
2. Kim, J., Shin, N., Jo, S.Y., Kim, S.H.: Method of intrusion detection using deep neural network. In: 2017 IEEE International Conference on Big Data and Smart Computing (BigComp) (2017). https://doi.org/10.1109/BIGCOMP.2017.7881684
3. Santosh Kumar, S., Kannan, M., Vignesh, B., Rajarajan, S.: Intrusion detection system using deep learning. Int. J. Eng. Res. Technol. (IJERT) **9**(5), 8–13 (2021). ISSN: 2278-0181 Published by, www.ijert.org ICRADL - 2021 Conference Proceedings.

4. Anuradha, K., Nirmala Sugirtha Rajini, S., Bhuvaneswari, T., Vinod, V.: TCP/SYN Flood of Denial of Service (DOS) Attack Using Simulation. Test Eng. Manage., 14553–14558 (2020). ISSN 0193-4120

5. Praneeth, V., Kumar, K.R., Karyemsetty, N.: Security: intrusion prevention system using deep learning on the internet of vehicles. Int. J. Saf. Secur. Eng. **11**(3), 231–237 (2021)

6. Vijayakumar, R, Alazab, M., Soman, K.P., Poornachandran, P., Al-Nemrat, A., Venkatraman, S.: Deep Learning Approach for Intelligent Intrusion Detection System. IEEE Access. 7, pp. 41525-41550 (2019).https://doi.org/10.1109/ACCESS.2019.2895334

7. Ahmad, Z.: Network intrusion detection system: a systematic study of machine learning. Emerg. Telecommun. Technol. **32**, e4150 (2020)

8. Azhagiri, M., Rajesh, A., Karthik, S.: Intrusion detection and prevention system: technologies and challenges. Int. J. Appl. Eng. Res. **10**(87), 1–13 (2015). ISSN 0973-4562

9. Mudzingwa, D., Agrawal, R.: A study of methodologies used in intrusion detection and prevention systems (IDPS). IEEE Access, pp. 1–6 (2012). 978-1-4673-1375-9/12

10. Nada, J.A., Al-Mosa, M.R.: A proposed wireless intrusion detection prevention and attack system. In: IEEE International Arab Conference on Information Technology (ACIT), Werdanye, Lebanon, 28 November 2018–30 November 2018, pp. 1–5 (2018). https://doi.org/10.1109/ACIT.2018.8672722

Classification of Medical Datasets Using Optimal Feature Selection Method with Multi-support Vector Machine

S. Silvia Priscila[1(✉)] and C. Sathish Kumar[2]

[1] Department of Computer Science, Bharath Institute of Higher Education and Research (BIHER), Chennai, Tamilnadu, India
silviaprisila.cbcs.cs@bharathuniv.ac.in
[2] Department of Computer Science, Bishop Heber College (Autonomous), Affiliated to Bharathidasan University, Tiruchirappalli, Tamilnadu, India
csathish@bhc.edu.in

Abstract. Automated Diagnosis in healthcare is becoming an interesting study in recent time among the data scientists to predict and diagnose the conditions in patients. In this manner, analysis of plays a major part in detection and classification of disease and accurately diagnose the medical condition in patients. Most of the data mining task is held up with poor classification accuracy due to the presence of redundant or irrelevant data items. In this research, the issue of poor classification accuracy is addressed and is solved by developing a framework that involves a series of stages. This includes pre-processing, feature extraction and classification of data items. The study uses Optimal Feature Selection Method (OFSM) as its feature selection tool and Multi-Support Vector Machine as its classification tool. The experimental validation is carried out to study the efficacy of the proposed method over various datasets and the outputs are evaluated in terms of accuracy, specificity, sensitivity and f-measure.

Keywords: Multi-Support Vector Machine · Classification · Chronic Kidney Disease · DE · OFSM

1 Introduction

Biomedical computing offers a significant role in the field of healthcare and this includes several theoretical models for the diagnosis of automatic diagnostic frameworks. In healthcare systems, there exist various problems on automated diagnostic framework that includes its cost, multiple alternative therapies, inadequate diagnostic information etc. [1]. Hence the researchers used various techniques on classification to assists the physicians to facilitate and check medical diagnosis and to reduce the vulnerability of diseases [2]. The majority of the classification model operates by optimal selection of features and such selects boost the classification process by securing the primitive information [3, 4].

© The Author(s), under exclusive license to Springer Nature Switzerland AG 2022
S. Rajagopal et al. (Eds.): ASCIS 2022, CCIS 1759, pp. 220–232, 2022.
https://doi.org/10.1007/978-3-031-23092-9_18

In order to determine the type of disease and to assist the surgical notions, it is necessary to optimally classify the type and nature of disease [5]. The decision tree is the first classifier used in medical history for the diagnosis of diseases [7]. Machine Learning (ML) is also applied as a supervised tool for the classification of type of disease [9]. Among the classification tools, the SVM is the best-known supervised classification model which maps the sample vector into a space onto high dimensions and searches for an ideal isolation hyperplane to classify the type. The support vector machine acts as a pattern identification technique that is used commonly as machine learning technique for various disease classification [8] [10]. Network-based SVM (NSVM) is an enhancement model that overcomes the limitations of the classification of SVM and provides effective class of the classified samples [11–13].

It is impossible to analyze the data with redundant and incomplete items because of the existence of huge volume of data in real time [23]. Feature Selection (FS) is a most appropriate technique that removes the replicated and undesired features and provides the most insightful final data variables, leading to successful prediction or classification. The objective is to minimize the amount of features in order to minimize the area size directly and allow classification models to use only the necessary features. This is regarded as an optimization problem and it is fixed using support vector machine [23, 24]. SVM acts as a generalized algorithm in making decisions to diagnose type of disease. It avoids the problems associated with the high-dimensional features with overfitting issue and it further reduces the cost of computation.

The major purpose of this research is discussed in the subsequent sections: In this paper, a framework that consists of a pre-processing, feature extraction using optimal feature selection model (OFSM) and classification of data items using multi-support vector machine is developed.

2   Related Works

The MRI classification of coded brain structures has primarily been tested for patient monitoring and examination of different brain conditions. In an audit of the best pro-grammed methods accessible from the brain structure to the complete brain percolation techniques, the research by Villa et al. [16] showed specific segmentation strategies. No single programmed segmentation model has been developed that will enhance normal clinical work on a precise characterization of the brain structures. The next step should concentrate primarily on the integration of multi- strategies with methodologies that are focused on learning. In text mining, the ML system is used to investigate doctor studies focused on cancer, which have been partly studied.

In enhancing data extraction out of cancer data, Napolitano et al. [17] suggested some rules for pre-trained breast cancer reports. The general objective of Molina et al. [18], in view of the revelation of repeated trends is to distinguish time schemes. First, the numerical time arrangements have been transformed into standard time groups in which the images are supposed to characterize the respective ideas in space. These images may be characterized using either the open or expert domain information.

Tosas et al. [19] presented another worldview of the creation of an activity of clinical classification from different data sources to anticipate a recovery of patients. Various classification strategies embrace a metric of each unit which must be usable during prediction.

In the present scenario, chronic data was graded as ordinary, fringe or obsessed in terms of clinical suggestions for disease according to De Bruin et al. [20]. The classification results often test the built-in fuzzy sets where instructions are used as rules for classification of data from time to time.

The ML models for the detection of CKD are considered by Salekins and Stankovic [21] to have 24 prediction parameters. The study focuses on the cost-accuracy trade-off in order to identify the most accurate and least expensive reliable CKD prediction model.

Yildirim et al. [22] investigate the effect of data imbalance while developing the CKD model. The tests showed that the sampling models would increase the classification performance, and a significant variable affects the multi-computer perception.

Elhoseny, M., et al. [26] proposed the Density based Feature Selection using ant colony optimization algorithm for CKD as an intelligent classification method. Before the ACO-based classifier construction, the given intelligent system uses DFS to remove invalid or redundant features.

Compared to other algorithms while classifying the different stages for patients with CKD, Rady, E. H. A., and Anwar, A. S. [27] found that the Probabilistic Neural Networks (PNN) algorithm provides the overall maximum classifier accuracy of 96.7%. But the Multilayer Perceptron requires a short execution period, while the PNN takes 12 s to complete the study. The above algorithms were correlated to classifier accuracy depending on the number of correctly identified phases for patients with CKD, the time it took to construct the model as well the time it took for testing it.

Subasi et al. [28] used a variety of ML classifiers that were experimentally tested on the data set from UCI Repository and the results were compared to those published in latest literature. The results are presented quantitatively and qualitatively and the observations show that the random forest classifier performs near-optimally in identifying CKD patients.

Random forest also was used by Qin, J., et al. [29] to obtain the highest results, with 99.75% diagnostic precision. It was suggested an optimized model which incorporates random forest and logistic regression with perceptron, that can averagely attain a 99.83% accuracy after simulating ten times, after evaluating the misclassified instances produced by the existing models.

The SVM algorithm was used to detect CKD by Polat, H., et al. [30]. To minimize the dimension of the CKD dataset, two basic forms of feature selection strategies namely wrapper and filter approaches were chosen to diagnose the disease. Classifier subset evaluator with greedy stepwise search engine and wrapper subset evaluator with Best First search engine were used in the wrapper method.

3   Proposed Method

Data Classification is another method which involves different information sorting techniques and conditions within a storage capacity or a database. This is done essentially using a database or a business knowledge program which enables information to be examined, recognized and isolated.

With the aid of an optimal method of extraction, the existing medical classification technique used hybrid classifier. The efficiency is improved and time complexity issues are minimized significantly by the modern classification model, The presented model applies OFSM (Optimal Feature Selection Method) with M-SVM to address these daunting challenges. In this case, the input dataset is preprocessed. Feature selection is then carried out with OFSM from the pre-processed results. Finally, the classification task is conducted using the M-SVM system for clinical data. Figure 1 shows the overall classification process.

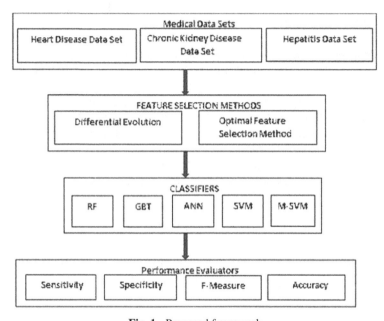

Fig. 1. Proposed framework

Preprocessing

The unprocessed medical input data is provided as input for preprocessing. These unprocessed results tend to be very noisy, with no values and inconsistencies. Classification accuracy is influenced by the dominance of these unprocessed results. Unprocessed data can be preprocessed to improve the standard of patient data.

Preprocessing in this article is more important in order to obtain data from non-numerical information in the context of a mathematical structure. For additional information, non-numerical data is collected and the arithmetic data collection is retrieved.

The pre-processing removes missing values from the input dataset. The discrete traits are built by synchronizing the models if continuous features tends to exist. The pre-processing further aims to reduce the presence of missing and noisy values in each instances using data cleaning operation. It further avoids the inconsistencies in the input dataset. The missing values are replaced with the value 0 and it gets transformed to make the data suitable for the process of mining. The values are further normalized via coding in data transformation process and hence the values take the binary form 0 or 1.

Dataset Description Three datasets from medical domain are taken for experimentation. Dataset for Heart disease, CKD dataset and Hepatitis dataset are used in this proposed work. All these datasets are available in the UCI machine learning repository. The Cleveland Heart disease dataset has 76 attributes and 303 instances. But all the published experiments concentrate only on 14 attributes. The CKD dataset consists of 24 attributes plus a class attribute that finds out the presence or not of CKD. 400 samples of data are given in CKD dataset. The hepatitis dataset contains 19 attributes and 155 instances.

Feature Selection Using Differential Evolution Optimization

One type of evolutionary algorithmic ways is Differential evolution (DE) in which feature exploration is based on ant colony optimization. DE features various actions, including 1) the capacity to manage multimodal, nonlinear and non-differentiable values, 2) parallelization that deals with high computational costs, 3) ease of use, and 4) good convergence properties. DE, like Genetic Algorithm, makes use of elements such as mutation, crossover, and selection. Performance of DE is subject to how the target vector and difference are handled during the searching operation in order to obtain a task vector. DE is a population-based metaheuristic technique for solving optimization problems using numerical vectors.

Feature Selection Using Optimal Feature Selection Method

Instead of mutation and crossover, Optimal Feature Selection Method (OFSM), encodes solutions to reduce the computational time in order of optimal classification on medical datasets. The process of OFSM is as follows:

Stage 1: Encoding of Solution

Each specific solution from the population is represented as binary string. The solution length is equal to various features in the datasets. The binary code 1 indicates that the feature is selected and vice versa. Thus $S = [F_1, F_2, \ldots, F_m]$ with m being the features of different datasets.

Stage 2: Initial Population

Set total population size of the OFSM as 50, where it produces random solution varying between 0 and 1 with real values. The real valued solution is then converted to binary value using the following digitization step:

$$S_{p,q}^{(i)} \begin{cases} 1 & S_{p,q}^{(i)} > rand \\ 0 & otherwise \end{cases} \tag{1}$$

where.

Rand - uniformly distributed random number between [0,1].

Stage 3: Fitness Function

This process measures a single positive integer output. The fitness of the obtained solution is formulated as below that assists M-SVM to correctly perform instance classification that with lesser classifier error.

$$fitness(S_p^{(i)}) = Error\_rate(S_p^{(i)}) \tag{2}$$

The solution obtained is the error rate of a classifier, which is otherwise defined as the testing error rate:

$$Error\_rate\left(S_p^{(i)}\right) = 100X \frac{Number\ of\ mis - classified instances}{Number\ of\ records} \tag{3}$$

Stage 4: Finding New Solutions

Based on the fitness values, the best and worst solution is identified to produce new solution. The solution with the lowest value of the fitness stage is regarded as the best solution because it is obtained with a lesser error rate at a generation i. Here, $s_{wt}^{(i)}$ represents the worst solution and $s_{bt}^{(i)}$ represents the best solution at an iteration i. With these constraints, the qth position of an old solution $s_{p,q}^{(i)}$ is hence given as below:

$$s_{p,q}^{(i)} = s_{p,q}^{(i)} + A\left|s_{bt,q}^{(i)} - s_{p,q}^{(i)}\right| + B|s_{wt,q}^{(i)} - s_{p,q}^{(i)}| \tag{4}$$

When random numbers A and B lie in the range of 0 to 1, then digitalization process transforms real into binary values for every position of the subsequent generation $i + 1$ based on following equation:

$$S_{p,q}^{(i)} \begin{cases} 1 & S_{p,q}^{(i+1)} > rand \\ 0 & otherwise \end{cases} \tag{5}$$

Stage 5: Termination Criteria

The termination criteria is satisfied when any one of the given condition is achieved:
1) fitness rate. 2) Threshold value of the iteration process and 3) overall count of iterations.

Algorithm of OFSM.

1: Start
2: Encode the solution
3: Generate initial populations
4: Evaluate the fitness function in terms of error rate
$fitness(S_p^{(i)}) = Error\_rate\ (S_p^{(i)})$.
5: Find the new solutions using the fitness function

$$s_{p,q}^{(i)} = s_{p,q}^{(i)} + A\left|s_{bt,q}^{(i)} - s_{p,q}^{(i)}\right| + B|s_{wt,q}^{(i)} - s_{p,q}^{(i)}$$

6: Convert the solutions to binary form

$$S_{p,q}^{(i)} \begin{cases} 1 & S_{p,q}^{(i+1)} > rand \\ 0 & otherwise \end{cases}$$

7: End

M-SVM Classification

M-SVM is a useful data classification technique. While Neural Networks are considered more user-friendly than this, they often produce unsatisfactory outcomes. In general, a classification task consists of training and evaluating results, consisting of such data instances [21]. There is one objective value and multiple characteristics in every instance of the training package. The aim of M-SVM is to generate a model which predicts the objective function of data instances provided in a test set only by the attributes [8].

Classification in M-SVM is a working example for monitoring learning. Known labels help to determine whether or not the device works properly. This knowledge leads to the right answer, validates the system's accuracy or is used to assist the system in proper action. One phase in the M-SVM classification includes identifying the known groups closely. This is called collection of functions or extraction of functionality. Even if unknown samples are not required, feature collection and M-SVM classification together will be beneficial. It can be used to classify key sets involved in any classification process [8].

A hyperplane may be used to split the data while the data is linear. But usually the data is non-linear and there are inseparable datasets. To move this kernel, the input data is mapped to a high-dimensional area in a non-linear way.

The data points are converted to a high dimensional space by the nonlinear mapping $\varphi(x)$, which solves the nonlinear problem between classes x_i. This helps to separate points using the mark y_i in the solution space. M-SVM solves the resulting problem with the function derived from data x_i of N-point and is shown as follows:

$$\min_{w, b, \epsilon_i} 0.5 w^T w + c \sum_{i=1}^{N} \epsilon_i$$

$$\text{s.t.} y_i \left(w^T \Phi(x) + b \right) \geq 1 - \epsilon_i$$

where,

ϵ_i - slack variables and.

$c \geq 0$ – tradeoff factor.

A dual Lagrangian optimizes M-SVM and it is expressed as below:

$$\min_{\alpha} 0.5 \sum_{i=1}^{N} \sum_{J=1}^{N} y_i y_j K(x_i, x_j) \alpha_i \alpha_j - \sum_{j=1}^{N} \alpha_i$$

$$0 \leq \alpha_i \leq C$$

$$\text{s.t. } \sum_{i=1}^{1} \alpha_i y_i = 0$$

where

K - kernel vector.

$K(x_i, x_j) = \; < \varphi(x_i), \varphi(x_j) >$ with $< \varphi(x_i), \varphi(x_j) >$

Hence for a data point x, the predicted class from the text document is given as below:

$$sign(\sum_{j=1}^{N} \alpha_i y_i K(x, x_i) + b)$$

At the end of the classification, undesirable data samples are extracted using M-SVM, which eliminates support vectors that are not important. The prediction limits are then graded according to consistent and most important characteristics.

For M-SVM classification with twice parameterized trigonometric kernel function [25] is expressed with dual formulation:

$$\min_{\alpha_i} \sum_{i=1}^{1} \alpha_i - \frac{1}{2} \sum_{i=1}^{1} \sum_{j=1}^{1} \alpha_i \alpha_j y_i y_j K(x_i, x_j)$$

where $0 \le \alpha_i \le C$, for all i;

$$\sum_{i=1}^{1} \alpha_i y_i = 0$$

When the amount of training points is great, training SVM becomes very demanding. The twice parameterized trigonometric kernel function helps in locating the solution within the best known bound that eases the process of classification within the limits and the solution tends to remain within bound. Therefore no extra-bound solutions are obtained and it reduces the iteration bound.

Transforming the data to a function space enables a similarity measure to be defined on the basis of the dot product. Pattern recognition can be easy [1] if the function space is selected appropriately.

$$(X1.X2) \leftarrow K(X1, X2) = \{\phi(X1).\phi(X2)\}$$

The definition of the kernel function is not the high-dimensional feature space, but allows for the application of the input region. Therefore, it is not necessary to determine the inner product in the function space. The algorithm should map the input field attributes to the function space. In SVM and its output, the kernel is important. The Kernel Hilbert Spaces is reproduced.

$$(K(X1, X2) = \{\phi(X1).\phi(X2)\}$$

The kernel then represents a valid internal product. With an entry space, the training set cannot be separated linearly. In the functional space, the training set is linearly separable. The kernel trick is referred to as [8, 12].

4   Results and Discussions

In this section, a simulation of the proposed model on different datasets collected from UCI repository that includes heart disease, CKD and hepatitis is provided. The proposed algorithm is simulated in a high end computing system running on i7 processor with 8 GB RAM. The performance of the recommended model is tested under classification accuracy, specificity, sensitivity and f-measure.

Table 1 presents the comparative performance results of heart disease dataset using different classifiers and two feature selection methods.

Table 1. Metrics results comparison of classifiers using DE and OFSM algorithm (heart disease dataset)

FS methods	Sensitivity (%)					Specificity (%)				
	LR	RF	NB	SVM	M-SVM	LR	RF	NB	SVM	M-SVM
DE	72.52	71.26	69.52	73.43	75.46	70.51	72.67	74.18	76.53	78.71
OFSM	91.57	93.72	93.85	94.25	96.14	90.14	92.17	93.85	94.74	96.43
FS methods	F-MEASURE (%)					ACCURACY (%)				
	LR	RF	NB	LR	RF	LR	LR	RF	SVM	LR
DE	67.23	69.26	DE	67.23	69.26	DE	67.23	69.26	DE	67.23
OFSM	88.45	91.46	OFSM	88.45	91.46	OFSM	88.45	91.46	OFSM	88.45

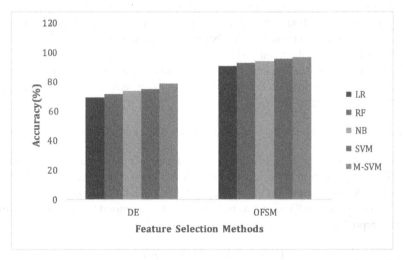

Fig. 2. Accuracy comparison of classifiers vs. feature selection methods (heart disease dataset)

Figure 2 presents the comparison of classifiers and feature selection strategies for the heart disease data set with respect to accuracy metric. Other classifiers like LR, RF, NB and SVM have accuracy values of 90.71%, 92.76%, 93.93%, and 95.47%, respectively, while the proposed OFSM + M-SVM based feature selection technique gives the best accuracy value of 96.47% (Refer Table 1).

Table 2 presents the comparative performance results of CKD dataset using different classifiers and two feature selection methods.

Table 2. Metrics results comparison of various classifiers using de and ofsm algorithm (ckd disease dataset)

FS methods	Sensitivity (%)					Specificity (%)				
	LR	RF	NB	SVM	M-SVM	LR	RF	NB	SVM	M-SVM
DE	68.96	71.68	70.87	79.25	83.58	68.41	71.16	74.14	80.16	83.18
OFSM	91.61	93.73	93.32	95.78	96.64	87.49	90.64	92.67	94.57	95.73

FS methods	F-Measure (%)					Accuracy (%)				
	LR	RF	NB	LR	RF	LR	LR	RF	SVM	LR
DE	70.34	68.94	DE	70.34	68.94	DE	70.34	68.94	DE	70.34
OFSM	88.62	92.16	OFSM	88.62	92.16	OFSM	88.62	92.16	OFSM	88.62

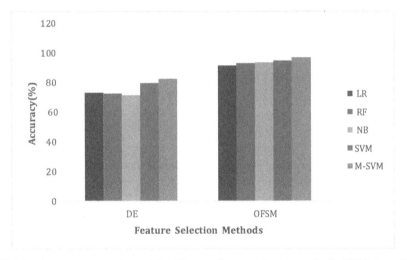

Fig. 3. Accuracy comparison of classifiers vs. feature selection methods (CKD dataset)

Figure 3 presents the comparison of classifiers and feature selection strategies for the CKD data set with respect to accuracy metric. Other classifiers like RF, GBT, ANN, and SVM have accuracy values of 91.64%, 93.27%, 93.72%, and 94.51%, respectively, while the proposed OFSM + M-SVM based feature selection technique gives the best accuracy value of 97.14% (Refer Table 2).

Table 3 presents the comparative performance results of Hepatitis disease dataset using different classifiers and two feature selection methods.

Table 3. Metrics results comparison of various classifiers using de and ofsm algorithm (hepatitis disease dataset)

FS methods	Sensitivity (%)					Specificity (%)				
	LR	RF	NB	SVM	M-SVM	LR	RF	NB	SVM	M-SVM
DE	80.86	79.92	83.68	78.05	80.64	75.51	77.46	78.62	79.15	81.43
OFSM	94.31	94.14	95.72	90.77	96.76	80.46	82.61	84.74	87.63	93.51

FS methods	F-Measure (%)					Accuracy (%)				
	LR	RF	NB	LR	RF	LR	LR	RF	SVM	LR
DE	76.23	80.32	DE	76.23	80.32	DE	76.23	80.32	DE	76.23
OFSM	80.47	84.65	OFSM	80.47	84.65	OFSM	80.47	84.65	OFSM	80.47

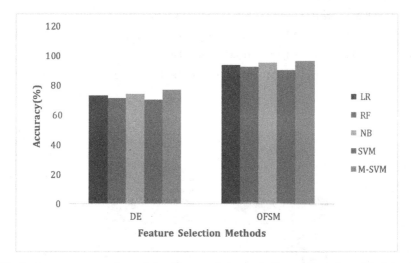

Fig. 4. Accuracy comparison of classifiers vs. feature selection methods (hepatitis dataset)

Figure 4 presents the comparison of classifiers and feature selection strategies for the Hepatitis disease data set with respect to accuracy metric. Other classifiers like LR, RF, NB and SVM have accuracy values of 93.57%, 92.63%, 95.15%, and 90.43%, respectively, while the proposed OFSM + M-SVM based feature selection technique gives the best accuracy value of 96.61% (Refer Table 3).

5   Conclusions

In this paper, the OFSM based M-SVM is utilized to improve the classification of disease in humans that includes heart disease, kidney disease and liver disease. The dataset following the series of stages in the proposed model including pre-processing, feature selection and classification enables improved classification of instances than existing methods. The OFSM obtains optimal features from the input dataset that improves the accuracy of classifier than existing methods. The M-SVM on other hand classifies with higher precision than other methods. The simulated outputs present that the proposed OFSM-M-SVM gives enhanced classification accuracy, specificity, sensitivity and f-measure. In future, the use of deep learning on large datasets could be applied to enhance the efficiency of OFSM and the classifier.

References

1. Hassan, C.A.U., Khan, M.S., Shah, M.A.: Comparison of machine learning algorithms in data classification. In: 2018 24th International Conference on Automation and Computing (ICAC), pp. 1–6. IEEE, September 2018
2. Kling, C.E., Perkins, J.D., Biggins, S.W., Johnson, C.K., Limaye, A.P., Sibulesky, L.: Listing practices and graft utilization of hepatitis C–positive deceased donors in liver and kidney transplant. Surgery 166(1), 102–108 (2019)
3. Khadidos, A., Khadidos, A.O., Kannan, S., Natarajan, Y., Mohanty, S.N., Tsaramirsis, G.: Analysis of COVID-19 Infections on a CT Image Using DeepSense Model. Frontiers in Public Health, 8 (2020)
4. Owada, Y., et al.: A nationwide survey of Hepatitis E virus infection and chronic hepatitis in heart and kidney transplant recipients in Japan. Transplantation 104(2), 437 (2020)
5. Mariappan, L.T.: Analysis on cardiovascular disease classification using machine learning framework. Solid State Technol. 63(6), 10374–10383 (2020)
6. Reyentovich, A., et al.: Outcomes of the Treatment with Glecaprevir/Pibrentasvir following heart transplantation utilizing hepatitis C viremic donors. Clin. Transplant. 34(9), e13989 (2020)
7. Raja, R.A., Kousik, N.V.: Privacy Preservation Between Privacy and Utility Using ECC-based PSO Algorithm. In Intelligent Computing and Applications, pp. 567–573. Springer, Singapore (2021). https://doi.org/10.1007/978-981-15-5566-4_51
8. Gidea, C.G., et al.: Increased early acute cellular rejection events in hepatitis C-positive heart transplantation. J. Heart Lung Transplant. 39(11), 1199–1207 (2020)
9. Ramana, B.V., Boddu, R.S.K.: Performance comparison of classification algorithms on medical datasets. In: 2019 IEEE 9th Annual Computing and Communication Workshop and Conference (CCWC), pp. 0140–0145. IEEE, January 2019
10. Lazo, M., et al.: Confluence of epidemics of hepatitis C, diabetes, obesity, and chronic kidney disease in the United States population. Clin. Gastroenterol. Hepatol. 15(12), 1957–1964 (2017)
11. Gowrishankar, J., Narmadha, T., Ramkumar, M., Yuvaraj, N.: Convolutional neural network classification on 2d craniofacial images. Int. J. Grid Distributed Comput. 13(1), 1026–1032 (2020)
12. Ariyamuthu, V.K., et al.: Trends in utilization of deceased donor kidneys based on hepatitis C virus status and impact of public health service labeling on discard. Transpl. Infect. Dis. 22(1), e13204 (2020)
13. Yuvaraj, N., Vivekanandan, P.: An efficient SVM based tumor classification with symmetry non-negative matrix factorization using gene expression data. In 2013 International Conference on Information Communication and Embedded Systems (Icices), pp. 761–768. IEEE, February 2013
14. Bowring, M.G., et al.: Center-level trends in utilization of HCV-exposed donors for HCV-uninfected kidney and liver transplant recipients in the United States. Am. J. Transplant. 19(8), 2329–2341 (2019)

15. Wasuwanich, P., et al.: Hepatitis E-Associated Hospitalizations in the United States: 2010–2015 and 2015–2017. J. Viral Hepatitis **28**(4), 672–681 (2021)
16. González-Villà, S., Oliver, A., Valverde, S., Wang, L., Zwiggelaar, R., Lladó, X.: A review on brain structures segmentation in magnetic resonance imaging. Artif. Intell. Med. **73**, 45–69 (2016)
17. Napolitano, G., Marshall, A., Hamilton, P., Gavin, A.T.: Machine learning classification of surgical pathology reports and chunk recognition for information extraction noise reduction. Artif. Intell. Med. **70**, 77–83 (2016)
18. Molina, M.E., Perez, A., Valente, J.P.: Classification of auditory brainstem responses through symbolic pattern discovery. Artif. Intell. Med. **70**, 12–30 (2016)
19. Last, M., Tosas, O., Cassarino, T.G., Kozlakidis, Z., Edgeworth, J.: Evolving classification of intensive care patients from event data. Artif. Intell. Med. **69**, 22–32 (2016)
20. de Bruin, J.S., Adlassnig, K.P., Blacky, A., Koller, W.: Detecting borderline infection in an automated monitoring system for healthcare-associated infection using fuzzy logic. Artif. Intell. Med. **69**, 33–41 (2016)
21. Salekin, A., Stankovic, J.: Detection of chronic kidney disease and selecting important predictive attributes. In: 2016 IEEE International Conference on Healthcare Informatics (ICHI), pp. 262–270. IEEE, October 2016
22. Yildirim, P.: Chronic kidney disease prediction on imbalanced data by multilayer perceptron: Chronic kidney disease prediction. In: 2017 IEEE 41st Annual Computer Software and Applications Conference (COMPSAC), vol. 2, pp. 193–198. IEEE, July 2017
23. Wong, G.L.H., et al.: Chronic kidney disease progression in patients with chronic hepatitis B on tenofovir, entecavir, or no treatment. Aliment. Pharmacol. Ther. **48**(9), 984–992 (2018)
24. Kaul, D.R., Tlusty, S.M., Michaels, M.G., Limaye, A.P., Wolfe, C.R.: Donor-derived hepatitis C in the era of increasing intravenous drug use: a report of the Disease Transmission Advisory Committee. Clin. Transplant. **32**(10), e13370 (2018)
25. Bouafia, M., Yassine, A.: An efficient twice parameterized trigonometric kernel function for linear optimization. Optim. Eng. **21**(2), 651–672 (2019). https://doi.org/10.1007/s11081-019-09467-w
26. Elhoseny, M., Shankar, K., Uthayakumar, J.: Intelligent diagnostic prediction and classification system for chronic kidney disease. Sci. Rep. **9**(1), 1–14 (2019)
27. Rady, E.H.A., Anwar, A.S.: Prediction of kidney disease stages using data mining algorithms. Inform. Med. Unlocked **15**, 100178 (2019)
28. Subasi, A., Alickovic, E., Kevric, J.: Diagnosis of chronic kidney disease by using random forest. In: CMBEBIH 2017, pp. 589–594. Springer, Singapore (2017). https://doi.org/10.1007/978-981-10-4166-2_89
29. Qin, J., Chen, L., Liu, Y., Liu, C., Feng, C., Chen, B.: A machine learning methodology for diagnosing chronic kidney disease. IEEE Access **8**, 20991–21002 (2019)
30. Polat, H., Mehr, H.D., Cetin, A.: Diagnosis of chronic kidney disease based on support vector machine by feature selection methods. J. Med. Syst. **41**(4), 55 (2017)

Predicting Students' Outcomes with Respect to Trust, Perception, and Usefulness of Their Instructors in Academic Help Seeking Using Fuzzy Logic Approach

R. K. Kavitha$^{(\boxtimes)}$, N. Jayakanthan, and S. Harishma

Department of Computer Applications, Kumaraguru College of Technology, Coimbatore, India
kavitha.rk.mca@kct.ac.in

Abstract. An instructor's persona and efficiency contribute significantly to predicting the performance outcome of the students during examinations. The primary objective of this paper is to realize in what way fuzzy logic can be applied to predict the outcome of student's performance with three parameters (i.e.) trust, perception, and usefulness of the instructor while seeking help in academics. Fuzzy logic makes decisions based on the rules and ambiguous data given to the model. It is used to handle partial truth where the range varies from absolutely true and absolutely false. Here, the predictions were made using a Mamdani-type fuzzy logic method with three inputs and one output. The study used a descriptive survey research model. Questionnaires were used as a research instrument in the study and a predictive model using the Fuzzy Logic approach was designed. Data collected from 1250 students belonging to various colleges were used in the study. Analysis was done using the python language and the Fuzzy inference system was designed using MATLAB. It was found that the study variables 'trust in instructor' and 'instructor usefulness' were highly correlated. With the input variables trust, perception, and usefulness of instructors, the output variable 'end semester performance' was predicted using the model.

Keywords: Fuzzy logic · Outcome prediction · Instructors · Student-teacher relationship

1 Introduction

Nowadays, education is extremely important for everyone to create a knowledgeable and strong society. Right education supports the student community to find sufficient career prospects soon. Decent education guides the student to take up and understand career aspirations and achieve high-level positions at work. Outcomes in education always depend on the learning process [1].

The teacher's role and efficacy will be useful in forecasting the students' performance in examinations. Teachers will exert a great influence on students thus affecting their careers, normally in the best way and sometimes for worse [4]. If analyzed carefully,

© The Author(s), under exclusive license to Springer Nature Switzerland AG 2022
S. Rajagopal et al. (Eds.): ASCIS 2022, CCIS 1759, pp. 233–243, 2022.
https://doi.org/10.1007/978-3-031-23092-9_19

the teachers influence the students by the way of their interaction and the extent they make the students comfortable in approaching them for academic support. The student's perception, trust in an instructor and its usefulness shall impact the way students perform in that course [7]. The most important factor in succeeding in a course is the instructor itself and the perception the student has of the instructor directly or indirectly impacts their perception of the course as well. Good teaching skills and a positive attitude will bring out positive outcomes among students.

Earlier studies have indicated that emotional experiences have an effect on students' enthusiasm, subject understanding, and accomplishment, although the emotional skills are inspired by means of personality as well as classroom traits [8, 9]. The purpose of this study is to describe an efficient method to predict the performance of students in end-semester examinations centered on fuzzy logic, which will support the faculty to judge the students' performance in advance and take corrective measures.

2   Literature Review

BUilding and fostering trusting relationships between students and teachers is crucial for establishing a stress-free learning atmosphere. No matter what the mode of education is (i.e., online, offline or hybrid), the relationship between student and teacher is the key to a positive outcome. A learner who believes to have a strong association with the teacher, approaches them frequently, is most likely to develop a deeper sense of trust towards that instructor or teacher and they perceive criticisms in a constructive manner [11, 13]. Mustafa Agaoglu [1] study in educational mining aimed at shaping student's performance. The course evaluation feedback obtained from the students was identified as one of the conventional tools to assess instructors' performance centered on students' perceptions. Four classification techniques were used in the research to create classifier models: decision trees, discriminant analysis, support vector machines, and artificial neural networks. Students' performances were related to the dataset which consisted of their replies to a course assessment questionnaire. The obtained responses were analyzed considering metrics namely recall, accuracy, precision, and specificity. Tripti et al. applied various classification methods to construct a performance prediction model focused on parameters such as social integration, academic assimilation, and emotional abilities of students which have not been considered so far. Bipin Bihari Jayasingh introduced a sample analysis done for a specific institution, in certain settings for batch and set of students [10]. The experiment data was gathered with the help of a questionnaire tried by two groups of students consisting of questions relating to Inquiry centered and deductive learning. The research model was built and analyzed two times and was executed using attributes like relevance. The results were visualized through bar charts exhibiting two sets of learners with various learning characteristics. In a study[14] conducted at a self-funded institution in Hong Kong where Moodle and Microsoft Team are the main teaching tools, important elements in determining undergraduate students' satisfaction with utilising ERL across departments were explored.. The goal of Dueas et al. was to gather more knowledge on the relationships between students' socioemotional variables, help-seeking behavior, and attitudes. The results of this research highlight the significance of psycho-emotional elements in academic help-seeking strategies and how they may affect students' final help-seeking behaviour [15]. Everyone has a perception of everything either positive or negative and everyone has different perceptions of the same thing, this perception affects how we view things in our daily life and it's the same in the case of education as well. There are a few aspects with which a student's perception of the instructor is determined: the usefulness of the teacher in the class, the personal interactions outside class, helpfulness, knowledge, etc. [12]. The study by Qayyum, A. analyzed students' opinions and preferences for taking academic help from peers and faculty. Students' attitudes regarding looking for help were analyzed [1]. Factor analysis outcomes displayed that about six attitudinal parameters inspired the students to get assistance from their friends and teachers.

In real-time, there are chances of encountering cases where it is not possible to come up with a decision, whether true or false. In such cases, Fuzzy logic comes handy which offers flexibility for reasoning [3, 7]. In this way, deviation or unlikeness can be dealt with. Regarding the fuzzy logic concept, there is no concept of perfect truth or false, instead, it has a range of values more like partially true or partially false [6]. Basically, Fuzzy logic is a concept where human-like thinking is embedded into a machine [2].

Fuzzy logic's architecture consists of four main parts as shown in Fig. 1.

Rules: Here the set of rules is given using if-then conditions which are fed into the system by the designer to provide a decision-making system to deliver the desired output.

Fuzzifier: Fuzzifier converts inputs as fuzzy sets. Crisp inputs are the precise inputs calculated by sensors and sent to the control system for data handling. Input data may be temperature, pressure, rpm's, etc. [5].

Inference engine: Inference is the process of drawing a certain conclusion from data and logic. This is where the decision-making takes place. It compares the present fuzzy input regarding each rule thus ignoring the unrelated ones. Following, the provided rules are merged to produce the output.

Defuzzifier: The inference engine's fuzzy output set is converted to a crisp value by the defuzzifier.. Various defuzzification techniques are available and the best suitable one is used to decrease the error.

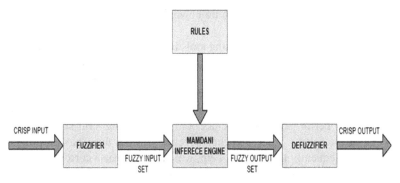

Fig. 1. Fuzzy Logic Architecture

Two kinds of fuzzy inference systems namely Mamdani FIS and Sugeno FIS. Here in this research Mamdani FIS is used.

Mamdani FIS: The outcome in this case will be derived from the collection of implication rules that people feed into the system. This inference framework is used in this investigation.

Six steps must be taken in order to calculate the output of this FIS given the inputs: The initial step is to choose a set of fuzzy rules. To establish the rule strength, fuzzify the inputs using the input membership functions, then combine the fuzzified inputs in accordance with the fuzzy rules. Find the effect of the rule by combining the rule strength and the output membership function. After combining the results to produce it, defuzzify the output distribution.

3 Proposed Work

The main goal of the suggested approach is to create a model that can predict students' performance based on the study variables trust, perception, and usefulness of instructor's help while seeking academic help. Research questions formulated for this study are as follows:

1. Which medium is preferred by the students to seek academic help?
2. To develop a fuzzy logic model which predicts the student's performance in the final examinations centered on the three variables namely trust, perception and usefulness of instructors while seeking academic help.

Data for the research was collected from around 1250 undergraduate and postgraduate students from both engineering and arts colleges in south India. A survey method was used in this study. Data was gathered with the help of Microsoft forms. Students were questioned about the communication options which they normally use to get in touch with friends or instructors for requesting academic-related help. Linkert scale was used to rate the questions. The research framework implemented in this paper is shown in Fig. 2.

The collected data was analyzed using tools link Python and Matlab. It was planned to use a fuzzy logic approach to foresee the performance of the students in end semester examinations depending on their response to the parameters namely trust, perception, and usefulness of instructors while seeking academic help. The three criteria in this case were chosen because teachers' personalities have a significant influence on everything from pupils' academic performance in the classroom to their long-term success. Students' perceptions of a teacher's value and their level of trust in them have a proportional impact on how frequently they ask for help, which in turn has a corresponding impact on their academic performance.

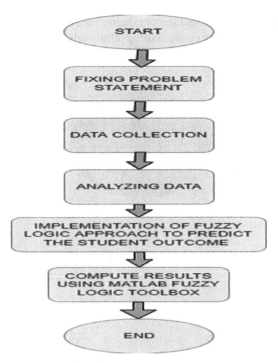

Fig. 2. Research framework

4 Results and Discussions

Data collected from 125 students from various colleges in south India was analyzed and the results are given below. Demographics of the collected data are shown in Figs. 3 and 4. Around 50% female and 49% male responded to the questionnaire. Figure 4 represents the preferred mode of study by the students. It can be observed that around 59% of respondents preferred to seek help from their friends and teachers in offline

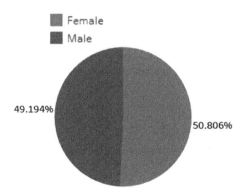

Fig. 3. Gender distribution

mode. Also, Figs. 5 and 6 states that students prefer informal medium like WhatsApp or social media while seeking help online. During offline help-seeking, no major preference between formal or informal mediums is noticed.

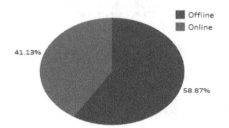

Fig. 4. Preferred mode of study

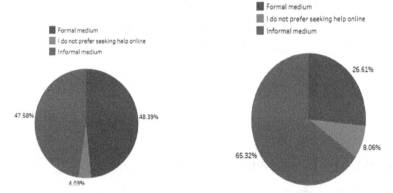

Fig. 5. Preferred medium-online   **Fig. 6.** Preferred medium-offline

	Self reliance	Frequency	Perception	Trust	Usefulness	Outcome
self reliance	1					
frequency	-0.02228	1				
perception	0.14396	0.14564	1			
Trust	-0.01758	0.05981	-0.07650	1		
usefulness	-0.09347	0.10625	-0.00959	0.70195	1	
Outcome	0.02519	0.21551	0.02569	0.55551	0.62455	1

Fig. 7. Correlation between variables

The statistical association between two variables is indicated as their correlation. Also, it is crucial to find and quantify the extent to which the variables in the dataset are dependent upon each other. It is clear from Fig. 7 that the variables "Trust" and "Usefulness" have a strong correlation of 0.7. The variables 'Usefulness' and 'good outcome of requesting aid' have the second-highest correlation. Additionally, there is a strong association between "Trust" and "Result of Seeking Help."

A fuzzy model was developed for this research. This model as found in Fig. 8 has three inputs namely: Trust, perception, and usefulness of the instructors while seeking help and student performance in exams as the outcome and it is shown in the FIS diagram below.

The input and output variables with the range values used in the model are shown in Tables 1 and 2. A triangular member function is used here, for the three inputs and one output as well.

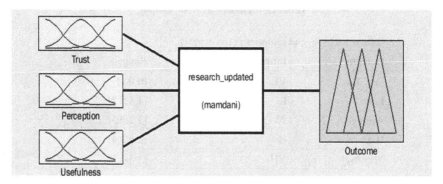

Fig. 8. Fuzzy Interface System

Table 1. Member functions-Input

Input variables		
Trust on instructors	Linguistic variable	Range
Strongly disagree	SD	[0 0 1]
Disagree	D	[1 1.5 2]
Neutral	N	[2 2.5 3]
Agree	A	[2.5 3 4]
Strongly agree	SA	[3.5 4 5]
Perception on instructors	**Linguistic variable**	**Range**
Negative	NG	[0 0.5 1]
Neutral	N	[1 2 3]
Positive	P	[2.5 3.5 5]
Usefulness of instructors	**Linguistic variable**	**Range**

(continued)

Table 1. (*continued*)

Input variables		
Trust on instructors	Linguistic variable	Range
Strongly disagree	SD	[0 0 1]
Disagree	D	[1 1.5 2]
Neutral	N	[2 2.5 3]
Agree	A	[2.5 3 4]
Strongly agree	SA	[3.5 4 5]

Table 2. Member functions-Output

Output variable (end semester performance)		
Outcome	Linguistic variable	Range
Very low	VL	[0 0 1]
Low	L	[1 1.5 2]
Average	AVG	[2 2.5 3]
High	H	[2.5 3 4]
Very high	VH	[3.5 4 5]

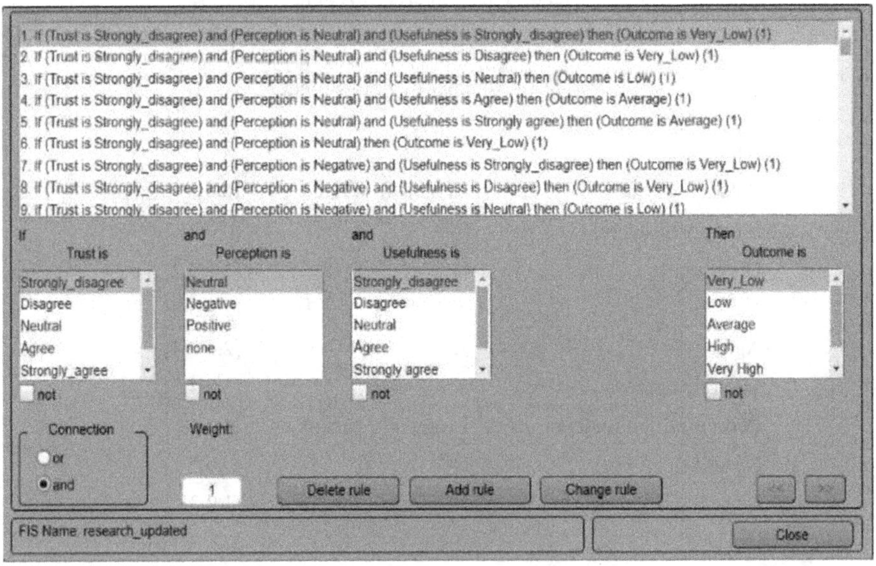

Fig. 9. Rules

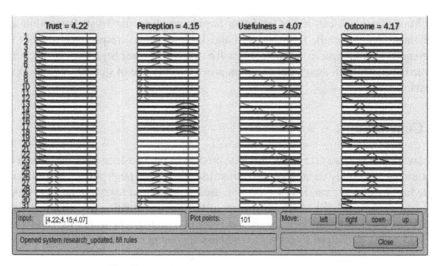

Fig. 10. Prediction for first set of input variables

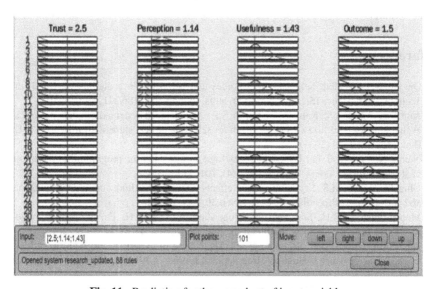

Fig. 11. Prediction for the second set of input variables

After analyzing the data collected the following rules have been framed as shown in Fig. 9. These rules were used in predicting data when a new set of values were given for the input variables. These rules will help us predict how the outcome will be with the three input variables.

Figure 10 predicts the outcome (end-semester results) when the value of trust, perception and usefulness is given. Here Trust = 4.22 (Strongly agree), Perception = 4.15 (Positive) and Usefulness = 4.07 (Strongly agree) and hence the outcome predicted is 4.17 which according to the linguistic variable means the outcome will be "Very high".

From Fig. 11, it can be inferred that the inputs given for Trust, Perception and Usefulness 2.5 (Neutral), 1.14 (Neutral) and 1.43 (Disagree) respectively predict the outcome as 1.5 which means the outcome will be low. Hence the instructors can take some corrective action from their side so as to improve the outcome of students' help-seeking behavior.

5 Conclusion

THis work introduces a fuzzy logic model to predict the performance outcome of students in examinations. Study variables namely trust, usefulness, and perception of help-seeking behavior of students from instructors were used as input to a fuzzy model. The model outcome shall be helpful to the instructors to foresee the situation and take necessary measures. When a student feels that he has less trust and finds the instructor less useful, the student can be helped by trying to establish a good connection with the instructor. Also, it can be inferred that the students prefer to seek academic help from the instructors in offline mode. When students feel comfortable with and trust their teachers, they are more likely to ask for assistance, which encourages interest in the subject and leads to greater results.

References

1. Qayyum, A.: Student help-seeking attitudes and behaviors in a digital era. Int. J. Educ. Technol. High. Educ. **15**(1), 1–16 (2018). https://doi.org/10.1186/s41239-018-0100-7
2. Ajoi, T.A., Gran, S.S., Kanyan, A., Lajim, S.F.: An enhanced systematic student performance evaluation based on fuzzy logic approach for selection of best student award. Asian J. Univ. Educ. **16**(4), 10–20 (2021)
3. Namli, N.A., Şenkal, O.: Using the fuzzy logic in assessing the programming performance of students. Int. J. Assess. Tools Educ. **5**(4), 701–712 (2018)
4. Ulug, M., Ozden, M.S., Eryilmaz, A.: The effects of teachers' attitudes on students' personality and performance. Procedia Soc. Behav. Sci. **30**, 738–742 (2011)
5. Mohd Adnan, M.R.H., Sarkheyli, A., Mohd Zain, A., Haron, H.: Fuzzy logic for modeling machining process: a review. Artificial Intelligence Review **43**(3), 345–379 (2015)
6. Khan, A.R., Amin, H.U., Rehman, Z.U.: Application of expert system with fuzzy logic in teachers 'performance evaluation'. International Journal of Advanced Computer Science and Applications **2**(2) (2011)
7. Ivanova, V., Zlatanov, B.: Implementation of fuzzy functions aimed at fairer grading of students' tests. Educ. Sci. **9**(3), 214 (2019)
8. Frasson, C., Chalfoun, P.: Managing learners affective states in intelligent tutoring systems. In: Advances in intelligent tutoring systems. Springer, Berlin, pp. 339–358 (2010)
9. Piad, K.C., Dumlao, M., Ballera, M.A., Ambat, S.C.: Predicting IT Employability Using Data Mining Techniques. In: 3rd International Conference on Digital Information Processing, Data Mining, and Wireless Communications (2016)
10. Jayasingh, B.B.: A Data Mining Approach to Inquiry Based Inductive Learning Practice in Engineering Education. In: IEEE sixth International Conference on Advanced Computing (2016)
11. Martín-Arbós, S., Castarlenas, E., Dueñas, J.M.: Help-seeking in an academic context: a systematic review. Sustainability **13**, 1–16 (2021)

12. Ho, I.M.K., Cheong, K.Y., Weldon, A.: Predicting student satisfaction of emergency remote learning in higher education during COVID-19 using machine learning techniques. PLoS ONE **16** (2021)

13. Ku, H.Y., Tseng, H.W., Akarasriworn, C.: Collaboration factors, teamwork satisfaction, and student attitudes toward online collaborative learning. Comput. Hum. Behav. **29**(3), 922–929 (2013)

14. Ho, I., Cheong, K.Y., Weldon, A.: Predicting student satisfaction of emergency remote learning in higher education during COVID-19 using machine learning techniques. PLoS ONE **16** (2021)

15. Dueñas, J.M, Camarero-Figuerola, M., Castarlenas, E.: Academic help-seeking attitudes, and their relationship with emotional variables. Sustainability **13**(11) (2021)

Smart Computing

Automatic Cotton Leaf Disease Classification and Detection by Convolutional Neural Network

Hirenkumar Kukadiya$^{(\boxtimes)}$ ⓘ and Divyakant Meva ⓘ

Marwadi University, Rajkot 360003, Gujarat, India
hirenkumar.kukadiya111474@marwadiuniversity.ac.in

Abstract. One of the main causes of low yield and the destruction of cotton plant growth is the attack of leaf disease. In any crops like cotton, groundnut, potato, tomato identification and detection of leaf diseases controlling the spread of an illness early on is essential, as is help to get the maximum crop production. For developing nations, it costs more to classify and identify cotton leaf disease through professional observation using only one's eyes. Therefore, offering software or application-based solutions for the aforementioned tasks will be more advantageous for farmers in order to boost agricultural production and develop their economies. This research presents a convolutional neural network approach based on deep learning that automatically classifies and distinguishes cotton leaf diseases. The existing lots of work has been done on leaf diseases that are commonly occurring in many crops, but in this work an effective and reliable method for identifying cotton leaf diseases was proposed. The suggested method successfully classifies and detects three important cotton leaf diseases, which are very difficult to control if not discovered at an early stage. The suggested model for identification and classification uses convolutional neural networks of cotton leaf diseases with training and testing accuracy accordingly 100% and 90%.

Keywords: Agriculture · Application · Cotton diseases detection · CNN classifier · Deep learning · Neural network

1 Introduction

State with the largest cotton production in India is Gujarat. The decrease in cotton productivity is cotton diseases. In a Gujarat state especially on the "Saurashtra Region" around 85–90% of diseases, including Bacterial blight and Alternaria leaf spot, mostly affect cotton plant leaves.

Several image processing ideas, including image filtering, image segmentation, and feature extraction, can be used to find illnesses on leaves. The three main types of diseases affecting the plant are bacterial disease, fungal disease, and viral disease. There are different stages of cotton to grow from land such as seedling, cotyledons, cotton bolls, mature cotton leaves. At any stage of cotton diseases can affect.

The most important commercial crops cultivated in India is cotton and it is also termed as "White Gold". The major use of cotton in India, used in textile industry. In the

S. Rajagopal et al. (Eds.): ASCIS 2022, CCIS 1759, pp. 247–266, 2022.
https://doi.org/10.1007/978-3-031-23092-9_20

Table 1. A list of the states in India that produce cotton by agro-ecological zone.

Zone	Name of states
Northern zone	Haryana, Punjab and Rajasthan
Central zone	Maharashtra, Gujarat and Madhya Pradesh
Southern zone	Andhra Pradesh, Telangana, Karnataka and Tamil Nadu

world, India is 2nd largest cotton consumer. Here is a list of Indian states that produce cotton (Table 1).

With proper management strategies such as fungicides, pesticides and chemical application s to control of diseases which interns improve quality. Agriculture is essential for increasing the gross domestic product of any country (GDP). By 2050, worlds need to increase food production by as estimated 70%. For agriculture product the first step in preventing crop loss and reduction in agricultural product quantity is the diagnosis of plant diseases. In the developing countries manually detection of plant diseases is very difficult. To increase agriculture productivity for farmers need fast and accurate plant diseases detection system.

The work exposed to automatic disease classification and detection on cotton leaves in the paper. One of the important agricultural industries that affects a country's economy is cotton. Here showing the details of National and Internationals details of cotton for Import, Export, Consumption and Production (Figs. 1, 2, 3, 4, 5 and 6).

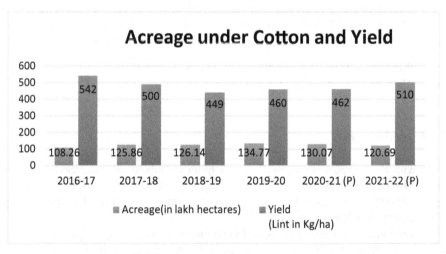

Fig. 1. Acreage under cotton and yield

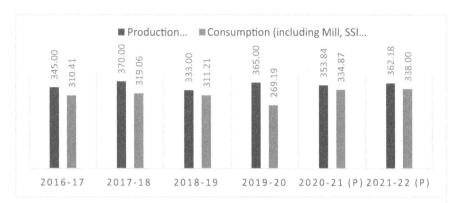

Fig. 2. Years of production and consumption of cotton

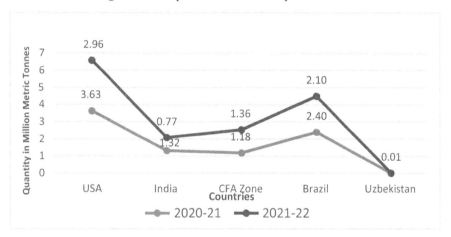

Fig. 3. Country-wise export of cotton

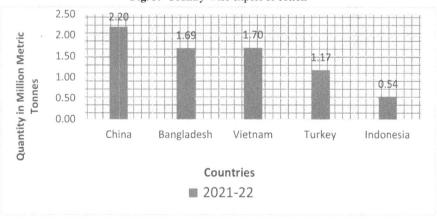

Fig. 4. Country-wise imports of cotton

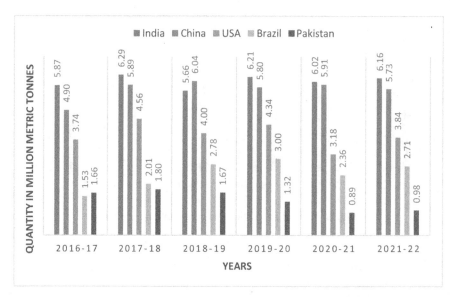

Fig. 5. Country-wise production of cotton

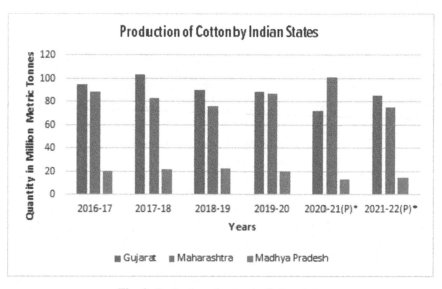

Fig. 6. Production of cotton by Indian state

2 Literature Review

1) (Brahimi et al. 2018) This paper is about diseases detection of plant and visualization of saliency map. In this paper author presented about deep learning based algorithm that is convolutional neural network using plant village dataset for diseases classification of plant. For this work classification accuracy of plant diseases was 99.76% [8].

2) (Nkemelu et al. 2018) This paper presented about plant seedlings classification. In this paper total 12 species with 4275 images were used. For classification of plants seedlings used traditional algorithms and convolutional neural network were used. For this paper CNN used with attention and OpenCV. CNN with attention has achieved accuracy 80.21% and CNN with OpenCV for background segmentation provided accuracy 92.60% [23].

3) (Bao et al. 2020) This paper discussed about plant species identification using leaf patterns using a convolutional neural network and a histogram of oriented gradient features space. In this paper for classification purpose used support vector machine algorithm (SVM) and for the sake of recognition convolutional neural network (CNN) algorithm was used. For this paper there was two types of dataset used one is Swedish public leaf and another is Flavia leaf dataset. For this work total 8180 images used and achieved accuracy of provided dataset was 94.17% [7].

4) (Rao and Kulkarni 2020) This paper discussed using For the detection and categorization of plant leaf diseases, use digital image processing. In this study, a MATLAB simulation tool was utilized to detect and categories plant leaf diseases and images taken from plant village dataset for analysis also provided accuracy more than 90% [27].

5) (Johannes et al. 2017) This paper discussed about using mobile capture device diagnosis of automatic plant diseases for wheat crop. In this paper there were three wheat disease analyses-septoria, rust and tan spot. Using more than 5 mobile devices this analysis was done and more than 3500 images used for diagnosis of plant diseases. In this paper for wheat diseases showing average accuracy between 88% to 81% [16].

6) (Gogul and Kumar 2017) This paper presented using transfer learning and convolutional neural networks (CNN) for flower species recognition system. In this paper images acquired using mobile phone. Machine learning classifiers like logistic regression or random forest are utilized for greater accuracy rates. For feature extraction using overfeat, Inception-V3 and Xception architectures used and for this three architectures provided accuracy 73.05%, 93.41% and 90.60% [12].

7) (Shobana 2020) The proposed research paper about classification of plants using machine learning algorithm. In this paper SVM and ANN algorithm was used. For classification of plant SVM provided accuracy 98.00% and ANN provided accuracy 92% also plant condition for classification was fresh and wilted [28].

8) (Tulshan n.d.) This paper presented using machine learning algorithm for diseases detection of plant leaf. For classification of plant leaf KNN algorithm was applied. Accuracy of proposed algorithm and its implementation has shown 98.56%. All of the experiments in this paper's classification phases, including pre-processing, image segmentation, extraction of features, and KNN classifiers, were carried out

using MATLAB tools. For Classification total 75 plants leaves sample collected. In this paper the work was done about different diseases like White flies, powdery mildew, downy mildew, and mosaic virus, leaf miner for exact diseases name for leaf diseases used KNN classifier [31].

9) (Ramesh and Vydeki 2018) This paper discussed about utilizing machine learning for rice blast disease detection and classification. For this work 300 images was used with two module training and testing. For blast infected images provide an accuracy of 99% and normal images provide an accuracy 100% during training phase. Also during testing phase provide an accuracy 90% and 86% for the disease and healthy images [26].

10) (Singh 2019) This paper discussed about image segmentation based on particle swarm optimization for diseases detection of sunflower. In this study classification of sunflower diseases is done using particle swarm optimization and classification accuracy of this algorithm is 98.00%. For this paper different image processing steps are applied also images taken from the digital camera for different types of leaves [30].

11) (Dyrmann et al. 2016) This paper discussed about deep convolutional neural network for classification of 22 plant species. For this work there were 10,413 images taken for experiments. The network provided accuracy of 86.2% for classification [11].

12) (Arnal Barbedo 2019) This paper presented for deep learning diseases identification of plant separate spots and lesions. Images for this study were taken with a variety of devices, including smartphones, small cameras, and DLSR cameras. And from 1 to 24 mega pixels of their resolutions range. For this paper experiments was run on GPU. Using transfer learning algorithm like GoogLeNet, CNN for severely diseased classification accuracy detected 85% [5].

13) (Ferentinos 2018) This paper discussed about plant diseases detection and diagnosis using deep learning models. In this paper total 87,848 images taken from public dataset. Images were divided into 58 distinct classes including healthy and diseased. For this paper deep learning based VGG convolutional neural network used. For this model achieved 99.53% of higher accuracy. For plant diseases detection and diagnosis used GPU to train the model [11] (Table 2).

3   List of Cotton Diseases

FOR farmers to recognize various diseases that affect crops and nutritional deficiencies in crops. There are several diseases affected on cotton leaves. There are primarily three types of diseases that affect cotton plant leaves, and they are as follows:

a) Fungal Disease: Leaf spot, Anthracnose
b) Viral Diseases: Leaf Roll, Leaf Curl, Leaf Crumple
c) Bacterial Diseases: Lint Degradation, Bacterial Blight, Crown Gall (Table 3).

Table 2. Summarizes numerous studies carried out to find diseases in plants

Application/Authors	Dataset			Model	Accuracy
	Name of crop	Dataset name	No of image		
(Brahimi et al. 2018)	14 species	Plant Village	55038	Backpropagation, CNN	99.76%
(Nkemelu et al. 2018)	12 species	Aarhus University Signal Processing group, in collaboration with University of Southern Denmark	4275	CNN with Open CV	92.60%
(Bao et al. 2020)	Plant species	Swedish and Flavia leaf data set	5825	CNN, SVM	95.6%, 88.7%
(Rao and Kulkarni 2020)	Sugar beet	Plant Village	54306	GLCM	91.74%
(Johannes et al. 2017)	36 different wheat varieties	Field conditions	3637	Naïve-Bayes	80%
(Gogul and Kumar 2017)	Flower species	FLOWERS17 dataset and FLOWERS102 dataset from the Visual Geometry group at University of Oxford	8189	CNN	97.5%
(Shobana 2020)	Wheat, rice	Plant Village	100	SVM, ANN	98%, 92%
(Tulshan n.d.)	Plant leaf	Real Field	225	SVM, KNN	97.6%, 98.56%
(Ramesh and Vydeki 2018)	Rice	Real Field	300	ANN	90%
(Singh 2019)	Sunflower leaf	Real Field	100	swarm optimization algorithm	98.0%
(Mohanty et al. 2016)	14 crop species	Plant Village	54306	CNN	99.35%

(continued)

Table 2. (*continued*)

Application/Authors	Dataset			Model	Accuracy
	Name of crop	Dataset name	No of image		
(Ferentinos 2018)		laboratory conditions images or field conditions images	87848	VGG AlexNetO WTBn	99.53% 99.49%
(Shrivastava and Pradhan 2021)	Rice	Indira Gandhi Agricultural University's agricultural field, Raipur, Chhattisgarh, India	619	SVM	94.68%

Table 3. List of cotton diseases and its symptoms.

No	Cotton disease name	Symptoms
1	Alternaria blight	– On plants, the disease's earliest symptoms are small, round or irregularly shaped, dark-brown spots that range in diameter from 0.5 to 10 mm and have concentric rings on their upper surfaces – In advance stage, the spots dry with grey centre which cracks and some of them drop down giving target board appearance. The spots get coalesced and formed a big patch and such leaves look like burnt or blighted, which results in defoliation. Few spots are also noticed on the petiole, stem, and bolls
2	Bacterial Blight Leaf	– The initial symptoms are round to elongate lesions on cotyledons (seedling phase), initially deep green and water-soaked and laterdrying to brown – The foliar phase of the bacterial blight (Angular leaf spot and vein blight phase, As the older spots dry, their colour darkens to brown – Later the infection also extends to stem causing elongated grayish to black lesions (Black armphase)

(*continued*)

Table 3. (*continued*)

No	Cotton disease name	Symptoms
3	Cotton Leaf curl disease (CLCuD)	– The CLCuD-affected cotton plants show characteristic symptoms of thickening and darkening of veins when seen against sunlight called small vein thickening type (SVT) followed by distinct upward/downward curling – In addition, the damaged plants' leaves have thicker dark green veins as opposed to the translucent veins that healthy plants have – The whitefly, Bemisia tabaci, a vector of the virus, spreads the disease
4	Grey mildew	– The disease appears on the older leaves usually when the plants are reaching maturity – As the infection progresses leaves become yellowish-brown and fall off prematurely
5	Leaf Rust	– On both leaf surfaces, uredia in a yellowish-brown colour develops – On the leaf's upper surface, primary uredia are deeply embedded in the tissues, while secondary uredia are shallowly seated on the bottom surface – Rust disease caused losses that could have been prevented that were assessed to be 21.7% in Bunny Bt and 34.05% in RCH 2 BG II
6	Myrothecium leaf spot	– Myrothecium leaf spot became an important problem of Madhya Pradesh. Myrothecium disease produces light brown small, circular spots of 2–10 mm diameter with dark brown to purple margins – In severe cases, the lesion/spots coalesce to form large patches. Later the bigger spots may show shot hole and infected leaves may fall off – In favourable weather conditions, conspicuous rings of pinhead size and black sporodochia can be seen on the spots

(*continued*)

Table 3. (*continued*)

No	Cotton disease name	Symptoms
7	Root rot	– A yellow spot first appears on the lowest portion of the stem and then turns black, causing the seedlings to dry out – The rotting of secondary roots makes it simple to pluck out seedlings and plants that have been impacted – Most root tips have a discoloured, yellow, and sticky appearance – When the conditions are right, it's possible to discern tiny black dots that resemble sclerotia on the wood beneath the bark and in the spaces between the shredded bands of bark – The most similar symptom is abrupt wilting of plants with leaves still on them, followed by shredding of bark and dry or wet brown rot of the bottom stem
8	Red Leaf Spot Disease	Nitrogen concentration in leaves below 2% is a sign of nutritional insufficiency. Soil that has been flooded. The production of the anthocynin pigment in the leaf is caused by a drop in the minimum temperature below 150C

Table 4. State wise major cotton diseases of cotton in India.

Diseases name	States name of India
Alternaria Leaf Spot	Maharashtra, Gujarat, Karnataka
Anthracnose	South zone (Minor)
Bacterial Blight	Maharashtra, Gujarat, Karnataka
Cotton Leaf Curl	North Zone (Potential threat)
Cercospora Leaf Spots	Andhra Pradesh (Minor)
Grey Mildew	Central & South zone (Emerging)
Helminthosporium Leaf Spot	Andhra Pradesh (Minor)
Leaf Rust	Karnataka, Andhra Pradesh (Emerging)
Myrothecium Leaf Spot	Madhya Pradesh
Tobacco Streak Virus	Andhra Pradesh (Emerging)
Verticillium Wilt	Tamil Nadu, Karnataka

In India, for Cotton crop different diseases have been reported. In this table shown state wise major cotton diseases of cotton in India (Table 4).

In this proposed work on three diseases of cotton leaf that is Alternaria Blight, Bacterial Blight and Red Leaf Spot. Here showing the images with disease name (Fig. 7).

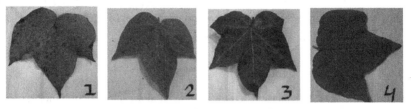

Fig. 7. 1) Cotton_Alternaria_Blight, 2) Cotton_Bacterial_Blight, 3) Cotton_Red_Leaf_Spot, 4) Cotton_Healthy_Leaves

Below figure showing the different diseases name images (Fig. 8).

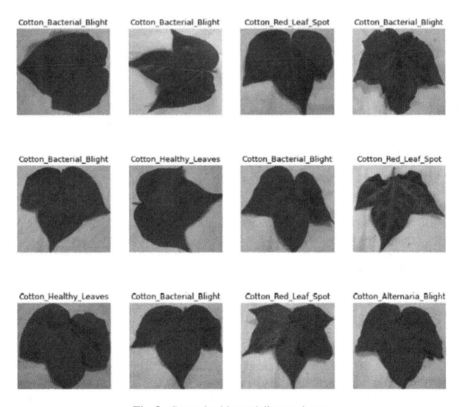

Fig. 8. Cotton healthy and diseases leaves

4 Materials and Methods

THE Proposed framework of cotton diseases classification and detection. In this proposed work, the real field images dataset used and modifications of images using data augmentation is presented, local transformation are performed using pre-trained model to the dataset. CNN based different transfer learning pre-trained model used for proposed system with real field images dataset. Then proposed model of CNN architecture along the hyper parameter proposed for training stages.

4.1 Dataset and Data Augmentation

In this proposed work, the dataset used for cotton leaf disease prediction model consists of 402 images consisting 4 different class of both healthy and diseased images. Images captured from real field using Mi 6A Mobile Device. Trained this model to detect disease of cotton plant. The resolution of images of 224 × 224 pixels. Each class has anywhere from 30 to 120 images. For more details dataset of cotton leaves are presented below (Table 5).

Table 5. Dataset used for classification

Crop name	Class	No of images
Cotton	Alternaria_Blight	50
	Bacterial_Blight	72
		45
	Red_Leaf_Spot	45
	Healthy_Leaves	235
Total		**402**

This vertical and horizontal flip, rotations in four different angles, and the generation of their trans-formations and responses were made to increase the data in order to avoid overfitting on the proposed training model and obtain more images from the original cotton leaf class from the real field dataset. 80% of the dataset was used for training, 10% for validation, and 10% for testing.

4.2 CNN Pre-trained Architectures

Six architectures were chosen in this study to carry out transfer learning: VGG16, VGG19, ResNet50, ResNet152, InceptionV3, DenseNet121. Hyper parameter were specified to carry out the training, as stated in the Table 6. The six models mentioned above VGG16, VGG19, ResNet50, ResNet152, InceptionV3, DenseNet121 were trained using transfer learning with 224 × 224 pixel input resolution. Weight selected for initialization from ImageNet training models. The global average pooling layer and a softmax layer with four classes are coupled to the feature map that was obtained at the end of the

CNN. All of the CNN layers were designated as trainable for deep learning in Transfer Learning.

4.3 Classification by Proposed CNN

In this proposed work, trained the neural network to represent a system using available data that includes particular matching of the system's input and outputs. A development of standard artificial neural networks that are CNN primarily utilized for applications involving repeated patterns in various areas of modeling space such as image recognition.

In this work six pre-trained CNN architecture used and these are compared with proposed CNN model that give more accurate result as compared to pre-trained model. Proposed CNN model build using tensorflow and keras framework. Here showing the work flow of proposed CNN model (Fig. 9).

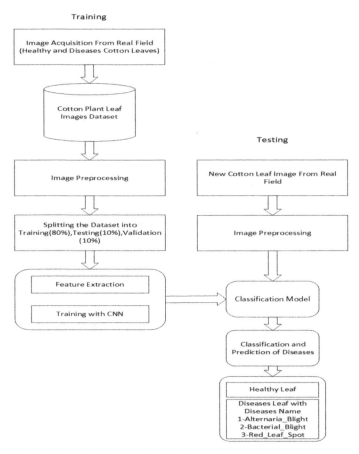

Fig. 9. Cotton leaf disease classification and recognition block diagram.

5 Results and Discussions of Research

In the experiments for the proposed study, there were primarily two sections. Pretrained models were utilized in the first half, and a CNN model was suggested in the second.

5.1 Pre-trained Model

Six pre-trained algorithms were utilized in this work. These algorithms are VGG16, VGG19, ResNet50, ResNet152, InceptionV3 and DenseNet121.

In above all the pre-trained algorithm used different parameters like learning rate, batch size, no of epoch, optimizer and save the best model functionality. Image size of cotton leaf 224 × 224 pixels used for all the algorithms. In this work all the experiments done using Google colaboratory which is provided by google with inbuilt GPU support.

Table 6. Showing the result and performance analysis of pre-trained model.

Parameters	VGG 16	VGG 19	ResNet 50	ResNet 152V2	Inception V3	DenseNet 121
Training Accuracy	0.83	0.84	0.53	0.62	0.58	0.87
Training Loss	0.46	0.43	1.05	0.99	0.98	0.34
Validation Accuracy	0.57	0.60	0.17	0.21	0.21	0.80
Validation Loss	1.01	1.31	1.66	9.72	8.58	0.79
Testing Accuracy	0.64	0.60	0.53	0.21	0.21	0.80
Testing Loss	0.92	1.31	1.22	16.67	19.16	0.79

For the cotton leaf diseases each model's accuracy and loss in figures, the performance of each model is represented graphically (Figs. 10, 11, 12, 13, 14 and 15).

Training and experimentation with accuracy and loss of deep learning architecture are conducted for the proposed CNN model, as shown specifically in the figure (Table 7 and Figs. 16, 17).

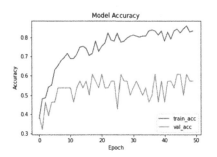
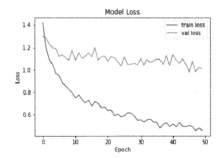

Fig. 10. Accuracy and loss of VGG16

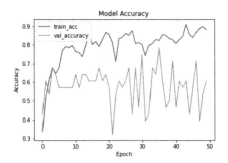
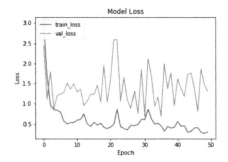

Fig. 11. Accuracy and loss of VGG19

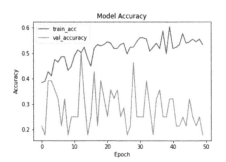
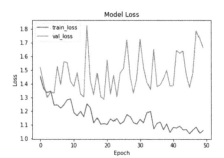

Fig. 12. Accuracy and loss of Resnet50

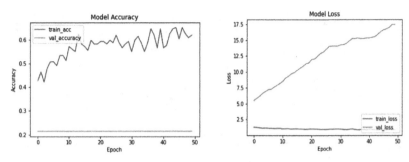

Fig. 13. Accuracy and loss of Resnet152V2

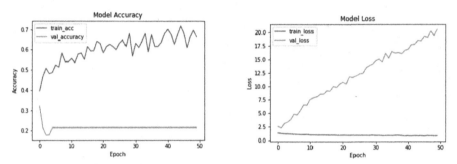

Fig. 14. The accuracy and loss of InceptionV3

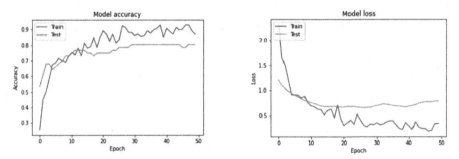

Fig. 15. Loss and accuracy for DenseNet121

Table 7. Result and performance analysis using proposed CNN model

Parameters	Proposed CNN model
Training Accuracy	1.0000
Training Loss	2.6086e−06
validation Accuracy	1.0000
Validation Loss	3.6051e−04
Testing Accuracy	0.9688
Testing Loss	0.3116
Training_Time	1 s 108 ms/step
Testing_Time	1 s 32 ms/step
Epoch	10

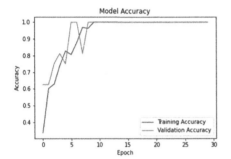
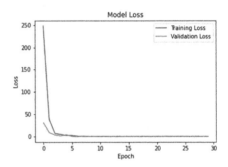

Fig. 16. Proposed model accuracy and loss

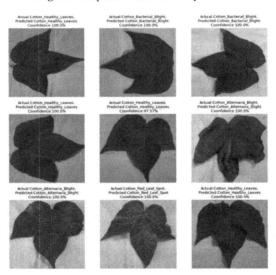

Fig. 17. Detection of diseases leaf with actual label, predicted label and confidence

6   Conclusion

IN this paper, Evaluation and comparison of six popular pre-trained models and proposed CNN model were presented with accuracy and its loss. This comparison was made with real field cotton leaf images dataset to perform an analysis.

The proposed model was implemented in TensorFlow and Keras Framewok with deep learning convolutional neural network. In this proposed convolutional neural network model given more accurate result as compared to pre-trained models.

The proposed model offers an accurate method for detecting cotton leaf diseases, which is useful for farmers and other agricultural users. In future, use more number of cotton leaf images from real field for work with different algorithms.

Declaration of Competing Interest.   The authors affirmed that they have no known financial or personal interests that would have appeared to have an impact on the work reported in this paper.

References

1. Adedoja, A., Owolawi, P.A., Mapayi, T.: Deep learning based on NASNet for plant disease recognition using leave images. In: IcABCD 2019 - 2nd International Conference on Advances in Big Data, Computing and Data Communication Systems, pp. 1–5 (2019). https://doi.org/10.1109/ICABCD.2019.8851029
2. Afifi, A., Alhumam, A., Abdelwahab, A.: Convolutional neural network for automatic identification of plant diseases with limited data. Plants **10**(1), 1–16 (2021). https://doi.org/10.3390/plants10010028
3. Ahmed, K., Shahidi, T.R., Irfanul Alam, S.M., Momen, S.: Rice leaf disease detection using machine learning techniques. In: 2019 International Conference on Sustainable Technologies for Industry 4.0, STI 2019, pp. 1–5, December 2019. https://doi.org/10.1109/STI47673.2019.9068096
4. Hussain, A., Ahmad, M., Mughal, I.A., Haider, A.: Automatic disease detection in wheat crop using convolution neural network. In: The 4th International Conference on Next Generation Computing, pp. 7–10 (2011). https://www.researchgate.net/profile/Altaf-Hussain-40/publication/343206552_Automatic_Disease_Detection_in_Wheat_Crop_using_Convolution_Neural_Network/links/5f1be49b299bf1720d627471/Automatic-Disease-Detection-in-Wheat-Crop-using-Convolution-Neural-Networr
5. Arnal Barbedo, J.G.: Plant disease identification from individual lesions and spots using deep learning. Biosys. Eng. **180**(2016), 96–107 (2019). https://doi.org/10.1016/j.biosystemseng.2019.02.002
6. Ashwinkumar, S., Rajagopal, S., Manimaran, V., Jegajothi, B.: Automated plant leaf disease detection and classification using optimal MobileNet based convolutional neural networks. Mater. Today: Proc. **51**(xxxx), 480–487 (2021). https://doi.org/10.1016/j.matpr.2021.05.584
7. Bao, T.Q., Kiet, N.T.T., Dinh, T.Q., Hiep, H.X.: Plant species identification from leaf patterns using histogram of oriented gradients feature space and convolution neural networks. J. Inf. Telecommu. 4(2), 140–150 (2020). https://doi.org/10.1080/24751839.2019.1666625
8. Brahimi, M., Arsenovic, M., Laraba, S., Sladojevic, S., Boukhalfa, K., Moussaoui, A.: Deep learning for plant diseases: detection and saliency map visualisation. In: Zhou, J., Chen, F. (eds.) Human and Machine Learning. HIS, pp. 93–117. Springer, Cham (2018). https://doi.org/10.1007/978-3-319-90403-0_6

9. Chen, J.W., Lin, W.J., Cheng, H.J., Hung, C.L., Lin, C.Y., Chen, S.P.: A smartphone-based application for scale pest detection using multiple-object detection methods. Electronics **10**(4), 1–14 (2021). https://doi.org/10.3390/electronics10040372

10. Dyrmann, M., Karstoft, H., Midtiby, H.S.: Plant species classification using deep convolutional neural network. Biosys. Eng. **151**(2005), 72–80 (2016). https://doi.org/10.1016/j.bio systemseng.2016.08.024

11. Ferentinos, K.P.: Deep learning models for plant disease detection and diagnosis. Comput. Electron. Agric. **145**, 311–318 (2018). https://doi.org/10.1016/j.compag.2018.01.009

12. Gogul, I., Kumar, V.S.: Flower species recognition system using convolution neural networks and transfer learning. In: 2017 4th International Conference on Signal Processing, Communication and Networking, ICSCN 2017, pp. 1–6 (2017). https://doi.org/10.1109/ICSCN.2017.8085675

13. Gonzalez-Huitron, V., León-Borges, J.A., Rodriguez-Mata, A.E., Amabilis-Sosa, L.E., Ramírez-Pereda, B., Rodriguez, H.: Disease detection in tomato leaves via CNN with lightweight architectures implemented in Raspberry Pi 4. Comput. Electron. Agric. **181** (2021). https://doi.org/10.1016/j.compag.2020.105951

14. Hang, J., Zhang, D., Chen, P., Zhang, J., Wang, B.: Classification of plant leaf diseases based on improved convolutional neural network. Sensors **19**(19), 1–14 (2019). https://doi.org/10.3390/s19194161

15. Jayswal, H.S., Chaudhari, J.P.: Plant leaf disease detection and classification using conventional machine learning and deep learning. Jayswal Chaudhari Int. J. Emerg. Technol. **11**(3), 1094–1102. (2020). www.researchtrend.net

16. Johannes, A., et al.: Automatic plant disease diagnosis using mobile capture devices, applied on a wheat use case. Comput. Electron. Agric. **138**, 200–209 (2017). https://doi.org/10.1016/j.compag.2017.04.013

17. Karthik, R., Hariharan, M., Anand, S., Mathikshara, P., Johnson, A., Menaka, R.: Attention embedded residual CNN for disease detection in tomato leaves. Appl. Soft Comput. J. **86** (2020). https://doi.org/10.1016/j.asoc.2019.105933

18. Kim, B., Han, Y. K., Park, J. H., Lee, J.: Improved vision-based detection of strawberry diseases using a deep neural network. Front. Plant Sci. **11**, 1–14 (2021). https://doi.org/10.3389/fpls.2020.559172

19. Krishnaswamy Rangarajan, A., Purushothaman, R.: Disease classification in eggplant using pre-trained VGG16 and MSVM. Sci. Rep. **10**(1), 1–11 (2020). https://doi.org/10.1038/s41598-020-59108-x

20. Kumar, M., Hazra, T., Tripathy, S.S.: Wheat leaf disease detection using image processing. Iv (n.d.)

21. Li, L., Zhang, S., Wang, B.: Plant disease detection and classification by deep learning - a review. IEEE Access **9**, 56683–56698) (2021). https://doi.org/10.1109/ACCESS.2021.3069646

22. Mohanty, S.P., Hughes, D.P., Salathé, M.: Using deep learning for image-based plant disease detection. Front. Plant Sci. **7**, 1–10 (2016). https://doi.org/10.3389/fpls.2016.01419

23. Nkemelu, D.K., Omeiza, D., Lubalo, N.: Deep convolutional neural network for plant seedlings classification (2018). http://arxiv.org/abs/1811.08404

24. Picon, A., et al.: Deep convolutional neural networks for mobile capture device-based crop disease classification in the wild. Comput. Electron. Agric. **161**, 280–290 (2019). https://doi.org/10.1016/j.compag.2018.04.002

25. Purbasari, I.Y., Rahmat, B., Putra PN, C.S.: Detection of rice plant diseases using convolutional neural network. IOP Conf. Ser. Mater. Sci. Eng. **1125**(1), 012021 (2021). https://doi.org/10.1088/1757-899x/1125/1/012021

26. Ramesh, S., Vydeki, D.: Rice blast disease detection and classification using machine learning algorithm. In: Proceedings - 2nd International Conference on Micro-Electronics and Telecommunication Engineering, ICMETE 2018, pp 255–259 (2018). https://doi.org/10.1109/ICMETE.2018.00063

27. Rao, A., Kulkarni, S.B.: A hybrid approach for plant leaf disease detection and classification using digital image processing methods. Int. J. Electr. Eng. Educ. (2020). https://doi.org/10.1177/0020720920953126

28. Shobana, K.B.: 3Odqwv &Odvvlilfdwlrq 8Vlqj 0Dfklqh /Hduqlqj $Ojrulwkp, 96–100 (2020)

29. Shrivastava, V.K., Pradhan, M.K.: Rice plant disease classification using color features: a machine learning paradigm. J. Plant Pathol. **103**(1), 17–26 (2021). https://doi.org/10.1007/s42161-020-00683-3

30. Singh, V.: Sunflower leaf diseases detection using image segmentation based on particle swarm optimization. Artif. Intell. Agric. **3**, 62–68 (2019). https://doi.org/10.1016/j.aiia.2019.09.002

31. Tulshan, A.S.: Plant leaf disease detection using machine learning (n.d.)

32. Warne, P.P., Ganorkar, S.R.: Detection of diseases on cotton leaves using K-mean clustering method. Int. Res. J. Eng. Technol. (IRJET) **2**(4), 425–431 (2015)

Analytical Review and Study on Emotion Recognition Strategies Using Multimodal Signals

Jaykumar M. Vala[1][✉] and Udesang K. Jaliya[2]

[1] Computer/IT Engineering, Gujarat Technological University, Ahmedabad, India
jayvala1629@gmail.com
[2] Department of Computer Engineering, Birla Vishvakarma Mahavidyalaya Engineering College, Gujarat Technological University, Ahmedabad, India

Abstract. Emotion is very important in the field of decision-making, human recognition, and the social intercourse. Multimodal emotion recognition is the promising research area of computing as well as sentiment analysis. Here, the information is carried out by the signals with various natures for making the emotion recognition systems accurately. Nowadays, the several robust emotion recognitions were developed for handling various languages and cultures. Hence, this has been complex because of potential applicability of the emotion recognizers over wide range of various scenarios. This work present survey of 50 papers based on emotion recognition strategies. In addition, thorough investigation is done based on the year of publication, adapted methodology, implementation tool, employed datasets, evaluation metrics, and values of evaluation metrics. On the other hand, the analysis of the methods with respect to the merits and demerits of the methods are presented. Finally, the issues of existing methods considering conventional emotion recognition strategies are elaborated to obtain improved contribution in devising significant emotion recognition strategy. Moreover, the probable future research directions in attaining efficient emotion recognition are elaborated.

Keywords: Emotion recognition · Multimodal signals · Deep learning · Fusion-based techniques · Classification accuracy

1 Introduction

Emotion is the physiological as well as mental state that results of various senses, and the thoughts [1]. Normally, positive emotions, like excitement, and satisfaction, whereas negative emotions, such as wrath and depression. However, the negative and positive emotions are containing visible influence on the individuals' behaviours. Emotion recognition is the important factor, which is applied in the field of effective computing [1, 14]. In order to obtain the effective environment for the man–machine interactions, the researchers have utilized several information that signifies the emotion [2]. Thus, the changes of people emotions may cause psychological, behavioural, and the physical changes. Posture, facial expression, physiological, and the voice signals may express some emotions independently [5–8]. Moreover, the emotional information is manifested

S. Rajagopal et al. (Eds.): ASCIS 2022, CCIS 1759, pp. 267–285, 2022.
https://doi.org/10.1007/978-3-031-23092-9_21

while the people communicating with the others. Presently, some of the researchers started their study on emotion recognition based on multimodal signals, but still the lack of key features and feature redundancy issues of multimodal fusion have to resolved [42].

The valence and the arousal space are the commonly employed dimensional space for the emotion recognition that defines the emotions based on non-activation or activation and negativeness or positiveness of the emotional state [7]. However, the dimension of the signals is broadly employed to describe the emotions based on machine learning techniques [7]. Regression and classification methods are studied well in the previous research works where valence or arousal space is utilized to allow the basic emotions [5]. However, some emotions are overlapped, and common emotional states are discriminated well based on classification [21]. In the recent years, several Deep Neural Networks (DNNs) are introduced in the affective computing and its results yield the better performance when compared to shallow techniques [13]. In addition, several multimodal architectures are also designed in order to leverage the two modality advantages, which is concluded to two categories as coordinate and joint [48].

The primary intention is to offer comprehensive survey of different emotion recognition strategies considering multimodal signals. Based on emotion categorization, the existing schemes are partitioned into deep learning, multimodal system, and fusion and so on. This survey considers classical techniques based on emotion recognition for the analysis. The survey is made by considering the publication year, employed methodology, performance measures, datasets utilized and implementation tool. Moreover, the performance evaluation measures are considered for evaluating the performance of the suggested emotion recognition methods. The conventional methods are classified into distinct approaches, and then, the survey is carried out for the exploitation of problems. Thus, it is considered as an inspiration for the future extension of effectual emotion recognition.

This article is arranged as follows: Sect. 2 elaborates survey of emotion recognition approaches and Sect. 3 shows the issues faced by conventional techniques. Section 4 discussed the analysis of techniques with respect to performance metrics, toolset, year of publication, and concludes the paper in Sect. 5.

2 Literature Survey

The review of numerous emotion recognition strategies is described in this section. Figure 1 depicts the classification of distinctive emotion recognition techniques. The techniques based on emotion recognition strategies are broadly categorized into four strategies, namely Deep learning, machine learning, fusion, and multimodal system. In addition, the deep learning-based techniques are categorized into Deep LSTM, NN, CNN, and DBN-based techniques, Auto encoder-based techniques. The brief illustration of the following techniques is given below:

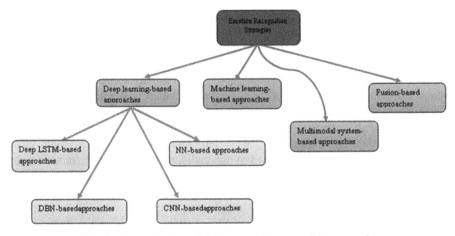

Fig. 1. Categorization of distinct emotion recognition strategies

2.1 Classification of Emotion Recognition Strategies

The research works considering various techniques utilized for emotion recognition are deliberated as follows,

2.1.1 Deep Learning Approaches

In this subsection, the deep learning approaches employed for emotion recognition are discussed below. Here, the deep learning approaches are further categorized into Deep LSTM, DBN, NN, auto encoder, and CNN approaches.

a) *Deep LSTM-based approaches*

The analysis of methods based on Deep LSTM for recognizing the emotion effectively using multimodal signal is deliberated below. Shizhe Chen *et al.* [2] developed multi-task strategy and temporal model for emotion recognition. Here, various deep learned and hand-crafted features were fused from several modalities, such as visual, textual, and acoustic modalities along with interlocutor influence was included for acoustic features. Then, the effectiveness of the temporal model, like LSTM-Recurrent Neural Network (RNN) and non-temporal model, which includes SVR was computed engineering to enhance the performance of the recognition system. Finally, the multi-task learning was introduced with numerous emotion dimensions for the collaborative prediction. Martin Wollmer *et al.* [5] presented context-sensitive method for recognizing the emotion using feature-level fusion of visual and acoustic cues. In addition, the bidirectional LSTM (BLSTM) networks were introduced to model the emotion evolution within the conversation. Moreover, the dimensional emotional labels were recognized for classifying both non-prototypical and prototypical emotional expressions in huge audio-visual dataset. Tengfei Song *et al.* [8] modelled Multi-Modal Physiological Emotion Database (MPED) for collecting Galvanic Skin Response (GSR), Electroencephalogram (EEG), respiration (RSP), and the Electrocardiogram (ECG) signal. These signals were recorded synchronously to describe six discrete emotions and the neutral emotion. Moreover, K Nearest Neighbors (KNN) as well as Support Vector Machine (SVM) classifiers were utilized for recognizing various emotions. In addition, the Attention-LSTM (A-LSTM) was introduced to boost the useful sequences and extracts more appropriate features effectively. Consequently, the correlations among EEG signals and participants' ratings were addressed. Guangxia Xu et al. [15] developed multimodal emotional classification approach for capturing users emotions in the social networks. Here, the textual, visual, and the audio information were extracted from the video. In addition, the hybrid model, named 3D Convolutional-Long Short-Term Memory (3DCLS) was employed to classify the text-enabled emotions. At last, the audio, text, and the video models were integrated for generating the emotional classification outputs. Jiaxin Ma et al. [43] developed multimodal residual LSTM (MMResLSTM) network for identifying the emotion. This approach was utilized to share the weights in every layer of LSTM for learning correlation among other physiological and EEG signals. In addition, the spatial paths were given by the residual network, whereas the temporal paths were provided using LSTM to learn the high-level features.

b) *DBN-based approaches*

The analysis of methods based on DBN practiced for emotion recognition using multimodal signals effectively is illustrated below. Dung Nguyen et al. [12] developed an approach for emotion recognition from various sources, like pose, facial expression, and the voice. Initially, features extraction was performed through cascading DBNs and 3-dimensional convolution neural networks (C3Ds) for modelling the temporal and spatial information. In addition, the feature-level fusion method was established using bilinear pooling theory for integrating audio and visual feature vectors. This fusion approach was utilized to allow component vectors that interacts each other effectively that results in in capturing intrinsic and complex associations expressively among component modalities. Wang Zhongmin et al. [42] employed deep learning approaches for fusing individual modalities to optimize psychophysiological features from multiple psychophysiological signal features. In addition, the bimodal DBN (BDBN) was established to represent the visual features, whereas other BDBN focused with high multimodal features obtained from two modalities. Hiranmayi Ranganathan et al. [35] developed DBN for the multimodal emotion recognition using emoFBVP dataset. Here, the multimodal signals, such as body gesture, face, physiological, and voice recordings were considered to find the emotion expressions. In addition, the database containing video and audio sequences of the actors by considering three various expression intensities with the skeletal tracking, and related physiological data. Then, the DBN models were described for generating multimodal features in the unsupervised way.

c) *NN-based approaches*

The research papers based on the NN approaches for emotion recognition using multimodal signals are discussed below: Panagiotis Tzirakis et al. [4] developed deep NN for end to end multimodal recognition. In addition, CNN was introduced for extracting the speech features, whereas the deep residual network was employed for visual modality.

Moreover, by considering the importance for extracting the features, the machine learning approach was required for modelling the context. However, the LSTM networks was utilized for solving the optimization issues. Han Zhiyan *et al.* [6] presented an multimodal emotion recognition method by considering facial expression and speech signal as the input. Initially, the feature of speech signal and facial expression was fused together based on back sampling algorithm to obtain sample sets. Then, BP neural network (BPNN) was introduced for the classification. Consequently, the differences among two classifiers were computed on the basis of double error difference selection method. At last, the majority voting rule was employed for getting the final recognition output. Eesung Kimy and Jong Won Shin [29] developed emotion recognition approach, which integrates the lexical and acoustic features for predicting emotion with the consideration of affect salient information. Here, the segment-level acoustic features were extracted using DNN, and then the utterance-level features were derived based on statistical functionals. In addition, the word-level lexical features were extracted using word2vec and lexicon-enabled dimensions. Consequently, the utterance-level lexical features were established on the basis of suitable weighting scheme. Finally, the lexical and acoustic features were interconnected using utterance level classification DNN for discriminating emotional states.

d) *Auto encoder-based approaches*

The analysis of methods based on auto encoder for finding the emotion using multimodal signals is deliberated below. Wei Liu *et al.* [1] developed an approach based on deep learning for emotion recognition. The steps followed in developed model were feature selection, supervised training, and the testing process. Initially, feature selection was performed based on Bimodal Deep Auto encoder (BDAE) for training purpose. Then, the linear SVM was employed for high-level feature extraction. At last, in testing phase, recognition results were obtained. Zhong Yin *et al.* [3] developed Multiple fusion layer-enabled Ensemble classifier of the Stacked Auto encoder (MESAE) in order to recognize the emotions. However, the SAE containing three hidden layers for filtering noise. In addition, the deep model was employed for achieving SAE ensembles. Consequently, the physiological features were partitioned to various subsets based on several feature extraction techniques where every subset are encoded based on SAE. After that, the derived SAE abstractions were integrated with physiological modality for creating encodings, which was then subjected to the three-layer adjacent-graph-driven network for the fusion. Finally, the fused features were utilized for recognizing the valence states or binary arousal. Jian Zhou *et al.* [14] developed convolutional auto-encoder (CAE) approach for multimodal emotion recognition. Initially, the fusion features of the multitype external physiological (EP) and multichannel EEG signal were obtained using trained encoder of CSE. Consequently, the obtained fused features were forwarded to trained Fully Connected Neural Networks (FCNNs) classifier for obtaining final emotion recognition outputs.

e) *CNN-based approaches*

This section describes the CNN-based approaches in emotion recognition collected from various existing research papers. Haiping Huang *et al.* [9] developed Ensemble Convolutional Neural Network (ECNN) model for emotion recognition. This approach was utilized to correlate among peripheral physiological signals and multi-channel EEG signals for improving the accuracy of emotion recognition. Initially, five convolution networks were introduced, and the plurality voting strategy was devised for designing ensemble model. Finally, this method classifies into four emotions. Tuan-Linh Nguyen *et al.* [17] presented convolutional neuro-fuzzy network for recognizing video clips emotions. This framework was the combination of fuzzy logic domain and CNN for extracting the features from text, audio, and visual modalities. Then, extracted feature sets was distinguished with CNN based on t-distributed Stochastic Neighbor Embedding. Thus, this approach generates the new rules for classifying the emotions. Min Seop Lee *et al.* [23] developed an emotion recognition approach using Photoplethysmogram (PPG) and Electromyogram (EMG) signals. Here, the arousal and valence were subdivided into four levels for classifying detailed emotions in which the previous methods partitioning the emotions into two levels. In addition, the CNN architecture was introduced to extract the signal features, and then classification was done to categorize the arousal and valence. Based on the EMG and PPG input signal, the segmentation was done and concatenated them to segment the signals. Dung Nguyen *et al.* [38] presented an approach based on C3Ds for modelling the information of spatio-temporal. Here, the multimodal DBNs was cascaded with spatio-temporal information for representing video and audio streams. In addition, the eNTERFACE multimodal emotion dataset was utilized for evaluating the performance of multimodal emotion recognition. Andrea K. Perez *et al.* [47] employed an approach for multimodal signals identification to recognize four human emotions, like anger, happiness, neutrality, and surprise in human robot interaction. Additionally, the multiclass classifier was introduced, which was performed using two uni-modal classifiers. Here, one classifier was utilized for processing input data from video signal, whereas other uses the audio. Moreover, the human emotions were detected on the basis of CNN using video data. Gaoyuan He *et al.* [49] developed multimodal emotion recognition system from three modalities. Initially, the residual network architecture was introduced in CNN for improving the performance of facial expression recognition. After that, the selection of video frames was done for tuning pre-trained model. Then, the emotion recognition was carried out based on SVM for predicting emotion labels. Consequently, the feature extraction was done, and then score level fusion was employed for combining multimodal information.

2.1.2 Machine Learning-Based Approaches

In this subsection, the machine learning approaches employed for emotion recognition are discussed below. Gyanendra K. Verma, and Uma Shanker Tiwary [13] presented Daubechies Wavelet Transform for detecting the emotions from the physiological signals. Here, thirteen emotions were recognized accurately through facial expression. Moreover, continuous 3D emotion approach was introduced to fuse the arousal, dominance, and valence primitives. In addition, the clustering framework was established to group the thirteen emotions to five clusters, and then the appropriate clusters were selected using Euclidean distance between several emotions in valence, dominance, arousal space. Kah Phooi Seng *et al.* [18] designed audio-visual emotion recognition system for improving recognition efficacy in video and audio paths. The visual path was designed based on Least-Square Linear Discriminant Analysis (LSLDA) and Bidirectional Principal Component Analysis (BDPCA) for reducing the dimensions and discriminating class. Then, the extracted visual features were forwarded to Optimized Kernel-Laplacian Radial Basis Function (OKL-RBF) neural classifier for classification. On other hand, the audio path was modelled based on spectral features and input prosodic features, and then the audio feature level fusion was done for determining emotion in audio signal. Finally, the output obtained from audio and visual modules were fused to get the final output. Rok Gajsek *et al.* [22] designed the multi-modal emotion recognition system to classify emotions. For audio sub-system, the cepstrum, spectral, and prosodic, features were chosen to form the feature vector, and then the SVM classifier was employed for producing scores for every emotional category. In addition, the new approach was introduced for the video sub-system to eliminate the issues caused by the facial landmarks. Yixiang Dai *et al.* [24] designed wearable biosensor network for multimodal emotion recognition. Here, the Reputation-based SVM (RSVM) algorithm was introduced for reducing the classification error. In addition, the reputations were computed by using correlation calculation by finding the similarity, and then the fuzzy membership degree was utilized for sample selection and the determination. Huge subjects and longer-time-scale signals was not analysed for better emotion recognition. Kazuhiko Takahashi *et al.* [25] modelled the computational emotion recognition approach based on multimodal physiological signals. Here, respiration rate, plethysmogram, skin temperature, and the skin conductance change were computed for evaluating negative, positive, and the neutral states. Moreover, the psychophysical experiments based on kanji words were performed for gathering the physiological signals. Finally, the emotion was recognized using random forests, multilayer neural networks, decision trees, and SVM were employed.

Marc Lanze Ivan C. Dy *et al.* [26] designed multimodal emotion recognition system based on spontaneous Filipino dataset. Facial and Acoustic feature points were extracted initially, and then the various feature sets were employed for each modality for finding the optimal feature set. However, the 12 distance features points were selected for better facial emotion recognition. Finally, fusion is performed for improving the classification accuracy in the emotion recognition system. Jing Chen *et al.* [33] introduced three-stage decision framework to recognize four emotions of the multiple subjects. The steps followed in the developed model were as follows. Initially, the subject group was identified where the test subject was mapped. Consequently, the emotion pool was determined, and then the emotions were predicted from the obtained emotion pool for test instance. Chen Wei *et al.* [44] presented EEG-enabled emotion recognition system to identify neutral, negative, and positive emotions. In addition, the time dependency property was considered during the emotion process. Furthermore, deep Simple Recurrent Units (SRU) network was introduced for grasping temporal information of the EEG, and for solving long-term dependencies problems in the normal Recurrent Neural Network (RNN). Additionally, the Dual-tree Complex Wavelet Transform (DT-CWT) was established for decomposing raw EEG to the five constituent sub-bands. At last, three ensemble methods were utilised for obtaining better classification performance. Jing Chen *et al.*

[45] presented three-stage decision method using physiological signals for recognizing emotions in multi-subject context. In addition, stage-divided method was introduced where every stage deal with the fine-grained goal for emotion detection. O. A. Ordonez-Bolanos *et al.* [40] presented emotion classification from peripheral and EEG signals. However, 40 different physiological signals were taken as the input classifying the emotions. Moreover, Improved Empirical Mode Decomposition (ICEEMD) decomposition was introduced for achieving better system performance.

2.1.3 Fusion-Based Approaches

The research papers based on the fusion-based approaches for identifying the emotions using multimodal signals are discussed below. Shahla Nemati *et al.* [19] presented hybrid multimodal data fusion from which visual and audio modalities were fused based on mapping. After that, the projected features were fused to cross-modal space, whereas textual modality based on Dempster-Shafer (DS) theory. Here, the experimentation was performed using DEAP dataset for getting the system improvement. Shahla Nemati [27] employed visual, audio, and the users' comments as the modalities for the video emotion recognition. Here, initial two modalities were synchronized, whereas the users' comments were not synchronized for making pure feature-level data fusion. In addition, the hybrid method was introduced for feature extraction, and then the Canonical Correlation Analysis (CCA) was employed to visual and audio modalities, and then users' comments outputs was integrated using decision-level fusion. ZhibingXie and Ling Guan [39] developed kernel entropy component analysis (KECA) to achieve enhanced performance with entropy computation. Then, the novel solution was employed by integrating information theoretic tools and information fusion theory. Finally, the developed model was given to the audio-visual emotion recognition. Zhibing Xie, and Ling Guan [41] developed an approach by integrating information fusion and kernel entropy component analysis for emotion recognition. After that, features fusion was realized based on information entropy descriptor, and was optimized with entropy computation. Moreover, the multimodal information fusion method was employed for recognizing audio emotion using Kernel Entropy Component Analysis (KECA).

2.1.4 Multimodal System-Based Approaches

This section describes the multimodal system-based approaches in emotion recognition collected from various existing research papers. ImenTayari-Meftah*et al.* [7] modelled multi-modal system, which facilitates the inter-systems exchanges and improves emotion interaction credibility among computers and the users. Then, the multimodal emotion was recognized through physiological data using the signal processing approaches. In addition, this approach permits to find the emotions, such as masked and simulated emotions. Chao Li *et al.* [11] presented multimodal attention-enabled Bidirectional Long Short Term Memory (BLSTM) for emotion recognition effectively. Initially, the original physiological signals from every channel was changed into spectrogram image to capture their frequency and time information. Then, the attention-driven Bidirectional (LSTM-RNNs) was introduced for obtaining optimal temporal features automatically. After that, the obtained features are subjected to the DNN for predicting probability function of for each channel. At last, the decision level fusion method was employed for predicting final emotion. Imen Tayari Meftah *et al.* [30] designed multimodal emotion recognition system, which has the capability for preventing depression. This approach used multidimensional vectors with the algebraic representation of the emotional states. However, the algebraic model was utilized to process the emotions, and allowed the fusion of the complementary information, like voice, physiological signals, and facial expression and so on. ImenTayari Meftah *et al.* [32] introduced multimodal approach where the information is obtained from various modalities and cues for emotion recognition. This framework employed the multidimensional model based on the representation of algebraic emotional states. In addition, infinity of emotions was represented in order to analyse and process these emotions. Imen Tayari Meftah*et al.* [36] presented multimodal approach for recognizing the emotions from facial expressions, physiological signals, and speech etc. Here, the algebraic representation was defined on emotional states based on multidimensional vectors. Moreover, the multidimensional model was the promising mathematical tool for emotion analysis. In addition, the information from various modalities was integrated for allowing more emotional states.

2.1.5 Other Approaches

The analysis based on other approaches for emotion recognition is elaborated in this subsection. Yingying Jiang *et al.* [10] presented data-enabled multimodal emotion information. Here, the mental health monitoring system based on real-time was considered for gathering the input signal. In addition, the multimodal features extraction parameters, such as EEG, text features, expression, and speech were included for better performance. Dazhi Jiang *et al.* [16] developed Probability and Integrated Learning (PIL) in order to tackle high-level human emotion recognition issues. Initially, the complex human emotions were analysed, and then, the PIL was adapted to compute confidence level of classification probability. Tauhidur Rahman and Carlos Busso [20] introduced unsupervised feature adaptation approach for reducing the mismatch among acoustic features. In addition, the system was trained and extracted the acoustic features from the unknown targeted speaker. Moreover, adaptation method used iterative feature normalization (IFN) framework for better recognition. Cristian A. Torres-Valencia *et al.* [21] designed Hidden Markov Models (HMM) for capturing dynamic signals for further emotional states processing based on valence and arousal. The main aim of this approach was to identify the information of EEG and physiological signals in emotion recognition task. Seunghyun Yoon *et al.* [28] presented multimodal dual recurrent encoder model for allowing the better understanding of the speech data. However, this framework was utilized to encode the text and audio sequence information based on dual RNNs. After that, the information obtained from the above-mentioned sources was combined based on feed-forward neural network model for predicting emotion class. Yelin Kim, and Emily Mower Provost [31] developed Informed Segmentation and Labeling Approach (ISLA) for enhancing the emotion recognition performance. This framework captured the speech variability in lower and upper face regions. However, signals were utilized for segmenting and classifying the facial emotion temporally.

Javier Gonzalez-Sanchez *et al.* [34] designed the Agent-Based Software Architecture (ABE) for recognizing emotions. This framework creates highly reusable, flexible, and the software components. In addition, sensing devices was integrated to ABE, like computer vision systems eye tracking systems, and the physiological sensors. Chun-Min Chang *et al.* [37] developed improved approach, named bootstrapped multi-view weighted kernel fusion for improving the recognition accuracy. In addition, two emotional corpora were introduced for various languages for further processing. However, the developed model obtained enhanced recognition in the valence attributes and regressing activation based on video and audio modalities across both databases. Additionally, the weighted kernel fusion used the additional power for emotional recognition. Morteza Zangeneh Soroush, and Keivan Maghooli [46] developed setting time intervals for processing the EEG signals, relative values of the nonlinear feature extraction, and the classification based on Dempster–Shafer theory (DST). Here, the EEG signals was taken from the standard dataset, and then using the features the classification was done based on DST for reducing uncertainty, and for achieving optimal results. Jie-Lin Qiu *et al.* [48] presented Deep Canonical Correlation Analysis (DCCA) for representing high-level coordination, and for making feature extraction from the eye movement and EEG data. Here, nonlinear transformations was jointly learned to increase correlation. Then, the DCCA was introduced with the high correlation to attain higher emotion classification accuracy Yimin Yang *et al.* [50] developed hierarchical network with the sub network nodes for discriminating neutral, positive, and the negative emotions. Here, each subnetwork node was embedded in network to form hundreds of the hidden nodes. The mammal cortex in brain was combined from sub network nodes for producing more reliable cognition.

3   Research Gaps and Issues

This section illustrates the gaps and issues faced by previous emotion recognition methods using multimodal signals. The research issues of deep learning approaches are discussed as follows: The method in [2] failed to consider other deep learned visual and audio features for enhancing baseline systems more effectively. Dynamic modelling of low-level features was not investigated using multimodal LSTM for improving the recognition rate better [5]. The method failed to consider other NN for identifying and enhancing the accuracy of the audio emotion [15]. The method in [43] does not consider other modalities, like labor concentration, sleep stages analysis, and the driving fatigue for better performance. In [35], real-time multimodal emotion recognition system was not considered based on deep learning architecture for enhancing classification accuracy. The method in [4] failed to include more modalities, such as physio for improving the performance of the emotion recognition. More efficient features were not identified in [6] for enhancing the performance of the system. In [1], the method does not investigate eye movement features for better system performance.

The effective data augmentation method was not considered for generating the feature vectors [3]. Other datasets were not considered in [14] for improving the stability of the system. Ensemble recurrent neural network was not considered in [9] for identifying the emotions due to peripheral physiological and EEG signals are time series data. The method [17] failed to consider other fuzzy operators in deep recurrent neuro-fuzzy network and deep convolutional neuro-fuzzy networks to improve the system performance.

The method in [47], detects the class accurately, but failed to enhance the interaction experience. In [49], another advanced score fusion techniques, such as logistic regression method was not included in popular FoCal toolkit for improving the system performance.

The challenges determined from machine learning approaches are given below: In [18], the method failed to find the window segment length, and the overlapped audio path percentage. Include other systematic method in order to select the appropriate parameters for better recognition [44]. The method in [45] does not included more suitable labelling strategy for improving the recognition rate. Other classification systems based on features was not tested to improve the generality and discernibility of the system [40]. The issues of fusion techniques are discussed as follows: The method [19] failed to consider DNN for enhancing the output obtained from textual modality. The gaps and issues identified by the multimodal system-based approaches are discussed as follows: End-to-end learning was not investigated to speed up the emotion recognition system performance [11]. The issues of other approaches are as follows: Advanced genetic programming principles were not considered in order to enhance the classification accuracy [16]. Transfer learning was not included for producing generalizable emotion recognition systems [31]. In [37], more factors, like elicitation styles, languages, and cultural backgrounds was not included to enrich modelling power of the fusion architecture. The active regions of scalp and selected channels was not analysed to better recognition rate [46].

4   Analysis and Discussion

The evaluation is performed based on various strategies adapted for emotion recognition in terms of year of publication, adapted methodologies, evaluation measures, software tools, and performance evaluation values.

4.1   Analysis with Respect to Publication years

The analysis using years is briefed wherein 50 research papers are being selected for study of emotion recognition using multimodal signals. The analysis in terms of publication year is depicted in Table 1. Out of the 50 papers surveyed, more research papers for emotion recognition are published in years 2017.

4.2   Analysis on the Basis of Strategies

The analysis using adapted emotion recognition strategies is elaborated in this subsection.

The strategies utilized for emotion recognition using multimodal signals is depicted in Fig. 2. Based on below figure, 25% of the researches employed machine learning techniques, whereas 15% of works considered CNN techniques for emotion recognition. In addition, 13% of researches are covered by each fusion, and multimodal system-based techniques, whereas 12% of the researches utilized Deep LSTM-based techniques. The auto encoder-based techniques are employed in 8% of the researches, and remaining 7% of researches use each of DBN, and NN techniques. From analysis, it noted that machine learning techniques are the broadly employed approaches for emotion recognition using multimodal signals.

Table 1. Analysis with respect to publication year

Published year	Number of research papers
2020	6
2019	7
2018	7
2017	8
2016	6
2015	1
2014	2
2013	3
2012	5
2011	1
2010	3

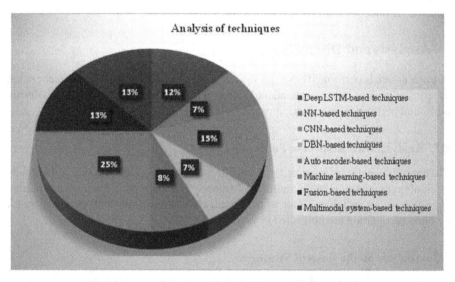

Fig. 2. Analysis of strategies based on emotion recognition

4.3 Analysis on the Basis of Implementation Tool

The analysis of conventional techniques using implementation tool adapted in the literary works are described in this sub-section. Figure 3 elaborate software tools employed to recognize the emotion effectively. The software tools adapted in different path optimization strategies are OpenSMILE toolkit, Tensorflow, HTK Toolbox, libsvm toolbox, MATLAB, Wavelet toolbox, Python, WEKA data mining toolkit, HMM toolbox, Keras, New information theoretic tool, and ANVIL tool. From Fig. 3, it is observed that

OpenSMILE toolkit is commonly adapted software tool for recognizing emotion using multimodal signals.

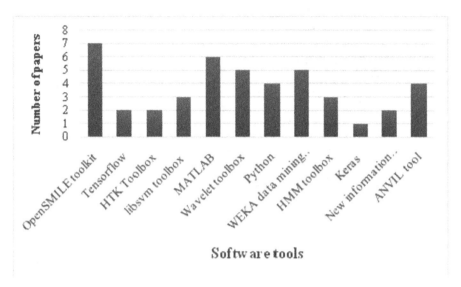

Fig. 3. Analysis devised with respect to implementation tools

4.4 Analysis in Terms of Employed Datasets

This sub-section analysed the datasets utilized by various research works. Figure 4 illustrates the datasets utilized for emotion recognition. The most commonly used datasets in the emotion recognition are SEED dataset, DEAP dataset, Interactive Emotional Dyadic Motion Capture (IEMOCAP) dataset, Multimodal Affective dataset, eNTER-FACE dataset, RML emotion dataset, Acted Facial Expressions in the Wild (AFEW), RECOLA dataset, emoFBVP dataset, and Filipino emotion dataset. From Fig. 4, it is clear that DEAP datasetis most frequently used datasets.

4.5 Analysis on the Basis of Evaluation Measures

The analysis based on evaluation measures for emotion recognition using multimodal signals is illustrated in the subsection using Table 2. The frequently employed evaluation measures are accuracy, F1-measure, and recognition rate. Other metrics include Root Mean Square (RMSE), Pearson Correlation Coefficient (PCC), Concordance correlation coefficient (CNN), time, standard deviation, loss function, frequency, precision, True Positive Rate (TPR), recall, specificity, reputation, and amplitude, which are employed in the emotion recognition strategies for computing the performance of each method.

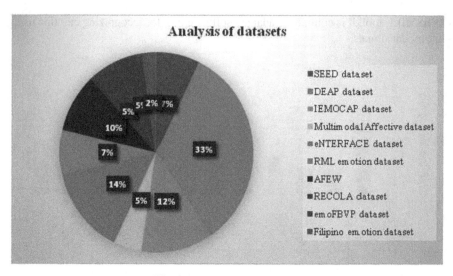

Fig. 4. Analysis using datasets

Table 2. Analysis devised on the basis of evaluation measures

Performance metrics	Number of research papers
Accuracy	[1, 3, 7–12, 14–17, 19–24, 26–31, 33, 35, 38, 41–48]
RMSE	[2]
F1-measure	[3, 5, 8, 11, 16, 19, 27, 44]
Recognition rate	[6, 7, 18, 25, 30, 32]
Time	[8, 44]
Reputation	[24]
Loss function	[10, 15]
Pearson Correlation Coefficient	[2]
Concordance correlation coefficient	[2]
Frequency	[12, 17]
Precision	[16, 19, 44, 49]
Recall	[16, 19, 22, 44]
Standard deviation	[8, 17, 24, 48]
True Positive Rate	[19]
Specificity	[19]
Amplitude	[42]

4.6 Analysis Using Evaluation Measures Values

The analysis devised using evaluation measures values are illustrated. The analysis based on accuracy, and F1-measure is depicted in the tabular format.

4.6.1 Analysis Using Accuracy

The analysis based on the values of accuracy is discussed in the below section. Table 3 shows the accuracy parameter analysis by considering four ranges as, 60%–70%, 70%–80%, 80%–90%, and 90%–99%. From the below table, research papers [1, 12, 14, 23, 35, 41, 43, 46, 47] had achieved highest accuracy with range 90%–99%, whereas [20, 30, 48] had achieved less accuracy at 60%–70%, respectively.

Table 3. Analysis based on accuracy

Accuracy (%)	Number of papers
60–70	[20, 30, 47]
70–80	[7, 11, 21, 24, 28, 29, 32, 33, 42, 44, 45]
80–90	[9, 13, 17, 26, 27, 31, 38]
90–99	[1, 12, 14, 23, 35, 41, 43, 46, 48]

4.6.2 Analysis Using F1-Measure

The analysis on the basis of values of F1-measure is elaborated in this subsection. Table 4 details the evaluation of the F1-measure parameter with three ranges. Based on the table, it is evaluated that paper [5, 11, 19, 27] required maximal F1-measure for emotion recognition using multimodal signal.

Table 4. Analysis based on F1-measure

F1-measure (%)	Number of papers
70–80	[5, 11, 19, 27]
80–90	[3]
90–99	[8, 16, 44]

5   Conclusion

In: this survey, several techniques are being adapted for emotion recognition using multimodal signals, and are categorized as Deep LSTM, NN, CNN, DBN-based techniques, Auto encoder-based techniques, machine learning-based techniques, fusion, and multimodal system based on certain criterions. The main aim of this review is to partition the conventional approaches on the basis of years of publication, methodologies adapted, employed datasets, evaluation measures and software tools, and the values of performance metrics by considering 50 papers based on the emotion recognition using multimodal signals. Additionally, the gaps and issues of the research works based on emotion recognition are elaborated in briefer manner in order to suggest effectual future scope. From analysis, it is clearly reviewed that machine learning - is mostly used techniques in the research papers. Likewise, OpenSMILE toolkit is the widely used toolset in existing papers, whereas the frequently employed dataset is DEAP dataset. Moreover, accuracy, F1-measure, and recognition rate are metric used in most of the research papers. In addition, there are some of the main drawbacks which should to be solved in the near future by employing novel emotion recognition strategies.

References

1. Liu, W., Zheng, W.-L., Lu, B.-L.: Emotion recognition using multimodal deep learning. In: Hirose, A., Ozawa, S., Doya, K., Ikeda, K., Lee, M., Liu, D. (eds.) ICONIP 2016. LNCS, vol. 9948, pp. 521–529. Springer, Cham (2016). https://doi.org/10.1007/978-3-319-46672-9_58
2. Chen, S., Jin, Q., Zhao, J., Wang, S.: Multimodal multi-task learning for dimensional and continuous emotion recognition. In: Proceedings of the 7th Annual Workshop on Audio/Visual Emotion Challenge, pp. 19–26, October 2017
3. Yin, Z., Zhao, M., Wang, Y., Yang, J., Zhang, J.: Recognition of emotions using multimodal physiological signals and an ensemble deep learning model. Comput. Methods Programs Biomed. **140**, 93–110 (2017)
4. Tzirakis, P., Trigeorgis, G., Nicolaou, M.A., Schuller, B.W., Zafeiriou, S.: End-to-end multimodal emotion recognition using deep neural networks. IEEE J. Sel. Top. Signal Process. **11**(8), 1301–1309 (2017)
5. Wöllmer, M., Metallinou, A., Eyben, F., Schuller, B., Narayanan, S.: Context-sensitive multimodal emotion recognition from speech and facial expression using bidirectional LSTM modeling. In: Proceedings of INTERSPEECH, Makuhari, Japan, pp. 2362–2365 (2010)
6. Han, Z., Wang, J.: Feature fusion algorithm for multimodal emotion recognition from speech and facial expression signal. In: Proceedings of MATEC Web of Conferences. EDP Sciences, vol. 61, p. 03012 (2016)
7. Meftah, I.T., Le Thanh, N., Amar, C.B.: Multimodal approach for emotion recognition using a formal computational model. Int. J. Appl. Evol. Comput. (IJAEC) **4**(3), 11–25 (2013)
8. Song, T., Zheng, W., Lu, C., Zong, Y., Zhang, X., Cui, Z.: MPED: a multi-modal physiological emotion database for discrete emotion recognition. IEEE Access **7**, 12177–12191 (2019)
9. Huang, H., Hu, Z., Wang, W., Wu, M.: Multimodal emotion recognition based on ensemble convolutional neural network. IEEE Access **8**, 3265–3271 (2019)
10. Jiang, Y., Li, W., Hossain, M.S., Chen, M., Alelaiwi, A., Al-Hammadi, M.: A snapshot research and implementation of multimodal information fusion for data-driven emotion recognition. Inf. Fusion **53**, 209–221 (2020)

11. Li, C., Bao, Z., Li, L., Zhao, Z.: Exploring temporal representations by leveraging attention-based bidirectional LSTM-RNNs for multi-modal emotion recognition. Inf. Process. Manage. **57**, 102185 (2020)
12. Nguyen, D., Nguyen, K., Sridharan, S., Dean, D., Fookes, C.: Deep spatio-temporal feature fusion with compact bilinear pooling for multimodal emotion recognition. Comput. Vis. Image Underst. **174**, 33–42 (2018)
13. Verma, G.K., Tiwary, U.S.: Multimodal fusion framework: a multiresolution approach for emotion classification and recognition from physiological signals. Neuro Image **102**, 162–172 (2014)
14. Zhou, J., Wei, X., Cheng, C., Yang, Q., Li, Q.: Multimodal emotion recognition method based on convolutional auto-encoder. Int. J. Comput. Intell. Syst. **12**(1), 351–358 (2018)
15. Xu, G., Li, W., Liu, J.: Social emotion classification approach using multi-model fusion. Future Gener. Comput. Syst. **102**, 347–356 (2020)
16. Jiang, D., et al.: A probability and integrated learning based classification algorithm for high-level human emotion recognition problems. Measurement **150**, 107049 (2020)
17. Nguyen, T.-L., Kavuri, S., Lee, M.: A multimodal convolutional neuro-fuzzy network for emotion understanding of movie clips. Neural Netw. **118**, 208–219 (2019)
18. Seng, K.P., Ang, L.M., Ooi, C.S.: A combined rule-based & machine learning audio-visual emotion recognition approach. IEEE Trans. Affect. Comput. **9**(1), 3–13 (2016)
19. Nemati, S., Rohani, R., Basiri, M.E., Abdar, M., Yen, N.Y., Makarenkov, V.: A hybrid latent space data fusion method for multimodal emotion recognition. IEEE Access **7**, 172948–172964 (2019)
20. Rahman, T., Busso, C.: A personalized emotion recognition system using an unsupervised feature adaptation scheme. In: 2012 IEEE International Conference on Acoustics, Speech and Signal Processing (ICASSP), pp. 5117–5120. IEEE, March 2012
21. Torres-Valencia, C.A., Garcia-Arias, H.F., Lopez, M.A.A., Orozco-Gutiérrez, A.A.: Comparative analysis of physiological signals and Electroencephalogram (EEG) for multimodal emotion recognition using generative models. In: proceedings of 2014 XIX Symposium on Image, Signal Processing and Artificial Vision, pp. 1–5. IEEE, September 2014
22. Gajsek, R., Struc, V., Mihelic, F.: Multi-modal emotion recognition using canonical correlations and acoustic features. In: Proceedings of 20th International Conference on Pattern Recognition, pp. 4133–4136. IEEE, August 2010
23. Lee, M.S., Cho, Y.R., Lee, Y.K., Pae, D.S., Lim, M.T., Kang, T.K.: PPG and EMG based emotion recognition using convolutional neural network (2019)
24. Dai, Y., Wang, X., Li, X., Zhang, P.: Reputation-driven multimodal emotion recognition in wearable biosensor network. In: Proceedings of IEEE International Instrumentation and Measurement Technology Conference (I2MTC), pp. 1747–1752. IEEE, May 2015
25. Takahashi, K., Namikawa, S., Hashimoto, M.: Computational emotionrecognition using multimodal physiological signals: elicited using Japanese Kanji words. In: Proceedings of 35th International Conference on Telecommunications and Signal Processing (TSP), pp. 615–620. IEEE, May 2012
26. Dy, M.L.I.C., Espinosa, I.V.L., Go, P.P.V., Mendez, C.M.M., Cu, J.W.: Multimodal emotion recognition using a spontaneous Filipino emotion database. In: proceedings of 3rd International Conference on Human-Centric Computing, pp. 1–5. IEEE, August 2010
27. Nemati, S.: Canonical correlation analysis for data fusion in multimodal emotion recognition. In: proceedings of 9th International Symposium on Telecommunications (IST), pp. 676–681. IEEE, December 2018
28. Yoon, S., Byun, S., Jung, K.: Multimodal speech emotion recognition using audio and text. In: Proceedings of IEEE Spoken Language Technology Workshop (SLT), pp. 112–118. IEEE (2018)

29. Kimy, E., Shin, J.W.: DNN-based emotion recognition based on bottleneck acoustic features and lexical features. In: proceedings of International Conference on Acoustics, Speech and Signal Processing (ICASSP), pp. 6720–6724. IEEE (2019)

30. Meftah, I.T., Le Thanh, N., Amar, C.B.: Detectingdepression using multimodal approach of emotion recognition (2012)

31. Kim, Y., Provost, E.M.: ISLA: temporal segmentation and labeling for audio-visual emotion recognition. IEEE Trans. Affect. Comput. **10**(2), 196–208 (2017)

32. Meftah, I.T., Le Thanh, N., Amar, C.B.: Multimodalapproach for emotion recognition using an algebraic representation of emotional states. In: Proceedings of Eighth International Conference on Signal Image Technology and Internet Based Systems, pp. 541–546. IEEE, November 2012

33. Chen, J., Hu, B., Wang, Y., Dai, Y., Yao, Y., Zhao, S.: Three-stage decisionframework for multi-subject emotion recognition using physiological signals. In: Proceedings of IEEE International Conference on Bioinformatics and Biomedicine (BIBM), pp. 470–474. IEEE, December 2016

34. Gonzalez-Sanchez, J., Chavez-Echeagaray, M.E., Atkinson, R., Burleson, W.: ABE: an agent-based software architecture for a multimodal emotion recognition framework. In: Proceedings of Ninth Working IEEE/IFIP Conference on Software Architecture, pp. 187–193. IEEE, June 2011

35. Ranganathan, H., Chakraborty, S., Panchanathan, S.: Multimodal emotion recognition using deep learning architectures. In: 2016 IEEE Winter Conference on Applications of Computer Vision (WACV), pp. 1–9. IEEE, March 2016

36. Meftah, I.T., Thanh, N.L., Ben Amar, C.: Multimodal recognition of emotions using a formal computational model (2012)

37. Chang, C.-M., Su, B.-H., Lin, S.-C., Li, J.-L., Lee, C.-C.: A bootstrappedmulti-view weighted kernel fusion framework for cross-corpus integration of multimodal emotion recognition, In: Proceedings of Seventh International Conference on Affective Computing and Intelligent Interaction (ACII), pp. 377–382. IEEE (2017)

38. Nguyen, D., Nguyen, K., Sridharan, S., Ghasemi, A., Dean, D.: Deepspatio-temporal features for multimodal emotion recognition. In: 2017 IEEE Winter Conference on Applications of Computer Vision (WACV), pp. 1215–1223. IEEE, March 2017

39. Xie, Z., Guan, L.: Multimodal information fusion of audiovisual emotion recognition using novel information theoretic tools. In: proceedings of IEEE International Conference on Multimedia and Expo (ICME), pp. 1–6. IEEE, July 2013

40. Ordonez-Bolanos, O.A., et al.: Recognition of emotions using ICEEMD-based characterization of multimodal physiological signals. In: Proceedings of IEEE 10th Latin American Symposium on Circuits and Systems (LASCAS), pp. 113–116. IEEE, February 2019

41. Xie, Z., Guan, L.: Multimodal information fusion of audio emotion recognition based on kernel entropy component analysis. Int. J. Semant. Comput. **7**(1), 25–42 (2013)

42. Wang, Z., Zhou, X., Wang, W., Liang, C.: Emotion recognition using multimodal deep learning in multiple psychophysiological signals and video. Int. J. Mach. Learn. Cybern. **11**(4), 923–934 (2020)

43. Ma, J., Tang, H., Zheng, W.-L., Lu, B.-L.: Emotion recognition using multimodal residual LSTM network. In: Proceedings of the 27th ACM International Conference on Multimedia, pp. 176–183, October 2019

44. Wei, C., Chen, L.L., Song, Z.Z., Lou, X.G., Li, D.D.: EEG-based emotion recognition using simple recurrent units network and ensemble learning. Biomed. Signal Process. Control **58**, 101756 (2020)

45. Chen, J., et al.: Subject-independent emotion recognition based on physiological signals: a three-stage decision method. BMC Med. Inform. Decis. Mak. **17**(3), 167 (2017)

46. Soroush, M.Z., Maghooli, K.: A novel method of EEG-based emotion recognition using non-linear features variability and Dempster-Shafer theory. Biomed. Eng. Appl. Basis Commun. **30**(4), 1850026 (2018)

47. Pérez, A.K., Quintero, C.A., Rodríguez, S., Rojas, E., Peña, O., De La Rosa, F.: Identification of multimodal signals for emotion recognition in the context of human-robot interaction. In: Brito-Loeza, C., Espinosa-Romero, A. (eds.) ISICS 2018. CCIS, vol. 820, pp. 67–80. Springer, Cham (2018). https://doi.org/10.1007/978-3-319-76261-6_6

48. Qiu, J.-L., Liu, W., Lu, B.-L.: Multi-view emotion recognition using deep canonical correlation analysis. In: Cheng, L., Leung, A.C.S., Ozawa, S. (eds.) ICONIP 2018. LNCS, vol. 11305, pp. 221–231. Springer, Cham (2018). https://doi.org/10.1007/978-3-030-04221-9_20

49. He, G., Chen, J., Liu, X., Li, M.: The SYSU system for CCPR 2016 multimodal emotion recognition challenge. In: Tan, T., Li, X., Chen, X., Zhou, J., Yang, J., Cheng, H. (eds.) CCPR 2016. CCIS, vol. 663, pp. 707–720. Springer, Singapore (2016). https://doi.org/10.1007/978-981-10-3005-5_58

50. Yang, Y., Wu, Q.J., Zheng, W.L., Lu, B.L.: EEG-based emotion recognition using hierarchical network with subnetwork nodes. IEEE Trans. Cogn. Dev. Syst. **10**(2), 408–419 (2017)

An Image Performance Against Normal, Grayscale and Color Spaced Images

Atul Kumar[1], Radhesh Pandey[2], Kamal Kumar Srivastava[2(✉)], Sumit Awasthi[3], and Talha Jamal[4]

[1] Department of Computer Science and Engineering, Shri Ramswaroop Memorial College of Engineering and Management, Lucknow, India
[2] Department of Information Technology, Babu Banarasi Das Northern India Institute of Technology, Lucknow, U.P., India
`2007.srivastava@gmail.com`
[3] Tata Consultancy Services Private Limited, Lucknow, India
[4] Cognizant Private Limited, Lucknow, India

Abstract. Generally, an image matching belongs to comparing the two images, with the simple concept i.e. When the two images match or comparable and how can this similarity be measured? Fast and robust feature detection and image matching have always been a very major and challenging task in itself along with the applications. In this paper, we are using normal, grayscale and LAB color spaced images and measure the recital of contrasting approaches for image corresponding, i.e., SIFT, SURF, and ORB. For this purpose, we manually transform original images into grayscale and LAB color spaced images and compute all the parameters on the basis of which evaluation is done such as the total of distinct points in images, the match-up percentage. By this, we will show that which algorithm works best and more robust against each kind of image.

Keywords: Image matching · Scale-invariant feature transform (SIFT) · Speed Up Robust Feature (SURF) · Oriented FAST · Rotated BRIEF (ORB)

1 Introduction

Feature Detection and matching is a process of detecting and matching the distinct features in a given sequence of the image in order to match the entire images. It is always has been an important and challenging task in the field of computer vision and robotics and their application. An ideal technique for performing this process must be robust in every possible way like rotation, scale, illumination, noise, and affine transformations. According to the above-said statement, each and every feature should match up with a high likelihood [1, 2].

"Scale Invariant Feature Transform (SIFT) is a feature detector developed by Lowe in 2004 [3]". SIFT has proven itself a well-planned and logical algorithm for solving problems like object recognition but also it has shown a great drawback for real-time applications as it requires a large computational power [3, 4].

S. Rajagopal et al. (Eds.): ASCIS 2022, CCIS 1759, pp. 286–294, 2022.
https://doi.org/10.1007/978-3-031-23092-9_22

Speed up Robust Feature (SURF) technique, which is a probabilistic approach of a SIFT. It overcomes the drawback for SIFT by performing faster than SIFT without even altering the standard of feature points [6]. As both SIFT and SURF are descriptor and detector based, "Rublee et al. proposed an Oriented FAST and Rotated BRIEF (ORB) as another efficient alternative for SIFT and SURF [10]".

The whole paper is arranged in the following way: Sect. 2 summarizes the working of SIFT, SURF, and ORB. In Sect. 3, we explore the responsiveness of SIFT, SURF, and ORB against each normal, grayscale and LAB colored spaced image. Section 4 concludes the overall result of this paper.

2 Overview of Image Matching Techniques

2.1 SIFT

SIFT propound by Lowe has proven its best result in image rotations, passion, affine transformation, and viewpoint change while detecting features. It works by working into four stages or say steps [8].

- By using the Difference of Gaussian (DoG), assessment of scale-space extreme.
- Localization of distinct points by refining and eliminating the low contrast points.
- Orientation assignment of those distinct points based on the local image gradient.
- In last, a descriptor generator for computing the local image descriptor for each distinct point based on image gradient immensity and direction.

2.2 SURF

For finding the points of interest, SURF uses the BLOB filters, which is totally based on the Hessian matrix. It uses wavelet responses in both vertical and horizontal directions by applying adequate Gaussian Weights for orientation assignment and feature description. For finding the feature descriptor it works in a manner that points out a neighborhood around the key points and divides them into sub regions then for every sub region it collects and represents the wavelet responses. Already computed Laplacian Points during the detection are then used for underlying the interest points. Laplacian Signs are used for distinguishing the bright blobs on the dark background from the reverse case [5].

2.3 ORB

By some modifications in the BRIEF descriptor and FAST key point detector, a fusion of ORB can be extracted [7]. At the very beginning, it uses FAST to determine the key points. Then to find top N points it applies the Harris corner measure. As FAST is not able to compute orientation because it is a rotation variant, it computes the intensity weighted centroid of the patch with the located corner at the center. Then the direction of the vector from the corner point to the centroid gives the orientation [9, 14]. To improve the rotation invariance Moments are computed. In ORB, using the orientation of the patch rotation matrix is computed and then the BRIEF descriptor is steered according to the orientation [15, 16].

3 Experimental Results

In this section, we look over the responsiveness of SIFT, SURF, and ORB versus each normal, grayscale and LAB colored spaced image.

3.1 L*A*B* Color Space

"This color space is originally defined by CAE and specified by the International Commission on Illumination" [12, 13]. LAB color space consists of 3 channels in which one is for Luminance (Lightness) and the further two are a and b studied as chroma layers. A* and B* represents the following points:

- A* layer shows where the color falls along the RED-GREEN AXIS.
- A* negative values show GREEN while positive values show MAGENTA.
- B* layer indicates where the color falls along the BLUE-YELLOW AXIS.

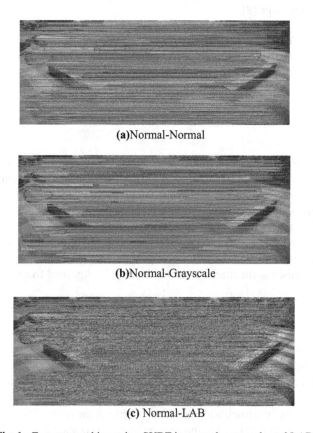

(a)Normal-Normal

(b)Normal-Grayscale

(c) Normal-LAB

Fig. 1. Feature matching using SURF in normal, grayscale and LAB

- B* negative values indicate BLUE and positive values indicate YELLOW.

The major characteristic of the LAB is that this is device unfettered [11, 14] which provides us the opening to communicate divergent colors over divergent devices.

After extracting all the key points from the image, we can calculate the matching ratio from them. The matching ratio is calculated [1] as follows:

$$MR = MC/MT * 100 \tag{1}$$

where MC is the number of correct matching pairs and MT is the total number of matching pairs in the image (Tables 1, 2, 3 and 4).

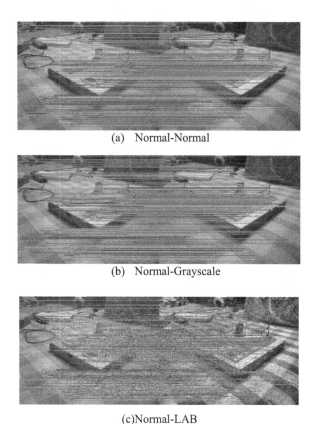

(a)   Normal-Normal

(b)   Normal-Grayscale

(c)Normal-LAB

Fig. 2. Feature matching using SIFT in normal, grayscale and LAB

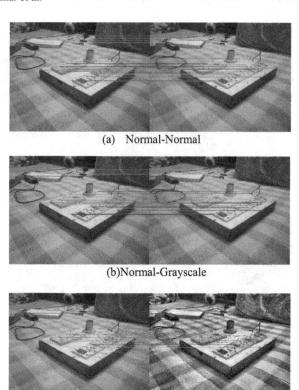

(a)   Normal-Normal

(b)Normal-Grayscale

(c)Normal-LAB

Fig. 3. Feature matching using ORB in normal, grayscale and LAB

Table 1. Results of Fig. 1, 2 and 3 (table for extracted key points numbers)

	Kpoint1 (normal)	Kpoint2 (grayscale)	Kpoint3 (LAB)
SURF	20181	20181	70426
SIFT	5669	5669	52053
ORB	500	500	500

Table 2. Results of matching ratio in Fig. 1, 2, and 3

	Matching ratio % (normal - normal)	Matching ratio % (normal - gray)	Matching ratio % (normal - lab)
SURF	50–55	33–37	50–55
SIFT	63–67	47–52	64–69
ORB	46–51	36–41	48–53

(a) Normal-Normal

(b) Normal-Grayscale

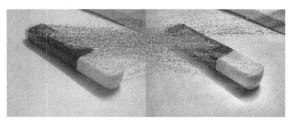

(c) Normal-LAB

Fig. 4. Feature matching using SURF in normal, grayscale and LAB

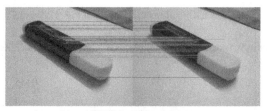

(a)   Normal-Normal

(b) Normal-Grayscale

(c)   Normal-LAB

Fig. 5. Feature matching using SIFT in normal, grayscale and LAB

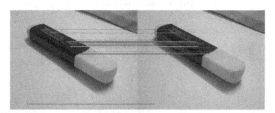

(a)   Normal-Normal

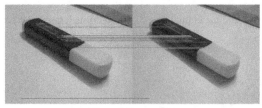

(b)   Normal-Grayscale

Fig. 6. Feature matching using ORB in normal, grayscale and LAB

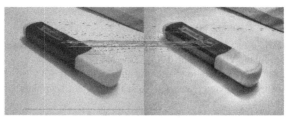

(c) Normal-LAB

Fig. 6. (*continued*)

Table 3. Results of Fig. 4, 5 and 6 (table for extracted keypoints numbers)

	Kpoint1 (normal)	Kpoint2 (grayscale)	Kpoint3 (LAB)
SURF	1314	1311	3012
SIFT	315	313	927
ORB	348	349	500

Table 4. Results of Figs. 4, 5 and 6 (table for extracted keypoints numbers)

	Matching ratio % (normal normal)	Matching ratio% (normal gray)	Matching ratio% (normal LAB)
SURF	58–63	42–47	62–67
SIFT	70–75	63–68	69–74
ORB	42–47	40–44	51–55

4   Conclusion

In this paper, we have collated three divergent image matching approaches for unlike images such as normal; grayscale and LAB color spaced images. For this purpose, we applied, grayscale and LAB color spaced modification on initial images and present the matching assessment variables such as the number of distinct points in images as the above figure shows, the matching ratio for each algorithm. As a above analysis and result we have found that manifest SIFT performs was the best in most scenarios among all the above test results as shown in analysis. After all the observation, we showed that the LAB color spaced images might give better results than using normal and grayscale images for image matching. In ORB, the features are largely settled around objects in the middle of the image while in SURF; SIFT keypoint detectors are allocated across the image. We have found that the feature points increase and the percentage of the number of matches also increases. Thus, we have found that the feature point's detection increases very well as our experimental result shows.

References

1. Moghaddam, B., Nastar, C., Pentland, A.: A Bayesian similarity measure for deformable image matching. Image Vis. Comput. **19**(5), 235–244 (2001)
2. Shan, B.: A novel image correlation matching approach. JMM **5**(3), 268–275 (2010)
3. Lowe, D.G.: Distinctive image features from scale-invariant keypoints. Int. J. Comput. Vis. **50**(2), 91–110 (2004)
4. Karami, E., Shehata, M., Smith, A.: Image identification using SIFT algorithm: performance analysis against different image deformations. In: Proceedings of the 2015 Newfoundland Electrical and Computer Engineering Conference, St. John's, Canada, November 2015
5. Ke, Y., Sukthankar, R.: PCA-SIFT: a more distinctive representation for local image descriptors. In: Proceedings of CVPR, vol. 2, pp. 506–513 (2004)
6. Bay, H., Tuytelaars, T., Van Gool, L.: Speeded-up robust features (SURF). Comput. Vis. Image Underst. **110**(3), 346–359 (2008)
7. Calonder, M., Lepetit, V., Strecha, C., Fua, P.: BRIEF: binary robust independent elementary features. In: Daniilidis, K., Maragos, P., Paragios, N. (eds.) ECCV 2010. LNCS, vol. 6314, pp. 778–792. Springer, Heidelberg (2010). https://doi.org/10.1007/978-3-642-15561-1_56
8. Rublee, E., Rabaud, V., Konolige, K., Bradski, G.: ORB: and efficient alternative to SIFT or SURF. In: IEEE International Conference on Computer Vision (2011)
9. Fischler, M., Bolles, R.: Random sample consensus: a paradigm for model fitting with applications to image analysis and automated cartography. Commun. Assoc. Comput. Mach. **24**(6), 381–395 (1981)
10. Hunter, R.S.: Photoelectric color-difference meter. JOSA **38**(7), 661 (1948). (Proceedings of the winter meeting of the optical society of America)
11. Hunter, R.S.: Accuracy, precision, and stability of new photo-electric color-difference meter. JOSA **38**(12), 1094 (1948). (Proceedings of the thirty-third annual meeting of the optical society of America)
12. Kwon, O.S., Ha, Y.H.: Panoramic video using scale-invariant feature transform with embedded color-invariant values. IEEE Trans. Consum. Electron. **56**(2), 792–798 (2010)
13. Karami, E., Prasad, S., Shehata, M.: Image matching using SIFT, SURF, BRIEF and ORB: performance comparison for distorted images
14. Katiyar, V., Srivastava, K.K., Kumar, A.: Applying adaptive strategies for website design improvement. In: Wyld, D., Zizka, J., Nagamalai, D. (eds.) Advances in Computer Science, Engineering & Applications. AISC, vol. 166, pp. 857–867. Springer, Heidelberg (2012). https://doi.org/10.1007/978-3-642-30157-5_85
15. Dwivedi, N., Srivastava, K., Arya, N.: Sanskrit word recognition using Prewitt's operator and support vector classification. In: 2013 IEEE International Conference ON Emerging Trends in Computing, Communication and Nanotechnology (ICECCN), pp. 265–269 (2013). https://doi.org/10.1109/ICE-CCN.2013.6528506
16. Kumar, A., Katiyar, V., Chauhan, B.K.: Text summarization in Hindi language using TF-IDF. In: Mallick, P.K., Bhoi, A.K., Barsocchi, P., de Albuquerque, V.H.C. (eds.) Cognitive Informatics and Soft Computing. Lecture Notes in Networks and Systems, vol. 375. Springer, Singapore (2022). https://doi.org/10.1007/978-981-16-8763-1_25

Study of X Ray Detection Using CNN in Machine Learning

Neeraj Bhargava[1], Pramod Singh Rathore[2]([✉]), and Apoorva Bhowmick[3]

[1] School of Engineering and System Sciences, MDS University, Ajmer, India
[2] Aryabhatta College of Engineering & Research Center, Ajmer, India
pramodrathore88@gmail.com
[3] MDS University, Ajmer, India

Abstract. The coronavirus spread that started in Wuhan, China and spread across the world, affecting the best of the healthcare systems from the Lombardy region of Italy to India, the US, and the UK, required accurate diagnosis. A rapid assessment to ascertain whether or not a patient has COVID-19 is required by frontline clinicians. In this paper, we propose to deduce the presence of COVID-19 using X-ray images of the lungs through feature extraction. A convolution network model is built for binary classification of images into corona positive and negative using the deep learning framework on Python, Keras. Various studies using different classifiers such as CART, XGB-L and XGB Tree were studied, which used machine learning for detection of COVID-19 and yielded a very accurate diagnosis. In this particular CNN model, Google Colab is used to execute the algorithm. The dataset is trained and the validation accuracy obtained is more than 96%. This is a very cost-effective way of using machine learning for the classification of infected and non-infected cases since working on Google Colab doesn't require enormous computational resources.

Keywords: CNN · Feature extraction · COVID-19 · X-ray

1 Introduction

A series of instances of pneumonia with an obscure reason were accounted for in the Wuhan, Hubei area of China; it was. discovered to be Severe Acute Respiratory Syndrome Coronavirus-2 (SARS-CoV-2) which caused major public health concerns.

As per the new statistics, the confirmed cases in the United States and India are still on the rise. On January 13, 2020, the WHO also declared COVID-19 to be the sixth global health crisis of concern, following H1N1 (2009), Ebola in West Africa (2014), Democratic Republic of Congo (2019), and Zika (2016).

It was additionally found that the novel coronavirus based pneumonia shares similarity with the Middle East respiratory condition (MERS) and has the capability of causing acute respiratory distress syndrome (ARDS). The rapid rates of infection transmission are due to the slow onset of symptoms, consequently empowering inescapable transmission by asymptomatic carriers. Radiological imaging of pneumonia infliction due

© The Author(s), under exclusive license to Springer Nature Switzerland AG 2022
S. Rajagopal et al. (Eds.): ASCIS 2022, CCIS 1759, pp. 295–303, 2022.
https://doi.org/10.1007/978-3-031-23092-9_23

to coronavirus uncovers the obliteration of lung parenchyma which incorporates broad union and interstitial inflammation as recently revealed in other COVID diseases.

Reverse transcription-polymerase chain reaction (RT-PCR) when measured for swabs taken from the upper part of the throat behind the nose is mostly used for coronavirus contamination. At the beginning of the pandemic, the high misleading negative rate, lack of Reverse Transcriptase-Polymerase Chain Reaction tests, and duration of the test results limited the early determination of contaminated patients. Chest X-rays and computed tomography can appropriately picture the lungs of coronavirus disease.

Chest X-Rays and Computed Tomography are better able to represent the spatial area of the presumed pathology along with the degree of damage in comparison to swab tests. Certain advantages of imaging could be its great responsiveness, a quick completion time, and the ability to visualise the degree of contamination in the lungs. The inconvenience is caused mostly due to low explicitness; the severity of lung infection makes it challenging to differentiate between various types of lung infection. Radiologists can improve symptomatic precision with the help of computer-aided diagnostic (CAD) frameworks.

Presently, specialists are utilising the hand-made or learned features that depend on geometry, texture, and morphological attributes of the lung for recognition of infection. The application of AI in the area of clinical imaging has become famous for the innovation headway and improvement of profound learning. The artificial intelligence-based framework, when checked and tried, results in the critical identification and administration of patients impacted by the coronavirus. Moreover, the AI picture assessment could help the radiologists to diagnose after a thorough evaluation (Table 1).

Table 1. Country-wise cases and death counts [1]

X-Ray	X-Ray	X-Ray
United States	75,271,402	905,661
India	40,858,241	493,218
Brazil	25,040,161	625,948
France	18,476,227	130,278
UK	16,333,980	155,317
Russia	11,502,657	329,443
Turkey	11,343,693	86,871
Italy	10,683,948	145,537

A. *Convolutional Neural Network*

The CNN model has following layers:

- *Input layer.* The size of the image given to input layers is $224 \times 224 \times 3$.
- *Convolutional layer* - The convolution layer is central to convolution network. The network's computational load is managed by this layer.
- *Pooling layer.* When input is shifted or rotated, a variance may be obtained in the activation map. The pooling layer is therefore added to avoid this variance; it also reduces the required no. of parameters and computations. To prevent over fitting, a dropout layer is added.
- *Dense layer.* The result of the pooling layer was straightened to a one dimensional vector in order to give input to the dense layer. This layer refreshes load so that it had the option to anticipate the probabilities of the class that input belongs to (Figs. 1, 2 and 3).

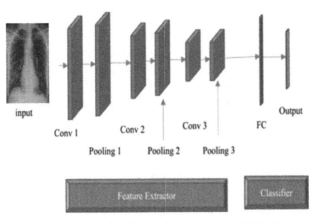

Fig. 1. Convolution Neural Network model (CNN) [2]

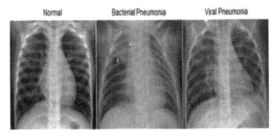

Fig. 2. X-Ray of healthy and pneumonic patients [3]

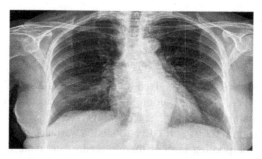

Fig. 3. SARS corona-virus affected lungs [6]

B. *Non-linear operations*

  i.   *Sigmoid* - The non-linear operation of sigmoid can be expressed in numerical form as $\sigma(\kappa) = 1/(1 + e^{-\kappa})$. It takes a genuine esteemed number and "squashes" it into a reach somewhere in the range of 0 and 1. In any case, atruly unfortunate characteristic of sigmoid is the slope comes around zero when the initiation is at one or the other end.
  ii. *Tanh* - Tanh squashes a genuine esteemed number to the reach $[-1, 1]$. Similar to the sigmoid operation the activation saturates, however - in contrast to the sigmoid neurons - its result is zero focused.
  iii. *ReLU* - Rectified Linear Unit (ReLU) activation function is used in the process. It transforms the input received in a node in a non-linear fashion.

The values for the feature map can be calculated using equation,

$$G[m, n] = (i \times f)[m, n] = \sum j \sum kf[j, k]i[m - j, n - k].$$

Here the input image is denoted by i and the filter by f, m and n are the indices of rows and columns of resultant matrix respectively.

As compared to tanh and sigmoid, more reliability is on ReLU as convergence can be accelerated six fold. Adaptive learning rates can rectify the fragility of ReLU during training (Table 2).

Table 2. Parameters for different algorithms

Classifier	Sensitivity	Specificity	Accuracy
XGB-Tree	100%	100%	100%
XGB-L	100%	100%	100%
KNN	89.71%	100%	95%
CART (DT)	100%	100%	100%

C. *Other classifiers and approaches used for the specific purpose include:*

1. *Support Vector Machine (SVM)* - Support Vectors are data points nearer to the hyper plane and impact its position and direction. Hyper plane in SVM isolates different classes such that the distance between them is maximized. In the event that the classes are distinguished on a non-linear basis, SVM changes the lower layered information into a greater aspect utilizing non-straight Kernel capacity like Radial Basis Function, Sigmoid and thereafter performs classification.

2. *Gradient Boost Decision Tree (XGBoost):* Chen and Guestrin proposed XGBoost as an ensemble algorithm based on Gradient boost decision trees. XGBoost utilizes a standardized objective function to lessen intricacies of the model and forestall over fitting. XGBoost enhances productivity, flexibility and adaptability as a gradient boosting algorithm. Lately, XGBoost shows great execution in various Machine Learning (ML) problems where it is broadly utilized by specialists. In order to remove the residual errors of past models, it works to add new model to the existing ones.

3. *Classification and regression tree (CART)* - The algorithm helps to predict target variable values based on other values. It is, therefore, a decision tree where every fork becomes a split in a predictor variable and at the end of every node has a prediction for target variable.

2 Literature Review

HongZhou Lu (2020), in their review, made the disclosures about the novel coronavirus due to its similarity to the SARS infection of 2003. This coronavirus can be identified in lung liquid, blood and throat swab tests of the patients. In people, these viruses are among the range of infections that cause the normal cold, as well as more serious respiratory illnesses like SARS and MERS.

Barstugan et al. proposed an AI approach for SARS COV-2 characterization from computed tomography scans. Patches in a variety of sizes (1616, 3232, and 6464) were extracted from 150 computed tomography scans.

Zhi-Min Chen (2020) [10] in their review gave results about the contamination affecting young ones. Children are no longer immune to the infection, and they, along with people over a certain age who have co-morbidities, are at risk.

Breiman (1984) first proposed the decision tree (DT) algorithm, a predictive model of machine learning. It is a learning algorithm for a huge amounts of input data that can be used for data mining. It predicts the class label based on several input variables. A classifier can compare and check for similarities in a dataset for a decision tree. It is then ranked into disti nct classes.

L. Hussain (2020) [1] deduced a comparative analysis on obtaining results using four different classifiers: XGB-L, XGB-Tree, CART (DT), and K-Nearest Neighbour machine learning algorithms and characterization of features for COVID-19.

These classifiers provided near-perfect accuracy for all performance measures, including the top four ranked parameters of compactness, standard deviation, thin ratio, and perimeter. It demonstrates the huge distinction between the two groups.

2.1 Methods

A. *Dataset*-The data for COVID-19 Chest X-Ray images is downloaded from GitHub. The images with only PA view i.e. Posterior-anterior view were taken for training and testing. Kaggle is the other source for data related to chest X-ray images dataset. The sample contains images related to non-COVID viral pneumonia, bacterial pneumonia, and normal Chest X-rays. A stratified sampling method is used to split the dataset into 80% and 20% ratio for training and testing data. Further, we use the training data instead the whole dataset for feature selection.

B. *Proposed work*-Building a classifier using CNN to differentiate between other viral diseases and corona virus.

  i.   Classification - Training the classifier with both sets of images for Covid-19 infected as well as non-infected cases.
  ii.   Reasoning - Class Activation maps that can be done using Grad-CAM algorithm and generate Saliency maps.
  iii. Visualization - Heat maps can be drawn to ascertain which part is infected due to virus.

While using Deep learning Models with medical data, the reason for the obtained results must be comprehended.

3 Algorithm CNN Model Algorithm Model = Sequential()

```
model.add(Conv2D(filters=32, kernel_size=(3,3), activation= 'relu', input_shape=(224,224,3)))

model.add(Conv2D(filters=64,kernel_size=(3,3), activation= 'relu'))

model.add(MaxPool2D()) model.add(Dropout(rate=0.25))

model.add(Conv2D(filters=64,kernel_size=(3,3), activation= 'relu'))

model.add(MaxPool2D())
model.add(Dropout(rate=0.25))

model.add(Conv2D(filters=128, kernel_size=(3,3),activation= 'relu'))

model.add(MaxPool2D()) model.add(Dropout(rate=0.25))
```

4 Flowchart

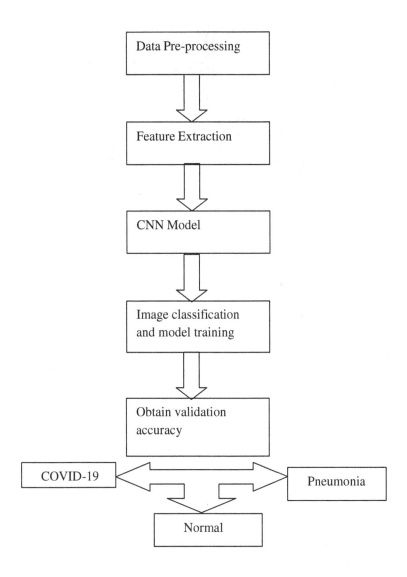

5 Experiment and Results

We trained the model by calling the final generator function. Validation data comes from a validation generator. We started with a baseline accuracy of 50% for validation as we ran one epoch. And as we run 10 epochs, we achieve training accuracy of 95.31% and validation accuracy of 96.67%. We obtained the following plot for True +ve, False − ve, False +ve, and True −ve cases.

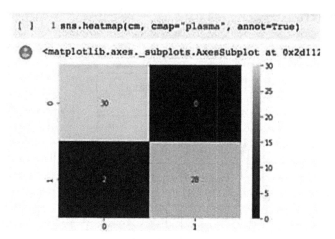

```
[ ]    1 sns.heatmap(cm, cmap="plasma", annot=True)
```

`<matplotlib.axes._subplots.AxesSubplot at 0x2d11;`

6 Workflow

Given below is the workflow and steps used in the study:

Initialization: In order to process the X-ray images available in different sizes by algorithms, we resize them to 224 224 3 dimensions. The number 3 represents the RGB.

Training: For training, we use the Keras image data generator library to make data ready for the model. We will rescale the data for augmentation by the factor of 1/255 for

Validation: We will create a similar generator function for validation data. For validation purposes, 20% of the model is used and 80% of it is used for constructing the model for training.

Data Labeling: It gives a label of "0" for positive COVID cases and "1" for negative cases.

To approve the model developed, the preparation dataset was split with 80% for building the model and 20% for approval of the built model. The test dataset was not displayed to the model at the time of the training process and was utilised to chec k the genuineness of the developed model.

Developing a Convolutional Neural Network

Input layer. The size of the image given to the input layers is 224 224 3.

It is central to the Convolution Neural Network that carries the primary part of the network's computational burden.

Here we work on Google Colab, wherein we import certain libraries like matplotlib.pyplot, keras, and layers. Thereafter, we try to build a CNN-based sequential model in Keras. We work with multiple layers in CNN, with each layer having a number of filters having a layered architecture. We will create 3–4 CNN layers followed by classification layers.

32 Filters Are Used

The CNN algorithm helps to extract 32 features in a 2D convolution with the help of a kernel and filter. As the filter scans over the whole image, a dot product is obtained at each site covered by the filter. Feature maps or activation maps are generated due to this process.

7   Conclusion

The approach proposed here decreases the recognition time drastically while accomplishing satisfactory accuracy, a predominant benefit for the development of real-time or near-real-time inferences in clinical applications. In this particular CNN model, Google Colab is used to execute the algorithm. The dataset is trained and the validation accuracy obtained is more than 96%. This is a very cost-effective way of using machine learning for the classification of infected and non-infected cases since working on Google Colab doesn't require enormous computational resources.

References

1. Hussain, L., et al.: Machine-learning classification of texture features of portable chest X-ray accurately classifies COVID-19 lung infection
2. Li, Q., Guan, X., Wu, P., Wang, X., Zhou, L., Tong, Y.: Early transmission dynamics in Wuhan, China, of novel coronavirus-infected pneumonia. N. Engl. J. Med. (2020)
3. Xie, X., Zhong, Z., Zhao, W., Zheng, C., Wang, F., Liu, J.: Chest CT for typical 2019-nCoV pneumonia: relationship to negative RT-PCR testing. Radiology (2020)
4. Zargari Khuzani, A., Heidari, M., Shariati, S.A.: COVID-Classifier: an automated machine learning model to assist in the diagnosis of COVID-19 infection in chest X-ray images. Sci. Rep. **11,** 9887 (2021)
5. Wang, S., et al.: A deep learning algorithm using CT images to screen for corona virus disease (2020)
6. Kumar, R., et al.: Accurate prediction of COVID-19 using chest X-ray images through deep feature learning model with SMOTE and machine learning classifiers (2020)
7. Chavez, S., Long, B., Koyfman, A., Liang, S.Y.: Coronavirus Disease (COVID-19): a primer for emergency physicians. Am. J. Emerg. Med. **44**, 220–229 (2021)
8. Liu, H., Liu, F., Li, J., Zhang, T., Wang, D., Lan, W.: Clinical and CT imaging features of the COVID-19 pneumonia: Focus on pregnant women and children. J. Infect. **80**, e7–e13 (2020)
9. Rothan, H.A., Byrareddy, S.N.: The epidemiology and pathogenesis of coronavirus disease (COVID-19) outbreak. J. Autoimmun. **109**, 102433 (2020)
10. Wu, F., et al.: A new coronavirus associated with human respiratory disease in China. Nature **579**(7798), 265–269 (2020). https://doi.org/10.1038/s41586-020-2008-3. Epub 2020 Feb 3. Erratum in: Nature 2020 Apr; 580(7803):E7. PMID: 32015508; PMCID: PMC7094943

Smart Healthcare Surveillance System Using IoT and Machine Learning Approaches for Heart Disease

Santanu Basak[✉] and Kakali Chatterjee

Department of Computer Science and Engineering, National Institute of Technology Patna,
Patna 800005, Bihar, India
{santanub.ph21.cs,kakali}@nitp.ac.in

Abstract. The Internet of Things (IoT) and Machine Learning (ML) based Smart Healthcare Surveillance System (SHSS) enhances the monitoring service quality of the present healthcare sectors. Efficient SHSS for specially heart disease is a challenging task. It involves collecting data of vital parameters of the body from different sensors (wearable sensors, implanted sensors), then filtering that to remove less important data, and finally data analyzing for taking the decision to provide proper treatment. Diseases can be caused by changing lifestyle or changing in lifestyle may be the symptom of a disease. IoT can provide services not only for detecting heart disease for future but also it can serve in emergency situations. The primary goal of this surveillance system is to monitor changes in a patient's health in order to predict heart disease and deliver appropriate medicine via an automated procedure in the real-time environment. The SHSS uses edge layer to provide real-time services and the cloud layer for further latency tolerable analysis. Security and privacy are inevitable part of SHSS as it works with sensitive data of the patients. So, data security and user access mechanism should be involved. In this paper we have proposed an architecture of SHSS for heart disease, and discussed and analyzed the efficiency of different ML algorithms for making prediction of heart disease.

Keywords: Smart Healthcare Surveillance System · Internet of Things (IoT) · Machine learning · Edge computing · Supervised learning

1 Introduction

Increasing numbers of patients of heart disease day by day, result in increasing load for a existing system. To overcome this situation involvement of specialist should also be increased. On the other hand time is the most important factor for the heart patients as quick action is required to handle the emergency situations. An efficient SHSS is capable to resolve both issues by providing different services such as monitoring, remote treatments, taking action autonomously and handling real-time situations. The cloud based SHSS is capable of storing huge data, and processing the data faster but due to higher latency, jitter, and power consumption it may insecure the life of the patients in

© The Author(s), under exclusive license to Springer Nature Switzerland AG 2022
S. Rajagopal et al. (Eds.): ASCIS 2022, CCIS 1759, pp. 304–313, 2022.
https://doi.org/10.1007/978-3-031-23092-9_24

emergency situations. To overcome these issues, edge computing was introduced, where end devices are capable of storing data, and processing the data [16]. Alternatively it can be said, the edge devices are able to store, and process data but there are some limitations, because of the resource constraint. Otherwise the quality and the cost of the Healthcare sector will change using IoT-Edge-Cloud based systems [12]. Apart from that there should be a module that provides data security and protection from unauthorized access as clinical data is sensitive [9].

Contribution of research in this paper is as follows.

– An IoT-Edge-Cloud enabled architecture of Smart Healthcare Surveillance System for heart disease is proposed. The Edge device plays a major role for managing real-time situations and makes the system more efficient by reducing computation and transmission overhead.
– The proposed architecture provides data security to protect patient's sensitive information.
– An access mechanism has been proposed with the architecture to stop unauthorized access.
– Different ML classifiers have been used with a dataset of heart disease to analyze the efficiency.

The rest part of the paper is organized as follows: Sect. 2 presents related works. The proposed architecture is discussed in Sect. 3. In Sect. 4 result analysis is discussed. Section 5 concludes the work.

2 Related Works

An IoT based healthcare system is proposed in [4, 14], able to monitor and track patient, staff, biomedical devices, and handle emergency situations. This smart system provides the interaction environment for smart mobile where local and remote users can access patient's physiological and environmental data from the control center. A healthcare system based on IoT to support physiological study uses improved particle swarm optimization (PSO) and provides an early warning system to detect physical abnormality in advance is discussed in [2]. A low cost, low powered, lightweight, wearable device for the guidance and improving the daily life where data coming from IoT devices is stored, processed, and analyzed at the cloud is presented in [1, 3, 5]. A framework for IoT-cloud to support the patients of Intensive Care Unit (ICU) provides a real-time alert generation system is proposed in [6], where collected data from heterogeneous sensors is stored, extracted, and analyzed in the cloud server. Another IoT-cloud based framework for healthcare solutions to predict vulnerabilities of health during workout time in real-time, is introduced in [7], where the data accumulating layer collects physiological, environmental, dietary, behavioral data and sends it to the cloud for storing, through a secure channel. Then the data categorization layer uses a feature extraction mechanism and the data abstraction layer provides abstraction using temporal mining techniques, and also measures the vulnerability level. The predictive layer uses Artificial Neural Network (ANN) for monitoring, learning, prediction and mathematical foundation helps in prediction of vulnerability. Authors in [8] have proposed a gateway (UT-GATE) with high-processing power and parallel processing features for edge layer (intermediary intelligence geo-distributed layer) works as protocol translator between sensor node and cloud and provides services like data filtering, data analysis, real-time data processing for high priority tasks to handle medical emergencies, and embedded data mining. It supports streaming based transmission for getting real-time response. A Fully Homomorphic Encryption (FHE) and machine learning based EoT framework for smart health surveillance is presented in [9]. It manages biosignal data by aggregating, monitoring, performing real-time analysis, and detecting abnormality, where data is analyzed in encrypted form using FHE. An IoT based healthcare system with cross-domain support and the attribute-based encryption controls prevents unauthorized access of patient's data in normal situations and during emergency situations a break-glass access mechanism is designed in [10]. It also uses deduplication techniques to remove redundant data which helps in reducing transfer overhead. This paper [11] presents a lightweight HealthFog framework that manages heart patient's data, where Edge device uses deep learning to analyze heart disease automatically. The power consumption, bandwidth utilization, latency, jitter, and execution time is low with high accuracy but the result is unreliable when the confidence is considered below 50%. A smart real-time health monitoring system is developed in [15], where body information like temperature, humidity, motion are collected from wearable devices accurately and transferred to the smartphone for providing health support in advance. To handle one of the COVID-19 pandemic challenges for the patients of ICU (Intensive Care Unit), an IoT-cloud based healthcare platform (PAR) is introduced in [17]. It uses integrated wearable unobtrusive sensors and provides real-time remote monitoring and emergency situation handler.

3 Proposed Architecture

In this section a proposed architecture of Smart Healthcare Surveillance System for heart disease has been discussed.

The Architecture (see Fig. 1) consists of three layers, Data Generation Layer, Edge Layer, and Cloud Layer.

Data Generation Layer: This Layer is responsible for generating different physiological parameters like respiratory system, heart's rhythm and electrical activity, heart rate, blood pressure, body temperature, oxygen saturation. Respiratory system related data is generated from the Respiration Rate (RR) sensor, heart's rhythm and electrical activity related data is generated from Electrocardiograph (ECG) sensor, generated data from Heart Rate (HR) sensor is used to calculated the heart rate per minute (BPM) using the first pulse value (FPV), list pulse counter value (LPCV), single pulse time (SPT), and Ten pulse time (TPT) as it is discussed in [19]:

$$TPT = FPV \check{\ } LPCV \tag{1}$$

$$SPT = TPT/10 \tag{2}$$

$$BPM = 60/STP \tag{3}$$

Data coming from Blood Pressure (BP) sensor is used to measure the mean arterial pressure (MAP) using diastolic blood pressure (DBP), blood pressure (BP) as evaluated in [20]:

$$MAP = (BP - DBP) * 0.3 + DBP \tag{4}$$

Data of Body Temperature (BT) sensor is calculated as it is described in [19]:

$$Temperature = 32 + (Outputvolt. * 1.8) \tag{5}$$

The oxygen saturation level (SpO2) is estimated using oxyhaemoglobin (OH) and deoxyhaemoglobin (DH) as formulated in [20]:

$$SpO2 = OH/DH \tag{6}$$

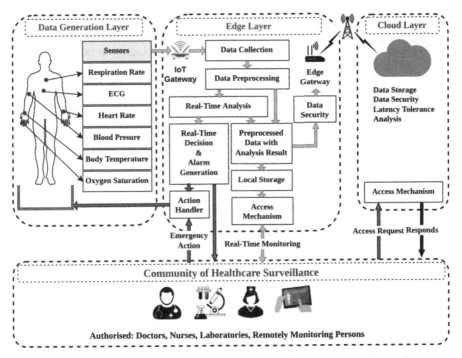

Fig. 1. Proposed architecture of smart healthcare surveillance system for heart disease

The data from RR sensor is used for predicting symptoms of chronic respiratory diseases, asthma and chronic obstructive pulmonary disease, the data from ECG sensor is used for predicting the primary diagnosis of certain heart diseases, the data from HR sensor and BT sensor are used for detecting the heartbeat of the patient in order to monitor the risk of heart attack, the data from SpO2 sensor is used for oxygen level in blood. All the physiological data is sent to the Edge Layer.

Edge Layer: This Layer mainly performs computation for early detecting and takes required action. The Data Collection module collects all the data coming from Data Generation Layer using IoT Gateway and performs preprocessing for data filtering and data aggregation which makes the real-time analysis faster. After analysis is done the decision making module decides if any immediate action is required and depending on the decision the alarm is raised. If an alarm is raised a notification is sent to all communities of the healthcare and also to the autonomous system that is able to handle the emergency situation in real-time. If an alarm is not raised then data and analysis result is stored in local storage of Edge Layer and also sent to the Cloud Layer. The access mechanism ensures access control for the community of healthcare.

Cloud Layer: This layer is responsible for storing data and performing further analysis that is latency tolerable. The access mechanism also ensures access control for the community of healthcare. The decision of latency tolerance analysis is sent to the community of healthcare form taking action if required.

Data Security: Integration of security takes an important role for an application. It is also a crucial phase for an application development life cycle as it is not necessary during design phase. A framework of security engineering based process is introduced in [23] to reduce the identified security threads. Requirement engineers finds different constraints for providing security. That task involves identifying risks of the threads. Improper design increases cost of development or vulnerability. Providing data security at edge also a challenging role. Physiological data is sensitive and requires proper techniques to maintain confidentiality also to stop unauthorized access. So data encryption, access control mechanism are required to ensure that. A light weight privacy preservation scheme based on Paillier cryptosystem is proposed in [24]. This cryptosystem uses operations as exclusive-OR and generates random ciphers.

Access Mechanism: Clinical data is very sensitive as it is the foundation of treatments. One of the major issues is transmitting those data through wireless network [13]. So communication process should ensures confidentiality, authenticity, and integrity. It should also able to resist vulnerable attacks with low transmission, computational overhead. Sending sensed data to the cloud securely is the biggest challenge. Any modification of such sensitive data make the patient's life in danger. To avoid such situation a secure communication is required [24]. The asymmetric key cryptography such as Elliptic Curve Cryptography (ECC) based authentication technique can be used but communication overhead is high for distributing public key [21]. Therefore the Identity (ID) based authentication technique was introduced in [22], but it is also not suitable for high time complexity. Biometric based authentication scheme is proposed in [24].

4   Result Analysis

In this section accuracy related analysis results have been discussed for different ML algorithms which can be used in proposed architecture to predict heart disease.

Different machine learning algorithms such as Logistic Regression, Random Forest, Gaussian NB, K-Nearest Neighbors (KNN), Decision Tree, Support Vector Machines are used with heart disease dataset of kaggle [18]. The dataset is described in Table 1.

Table 1. Description of Heart Disease Dataset

Sl. no.	Name of the attribute	Description
1	Age	Patient's age in years
2	Sex	Male, Female
3	ChestPainType	ASY = Asymptomatic, ATA = Atarax, NAP = Naproxen, TA = Typical angina
4	RestingBP	Resting blood pressure
5	Cholesterol	Value of cholesterol
6	FastingBS	Fasting blood sugar
7	RestingECG	LVH = Left ventricular hypertrophy, Normal, ST = ST segment
8	MaxHR	Maximum heart rate
9	ExerciseAngina	N = No, Y = Yes
10	Oldpeak	ST depression induced by exercise relative to rest
11	ST_Slope	Up, Flat, Down
12	HeartDisease	Prediction of heart disease (0 = No and 1 = Yes)

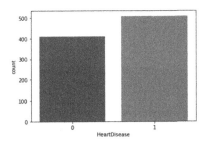

Fig. 2. Data distribution of target class.

Before training the model with a predefined dataset it is processed in several steps for preprocessing. Dataset does not contain any missing value or null value, so further fields containing non-numerical data are identified and converted to numeric forms using LabelEncoder of sklean python library. Next data is scaled using StandardScaler of sklearn python library in-order to achieve mean as 0 and standard deviation as 1, otherwise features having higher value may dominate the trained model. Figure 2 shows that the data is almost balanced for the target class, so it is not required to balance data for the target class. The features are Age, Sex, ChestPainType, RestingBP, Cholesterol, FastingBS, RestingECG, MaxHR, ExerciseAngina, Oldpeak, and ST_Slope. The features are selected using correlation coefficient (see Fig. 3). The highest correlated value is −0.56 for ST_Slope with HeartDisease and lowest correlation value is 0.057 for RestingECG. No features are not much less correlated with target class, HeartDisease. So all the features are selected for the experiment.

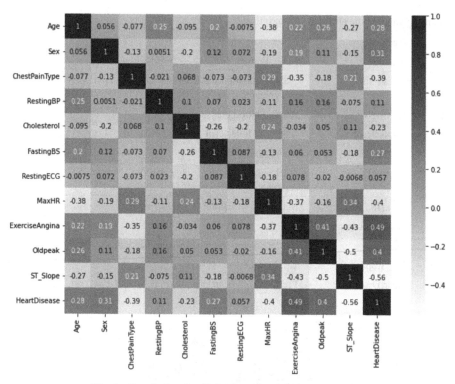

Fig. 3. Correlation Coefficient matrix of different features.

Table 2 shows different analysis results of different algorithms. In the confusion matrix (see Fig. 4), 0 denotes false-class and 1 denotes true-class. If prediction is correctly predicted for true-class or positive-class then it is defined as True Positive (TP), similarly if prediction is correctly predicted for false-class or negative-class, it is defined as True Negative (TN) but if prediction is wrongly predicted for true-class or positive-class, is denoted as False Positive (FP) and otherwise it is False Negative (FN).

Table 2. Analysis results of different algorithms.

Classifiers	TP	TN	FP	FN	Accuracy
Logistic Regression	46.20%	40.22%	6.52%	7.07%	86.4%
Random Forest	48.91%	43.48%	3.26%	4.35%	92.4%
Gaussian NB	47.83%	40.76%	5.98%	5.43%	88.6%
KNeighbors	45.65%	33.15%	13.59%	7.61%	78.8%
Decision Tree	44.57%	40.22%	6.52%	8.7%	84.8%
Support Vector Machines	47.28%	40.22%	6.52%	5.98%	87.5%

Figure 4a shows the confusion matrix for Logistic Regression where TP is 46.20%, TN is 40.22%, FP is 6.53%, and FN is 7.07%. Figure 4b shows the confusion matrix for Random Forest classifier where TP is 48.91%, TN is 43.48%, FP is 3.26%, and FN is 4.35%. Figure 4c shows the confusion matrix of Gaussian NB classifier where TP is 47.83%, TN is 40.76%, FP is 5.98%, and FN is 5.43%. Figure 4d shows the confusion matrix of K-Nearest Neighbors (KNN) classifier where TP is 45.65%, TN is 33.15%, FP is 13.59%, and FN is 7.61%. Figure 4e shows the confusion matrix of Decision Tree classifier where TP is 44.57%, TN is 40.22%, FP is 6.52%, and FN is 8.7%. Figure 4f shows the confusion matrix of Support Vector Machines classifier where TP is 47.28%, TN is 40.22%, FP is 6.52%, and FN is 5.98%.

$$Accuracy = (TP + TN)/(TP + TN + FP + FN) \tag{7}$$

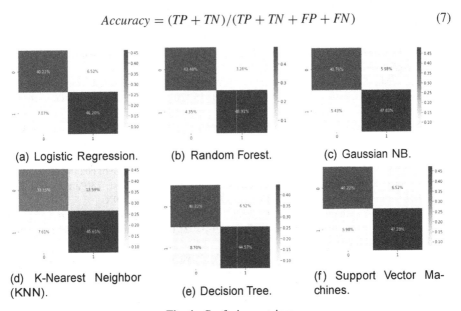

(a) Logistic Regression.

(b) Random Forest.

(c) Gaussian NB.

(d) K-Nearest Neighbor (KNN).

(e) Decision Tree.

(f) Support Vector Machines.

Fig. 4. Confusion matrices

5   Conclusion

In this research an architecture of IoT and ML based Smart Healthcare Surveillance System for heart disease is proposed. This architecture consisting three layers which are discussed with required component of each layer. The current work is focused on the ML algorithms for prediction of heart disease, further we will work on the data security and access mechanism. A heart disease related dataset is used for analysing efficiency using ML algorithms such as Logistic Regression, Random Forest, Gaussian NB, K-Nearest Neighbors (KNN), Decision Tree, Support Vector Machines. All of these gives good accuracy but Random Forest gives 92.4% as accuracy level which the best with compare to all. Rates for TP, TN, FP, and FN shows no model is biased with the current dataset.

References

1. Jara, A.J., Alcolea, A.F., Zamora, M.A., Skarmeta, A.F.G., Alsaedy, M.: Drugs interaction checker based on IoT. In: 2010 Internet of Things (IOT), pp. 1–8 (2010). https://doi.org/10.1109/IOT.2010.5678458
2. Sung, W.T., Chiang, Y.C.: Improved particle swarm optimization algorithm for android medical care IOT using modified parameters. J. Med. Syst. **36**(6), 3755–3763 (2012). https://doi.org/10.1007/s10916-012-9848-9
3. Yang, G., et al.: A health-IoT platform based on the integration of intelligent packaging unobtrusive bio-sensor, and intelligent medicine box. IEEE Trans. Ind. Inform. **10**(4), 2180–2191 (2014). https://doi.org/10.1109/TII.2014.2307795
4. Catarinucci, L., et al.: An IoT-aware architecture for smart healthcare systems. IEEE Internet Things J. **2**(6), 515–526 (2015). https://doi.org/10.1109/JIOT.2015.2417684
5. Abdelgawad, A., Yelamarthi, K., Khattab, A.: IoT-based health monitoring system for active and assisted living. In: Gaggi, O., Manzoni, P., Palazzi, C., Bujari, A., Marquez-Barja, J.M. (eds.) GOODTECHS 2016. LNICSSITE, vol. 195, pp. 11–20. Springer, Cham (2017). https://doi.org/10.1007/978-3-319-61949-1_2
6. Bhatia, M., Sood, S.K.: Temporal informative analysis in smart-ICU monitoring: M-HealthCare perspective. J. Med. Syst. **40**(8), 1–15 (2016). https://doi.org/10.1007/s10916-016-0547-9
7. Bhatia, M., Sood, S.K.: A comprehensive health assessment framework to facilitate IoT-assisted smart workouts: a predictive healthcare perspective. Comput. Ind. **92–93**, 50–66 (2017). https://doi.org/10.1016/j.compind.2017.06.009. ISSN 0166-3615
8. Rahmani, A.M., et al.: Exploiting smart e-Health gateways at the edge of healthcare Internet-of-Things: a fog computing approach. Future Gener. Comput. Syst. **78**(Part 2), 641–658 (2018). https://doi.org/10.1016/j.future.2017.02.014. ISSN 0167-739X
9. Alabdulatif, A., Khalil, I., Yi, X., Guizani, M.: Secure edge of things for smart healthcare surveillance framework. IEEE Access **7**, 31010–31021 (2019). https://doi.org/10.1109/ACCESS.2019.2899323
10. Yang, Y., Zheng, X., Guo, W., Liu, X., Chang, V.: Privacy-preserving smart IoT-based healthcare big data storage and self-adaptive access control system. Inf. Sci. **479**, 567–592 (2019). https://doi.org/10.1016/j.ins.2018.02.005. ISSN 0020-0255
11. Rathee, G., Sharma, A., Saini, H., Kumar, R., Iqbal, R.: A hybrid framework for multimedia data processing in IoT-healthcare using blockchain technology. Multimed. Tools Appl. **79**(15–16), 9711–9733 (2019). https://doi.org/10.1007/s11042-019-07835-3

12. Tuli, S., et al.: HealthFog: an ensemble deep learning based smart healthcare system for automatic diagnosis of heart diseases in integrated IoT and fog computing environments. Future Gener. Comput. Syst. **104**, 187–200 (2020). https://doi.org/10.1016/j.future.2019.10.043. ISSN 0167-739X

13. Guo, X., Lin, H., Wu, Y., Peng, M.: A new data clustering strategy for enhancing mutual privacy in healthcare IoT systems. Future Gener. Comput. Syst. **113**, 407–417 (2020). https://doi.org/10.1016/j.future.2020.07.023. ISSN 0167-739X

14. Aujla, G.S., Jindal, A.: A decoupled blockchain approach for edge-envisioned IoT-based healthcare monitoring. IEEE J. Sel. Areas Commun. **39**(2), 491–499 (2021). https://doi.org/10.1109/JSAC.2020.3020655

15. Lee, S., et al.: All-day mobile healthcare monitoring system based on heterogeneous stretchable sensors for medical emergency. IEEE Trans. Ind. Electron. **67**(10), 8808–8816 (2020). https://doi.org/10.1109/TIE.2019.2950842

16. Singh, A., Chatterjee, K.: Securing smart healthcare system with edge computing. Comput. Secur. **108**, 102353 (2021). https://doi.org/10.1016/j.cose.2021.102353. ISSN 0167-4048

17. Filho, I.d.M.B., Aquino, G., Malaquias, R.S., Girão, G., Melo, S.R.M.: An IoT-based healthcare platform for patients in ICU beds during the COVID-19 outbreak. IEEE Access **9**, 27262–27277 (2021). https://doi.org/10.1109/ACCESS.2021.3058448

18. Fedesoriano: Heart Failure Prediction Dataset, Version 1, 10 September 2021. https://www.kaggle.com/fedesoriano/heart-failure-prediction. Accessed 02 Jan 2022

19. Mahamud, M.S., Islam, M.M., Rahman, M.S., Suman, S.H.: CUSTODY: an IoT based patient surveillance device. In: Arai, K., Bhatia, R., Kapoor, S. (eds.) FTC 2018. AISC, vol. 880, pp. 225–234. Springer, Cham (2019). https://doi.org/10.1007/978-3-030-02686-8_18

20. Sahu, M.L., Atulkar, M., Ahirwal, M.K., Ahamad, A.: Vital sign monitoring system for healthcare through IoT based personal service application. Wirel. Pers. Commun. **122**(1), 129–156 (2021). https://doi.org/10.1007/s11277-021-08892-4

21. Lim, M.-H., Yeoh, C.-M., Lee, S., Lim, H., Lee, H.: A secure and efficient three-pass authenticated key agreement protocol based on elliptic curves. In: Das, A., Pung, H.K., Lee, F.B.S., Wong, L.W.C. (eds.) NETWORKING 2008. LNCS, vol. 4982, pp. 170–182. Springer, Heidelberg (2008). https://doi.org/10.1007/978-3-540-79549-0_15

22. Yang, J.-H., Chang, C.-C.: An ID-based remote mutual authentication with key agreement scheme for mobile devices on elliptic curve cryptosystem. Comput. Secur. **28**, 138–143 (2009). https://doi.org/10.1016/j.cose.2008.11.008

23. Chatterjee, K., Gupta, D., De, A.: A framework for development of secure software. CSI Trans. ICT **1**, 143–157 (2013). https://doi.org/10.1007/s40012-013-0010-8

24. Chatterjee, K.: An improved authentication protocol for wireless body sensor networks applied in healthcare applications. Wirel. Pers. Commun. **111**(4), 2605–2623 (2019). https://doi.org/10.1007/s11277-019-07005-6

Detection of the Affected Area and Classification of Pests Using Convolutional Neural Networks from the Leaf Images

Bhasker Pant[1], Durgaprasad Gangodkar[1], Dibyahash Bordoloi[1(✉)], and Ankur Dumka[1,2]

[1] Department of Computer Science and Engineering, Graphic Era Deemed to be University, Dehradun, Uttarakhand 248002, India
{bhaskerpant,dibyahashbordoloi}@geu.ac.in, ankurdumka@wit.ac.in
[2] Department of Computer Science and Engineering, Women Institute of Technology, Dehradun, Uttarakhand 248001, India

Abstract. Insect infestation is the primary threat to vegetable crops. Using effective insecticides is one method for preventing pest infestation. The success of any effort to safeguard crops relies on their discovery of the pest or their presence as soon as possible. In the beginning, pests were identified by hand. This is a lengthy process that needs constant oversight from professionals. The infestation must be inspected, and the various pests must be classified, using an automated pest detection system. Pests and plant diseases may be identified and located with the help of a wide variety of modern tools and approaches. There is a high degree of efficiency and dependability in the use of image processing techniques in these methods. Before calculating the impacted area in the picture, the suggested model determines whether the leaf has been harmed. Then, convolutional neural networks were used to classify the found pest's location. By determining what proportion of the surface is infected, one may gauge the extent of the problem and act accordingly.

Keywords: Segmentation · Localised interest · Convolution neural networks · Insect identification

1 Introduction

Virtual Insect infestation is the primary threat to vegetable crops. Using effective insecticides is one method for preventing pest infestation. The success of any effort to safeguard crops relies on their discovery of the pest or their presence as soon as possible. In the beginning, pests were identified by hand. This is a lengthy process that needs constant oversight from professionals. The infestation must be inspected, and the various pests must be classified, using an automated pest detection system. Pests and plant diseases may be identified and located with the help of a wide variety of modern tools and approaches. There is a high degree of efficiency and dependability in the use of image processing techniques in these methods. Before calculating the impacted area in

© The Author(s), under exclusive license to Springer Nature Switzerland AG 2022
S. Rajagopal et al. (Eds.): ASCIS 2022, CCIS 1759, pp. 314–322, 2022.
https://doi.org/10.1007/978-3-031-23092-9_25

the picture, the suggested model determines whether the leaf has been harmed. Then, convolutional neural networks were used to classify the found pest's location. By determining what proportion of the surface is infected, one may gauge the extent of the problem and act accordingly.

First, let's set the scene. Agriculture is a major industry in Sri Lanka's Batticaloa District, located in the country's eastern region. Agriculture is the primary source of income for more than 60% of the population. That's why boosting agricultural yields is so crucial. The Batticaloa area is known for its diverse vegetable crops. Women's Finger Tomatoes Long Beans Brinjal Squash Chili Onion But the "pest infestation" on food plants is one of the most pressing issues right now. Identifying the indications of pests, which may be seen on the leaves of damaged or diseased vegetable plants, is crucial to the fruitful production of crops. The only method to counteract the damage caused by these bugs is using pesticides. Using pesticides may get rid of some types of insects. Increasing the usage of pesticides has devastating effects on agricultural output, the environment, natural resources, and animals that come into contact with the chemicals. Chemical pesticides have a negative impact on soil biodiversity. Early pest detection is a primary area of investigation for us. The pictures are from a combination of camera captures and downloads from imagenet.org and other sources on the web. So, before the picture content can be retrieved by the image processing techniques, the images must undergo some kind of preprocessing.

This research proposes a method for automatically identifying infected leaves and classifying the presence of the pest in photos of leaves from different plants. Next, a convolutional neural network based on image processing provides a straightforward and powerful approach to pest categorization.

There are a number of factors that make it challenging to identify the pests that plague vegetable fields, including the bugs' complex articulation, their varied size and coloration, and the fact that some of them are visually challenging despite their otherwise simple anatomy. Recognizing pests in still photographs using an automated approach raises the difficulty level of the job. Different angles, a cluttered backdrop, and transformations like rotation, noise, etc. may be applied to an image of an annoying bug. Since intra-pest differences make it hard to distinguish the kind of pest, it is possible that two photos of the same insect are distinct [2]. We need to offer a good segmentation approach to deal with these issues. When it comes to pattern recognition, picture retrieval, and minimal surveillance, image segmentation is often the most important task involved. Segmentation's end product is employed mostly for comprehending picture material and identifying visual things by pinpointing the area of interest [13]. To isolate the leaf area when a pest is present, this research makes use of a colour transformation methodology for image pre -processing and an adaptive thresholding approach. The properties of the impacted and pest areas were also taken into account. MATLAB 2014a is used to implement the strategy.

The study's primary aims are to:

- Collect a dataset consisting of photographs of vegetable gardens.
- To count the types of insect pests included in the data collection.
  The goal is to create a model that can determine whether or not a leaf has been harmed by pests by analysing its texture.

- To determine the most effective segmentation technique for the targeted area in insect detection.
- Constructing a model for a classification technique and setting it up for recognition.
- Assess and examine the findings of the categorization.

Below is a breakdown of the remaining sections of the paper: Part II explains what others have done along the same lines in the same issue space. The suggested approach and the results of the sequential procedures are described in further detail in Section (II-A). The experimental setup for the classification is then described in Section (III), followed by the findings and discussion in Section (II-B). The last part (IV) summarises the categorization outcomes and suggests further study directions based on our findings.

2 Instrumentation and Materials

IN this part, we will discuss a few recent efforts that have contributed to the issue space. It also describes the experimental setup for the classification tests and gives a short introduction of alternative segmentation approaches for detecting the items supplied in the leaf pictures.

The images were then classified by the system, which included features like region detection and representation using SIFTs or SURFs (speeded-up robust feature descriptors), codebook construction to make the descriptors a fixed-length vector in the histogram space, and support vector machine multi-class classification of the feature histograms (SVMs). In addition, the classification used histograms of oriented gradient descriptors (HOG). The closest neighbour method was employed as a baseline classifier and compared to SVM-based classifiers. They divided the outcomes of their experiments into three groups. Comparing the SIFT and SURF descriptors' effectiveness in the bag-of-words technique to insect pest classification in paddy fields is the first task. In this method, similar images from the same class were broken down into local patches and used to extract SIFT or SURF characteristics. After that, a visual codebook was created to quantify these characteristics, with like-class descriptors shown as a bag-of-words.

The efficacy of the HOG traits was evaluated in the second group by pest categorization testing. In defence of this method, they claimed that all HOG parameters were stable across all pest types. The 128×128 pixel detection window was split into 225 blocks, 15 across and 15 down. There are a total of 32 values in each block, distributed over 4 cells with an 8-bin histogram. That makes the total size of the vector 7200, or 15 rows by 15 columns by 4 cells per block by 8 histograms. Finally, the effectiveness of SIFT and SURF features when combined with HOG was analysed.

According to their experiments, the HOG descriptors perform noticeably better than the currently available local invariant features, SIFT and SURF, when it comes to classifying paddy field insect pests. When HOG descriptors are used in conjunction with SURF features, classification accuracy improves to about 90%. For its efficiency and ease of use, the linear SVM was the classifier of choice throughout the research.

A customised mask is utilised to detect pests, and then the average filtering is used. This filtered picture is then convolved using what's hiding behind it, the mask. The categorization is then done into two categories, whiteflies and aphids, by extracting the area characteristics and grey co-occurrence matrix properties. For the purpose of identification, they have taken into account aspects of the area, such as the standard deviation and the contrast. The SVM classifier was employed once again to make the labelling decision.

More early detection of the pest is being identified with greater accuracy, as shown by the data. They made two groups, "affected" and "unaffected," from the pictures they collected. Whiteflies and aphids are the two main types of pests in this group. The outcome proves that the SVM training was carried out accurately to a one hundred percent degree.

An method for locating and categorising these pests was devised by the authors of [4]. Their cutting-edge technology offers a quick, efficient, and straightforward approach to pest detection. They provide a straightforward and efficient approach to pest identification based on image processing using a neural network. Images are shrunk and turned to grayscale after being obtained. Region attributes and grey covariance matrix properties are only two examples. Parameters like entropy, mean, standard deviation, and contrast are among those derived from a picture. The Neural Networks classifier takes these characteristics as inputs. The features of the input picture are retrieved and used as input to train the network. Diseases are classified using a feed-forward network. The network was constructed using both damaged and unharmed photos. Their findings show that various measures of dispersion and dissimilarity (such as standard deviation, contrast, variance, and entropy) are distinct. Finding out if the pest is a whitefly or an aphid is the next step once a leaf has been infested. They are inputs to a feedback neural network that represent derived features and provide a binary value of zero or one. Affected images are represented by a 1, whereas unaffected images are deemed 0.

As far as the writers are concerned, their approach is just as lucrative and easy. It's also possible to draw the conclusion that early detection of parasites may save pesticide consumption by as much as 80%.

In [15], the authors suggest inspecting crops for signs of pest infestation and then categorising the types of pests found on the crops. The suggested method estimates the quantity of whiteflies on each leaf by counting the bugs that have settled there. In this paper, we offer a technique for the automated detection and identification of whiteflies on plant leaves. Preprocessing colour photos requires a lot of space and effort. To facilitate their manipulation and reduce storage needs during processing, pictures are often transformed to grayscale. The resulting black-and-white pictures after applying the following equation to them.

$$\text{Intensity}(I, x, y) = 0.2989 * B + 0.5870 * G + 0.1140 * B$$

Images were scaled using bi-cubic interpolation, which produces more natural results than bilinear interpolation or closest neighbour scaling. The typical filtering method used. Morphological operators are used to determine the picture's background, which is then removed from the original image to reveal any pests present. The final picture will consist entirely of pixels with the value 1 for the foreground items and 0 for the background. They claimed that their approach outperforms other segmentation methods like watershed and Gaussian mixture segmentation. The execution time of these algorithms grows exponentially because of the enormous number of sophisticated mathematical operations they perform, including division, multiplication, and the mean. Therefore, the suggested strategy enhances efficiency and produces superior outcomes. The noise was cleaned up with the help of the erosion algorithm. The next step, after the elimination of background noise, was to enhance the pest detection using the dilation algorithm segmentation. As part of the feature extraction procedure, we compute the grey level co-occurrence matrix (GLCM) and the regional attributes of the pictures. The support vector machine was trained using these features in order to classify images. To determine how many bugs there were per square metre of cropland, researchers employed Moore's neighbourhood tracing technique and Jacob's halting criteria.

Detection models for plant diseases were created in [12]. As RGB is used for colour production and this is for the colour descriptor, the input RGB picture has first been transformed to HSI. Next, the picture is segmented, and the relevant regions are retrieved; finally, the green pixels are masked and removed using a certain threshold value. The SGDM matrices are then used to derive the texture statistics. The last step is a check for leaf diseases.

Using correlation-based feature selection (CFS) and the incremental backpropagation learning network, the authors of [8] suggested an autonomous diagnostic method for the categorization of tea pests (IBPLN). The authors collected data on eight significant pests from several tea garden records in northern Bengal, India, to construct a database. There are a total of 609 records in the database, divided into 8 categories and characterised by 11 nominal qualities (signs and symptoms). Machine learning techniques were used to accomplish the categorization. Both the whole feature set and a subset were used to evaluate the categorization results. Findings from their study suggest that CFS may be used to shrink the feature vector, and that CFS combined with IBPLN can be used to a wide variety of classification issues.

[6] proposes a technique for detecting pests in both greenhouse and agricultural settings while requiring less computing complexity. Images are captured and then transformed from RGB to brightness and chroma components (YCbCr). Whiteflies are separated from the backdrop of the transformed picture using mixture models and watershed segmentation methods. The execution time of these algorithms grows exponentially because of the enormous number of mathematical operations they need, such as divisions, multiplications, and averaging. The erosion algorithm was used to get just whiteflies. To further clarify the segmented whiteflies, we additionally apply picture enhancement in the form of dilatation. Moore Neighbor tracing and Jacob stopping criteria are used in the implementation of the counting technique for the whitefly population on each impacted leaf. Whiteflies can be isolated with only two subtraction operations and a pixel comparison using the RDI technique, which is based on their illustrative experience. They claim that numerous aspects have been considered in order to validate the accuracy of the algorithm, including the whiteflies in the area and the fluctuating light intensity that illuminates the leaf.

Due of the computing difficulty involved in processing photos, most studies choose to use grayscale images instead of RGB. In addition, while implementing different neural network topologies for the classification job, regional features are often prioritised.

First, the camera in the garden captures colour photographs of the leaves (RGB), and further images are retrieved from imagenet.org. Images are first transformed from the RGB colour system to an HSV representation (saturation hue value). Color creation works best in RGB format. The HSV model is, nonetheless, a great resource for understanding how colours are perceived. Pure colour, or hue, is one of the attributes of colour that specifies how we see colour. Saturation is the degree to which a colour is pure or how much white light is added to it, and value is the intensity of that light. Additional evaluation is performed using the Hue component, and the colour transformation structure is then applied. The Saturation and Value components are then taken out since they contribute nothing to the overall picture.

The masking method involves setting the pixel value of a picture to zero or another background value. In this case, we're interested in finding areas where the dominating hue is green. This is done in accordance with the threshold value that has been determined for these pixels. If a certain pixel's green intensity component is below a certain threshold, the pixel's intensity is reduced to zero.

After the background was removed, the area of interest and the HSV components. The threshold value for background subtraction is calculated using the level of the image's value component. The threshold value changes depending on the quality of the image and the circumstances under which it was captured. For these reasons, the threshold value is changed for each image.

Small imperfections in a picture may be patched up using morphological image processing. The bwareaopen procedure eliminates from a binary picture all linked components (objects) of fewer than 08 pixels in size.

To identify the pest-infested area in the leaf photograph, a morphological closure operation is first applied, and then a filling operation is performed. To do this, we measured how far apart the centres of mass were for each item throughout the whole length of the boundary pixels. Then, the picture is patched together with a few missing spots determined by the chosen range. Consideration of area attributes for pest detection: (iii)

Area, eccentricity, Euler number, and other attributes of regions were determined at this stage. The bw boundaries boundary-tracing tool was then used to properly pick the pest-infested zones (calculated under the region properties). The result of this process is shown below.

The final picture produced following morphological processing of the leaf image (with pest region). Operations the areas of the pest identified in the impacted leaf photos vary with the region attributes and the bounding box choice. One goal of the study is to determine the severity of pest assault on a leaf by counting the number of insects on a leaf.

3   Convolutional Neural Network-Based Classification Model

THE development of a classification model is required for pest detection based on leaf images. A Matlab "MatConvNet" package was used to construct the classification model. MatConvNet is a MATLAB toolbox for working with convolutional neural networks (CNN). Both ease of use and adaptability have been prioritised in the development of the toolkit. Easy-to-use MATLAB functions are introduced to facilitate the construction of CNNs; they include methods for computing linear convolutions with filter banks, pooling capabilities, and more. MatConvNet facilitates fast computation of CPUs and

GPUs to create complicated models on big data sets like ImageNet ILSVRC, allowing for quick prototyping of novel CNN architectures. To train and evaluate the model, we have employed a computational architecture based on central processing units (CPUs). Matconvnet-1.0-beta-17 and Matlab R2014a were used in the development and testing phases, respectively.

This study took into account the following five groups of pest pictures.

Separate the data set for the classification model into training, testing, and validation sets. Seventy percent of the photos in each category were chosen for training, while the remaining thirty percent were used for testing. Thereafter, 70% of training photos were utilised to construct the training model, while the remaining 30% were used to construct the validation model. And the results of the classifications that were performed using the testing photos and the training model.

3.1 Setting up a MatConvNet to Create a Training Model from the Dataset

MODel construction from scratch and transfer learning are the two most popular applications of deep learning. Both methods are useful and may be used in a variety of contexts to facilitate extensive learning. For very particular jobs for which there are no suitable pre-existing models, developing and training a model from scratch is the best option. An issue with this method is that it often needs a big volume of data to get reliable conclusions. Due to insufficient data, we were unable to start the training process with a blank slate using the dataset we were using. With these pre-trained networks, the training model may be constructed directly from the dataset. To construct the training network models, there are several accessible pre-trained networks to choose from [14]. Some examples are alexnet, vgg16, resnet18, and others.

4 Conclusions and Recommendations

THE fraction of correctly classified test photos, as determined by the following formula.

Rate = The classification success rate was determined by using the deployed training model. The percentages based on the categories given below.

Aspect of pests, Sum of all test images, Accuratelycategorised images, Classification Frequency The percentage of flea beetles (197 out of 151), the June beetle, 266–221 (83.08%), Female insect 71.73% 283 votes, To eliminate insects, 156 out of 104 (66.67)

Pests that leave ugly marks on plants: 89.5865.17, According to the data shown above, tarnish plant bugs have a rather low percentage of accurate categorization. Due to the fact that the only real difference between squash bugs and tarnish plant bugs is their outside coloration. Therefore, majority of the pictures tested for tarnish plant bugs were incorrectly labelled as squash bugs. Furthermore, fewer photographs of each pest species were taken. Because of this, the categorization success rate may vary from study to study.

A classification model constructed utilising the convolutional neuron network is proposed in our study as a means to locate the afflicted region, detect the amount of pests, and identify the kind of insect pest. Many issues have arisen from the implementation of an image processing-based pest identification system. Minor adjustments might cause enormous problems. The image's hue, brightness, contrast, and other attributes may shift when the light changes. In addition, the approach does not provide complete assistance for pest region detection for these reasons, thus the job is only semi-automated for pest detection before the categorization process continues.

An further challenge is that a larger convolution neural network classification success rate requires more examples of each kind of pest. This is why a training model is often constructed using pre-trained network models. The similarities between pests of various classes also played a role in determining the latter's classification.

MatConvNet (matconvnet-1.0-beta17) is the Convolution neural network implementation we've evaluated for this study, although there are newer versions with expanded versions of convolution neural networks that may be used for object identification, such as R-CNN, Fast R-CNN, and Faster R-RCNN. More processing capacity, such as GPU based computer architecture rather than CPU based architecture, is required to realise the newest feature benefits. If you want a better classification rate, you might look at using CUDA, a parallel computing platform, and other image processing toolboxes. Work with massive datasets is something we want to prioritise in the future.

Finally, this study allows for the detection of pests at an earlier stage than ever before. In this way, we may lessen our reliance on harmful chemicals. Image processing techniques provide for more precision than traditional manual procedures. More study is required in this area before we can make recommendations for pesticides based on the impacted pattern and the identification of the pest species.

References

1. Rajan, P., Radhakrishnan, B., Suresh, L.P.: Detection and classification of pests from crop images using support vector machine. In: 2016 International Conference on Emerging Technological Trends (ICETT), pp. 1–6. IEEE, October 2016
2. Xie, C., et al.: Multi -level learning features for automatic classification of field crop pests. Comput. Electron. Agric. **152**, 233–241 (2018)
3. Alfarisy, A.A., Chen, Q., Guo, M.: Deep learning based classification for paddy pests & diseases recognition. In: Proceedings of 2018 International Conference on Mathematics and Artificial Intelligence, pp. 21–25, April 2018
4. Xiao, D., Feng, J., Lin, T., Pang, C., Ye, Y.: Classification and recognition scheme for vegetable pests based on the BOF-SVM model. Int. J. Agric. Biol. Eng. **11**(3), 190–196 (2018)
5. Liu, Z., Gao, J., Yang, G., Zhang, H., He, Y.: Localization and classification of paddy field pests using a saliency map and deep convolutional neural network. Sci. Rep. **6**(1), 1–12 (2016)
6. Boniecki, P., et al.: Neural identification of selected apple pests. Comput. Electron. Agric. **110**, 9–16 (2015)
7. Yadav, I.C., Devi, N.L.: Pesticides classification and its impact on human and environment. Environ. Sci. Eng. **6**, 140–158 (2017)
8. Durgabai, R.P.L., Bhargavi, P., Jyothi, S.: Classification of cotton crop pests using big data analytics. In: Jyothi, S., Mamatha, D.M., Satapathy, S.C., Raju, K.S., Favorskaya, M.N. (eds.) CBE 2019. LAIS, vol. 15, pp. 37–45. Springer, Cham (2020). https://doi.org/10.1007/978-3-030-46939-9_4
9. Suthakaran, A.: Detection of affected area, pests and classification of pests using convolutional neural networks from the leaf images. Doctoral dissertation (2019)

10. Singh, J., Kad, S., Singh, P.D.: implementing fog computing for detecting primary tumors using hybrid approach of data mining. In: Baredar, P.V., Tangellapalli, S., Solanki, C.S. (eds.) Advances in Clean Energy Technologies. SPE, pp. 1067–1080. Springer, Singapore (2021). https://doi.org/10.1007/978-981-16-0235-1_83

11. Seth, J., Nand, P., Singh, P., Kaur, R.: Particle swarm optimization assisted support vector machine based diagnostic system for lung cancer prediction at the early stage PalArch's. J. Archaeol. Egypt/Egyptol. **17**(9), 6202–6212 (2020)

12. Singh, J., Kad, S., Singh, P.: Comparing Outcome of Fog Computing with Cloud Computing for detecting diseases in Healthcare. Solid State Technol. **1**, 5727–5740 (2020)

13. Angurala, M., Bala, M., Bamber, S.S., Kaur, R., Singh, P.: An internet of things assisted drone based approach to reduce rapid spread of COVID-19. J. Saf. Sci. Resilience **1**(1), 31–35 (2020)

14. Singh, D., Singh, P., Kaur, R.: Applying hybrid classification data mining techniques to improve lung cancer diagnosis. Int. J. Comput. Sci. Eng. **9**(1), 92–98 (2020)

Early-Stage Detection Model Using Deep Learning Algorithms for Parkinson's Disease Based on Handwriting Patterns

Jainish Savalia[1], Shivani Desai[1(✉)], Rebakah Geddam[1], Pooja Shah[1], and Hitesh Chhikaniwala[2]

[1] Institute of Technology, Nirma University, Ahmedabad, India
{19bce240,shivani.desai,rebakah.geddam,
pooja.shah}@nirmauni.ac.in
[2] Adani Institute of Infrastructure Engineering, Ahmedabad, India

Abstract. Early detection of degenerative diseases is crucial in medical science. Disease like Parkinson's Disease is a neurological disorder affecting the brain control over the limbs and in turn affecting motor skills. Parkinson patients suffer from tremors and low dopamine levels resulting in anxiety and depression. Thus, an early diagnosis for such diseases become vital. But in many of the cases, by the time a clear diagnosis can be made, the disease has been progressed significantly. The most common and early symptom among all is the loss of motor control. Thus, the progression in loss of motor control can be easily detected using a computer aided system for quicker diagnosis. The proposed CNN model with an accuracy 84 for cross fold of 40% for the kinematics detection of a person with Parkinson in early stage using images and signals collected by a smart pen and tablet.

Keywords: Parkinson's detection · Handwritten tasks · Sensor pen · Convolution Neural Network - Bidirectional Long Short Term Memory (CNN-BLSTM)

1 Introduction

Parkinson's disease is a neuro degenerative condition that progresses over time which affects the neurological working system and impairs movement, and its basic symptoms are weakening muscles. Lower levels of dopamine are found in people with this disease. This condition is distinguished by both motor and non-motor symptoms. Tremor, stiffness, slowness of movement, dyskinesia, and speaking and swallowing difficulties are among the motor symptoms [15]. Non-motor symptoms include sleep, perception, anxiety, depression, lethargy, compulsive, autonomic, and attention issues. Different people may experience these symptoms to varying degrees and in different combinations [10].

In addition to brain scans, tests like the unified Parkinson's disease rating scale (UPDRS) can be carried out to diagnose this disease [15]. The diagnosis require an expert doctor along with expensive diagnostic methods. Therefore, for the diagnosis of Parkinson's disease, we need a computer system aiding in the decision-making process.

S. Rajagopal et al. (Eds.): ASCIS 2022, CCIS 1759, pp. 323–332, 2022.
https://doi.org/10.1007/978-3-031-23092-9_26

With the advancement in cellular technology, we can collect handwriting data using an electronic pen, which has several features to measure important data, which helps to identify the disease. This paper propose a computer aided system which can collect handwriting data which is in the form of signals (time series data) and apply Deep Learning algorithms and classify the signals.

In the paper by Pereira et al. [12] have proposed encoding the data set in a form of matrix of X and Y representation. The image generated from the signal data has all the attributes captured by the pen. In order to predict PD using CNNs, Moetesum et al. [8] used the handwriting's static visual qualities (a visual representation of the drawing).The input data epitomized from the three representations of the input data, they isolate the discriminating visual characteristics (the raw image, median filter residual image, and edge image). Three CNNs merge their derived features into a single SVM for classification. For the classification of PD, Khatamino et al. [7] developed a CNN model using both dynamic features and static visual qualities from hand-writing drawings. A novel method for detecting PWP (People with Parkinson) generated on networks models using Echo State has been proposed by Gallicchio et al. [3] DL algorithm using time series data was recorded using a pen & tablet.

When time series data is involved, it is necessary to have fixed-dimension data of a certain length (time). In order to fulfil this requirement, normalisation of time series with the fixed dimension representation is done [12]. Dataset collection and preparation are discussed in Sect. 5.1. Spectrograms (5.2) are used to deal with the irregular size of the time series data. In this paper we have discussed ways to use these conversion methods to train the CNN-BLSTM model, and its possible demerits, with an approach to tackle them using data augmentation.

2 Literature Survey

Table 1 shows the literature survey of various papers having different parameters like parameters of Pen, methodology, input, outcome, and limitations.

As discussed in the introduction, differentiating on the basis of signals is an easy and efficient task to classify between PD and non-PD patients. As shown in Table 1, techniques like CNN for handwritten images [19], various ML algorithms [5] for the signals from the pen, LSTM and BLSTM [13] transfer learning using ImageNet, CIFAR-10, LeNet, VGG16 [1], and various statistical tests [22] are used to determine the disease. Although CNN is used extensively for image recognition, it cannot tell apart between the images due to the images having very little difference in handwriting. On the other hand, by applying ML approaches to data based on the traits of writing, it is possible to readily distinguish between them and uncover patterns within them. Finding recurring patterns in signals is a strong suit of deep learning algorithms. Transfer learning is an additional approach. However, it is more difficult to achieve good results than ML techniques because there is no prior domain to adapt from. On the other hand, models like VGG16 can be employed to achieve satisfactory results. In this paper, we have combined the functionality of CNN and BLSTM to achieve higher accuracy. Statistical tests like t-test, 2-tailed test, Chi-square test, and Mann Whitney U test are used to do tremor assessment to look out for the potential of breaykinesia and micrographia. For this, tests have to be designed in such a way that a distinction can be made.

Table 1. State of Art in the field of PD detection techniques

Methodology	Pen parameters	Input	Results	Ref.
Two CNN architec-ture: for feature extraction and for classification	-	Images of handwriting	The total accuracy obtained by all the Modeling is 96.67%	[19]
Arduino scheduled on IDE in different programming languages	Accelerometer and gyroscope	Signals obtained from accelerometer and gyroscope	The overall accuracy obtainedover is nearby 99.9%	[5]
Deep learning strategies like LSTM and BLSTM	X, Y, Z, Pressure, altitude, azimuth, time Stamp, pen position	Signals, images	Out of all CNN-BLSTM model has given a accuracy of (83.33%)	[16]
Three CNN architecture: ImageNet, CIFAR-10, LeNet, OPF	Microphone, Finger Grip, Axial Pressure of ink Refill, Tilt and Acceleration in "X direction", Tilt and Acceleration in "Y direction", Tilt and Acceleration "Z direction", Refill pressure sensor, Grip pressure sensor, Writing pressure sensor	Images, signals	Opf for meandors 92.86% Opf for spiral is 82.1%	[13].

3 Material and Methods

More than 1% of adults over 60 have PD, which is among the most prevalent neuro degenerative conditions (it is second only to Alzheimer's disease in prevalence) [17]. Parkinson's disease cannot currently be objectively assessed, hence there is a high risk of misdiagnosis, especially when performed by a nonspecialist: A 20% chance of a false-positive diagnostic is possible [14]. The accuracy of the diagnosis can be improved by carefully examining the primary symptoms, such as tremor, bradykinesia, and stiffness. However clinical judgments might be impacted by the doctor's subjective judgement. Tools for medical decision aid are particularly intriguing since they can improve objectivity and aid in an early diagnosis. Thus a computer aided diagnostic system can help increase diagnosis for PD in early stage. Our goal is to gather required data and design a model that will enable classification to be done more accurately.

4 Proposed Model

This section includes the proposed model for detecting the handwriting kinematics. The first phase is data Acquisition using the medical aided tool, Pre-processing the data but eliminating null values, Zero values, and unexpected pattern. The dominant features are selected by using cross entropy and classification using CNN model. The data is collected from the tablet in form of images (pixel matrix), Time series data from gyroscope, Accelerometer, Pressure sensors from the finger tip. The model is generated on fusion of image and TSD signals. The signals are converted to image of different resolution. The different model comparison of models was generated on 256, 384 resolution.

Starting task include continuous movement of the hand to draw pattern in form of circles. Through the remaining tasks, repetition of words is seen, which detects micrographia. As shown in the Fig. 1, we propose a CNN architecture where CNN extracted features are analysed to get predictions on time series data. The gradient optimiser ADAM is processed for dominant feature. The model is trained for a batch size of 4, image size is 128, with learning of 0.002 for 30 epoch. The efficient net (EfficientNET-B7) model is also implemented for auto scaling and multi classification of images for transfer learning method. The existing models has taken into consideration of one particular data set of a certain handwriting signals, this differs in the proposed model as Time series signal and image fusion is implemented.

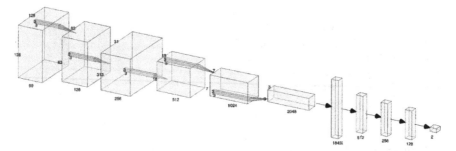

Fig. 1. Proposed model

5 Data Acquisition

The PD data is acquired from the healthy and PD persons using the following tool:

5.1 Medical Aid Tool: Intelligent Pen & Tablet

As shown in Fig. 2, a digital pen provides features which are accelerometer and gyroscope data, finger grip pressure, axial pressure, altitude, and the azimuth angle with respect to the writing surface, and a tablet provides a surface to write on and collectively collect different data. The pen consists of 6 different channels. Measurements collected from the pen are:

- Finger grip pressure
- Axial pressure
- Altitude & Azimuth angle with respect to the writing surface
- Writing position (tilt) in X, Y & Z axis
- Acceleration in X, Y & Z axis
- Time stamp

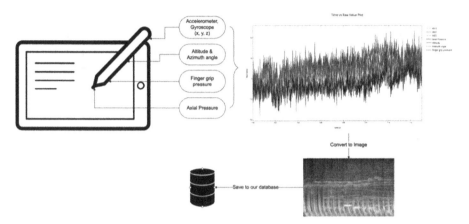

Fig. 2. Data collection procedure

The dataset used in this paper is called the NewHandPD dataset [13]. It comprises of a total of 66 subjects, a combination of 35 healthy and 31 patients. Each person was instructed to draw 12 examinations, including left and right handed diadochokinesis, two circled movements as mentioned in earlier section. The tasks are as follows: four spirals, four meanders, and four circles. Along with these images, the pen also recorded the signals from all the 12 test. Thus each individual subject has 9 images and 12 signals recorded.

5.2 Data Processing

Our dataset contains a table wherein rows show the time and columns have the data for a specific feature collected by the Intelligent pen. Our first approach is *Concatenation Approach*, a single image of 256 resolution is reconstructed from a time series data of length "n" [12]. Here we have prepared 7 tasks, so it is a hyper-parameter which can change. Let it be k in general. After all, the whole data (n × k) matrix is transformed into one image by concatenating the n rows. into one vector and then reshaping them into a square matrix of size $\sqrt{2}\, n * k$.

This matrix is then resized to 64 × 64 using the Lanczos resampling method [4].

Spectrogram based approach [6] computes Short Time Fourier Transformations (STFT) on cascading signal broken into different windows. The window width and frame size is depends on the frequency of signal [11]. The experimentation using black-man windowing with a window frame of 256 and an extending rate of 50% provides the best spectrogram resolution. The height and width of the image are derived from the number of the frequencies and the number of time bins (length of the signal in the spectrogram). The value of the pixel is the value in the spectrogram. In the form of logarithmic Values then normalised as an index of [0, 1]. This image is then resized to 64x64 using the same Lanczos resampling method [4] used in other approaches.

5.3 Data Augmentation

As our data set is small, our model will tend to over fit the training set [18]. Deep Learning is known to perform well when the data set is large. In order to deal with over fitting, two strategies can be implemented. One is data augmentation [21] and the other is transfer learning [9]. In this paper, data augmentation has been discussed.

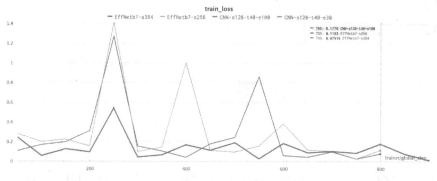

Fig. 3. Comparison of training loss between multiple models used

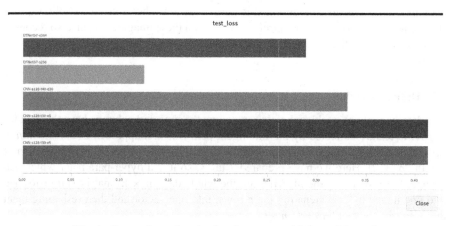

Fig. 4. Comparison of testing loss between multiple models used

The dataset size can be increased by generating synthetic data from the available dataset. The over fitting model increase accuracy but a reframed augmentation will

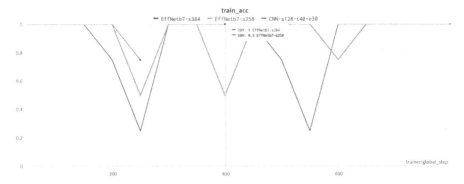

Fig. 5. Training accuracy between multiple models used

decrease the effect on over fitting. The two augmentation method in the are of computer vision geometric transformation (Scaling, altering the values, angel rotation or mirroring) and noise addition [18]. The time series data uses time-wrapping, Jittering, scaling. The time series data is framed into smaller windows.

Jittering is a way to induce calculated noise in order to make the image look different. We add Gaussian noise with $\mu = 0$ to it as it doesn't affect the average amplitude [20]. Standard deviation will decide the intensity of the noise. Less noise has almost no effect and more noise may alter the image totally that it is difficult to interpret and classify by the model.

A random scaling of amplifying the data in an window by a scalar unit [18]. The sensor data artifacts is multiplicative generated in the stimulation.

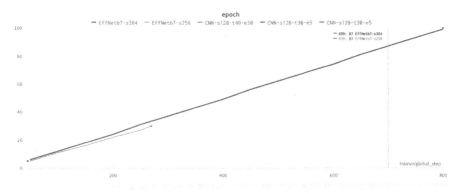

Fig. 6. Number of epochs on different models

Generating random sampling of data by applying mean to the time series data [2]. A variable length of data set is trained for the same class label. assigning weights to the data to calculate the optimising function. The initial weight is assigned to 0.5, the nearest neighbour is sampled using Dynamic Time Warping (DTW). The weights are adjusted to 0.15 and randomly selected. The rest of the data carries a weight of 0.2. The

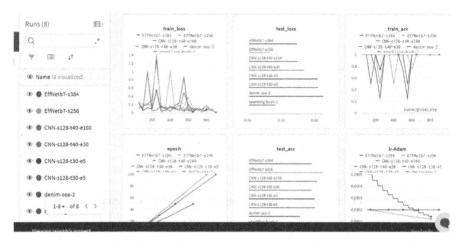

Fig. 7. Results of all models used

complexity of algorithms has considered the Convolution network model with different resolution taken into considerations for various epochs.

6   Results and Discussions

This section includes Comparison of training loss, testing loss, and training accuracy between the multiple models like EffNetb7-s3, EffNetb7-s2, CNN-s128-t40-e100, and CNN-s128-t40-e100 which are shown in Fig. 3, 4, and 5.

Figure 6 shows the number of epochs on different models and Fig. 7 shows the results of all the models used in this paper.

Model	Runtime	batch_size	epochs	img_size	lr	max_epoc	num_work	optimizer	precision	weight_de	epoch	lr-Adam	test_acc	test_loss	train_acc	train_loss	trainer
EffNetb7-s384	3907	4	100	384	0.0005			1	adam		0.000001	100	0.000141	0.848485	0.288392	1	0.079164	800
EffNetb7-s256	3157	4	100	256	0.0002			1	adam		0.000001	100	0.000123		1	0.124121	1	0.115279	800
CNN-s128-t40-e30	955	4		128	0.0002	30		1			32	30	0.0002	0.846154	0.330547	0.75	0.540777	270
CNN-s128-t30-e5	208	4		128	0.0002	5		1			32	5	0.0002	0.884615	0.412924			45
CNN-s128-t30-e5	228	4		128	0.0002	5		1			32	5	0.0002	0.884615	0.412924			45

Fig. 8. Summary table with various parameters on all the models

A part from these results, Fig. 8 shows the summary table having various parameters like run time, batch size, epochs, image size, optimizer, precision, testing accuracy, testing loss, training accuracy, etc. on all the models mentioned above.

7   Conclusion

The Early detection of features in Parkinson's Person helps in early diagnosis. The tremors in upper limbs resulting in difficulty in handwriting patterns. The medical aided too helps to analyse the difference between healthy people and People with Parkinson. The aided tool can also be used remotely and the pat tern can be shared for the analysis.

The pattern task were not repeated at the same task level with every user for validating the proposed model. The proposed model has classified with an accuracy of 84 at a cross fold of 30:70 using DL Algorithm. The future scope of extending the model can be used for bio-metric authentication purposes and cognitive behavioural analysis.

References

1. Diaz, M., Ferrer, M.A., Impedovo, D., Pirlo, G., Vessio, G.: Dynamically enhanced static handwriting representation for Parkinson's disease detection. Pattern Recogn. Lett. **128**, 204–210 (2019)
2. Fawaz, H.I., Forestier, G., Weber, J., Idoumghar, L., Muller, P.A.: Data augmentation using synthetic data for time series classification with deep residual networks. arXiv preprint arXiv: 1808.02455 (2018)
3. Gallicchio, C., Micheli, A.: Deep tree echo state networks. In: 2018 International Joint Conference on Neural Networks (IJCNN), pp. 1–8. IEEE (2018)
4. Huzaifah, M.: Comparison of time-frequency representations for environmental sound classification using convolutional neural networks. arXiv preprint arXiv:1706.07156 (2017)
5. Júnior, E.P., et al.: Intelligent sensory pen for aiding in the diagnosis of Parkinson's disease from dynamic handwriting analysis. Sensors **20**(20), 5840 (2020)
6. Khan, N.A., Jafri, M.N., Qazi, S.A.: Improved resolution short time Fourier transform. In: 2011 7th International Conference on Emerging Technologies, pp. 1–3. IEEE (2011)
7. Khatamino, P., Cantürk, İ., Özyılmaz, L.: A deep learning-CNN based system for medical diagnosis: an application on Parkinson's disease handwriting drawings. In: 2018 6th International Conference on Control Engineering & Information Technology (CEIT), pp. 1–6. IEEE (2018)
8. Moetesum, M., Siddiqi, I., Vincent, N., Cloppet, F.: Assessing visual attributes of handwriting for prediction of neurological disorders—a case study on Parkinson's disease. Pattern Recogn. Lett. **121**, 19–27 (2019)
9. Mormont, R., Geurts, P., Marée, R.: Comparison of deep transfer learning strategies for digital pathology. In: Proceedings of the IEEE Conference on Computer Vision and Pattern Recognition Workshops, pp. 2262–2271 (2018)
10. Nilashi, M., Ibrahim, O., Ahani, A.: Accuracy improvement for predicting Parkinson's disease progression. Sci. Rep. **6**(1), 1–18 (2016)
11. Nisar, S., Khan, O.U., Tariq, M.: An efficient adaptive window size selection method for improving spectrogram visualization. Comput. Intell. Neurosci. **2016** (2016)
12. Pereira, C.R., et al.: Handwritten dynamics assessment through convolutional neural networks: an application to Parkinson's disease identification. Artif. Intell. Med. **87**, 67–77 (2018)
13. Pereira, C.R., Weber, S.A., Hook, C., Rosa, G.H., Papa, J.P.: Deep learning-aided Parkinson's disease diagnosis from handwritten dynamics. In: 2016 29th SIBGRAPI Conference on Graphics, Patterns and Images (SIBGRAPI), pp. 340–346. IEEE (2016)
14. Rizzo, G., Copetti, M., Arcuti, S., Martino, D., Fontana, A., Logroscino, G.: Accuracy of clinical diagnosis of Parkinson disease: a systematic review and metanalysis. Neurology **86**(6), 566–576 (2016)
15. Sharma, R., Gupta, A.K., et al.: Voice analysis for telediagnosis of Parkinson disease using artificial neural networks and support vector machines. Int. J. Intell. Syst. Appl. **7**(6), 41 (2015)
16. Taleb, C., Likforman-Sulem, L., Mokbel, C., Khachab, M.: Detection of Parkinson's disease from handwriting using deep learning: a comparative study. Evol. Intell. 1–12 (2020)

17. Tysnes, O.B., Storstein, A.: Epidemiology of Parkinson's disease. J. Neural Transm. **124**(8), 901–905 (2017)
18. Um, T.T., et al.: Data augmentation of wearable sensor data for Parkinson's disease monitoring using convolutional neural networks. In: Proceedings of the 19th ACM International Conference on Multimodal Interaction, pp. 216–220 (2017)
19. Vatsaraj, I., Nagare, G.: Early detection of Parkinson's disease using contrast enhancement techniques and CNN. Int. J. Eng. Res. Technol. **10**(5) (2021)
20. Wang, F., Zhong, S., Peng, J., Jiang, J., Liu, Y.: Data augmentation for EEGased emotion recognition with deep convolutional neural networks. In: Schoeffmann, K., Chalidabhongse, T.H., Ngo, C.W., Aramvith, S., O'Connor, N.E., Ho, Y.-S. (eds.) MMM 2018. LNCS, vol. 10705, pp. 82–93. Springer, Cham (2018). https://doi.org/10.1007/978-3-319-73600-6_8
21. Wen, Q., et al.: Time series data augmentation for deep learning: a survey. arXiv preprint arXiv:2002.12478 (2020)
22. Zham, P., et al.: A kinematic study of progressive micrographia in Parkinson's disease. Front. Neurol. **10**, 403 (2019)

Farmright – A Crop Recommendation System

Dviti Arora[✉], Sakshi, Sanjana Drall, Sukriti Singh, and Monika Choudhary

Computer Science and Engineering, Indira Gandhi Delhi Technical University for Women, Delhi, India

{dvitiarora125btcse18,sakshi097btcse18,sanjana107btcse18,
sukritisingh111btcse18,monikachoudhary}@igdtuw.ac.in

Abstract. Agriculture is extremely vital to our economy and boosting the development of this sector always adds up to the economic & political value of our country. Health of all the crops grown is affected by various aspects including technological, biological, and environmental factors. The environmental facet particularly has been drastically changing, posing challenges in front of the peasants. They face a significant difficulty in determining the optimal crop for their farming region to maximize productivity and profit. For Indian farmers, there is no existing reliable recommendation mechanism. Giving an address to this issue, the study proposes a crop recommendation system based on a multi-label classification model which considers the location of peasants, composition of soil, and weather characteristics, and provides a ranked list of suggested crop seed to be produced for greater yield. Researchers compare many algorithms based upon the performance criteria and capabilities to develop the best recommendation model for crops. With a precision of 82.74%, a recall of 80.92%, and an F1 score of 78.67%, the most optimal model was revealed to be an RF Technique. The trained model proved advantageous in catering the farmers with a ranked list of crops deployed along with an interface for better user experience.

Keywords: Crop recommendation · Agriculture · Multi-label classification · Random Forest Algorithm · Soil characteristics · Climate properties · Chatbot

1 Introduction

Agronomy and cultivation are a crucial part of our economic sector acting as the lifeblood of rural households with 70% [20] of them depending on agriculture for their livelihoods. This sector accounts for about 13.7% [11] of India's total GDP. It is the largest employment sector that employs more than 57% [11] of the population making up about two-thirds of the working population in India. It also impacts international trade, food grain supply, and input to other industrial sectors. This increasing demand can only be met by increasing agricultural production. So, there is raising pressure on the country's smallholders to meet the demand for food grain requirement. With that in mind, we focus on dramatic changing factors such as weather and soil that affect plant health. Farm owners today confront considerable challenges in picking the best crop for their sowing acreage in order to increase output and profit. They need to choose the best

© The Author(s), under exclusive license to Springer Nature Switzerland AG 2022
S. Rajagopal et al. (Eds.): ASCIS 2022, CCIS 1759, pp. 333–345, 2022.
https://doi.org/10.1007/978-3-031-23092-9_27

harvest for their land. They have always tried to pick desirable characteristics in seed and harvest for many years, upgrading the plant quality and quantity for agricultural reasons. They started looking for crop types with shorter growing seasons, larger seeds, and fruits. Agricultural technology has given rise to a diverse range of food, fruit, feed, and fiber production options. In all manner of ways, technology makes our life easier and more fun by lowering the amount of efforts and time we spend on necessary tasks such as food production. Farmers sometimes fail to select the appropriate crops and sowing locations depending on environmental considerations. This became a research area to heighten the knowledge and improve agricultural technology. Studies tried to improve the crop selection methods & emulsifying it with technology. The selection method requires the latest data & knowledge about agricultural tendencies which lacked in recent studies. Since there are myriad factors affecting the process of growing a crop, the complexity of agricultural technology proliferates. For Indian farmers, there is no official trustworthy agricultural advisory system as of now. If you choose the wrong crop or seeding area, your investment, resources, and efforts will be wasted. An equally notable problem these days is the decreasing proportion of farmers who cultivate large areas. Farmers are afraid of mass planting due to unpredictable yields, erratic weather, and lack of assets. Keeping this in view, researchers have been trying to devise ways that can help mitigate the problems and boost the sector. Various technologies are used in the process with Machine Learning [7] being the most used one. ML models are trained using the agricultural data like temperature, rainfall, soil type and properties, traditionally grown crops in the concerned area, production per unit area of previous decades so that they can recommend the most suitable crop.

This paper aims at proposing a crop recommendation system called FarmRight, to tackle such problems. The system takes in parameters that affect the growth of crops as input and recommends the most favourable crop as output using Machine Learning algorithms [3]. The recommendation system employs a supervised learning task viz. Multi-label classification in which an occurrence in the training data is linked to one or more mutually non-exclusive class labels. To determine the best accurate crop recommendation model, researchers compare multiple algorithms based on their performance criteria. A Random Forest Algorithm was shown to be the best accurate model, with a precision of 82.74 percent, recall of 80.92 percent, and an F1 score of 78.67 per cent. The model trained up to this point proved advantageous in catering the farmers with a ranked list of recommended crops.

By the same token, this paper is organised along these lines, in Sect. 2, a brief review towards some related work on crop recommendation systems is presented. Section 3 contains the details about the solution that the paper aims at proposing, followed by Sect. 4 which explains the steps followed for making the model. Implementation results are presented and discussed in Sect. 5. Section 6 concludes and tells about the future scope of the paper.

2   Background and Literature Review

GiVen the importance of agriculture in our economy, researchers have been trying to come up with methods that would help this sector boost. Various techniques have been used starting from use of sensors to ensembling approach of Machine Learning. Vijayabaskar et al. [19] develops a project to determine soil fertility and proposes that crops should be planted based on sensor readings. Users can share information and receive assistance from specialists in a "farmer chat" created by the writers. It allows farmers to assess their land's fertility and plant the most productive and profitable crop. It also offers information on the type of fertilizer to use on the soil as well as the location of a fertilizer store nearby. Patel et al. [13] collected data from Indian Government Soil testing card website and experimented on the data using R programming to build a Land Recommendation System(LSR) which recommends crops predicted on different parameters. Indira et al. [4] proposed a recommendation system based on machine learning to increase agricultural yield. Multiple algorithms used include MobileNet, which identifies disease using image leaf, XGBoost which suggests crop on the basis of local rainfall and soil properties and Random Forest to predict fertilizer values. Prakash et al. [18] collected soil moisture, pH, temperature and humidity values from field with the help of sensors and sent to cloud using Node MCU. Data in cloud was used to analyze different ML algorithms and compared their prediction accuracy. S Pudumalar et al. [14] developed a crop recommendation system using the technique of data mining that will assist cultivators in choosing the appropriate crop based on soil requirements to boost production and profit. Precision farming is an improved cultivation approach that employs explored datasets on soil properties, soil type, and yield data to advise cultivators on the suitable crop for their sowing area. This solution is a system of recommendation that uses algorithms such as CHAID, KNN, Naive Bayes etc.as learners. Banerjee et al. [1] build an proficient and potent crop recommendation system taking in account various parameters such as soil type and nature, terrain and rainfall pattern using fuzzy logic for West Bengal. Liu et al. [10] the author suggests a clustering centre optimised technique using the Synthetic Minority Over-sampling Technique (SMOTE) to experiment on imbalanced soil data. The procedure begins by examining the original sample points and selecting density based grouping centres. The clustering centre is then used to generate minority samples in order to balance out the data distribution. Finally, for accurate prediction, the ensemble approach is employed to train the prediction model. Kumar et al. [8] suggested the Crop Selection Method (CSM) as a method for solving crop selection problems which also uses machine learning techniques. The proposed strategy has the potential to increase crop net production rates. Sujjaviriyasup et al. [16] proposed SVM model for forecasting exports of agricultural products and ARIMA was utilised as a benchmark to assess other developed models, and Thailand's Pacific white shrimp export data and data on chicken produced in Thailand were used. Ramya et al. [15] aims at providing a Climate Smart and agriculture decision-making platform for changing climate that affects agriculture. Using data and analytics, they were able to predict and mitigate the impact of catastrophic weather events on global finance and the Economic Dimensions of Climate Change all over the world. Kulkarni et al. [9] projected that a crop recommendation system based on the ensembling approach of ML would be built to boost agricultural productivity. It aims at designing a system for recommending the precise selection of seed based on multiple soils and climatic factors is the goal of this research work. The purpose of the research is to increase crop productivity by using the ensembling technique to provide high-accuracy and efficient predictions. The research work presented by Teja et al. [17] includes a website integrated with ML algorithms such as K-Nearest Neighbour (KNN), Naïve Bayes, SVM algorithm, etc., and historical weather data to find the most profitable crop under current weather conditions. As Machine Learning algorithms advanced, Jeong et al. [5] investigated RF regression effectiveness and predicted complicated crop yield responses. They discovered that RF performs well in predicting yields for all plants and areas studied. The findings of this study suggest that RF algorithms have a lot of potential as a statistical modeling tool for yield prediction. In every performance measure evaluated, RF results outperformed the MLR benchmark. The most significant observation was the mean square error of all test cases in the RF model ranged from 6 percent to 14 percent of the mean observed yield, while these values ranged from 14 percent to 49 percent of the compared model. The study of Banjara et al. [2] shows how diversifying the rice-wheat crop system can improve the rice produce and increase profits in Indo-Gangetic Plain region. Rice–berseem–cowpea fodder and rice– potato–green gram were found the most appropriate sequence of cropping. This was found with the the help of nutrient content analysis and calculating nutrient uptake by grain and straw. Krishna et al. [6] studies and examines crop–climate relationships in India using historical production data for major crops (rice, groundnut, wheat, sugarcane, and sorghum), as well as aggregate pulses, food grain, oil seed and cereal production.

Above said approaches worked well but some limitations were tagged along such as the set of crops they could predict was limited to few crops only as in [9] though there are more than hundreds of crops that are grown in India. Moreover, dataset used focused on data from few locations as in [14] and [19]. Algorithms used and the accuracy of the model were not mentioned clearly as in [19].

3 Proposed Solution

AgricUlturE-DEPEndENT countries, such as India, rely on agriculture for economic growth. As the country's population grows, so does its reliance on agriculture, which impairs subsequent economic growth. Therefore, it is necessary to increase the yield of crops. Some biological procedures along with a few chemical techniques can find solutions to this problem. Additionally, a crop recommendation model is needed to improve seasonal crop yield by recommending a list of acceptable crops based on location, soil, and climatic parameters. To improve crop productivity and facilitate correct decision-making for the selection of crops, this project proposes a recommendation system that recommends a list of apt crops based on the location, climate, and field properties using Multi-Label Classification techniques. The selection of crops is dependent on various parameters. The datasets used have been collected based on these affecting factors and include the soil properties (Macronutrients and soil pH levels) for all districts in India, the agro-climatic factors such as precipitation and temperature, and the district wise crop distribution for all states of India. These datasets obtained from different sources have been merged to create one master dataset. The master dataset contains instances associated with about 124 different crops ranging from food and non-food crops to crops grown in different seasons in different parts of India. This dataset obtained is then used to train different machine learning classification models using two multi-label classification techniques, Binary Relevance and Classifier Chain. To find the most appropriate model, different performance metrics corresponding to each model such as recall, precision, f1 score, and hamming loss are compared. For the crop recommendation system, the model with the lowest hamming loss and significantly high precision, recall, and f1 score is preferred. After finding the best possible model, it can be used by the users to give a recommended list of crops if they enter their location, soil characteristics of their land, and the climatic variable such as rainfall and temperature. This system can help in giving the farmers/ users a more personalized experience in deciding crops according to their location and land parameters. It also provides a user-friendly way to assist in the right crop selection decisions. Another benefit of the system proposed is that it doesn't restrict its results to 1 or 2 crops, but with the help of multi-classification techniques gives a wide range of crops to choose from. Our model can potentially predict around 124 crops (Fig. 1).

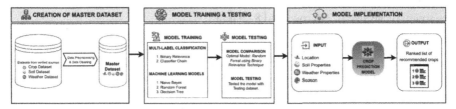

Fig. 1. Workflow diagram

4 Methodology

4.1 Data Collection

THERE are four categories into which major crops in India can be divided into viz. Food Grains such as Wheat, Maize, Rice, Pulses, Millets, etc., Cash Crops including Jute, Cotton, Sugarcane, Oilseeds and Tobacco, Plantation Crops such as Coconut, Rubber, Coffee and Tea and Horticulture crops including Fruits and Vegetables. The yield potential of the crops, in particular, depends on the soil characteristics of the land and the climate. Adequate nutrition of plants is critical for the optimal production of crops. Primary macronutrients are very vital for the yield quality enhancement of crops. Nitrogen (N), phosphorous (P), and potassium (K) are the three primary elements that must be consumed in large quantities. Soil pH is an important variable in soils because it regulates numerous chemical and biological activities. It refers to the soil's acidity or basicity/alkalinity. In agriculture, soil pH is important because it regulates plant nutrition availability by controlling the chemical forms of various nutrients and their chemical interactions[12]. As a result, the soil pH has a significant impact on soil and crop yield. The monsoon, which originates from the Indian and Arabian Seas, is vital to India's agriculture. As the climate changes, farmers are unprepared for changes in the rainfall cycle, magnitude, and timing. Soil moisture evaporates quickly in arid climates, reducing water available for agricultural production. Climate change has an impact on groundwater levels in different parts of the world.

Therefore, the following datasets were collected from different sources:

Crop Dataset [21]. This crop dataset contains the distribution of crops in different regions and the production statistics. The data can be utilized to study and analyze crop production, contribution to regional production, agricultural climate zone performance, crop growth pattern and high yield production for crops, and diversification. The dataset has approximately 246091 rows and 7 columns. Source of this dataset is Open Government Data (OGD) Platform India [22].

Soil Dataset [21]. This dataset sourced by the DoAFW [23] contains the percentage of Macro-nutrients in a particular district based on the year cycle. Macro Nutrients comprises Organic carbon(OC), Potassium(K), Nitrogen(N), and Phosphorus(P). It also includes the percentage of Acidity, Neutrality, and Alkalinity of the soil in a particular district year-wise. The pH is tested and categorized based on the acidic, basic, and neutral elements found in the soil, such as Acid Sulphate, Calcium, Magnesium, Sodium, etc. The idea is to take the average of acidic, basic, and neutral percentages for our dataset. Its approximate size is 748 rows and 8 columns.

Climate Dataset. The climate dataset contains monthly readings of a particular Geographic coordinate (District-wise) taken in a year. The Agro-Climatic parameters include: Temperature at 2 m (°C), Precipitation Corrected (mm). The dataset had around 14212 instances. This dataset was collected from API from NASA Prediction Of Worldwide Energy Resources (POWER) [24] (Fig. 2).

CROP DATA SET				CLIMATE		SOIL PROPERTIES							LABEL
State_Name	District	Season	Prod/Area	Temp	Rainfall	N	P	K	OC	Acidic	Neutral	Basic	Crop
ANDAMAN An	NICOBAR	Kharif	0.3316710	27.5725	9.145	99.11	78.16	89.89	0.6596	0	8.53	0	Arecanut
ANDAMAN An	NICOBAR	Kharif	0.3316710	27.5725	9.145	99.11	78.16	89.89	0.6596	35.27	8.53	56.2	Other Kharif
ANDAMAN An	NICOBAR	Kharif	0.3316710	27.5725	9.145	99.11	78.16	89.89	0.6596	35.27	8.53	56.2	Rice
ANDAMAN An	NICOBAR	Whole Year	0.2205095	27.5725	6.08	99.11	78.16	89.89	0.6596	35.27	8.53	56.2	Banana
ANDAMAN An	NICOBAR	Whole Year	0.2205295	27.57	6.08	99.11	78.16	89.89	0.6596	35.27	8.53	56.2	Cashewnut
ANDAMAN An	NICOBAR	Whole Year	0.2205295	27.57	6.08	99.11	78.16	89.89	0.6596	35.27	8.53	56.2	Coconut
ANDAMAN An	NICOBAR	Whole Year	0.2205295	27.57	6.08	99.11	78.16	89.89	0.6596	35.27	8.53	56.2	Dry ginger
ANDAMAN An	NICOBAR	Whole Year	0.2205295	27.57	6.08	99.11	78.16	89.89	0.6596	35.27	8.53	56.2	Sugarcane
ANDAMAN An	NICOBAR	Whole Year	0.2205295	27.57	6.08	99.11	78.16	89.89	0.6596	35.27	8.53	56.2	Sweet potato
ANDAMAN An	NICOBAR	Whole Year	0.2205295	27.57	6.08	99.11	78.16	89.89	0.6596	35.27	8.53	56.2	Tapioca

Fig. 2. Master dataset made by combining crop, soil and climate datasets

4.2 Data Preprocessing

THE second stage of the proposed solution was to preprocess the data and the steps followed were:

- Removing rows with missing values in crop dataset.
- Replacing missing values in columns with mean of the adjacent states in soil dataset as per the Map of India, 2021.
- Adding columns corresponding to each season for the climate dataset.
- Making state and district names consistent in all 3 datasets for merging.
- Label Encoding the categorical columns such as state, district, season, and One Hot Encoding the Crop Label.

- Merging the 3 datasets on the columns State, District, and Year and dropping duplicate and unrequired columns to get the Master Dataset.

This resulted in the creation of a master dataset which had attributes: State, District, Season, Temperature, Rainfall, percentage of macronutrients (N, P, OC, K), and pH values categorized into Acidic, Basic, and Neutral percentages present and crop name as the Label. Now, the master dataset has 242361 rows with 14 columns.

4.3 Multi-label Classification

WHen given an input, classification refers to a predictive modelling problem in which a class label is obtained as an output. This differs from regression situations in which a numeric value is predicted. In most classification problems, a single label is predicted. It could also refer to estimating the likelihood of two or more different class designations. In such certain cases, the classes are mutually exclusive, which means the classification task believes the input belongs to only one class. However, there are times when more than one class label needs to be predicted. In this sense, class labels are mutually nonexclusive. These tasks are known as multiple label classification. Multi-label categorization produces zero or more labels as an output for every sample of input. It is assumed that the output labels can be defined as a function of the inputs. In our system, since we aim to recommend a list of crops, i.e. we need multiple crop predictions, multi-label classification is an apt technique. For single-label classification tasks, most classical learning methods are designed. As a result, numerous approaches in the literature reduce the multi-label problem to a series of single-label problems that can be addressed using current single-label algorithms. Most traditional learning methods are developed for single-label classification tasks. As a result, numerous approaches in the literature reduce the multi-label problem to a series of single-label problems that can be addressed using current single-label algorithms. Here, we have considered two techniques of multi-label classification:

Binary Relevance. Here, an ensemble of single-label binary classifiers is used and trained for every single class. Every single classifier determines whether or not an instance belongs to a specific class. To produce the multi-label result, all predicted classes are considered simultaneously. This is a common strategy since it is straightforward to implement, but it ignores any potential relationships between class labels.

Classifier Chains. In this case, a chain of n binary classifiers is formed, where n is the number of possible class labels and each classifier uses the predictions of all its predecessors. This allows us to account for label correlations in this way.

4.4 Models Used

Since we had got labeled data, some of the supervised classification algorithms considered were:

Naive Bayes. The Naive Bayes classifier is a straightforward heuristic classifier that employs Bayes' theorem (from Bayesian statistics) and the strong naive independent hypothesis. This technique uses classifier models to assign class labels to examples that are represented as vectors of feature values, with the class labels coming from a finite set. It is a collection of algorithms rather than a single algorithm based on a common premise. All naive Bayes classifiers assume that the value of one attribute is independent of the value of any another attribute given the class variable. Because Naive Bayes is useful for multidimensional information, it is taken into account in this scenario. For our system, we have considered two Naive Bayes classifiers, namely Multinomial Naive Bayes and Gaussian Naive Bayes.

Decision Tree. Decision trees use a tree structure to gather information. For better clarity and understanding, this tree structure can alternatively be represented as a series of discrete rules. The flexibility to use different subsets of attributes and decision rules at different phases of categorization gives decision tree classifiers an advantage. A root node, internal and leaf nodes, and branches make up a standard decision tree. The leaf node represents the class that will be allocated to a sample. Each internal node in a tree represents an attribute, while branches represent feature combinations that lead to classifications. The decision tree divides the population of data into smaller segments, allowing for more accurate predictions.

Random Forest. RFA is a tree ensemble method-based machine learning bagging approach. It creates a series of trees based on randomly subsampled attributes. The result of RFA is the average value of individual tree projections. Because RFA uses random sub-sampled features, it can be used in high-dimensional input predictors.

4.5 Model Training and Performance Metrices

THE dataset has been split into training and testing samples in the ratio 70:30. The partitioning of the dataset and the availability of testing data aid in the evaluation of the model's performance. The training data is then given as input to each of the classifiers independently. After successfully training and testing, the following evaluation metrics were considered to evaluate the performance of the models and for the comparison of their performance:

Hamming Loss. Hamming-Loss is an example-based metric that measures the percentage of labels that are wrongly predicted or the proportion of incorrect labels to the total number of labels.

Precision. It is the propensity of a classification model to identify only the pertinent data points. It's strategically calculated by dividing the count of genuine positives by the total number of true positives plus false positives.

Recall. A classification model's capacity to find all relevant examples bounded in a data collection. The count of true positives divided by the count of true positives added to the count of false negatives is called recall.

F1 Score. The F1 Score is a means to integrate precision and recall into a single metric that accounts for both. It's the harmonic mean of the precision and recall of a classifier's predictions, therefore it's an overall measure of the quality of the prediction.

5   Results and Discussions

To find the performance of our models, we tested the models using the testing data. The performance metrics were observed for each of the models. It was observed that both the Naive Bayes algorithms, Multinomial Naive Bayes and Gaussian Naive Bayes had extremely low F1 scores, indicating that the model wasn't performing very well. Whereas, the Random Forest Algorithm using the Binary Relevance technique returned the least hamming loss and high values of recall, precision, and F1 score. RFA proved to be efficient for our use case due to the very large dataset. Since we have a large dataset, and a variety of features, a lot of rules can be induced from it. Random forest has the ability to discover all the rules in the dataset as it creates multiple trees while training, hence it is able to cover all existing rules/patterns in the dataset, thus giving better accuracy. We also observe that binary relevance technique gives the most optimal results. Being the most simple multi-label classification technique, it is easily parallelized for our large dataset. It only needs one-step learning and is able to optimize several loss functions. Hence, it can be concluded that the RFA with Binary Relevance is the most suited algorithm for our proposed solution (Tables 1 and 2).

Table 1.   Performance evaluation for binary relevance

Model	Hamming Loss	Precision	Recall	F1-Score
Multinomial NB	30.02	11.39	61.64	17.26
Gaussian NB	07.72	37.74	55.96	39.34
Decision Tree	02.76	77.22	79.25	75.15
Random Forest	02.23	82.72	80.92	78.76

Table 2.   Performance evaluation for classifier chain

Model	Hamming Loss	Precision	Recall	F1-Score
Multinomial NB	39.95	08.26	42.75	12.49
Gaussian NB	18.97	18.15	63.13	26.13
Decision Tree	02.80	77.98	78.33	74.49
Random Forest	02.49	82.00	79.89	77.35

FarmRight, the crop recommendation model, is further integrated with a website to provide an interface to the users for greater accessibility and usage. Farmers can visit the "Farm Right" website and get to know which is the most suitable crop for his land by filling details about the farmer's land and other properties. It also caters with a Load Properties button that auto-fills the common soil and weather properties' values from the database, to abstract the users from the technical details such as pH and NPK values. It uses the built crop-recommendation model FarmRight to recommend a list of crops as an output. The website provides a brief detail of the problems faced by farmers of our country (Figs. 3 and 4).

Fig. 3. FarmRight Website

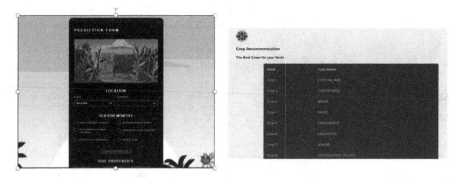

Fig. 4. User Input and Output

Along with this it has a chatbot "KrishiBot" which enables users to explicitly ask their queries regarding chat recommendation system and the workflow and get the best answers. The chatbot is implemented using NLP using a set of intents and responses that helps to answer queries asked by the user (Fig. 5).

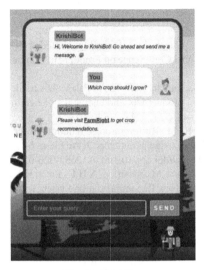

Fig. 5. KrishiBot

6 Conclusion and Future Scope

India is a country where agriculture plays a vital part. The country prospers in the prosperity of the peasants. As a result, our study assists farmers in sowing the appropriate seeds based on soil requirements and climatic factors in order to boost productivity and benefit from strategies like these. This allows farmers to plant the right crops to increase yields and increase the overall productivity of the land. The project aims at implementing multi-label classification on the collected dataset using different algorithms to find the best fit algorithm for the recommendation system. To determine the best accurate model, paper compares different algorithms based on their performance criteria. A Random Forest Algorithm was discovered to be the most accurate model, with a precision of 82.74 percent, a recall of 80.92 percent, and an F1 score of 78.67 percent. The trained model proved beneficial in assisting the farmers with a ranked list of crops deployed along with an interface for better user experience.

In future, recently updated datasets with more attributes like fertilizers added and humidity could be used for prediction of crops. We can further look for other model building techniques and model tuning like hyperparameter tuning can be performed as well. Also, the website could be made multilingual, connecting to experts and helpline for scalable use. The chatbot capabilities can be enhanced to handle extensive and complex queries for better user experience. Along with this, fertilizer recommendation, crop disease detection and profit made, depending upon region and crop chosen by the user can be added as another feature in the website.

References

1. Banerjee, G., Sarkar, U., Ghosh, I.: A fuzzy logic-based crop recommendation system. In: Proceedings of International Conference on Frontiers in Computing and Systems, pp. 57–69. Springer (2021)
2. Banjara,T.R., Bohra, J.S., Kumar, S., Ram, A., Pal, V.: Diversification of rice–wheat cropping system improves growth, productivity and energetics of rice in the Indo-Gangetic plains of India. Agric. Res. 11(1), 48–57 (2021)
3. Elavarasan, D., Vincent, P.M.D.R.: A reinforced random forest model for enhanced crop yield prediction by integrating agrarian parameters. J. Ambient. Intell. Humaniz. Comput. 12(11), 10009–10022 (2021). https://doi.org/10.1007/s12652-020-02752-y
4. Indira, D.N.V.S.L.S., Sobhana, M., Swaroop, A.H.L., Phani Kumar, V.: KRISHI RAKSHAN - A Machine Learning based New Recommendation System to the Farmer. In: 6th International Conference on Intelligent Computing and Control Systems (ICICCS), pp. 1798–1804. IEEE Xplore (2022)
5. Jeong, J.: 2016 Random forests for global and regional crop yield predictions PLoS ONE 11(6), e0156571 (2016)
6. Krishna Kumar, K., Rupa Kumar, K., Ashrit, R., Deshpande, N., Hansen, J.: Climate impacts on Indian agriculture. Int. J. Climatol.: J. R. Meteorol. Soc. 24(11), 1375–1393 (2004)
7. Kumar, R., Singhal, V.: IoT enabled crop prediction and irrigation automation system using machine learning. Recent Advances in Computer Science and Communications (Formerly: Recent Patents on Computer Science) 15(1), 88–97 (2022)
8. Kumar, R., Singh, M., Kumar, P., Singh, J.: Crop selection method to maximize crop yield rate using machine learning technique. In: 2015 International Conference on Smart Technologies and Management for Computing, Communication, Controls, Energy and Materials (ICSTM), pp. 138–145. IEEE (2015)
9. Kulkarni, N., Srinivasan, G., Sagar, B., Cauvery, N.: Improving crop productivity through a crop recommendation system using ensembling technique. In: 2018 3rd International Conference on Computational Systems and Information Technology for Sustainable Solutions (CSITSS), pp. 114–119. IEEE (2018)
10. Liu, A., Lu, T., Wang, B., Chen, C.: Crop recommendation via clustering center optimized algorithm for imbalanced soil data. In: 2020 5th International Conference on Control, Robotics and Cybernetics (CRC), pp. 31–35. IEEE (2020)
11. Malik, A., Kumar, R.: An overview on agriculture in India. Int. J. Mod. Agric. 10(2), 2087–2095 (2021)
12. Odutola Oshunsanya, S.: Introductory Chapter: Relevance of Soil pH to Agriculture. Soil pH for Nutrient Availability and Crop Performance, IntechOpen, London (2019). https://doi.org/10.5772/intechopen.82551
13. Patel, K., Patel, H.: A state-of-the-art survey on recommendation system and prospective extensions. Comput. Electron. Agric. 178 105779 (2020)
14. Pudumalar, S., Ramanujam, E., Rajashree, R., Kavya, C., Kiruthika, T., Nisha, J.: Crop recommendation system for precision agriculture. In: 2016 Eighth International Conference on Advanced Computing (ICoAC), pp. 32–36. IEEE (2017)
15. Ramya, M., Balaji, C., Girish, L.: Environment change prediction to adapt climate-smart agriculture using big data analytics. Int. J. Adv. Res. Comput. Eng. & Technol. (IJARCET) 4(5) (2015)
16. Sujjaviriyasup, T., Pitiruek, K.: Agricultural product forecasting using machine learning approach. Int. J. Math. Anal. 7(38), 1869–1875 (2013)
17. Teja, M.S., Preetham, T.S., Sujihelen, L., Christy, Jancy, S., Selvan, M.P.: Crop recommendation and yield production using SVM algorithm. In: 6th International Conference on Intelligent Computing and Control Systems (ICICCS), pp. 1768–1771 (2022)

18. Varun Prakash, R., Mohamed Abrith, M., Pandiyarajan, S.: Machine learning based crop suggestion system. In: 6th International Conference on Intelligent Computing and Control Systems (ICICCS), pp. 1355–1359. IEEE Xplore (2022)
19. Vijayabaskar, P., Sreemathi, R., Keertanaa, E.: Crop prediction using predictive analytics. In: 2017 International Conference on Computation of Power, Energy Information and Communication (ICCPEIC), pp. 370–373. IEEE (2017)
20. India at a Glance, FAO in India. https://www.fao.org/india/fao-in-india/india-at-a-glance/en/. Accessed 28 Jan 2022
21. FarmRight, Github. https://github.com/Know-and-Grow/FarmRight-A-Crop-Recommendation-System. Accessed 31 Aug 2022
22. Open Government Data (OGD) Platform India. https://data.gov.in/. Accessed 10 Feb 2022
23. Department of Agricultural Cooperation & Farmers Welfare Homepage. https://agricoop.nic.in/en. Accessed 18 Feb 2022
24. NASA Prediction Of Worldwide Energy Resources (POWER). https://power.larc.nasa.gov/. Accessed 01 Mar 2022

Corn Leaf Disease Detection Using RegNet, KernelPCA and XGBoost Classifier

Tejas Chauhan[1], Vijay Katkar[1(✉)], and Krunal Vaghela[2(✉)]

[1] Department of Computer Engineering, Marwadi University, Rajkot, India
{tejas.chauhan,vijay.katkar}@marwadieducation.edu.in
[2] Department of Information Technology, Marwadi University, Rajkot, India
Krunal.vaghela@marwadieducation.edu.in

Abstract. India is a developing nation, and agriculture is essential to the health of its economy as a whole. Given the importance of the agriculture sector, there is a need to improvise crop maintenance systems and deal with the effects of Diseases (Bacterial, Viral, Fungal) on crop production. It requires continuous monitoring as well as large team of experts for physical observation. Farmers do not always have access to adequate facilities or even know how to contact experts. Also large farms require a significant time investment and substantial cost to consult experts. Plant diseases also pose a threat to the income of smallholder farmers. Detecting diseases in each crop is a complex task and it consumes a lot of time for farmers to look after the maintenance of crops. Thus, farmers need a technology that can help them in maintaining the crop in an efficient manner. It is easier, quicker, and less expensive to automatically detect diseases by only examining the symptoms on plant leaves. In this paper, we present a technique to detect the disease on a Corn plant using leaf images and Transfer Learning. The proposed approach extracts features of leaf images using assorted pre-trained models of RegNet and it reduces the dimensionality of extracted feature set by utilising Kernel-PCA. For classification of the diseases it makes use of XGBoost classifier. The study proves that the proposed approach can achieve the accuracy of 96.74% considering different parameters. One such intelligent system can help not only the farmers, but can be helpful to Insurance Agents, Government Agencies and other organisations working for the betterment of farmers.

Keywords: Agriculture · Artificial intelligence · Deep learning · Disease detection · Machine learning · RegNet

1 Introduction

India's economy is heavily reliant on agriculture. A significant portion of the nation's overall labour force is employed in agricultural and related sector activities and contributes significantly to the country's Gross Value Added (GVA). Considering how important the agriculture industry is, there is a need of focussing on the effects of Diseases (Bacterial, Viral, Fungal) on the production of the crops.

S. Rajagopal et al. (Eds.): ASCIS 2022, CCIS 1759, pp. 346–361, 2022.
https://doi.org/10.1007/978-3-031-23092-9_28

Commonly found Diseases (Bacterial, Viral, Fungal) in cereal crops are: Bacterial blight, leaf streak, blast, common rust, gray leaf spot, brown spot, powdery mildew. These causes delayed flowering, panicles small and not completely exerted or partially filled grains [1]. Physical observation by experts requires a large team as well as continuous monitoring. Farmers do not always have access to adequate facilities or even know how to contact experts. Consulting experts costs very high with large farms, Time consuming too. The financial security of smallholder farmers is also threatened by plant diseases (Fig. 1).

Fig. 1. Common diseases of cereal crop

Using leaf images to detect plant diseases, conventional image processing approaches produced acceptable results and performance, but they were only capable of working with tiny data sets and providing theoretical outcomes [2]. Since Artificial Intelligence and Deep Learning has completely changed the field of computer vision, particularly the areas of image classification and object detection, it is now thought to be a promising tool to enhance such automated systems in order to achieve better results, broaden the scope of diseases, and implement useful real-time plant disease detection systems [2]. However, it is not the easy task as the forms of the data are changing very dynamically and huge in numbers as well as storage space. In the last few years, the types of datasets have seen a significant transformation, with text datasets giving way to image datasets and, more recently, video datasets becoming popular in the field of study. As a result, with technological revolutions, there is a requirement for developing numerous intelligent systems in all aspects of daily life. The automatic detection of diseases by merely looking at the symptoms just on plant leaves makes it simpler, faster, and less expensive [3].

Artificial Intelligence, very well known as Machine Intelligence is a system to interpret an information correctly, learn it, evaluate it and execute the findings to complete the defined task using flexible adaptation [4]. Shortly, Artificial Intelligence is a machine that learns from the information and solves the given problem. However. it is achieved by utilising the problem-solving abilities of Human Brains that helps to design and deploy new intelligent systems. Ultimately, Artificial intelligence is a union of technology with science like Biology, Computer Science, Engineering, Linguistics, Mathematics and

Psychology where merging two or more domains results in intelligent systems [4]. Artificial intelligence's main objective is to create intelligent systems that can learn, assess, and produce solutions to problems.

With the expansion in the size of information, it is utmost required that to develop smart systems that can analyse such information for technological progress. Machine learning, an application of an Artificial Intelligence which allows the system to study the required and valuable information automatically as well as independently without being dependent on any external resources [5]. Machine learning build a mathematical model of datasets known as "training data", that can be used for developing some intelligent techniques later. Machine learning is also known as Predictive Analytics. Machine learning is categorised as: a) Supervised Learning, where training data consists of inputs and the expected output based on inputs and b) Unsupervised Learning, where training data consist of only inputs and determining outputs is bit difficult [5].

For plant disease identification using typical computer vision methods, features must be manually chosen before classification judgments can be made [6, 7]. Feature Engineering (FE) is a time-consuming and complicated process that must be adjusted whenever the problem or dataset changes [7]. As a result, FE is a costly endeavour that dependent on expert knowledge and does not scale well. The elimination of the need for FE is one of the most significant benefits of using Deep Learning (DL) in image processing. Deep convolutional networks, in contrast, automatically pick up the most crucial features through layered interpretation of visual information.

DL expands on traditional ML by incorporating more "depth" (complexity) into the model and modifying the input using various functions that enable hierarchical data representation through several levels of abstraction [8]. If there are sufficiently substantial datasets characterising the problem, these complicated models are employed in DL to enhance classification precision or reduce regression error. Depending on the network architecture being utilised, DL can have a variety of different components (such as convolutions, pooling layers, fully linked layers, gates, memory cells, activation functions, encode/decode schemes, etc) [8].

An output, such as a crop-disease pair, can be produced by deep neural networks by mapping an input, such as a picture of a sick plant, to an output. The mathematical processes that make up a neural network's nodes take numerical inputs from incoming edges and output numerical results as outgoing edges. The input layer is mapped to the output layer via deep neural networks, which are merely stacks of layers of nodes. Making sure that the network's structure, nodes, and edge weights appropriately map the input to the output is the challenging phase of creating a deep network [9]. Deep neural networks are trained by adjusting the network parameters so that the mapping gets better during the course of training.

While training large neural networks can be very time-consuming, the requirement of heigh performance computing resources and longer training time associated with DL is a disadvantage. However, testing takes less time than other ML-based methods. Other drawbacks include issues that may arise when using pre-trained models on small or significantly different datasets, optimisation issues due to the models' complexity, and hardware constraints. Recent research work demonstrates that it can be overcome using the different Deep Learning (DL) approaches.

With the non-ending problem of global warming as food shortage, it is very much important that we care about trees and plants. However, majority of the trees or plants are cut down owing to many reasons. One such reason is the plants suffer from various diseases. If they are not provided proper medication on time, their growth stops and ultimately, they are cut down. It is utmost important to detect the disease in the plants so that they can be nurtured properly. In this, paper, we present a technique to detect the disease on a Corn Leaf. The proposed approach extracts features using pre-trained models of RegNet, it further reduces the feature set by Kernel-PCA and for classification of the diseases it makes use of XGBoost classifier.

This paper is organised as follows: Sect. 2 provides a review on related works, Sect. 3 describes the proposed system, Sect. 4 describes the results and finally Sect. 5 concludes the paper.

2   Related Works

One of the key elements that maintains the framework for future system improvement and development is the literature review research of existing methodologies. Consequently, a review has been created in order to learn more about the methods or tools now in use for detecting plant leaf diseases.

In [10], the authors have focused on automatic detection of disease on maize leaf as well as an improvement in accuracy level. The authors employed the enhanced GoogLeNet and Cifar10 models based on deep learning to recognise the leaf disease in order to increase the identification accuracy of maize leaf diseases and decrease the number of network parameters. Later, two improved models were used to train and evaluate nine different types of maize leaf images by changing the parameters, changing the pooling combinations, adding dropout operations and Relu functions, and reducing the number of classifiers [10]. In comparison to VGG and AlexNet, the improved models had a much lower number of parameters. While the Cifar10 model's accuracy was 98.8%, that of the GoogLeNet model was 98.9%. In 8 out of 9 maize leaves, the models operated effectively and achieved a better accuracy level.

In [11], Rice sheath blight, rice brown spot, and rice stem borer symptoms were the three types of rice illnesses and pests that the authors successfully identified by video analysis. The authors first focused on extracting frames from the video, providing the frames for detection of crop and all the correctly detected crops were then used for further processing. The proposed set of video detection measures by the authors was compatible with the image training model. Additionally, they created a unique DCNN backbone network for video detection that was appropriate for detecting videos of rice [11]. According to the findings, VGG16, ResNet-50, and ResNet-101 did a poor job of detecting objects in somewhat hazy photos. Moreover, the same dataset and video were tested using Yolo-3 model which resulted in consistent performance even with the blurry images.

In [12], the authors have specifically focused on Northern Maize Leaf Blight; a disease that is most commonly seen in maize leaves. The authors have considered on the live field images. The entire implementation was in 3 steps [12]. In the first step, the authors pre-processed the images to resolve the issues of object detection due to high intensity of light or any other factors. In the second step, a Region Proposal Network (RPN) was used to mark the regions with boxes wherever the model assumes the presence of disease. Moreover, a transmission module was defined to fine tune all the marked images to filter and delete the wrongly marked images. In the third step, the model took all the remaining images as an input, tested with the given parameters and stored all correctly detected images. The entire implementation achieved about 92% accuracy level.

In [13], the authors presented simple way of detecting the disease on maize leaf using simple CNN model. The authors mainly focused on 4 parameters of a leaf like healthy, cercospora, common rust and northern leaf blight. The implementation was in 2 stages. In the first step, the feature extraction process was initiated using different CNN models like AlexNet, VGG, VGG-19, GoogleNet, Inception-V3, Resnet50 and Resnet101. In the second step, the authors used machine learning techniques like support vector machine, k-nearest neighbourhood and decision trees for classification process. The authors used about 200 different maize leaf images. On implementing each set of featured images available after first step with each machine learning technique, it was found that the features extracted by AlexNet and classified using support vector machine attained the highest level of accuracy of 95%.

In [14], the authors have proposed a deep learning approach to recognize and classify the paddy crop variety-wise biotic and abiotic stress. Authors have considered 5 different petty crops with 11 classes of stresses and one healthy class to be recognized and classified by using five separate VGG-16 CNN models. Authors have achieved maximum average classification accuracy of 95.08% for paddy crop variety called Mugad-101 and minimum average classification accuracy of 90.75% for paddy crop variety called Jaya. Concluding the approach, trained models achieve average classification accuracy of 92.89% on paddy crop variety-wise biotic and abiotic stresses.

In [15], author have used PlantVillage dataset and four different DL models (InceptionV3, InceptionResnetV2, MobileNetV2, EfficientNetB0) for the detection of plant leaf diseases. Authors have tested all DL models on 3 variations of image dataset as color, grayscale, and segmented, with different combinations of train-test split as 80–20, 70–30, and 60–40. The results were ranging from minimum accuracy of 93.21% with grayscale image having 70–30 train-test split on MobileNetV2 to maximum accuracy of 99.78% with segmented image having 80–20 train-test split on EfficientNetB0. The highest average classification accuracy that authors have achieved is 99.56% with EfficientNetB0, which also took less training time compared to the other models used in the paper.

In [16], authors have proposed a hybrid model for plant disease detection. The model is based on Convolutional Autoencoder (CAE) and Convolutional Neural Network (CNN). In the proposed approach dataset images were first given to encoder network of CAE to find compressed domain representation of leaf images and then it has been fed up to CNN for the classification. Authors have claimed to have very less number of training parameters and significantly less time to train the model due to having less number of features because of dimensionality reduction using CAE. The proposed model has achieved training accuracy of 99.35% and testing accuracy of 98.38% on dataset having bacterial spot disease present in peach plants, extracted from the PlantVillage dataset.

In [17], authors have proposed an approach with EfficientNetB0 architecture, which was implemented as telegram bot. A dataset with 2414 images of wheat fungi diseases (WFD2020) with 7 classes was used by authors in this paper. To achieve better performance authors have tested multiple implementation techniques like transfer learning, dataset stratification, and augmentation. A network with a training method based on the augmentation and transfer of image styles managed to reach the best accuracy of 94.2%. The telegram bot was created using the proposed recognition model. Telegram application, enables us to utilise this service both in the lab with a stationary computer and in the field using mobile devices.

3 Methodology

See (Fig. 2)

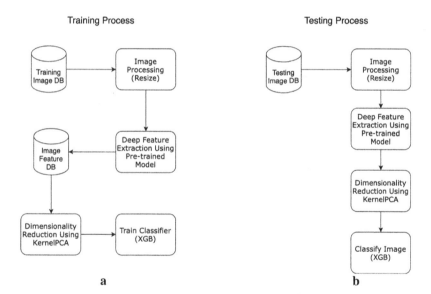

Fig. 2. (a) Proposed Training Process (b) Proposed Testing Process

Proposed System for developing corm or maze leaf disease detection system is briefly explained with the help of following algorithm:

Algorithm: Train corm or maze leaf disease detection classifier
Input:
M ← Pre-Trained RegNet Model
IMG ← Set of images belonging to different diseases and healthy leaf category
Output:
XGB ← Trained XGBoost Classifier
Procedure:
Resized_Image ← []
For every Image in IMG do
Resized_Image ← Resized_Image U Resize (Image)
End for
Deep_Features_Set ← []
For every Image in Resized_Image do
Deep_Features ← Output of Model 'M' after Image as input
End for
Spilt Deep_Feature_Set into two parts (Training_Feature_Set and Testing Feature Set)
Train XGBoost Classifier using Training_Feature_Set
Evaluate XGBoost Classifier using Testing_Feature_Set

3.1 Deep Feature Extraction

DeeP feature extraction is the technique of extracting image features from the deep levels of a CNN, and deep features are the features themselves. Steps include putting data into a Pre-trained CNN model and obtaining activation values from the fully connected layer, located at the output of the network, or from the multiple pooling layers distributed throughout the design. Using a various version of the RegNet model, experiments were conducted to see how well the proposed system works.

3.2 RegNet

Many variations of the ResNet have shown exceptional performance in computer vision-based quests. While the modest shortcut connection technique is effective in facilitating gradient flow between construction blocks, the additive nature of the function prevents it from being used to re-explore possibly complementary features. To solve this problem, Jing Xu et al. [18] suggested feeding the ResNet the output of a regulator module that acts as a memory component to retrieve complimentary features. Convolutional RNNs, used to make up the regulator module, have been found to be effective at extracting Spatiotemporal data. RegNet was chosen as the name of the new Regulated Network system.

3.3 Kernel PCA

Principal Component Analysis (PCA) is a form of factor investigation. Because of this, we can lower the size of the data set without suffering from significant loss of detail

[19]. PCA finds a small number of orthogonal linear blends of the original variables that account for the most variance, hence decreasing the dimensionality. When analysing data, PCA uses a linear approach. In other words, it can only be used on linearly separable datasets. If your data can be neatly split up into linear categories, then this method will work wonderfully for you. However, we might not get the best dimensionality reduction if we apply it to non-linear datasets. With kernel PCA, the dataset is projected onto a higher dimensional feature space, where the features can be linearly separated. It's conceptually close to Support Vector Machines [20].

3.4 XGBoost Classifier

One of the most well-known gradient boosting approaches, eXtreme Gradient Boosting (XGBoost) improves both the effectiveness and speed of tree-based classification. In Ensemble Learning, it is classified as a Boosting method. For improved classification accuracy, ensemble learning combines numerous models into a single set of predictors. With the Boosting approach, newer models attempt to fix the mistakes of older models by giving more weight. Gradient boosting strategies optimises the loss function, as opposed to other boosting algorithms that upsurge the weights of misclassified twigs. XGBoost's generalisation abilities are enhanced by the application of advanced regularisation (L1 and L2), making it a more regularised variant of Gradient Boosting [21].

4 Experimental Results

This section explains the experimental setup and performance of the proposed approach for corn leaf disease detection. The results are examined in multiple different measures like accuracy, f1 score, precision, recall, sensitivity and specificity. Details of the experiments and result analysis are in the subsequent sections.

4.1 Implementation Data

The proposed approach extracts features using pre-trained models of RegNet architectures, it further reduces the feature set by Kernel-PCA and for classification of the diseases it makes use of XGBoost classifier. This approach is tested on the Corn or Maize Leaf Disease Dataset created by utilizing the well-known PlantVillage and Plant-Doc datasets [22, 23]. Images that were not deemed to be valuable during the dataset's creation have been removed. The final dataset consists of 4188 images in total, which are separated into four categories (Common Rust, Gray Leaf Spot, Blight, Healthy) that are described with image count in Table 1. Oversampling was made to overcome the problem of class imbalance.

To obtain the best results, which are described in the following section, multiple readings with all RegNet models of the X-series and Y-series (Listed in Table 2), with varying values of components in Kernel-PCA and variations in the values of estimators, gamma, and learning-rate for XGBoost Classifier, were conducted.

Table 1. Dataset description.

Disease	Image count
Common Rust	1306
Gray Leaf Spot	574
Blight	1146
Healthy	1162

Table 2. RegNet X and Y series models list.

RegNet series	List of RegNet models
RegNet X-Series	RegNetX002, RegNetX004, RegNetX006, RegNetX008, RegNetX016, RegNetX032, RegNetX040, RegNetX064, RegNetX080, RegNetX120, RegNetX160, RegNetX320
RegNet Y-Series	RegNetY002, RegNetY004, RegNetY006, RegNetY008, RegNetY016, RegNetY032, RegNetY040, RegNetY064, RegNetY080, RegNetY120, RegNetY160, RegNetY320

4.2 Results Analysis

The proposed approach is tested on multiple parameters: accuracy, F1-score, precision, recall and specificity. Equations (1) through (5) define measures used to gauge how well a trained XGBoost classifier can identify and categorise diseases in plant leaves.

$$Accuracy = \frac{(TP + TN)}{(TP + FP + TN + FN)} \tag{1}$$

$$F1 = 2 * \frac{Precision * Recall}{(Precision + Recall)} \tag{2}$$

$$Precision = \frac{TP}{(TP + FP)} \tag{3}$$

$$Recall = \frac{TP}{(TP + FN)} \tag{4}$$

$$Specificity = \frac{TN}{(TN + FP)} \tag{5}$$

The maximum micro-average accuracy of 0.9674 and F1-score of 0.9349 is obtained when RegNetX320 is used to extract deep features, whereas the minimum micro-average accuracy of 0.9473 and F1-score of 0.8946 is obtained when RegNetX002 is used to extract deep features. All other RegNet models are having results in between the range of minimum and maximum listed with RegNetX002 and RegNetX320 respectively. Leaf disease category wise and overall micro-average of accuracy, f1 score, precision, recall and specificity for all RegNet models as deep feature extractor, KernelPCA as dimensionality reducer and XGBoost as Classifier are given in tables from Table 3, 4, 5, 6, 7, 8, 9, 10, 11, 12, 13 to Table 14. These tables consider accuracy, f1 score, precision, recall and specificity as M1, M2, M3, M4 and M5 respectively, and disease category Blight, Common Rust, Gray Leaf Spot, and Healthy as Cls1, Cls2, Cls3, Cls4, with micro-average as mAvg.

Table 3. RegNetX002 & RegNetX004 results

	RegNetX002					RegNetX004				
	Cls1	Cls2	Cls3	Cls4	mAvg	Cls1	Cls2	Cls3	Cls4	mAvg
M1	0.9042	0.9783	0.9240	0.9777	0.9460	0.8467	0.9725	0.8787	0.9840	0.9205
M2	0.8011	0.9556	0.8551	0.9558	0.8921	0.7022	0.9427	0.7607	0.9680	0.8410
M3	0.8343	0.9786	0.8163	0.9450	0.8921	0.6836	0.9861	0.7494	0.9692	0.8410
M4	0.7704	0.9337	0.8977	0.9668	0.8921	0.7219	0.9031	0.7724	0.9668	0.8410
M5	0.9489	0.9932	0.9328	0.9813	0.9640	0.8884	0.9957	0.9140	0.9898	0.9470

Table 4. RegNetX006 & RegNetX008 results

	RegNetX006					RegNetX008				
	Cls1	Cls2	Cls3	Cls4	mAvg	Cls1	Cls2	Cls3	Cls4	mAvg
M1	0.9189	0.9764	0.9381	0.9891	0.9556	0.9246	0.9738	0.9425	0.9815	0.9556
M2	0.8304	0.9523	0.8821	0.9783	0.9112	0.8475	0.9461	0.8894	0.9630	0.9112
M3	0.8711	0.9634	0.8403	0.9746	0.9112	0.8586	0.9756	0.8558	0.9617	0.9112
M4	0.7934	0.9413	0.9284	0.9821	0.9112	0.8367	0.9184	0.9258	0.9642	0.9112
M5	0.9608	0.9881	0.9413	0.9915	0.9704	0.9540	0.9923	0.9481	0.9872	0.9704

Table 5. RegNetX016 & RegNetX032 results

	RegNetX016					RegNetX032				
	Cls1	Cls2	Cls3	Cls4	mAvg	Cls1	Cls2	Cls3	Cls4	mAvg
M1	0.9157	0.9693	0.9381	0.9917	0.9537	0.8819	0.9706	0.9042	0.9789	0.9339
M2	0.8316	0.9372	0.8795	0.9833	0.9074	0.7643	0.9403	0.8111	0.9579	0.8678
M3	0.8316	0.9624	0.8551	0.9871	0.9074	0.7634	0.9577	0.7990	0.9566	0.8678
M4	0.8316	0.9133	0.9054	0.9795	0.9074	0.7653	0.9235	0.8235	0.9591	0.8678
M5	0.9438	0.9881	0.9489	0.9957	0.9691	0.9208	0.9864	0.9311	0.9855	0.9559

Table 6. RegNetX040 & RegNetX064 results

	RegNetX040					RegNetX064				
	Cls1	Cls2	Cls3	Cls4	mAvg	Cls1	Cls2	Cls3	Cls4	mAvg
M1	0.9036	0.9706	0.9227	0.9872	0.9460	0.9195	0.9815	0.9368	0.9885	0.9566
M2	0.8021	0.9403	0.8504	0.9747	0.8921	0.8346	0.9627	0.8788	0.9768	0.9132
M3	0.8248	0.9577	0.8230	0.9649	0.8921	0.8595	0.9714	0.8427	0.9844	0.9132
M4	0.7806	0.9235	0.8798	0.9847	0.8921	0.8112	0.9541	0.9182	0.9693	0.9132
M5	0.9446	0.9864	0.9370	0.9881	0.9640	0.9557	0.9906	0.9430	0.9949	0.9711

Table 7. RegNetX080 & RegNetX120 results

	RegNetX080					RegNetX120				
	Cls1	Cls2	Cls3	Cls4	mAvg	Cls1	Cls2	Cls3	Cls4	mAvg
M1	0.9310	0.9738	0.9496	0.9923	0.9617	0.9304	0.9764	0.9438	0.9872	0.9595
M2	0.8612	0.9475	0.9006	0.9846	0.9234	0.8611	0.9515	0.8911	0.9742	0.9189
M3	0.8679	0.9512	0.8861	0.9897	0.9234	0.8601	0.9784	0.8633	0.9818	0.9189
M4	0.8546	0.9439	0.9156	0.9795	0.9234	0.8622	0.9260	0.9207	0.9668	0.9189
M5	0.9566	0.9838	0.9609	0.9966	0.9745	0.9532	0.9932	0.9515	0.9940	0.9730

Table 8. RegNetX160 & RegNetX320 results

	RegNetX160					RegNetX320				
	Cls1	Cls2	Cls3	Cls4	mAvg	Cls1	Cls2	Cls3	Cls4	mAvg
M1	0.9361	0.9789	0.9438	0.9904	0.9623	0.9432	0.9853	0.9527	0.9885	0.9674
M2	0.8691	0.9570	0.8927	0.9808	0.9246	0.8824	0.9702	0.9095	0.9770	0.9349
M3	0.8925	0.9787	0.8531	0.9821	0.9246	0.9151	0.9843	0.8712	0.9746	0.9349
M4	0.8469	0.9362	0.9361	0.9795	0.9246	0.8520	0.9566	0.9514	0.9795	0.9349
M5	0.9659	0.9932	0.9464	0.9940	0.9749	0.9736	0.9949	0.9532	0.9915	0.9783

We also used the findings from Multi-layer Perceptron classifier to compare the classification accuracy of XGBoost classifier with accuracy of base neural network model. This demonstrated the superiority of XGBoost over MLP and allowed us to reduce the overall complexity of the entire model. When used after KernalPCA in the proposed approach, Table 15 compares the average accuracy of the two classifiers.

The maximum accuracy with MLP as the classifier is 83.97% when RegNetY320 is used as the Feature Extractor model. The choice of a machine learning-based classifier with a significant improvement in the outcome is justified by XGBoost's highest accuracy of 96.74% when RegNetX320 is employed as the Feature Extractor model.

Table 9. RegNetY002 & RegNetY004 results

	RegNetY002					RegNetY004				
	Cls1	Cls2	Cls3	Cls4	mAvg	Cls1	Cls2	Cls3	Cls4	mAvg
M1	0.8966	0.9732	0.9183	0.9783	0.9416	0.9195	0.9808	0.9285	0.9847	0.9534
M2	0.7863	0.9457	0.8447	0.9562	0.8831	0.8329	0.9612	0.8657	0.9688	0.9068
M3	0.8142	0.9581	0.8037	0.9636	0.8831	0.8674	0.9738	0.8149	0.9842	0.9068
M4	0.7602	0.9337	0.8900	0.9488	0.8831	0.8010	0.9490	0.9233	0.9540	0.9068
M5	0.9421	0.9864	0.9277	0.9881	0.9610	0.9591	0.9915	0.9302	0.9949	0.9689

Table 10. RegNetY006 & RegNetY008 results

	RegNetY006					RegNetY008				
	Cls1	Cls2	Cls3	Cls4	mAvg	Cls1	Cls2	Cls3	Cls4	mAvg
M1	0.9144	0.9757	0.9259	0.9898	0.9515	0.8940	0.9738	0.9125	0.9885	0.9422
M2	0.8260	0.9504	0.8578	0.9795	0.9029	0.7763	0.9472	0.8343	0.9771	0.8844
M3	0.8413	0.9733	0.8235	0.9820	0.9029	0.8229	0.9558	0.7913	0.9722	0.8844
M4	0.8112	0.9286	0.8951	0.9770	0.9029	0.7347	0.9388	0.8824	0.9821	0.8844
M5	0.9489	0.9915	0.9362	0.9940	0.9676	0.9472	0.9855	0.9226	0.9906	0.9615

Table 11. RegNetY016 & RegNetY032 results

	RegNetY016					RegNetY032				
	Cls1	Cls2	Cls3	Cls4	mAvg	Cls1	Cls2	Cls3	Cls4	mAvg
M1	0.9017	0.9789	0.9151	0.9847	0.9451	0.9215	0.9789	0.9406	0.9866	0.9569
M2	0.7968	0.9573	0.8396	0.9689	0.8902	0.8437	0.9563	0.8853	0.9730	0.9138
M3	0.8251	0.9711	0.7945	0.9816	0.8902	0.8405	0.9945	0.8548	0.9768	0.9138
M4	0.7704	0.9439	0.8900	0.9565	0.8902	0.8469	0.9209	0.9182	0.9693	0.9138
M5	0.9455	0.9906	0.9234	0.9940	0.9634	0.9463	0.9983	0.9481	0.9923	0.9713

Table 12. RegNetY040 & RegNetY064 results

	RegNetY040					RegNetY064				
	Cls1	Cls2	Cls3	Cls4	mAvg	Cls1	Cls2	Cls3	Cls4	mAvg
M1	0.9240	0.9783	0.9361	0.9853	0.9559	0.8972	0.9630	0.9221	0.9891	0.9428

(*continued*)

Table 12. (*continued*)

	RegNetY040					RegNetY064				
	Cls1	Cls2	Cls3	Cls4	mAvg	Cls1	Cls2	Cls3	Cls4	mAvg
M2	0.8468	0.9561	0.8756	0.9704	0.9119	0.7839	0.9231	0.8551	0.9785	0.8857
M3	0.8545	0.9686	0.8523	0.9767	0.9119	0.8272	0.9613	0.7982	0.9675	0.8857
M4	0.8393	0.9439	0.9003	0.9642	0.9119	0.7449	0.8878	0.9207	0.9898	0.8857
M5	0.9523	0.9898	0.9481	0.9923	0.9706	0.9480	0.9881	0.9226	0.9889	0.9619

Table 13. RegNetY080 & RegNetY120 results

	RegNetY080					RegNetY120				
	Cls1	Cls2	Cls3	Cls4	mAvg	Cls1	Cls2	Cls3	Cls4	mAvg
M1	0.9183	0.9764	0.9246	0.9866	0.9515	0.9195	0.9732	0.9298	0.9872	0.9524
M2	0.8338	0.9521	0.8525	0.9734	0.9029	0.8376	0.9464	0.8618	0.9742	0.9049
M3	0.8492	0.9659	0.8337	0.9648	0.9029	0.8464	0.9464	0.8469	0.9818	0.9049
M4	0.8189	0.9388	0.8721	0.9821	0.9029	0.8291	0.9464	0.8772	0.9668	0.9049
M5	0.9514	0.9889	0.9421	0.9881	0.9676	0.9497	0.9821	0.9472	0.9940	0.9683

Table 14. RegNetY160 & RegNetY320 results

	RegNetY160					RegNetY320				
	Cls1	Cls2	Cls3	Cls4	mAvg	Cls1	Cls2	Cls3	Cls4	mAvg
M1	0.9176	0.9757	0.9310	0.9866	0.9527	0.9221	0.9706	0.9425	0.9872	0.9556
M2	0.8327	0.9505	0.8657	0.9734	0.9055	0.8411	0.9396	0.8900	0.9745	0.9112
M3	0.8470	0.9707	0.8426	0.9648	0.9055	0.8590	0.9676	0.8525	0.9720	0.9112
M4	0.8189	0.9311	0.8900	0.9821	0.9055	0.8240	0.9133	0.9309	0.9770	0.9112
M5	0.9506	0.9906	0.9447	0.9881	0.9685	0.9549	0.9898	0.9464	0.9906	0.9704

Table 15. Average accuracy of XGBoost and MLP Classifiers in proposed approach.

Feature extractor model	XGBoost classifier	MLP classifier
RegNetX002	0.9473	0.7944
RegNetX004	0.9518	0.7963

(*continued*)

Table 15. (*continued*)

Feature extractor model	XGBoost classifier	MLP classifier
RegNetX006	0.9556	0.8110
RegNetX008	0.9572	0.8052
RegNetX016	0.9572	0.8135
RegNetX032	0.9496	0.7989
RegNetX040	0.9572	0.8225
RegNetX064	0.9566	0.8155
RegNetX080	0.9617	0.8308
RegNetX120	0.9595	0.8135
RegNetX160	0.9623	0.8250
RegNetX320	0.9674	0.8327
RegNetY002	0.9559	0.7727
RegNetY004	0.9534	0.7720
RegNetY006	0.9569	0.7957
RegNetY008	0.9511	0.7982
RegNetY016	0.9569	0.7803
RegNetY032	0.9595	0.8231
RegNetY040	0.9559	0.7893
RegNetY064	0.9572	0.8103
RegNetY080	0.9642	0.8384
RegNetY120	0.9630	0.8301
RegNetY160	0.9601	0.8129
RegNetY320	0.9601	0.8397

5 Conclusion

Using leaf images and transfer learning, we present a method in this work for identifying the disease on a corn plant. The proposed method extracts features from leaf image data using a variety of pre-trained RegNet models, and Kernel-PCA is utilised to minimise the dimensionality of the obtained feature set. The diseases are classified using the XGBoost classifier. The research demonstrates that the suggested approach can achieve an accuracy of 96.74% when various factors are taken into account.

In addition to farmers, insurance agents, governmental agencies, and other organisations that aim to improve the lot of farmers can all gain from such an intelligent system.

Acknowledgement. Authors would like to acknowledge the supercomputing facility established by Gujarat Council of Science and Technology (GUJCOST) at the Marwadi University, Rajkot,

India. This work was carried out utilizing the PARAM Shavak supercomputer developed at the Center for Development of Advanced Computing (C-DAC).

References

1. Bari, B.S., et al.: A real-time approach of diagnosing rice leaf disease using deep learning-based faster R-CNN framework. PeerJ Comput. Sci. **7** (2021)
2. Loey, M., ElSawy, A., Afify, M.: Deep learning in plant diseases detection for agricultural crops: a survey. Int. J. Serv. Sci. Manag. Eng. Technol. **11**(2), 41–58 (2020)
3. Ashwinkumar, S., Rajagopal, S., Manimaran, V., Jegajothi, B.: Automated plant leaf disease detection and classification using optimal mobilenet based convolutional neural networks. Mater. Today Proc. **51**, 480–487. Elsevier Ltd (2021)
4. Baccouche, M., Mamalet, F., Wolf, C., Garcia, C., Baskurt, A.: Lncs 7065 – sequential deep learning for human action recognition. In: Human Behavior Understanding, pp. 29–39. Springer (2011). https://doi.org/10.1007/978-3-642-25446-8_4
5. Sabbar, W., Chergui, A., Bekkhoucha, A.: Video summarization using shot segmentation and local motion estimation. In: Innovative Computing Technology (INTECH), 2012 Second International Conference on, pp.190, 193 (2012)
6. Deshapande, A.S., Giraddi, S.G., Karibasappa, K.G., Desai, S.D.: Fungal disease detection in maize leaves using Haar Wavelet features. In: Information and Communication Technology for Intelligent Systems, pp. 275–286. Springer, Singapore (2019). https://doi.org/10.1007/978-981-13-1742-2_27
7. Kumar, S., Mishra, S., Khanna, P.: Precision sugarcane monitoring using SVM classifier. Procedia Comput. Sci. **122**, 881–887 (2017)
8. Kamilaris, A., Prenafeta-Boldú, F.X.: Deep learning in agriculture: a survey. Comput. Electron. Agric. **147**(February), 70–90 (2018)
9. Mohanty, S.P., Hughes, D.P., Salathe, M.: Using deep learning for image-based plant disease detection. Front. Plant Sci. **7** (2016)
10. Zhang, X., Qiao, Y., Meng, F., Fan, C., Zhang, M.: Identification of maize leaf diseases using improved deep convolutional neural networks. IEEE Access **6**, 30370–30377 (2018)
11. Li, D., et al.: A recognition method for rice plant diseases and pests video detection based on deep convolutional neural network. Sensors (Switzerland). **20** (2020)
12. Sun, J., Yang, Y., He, X., Wu, X.: Northern maize leaf blight detection under complex field environment based on deep learning. IEEE Access **8**, 33679–33688 (2020)
13. Syarief, M., Setiawan, W.: Convolutional neural network for maize leaf disease image classification. Telkomnika (Telecommun. Comput. Electron. Control) **18**, 1376–1381 (2020)
14. Anami, B.S., Malvade, N.N., Palaiah, S.: Deep learning approach for recognition and classification of yield affecting paddy crop stresses using field images. Artif. Intell. Agric. **4**, 12–20 (2020)
15. Hassan, S.M., Maji, A.K., Jasinski, M., Leonowicz, Z., Jasinska, E.: Identification of plant-leaf diseases using CNN and transfer-learning approach. Electronics (Switzerland). **10** (2021)
16. Bedi, P., Gole, P.: Plant disease detection using hybrid model based on convolutional autoencoder and convolutional neural network. Artif. Intell. Agric. **5**, 90–101 (2021)
17. Genaev, M.A., Skolotneva, E.S., Gultyaeva, E.I., Orlova, E.A., Bechtold, N.P., Afonnikov, D.A.: Image-based wheat fungi diseases identification by deep learning. Plants **10**, 8 (2021)
18. Xu, J., Pan, Y., Pan, X., Hoi, S., Yi, Z., Xu, Z.: RegNet: self-regulated network for image classification. IEEE Trans. Neural Netw. Learn. Syst. https://doi.org/10.1109/TNNLS.2022.3158966

19. Abdi, H., Williams, L.J.: Principal component analysis. WIREs Comput. Stat. **2**(4), 433–459 (2010)
20. Hoffmann, H.: Kernel PCA for novelty detection. Pattern Recogn. **40**(3), 863–874 (2007)
21. Chen, T., Guestrin, C.: Xgboost: a scalable tree boosting system. In: Proceedings of the 22nd ACM SIGKDD International Conference on Knowledge Discovery and Data Mining, pp. 785–794. Association for Computing Machinery (2016)
22. Singh, D., Jain, N., Jain, P., Kayal, P., Kumawat, S., Batra, N.: PlantDoc: a dataset for visual plant disease detection. In: Proceedings of the 7th ACM IKDD CoDS and 25th COMAD, pp. 249–253 (2020)
23. Arun Pandian, J., Geetharamani, G.: Data for: identification of plant leaf diseases using a 9-layer deep convolutional neural network. Mendeley Data. **1** (2019). https://doi.org/10.17632/tywbtsjrjv.1

A Machine Learning Algorithm-Based IoT-Based Message Alert System for Predicting Coronary Heart Disease

C Dhanamjayulu[1], Grandhi Venkata Suraj[1], Madicharala Nikhil[1], Rajesh Kaluri[2], and Srinivas Koppu[2(✉)]

[1] School of Electrical Engineering, Vellore Institute of Technology, Vellore 632014, India
{grandhivenkata.suraj2017,
madicharla.nikhil2017}@vitstudent.ac.in
[2] School of Information Technology and Engineering, Vellore Institute of Technology, Vellore 632014, India
rajesh.kaluri@vt.ac.in, srinukoppu@vit.ac.in

Abstract. Coronary illness is one of the most dependable reasons for death in the world today. The expectation of cardiovascular action is a basic test in the zone of clinical information examination. AI has ended up being viable in aiding in settling on choices and expectations from the huge amount of information created by specialists or Health associations. It is getting more support to foresee coronary illness with various Machine Learning methods and it additionally causes individuals to take future solutions for dodge. The proposed a novel procedure that objectives discovering basic features by applying Machine Learning techniques, achieving improved precision in the assumption for cardiovascular infirmity. The proposed algorithm has an accuracy of 95.5% with a F-measure of 0.95. The forecast model is given different mixes of features and a couple of known ensemble methods. It will deliver an improved demonstration level with a proximity level of 95% through the assumption model for coronary sickness. It is also compared with existing models like SVM, KNN, Logistic Regression, Decision tree, and Naive Bayes. Future more presents, with a ready framework utilizing it and the specialist recommendation.

Keywords: IoT · Machine Learning · Heart disease

1 Introduction

Heart disease affects the functions of the heart with blockage or reducing the coronary arteries, which are required to supply blood to the heart. In the modern era, still, cardiovascular disease (CVD) affecting many people's lives. There are a lot of technologies are available to diagnose CVD. Recent research developments find out different factors to cause a high risk of heart diseases such as pulse rate, high cholesterol, high blood pressure, and diabetes. These factors made attention to researchers develop machine learning-based models for the prediction of heart disease. The neural network-based

S. Rajagopal et al. (Eds.): ASCIS 2022, CCIS 1759, pp. 362–376, 2022.
https://doi.org/10.1007/978-3-031-23092-9_29

prediction is another method and used X^2-DNN statistical model to eliminate the irrelevant features whereas the conventional DNN uses an exhaustive search strategy [1, 2]. This model also removes over-fitting and under-fitting data sets. The authors proposed a multitask deep and wide neural network (MTDWNN) for predicting fatal complications of renal dysfunction. It is caused due to heart failure. It gives high accurate model [3]. Medical syndromes such as hypertension, cholesterol, etc. are important parameters to do classification and the prediction of heart disease data mining domain [4]. Machine Learning is the one of key models for the medical diagnosis of heart patients with factors such as smoking, age, sex, high cholesterol, high blood pressure, diabetes, and due to lack of physical activity. In [5] authors developed SVM (support vector machine) model to predict early heart disease with the limited dataset. Many researchers concentrated to develop prediction models for the prediction of heart disease. However, due to a lack of alert and alerting message system development for the patients, and lost their lives. The alarm system development is very important for the current world and we have proposed a model for the same.

In [6] authors developed a prediction model based on a neural network. It uses an Electronic health record for heart failure prediction which contains all the patient data. Also, the proposed models use the long-short-term memory (LSM) network model for robustness and efficiency.

In [7] authors proposed a parallel compressive sensing model for the multichannel synchronous acquisition of heart disease signals. This makes use of bio-sensors based on the IoT for heart failure prediction. The proposed model can reconstruct effectively the normal heartbeats from abnormal heartbeats to feed a four-channel synchronous model. The outcome of the paper was that hypertensive patients develop hypertensive heart disease. The benefits of the proposed model are highly feasible, is accurate, uses the filter to remove unwanted features, and gives a positive probability of patients who will suffer from heart disease [8]. In [9, 10] authors studied human oxidative stress which leads to various diseases like Alzheimer's, cancer, heart failure diabetes, and blood pressure. In [10] used a prediction model for early detection of Malignant Ventricular Arrhythmias (MVA) from sudden cardiac death (SCD) arrest.

The [11] main aim of the adapted system is to find the relationship between individual risk significant parameters and diabetes mellitus of metabolic syndrome (Met-S) using balanced training datasets. Also, this model [12] is to investigate the relative performance of machine learning methods. The prediction of such diseases caused due to several risk factors will help a lot to the people. In the modern era, different model has been developed for human heart disease prediction in the domain of data mining and neural networks. To classify the intention of heart diseases various classifiers are employed such as SVM, K -Nearest Neighbor Algorithm (KNNA), Genetic Algorithm, Optimized models, Naïve Bayes model, and Decision Trees. The blood pressure disease which causes heart stroke is a major challenge or threat to human health [13]. Some of the developments are based on the clinical course of cystic fibrosis (CF) lung disease which is induced by serious issues of lung function. Pulmonary diagnosis is used to test lung function and is monitored routinely through testing, preventing which helps hundreds of safety measurements over the lifespan of an individual patient [14].

The ECG data is mainly used to find the abnormalities causing heart problems. The need for a machine-learning algorithm to compare the current method with a new ECG-based prediction algorithm for evaluating physiologic diseases. The main intention of developing new ECG- detection models is to improve the rate of detection of heartbeats despite irregular heart disease [15].

In [16] authors used deep learning techniques for cardiovascular disease prediction to reduce misdiagnosis. The proposed model considered different parameters to obtain robust health. The exponentials show that the developed models produced decent results compared with existing models. However, this model is considered a limited data set. [17] Cardiovascular diseases are very dangerous and highly sensitive. Due to this, it is very important to handle it with high care while predicting the disease. The estimation of risk significant factors that makes early predictions in mortality patients is critical while making a clinical decision in intensive diagnosis.

In [18] authors adapted a hybrid model to improve the efficiency of the support vector machine with an accuracy of 3.3%. The proposed model produces better results compared with existing models with maximum accuracy of 91.83%. In [19] Maximum Heart Rate (MHR) is used to design patient prescriptions and monitor fitness. The introduced technique uses age as a significant feature for predicting.

Using the CNN model, they achieved 65% accuracy [20]. As nowadays doctors and as well as patients were more aware of computer knowledge and can easily access it at any time. So, computers are used profoundly in the medical industry, giving more Opportunities. They can study many possible methods and challenges faced in prediction [21]. An improved random forest technique has been used for the prediction of heart disease based on parameters in the apache spark framework in the domain of big data analytics. In [23–26] authors It shows that data mining techniques SVM is the best out of Decision Tree, Naïve Bayes, Multilayer Perceptron, K-Nearest Neighbor, Single Conjunctive Rule Learner, Radial Basis Function]. The output of the paper strengthens the idea of the application of machine learning in the early detection of diseases [27–30]. Several deep learning based methods to predict cardiac arrhythmia by using several transform techniques are presented in [31–35].

The article is designed as follows, Sect. 2 presents an implementation of the proposed methodology, Sect. 3 shows the results and discussion with highlights, Sect. 4 describes the comparative analysis, and finally, Sect. 5 presents a conclusion.

2   Methodology

The proposed model is shown in Fig. 1. In this process, it will take the input data set which contains, age, gender, blood pressure, cholesterol, smoking habits & ancestors' heart disease. The algorithm is used in this method is a random forest which helps to predict the needs of this article. Unpredictable boondocks or subjective decision woods are a social event learning technique for gathering, backsliding, and various endeavors that work by building an immense number of decision trees at getting ready time and yielding the class that is the strategy for the classes or mean estimate of the individual trees. Random choice backwoods right for choice trees' propensity for overfitting to their preparation set and it will send this data into pre-processing which is the first step in machine learning & here it checks if there are any duplicate values and removes & sends into the second step which is feature selection in this process it contains some limits of the dataset by comparing the values it will send to the prediction which gives the result. From the processing of data from prediction using IoT, the values from this will be stored in a cloud. The alert message and doctor's suggestion will send to the respective mail id

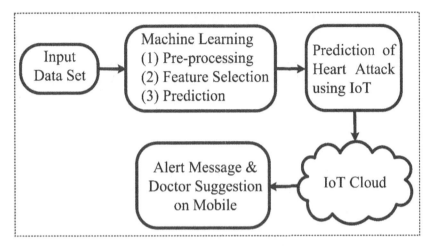

Fig. 1. Machine learning-based IoT based Message Alert system

The process carried out by the model can be explained by the flow chart shown in Fig. 2. Training set and the test set, the predicted output we export the excel file containing the phone numbers from the data set corresponding to the heart attack prone patients. Now, this data is given to the cloud and activated the cloud to send the alert messages to the patients shown in Fig. 2.

3   Implementation of Random Forest

The machine learning algorithm is used in the Random Forest. In this, the data set is divided into various decision trees based on the characteristics and merges them to give the most accurate prediction. The more unmistakable number of trees in the forest area prompts higher precision and thwarts the issue of over-fitting. This uses both classification and regression in machine learning. It additionally requires some training when contrasted with different calculations and predicts yield with high precision, in any event, for the enormous dataset it runs productively. Even though a large data are missing it gives an accurate prediction.

3.1   Mathematical Model

This outfit classifier constructs a few choice trees and consolidates them to get the best outcome. Tree learning predominantly applies bootstrap conglomerating or sacking. For

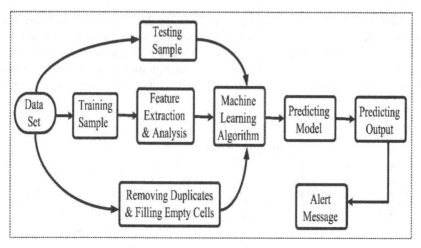

Fig. 2. Flow chart of ML-based IoT

a given information, X = {x1, x2, x3, ..., xn} with reactions Y = {x1, x2, x3, ..., xn} which rehashes the packing from b = 1 to B as demonstrated in Eq. 1.

$$j = \frac{1}{R} \sum_{b=1}^{B} fb(x^1)$$ (1)

The uncertainty of expectation on this tree is made through its standard deviation as demonstrated in Eq. 2

$$\sigma = \sqrt{\frac{\sum_{b=1}^{B} (fb(x^1) - f)^2}{B - 1}}$$ (2)

4   Implementation of ML-Based IoT

The proposed Machine learning-based IoT cloud model can be implemented in the following manner. The data pre-processing stage will be initialized, calculation of random forest with multiple datasets, prediction features, and testing.

4.1   Data Pre-processing

In this step, it becomes familiar with the data set and identifies any duplicates and missing data. Here we used 13 data Attributes and fill the missing data with the most suitable values and remove the duplicates and make the dataset more accurate. It represented the parameters that are used to say the dependability of the model on the attribute. In the table, the mean and correlation values are taken into account for which describes the data set more clearly. And the correlation directly depends on the fact to which extent the attribute affects the model output, i.e. if an attribute has a high correlation, then the model is said to be more dependent on a particular attribute.

4.2 Fitting the Random Backwoods Calculation to the Training Set

It will train the training and testing sets. Which are key points in the prediction. It includes the Algorithm: It divides the dataset into many decision trees like d1, d2, d3, etc. it can also be called baggage and chooses the best of it by voting.

4.3 Predicting the Test Result

The above results of all decision trees are considered and give the output as a prediction as several patients are likely to be affected by a heart attack. It is done by analyzing the test and training sets shown in Table 1.

Table 1. Attribute analysis with various metrics

Attribute	Mean	Standard deviation	Min	Max	Correlation
Age	54.366337	9.082101	29.000000	77.000000	0.225439
Sex	0.683168	0.466011	0.000000	1.000000	0.280937
Cp	0.966997	1.032052	0.000000	3.000000	0.433798
Trestbps	131.62376	17.538143	94.000000	200.000000	0.144931
Chol	246.264026	51.830751	126.00000	564.000000	0.085239
Fbs	0.148515	0.356198	0.000000	1.000000	0.028046
Restecg	0.528053	0.525860	0.000000	2.000000	0.137230
Thalach	149.6468	22.905161	71.000000	202.00000	0.421741
Exang	0.326733	0.4697	0.000000	1.000000	0.436757
old peak	1.039604	1.161075	0.000000	6.200000	0.430696
Slope	1.399340	0.616226	0.000000	2.000000	0.345877
Ca	0.729373	1.022606	0.000000	4.000000	0.391724
Thal	2.313531	0.612277	0.000000	3.000000	0.344029

4.4 Test Accuracy of the Result

In this step, the accuracy is calculated by several correct predictions that match the dataset and gives its accuracy. It very well may be appeared in exactness and the F1 score. The formulas for accuracy, recall, precision, and f1 score are given in Eqs. 3, 4, 5 and 6 respectively. By using the confusion matrix, the model evaluation is executed. Four outcomes are generated by the confusion matrix, namely TN-True Negative, TP-True Positive, FN-False Negative, and FP -False Positive.

$$Accuracy = \frac{TP + TN}{(TP + TN + EP + FN)-} \tag{3}$$

$$Recall = \frac{TP}{(TP + TN)-} \tag{4}$$

$$Precision = \frac{TP}{(TP + FP)-} \tag{5}$$

$$F1 = 2 * \frac{(Precision * Recall)}{(Precision * Recall)} \tag{6}$$

4.5 Visualizing the Test Set Result

IT is being visualized as a bar plot. And it is compared with the existing models to show that it is better among them. It is shown in Fig. 10. In this, they mostly plot bar graphs to analyze the outputs.

4.6 Results and Discussion

In the UCI Dataset, we used the parameters like Age, Sex, cp, Resting blood pressure (trestbps), thali (maximum heart rate), Chol (cholesterol), resting (resting ECG), exang (exercised induced angina), ca, Old peak (ST depression induced by exercise relative to rest), slope, Thal, etc. Now we analyze how each parameter affects the heart attack to occur by the bar graph between the parameter and the prediction results. And also, compared with some of the other algorithms to show that our algorithm is the best based on prediction accuracy. Here for the bar plot, we use a seaborn kit from python. As displayed in Table 1 we showed how the individuals are correlated with the prediction and we can also see that the fbs is very less affecting the prediction output. Now we see the same dependability of the prediction model on values in the bar plot.

The prediction fashions are advanced by the usage of thirteen features and the accuracy is calculated for modeling strategies. The great category techniques are listed in Table 2. The Table 2 presents the comparison concerning the accuracy, precision, and F-measure. The highest accuracy is accomplished with the aid of the random forest technique in evaluation with the present methods.

Table 2. Comparison of models based on accuracy and f1 score

Model Name	Accuracy	F-Measure
DT	81.97	0.82
RF	**95.25**	**0.95**
SVM	81.97	0.82
NB	85.25	0.84
KNN	67.21	0.67
LR	85.25	0.85

In Fig. 3, it can seem that women and men were taken into consideration in our data set. As we can see the below bar plot depicts the relation between the sex and the target or predicted output. We can infer that the sex = 0 i.e. the woman is more affected by the heart attack. Not only sex but we also considered the other attributes while predicting. So, drew bar plots of certain attributes showing the category of patients prone to coronary disease concerning the given attribute.

In Fig. 4, the patient with 0 chest pain is less prone to a heart attack. Here the chest pain indicates the severity of the heart attack. The one with high chest pain is highly prone to a heart attack shown in Fig. 4. In Fig. 5 the patient with respect to 0 and 1 are more prone to heart disease. It means the ECG values when a patient is resting and low ECG values have a high risk of getting a heart attack.

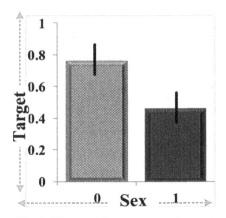

Fig. 3. The graph between sex and output

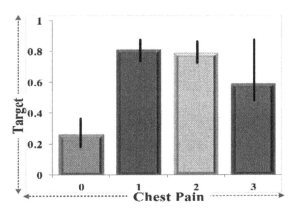

Fig. 4. Bar-plot cp (chest pain) vs target

In Fig. 6 the patient who does exercise daily is less affected by a heart attack. One who is maintaining a good diet and daily workouts are less prone to heart attacks as he burns sufficient calories to keep fat deposits less in the heart walls. The accumulation of fat in heart walls leads to a heart attack or other heart-related diseases. In Fig. 7 if a patient has ca = 4 heart attack cases are more. It states the blockage of the vessels due to fat. If the vessels are blocked then the heart function becomes less due to the unstable flow of blood in the vessels. This value of ca shows the severity of the vessel's functioning. So, the high value of ca leads to a heart attack. In Fig. 8. The cases with a slope of 2 are more affected by heart disease. The slope is a direct relation to the heart attack. It shows the peak value of the blood pressure during the exercises.

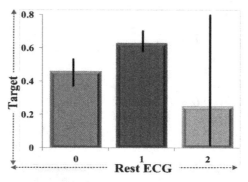

Fig. 5. RestECG vs target

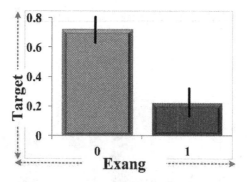

Fig. 6. Exang vs target

5   Comparison of Models

It shows that the random forest is the most accurate in the prediction of getting a heart attack in a person. Figure 10 shows the random forest is giving 95% of accuracy with the UCI Dataset. By the comparison from Table 3.

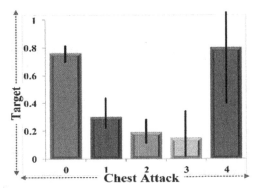

Fig. 7. CA vs target

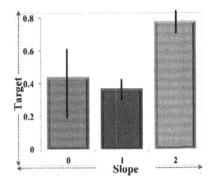

Fig. 8. Slope vs target

It can draw this plot shows the superiority of our model over the other models. We can now show that our product is the best out of the others. The accuracy is calculated as the percentage number of total heart attack patients in a dataset to the number predicted by the proposed model. As stated earlier as best of existing is shown in Fig. 10 below and also the attributes used in the model provided the best results. As shown above, in the Table 2 the description of the dataset used comprised of the 12 attributes are classified based on the feature selection of the machine learning algorithm and made an accurate prediction of the heart disease development inpatient when compared to the existing models. The Thal vs target is presented in Fig. 9.

Table 3 presents a comprehensive comparison made on accuracy and F-measure with similar kinds of algorithms. The proposed Random Forest algorithm provides more accuracy and F measure compared to existing algorithms such as DNN, FFT, DTA, CNN,

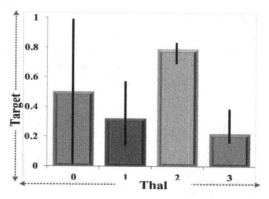

Fig. 9. Thal vs target

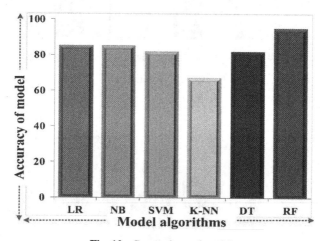

Fig. 10. Comparison of models

and NBDT predict with less accuracy. The CNN [20] has 67.21% accuracy with an F-measure value of 0.67, and the DNN & FFT [1, 4] have the same amount of accuracy(i.e, 81.97%) with an F-measure value of 0.82, The DTA [13] has 85.25% accuracy with an F-measure value of 0.84, The NBDT [23] has 85.25% accuracy with an F-measure value of 0.85, and where has proposed RF has greater accuracy 95.25% with an F-measure value of 0.95. The proposed RF algorithm provides a higher amount of accuracy compared to existing algorithms and graphically is represented in Fig. 11.

Table 3. Comparison of Models based on accuracy and f1 score proposed with existing algorithm

Ref.	Algorithms	Accuracy (%)	F-measure
[1]	DNN	81.97	0.82
[4]	FFT	81.97	0.82
[13]	DTA	85.25	0.84
[20]	CNN	67.21	0.67
[23]	NBDT	85.25	0.85
Proposed	**RF**	**95.25**	**0.95**

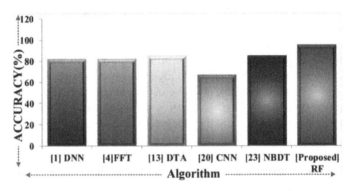

(a) Algorithms vsAccuracy

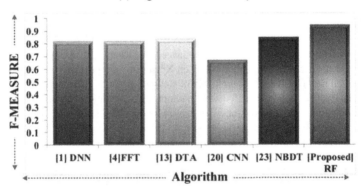

(b) Algorithms vs F-measure

Fig. 11. Comparison of the proposed algorithm with existing algorithms

6 Conclusion

Figuring out the planning of uncooked clinical consideration information of coronary heart experiences will help a long time saving of living spirits and early acknowledgment of oddities in heart conditions. Structure learning procedures had been used in this work to manage rough information and offer an immaculate course of action toward the coronary ailment. Coronary heart disease forecast is troublesome and essential inside the logical territory. Be that as it may, the mortality charge can be remarkably controlled if the confusion is identified at the early degrees and protection measures are embraced when practical. Likewise, an augmentation of this notice is remarkably ideal to guide the examinations to genuine worldwide datasets in inclination to simply hypothetical methodologies and recreations. The random forest ends up being very exact in the forecast of coronary illness. The future course of these investigations might be performed with different combos of machines acquiring information on methodologies to better expectation techniques. Also, new trademark determination methods can be progressed to get a more extensive impression of the broad highlights to blast the presentation of coronary illness forecast. The proposed algorithm is compared with other existing techniques and is found to be more effective in obtaining results. The graphical representations are made in detail. The alert system we encrypted in the model is the most helpful part which gives an alarm to the user before he faces a bad situation. By this, we can decrease the deaths of patients due to heart attacks before it's too late as in some persons it takes a lot of time to even know they are facing heart disease nowadays. In future work, it can be updated with more advanced algorithms and provide cloud-based monitoring of heart rate and provide necessary action and treatment as per the situation.

References

1. Ali, L., Rahman, A., Khan, A., Zhou, M., Javeed, A., Khan, J.A.: An automated diagnostic system for heart disease prediction based on X^2 statistical model and optimally configured deep neural network. IEEE Access **7**, 34938–34945 (2019)
2. Severino, P., et al.: Ischemic heart disease pathophysiology paradigms overview: from plaque activation to microvascular dysfunction. Int. J. Mol. Sci. **21**(21), 8118 (2020)
3. Javeed, A., Zhou, S., Yongjian, L., Qasim, I., Noor, A., Nour, R.: An intelligent learning system based on random search algorithm and optimized random forest model for improved heart disease detection. IEEE Access **7**, 180235–180243 (2019)
4. Zhang, J., et al.: Coupling a fast fourier transformation with a machine learning ensemble model to support recommendations for heart disease patients in a telehealth environment. IEEE Access **5**, 10674–10685 (2017)
5. Karanasiou, G.S., et al.: Predicting adherence of patients with HF through machine learning techniques. Healthcare Technol. Lett. **3**(3), 165–170 (2016)
6. Jin, B., Che, C., Liu, Z., Zhang, S., Yin, X., Wei, X.: Predicting the risk of heart failure with EHR sequential data modeling. IEEE Access **6**, 9256–9261 (2018)
7. Cheng, X., Feng, S., Li, Y., Gui, G.: Research on parallel compressive sensing and application of multi-channel synchronous acquisition of heart sound signals. IEEE Access **7**, 30033–30041 (2019)
8. Chang, W., Liu, Y., Wu, X., Xiao, Y., Zhou, S., Cao, W.: A new hybrid XGBSVM model: application for hypertensive heart disease. IEEE Access **7**, 175248–175258 (2019)

9. Chen, J., Valehi, A., Razi, A.: Smart heart monitoring: early prediction of heart problems through predictive analysis of ECG signals. IEEE Access **7**, 120831–120839 (2019)
10. Verma, N., Singh, H., Khanna, D., Rana, P.S., Bhadada, S.K.: Classification of drug molecules for oxidative stress signalling pathway. IET Syst. Biol. **13**(5), 243–250 (2019)
11. Lai, D., Zhang, Y., Zhang, X., Su, Y., Heyat, M.B.B.: An automated strategy for early risk identification of sudden cardiac death by using machine learning approach on measurable arrhythmic risk markers. IEEE Access **7**, 94701–94716 (2019)
12. Perveen, S., Shahbaz, M., Keshavjee, K., Guergachi, A.: Metabolic syndrome and development of diabetes mellitus: predictive modeling based on machine learning techniques. IEEE Access **7**, 1365–1375 (2018)
13. Zhang, B., Ren, J., Cheng, Y., Wang, B., Wei, Z.: Health data driven on continuous blood pressure prediction based on gradient boosting decision tree algorithm. IEEE Access **7**, 32423–32433 (2019)
14. Szczesniak, R.D., Brokamp, C., Su, W., Mcphail, G.L., Pestian, J., Clancy, J.P.: Improving detection of rapid cystic fibrosis disease progression-early translation of a predictive algorithm into a point-of-care tool. IEEE J. Trans. Eng. Health Med. **7**, 1–8 (2018)
15. Choi, K.H., et al.: Comparison of current and novel ECG-independent algorithms for resting pressure derived physiologic indices. IEEE Access **7**, 144313–144323 (2019)
16. Junejo, A.R., Shen, Y., Laghari, A.A., Zhang, X., Luo, H.: Molecular diagnostic and using deep learning techniques for predict functional recovery of patients treated of cardiovascular disease. IEEE Access **7**, 120315–120325 (2019)
17. Miao, F., et al.: Predictive modeling of hospital mortality for patients with heart failure by using an improved random survival forest. IEEE Access. **6**, 7244–7253 (2018)
18. Ali, L., et al.: An optimized stacked support vector machines based expert system for the effective prediction of heart failure. IEEE Access **7**, 54007–54014 (2019)
19. Matabuena, M., Vidal, J.C., Hayes, P.R., Saavedra-García, M., Huelin Trillo, F.: Application of functional data analysis for the prediction of maximum heart rate. IEEE Access. **7**, 121841–121852 (2019)
20. Ambekar, S., Phalnikar, R.: Disease risk prediction by using convolutional neural network. In: 2018 Fourth International Conference on Computing Communication Control and Automation (ICCUBEA), pp. 1–5. IEEE (2018)
21. Shanmugasundaram, G., Malar Selvam, V., Saravanan, R., Balaji, S.: An investigation of heart disease prediction techniques. In: 2018 IEEE International Conference on System, Computation, Automation and Networking (ICSCA), pp. 1–6. IEEE (2018)
22. Saboji, R.G.: A scalable solution for heart disease prediction using classification mining technique. In: 2017 International Conference on Energy, Communication, Data Analytics and Soft Computing (ICECDS), pp. 1780–1785. IEEE (2017)
23. Priyanka, N., Ravi Kumar, P.: Usage of data mining techniques in predicting the heart diseases—Naïve Bayes & decision tree. In: 2017 International Conference on Circuit, Power and Computing Technologies (ICCPCT), pp. 1–7. IEEE (2017)
24. Kohli, P.S., Arora, S.: Application of machine learning in disease prediction. In: 2018 4th International Conference on Computing Communication and Automation (ICCCA), pp. 1–4. IEEE (2018)
25. Pouriyeh, S., Vahid, S., Sannino, G., De Pietro, G., Arabnia, H., Gutierrez, J.: A comprehensive investigation and comparison of Machine Learning Techniques in the domain of heart disease. In: 2017 IEEE Symposium on Computers and Communications (ISCC), pp. 204–207. IEEE (2017)
26. Aditya K., Gupta, D., de Albuquerque, V.H.C., Sangaiah, A.K., Jhaveri, R.H.: Internet of health things-driven deep learning system for detection and classification of cervical cells using transfer learning. J. Supercomput. Springer (2020). https://doi.org/10.1007/s11227-020-03159-4

27. Reddy, G.T., et al.: Analysis of dimensionality reduction techniques on big data. IEEE Access **8**, 54776–54788 (2020)

28. Reddy, G.T., Reddy, M.P.K., Lakshmanna, K., Rajput, D.S., Kaluri, R., Srivastava, G.: Hybrid genetic algorithm and a fuzzy logic classifier for heart disease diagnosis. Evol. Intel. **13**(2), 185–196 (2019). https://doi.org/10.1007/s12065-019-00327-1

29. Rupa, C., et al.: Medicine drug name detection based object recognition using augmented reality. Front. Public Health. **29**(10), 881701 (2022)

30. Chowdhary, C.L., Khare, N., Patel, H., Koppu, S., Kaluri, R., Rajput, D.S.: Past, present and future of gene feature selection for breast cancer classification–a survey. Int. J. Eng. Syst. Model. Simul. **13**(2), 140–153 (2022)

31. Sarra, R.R., Dinar, A.M., Mohammed, M.A., Abdulkareem, K.H.: Enhanced heart disease prediction based on machine learning and χ2 statistical optimal feature selection model. Designs. **6**(5), 87 (2022)

32. Fathima, M.D., Justin Samuel, S., Natchadalingam, R., Vijeya Kaveri, V.: Majority voting ensembled feature selection and customized deep neural network for the enhanced clinical decision support system. Int. J. Comput. Appl. 1–11 (2022)

33. Tejamma, M., Jayakumar, N., Patil, S.: A model based on convolutional neural network (CNN) to predict heart disease. J. Algebr. Stat. **13**(3), 2360–2367 (2022)

34. Sahoo, S., Dash, P., Mishra, B.S.P., Sabut, S.K.: Deep learning-based system to predict cardiac arrhythmia using hybrid features of transform techniques. Intell. Syst. Appl. **16**, 200127 (2022)

35. Ullah, N., Khan, M.S., Khan, J.A., Choi, A., Anwar, M.S.: A robust end-to-end deep learning-based approach for effective and reliable BTD using MR images. Sensors. **22**(19), 7575 (2022)

Development of Predictive Models of Diabetes Using Ensemble Machine Learning Classifier

Madhubrata Bhattacharya[1(✉)] and Debabrata Datta[2]

[1] Department of Physics, The Heritage College, Kolkata, India
madhubrata.bhattacharya@thc.edu.in
[2] Department of Information Technology, Heritage Institute of Technology, Chowbaga Road, Anandapur, Kolkata 700107, India
debabrata.datta@heritageit.edu

Abstract. The discovery of knowledge from medical database using machine learning approach is always beneficial as well as challenging task for diagnosis. Diabetes if left undiagnosed can affect many other organs (e.g., kidney and liver) of human body and this particular disease is very common in all ages young to adult. Several researchers have attempted to predict via classification algorithms of machine learning. However, ensemble learning approach of classification of diabetes is missing in the parlour of classification algorithms of diabetes, indicating a research gap. This work presents classification algorithms for the prediction of diabetes based on machine learning using ensemble classifiers and in our work four classifier models, viz., (a) Random Forest (RF), (b) Bagging, (c) AdaBoosting and Gradient Boosting are used. Classification of the diabetic such as non-diabetic (labelled as 0) and diabetic (labelled as 1) of ensemble classifiers implemented for the present work is reported using metrics such as precision, recall, accuracy and F1-score. Results show that numerical value of accuracy of random forest model is 0.75 whereas accuracy of Bagging, AdaBoosting and Gradient Boosting ensemble classifiers is 0.72, 0.71 (0.75 with best parameter) and 0.75 (0.76 with best parameter) respectively. Accuracy of Gradient Boosting ensemble classifiers with respect to prediction of diabetes being 0.82, it can be mentioned that Gradient Boosting is the best among all other ensemble classifiers attempted to predict diabetes. A PYTHON code "ENSEMBLE" has been developed for our computation. Our future task towards the classification of diabetes will be based on metaheuristic algorithms and deep learning.

Keywords: Diabetes · Ensemble learning · Random Forest · Bagging · Ada Boosting · Gradient Boosting

1 Introduction

Diabetes Mellitus is an extensive disease in which the hormone insulin producing capacity of the body becomes affected. It increases the glucose level in the blood due to abnormal carbohydrate metabolism which in turn affects the vital organs of human body causing other health disorders. Diabetes is broadly classified into four categories such as

S. Rajagopal et al. (Eds.): ASCIS 2022, CCIS 1759, pp. 377–388, 2022.
https://doi.org/10.1007/978-3-031-23092-9_30

Type-I, Type-II, Gestational and Pre-diabetes. Type-I is sometimes called as the "insulin-dependent" diabetes [1], Type-II is known as "insulin resistance" diabetes [1] which is usually diagnosed later on for most of the cases. During pregnancy, the insulin blocks the hormones and Gestational (Type III) diabetes occurs. When the blood sugar level goes above the normal level, it is called Pre-diabetes.

With the advent of technology, analysis of medical data is extremely important. Usage of artificial intelligence, machine learning and deep learning algorithms provide very useful tools to develop predictive models in the field of medical science. This helps in the overall advancement in the public health industry [2]. Supervised and unsupervised machine learning (SAUML) methods have been extensively used in the area of diabetes prediction via classification. Some of the techniques used are identification of patterns, analysis of cluster and classification approach [3]. Scientists have shown that ML algorithm [4, 5] works well in classifying and diagnosing diseases. Orabi et al. [6] and World Health Organization (WHO) [7] designed a model based on ML to predict diabetes. Nai-arun and Moungmai [8] have performed comparative study of classifiers for risk of diabetes. Bamnote, M.P., et al. [9] used Genetic programming (GP) for analysing the diabetic database. Bansal et al., [10] illustrated the performance of K- Nearest neighbour (KNN) classifier and particle swarm optimization (PSO) to predict diabetes mellitus. Saxena, Khan, and Singh [11] also have implemented KNN algorithm as classifier of diabetic mellitus. Complications in diabetes are predicted by Dagliati et al. Aljumah et al. [12] in which they have used Support Vector Machine (SVM) algorithm to frame a predictive analysis model. In our previous work [13] we have applied Naïve Bayes (NB), SVM, RF, KNN and Decision Tree (DT) algorithms as machine learning classifier models for prediction of diabetes where we had shown DT was the best among other algorithms with respect to the accuracy of the models.

ML algorithms set up models from the given dataset. This process is known as learning or training. The learning algorithms can establish a group of classifiers and new data points can be classified on the basis of the prediction of the classifiers. This is known as ensemble learning or committee based learning [14]. Ensemble learning is an approach to ML which founds better prognostic execution by merging the prognosis from various models compared to an individual model. Ensemble learning methods consist of three main classes- bagging, stacking, and boosting. In bagging different predictions from the classifiers are averaged out to make the final prediction. In stacking the model is enabled to learn the use of combined predictions provided by the learner classifiers and a final model is prepared which gives the accurate prediction. In boosting, multiple weak learners are combined sequentially and improve the observation iteratively. In this context, some recent researches can be mentioned. In [15], four ML models DT, Artificial Neural Network (ANN), Logistic Regression (LR) and NB are employed by Prema and Push-palatha. In the present work, authors have applied random forest, bagging and boosting (AdaBoosting (AB) and Gradient Boosting (GB)) techniques and results showed that performance of classification using these ensemble learnings improves gradually from RF to GB and this implies that GB is the best ensemble learning classifier compared to other ensemble learning methods. A literature review of the diagnosis methodologies for diabetes evidenced that among many data mining algorithms used for the said process, 85% are of supervised approaches and 15% are of unsupervised approaches. Another work carried out by Iyer and Sumbaly for analysis of diabetes prediction presents the models multi-layered perceptron (MLP), DT and NB [16]. Their study showed that NB method has clear advantage over other methods while using Pima dataset for diabetes.

Our research work develops the predictive ensemble learning classifier models to predict diabetes through classification using Bagging, AB, GB and RF algorithms. The remaining part of the paper is organized into various sections. Subsection 1.1 describes our research aims and objectives. Section 2 presents mathematical background of four ML techniques implemented in the present study. Section 3 describes the details of the input data set used [17]. Section 4 present the exploratory data analysis as pre-processing of the input dataset. We have discussed the results of our models in Section 5 and the conclusions and future work with a short summary of the work are presented in Section 6.

1.1 Aims and Objectives

Research aim – To detect diabetes using machine learning ensemble algorithms using python programming language. Detection of diabetes being either absent (labelled 0) and present (labelled 1) ensemble algorithms here used as classifier.

Research Objectives – The objectives of the present study are as follows:

(i) To analyse critically the ways python language is used to detect diabetic
(ii) To apply data exploration and interpretation critically in python language for health problem detection.

2 Mathematical Background of Various Classifier Models Used

The focus of our study is to implement ensemble learning which helps to improve machine learning results by a combination of several models. The backbone of the ensemble learning concept is to learn a set of classifiers as experts and then to allow them to vote to produce one predictive powerful model. The main advantage of ensemble learning is that it has higher predictive accuracy. However, ensembles are difficult to interpret implying as one of its cons. Mathematics behind all ensemble learning algorithms are not unique and hence description of each ensemble learning is mandatory before its application in respective areas. Subsections 2.1–2.4 presents mathematics behind ensemble learning.

2.1 Bagging

Basic math behind bagging method of ensemble learning is based on bootstrapping in which sample with replacement takes place. That is why bagging or bootstrap aggregating [18, 19] is one of the ensemble methods used for classifier problems which fits multiple base classifiers on random subsets of data. All sampling is done at sampling with replacement. In bagging different predictions from the classifiers are averaged out to make the final prediction. A model is said to have high variance provided the model changes a lot with changes in training data resulting the possibility of reducing over-fitting of data. If we consider a training set having p observations and q features the following steps are to be performed:

Step 1: A random data is selected without replacement from the training set.

Step 2: A subset, chosen randomly, consisting of q features constructs the model using the selected observations.

Step 3: The feature, out of the q features which offers the best split is chosen to split the node.

Step 4: Repetition of Steps 2 & 3.

2.2 Ada Boosting (AB)

Boosting introduces the concept of combining multiple weak learners to get a strong learner [20, 21]. In adaptive boosting (AdaBoosting) weightage is given to the misclassified points. The weightage of misclassified points increases from stage to stage. Decision trees (with level one) are the basic algorithms used in Ada Boost. The tree is adjusted iteratively towards the incorrect predictions and thus giving better accuracy than RF. The algorithm of AB can be represented as:

Step 1: For a dataset with N number of samples, let us initialize the weight of each data point with $w_i = \frac{1}{N}$. Dataset is processed and equal weight is assigned to every data point.

Step 2: For m = 1 to M:

(a) Sample the dataset using the weights $w_i^{(m)}$ to obtain training samples x_i. *Fit a classifier K_m using all the training samples x_i.*

(b) Compute $\eta = \dfrac{\sum_{y_i \neq K_m(x_i)} w_i^{(m)}}{\sum_{y_i} w_i^{(m)}}$, where y_i is the ground truth value of the target variable and $w_i^{(m)}$ is the weight of the sample I at iteration m.

(c) Compute $\beta_m = \frac{1}{2} ln \frac{1-\theta}{\theta}$. The processed dataset is given as input to the classifier and the data which are not correctly classified are recognized.

Step 3: Weight of the incorrect data points are updated by $w_i^{(m+1)} = w_i^{(m)} e^{-\beta_m y K_m(x)}$.

Step 4: New predictions computed by $K(x) = sign\left[\sum_{m=1}^{M} \beta_m y K_m(x)\right]$.

2.3 Gradient Boosting (GB)

The main idea behind this algorithm is to build models sequentially and these subsequent models try to reduce the errors of the previous model. This is done by building a new model on the errors or residuals of the previous model. Gradient boosting mechanism develops incremental process and steps up the program according to optimization of loss function F [22]. Detection and rectification of errors improves the accuracy. Optimal prognosis of the outcome is achieved after the analysis and measurements of the errors from these calculations. Loss function F analyses and calculates the Model Learners. Base learners are added to all steps and F is reduced for optimum accuracy. A gradient boosting classifier is used when the target column is binary. Mathematically, the first step of optimization of Loss function F can be written as $U_0 = arg \min_{\gamma} \sum_{i=1}^{n} F(y_i, \gamma)$, γ is the predicted value.

The algorithm of Gradient Boosting method is as follows:

Step 1: A sample of target values as M is considered and the error E is estimated.

Step 2: The weights are updated and adjusted to reduce the error E.

Step 3: $M[x] = p[x] + \alpha E[x]$

Step 4: Loss function F analyses and calculates the Model Learners.

Step 5: Repetition of Steps 3 & 4.

2.4 Random Forest (RF) Classifier

RF classifier is based on supervised machine learning approach. The ensemble learning is the basic concept on which learning algorithm of RF is based [19]. In RF classifier, decision trees are applied on various data points of the input dataset and then average performance of all decision trees (DT) is estimated to improve the accuracy of the dataset. As we increase the number of base learners (k), the variance will decrease. When we decrease k, variance increases. But bias remains constant for the whole process. k can be found using cross-validation. Mathematical structure of random forest algorithm can be depicted as:

Random forest= DT(base learner) + bagging(Row sampling with replacement)+ feature bagging(column sampling) + aggregation(mean/median, majority vote). Therefore, having a large number of trees in the forest, higher precision can be achieved and over fitting problems can be avoided. The main idea behind this algorithm is to build models sequentially and these subsequent models try to reduce the errors of the previous model. The algorithm of random forest can be represented as:

Step 1: Data points are selected from the training set {Tr} randomly.

Step 2: DT associated with the selected data points are constructed.

Step 3: N is to be chosen to build the appropriate decision tree.

Step 4: Repetition of Steps 1 & 2.

3 Input Dataset Description

PIMA Indians dataset [17] of diabetes taken from UCI repository is used for this study because it is publicly available. Total number of 768 cases (all women) with eight different features are recorded through clinical examinations. It is observed that only 268 of them are diabetic. The features of a typical sample of diabetic patient are age, number of times pregnant, plasma glucose, blood pressure, skin thickness, serum insulin, body mass index (BMI) and diabetic pedigree function. Figure 1 shows the outline of features. Sample values of all dataset of 768 data have been checked and there is no missing values found in the dataset (missing values are checked by isnull() function of PYTHON).

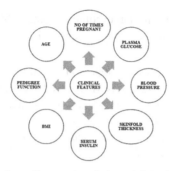

Fig. 1. Input Feature description of diabetic dataset

4 Exploratory Data Analysis (EDA)

Sample counts are shown in a bar plot (Fig. 2) that indicates how our dataset is divided into non-diabetic class (0) and diabetic class (1).

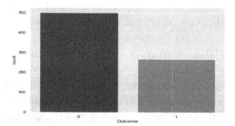

Fig. 2. Count of non-diabetic and diabetic

We have plotted the histogram of all features to know their statistical distribution, which helps authors to take decisions that whether scaling towards normalization is required or not. Scaling is one of the important issue for machine learning models to implement. The distribution of all features is scaled to normal distribution and reason behind this to make the features independent of one another. Figure 3 shows the distribution of feature data.

Before proceeding further to implement of any model, we have carried out correlation analysis of input features and that has been carried out by heat map module of python and the heat map plot is as shown in Fig. 4. Next attempt of EDA is to split the input dataset into training and testing and accordingly input dataset is splitted into training and testing dataset. For this purpose, 70% of the input data is considered as training and 30% of the input data is taken into as testing size. This kind of partitioning of input data into training and testing is achieved by train_test_split module of scikit learn of python and this is executed by random state = 0 of this module.

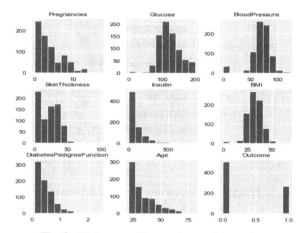

Fig. 3. Histogram of feature data and target data

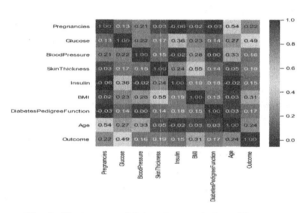

Fig. 4. Heat map explaining the correlation of features

In order to know the importance of features we have executed feature engineering task for random forest model only because all other models (Bagging, AdaBoosting and Gradient Boosting) this task will be same. Feature engineering extracts the relevant features to be used for training and testing and by this computational speed of training and testing can be increase. Figure 5 presents the visualization of feature set importance for RF classifier model.

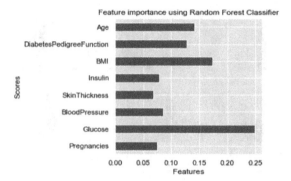

Fig. 5. Feature set representation of Random Forest Classifier

5   Results and Discussions

Results of our work are as follows: In this work we have used four classifier models - Bagging, Ada Boosting, Gradient Boosting and Random Forest. Due to the nature of target problem of classification, each model of ensemble learning is used here as classifier. Initially all ensemble learning models are implemented respectively to obtain the accuracy of classification task. But changing the value of some parameters of an ensemble learning model can improve the accuracy. With a view to this we have changed the parameters to their best values. Table 1 shows the best parameters with accuracies of the classifier models. The performance report of the classifier models of non-diabetic (label 0) and diabetic (label 1) are carried out using confusion matrix which has been used further to compute parameters of performance such as precision, recall and accuracy. The outcome of this task is presented in details in Table 2. The performance of a classification model at all classification thresholds is visualized by a graph known as receiver operating characteristic (ROC) curve. A typical ROC curve is as shown in Fig. 6. ROC curve plots two parameters named as true positive rate (TPR) and false positive rate (FPR) which are defined as

$$TPR = \frac{TP}{TP + FN}, \; FPR = \frac{FP}{FP + TN},$$

where, TP = True positive, FP = False positive, TN = True negative and FN = False negative

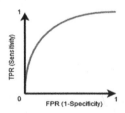

Fig. 6. Receiver Operating Characteristic (ROC) curve

Interpretation of ROC curve can be given as follows: Lower the classification threshold more the items are classified as positive, thus one can increase both False Positives and True Positives. Figure 7 presents ROC curves of present work of ensemble learning classifier models such as Bagging, AdaBoosting and Gradient Boosting.

Table 1. Best parameters of different Classifier Models

Classifier model	Best parameters	Accuracy
Bagging	'max_features':1.0, 'max_samples':0.5, 'n_estimators': 30	0.72
Ada Boosting	"learning_rate": 0.1, "n_estimators": 50	0.75
Gradient Boosting	"learning_rate":0.1, "max_depth": 4, "max_features": "sqrt", "n_estimators": 100	0.76

Table 2. Classification Report of different Classifier Models

Classifier model	Confusion matrix	Outcome	Precision	Recall	Accuracy
Random Forest	$\begin{bmatrix} 129 & 22 \\ 35 & 45 \end{bmatrix}$	0	0.79	0.85	0.75
		1	0.67	0.56	0.61
Bagging	$\begin{bmatrix} 132 & 19 \\ 45 & 35 \end{bmatrix}$	0	0.75	0.87	0.72
		1	0.65	0.44	0.52
Bagging Model with best parameters	$\begin{bmatrix} 131 & 20 \\ 38 & 42 \end{bmatrix}$	0	0.78	0.87	0.80
		1	0.68	0.53	0.59
Ada Boosting with best parameters	$\begin{bmatrix} 134 & 17 \\ 41 & 39 \end{bmatrix}$	0	0.77	0.89	0.75
		1	0.70	0.49	0.57
Gradient Boosting with best parameters	$\begin{bmatrix} 125 & 26 \\ 32 & 48 \end{bmatrix}$	0	0.80	0.83	0.76
		1	0.65	0.60	0.62

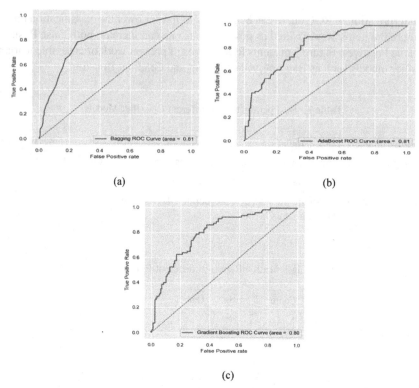

(a)   (b)

(c)

Fig. 7. ROC curve of (a) Bagging Classifier, (b) Ada Boosting, (c) Gradient Boosting

6 Conclusions

The prevalence of Diabetes worldwide has increased significantly over the years. It can be predicted and detected in early stages using machine learning models. In the present work, ensemble learning algorithms used as classifier for the prediction of Diabetes have been developed and implemented. It is evident from the experimental investigation that Gradient Boosting classifier excels over Ada Boosting, Bagging and Random Forest methods. The best estimator is decided on the basis of accuracy metric. The reason behind excel performance of Gradient Boosting is that this learning proceeds slowly, aggregates all weak learners towards reduction of variance by row as well as column sampling. In future, this work can be extended with deep learning (convolutional recurrent neural network model) because of time involvement for following up of diabetic status of a patient. Our future work of classification of diabetic will also be towards promotion of metaheuristic algorithms so that risk informed decision making of classification of diabetic can be achieved (an innovative research domain in health care sector using Artificial Intelligence) to reduce misclassification.

References

1. Rani, S., Kautish, S.: Association clustering and time series based data mining in continuous data for diabetes prediction. In: Second International Conference on Intelligent Computing and Control Systems (ICICCS) (2018)
2. IDF DIABETES ATLAS, 8th edn. International Diabetes Federation, 2017. [Onine]. https://diabetesatlas.org/. Accessed 15 December 2018
3. Sisodia, D., Sisodia, D.S.: Prediction of diabetes using classification algorithms. Procedia Comput. Sci. **132**, 1578–1585 (2018)
4. Shailaja, K., Seetharamulu, B., Jabba, M.A.: Machine learning in healthcare: a review. In: 2018 Second International Conference on Electronics, Communication and Aerospace Technology (ICECA), pp. 910–914. IEEE (2018)
5. Sarwar, M.A., Kamal, N., Hamid, W., Shah, M.A.: Prediction of diabetes using machine learning algorithms in healthcare. In: 2018 24th International Conference on Automation and Computing (ICAC), pp. 1–6. IEEE (2018)
6. Orabi, K.M., Kamal, Y.M., Rabah, T.M.: Early predictive system for diabetes mellitus disease. In: Industrial Conference on Data Mining. Springer, pp. 420–427 (2016)
7. Global Report On Diabetes Who Library: Cataloguing-in-Publication Data Global report on diabetes (2016)
8. Nai-arun, N., Moungmai, R.: Comparison of classifiers for the risk of diabetes prediction. Procedia Comput. Sci. **69**, 132–142 (2015)
9. Pradhan, M., Bamnote, G.R.: Design of classifier for detection of diabetes mellitus using genetic programming. Adv. Intell. Syst. Comput. **1**, 763–770 (2014). https://doi.org/10.1007/978-3-319-11933-5
10. Bansal, R., Kumar, S., Mahajan, A.: Diagnosis of diabetes mellitus using PSO and KNN classifier. In: 2017 International Conference on Computing and Communication technologies for Smart Nation (IC3TSN), pp. 32–38 (2017)
11. Krati Saxena, D., Khan, Z., Singh, S.: Diagnosis of diabetes mellitus using k nearest neighbor algorithm. Int. J. Comput. Sci. Trends Technol. **2**(4) (2014)
12. Dagliati, A., et al.: Machine learning methods to predict diabetes complications. J. Diabetes Sci. Technol. **12**(2), 295–302 (2018)
13. Bhattacharya, M., Datta, D.: Performance evaluation of predictive machine learning models for diabetic disease using python. In: 2022 IEEE 3rd Global Conference for Advancement in Technology (GCAT) (2022). ISBN-978-1-6654-6855-8
14. Kavakiotis, I., Tsave, O., Salifoglou, A., Maglaveras, N.: Machine learning and data mining methods in diabetes research. Comput. Struct. Biotechnol. J. **15**, 104–116 (2017)
15. Prema, N.S., Pushpalatha, M.P.: Prediction of gestational diabetes mellitus (GDM) using classification. In: 2017 IEEE International Conference on Science, Technology, Engineering and Management (ICSTEM). Coimbatore (2017)
16. Iyer, A., Jeyalatha, S., Sumbaly, R.: Diagnosis of diabetes using classification mining techniques. Int. J. Data Min. Knowl. Manag. Process. **5**, 1–14 (2015). https://doi.org/10.5121/ijdkp.2015.5101, arXiv:1502.03774
17. PIMA Indian Diabetes Dataset, An open dataset. UCI Machine Learning Repository. [Online]. http://ftp.ics.uci.edu/pub/machine-learnigdatabases/pima-indians-diabetes/
18. Breiman, L.: Bagging predictors. Mach. Learn. **24**, 123–140 (1996)
19. Louppe, G.: Understanding random forests: from theory to practice. PhD Thesis, University of Liege (2014)
20. Salman, R., Alzaatreh, A., Sulieman, H., Fisal, S.: A Bootstrap framework for aggregating within and between feature selection methods. Entropy (Basel, Switzerland) **23**(2), 200 (2021). https://doi.org/10.3390/e23020200

21. Ayinala, M., Parhi, K.K.: Low complexity algorithm for seizure prediction using Adaboost. In: Proceedings of International Conference IEEE-Engineering in Medicine and Biology Society, pp. 1061–1064 (2012)
22. Friedman, J.H.: Stochastic gradient boosting. Comput. Stat. Data Anal. **38**(4), 367–378 (2002)

Clustering and Association Rule Mining of Cardiovascular Disease Risk Factors

Zahiriddin Rustamov[(✉)] [iD]

University of Malaya, 50603 Kuala Lumpur, Malaysia
contact@zahiriddin.com

Abstract. Cardiovascular diseases (CVDs) are the leading cause of death globally, with millions of lives lost yearly. CVDs are a group of disorders of the heart and blood vessels. Although there are no exact causes of CVDs, there are risk factors associated that increase the likelihood of getting CVDs. Clustering and association rule mining are among the methods used for pattern discovery. However, not much research has been proposed to compare clustering and association algorithms regarding risk factors of CVDs. Hence, this study presents a comparative analysis of clustering and association on the risk factors of CVDs to assess which factors are significant. The Framingham Heart Study dataset was used for clustering and association rule mining. The clustering results using three clusters show that older age, high BMI, and high systolic blood pressure are the significant risk factors. Smoking and hypertension are among the risk factors contributing to angina and heart attack based on association analysis with minimum support, minimum confidence, and maximum items of 25%, 60% and 4, respectively. This study successfully adopted clustering and association for pattern discovery to assess the most critical risk factors of CVDs.

Keywords: Association rule mining · Cardiovascular diseases · Clustering

1 Introduction

Cardiovascular diseases (CVDs) are the leading cause of death globally, with millions of lives lost annually. CVDs are a group of disorders of the heart and blood vessels. Examples of CVDs include heart disease, angina pectoris and heart attack. CVDs are caused by a combination of risk factors that can be modified and those that cannot be modified [1]. For example, age and gender are risk factors that cannot be altered. On the other hand, smoking and alcohol consumption are among the risk factors that can be changed through individual behaviour. Many studies have been conducted in the field of CVDs to assist patients by adopting techniques such as classification, clustering, and association rule mining [2–4]. Clustering aims to divide a collection of observations into separate groups called clusters so that the observations in the clusters have similarities. Association rule mining can be helpful for assisting physicians by discovering the underlying relationship of diseases based on risk factors [2, 5].

© The Author(s), under exclusive license to Springer Nature Switzerland AG 2022
S. Rajagopal et al. (Eds.): ASCIS 2022, CCIS 1759, pp. 389–396, 2022.
https://doi.org/10.1007/978-3-031-23092-9_31

Most of the studies around CVDs are focused on predicting the presence of CVDs. However, little research has been conducted using data mining techniques such as clustering and association rules to uncover the critical risk factors associated with CVDs. Moreover, clustering and association rules are among the methods to perform pattern discovery on data in finding similarities between observations and associations between observations. However, not much research has been conducted to compare clustering and association rules to explore the risk factors of CVDs. Hence, this study proposes a comparative study to compare clustering and association rule mining using the cardiovascular disease patient dataset based on the various risk factors.

2   Literature Review

This section will discuss the related literature using association rules and clustering techniques on CVDs. Association rule mining is among the well-established techniques in data mining. In its essence, rules that fulfil the minimum support and confidence levels are extracted. The rules generated by association rules consist of two parts: an antecedent (if) and a consequent (then). This study expresses the rules in the form of: LHS (left-hand side) = > RHS (right-hand side). This rule expresses that the consequent set is likely to occur whenever the antecedent set occurs. Support and confidence are two measures of the rules where support indicates the frequency of items in the data and confidence indicates the number of times the if-then statements are found true [5, 6]. The Apriori algorithm has become a standard method in association rule mining. The algorithm uses a transactional dataset to construct frequent item sets with the user-specified minimum support and minimum confidence levels.

[6] proposed a study to detect factors contributing to heart disease in males and females using association rule mining. The study adopted the UCI Cleveland dataset to investigate the factors which contribute to heart disease. The results indicate that females are seen to have less chance of heart disease than males. Moreover, resting ECG being hyper was a significant factor for females. Also, it was found that factors such as asymptomatic chest pain and exercise-induced angina indicate the presence of heart disease. [7] presented a data mining system using association analysis based on the Apriori algorithm to assess heart event-related risk factors. The events considered were heart attack, percutaneous coronary intervention, and coronary artery bypass graft surgery. A total of 369 observations were collected from heart disease patients in Paphos General Hospital of Cyprus, with most patients having more than one event. The results extracted from the association rules indicate that sex, smoking, highdensity lipoprotein, glucose, family history and hypertension were the most critical risk factors. [3] proposed a study to explore the risk factors using association rule mining by adopting four datasets related to heart disease: Cleveland, Hungarian, Long Beach and Switzerland UCI. The results from the association show that high cholesterol, sex, and asymptotic chest pain provided the highest confidence values.

Clustering is a pattern discovery tool for dividing observations into separate groups called clusters in which observations in each cluster tend to be similar to each other. A good clustering method produces high-quality clusters with minimum intra-cluster and maximum inter-class distance. [2] proposed a study to group CVD patients to determine the importance of various risk factors using two clusters. The study applied the

K-Medoids algorithm for clustering. The study used secondary data from the blood tests of patients obtained from a private hospital in Jakarta. The data consisted of 644 observations and eight variables. The results indicate that the second cluster had higher rates of cardiovascular complications, with significant risk factors being age, uric acid, cholesterol, and glucose at higher-than-normal levels. [8] presented a study to cluster cardiovascular phenotypes in patients with type 2 diabetes and atherosclerotic CVD. The study adopted data from the Trial Evaluating Cardiovascular Outcomes with Sitagliptin study with 14,671 observations with 40 baseline variables. The study performed cluster analysis with associations between clusters and outcomes such as cardiovascular death, nonfatal heart attack, nonfatal stroke and unstable angina assessed by Cox proportional hazards models. The results show four clusters, starting with Caucasian men with a high prevalence of coronary artery disease in the first cluster; Asian patients with a low BMI in the second cluster; women with noncoronary atherosclerotic CVD in the third cluster; and patients with heart failure and kidney dysfunction in the last cluster.

None of the existing research focused on comparing clustering and association rule mining algorithms on the risk factors of CVDs. Hence, this study aims to perform clustering and association based on the risk factors of CVDs.

3   Methodology

Figure 1 shows the proposed research design for this study.

Fig. 1. Research design of this study.

3.1   Description of Dataset

This study adopts the Framingham Heart Study dataset to perform clustering and association. The Framingham Heart Study is a study of the aetiology of CVD among individuals in Framingham, Massachusetts. The dataset collection lasted 24 years, from 1948 to 1972, where each patient was examined three times for the outcome of CVD events. The dataset contains 11,627 observations with a total of 39 attributes. This study will select three interval variables as the risk factors for performing the clustering of CVDs. The critical risk factors mentioned in studies related to CVDs are age, BMI, and blood pressure [9–11]. Hence, this study aims to cluster the observations using these variables. Table 1 shows the selected variables for clustering along with their roles, measurement scales and descriptions.

Transactional data is required for association rule mining. The dataset has a "RAN-DID" variable denoting a unique identification number for each patient. Moreover, there

Table 1. Selected variables and their descriptions for clustering.

Variable	Role	Measurement Level	Description
AGE	Input	Interval	Age of patient at the exam in years
BMI	Input	Interval	Body Mass Index of the patient in kg/m^2
SYSBP	Input	Interval	Systolic Blood Pressure of patient in mmHg
CVD	Target	Binary	Presence or absence of CVD in the patient

are several binary risk factors, including the patient's status of a smoker, diabetic and hypertensive, and whether the patient had angina, heart attack or stroke. This study uses association rule mining to find associations between the risk factors and individual CVDs. Table 2 shows the attributes for association analysis, their roles, measurement scales and descriptions.

Table 2. Selected variables and their descriptions for association rule mining.

Variable	Role	Measurement Level	Description
RANDID	ID	Interval	Unique identification number for each patient
RISK	Target	Nominal	Type of risk factor or disease; Constructed using the variables of smoking, diabetes, hypertension, angina pectoris, heart attack and stroke

3.2   Data Exploration and Preprocessing

An essential step in any data mining project is to perform exploratory analysis to analyze for dirty data as clustering algorithms are sensitive to outliers [12]. Hence, we will conduct exploratory analysis to assess the data quality for missing values and outliers. This study uses Talend Data Preparation v2.1.1 for data preprocessing.

3.3   Clustering

This study adopts SAS Enterprise Miner 15.1 for performing clustering and association. The Cluster and Segment Profile nodes will be used for the cluster analysis as shown in Fig. 2. The cleaned dataset will be supplied to the Cluster node.

Fig. 2. Process of Clustering in SAS Enterprise Miner.

3.4 Association Rule Mining

The constructed transactional dataset will be supplied to the Association node to perform association rule mining, as shown in Fig. 3. This study adopts the minimum confidence and minimum support percentage as 60% and 25%, respectively. The 60% minimum confidence tells us that 60% of the time, if the antecedent occurs, the consequent occurs as well. Therefore, establishing a relationship above the fifty-fifty chance. The 25% minimum support shows that the rule has been observed in more than a quarter of the total transactions.

Fig. 3. Process of Association Rule Mining in SAS Enterprise Miner.

4 Results and Discussion

This study performed clustering and association on CVD patients using SAS Enterprise Miner 15.1. Three clusters were specified for cluster analysis. Figure 4 shows a three-dimensional scatter plot of systolic blood pressure, BMI, and age between the three segments. Cluster 1 contains observations with older age, low BMI, and high systolic blood pressure. In contrast, Cluster 2 includes observations with younger age, low BMI, and low systolic blood pressure. Lastly, Cluster 3 contains observations with older age, high BMI, and high systolic blood pressure.

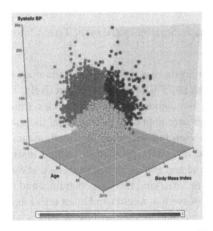

Fig. 4. Three-Dimensional Scatter Plot of Age, BMI and Systolic BP based on Clusters.

Next, we performed profiling to understand the individual clusters' variable distributions to the overall variable distribution, including the target variable, CVD, to see whether the variables signify any importance as a risk factor to the target attribute.

Figure 5 shows the segment profile of the three clusters and three interval variables against their total distribution with the distribution of the target attribute as the pie chart. We can instantly perceive that Clusters 1 and 3 have a higher proportion of positive CVD observations, as indicated in the outer pie chart. Furthermore, in Cluster 1, the age and systolic blood pressure have higher than average distribution, meaning that older patients with high systolic blood pressure may be at higher risk. Similarly, in Cluster 3, the BMI and systolic blood pressure variables have higher than average distribution, indicating that high BMI and high systolic blood pressure may significantly contribute to CVDs. On the other hand, in Cluster 2, the variables systolic blood pressure and age are lower than average, and BMI follows almost a normal distribution, indicating that younger patients with lower systolic blood pressure and normal BMI (i.e., between 18.5 and 24.9) are at lower risk of CVDs.

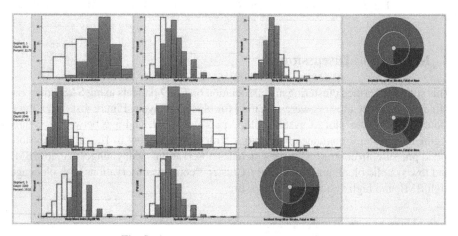

Fig. 5. Segment Profile of the Three Clusters.

For the association analysis, we specified the minimum support, minimum confidence, and maximum items as 25%, 60% and 4, respectively. This study also considered lift as a metric to assess association rules as it provides a measure of the importance of the rules. A lift value greater than one indicates that the rule antecedent and the rule consequent appear more often together than expected, meaning the occurrence of the antecedent has a positive effect on the occurrence of the consequent. We aim to consider those rules with a lift of one and above, as it assures us that our rules are not coincidental. Table 3 shows the rules satisfying the set constraints and their support, confidence, and lift values. We can observe that angina and heart attack have the highest lift values, indicating that if a patient has angina, they will likely have a heart attack, and vice versa. Similarly, Rules 1 and 2 indicate that if a patient is smoking and hypertensive, they are likely to have a heart attack and angina, respectively. It is commonly known that smoking causes blood to thicken and form clots inside veins and arteries; as a result, it increases the risk of heart attacks. In Rule 8, we can observe that if a patient is a smoker and has angina, the likelihood of a heart attack is significant, with 84.62% of patients in the dataset having the phenomenon. Rules 13 and 14 provide considerable insight into smokers and hypertensive patients as they.

have a higher risk of angina and heart attack, indicating that hypertension and smoking are significant risk factors. However, diabetes was not observed in any of the rules suggesting that it may not be a signfiicant risk factor based on the set rule constraints.

Table 3. Generated Rules using Association Rule Mining.

Rules	Support (%)	Confidence (%)	Lift
1{hypertensive} = > {angina}	45.45	62.50	1.09
2{smoker} = > {heartattack}	45.45	62.50	1.09
3{angina} = > {hypertensive}	45.45	78.95	1.09
4{heartattack} = > {smoker}	45.45	78.95	1.09
5{heartattack} = > {angina}	42.42	73.68	1.28
6{angina} = > {heartattack}	42.42	73.68	1.28
7{hypertensive, heartattack} = > {angina}	33.33	84.62	1.47
8{smoker, angina} = > {heartattack}	33.33	84.62	1.47
9{smoker, heartattack} = > {angina}	33.33	73.33	1.27
10 {hypertensive, angina} = > {heartattack}	33.33	73.33	1.27
11 {heartattack, angina} = > {hypertensive}	33.33	78.57	1.08
12 {heartattack, angina} = > {smoker}	33.33	78.57	1.08
13 {smoker, hypertensive} = > {angina}	27.27	60.00	1.04
14 {smoker, hypertensive} = > {heartattack}	27.27	60.00	1.04

5   Conclusion

This study performed clustering and association analysis on the risk factors of CVDs to assess which risk factors are significant in CVDs. The Framingham Heart Study dataset was used for clustering and association rule mining. Three interval variables that may be risk factors were selected for clustering. A transaction dataset was constructed using seven features from the dataset to be used for association analysis. Data exploration was performed to improve the data quality by handling missing values and outliers in the selected attributes. Three clusters were generated for clustering. For association, the constraints set were minimum support, minimum confidence level and maximum items as 25%, 60% and 4, respectively. The clustering results indicate that older age (i.e., seniors), high BMI (i.e., obesity), and high systolic blood pressure are the significant risk factors for CVDs. The association analysis results indicate that smoking and hypertension are important risk factors, increasing the risk of angina and heart attack. Future works should consider adopting other available datasets to compare the results obtained and utilize clinical parameters to enhance the value of the study.

References

1. Cardiovascular Diseases: https://www.who.int/health-topics/cardiovascular-diseases, last accessed 2022/06/21
2. Irwansyah, E., Pratama, E.S., Ohyver, M.: Clustering of cardiovascular disease patients using data mining techniques with principal component analysis and K-medoids clustering of cardiovascular disease patients using data mining techniques with principal component analysis and K-medoids (2020). https://doi.org/10.20944/preprints202008.0074.v1
3. Khare, S., Gupta, D.: Association rule analysis in cardiovascular disease. In: Proc. 2016 2nd Int. Conf. Cogn. Comput. Inf. Process. CCIP 2016 (2016). https://doi.org/10.1109/CCIP.2016.7802881
4. Yang, L., et al.: Study of cardiovascular disease prediction model based on random forest in eastern China. Sci. Rep. **10**, 1–8 (2020). https://doi.org/10.1038/s41598-020-62133-5
5. Rai, A.: Association Rule Mining: An Overview and its Applications: https://www.upgrad.com/blog/association-rule-mining-an-overview-and-its-applications/
6. Nahar, J., Imam, T., Tickle, K.S., Chen, Y.P.P.: Association rule mining to detect factors which contribute to heart disease in males and females. Expert Syst. Appl. **40**, 1086–1093 (2013). https://doi.org/10.1016/j.eswa.2012.08.028
7. Karaolis, M., Moutiris, J.A., Papaconstantinou, L., Pattichis, C.S.: Association rule analysis for the assessment of the risk of coronary heart events. In: Proc. 31st Annu. Int. Conf. IEEE Eng. Med. Biol. Soc. Eng. Futur. Biomed. EMBC 2009, pp. 6238–6241 (2009). https://doi.org/10.1109/IEMBS.2009.5334656
8. Sharma, A., et al.: Cluster analysis of cardiovascular phenotypes in patients with type 2 diabetes and established atherosclerotic cardiovascular disease: a potential approach to precision medicine. Diabetes Care **45**, 204–212 (2022). https://doi.org/10.2337/DC20-2806
9. Khan, S.S., et al.: Association of body mass index with lifetime risk of cardiovascular dis-ease and compression of morbidity. JAMA Cardiol. **3**, 280–287 (2018). https://doi.org/10.1001/jamacardio.2018.0022
10. Rodgers, J.L., Jones, J., Bolleddu, S.I., Vanthenapalli, S., Rodgers, L.E., Shah, K., Karia, K., Panguluri, S.K.: Cardiovascular risks associated with gender and aging. J. Cardiovasc. Dev. Dis. 6 (2019). https://doi.org/10.3390/jcdd6020019
11. Yano, Y., et al.: Association of daytime and nighttime blood pressure with cardiovascular disease events among African American Individuals. JAMA Cardiol. **4**, 910–917 (2019)
12. Helm, M.: Use this clustering method if you have many outliers|by Martin Helm|Towards Data Sci. https://towardsdatascience.com/use-this-clustering-method-if-youhave-many-outliers-5c99b4cd380d, last accessed 2022/06/22

Improving Architectural Reusability for Resource Allocation Framework in Futuristic Cloud Computing Using Decision Tree Based Multi-objective Automated Approach

Husain Godhrawala(✉) ⓘ and R. Sridaran ⓘ

Faculty of Computer Applications, Marwadi University, Rajkot, India
husain_hq@yahoo.com, sridaran.rajagopal@marwadieducation.edu.in

Abstract. Cloud computing is a highly popular computing technique. Cloud combined with IoT, fog, edge, and mist computing in 5G networks gives us realtime and highly predictive responses leading to a better and smart life. It requires a highly robust and integrated cloud administration, especially cloud resource allocation. Artificial intelligence and machine learning can be easily implemented along cloud design patterns for efficient resource allocation. In this paper we discuss multi-tenant cloud resource allocation problem. We propose to use a rule-based analysis pattern to dynamically reconfigure resource allocation processes. The pattern uses various attributes of clouds, resources, subscribers and requests along with heuristic data like configurations, policies, strategies, and methods to efficiently identify and apply rule of allocation. We implemented a decision tree to assist pattern to have automated decisions, which rule to follow. The pattern caters for multi-objectivity, simplifies architecture, enables the extension of the cloud framework and makes it possible to interact easily with cloud. This paper describes the architectural framework pattern, which learns from itself. This paper presents CK's object-oriented metrics comparisons of pattern-based object-oriented code. The comparison shows that object-oriented code improves code quality, making pattern-based code more maintainable, flexible, extendable and secure.

Keywords: Cloud design pattern · Decision tree · Multi objective approach · Dynamic resource allocation · Strategic behavior

1 Introduction

Cloud computing is a computing framework that represents the idea that a central ubiquitous facility can cater the computing needs of several organizations at the same time. It is a rapidly growing idea. With the advent of the Internet of Things (IoT), fog, edge, mist, and 5G networks, the future of computing is directed toward cloud computing. Cloud computing may be defined as "a model for enabling ubiquitous, online on demand resources that can be configured instantly to serve an incoming request." The characteristics of cloud computing have been discussed in detail by Singh et al. [1]. Five essential

© The Author(s), under exclusive license to Springer Nature Switzerland AG 2022
S. Rajagopal et al. (Eds.): ASCIS 2022, CCIS 1759, pp. 397–415, 2022.
https://doi.org/10.1007/978-3-031-23092-9_32

characteristics of cloud computing are On-demand self-service, broad network access, resource pooling, rapid elasticity, and measured service. Nowadays, cloud computing is a highly recommended computing technique.

1.1 Cloud Computing and Resource Allocation

Generally, a cloud provider engages in five activities mainly; they are Service Deployment, Service Orchestration, Cloud Service Management, Security, and Privacy. Figure 1 explains the activities undertaken by cloud service providers, especially service management. Resource management is more than a simple resource allocation process. Resource management includes provisioning virtual machines (VMs), assigning VMs, computing processes, networks, nodes, and storage resources on-demand to a set of applications in a cloud computing environment. Many factors, including revenue, available resource pool, energy consumption, dynamic nature, SLA protection, etc. play a vital role in deciding this strategy [2]. Numerous methods and algorithms exist for scheduling resources including genetic, heuristic, swarm, physical, evolutionary, etc.

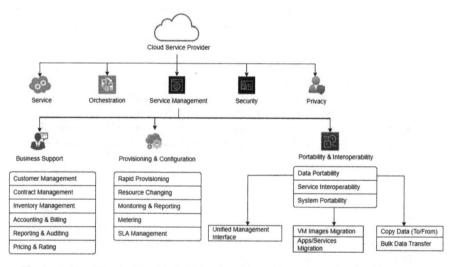

Fig. 1. A Cloud Service Provider's Major Activities with respect to Service Management

1.2 Cloud Design Patterns and Architecture

A design pattern (DP) is a method for implementing the object orientation. DPs are general repeatable solutions to a commonly occurring problem. Erich Gamma et al. [3] have popularized the concept of patterns widely. Chidamber and Kemerer [4] have proposed an object-oriented (OO) metric which can be used to compare the quality of code; good use of DP can improve these metrics. Kohls [5] identifies the benefits of the DP approach as a solution that improves an environment, identifies and points to serious problems, provides reusability and preservation of good solutions, reduces complexity, provides shared vocabulary and generates good design. Cloud computing faces problems like QoS, fault tolerance, energy consumption, etc. Dynamic changes in service requirements and reconfiguration in terms of location, time, activity, the interaction between agents, and communication also play a big part in the success of cloud computing, as noted by Baneli [6] et al. Thus, it requires a well-defined architectural framework and standard procedures that can be used to configure the cloud.

Cloud DPs are useful for building reusable, portable, reliable, scalable, and secure applications in the cloud. Cloud DPs can be defined as a general reusable solution to commonly occurring problems in cloud architecture. Microsoft Azure and Amazon Web Service (AWS) have prescribed various cloud DPs, and Arcitura also lists various cloud DPs. Thus, we find DP to be a great help in designing a better and simpler system.

1.3 Organization of Paper

This paper is further organized in the following manner. Section 2 enlists similar studies and a literature review. Section 3 defines the system model and resource allocation management. Section 4 presents a note on the pattern, automated decision process and numerical comparisons and results. Section 5 concludes the paper by giving a summary and notes on future directions.

2 Literature Review

Cloud DPs are seen more frequently than ever before. Hundreds of patterns prescribed for Architecture, Application Deployment, Sharing/Scaling Resources, Load Balancing/Resource Allocation, Data Management, VM & Hyper-visoring, Security, and other purposes are popular. Many research recommendations made related to cloud DPs. Some cloud DP-related papers are summarized below.

Christoph Fehling [7] in his doctoral dissertation argued that the results of properties affected due to commonly provisioned cloud resources are unknown. Each cloud provider has its own effect on provisioning. He proposed a design to capture architecture concepts to ensure technology independence and to gain persistent knowledge from these effects. He presented a method for carving structured patterns with textual and graphic designs along with human-understandable method descriptions. He suggested various usages of cloud patterns in research and industry applications.

Sousa et al. [8] studied how cloud professionals adopt patterns. They found that the adoption of some patterns is based on company characteristics and that the adoption of certain patterns leads to the adoption of other relevant patterns. Sukhpal Singh et al. [9] have identified cloud workload DPs and mapped them with QoS requirements. They have also discussed the process of cloud workload DPs along with problems in patterns and their terminologies in the cloud. Abdul et al. [10] have studied DPs in various cloud models, especially for SaaS clouds offering multi-tenancy. Kalra et al. [11] have presented implementation patterns for building a multi-tenant application in cloud environments. Jalawi [12] proposed a three-stage process for defining cloud patterns. This includes pattern discovery, pattern documentation, and pattern implementation. Shi et al. [13] argue that the time taken to allocate resources and the efficiency of resource allocation are inversely proportional. They advocated a pattern-based resource allocation to overcome this challenge. Ezugwu et al. [14] presented DPs for several classes of multi-component, multi-tenant cloud applications. They also proposed a component-based reference architectural model to describe a general-purpose scheduling system of multi-component applications. Reina et al. [15] proposed a DP for decision-making based upon a nature-inspired algorithm. Banijamali et al. [16] identified state of art architectural elements in cloud computing regarding IoT, including DPs, styles, views, quality attributes, and evaluation methodology. Saboor et al. [17] compared cloud microservices when clustered in a behavioral DP-based cluster against random distribution. They found that pre-distribution based on pattern classification reacts faster. Taibi et al. [18] surveyed FaaS patterns in clouds, and surveyed various aspects, including, a multivocal literature review and classified them according to benefits and issues. Leitner et al. [19] conducted a study on software development for FaaS applications. They found that developers use various application patterns to deal with the inherent limitations of FaaS platforms. Krupitzer et al. [20] presented an overview of DPs for self-adaptive systems regarding IoT. They have provided taxonomy on DPs, which can be applied similarly to IoT and cloud systems. Washizaki et al. [21] suggested that due to the proliferation of IoT and there is a need to have a fresh perceptive on system design. They classified IoT and non-IoT patterns and found that about only 53% patterns used in IoT architecture are relevant to IoT. Prieto et al. [22] used an incremental deployment model and Mannava [23] used a combination of certain cloud DPs. Both argue that cloud applications should support the dynamic reconfiguration of services in a distributed environment. Z Durdik [24] presents an idea of lightweight support for evaluating decisions and the documentation of rationale for DP applications. Sahly et al. [25] proposed a solution strategy method for selecting DP based on an appropriate recommendation for software engineering. Fortis et al. [26] provided an overview of a set of guidance and patterns which are used in MODAClouds projects. Liu et al. [27] presented SSI architecture in the blockchain environment, which advocates DP as a service model of deployment.

Gill et al. [28] discussed the effects of IoT, blockchain and artificial intelligence (AI) on cloud computing. They argue that resource provisioning in clouds, edge and fog computing paradigms is based on deep learning techniques to predict resource management. AI makes IoT and fog aware of the workload and continuously adapt to provide better QoS. Amongst various SLA and QoS requirements, they listed how AI can improve the performance of the cloud. They proposed a conceptual model for cloud futurology encompassing IoT, blockchain and AI to meet the challenges of smarter, safer and better computing. Madni et al. [29] presented a survey on advancement in resource allocation, they have listed AI-based methods including alert time-based resource allocation, cloudlet agent based, genetic algorithm, iterative algorithm, ACO, component based, auction based, swapping based and cluster-based AI algorithms. Joloudari et al. [30] presented AI, deep learning and machine learning (ML) based methods to optimize resource usage in cloud computing. They listed various techniques including Bayesian MDP, Bayesian P2PN (Supervised), RL IOT, RL 5GN, QL VCC, RL VCC (Reinforced Learning). They also discussed some fusion studies of Deep Reinforced Learning and how these techniques might help. Pirhoseinlo et al. [31] presented an AI-based framework for scheduling distributed systems. They devised a scheme to set subgoals for subsystems behaving within distributed systems. They used a hybrid approach of neural networks and genetic algorithms. Kumar et al. [32] presented an autonomic resource provisioning framework for clouds with decision-making capabilities to schedule the jobs at the best resources within the deadline and to optimize both the execution time and the cost simultaneously. This framework uses spider monkey optimization (SMO) algorithm based scheduling mechanism to solve a multi-objective optimization problem honoring various QoS parameters. Liu et al. [33] presented a hierarchical framework for resource allocation and power management in clouds. They used reinforced learning partially along with deep reinforced learning and long short term memory to achieve tradeoff between latency and power consumption. Wang et al. [34] presented a ML based framework for assisted resource allocation. They proposed beam allocation in a multi-user massive multiple-input-multiple-output (MIMO) system that outperforms conventional methods. They used K near neighbor algorithm to solve the assignment problem for multiclass classification problem. Daoud et al. [35] proposed AI-based method for energy reduction in cloud and IoT devices. This study used intelligent agents using Q reinforced learning to consolidate the VM migration. This method improves various QoS parameters including energy consumption, number of migrations, SLA decline and SLA violations. Zhang et al. [36] proposed ML-based resource allocation using auctions. This method uses the classification of ML to model and analyze the multi-dimensional cloud resource allocation problem. It further proposes two resource allocation prediction algorithms based on linear and logistic regressions. This proposed method provides Pareto optimal allocation solution on various QoS parameters including social welfare, allocation accuracy, and resource usage. Cheng and Li [37] proposed deep reinforcement learning-based resource provisioning and task scheduling. This method uses Q learning-based two staged Resource provisioning and Task Scheduling. It is designed to automatically generate the best long-term decisions by learning from the changing environment, such as user request patterns and realistic electric prices. Compared with existing algorithms, this method improves 320% energy cost efficiency. Ji et al. [38] discussed AI-based techniques in dynamically changing task scheduling environments in mobile edge cloud computing. Xu et al. [39] proposed a reinforcement learning method embedded in a smart contract to further minimize the energy cost. Experimental results with this method on Google cluster traces and realworld electricity prices show that this approach can reduce the datacenters' cost significantly compared with other benchmark algorithms by reducing energy costs by up to 50%. Alfakih et al. [40] proposed Task Offloading and Resource Allocation for Mobile Edge Computing by Deep Reinforcement Learning. This paper proposed reinforcement learning based state-action-reward-state-action (RL-SARSA) algorithm to solve the problem of resource management. This multi-objective optimizer handles issues like minimizing system cost, energy consumption and computing time delay. In comparison to Q learning (RL-QL) this approach works better. This method improves performance up to 8% in terms of consistency. Hou et al. [41] proposed a hierarchical task off loading strategy for handling delay tolerant and delay-sensitive cloud services. This method guaranties user quality of experience, low latency, and ultrareliable services. This method uses a multiagent deep deterministic policy gradient in a federated environment to train the model. In comparison to existing models, this model improves system processing efficiency and task completion ratio. Khayyat et al. [42] used deep learning based computational offloading for mobile edge cloud vehicles. This algorithm finds near optimal solution, using parallel deep neural networks. These networks work on local and remote execution approaches. Since, it finds near optimal solution, it is faster and easier to implement. This method also improves costs as the number of vehicles increases. This method also helps serve more road side units for the same costs.

Chidamber and Keremer have proposed the CK metric [4] to measure the object orientation in code. Besides this, many other researchers have proposed new OO metrics. Several OO metrics were surveyed by Genero et al. [43] and Chhabara [44]. The extension works include Li and Henry, Martin's Package Metric, Marchesi, Harrison, Bansiya, Genero, Brito e Abreu, Lorenz and Kidd, etc. Ghareb et al. [45] have explored a new framework for calculating hybrid system metrics for dynamic aspect-oriented and object-oriented programming. CK metrics are further discussed in Sect. 4.

2.1 Motivation and Need

Several cloud DPs exist for resource allocation, but for multiple cloud service providers and other agents acting as a single unit, the scenario changes altogether. While implementing a strategy for common goals, the methods and structures adopted by individual clouds may vary. This poses the question of how a common solution to a generic and repetitive problem can be proposed while keeping the internal structures and methods of all members independent of those of the team. According to [29] resource management is a much more holistic approach than resource allocation. Resource allocation management is not limited to allotting a resource to a tenant, but it is strongly related to issues like pricing, brokering, mapping, modeling, provisioning, and scheduling of resources. It is necessary to have a mechanism that leads to adherence to multiple sets of rules, pre-conditions, pre-qualifications, and other properties besides following generic cost-saving or revenue generation models.

AI and ML can help take better, faster and nonprejudiced automated decisions to implement the most appropriate strategy.

Using the DP architecture, a cloud becomes a better model for assigning a resource or a group or aggregate set of resources, to a request or set of requests. Any layer from Cloud, a Physical Resource, a Logical Resource, or any other mechanism may it be an IaaS, PaaS, SaaS, FaaS, or XaaS, can be abstracted, which can be individually or jointly mapped using a strategy function. Thus, we propose a DP, which helps in dynamically reconfiguring cloud resource allocation policy based on the individual parameters of the member clouds.

3 System Model

Godhrawala and Sridaran [46] studied a multi-objective resource allocation problem. The system model described by them is shown in Fig. 2.

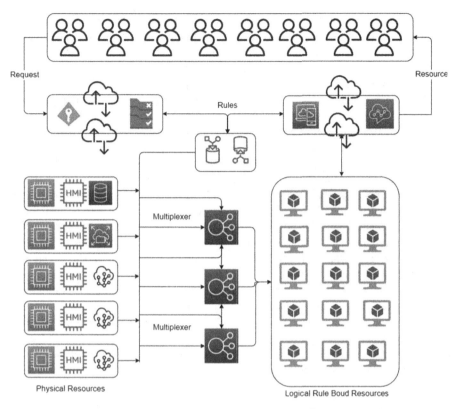

Fig. 2. Multitenant Cloud Resource Allocation Mechanism for Repeating Requests

We assume a pool of cloud service providers C, a pool of resources V across all clouds, and a pool of subscribing users S. Users may have contracts for guaranteed services or may participate in an auction for resources. We assume that multiple tenants subscribe to one, multiple, or all clouds at the same time. All clouds share a resource pool of resources and a scheduler. The subscribers send a set of requests R to the shared pool, which may be targeted to either open or repetitive. All the cloud service providers' respective strategies to the scheduler. Any subscriber can ask for any resource in any cloud that it subscribes to.

$C = \{c_i, i = 1...n\}$

$V = \{v_{ij}, i = 1...n, j = 1...m\}$ where i indicates resource id, j indicates optional cloud id.

$S = \{S_i, i = 1...n\}$

$R = \{r_{ij}, i = 1...n, j = 1...m\}$ where i indicates request id, j indicates subscriber id.

Providers act as a group serving subscribing clients. These requests are sent to the scheduler via a secure gateway. Each request is accompanied by a checklist of QoS properties that need to be satisfied by resources to serve the requests. The cloud physical resources are further divided into logical resources using a multiplexer. These logical resources are identified as a group of resources having a certain set of properties. These properties reflect various QoS parameters. These resources are then mapped along with the properties of incoming requests, and if the properties of requests and resources are matched, an allocation takes place and end-user computing is enabled using the connecting network. The mapping function P is defined as follows.

$P = \{p_{ij} = (r_{ij}, v_{ij}) \ni r_{ijp} \rightarrow v_{ijp}\}$ where r_{ijp} and v_{ijp} indicate respective QoS properties.

This is a two-stage problem. The first stage is the identification of the qualifying resources. The second stage is the actual allocation stage. The resource allocation problem is defined as a Stackelberg game between a pool of cloud service providers and a pool of subscribers. One of the qualifying resources is allocated to a request upon the successful mapping of properties. The optimization problem is defined as follows:

maximize profits r_{ijrev}, $\delta = \sum r_{ijrev}$, $\ni (r_{ijrev}, x) \in P, x \in V$

The qualifying criteria or the rules keep changing based on various factors like workload status, distribution of QoS viz. Workload, revenue generation, power availability, etc. Both requests and resources are renewed and their respective properties are updated based on heuristic data of their assignment history and the current status of the cloud configuration. The dynamic reconfiguration and allocation logic are updated using the strategy class. Furthermore, the behavior of the cloud is updated across all clouds and resources using the link_strategy function. This helps the cloud become self-configurable and self-driven. This is further discussed in the following Sect. 4.2.

Besides the resource allocation function, auxiliary mechanisms, including billing, security, and gateway control, are implemented through the validation process. Properties associated with requests and resources are updated continuously. A cycle of assignment, a reconfiguration of resources and updated properties are repeated over and over.

3.1 Problem Formulation

According to [46] three methods have been tested to optimize the performance of the cloud, they are EMA, Pivot and RSI price rebalancing methods. EMA optimizes revenue, RSI optimizes workload balancing and Pivot keeps both revenue and workload in equilibrium. Thus, our problem is to identify the three QoS parameters from heuristic data r_{ijxxx} and v_{ijxxx} revenue, workload and criticality of processes to decide what method of price balancing is to be automatically adopted so that these three conditions are satisfied. a) Cloud should generate optimum revenue, b) No process shall starve and c) Critical processes shall be honored. Thus, function is revised as maximize profits $\delta = \sum r_{ijrev}$, $\ni (r_{ijrev}, x) \in P, x \in V, A(r_{ijcri}) \rightarrow 1, (A(r_{ijxxx})) \in \{0,1\}$

4 Cloud Design Pattern for Dynamic Resource Allocation

Cloud-related DPs, are described for AWS by [47], for Microsoft Azure by [48] and real-life oriented cloud DPs by Earl et al. [49]. They are classified under various categories viz Sharing, Scaling, Elasticity, Reliability, Recovery, Data Management, Storage, Hypervisors, Monitoring, Provisioning, Security, etc.

4.1   Introduction to Rule-Based Analysis Pattern

We propose a rule-based analysis pattern for dynamically reconfiguring the resource allocation process for repeating requests. Besides multiple cloud service providers, it can be equally applied to the edge, fog and, IoT, etc. This pattern helps improve the architectural framework of the cloud and hence improves functionality and simplifies maintenance.

4.2   Discussions on the Proposed Pattern

This pattern is implemented using a dual queue, one queue for requests and one queue for resources. Requests and resources are stacked at their respective queues as they arrive. Any consistent method can be used to put requests and resources into queues viz. FCFS, priority-based, etc. Every request in the queue from the front will get a chance to acquire resources, given that resources are validated and satisfy the rules specified by the request. There may be special cases where the subscribing request overrides resource property, but a rule must explicitly declare that. All resources and requests are released after the completion of the allocation cycle. Requests and resources are either canceled or retired from the queue, or once again entered the queue based on the policy and properties. Since such dynamic nature of the pattern, it helps in refining allocation policies based upon heuristic data; instantaneously resulting in not only a resource allocation pattern but a cloud architecture pattern.

Decision Tree based Automized Strategy Selection of the Pattern. We implement the simplest of decision tree-based classifier to opt for an atomized selection of allocation strategy. We assign two properties to each request, critical and fixed denoted by r_{ijcri} and r_{ijfix}, respectively. Since, we are only considering two QoS attributes the final classification will be one of a) critical & fixed (CF), b) critical & auction (Cf), c) noncritical & fixed (cF), and d) non-critical & auction (cf). This tree needs only two decision nodes at most to decide on the appropriate strategy, as indicated by [46]. The algorithm is given in list 1, pattern code is given in list 2 below.

```
Input: Set of waiting requests with properties R Output: 1-
Classification, 2-Allocation Pairs based on classification
Process:
1. Start
2. Create root
3. Check if all properties are monogamous, if yes return tree with
most common label exit
4. Repeat a-c
a. Select most common property pᵢ
b. For each request property add branch corresponding to the test pi
and select best branch
c. Select subset branch to further propagate decision tree, till
leaf is reached
5. Declare Strategy based on classification as an associative rule
(cF->EMA, cf->EMA, CF->Pivot, Cf-> RSI)
6. If the rule is cF or cf define class ema
```

```
7. If the rule is CF, define class pivot
8. If the rule is Cf define class rsi
9. If class ema exists do action_ema
10. If class pivot exists do action_pivot
11. If class rsi exists do action_rsi
12. Stop
```

List 1. Pseudocode for generating decision tree-based classification

```
class strategy: public ema, rsi, pivot
{
ema e; pivot p; rsi r;
void setprice(ema)
{
// do allocation
}
void setprice(rsi)
{
// do allocation
}
void setprice(pivot)
{
// do allocation
}
};
```

List 2. Pseudocode for executing decision tree-based classification

Class Diagram. Following Fig. 3 shows the class diagram for this pattern. The clients create requests and the providers create resources. Both are queued along with the properties. Strategy is defined using the properties and history of allocations. A strategy class is used to configure the strategies of cloud service providers and subscribers. An assignment function is used to map resources and requests as they are queued. Once assignment occurs the allocation history is updated for both requests and resources and the billing process is initiated, ledgers of both client and provider are updated.

Dynamics and Transition of States for Request. Following Fig. 4 shows a state diagram or transition from one state to another state for Request. The states of the request may be loaded, validated, allocated, rearranged, updated, strategize, reloaded, and unloaded.

Following Fig. 5 shows a sequence diagram for the proposed pattern. The sequence of events includes request creation, resource creation, validation, assignment, configuration, billing and accounting, and loading and unloading.

Examples. Though there are many assignment problems existing, across all domains we limit our discussions to the following 3 examples with relevant rules and validations.

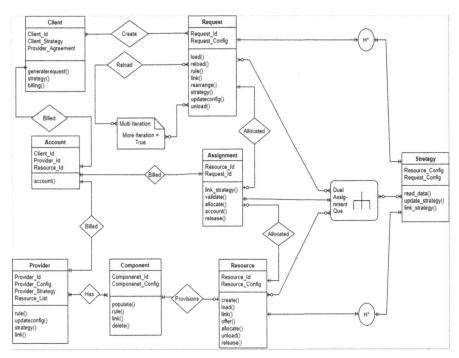

Fig. 3. Class diagram of a rule-based analysis pattern for dynamically reconfigure resource allocation process for repeating requests

- ☐ Railway Reservation (Ticketing) System: In this system, there are rules like types of tickets, class of travel, travel restrictions, etc. This problem has various constraints and raiders. Various types of tickets, primarily reserved and unserved, can be classified similar to contracted resources and open auction resources. These tickets can be further subdivided into various travel classes similar to various types of cloud services. There may be certain travel restrictions, including minimum distance to travel in a given travel class or minimum fare applicable in a given travel class, similar to country-specific law requirements. There may be suspended travel situations or diversion of routes and so forth. There may be a quota for senior citizens or ladies. Thus, various riders form a set of rules for booking. The berth allocation system in a train resembles resource allocation in a cloud. Likewise above criteria described for ticketing, there are various QoS parameters to adhere to in cloud computing. Hence, this pattern can be effectively used for that.
- ☐ Stock Market: A generic stock market is a two-way or double auction process. The stock exchanges and regulators enforce rules and validations like daily price limits like circuit filters, banning future trades based on OI calculations, etc. Further, there are events like bonus issues, splits, dividends, block/bulk deals etc. This system is a security allocation system based on a set of laws/rules, regulations, and validations and this pattern befits the same purpose. Stock exchanges and regulators enforce rules and validations including price limits, circuit filters, banning trades based on OI, etc.

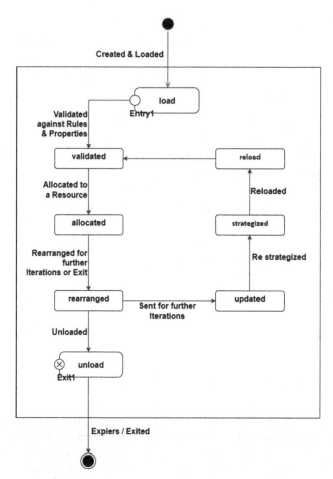

Fig. 4. State diagram of a rule-based analysis pattern for dynamically reconfigure resource allocation process for repeating requests

☐ Rolling Vacancy Employment/Recruitment System: In the rolling system, anyone can apply at any time for a given position, whenever the actual vacancy falls vacant the position is filled by selecting a candidate. The job types are either permanent or temporary/contractual. There may be a reservation policy (roster based) to fill in vacant positions. Only those candidates are selected who satisfy the qualifications regarding the open vacancy, validated through the recruitment process and who opt for salary structure and job location. This job assignment system is based on a set of qualifications, experience and salary constraints and this pattern effectively supports the purpose for that.

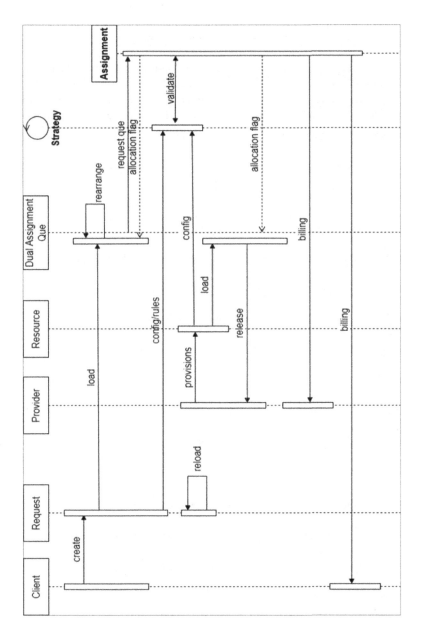

Fig. 5. Sequence Diagram of a rule-based analysis pattern for dynamically reconfigure resource allocation process for repeating requests

4.3 Results

The solution proposed by [46] is highly procedural and highly coupled. To reduce the coupling between objects and to promote and ease the maintenance of the code, OO techniques and DP are applied. The strategy pattern along with the observer and chain of responsibility is applied to ensure a better solution to the problem.

Numeric Comparisons. Table 1 shows the CK metric values for the above-mentioned primitive/procedural approach adopted. Table 2 shows the CK metric values of DPbased implementation. The data in Table 3 show improvements in every metric value. WMC is decreased by 4, nominal WMC is decreased by 15, DIC is decreased by 2, NOC is decreased by 5, and CBO is decreased by 4.

Table 1. CK metric values of Primitive/Procedural Approach

Class	WMC1	WMCv	DIT	NOC	CBO
Anonymous	1	1	0	0	0
Assignment	5	5	3	0	1
Client	6	6	0	1	1
Ema	1	1	0	1	1
Pivot	1	1	0	1	1
Provider	6	6	0	1	1
Queue	2	2	2	1	3
Request	6	6	1	2	3
Resource	6	6	1	2	3
Rsi	1	1	0	1	1
Strategy	10	10	2	0	5
Overall	45	45	9	10	20

Table 2. CK metric values of the OO/DP Approach

Class	WMC1	WMCv	DIT	NOC	CBO
anonymous	1	1	0	0	0
assignment	5	5	3	0	1
client	7	7	0	1	1
ema	0	0	0	0	1
pivot	0	0	0	0	1

(continued)

Table 2. (*continued*)

Class	WMC1	WMCv	DIT	NOC	CBO
provider	7	7	0	1	1
queue	omitted, implemented using request & resource que				
request	5	5	1	1	2
resource	5	5	1	1	2
rsi	0	0	0	0	1
strategy	**11**	**0**	**2**	**1**	**6**
Overall	**41**	**30**	**7**	**5**	**16**

Table 3. Improvements per module using DP Approach

Class	WMC1	WMCv	DIT	NOC	CBO
Anonymous	0	0	0	0	0
Assignment	0	0	0	0	0
Client	1	1	0	0	0
Ema	-1	-1	0	-1	0
Pivot	-1	-1	0	-1	0
Provider	1	1	0	0	0
Queue	-2	-2	-2	-1	-3
Request	-1	-1	0	-1	-1
Resource	-1	-1	0	-1	-1
Rsi	-1	-1	0	-1	0
Strategy	1	-10	0	1	1
Overall	-4	-15	-2	-5	-4

Discussions The data in above tables show improvements in every metric value, weighted methods per class is decreased in 6 classes, where as it increases in 2 classes, reducing 4 WMCs, indicting the simplification of module and encapsulation. Further weighted methods per class on a nominal weight basis increased in two modules and decreases on 6 modules reducing 15 WMC that indicates better encapsulation and security of data. The lower number of modules indicates more reusability and lower impact on inheriting child classes. The depth of inheritance is largely unaffected, but the omission of the que class reduces DIT, which indicates that the behavior of modules is more controlled and predictable. The lesser hierarchy of inheritance indicates that data are not affected by many other modules, thus it behaves predictably. The lesser hierarchy tree also indicates a simplified design. It protects the data in a better way. The number of children in each class is reduced in 6 classes where as it increases in 1 class, indicating that the abstraction of data is also improved in DP approach. The reduced number of better abstraction of classes. It reduces the chance of mishandling of subclasses or abstraction. The number of children classes also indicates the degree of impact by the parent module, thus lesser child classes reduce skewness in modules. Coupling between objects is reduced in 2 classes, increased in 1 class and due to omission of que class further reduction is observed. However, since all data modules are highly dependent on each other, there is less scope of reducing coupling. This reduces coupling between the object, thus helps in writing data independent code, the individual modules perform better.

Performance Analysis and Impact. Summarizing, reduced WMC indicates reusability and a lower impact on inheriting child classes. The reduced DIT indicates that behavior of the modules is controlled and predictable. Reduced NOC indicates that abstraction of data is improved. A reduced CBO indicates that data-independent code and better performing individual modules.

4.4 Remarks and Notes on the Pattern

The pattern is closely related to the Reservation and Use of Reusable Entities Pattern [50], Strategy Pattern [4], Parameterized (Adapted) Strategy Pattern [51], the Dynamic Reconfiguration of Autonomic Computing System [52] patterns. This pattern is a composite and compound pattern. It uses concepts described by various cloud DPs. This pattern is suitable for a multi-tenant environment. It is flexible enough to change the behavior of the allocation process, reconfigure resources and to allow dynamic handling of incoming requests. The pattern helps the cloud self-manage itself.

5 Conclusion and Summary

In this paper, we have discussed the resource allocation problem with various examples. We have discussed the multitenant cloud environment and the resource allocation problem associated with it. We have proposed a rule-based analysis pattern for dynamically reconfiguring the resource allocation process for repeating requests. We have explained the pattern; in terms of problems and solutions, including a class diagram, a state diagram, a sequence diagram, examples, and discussions including the potential use of the pattern and how ML can be used to dynamically reconfigure behavior of the pattern. We also list a few variations and related patterns. We have discussed how this pattern can be used in the cloud resource allocation problem in detail.

The proposed DP is a good automated reconfiguration pattern with a multi-objective outlook; allowing for integration with outer world entities. The strategy class can be used to identify, and analyze the situation. Based upon the cloud, resources and request configuration, a rule is selected to optimize resource allocation, and the resource management process and resource and request properties are updated accordingly.

Results of comparing CK metrics show that the object-oriented design pattern-based approach improves the code, improves the maintainability, and makes it simpler to revise the code. Since this pattern is aspect-oriented; it also helps maintain self-properties of the clouds by continuously maintaining the balance between requests and resources, making the clouds self-configurable, self-healing, self-aware, self-monitorable, selfoptimizing, and fault tolerant.

5.1 Future Work

Future work related to this work will be to study the ontology, framework, and architecture of the cloud. The pattern described in this paper can be further developed and defined in a structural form. Various other ML techniques may be tested to automize strategy selectin process. Other QoS parameters may also be tested for SLA guarantee. This pattern may be inspected against recurring tasks, randomly recurring tasks, periodically recurring tasks. Besides CK metrics, other OO metrics can be evaluated and studied for this pattern.

References

1. Singh, J., Dhiman, G.: A survey on cloud computing approaches. In: Materials Today: Proceedings. Science Direct (2021). https://doi.org/10.1016/j.matpr.2021.05.334
2. Singh, S., Chana, I.: A survey on resource scheduling in cloud computing: Issues and challenges. Journal of grid computing **14**(2), 217–264 (2016)
3. Gamma, E., et al.: Elements of Reusable Object-oriented Software. Pearson (2015)
4. Chidamber, S.R., Kemerer, C.F.: A metrics suite for object oriented design. IEEE Trans. Software Eng. **20**(6), 476–493 (1994)
5. Fard, M.V., et al.: Resource allocation mechanisms in cloud computing: a systematic literature review. IET Software **14**(6), 638–653 (2020)
6. Benali, A.E., Asri, B.: Towards rigorous selection and configuration of cloud services: research methodology. Int. J. Comput. Sci. Issues **17**(6), 77–81 (2020)
7. Fehling, C.: Cloud computing patterns: identification, design application (2015)
8. Sousa, T.B., Ferreira, H.S., Correia, F.F.: A survey on the adoption of patterns for engineering software for the cloud. IEEE Trans. Software Eng. **48**(6), 2128–2140 (2022). https://doi.org/10.1109/TSE.2021.3052177
9. Gill, S.S., Chana, I.: QoS based workload design patterns in cloud computing: a literature review. Int. J. Cloud-Comput. Super-Comput. **2**, 37–46 (2015). https://doi.org/10.21742/ijcs.2015.2.2.05
10. Abdul, A.O., et al.. Multi-tenancy design patterns in SAAS applications: a performance evaluation case study. Int. J. Digit. Soc. 17–20 (2018)
11. Kalra, S.: Implementation patterns for multi-tenancy. In: Proceedings of the 24th Conference on Pattern Languages of Programs (2017)
12. Alshudukhi, J. (2021). Pattern-based solution for architecting cloud-enabled software. Int. J. Adv. Appl. Sci. **8**, 9–19. https://doi.org/10.21833/ijaas.2021.08.002
13. Shi, J., et al.: Fast multi-resource allocation with patterns in large scale cloud data center. Journal of Computational Science **26**, 389–401 (2018)
14. Ezugwu, A.E., Eduard Frincu, M. Balarabe Junaidu, S.: Architectural pattern for scheduling multi-component applications in distributed systems. Int. J. Grid High Perf. Comput. **8**(1), 1–22 (2016)
15. Reina, A., et al.: A design pattern for decentralised decision making. PLoS ONE **10**, e0140950 (2015)

16. Banijamali, A., et al.: Software architectures of the convergence of cloud computing and the Internet of Things: A systematic literature review. Inf. Softw. Technol. **122**, 106271 (2020)

17. Saboor, A., Mahmood, A.K., Hassan, M.F., Shah, S.N.M., Hassan, F., Siddiqui, M.A.: Design pattern based distribution of microservices in cloud computing environment. In: 2021 International Conference on Computer and Information Sciences (ICCOINS), pp. 396–400 (2021) https://doi.org/10.1109/ICCOINS49721.2021.9497188

18. Ferguson, D., Méndez Muñoz, V., Pahl, C., Helfert, M. (eds.): CLOSER 2019. CCIS, vol. 1218. Springer, Cham (2020). https://doi.org/10.1007/978-3-030-49432-2

19. Leitner, P., et al.: A mixed-method empirical study of function-as-a-Service software development in industrial practice. J. Syst. Softw. **149**, 340–359 (2019)

20. Krupitzer, C., et al.: An overview of design patterns for self-adaptive systems in the context of the internet of things. IEEE Access **8**, 187384–187399 (2020)

21. Washizaki, H., et al.: Landscape of architecture and design patterns for Iot systems. IEEE Internet Things J. **7**(10), 10091–10101 (2020)

22. Zúñiga-Prieto, M., et al.: Dynamic reconfiguration of cloud application architectures. Softw. Pract. Exp. **48**(2), 327–344 (2018)

23. Mannava, V. T. Ramesh.: Design pattern for dynamic reconfiguration of component-based autonomic computing systems using RMI. Proc. Technol. **6**, 590–597 (2012)

24. Durdik, Z.: Architectural Design Decision Documentation through Reuse of Design Patterns. Vol. 14. KIT Scientific Publishing (2016)

25. Sahly, Eiman M. Omar M. Sallabi. Design pattern selection: A solution strategy method. In: 2012 ICCSII, IEEE (2012)

26. Fortiş, T.-F., Ferry, N.: Cloud patterns. In: Di Nitto, E., Matthews, P., Petcu, D., Solberg, A. (eds.) Model-Driven Development and Operation of Multi-Cloud Applications. SAST, pp. 107–112. Springer, Cham (2017). https://doi.org/10.1007/978-3-319-46031-4_11

27. Liu, Y., Lu, Q., Paik, H.-Y., Xu, X., Chen, S., Zhu, L.: Design pattern as a service for blockchain-based self-Sovereign identity. IEEE Softw. **37**(5), 30–36 (2020). https://doi.org/10.1109/MS.2020.2992783

28. Gill, S.S., et al.: Transformative effects of IoT, blockchain and artificial intelligence on cloud computing: Evolution, vision, trends and open challenges. Intern. Things **8**, 100118 (2019)

29. Madni, S., Shafie Abd Latiff, M., Coulibaly, Y.: Recent advancements in resource allocation techniques for cloud computing environment: a systematic review. Clust. Comput. **20**(3), 2489–2533 (2017)

30. Joloudari, J.H., et al.: Resource allocation optimization using artificial intelligence methods in various computing paradigms: A review. 12315 (2022)

31. Pirhoseinlo, A., Osati Eraghi, N. Akbari Torkestani, J.:. Artificial intelligence-based framework for scheduling distributed systems using a combination of neural networks and genetic algorithms. Mobile Inf. Syst. (2022)

32. Kumar, M., et al.: ARPS: An autonomic resource provisioning and scheduling framework for cloud platforms. IEEE Trans. Sustain. Comput. **7**(2), 386–399 (2021)

33. Liu, N., et al.: A hierarchical framework of cloud resource allocation and power management using deep reinforcement learning. In: 2017 IEEE 37th international conference on distributed computing systems (ICDCS). IEEE (2017)

34. Wang, J.-B., et al.: A machine learning framework for resource allocation assisted by cloud computing. IEEE Netw. **32**(2), 144–151 (2018)

35. Daoud, W.B., et al.: Cloud-IoT resource management based on artificial intelligence for energy reduction. In: Wireless Communications and Mobile Computing 2022 (2022)

36. Zhang, J., et al.: Machine learning based resource allocation of cloud computing in auction. Comput. Mater. Contin. **56**(1), 123–135 (2018)

37. Cheng, M., Li, J., Nazarian, S.: DRL-cloud: Deep reinforcement learningbased resource provisioning and task scheduling for cloud service providers. In: 2018 23rd Asia and South pacific design automation conference (ASP-DAC). IEEE (2018)
38. Ji, H., Alfarraj, O., Tolba, A.: Artificial intelligence-empowered edge of vehicles: architecture, enabling technologies applications. IEEE Access **8**, 61020–61034 (2020)
39. Xu, C., Wang, K., Guo, M.: Intelligent resource management in blockchain-based cloud datacenters. IEEE Cloud Comput. **4**(6), 50–59 (2017)
40. Alfakih, T., et al.: Task offloading and resource allocation for mobile edge computing by deep reinforcement learning based on SARSA. IEEE Access **8**, 54074–54084 (2020)
41. Hou, W., et al.: Multiagent deep reinforcement learning for task offloading and re-source allocation in Cybertwin-based networks. IEEE Internet Things J. **8**(22), 16256–16268 (2021)
42. Khayyat, M., et al.: Advanced deep learning-based computational offloading for multilevel vehicular edge-cloud computing networks. IEEE Access **8**, 137052–137062 (2020)
43. Genero, M., Piattini, M., Calero, C.: A survey of metrics for UML class diagrams. J. Object Technol. **4**(9), 59–92 (2005)
44. Chawla, Mandeep K. I. Chhabra: Implementation of an object oriented model to analyze relative progression of source code versions with respect to software quality. Int. J. Computer Applications **107**, 10 (2014)
45. Ghareb, M. I., Allen, G.: Quality metrics measurement for hybrid systems (aspect oriented programming—object oriented programming). Technium: Roman. J. Appl. Sci. Technol. **3**(3), 82–99 (2021)
46. Godhrawala, H. R. Sridaran: A dynamic Stackelberg game based multi-objective approach for effective resource allocation in cloud computing. Int. J. Inf. Technol. (2022) 1–16
47. Keery, S., Harber, C., Marcus , Y., Demiliani, O.S.: Implementing Azure Cloud Design Patterns: Implement Efficient Design Patterns for Data Management, High Availability, Monitoring And Other Popular Patterns On Your Azure Cloud. Packt Publishing Ltd (2018)
48. Erl, T., Cope, R., Naserpour, A.: Cloud Computing Design Patterns. Prentice Hall Press (2015)
49. Fernandez, E.B., Yuan, X.: An analysis pattern for reservation and use of reusable entities. In: Procs. of Pattern Languages of Programs Conference, PLoP99 (1999)
50. Sobajic, O., Moussavi Behrouz Far, M.: Parameterized strategy pattern. In: Proceedings of the 17th Conference on Pattern Languages of Programs (2010)
51. Mannava, V., Ramesh, T.: A novel adaptive re-configuration compliance design pattern for autonomic computing systems. Proc. Eng. **30**, 1129-1137 (2012)

Recent Trends in Modalities and Deep Learning Methods for Breast Cancer Detection

Iqra Nissar, Shahzad Alam, and Sarfaraz Masood[(✉)]

Department of Computer Engineering, Jamia Millia Islamia, New Delhi 110025, India
samasood@jmi.ac.in

Abstract. Automated and intelligent healthcare using deep learning has produced promising results in both diagnosis of diseases and precision medicine. Disease diagnosis without any human intervention has gained prominence among clinicians recently. Breast Cancer, the most prevalent type of cancer in women is the major cause of death among them. Therefore, its diagnosis is crucial in the early stage to lower the death rates. The use of medical imaging in the identification and diagnosis of breast cancer is highly recommended. The literature has offered several modalities, demonstrating a keen interest in several research areas. In pertinent medical domains, each modality has a significant role to play. This study has examined the benefits and drawbacks of various imaging techniques for diagnosing breast cancer, including mammography, ultrasound, and MRI. Using various imaging modalities, the techniques developed to make it easier to divide breast cancer into cancerous and non-cancerous classes. A quick insight into the modalities and subsequent machine learning and deep learning applications that have been widely used in the diagnosis of this disease is the major goal of this study.

Keywords: Breast cancer · Image modalities · Mammograms · Ultrasound · Deep learning

1 Introduction

Breast cancer is the highest incidence of malignant tumor found among women [1] and is the cause of the second leading cancer death globally. According to the statistics of the world health organization (WHO), there are 460,000 deaths each year worldwide out of 1,350,000 breast cancer cases [2], and in the United States alone, 268,600 breast cancer cases were reported in 2019 [3, 4]. In 2020, 2.3 million women were diagnosed with breast cancer, causing around 6,85,000 deaths worldwide [5]. This disease occurs when the cells of the breast become abnormal and divide uncontrollably [6]. Eventually, these abnormal cells form huge lumps of tissues, which ultimately becomes a tumor. The tumors developed, can either be benign or malignant. Benign tumors are non-cancerous tumors and are produced due to minor changes in the structure of the breast. On the other hand, malignant tumors are considered cancerous ones, the cells which divide uncontrollably, attack the tissue, and hence can enter the bloodstream, forming new tumors in other body parts.

S. Rajagopal et al. (Eds.): ASCIS 2022, CCIS 1759, pp. 416–434, 2022.
https://doi.org/10.1007/978-3-031-23092-9_33

Currently, there is no effective way that could prevent the occurrence of breast cancer. Extensive research is being carried out by researchers and medical professionals day in and day out, however, the best method for treating breast cancer is yet to be explored that could obtain the long-awaited treatment and also guarantees reliable evidence for its prevention. There are many factors by which breast cancer can occur. Some of these include ionizing radiation, prior family history of breast cancer, therapies involving hormone replacement during menopause, k line Felter syndrome, lack of exercise, obesity, and alcohol consumption.

Moreover, the disease can be grouped into five stages, O-IV. These stages are differentiated by the size of tumors which can be identified as invasive or non-invasive cancer. The survival chance decreases as the stage progresses to IV [7]. A huge amount of data is being generated day in and day out in the healthcare sector due to which radiologists may face problems to identify suspicious regions of cancer. So, to reduce the workload on medical professionals, different intelligent decision-making systems have been proposed in the literature that has always assisted radiologists in a better way, thus providing a second pair of eyes for clinicians. Early detection and correct diagnosis of breast cancer are very critical to avoid any sort of complications. It also plays a crucial role in breast cancer analysis. It is very important to detect breast cancer malignancies at early stages. The timely and effective treatment of this disease if done increases the survival probability and decreases the mortality rate. The content of this paper is structured as follows: Section 2 describes the various modalities that have been used from time to time for the BCD problem while Section 3 presents the various state-of-the-art deep learning (DL) based models proposed for this problem.

2   Medical Imaging Modalities for Analysis of BCD

In the literature, researchers have focused on medical images to provide better assistance to specialist radiologists. The different image modalities that have been used for breast cancer detection include Mammograms (MGs) [8], Ultrasound (US) [9], Magnetic Resonance Imaging (MRI) [10], Computed Tomography (CT), and Positron Emission Tomography (PET) [11], Histopathology [12] and Breast Thermography (BT) [13]. Systematic reviews show that the statistics published concerning medical imaging modalities have approximately 50% of mammogram datasets, 20% of ultrasound datasets, 18% of MRI datasets, and 8% of histopathological image datasets. The remaining datasets are either private or other modality datasets [14, 15]. Among all these imaging modalities, the most commonly used are mammograms [16–18]. The X-ray mammography is considered the primary screening tool for breast cancer detection, which is then followed by an ultrasound that performs a follow-up to acquire some more diagnostic information. For only special cases, MRI is used, but due to the high computational cost, its value for screening is still under debate. Thus, mammography and ultrasound are considered the effective modality for breast cancer screening in women whose age is under 40 years, as compared to the other methods e.g., biopsy. Figure 1 lists some well-known BCD image modalities.

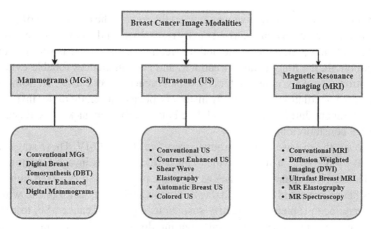

Fig. 1. Breast cancer image modalities.

2.1 Mammograms

IN the form of public datasets, mammogram datasets are easily available and accessible, thus making them the most frequently used imaging modality. Mammography is a diagnostic procedure in which low-intensity X-rays are used for breast examination and is currently the most recommended approach for screening due to its high reliability and low cost. The basic structure of mammograms is shown in Figure 2. These scans can reveal architectural defects, masses, microcalcifications, and bilateral asymmetry [19]. It has been proven that mammography is an effective method that reduces the mortality rate by 30%. Masses and microcalcifications are early indicators of breast cancer, which can be revealed through mammography. As evident from Figure 2, the cancerous tumors and microcalcifications appear brighter than the resting tissue of the breast. Thus, the diagnosis is easy and fast, if these images are analyzed by expert radiologists.

The mammograms that were used initially are called screen film mammograms (SFM). With the development in technology, the more advanced forms of mammograms are digital breast tomosynthesis (DBT), full-field digital mammograms (FFDMGs), and contrast-enhanced digital mammograms (CEDM). Each of these categories has been used widely for breast lesion classification as well as detection as shown in Figure 1.

2.2 Ultrasound

Although mammography is a highly adopted modality for early detection of breast cancer, there are certain health risks associated with mammograms which include overdosage of radiation and also ionizing radiation risks for both radiologists and patients. Moreover, this leads a large population in the range of 65% to 85% to unnecessary biopsy operations due to its low specificity [21, 22]. These unnecessary biopsy operations increase the hospitalization cost and also cause mental stress for individuals. Because of these limitations, the breast ultrasound modality is considered a better option for the analysis and detection of breast cancer [23].

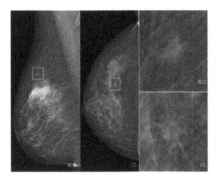 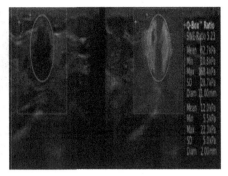

Fig. 2. Breast Mammogram [20].   **Fig. 3.** Left side: Grayscale 2D Ultrasound image; Right side: Shear-wave elastography image [24].

Ultrasound imaging modality is a relatively accessible, affordable, and non-ionizing method for lesion detection with the advantage of high sensitivity and specificity. In certain cases, X-ray mammography has limitations in lesion detection for dense breasts. However, ultrasound is an effective modality for women with dense breasts and breast mass differentiation as well. The ultrasound also imposes certain limitations such as limited reproducibility and operator dependency. When compared to mammography, it is shown in the literature that US image modality can increase the detection rate by 17% and decrease unnecessary biopsy operations by 40%. In medical terminology, US images are also called sonograms. These are used to detect the suspected lesions or regions of interest in the breast. The ultrasound images are used in three combinations, viz 2-D greyscale images, color ultrasound images with shear wave elastography (SWE) added features [24], and Nakagami-colored US images. The left side of Figure 3 shows the simple grayscale US image in which the black spot represents the irregular mass present in the breast. On the right side of Figure 3, the irregular mass appears in colors and has clear distinguishing boundaries. The colored images can detect regular masses in a better way. There are some other images other than SWE and Nakagami images that have also been reported in the literature.

2.3 MRI

MRI uses a magnetic field and radio waves for capturing detailed images of body tissues. It captures multiple images of a breast and combines them in a single image to provide a more detailed view. Figure 4 shows a sample breast MRI images.

In contrast to other image modalities, the MRI provides relatively higher sensitivity for lesion detection. Once cancer has been diagnosed, the radiologist or the doctors usually suggest undergoing MRI, since it provides a detailed view of breast tissue. Sometimes, MRI is used for suspicious breast tissue identification for biopsy purposes which is commonly called MRI-guided biopsy. The detection of breast lesions using an MRI provides high sensitivity [25] but with the limitation of the high cost associated with it [26]. However, other techniques are also introduced in MRI recently which provide

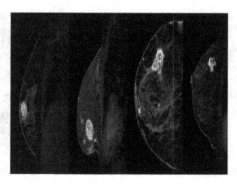

Fig. 4. Sample breast MRI image [44].

relatively high screening specificity and sensitivity in a shorter period with reduced cost [27, 28]. These include diffusion-weighted imaging (DWI) and ultrafast breast MRI (UFMRI). Table 1 lists the merits and demerits of each imaging modality.

Table 1. Image modalities for breast cancer.

Modalities	Pros	Cons
Mammograms	• Mammography is very economical and is generally the first approach for the diagnosis of breast cancer • Mammography is cost-effective and provides an efficient solution to capture breast tissue images • A huge number of digital MGs are available to train AI systems	• These are low-dose X-rays and have limited capabilities to capture micro calcifications due to the small sizes and distributed shape properties • MGs poses limitation in the diagnosis of breast cancer in dense breasts by missing cancerous tissues • Sometimes, small-sized microcalcifications are missed, thus additional procedures are required for accurate diagnosis
Ultrasound	• The US provides high flexibility in viewing breast lesions from various angles and orientations • It captures images in a real-time fashion, thus helping in reducing the chances of false negative cases • In this type of modality, the patients are not exposed to any kind of harmful radiation, and thus is considered a safe procedure, especially for pregnant women • Unlike mammography, US detects the breast cancer in dense breasts as well	• Unlike mammography, US images are of poor quality • It can mislead diagnosis if the scanner is not operated properly • Extracting the region of interest is not easy in US images

(*continued*)

Table 1. (*continued*)

Modalities	Pros	Cons
MRI	• It shows a detailed view of the internal tissues of the breast, thus can locate small breast lesions that can be missed by US and mammography • It does not expose patients to harmful radiation • It can detect suspicious regions in the breast that can be investigated further with biopsy, also called MRI-guided biopsy	• Unlike US or MGs which are very cost- effective, the MRI is a highly expensive method for screening breast cancer • It is usually the second option after the mammography • It is not recommended for pregnant women • To enhance the MRI images, usually, the contrasting agents are injected into patients which can cause allergies, especially for kidney patients, and thus it is not recommended in these cases

3 Present State-of-the-Art DL Methods for BCD

This section substantiates the recent state-of-the-art DL methods for early BCD as described in Figure 5. These models have been divided into 3 categories. The summary of these reviewed papers has been presented in Table 2.

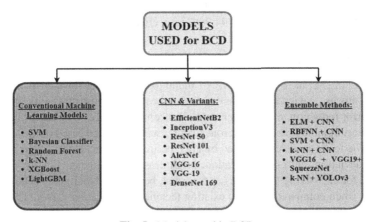

Fig. 5. Models used in BCD.

3.1 Conventional Machine Learning

In [29], the authors presented a machine learning approach along with image processing techniques to increase the chances of treatment and survival rate. For this framework, the input data used were the set of mammog ram images. The quality of images was improved by using the CLAHE algorithm. This technique is the improved version of basic histogram equalization, removes noise from images, and hence enhances the image quality. The second step in their framework was image segmentation, which was performed using the K-means algorithm where the image was divided into different segments, which helped in object and boundary location. Finally, the pre-processed images were classified using machine learning algorithms which include Bayesian classifier, fuzzy SVM, and random forest. The highest performance was reported by the fuzzy SVM classifier, the accuracy of which was around 96%.

The dataset used in this study [30], was gathered from a local hospital which contains 912 images (312 malignant and 600 benign). To obtain the ground truth, segmentation-based binarization was done. Also, the algorithm was developed for outline detection which enabled them to identify the image shapes. Certain parameters were set in the process of feature extraction. Finally, five machine learning classifiers were used: kNN, SVM, Random Forest, XGBoost, and LightGBM. The Bayesian optimization tree-structured Parzen estimator was used for optimization along with machine learning. 185 features were extracted from the images and saved in a tabular format with a CSV extension. A wavelet filter was used to remove the speckled noise. Out of 185 extracted features, 13 features were selected to train the machine learning algorithms. The feature selection was done using an embedded method that combines the qualities of filter and wrapper methods. The model was validated by a 10-fold cross-validation technique. Four metrics were used to assess the performance of the model, which include accuracy, F1 score, recall, and precision. The highest performance was produced by the LightGBM classifier with an accuracy of 99.86%, recall of 99.60%, the precision of 100%, and F1 score of 99.80%. The accuracy metric for K-NN, SVM, random forest, and XGBoost was 92.99%, 96.17%, 95.08%, and 94.96% respectively.

3.2 CNN & Variants

The authors in [31] have used the MIAS mammogram dataset for their work. For the denoising process, a wiener filter was employed, the main purpose of which was the mean squared error reduction, and to filter out noise from the images. For segmentation, the K-means technique was used. Numerous features were extracted based on the segmented images. The features were computed by area, perimeter, compactness, mean, variance, standard deviation, entropy, correlation, brightness, and diameter. Finally, CNN was employed for classifying the images into normal, benign, and malignant. The proposed technique when compared with the existing techniques performed better. The training accuracy of the proposed method was 96.94%, whereas the sensitivity and specificity were 96.23% and 98.32% respectively. The testing accuracy of CNN was reported as 97.14%, while the sensitivity and specificity were 96.52% and 98.88% respectively.

This work [32] is based on the concept of multi-stage transfer Learning (MSTL). Two ultrasound datasets were used in this study. First, the model was pre-trained on the ImageNet dataset which was then used for the classification of breast image datasets. The ultrasound images were subjected to augmentation which includes rotation and vertical flip. This resulted in increasing the training image dataset three-fold. During training, the weights of pre-trained models were fine-tuned excluding the last layer. The other parameters were kept the same as those of the pre-trained images. The number of epochs at each transfer learning stage was set to 50 after careful study of 20 to 150 ep ochs. Initially, the learning rate was set at 0.001. The batch size during training was taken as 16. The three optimizers were used along with models, stochastic gradient descent (SGD), Adam optimizer, and Adagrad. InceptionV3 and Adagrad together achieved an average accuracy of 92%, with an AUC of 0.981, F1 score of 0.945, specificity of 0.95, the sensitivity of 0.94, and loss of 0.208. While the EfficientNetb2 and Adagrad obtained an average accuracy of 90%, AUC of 0.992, F1 measure of 0.965, specificity of 0.97, sensitivity of 0.96, and loss of 0.207. The highest average test accuracy was reported on ResNet50 with Adagrad optimizer as 98%, with AUC of 0.999, F1-Measure of 0.989, specificity of 0.98, the sensitivity of 1, and loss of 0.030 respectively.

In this work [33], mini—the DDSM dataset was used to classify the images into normal, benign, and cancerous. The images were of different sizes, so the image resizing was done. There are generally two methods for resizing the images, cropping the border pixels and scaling them down. The literature has shown that scaling is a more reasonable choice than cropping. Also, the data augmentation was applied based on geometric transformations, which include zooming, rotation, and flipping. In their approach, commonly used CNN architectures were AlexNet, VGG16, and ResNet50. Some CNN models were pre-trained using the ImageNet dataset and some were trained from scratch. When trained from scratch, AlexNet and VGG16 obtained an accuracy of 65.89% and 37.56% respectively and when using pre-trained weights, the accuracy for VGG16 and ResNet50 was 65.70% and 62.26% respectively. Their study concluded that transfer learning models perform better than the network classifiers which are trained from scratch.

In this study [34], a probability-based deep learning methodology was implemented. The BUSI dataset was used which has three levels, normal, benign, and malignant. Their framework comprises of five steps, wherein the first step, data augmentation was done to increase the size of the training dataset. In the second step, the DarkNet-53 model was implemented which is the basis for the YOLOv3 object detection method. Combining Resnet's qualities avoids the gradient problem that arises from the too-deep neural network. In the third step, transfer learning was used for training purposes and the features were extracted from the Global Average Pooling (GAP) layer. The learning rate of the training model was 0.001, the batch size was 16, the number of epochs was set as 200 and the learning method used was stochastic gradient descent. In the fourth step, the optimization was done on the extracted features by two reformed optimization algorithms. These were grey wolf and differential evolution algorithms. Finally, the best-optimized features were fused into one feature vector, for which a probability-based serial approach was used. Their experiment reported the best accuracy of 99.1%.

In this work [35], a model was suggested that could lower the false positive rate (FPR), and false negative rate (FNR) and increase the MCC without altering the value of accuracy. To detect breast tumors, a modified network of YOLOv5 was used. In the initial stage, the rough white borders, artifacts, and pectoral muscles were removed. The elimination of white lines was done by cropping the image area by using some cropping function. For image enhancement, the CLAHE algorithm was used. The images were then subjected to the morphological procedure which is a set of non-linear procedures. Morphological operations remove the minor features from images while retaining the more extensive details. The images were annotated by using Roboflow an online source. Finally, all the versions of the Yolov5 network were employed. The proposed model was also compared with the YOLOv3 and faster RCNN. The YOLOv3 obtained an accuracy of 86%, Faster RCNN obtained an accuracy of 85.3%, whereas a modified YOLOv5x obtained the highest accuracy of 96.50%, FPR of 0.04, Map of 96%, FNR of 0.03 and MCC of 93.50%.

In this study [36], a transferable texture CNN deep learning method has been proposed for the classification of breast cancer using mammograms. In their work, three datasets were used v.i.z. DDSM, INbreast, and MIAS. To refine the details of edges and to adjust the contrast and standard brightness of the source images, the histogram equalization CLAHE method was used. Next, the TTCNN is presented which consists of two convolutional layers, the pooling layer and the 3rd convolutional layer directs the energy layer. Finally, a softMax layer was used with a fully connected layer. The performance of TTCNN was analyzed based on the deep features of several variants of pre-trained CNN models which include InceptionResNet-V2, VGG-16, Inception V3, VGG-19, ResNet 18, GoogleNet, ResNet-50, and ResNet-101. Finally, the extracted feature vectors were fused by the convolutional sparse image decomposition method (CSID). The best features of the model were selected by using the entropy-controlled firefly approach (ECfA). The proposed TTCNN model produced the best possible results on the DDSM dataset, with a specificity of 98.96%, a sensitivity of 99.19%, and an accuracy of 99.08%. On the INbreast dataset, the accuracy obtained is 96.82% with specificity and sensitivity of 97.68% and 95.99% respectively. On the MIAS dataset, the value of accuracy was 96.57%, with a specificity of 97.03% and a sensitivity of 96.11% respectively.

The authors in this study [37] focused on the principle of transfer learning. To avoid the problem of overfitting, data augmentation including reflection, rotation, scaling, and shifting was done to generate a new set of images. After the data augmentation step, the adaptive contrast enhancement technique was used, which improves the edge and curve visibility in each image part. Over the pre-processed images, the DL approaches: a modified version of ResNet-50 and NasNet-Mobile were employed, to learn useful and discriminative feature representations. Their suggested model produced an accuracy of 89.5%, precision of 89.5%, recall of 89.5%, and F1 score of 89.5% when ModRes was used along with oversampling, whereas for the NasNet-Mobile, the accuracy reached 70%, with a precision of 83.3%, F1-score of 62.5% and recall of 50%. Their proposed methodology (ModRes+oversampling) outperforms the existing models.

The authors [38] have presented a CAD system that holds great promise in cancer detection. They have used internal as well as the public dataset for their study. The dataset was split into two data pools, the first data pool for lesion detection and the second data pool for lesion classification. The images were augmented spatially by computing the square root, Laplacian of Gaussian, logarithm, exponential, wavelet and squared derivatives. For lesion detection, YOLOv3 and viola-Jones algorithms were used. For evaluating the breast lesion detection: intersection over union (IoU), recall, localization error (LE), precision, and F1-score were employed. For breast lesion classification: sensitivity, specificity and accuracy were used. In the test step, the IoU was 0.3986 ± 0.0540 for viola-Jones when taking the dataset with all augmentations and LE was 0.0959 ± 0.0162. For YOLOv3, when considering LN+ spatial augmentations, IoU was $0.5442 \pm$

Table 2. Models on breast cancer detection

Author/ year	Images used	Purpose	Dataset	Methodologies	Evaluation parameters
S. Chaudhury et al. [29], 2022	MGs	Classification of images into benign, normal and malignant	MIAS	CLAHE + Image Segmentation (K-means Algorithm) + Fuzzy SVM, Bayesian Classifier, Random Forest	Accuracy: 96% Sensitivity: 95% Specificity: 93% Precision: 95% Recall: 95%
E. Michael et al. [30], 2022	US	Classification into benign and malignant lesions	Proposed Dataset	**Pre-Processing:** Wavelet filter BO-TPE (Bayesian optimization-Tree structured Parzen Estimator) **Classification:** SVM, k-NN, RF, XGBoost, LightGBM	**LightGBM:** Accuracy: 99.86% Precision: 100.00% Recall: 99.60% F1-score: 99.80%
U Albalawi et al. [31], 2020	MGs	Classification of images into benign, normal and malignant	MIAS	**Pre-Processing:** Weiner Filter Segmentation using Thresholding Mass Detection: K-means **Classification:** CNN	Accuracy: 97.143% Sensitivity:96.522% Specificity:98.883%

(continued)

Table 2. (*continued*)

Author/ year	Images used	Purpose	Dataset	Methodologies	Evaluation parameters
G. Ayana et al. [32], 2022	US	Classification of US images into benign and malignant	Mendeley dataset MT-Small-Dataset	**MSTL** (Multistage Transfer Learning) Using EfficientNetB2, InceptionV3, and ResNet50 **Optimizers:** Adam, Adagrad, and SGD (Stochastic Gradient Descent)	**Resnet50 + Adagrad:** Best Accuracy: 99 ± 0.612% Loss: 0.03 AUC: 0.999 Specificity:0.98 Sensitivity: 1 F1- measure:0.989
S. Mohapatra et al. [33], 2022	MGs	Classification into benign, normal and cancerous images	mini-DDSM	**For Resize:** Scaling Augmentation: Rotation, Flipping, Zooming **Classification:** AlexNet, VGG-16, ResNet Optimizer: Adam	**Pre-Trained VGG16:** Epochs = 50 Spe:0.9035% Sen:0.9124% Accuracy: 0.6570%
K. Jabeen et al. [34], 2022	US	Classification into normal, benign and malignant	BUSI	**Data Augmentation:** (Horizontal flip, vertical flip, and rotate 90) + **Pre-Trained** DarkNet-53 Feature Selection: Reformed Differential Evaluation (RDE) and Reformed Gray Wolf (RGW)	Best Accuracy: 99.1%

(*continued*)

Table 2. (*continued*)

Author/ year	Images used	Purpose	Dataset	Methodologies	Evaluation parameters
A. Mohiyuddin et al. [35], 2022	MGs	Detection and classification	CBIS- DDSM	CLAHE + Data Augmentation + YOLOv3, modified YOLOv5x, and Faster RCNN	**Using YOLOv5x:** mAP: 96%, Acc: 96.50% FPR: 0.04 FNR 0.03
S. Maqsood et al. [36], 2022	MGs	Classification into benign, normal and cancerous images	1) DDSM 2) INbreast 3) MIAS	**CLAHE** (Contrast Limited Adaptive Histogram Equalization) + **TTCNN** (Transferable Texture Convolutional Neural Network) Feature vectors fusion by: Convolutional sparse image decomposition Feature selection: Entropy-controlled firefly approach	**On DDSM dataset:** Specificity: 98.96% Sensitivity: 99.19% Accuracy: 99.08% **On INbreast dataset:** Accuracy: 96.82% Specificity:97.68% Sensitivity:95.99% **On MIAS dataset:** Accuracy: 96.57% Specificity: 97.03% Sensitivity: 96.11%
M. Alruwaili et al. [37], 2022	MGs	Classification into benign and malignant cases	MIAS	**Data Augmentation** (Rotation, Reflection, Shifting, and Scaling) Transfer Learning 1) MOD-RES 2) Nasnet-Mobile network	**Using MOD-RES:** Accuracy: 89.5% Precision: 89.5% Recall:89.5% F1-score: 89.5% **Using Nasnet-Mobile:** Accuracy: 70% Precision: 83.3% Recall:50% F1-score: 62.5%

(*continued*)

Table 2. (*continued*)

Author/ year	Images used	Purpose	Dataset	Methodologies	Evaluation parameters
Z.A. Magnuska et al. [38], 2022	US	Detection and classification	BUSI	**For Lesion Detection:** 1) Viola–Jones 2) YOLOv3 **For Classification** Weighted KNN Manual Segmentation dataset) Ensemble Subspace KNN (trained on YOLOv3 dataset) Median KNN (trained on Viola-Jones dataset)	**For Detection** IoU: $0.544 + 0.081$ LE: $0.171 + 0.009$ **For Classification Weighted KNN** Accuracy:85% Sensitivity:83.33% Specificity:87.50%
J.G. Melekoodappattu et al. [39], 2022	MGs	Classification of images into normal and abnormal classes	MIAS DDSM	**Pre-Processing:** Median Filter-For Noise Removal CLAHE-For Image Enhancement Dimensionality Reduction: UMAP (Uniform Manifold Approximation Projection) **Classification:** Ensemble (ELM, RBFNN, SVM, KNN to CNN)	**On MIAS Dataset** PPV: 0.936 NPV:1.000 SP:0.978 SE: 1.000 ACC:0.980 **On DDSM Dataset** PPV: 0.924 NPV:0.974 SP: 0.983 SE:0.932 ACC: 0.979

(*continued*)

Table 2. (continued)

Author/ year	Images used	Purpose	Dataset	Methodologies	Evaluation parameters
M. Ragab et al. [40], 2022	US	Classification into normal, benign and malignant	BUSI	**EDLCDS-BCDC** (Ensemble Deep-Learning-Enabled Clinical Decision Support System for Breast Cancer Diagnosis and Classification) Pre-processing: 1) wiener filtering, CLAHE, CKHA Feature Extraction: VGG16+ VGG-19+ Squeeze Net Classification: Cat Swarm Optimization + MLP	Epochs = 250 Accuracy: 97.52% Sensitivity:96.01% Specificity: 97.95% Precision:95.39%
I. D. Naranjo et al. [41], 2022	MRI	Classification	Private Dataset	Multiparametric radiomics with ADC values and individual BI-RADS descriptors for masses	Sens:88.6% Spe: 93.9% Acc:91.7%
A. Mohammed [42], 2022	MRI	Classification	BACH Dataset	Color deconvolution and color normalization Pre-trained CNN ResNet 50 ResNet 101 Densenet169	Resnet50: Acc: 0.85 Resnet101: Acc:0.88 Densenet169: Acc: 0.82 Ensemble (Resnet50 Resnet101 Densenet169): Acc: 0.925
Basem S. Abunaser et al. [43], 2022	MRI	Classification	BreakHis	Xception model	Precision: 97.60% Recall: 97.60% F1-Score: 97.58%

0.0808 and LE was 0.1706 ± 0.0094. For classification purposes: manual segmentation, viola-Jones and YOLOv3 classification subsets were used. The highest performance was shown by weighted k-NN when trained on the manual segmentation dataset with an accuracy of 85%, sensitivity of 83.33% and specificity of 87.50% respectively.

3.3 Ensemble Models

In this suggested method [39], the architecture consisted of four stages which include pre-processing, classification using CNN, feature extraction-based classification and finally the integration system. The most important step in image processing is denoising. This approach reduces the noise present in the images while preserving its key characteristics. So, for this purpose, a median filter was used. For additional pre-processing, the image enhancement was performed using the CLAHE method. The features were extracted by using the Gabor filter and multi-scale local binary patterns (LBP). For dimensionality reduction, Linear discriminant analysis and uniform manifold approximation and projection (UMAP) were used. Finally, the ensemble approach was used in which different classifiers were combined with the CNN model. K-NN, when ensembled with CNN, achieved a positive predicted value (PPV) of 88.5%, negative predicted value (NPV) of 97.8%, specificity of 96.7%, the sensitivity of 93.4% and accuracy of 96.1%. For the feature extraction-based method, LBP achieved an accuracy of 92.4%, PPV of 77.8%, NPV of 95.4%, specificity of 95.4% and sensitivity of 77.8%. The highest accuracy of 95.2% was reported when LBP was used along with UMAP, the PPV of which was 84.2%, NPV was 97.7%, specificity of 96.6% and sensitivity of 88.9%. For their work, they employed two datasets, MIAS and DDSM. For the MIAS dataset, the ensemble system achieved an accuracy of 98%, PPV of 93.6%, NPV of 100%, specificity of 97.8% and sensitivity of 100%. On the DDSM repository, the accuracy obtained was 97.9%, PPV was 92.4%, NPV was 97.4%, specificity was 98.3% and sensitivity was 93.2%.

This study [40] involves the use of a novel approach called EDLCDS-BCDC for breast cancer classification. Their proposed work involves the pre-processing of the original image dataset which was done in two stages: noise elimination and contrast enhancement. Extraction of noise is an important step in pre-processing because image features can be corrupted by noise. For this purpose, a wiener filter was used. The CLAHE technique was used for contrast enhancement. For image segmentation, the Chaotic Krill Herd (CKH) algorithm was applied. For the feature extraction process, an ensemble of VGG-16, VGG-19 and SqueezeNet was used. The generated feature vectors were fed to the multilayer perceptron (MLP). For optimal adjustment of weights of MLP, Cat Swarm Optimization (CSO) was used. Experiments were performed on varying the number of Epochs. It was shown that on 250 epochs, the highest accuracy of 97.52% was reported. Moreover, the sensitivity, specificity and precision were 96.01%, 97.95% and 95.39% respectively. The work done on MRI datasets is very less due to its high computational cost, however, some of the studies have employed deep learning on MRI for the detection of breast cancer [41–43]. The distribution of the various models reviewed in this study is illustrated in Figure 6, while Figures 7 and 8 present the distribution and usage statistics of various BCD datasets.

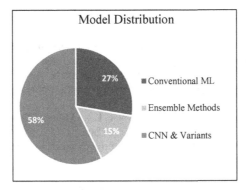

Fig. 6. Distribution of Models for BCD reviewed in this study.

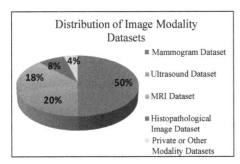

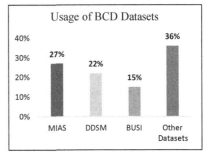

Fig. 7. Modality-wise BCD dataset distribution.   **Fig. 8.** Distribution of datasets usage.

4 Conclusion

Deep learning is cutting-edge technology in the field of medical imaging. It has been effectively used for several tasks related to medical image analysis, including the region of interest detection, segmentation, illness severity, and classification. In this work, many applications of deep learning and machine learning for the identification of breast cancer have been analyzed. The discussion of several imaging techniques, including mammograms, MRIs, and ultrasounds, has also been covered. The strength of this study in terms of machine learning algorithms is SVM, k-NN, and random forest, while CNN and its variants are in terms of deep learning architectures. Deep learning's standard summary of the detection process includes the following steps: (i) preprocessing of images to remove noise and artifacts; (ii) contrast enhancement and image segmentation; (iii) feature extraction; and (iv) classification. It is clear from the vast majority of current research that mammography is the most often employed imaging modality for the early diagnosis of breast cancer.

References

1. Nakamura, Y., Takada, M., Imamura, M., et al.: Usefulness and prospects of sentinel lymph node biopsy for patients with breast cancer using the medical imaging projection system. Front. Oncol. **11**, PMID: 34123842; PMCID: PMC8187896, Article ID 674419 (2021)
2. Network, C.G.A., et al.: Comprehensive molecular portraits of human breast tumors. Nature **490**(7418), 61 (2012)
3. DeSantis, C.E., Ma, J., Gaudet, M.M., Newman, L.A., Miller, K.D., Goding Sauer A., Jemal, A., Siegel, R.L: Breast cancer statistics. CA: A Cancer J. Clin. **69**(6), 438–451 (2019).
4. Man, R., Yang, P., Xu, B.: Classification of breast cancer histopathological images using discriminative patches screened by generative adversarial networks. IEEE Access **8**, 155362–155377 (2020)
5. https://www.who.int/news-room/fact-sheets/detail/breast-cancer, last accessed 2022/10/19.
6. Mambou, S.J., Maresova, P., Krejcar, O., Selamat, A., Kuca, K.: Breast cancer detection using infrared thermal imaging and a deep learning model. Sensors **18**(9), 2799 (2018)
7. Dey,B., Kumar, A.: A review article on breast cancer. Int. J. Pharm. Pharm. Res. **11**(2), 284–298 (2018)
8. Moghbel, M., Ooi, C.Y., Ismail, N., Hau, Y.W., Memari, N.: A review of breast boundary and pectoral muscle segmentation methods in computer-aided detection/diagnosis of breast mammography. Artif. Intell. Rev., 1–46 (2019)
9. Kozegar, E., Soryani, M., Behnam, H., Salamati, M., Tan, T.: Computer aided detection in automated 3-d breast ultrasound images: a survey. Artif. Intell. Rev. 1–23 (2019)
10. Murtaza, G., Shuib, L., Wahab, A.W.A., Mujtaba, G., Nweke, H.F., Al-garadi, M.A., Zulfiqar, F., Raza, G., Azmi, N.A.: Deep learning-based breast cancer classification through medical imaging modalities: state of the art and research challenges. Artif. Intell. Rev., 1–66 (2019)
11. Domingues, I., Pereira, G., Martins, P., Duarte, H., Santos, J., Abreu, P.H.: Using deep learning techniques in medical imaging: a systematic review of applications on CT and PET. Artif. Intell. Rev. **53**(6), 4093–4160 (2020)
12. Saha, M., Chakraborty, C., Racoceanu, D.: Efficient deep learning model for mitosis detection using breast histopathology images. Comput. Med. Imag. Graph. **64**, 29–40 (2018)
13. Moghbel, M., Mashohor, S.: A review of computer assisted detection/diagnosis (cad) in breast thermography for breast cancer detection. Artif. Intell. Rev. **39**(4), 305–313 (2013)
14. Murtaza, G., Shuib, L., Abdul Wahab, A.W., Mujtaba, G., Nweke, H.F., Al-garadi, M.A., Zulfiqar, F., Raza, G., Azmi, N.A.: Deep learning-based breast cancer classification through medical imaging modalities: state of the art and research challenges. Artif. Intell. Rev. **53**(3), 1655–1720 (2020)
15. Hadadi, I., Rae, W., Clarke, J., McEntee, M., Ekpo, E.: Diagnostic performance of adjunctive imaging modalities compared to mammography alone in women with non-dense and dense breasts: a systematic review and meta-analysis. Clin. Breast Cancer (2021)
16. Cheng, H.D., Cai, X., Chen, X., Hu, L., Lou, X.: Computer-aided detection and classification of microcalcifications in mammograms: a survey. Pattern Recogn. **36**(12), 2967–2991 (2003)
17. Cheng, H.D., Shi, X., Min, R., Hu, L., Cai, X., Du, H.: Approaches for automated detection and classification of masses in mammograms. Pattern Recogn. **39**(4), 646–668 (2006)
18. Suh, Y.J., Jung, J., Cho, B.J.: Automated breast cancer detection in digital mammograms of various densities via deep learning. J. Personalized Med. **10**(4), 211 (2020)
19. Tabl, A., Alkhateeb, A., ElMaraghy, W., Rueda, L., Ngom, A.: A machine learning approach for identifying gene biomarkers guiding the treatment of breast cancer. Front. Genet. **10**, 256 (2019)
20. Lang, K., Dustler, M., Dahlblom, V., Akesson, A., Andersson, I., Zackrisson, S.: identifying normal mammograms in a large screening population using artificial intelligence. Eur. Radiol. **31**(3), 1687–1692 (2021)

21. Jesneck, J.L., Lo, J.Y., Baker, J.A.: Breast mass lesions: computer-aided diagnosis models with mammographic and sonographic descriptors. Radiology **244**(2), 390–398 (2007)
22. Cheng, H.D., Shan, J., Ju, W., Guo, Y., Zhang, L.: Automated breast cancer detection and classification using ultrasound images: a survey. Pattern Recogn. **43**(1), 299–317 (2010)
23. Han, J., Li, F., Peng, C., Huang, Y., Lin, Q., Liu, Y., Cao, L., Zhou, J.: Reducing unnecessary biopsy of breast lesions: preliminary results with combination of strain and shear-wave elastography. Ultrasound Med. Biol. **45**(9), 2317–2327 (2019)
24. Youk, J.H., Gweon, H.M., Son, E.J.: Shear-wave elastography in breast ultrasonography: the state of the art. Ultrasonography **36**(4), 300 (2017)
25. Houssami, N., Cho, N.: Screening women with a personal history of breast cancer: overview of the evidence on breast imaging surveillance. Ultrasonography **37**(4), 277 (2018)
26. Greenwood, H.I.: Abbreviated protocol breast mri: the past, present, and future. Clin. Imag. **53**, 169–173 (2019)
27. van Zelst, J.C., Vreemann, S., Witt, H.J., Gubern-Merida, A., Dorrius, M.D., Duvivier, K., Lardenoije-Broker, S., Lobbes, M.B., Loo, C., Veldhuis W.: Multireader study on the diagnostic accuracy of ultrafast breast magnetic resonance imaging for breast cancer screening. Invest. Radiol. **53**(10), 579–586 (2018)
28. Heller, S.L., Moy, L.: MRI breast screening revisited. J. Magn. Reson. Imag. **49**(5), 1212–1221 (2019)
29. Chaudhury, S. et al.: Effective Image Processing and Segmentation-Based Machine Learning Techniques for Diagnosis of Breast Cancer. Computational and Mathematical Methods in Medicine, Hindawi (2022)
30. Michael E. et al.: An Optimized Framework for Breast Cancer Classification Using Machine Learning. BioMed Research International, pp. 1–18 (2022).
31. Albalawi,U, Manimurugan, S, Varatharajan, R.: Classification of breast cancer mammogram images using convolution neural network. Concurr. Comput. Pract. Exper. **34**, e5803 (2020)
32. Ayana, G. et al,: A novel multistage transfer learning for ultrasound breast cancer image classification. Diagnostics **12**, 135 (2022).
33. Mohapatra, S., Muduly, S., Mohanty, S., Ravindra, J.V.R., Mohanty, S.N.: Evaluation of deep learning models for detecting breast cancer using mammograms images. Sustain. Oper. Comput. **3**, 296–302 (2022)
34. Jabeen, K., Khan, M.A., Alhaisoni, M., Tariq, U., Zhang, Y.D., Hamza, A., Mickus, A., Damasevicius, R.: Breast cancer classification from ultrasound images using probability-based optimal deep learning feature fusion. Sensors **22**, 807 (2022)
35. Mohiyuddin, A. et al.: Breast tumor detection and classification in mammogram images using modified YOLOv5 network. Comput. Math. Methods Med., 1–16 (2022)
36. Maqsood, S., Damasevicius, R., Maskeli unas, R.: TTCNN: A breast cancer detection and classification towards computer-aided diagnosis using digital mammography in early stages. Appl. Sci. **12**, 3273 (2022)
37. Alruwaili,M., Gouda, W.: Automated breast cancer detection models based on transfer learning. Sensors **22**, 876 (2022)
38. Magnuska, Z.A., Theek, B., Darguzyte, M., Palmowski, M., Stickeler, E., Schulz, V., Kiebling, F.: Influence of the computer-aided decision support system design on ultrasound-based breast cancer classification. Cancers **14**, 277 (2022)
39. Melekoodappattu, J.G., Dhas, A.S., Kandathil, B.K., et al.: Breast cancer detection in mammogram: combining modified CNN and texture feature-based approach. J. Ambient Intell. Human Comput. (2022)
40. Ragab, M., Albukhari, A., Alyami, J., Mansour, R.F.: Ensemble deep-learning-enabled clinical decision support system for breast cancer diagnosis and classification on ultrasound images. Biology **11**, 439 (2022)

41. Daimiel Naranjo, I., Gibbs, P., Reiner, J.S., Lo Gullo, R., Thakur, S.B., Jochelson, M.S., Thakur, N., Baltzer, P.A.T., Helbich, T.H., Pinker, K.: Breast lesion classification with multi-parametric breast MRI using radiomics and machine learning: a comparison with radiologists performance. Cancers **14**, 1743 (2022)
42. Ammar, M., et al.: The impact of data processing and ensemble on breast cancer detection using deep learning. J. Comput. Commun. **1**(1), 27–37 (2022)
43. Basem S., Abunaser et al.: Breast Cancer Detection and Classification using Deep Learning Xception Algorithm. Int. J. Adv. Comput. Sci. Appl. (IJACSA) **13**(7) (2022)
44. Sheth, D., Giger, M.L.: Artificial intelligence in the interpretation of breast cancer on MRI. J. Magn. Reson. Imaging **51**(5), 1310–1324 (2020)

Development of Deep Learning-Based Predictive Models for Semen Quality Analysis

C. Shanthini$^{(\boxtimes)}$ and S. Silvia Priscila

Department of Computer Science, Bharath Institute of Higher Education and Research,
Chennai, India
rajeshshanthini@gmail.com,
silviaprisila.cbcs.cs@bharathuniv.ac.in

Abstract. Quality of the semen has a very important part of pregnancy. Sterility has many side causes and is one of the main reasons for the inability of the pairs. There is a way for detecting the ability of the semen which causes pregnancy by checking the quality of the sperm through clinical diagnosis. The overall concept of this work is to improve the prognostic methods for the national infertility monitoring system for accelerating and enabling the prevention, analysis, and follow-up of infertility. This work utilizes the WOA method for identifying the major features of the semen dataset. Deep Learning (DL) models like DT, RF, SVM and CNN are utilized for classifying the dataset. These methods are created for accomplishing the dependable and high grouping exactness of infertility analysis; anticipating original quality from a way of life data is becoming conceivable. The exhibition of the classifiers was evaluated on the basis of Accuracy, Precision and Recall values. The results shows that proposed CNN + WOA produces better results than other algorithms with Accuracy 95%, Precision 0.94 and Recall 0.89 respectively. The tool used for evaluation is python.

Keywords: Semen quality analysis · Precision · Recall · Accuracy · Deep Learning

1 Introduction

One of the major questions is the worldwide importance of public health strategies and projects to expand the population level and give reasonable, protected, and powerful administrations for families [1]. Sterility or its handling treatments can cause mental pressure, tension, and despondency. Over the most recent twenty years, concentrates on uncovering that there is a critical decrease in masculine infertility. Even though there are a few reasons for male infertility, the way of life is also the main reason. Accordingly, studying the impacts of Infertility and measuring progress in diminishing this issue becomes a major significant task. Infertility is one of the six parental illnesses/outcomes which has been disregarded everywhere [2].

Latest scientific examinations have noticed that the quality of semen has been decreasing because of this modern lifestyle. In this regard, a trial experiment was made in

S. Rajagopal et al. (Eds.): ASCIS 2022, CCIS 1759, pp. 435–445, 2022.
https://doi.org/10.1007/978-3-031-23092-9_34

detecting the quality of semen. The exhibition of the results has been diminished because of an expanded number of tests and the high dimensionality of elements/qualities in the dataset. Consequently, to address this problem, CNN's profound learning strategy, and WAO method for include the choice of anticipating semen quality.

Because of the advances in ML (Machine Learning) concepts, particularly the dependable and high categorization exactness of NN (Neural Network) in healthiness-related issues, anticipating original quality from the way of life data is becoming conceivable. Its ability in uncovering the nonlinear connection among various attributes can be utilized to appraise the quality of the semen. Imbalanced type datasets problems have been settled by utilizing feature selection techniques. For expanding the accuracy rate of the classifier, by decreasing the attributes dimension WOA strategy assumes a critical part. These techniques will diminish the execution time of the classification strategies, and enhance the accuracy value.

2 Literature Survey

Latest scientific examinations have noticed that the quality of semen in males is decreasing because of modern lifestyles and various environmental features. Clinical analysis of sperm features is one significant part of differencing the capability of semen for the event of pregnancy. Because of the advances in ML, particularly the dependable and high exactness of NN in well- being-related issues. Concerning this, a couple of research was made to detect the quality of the semen. These investigations were directed utilizing imbalanced type datasets, where the presentation results will more often than not be one-sided towards the majority case. Different examinations executed the gradient descent method for preparing the NN. The gradient descent method is a nearby preparation strategy that is inclined to stall out to neighbourhood minima. Abdulkerim M. Yibr et al. (2021) conducted a review for identifying semen quality. In this review, AAA (Artificial Algae Algorithm) is further developed utilizing a Learning-Based wellness assessment strategy proposed for preparing FFNN (Feed Forward Neural Network). Trial examinations were done to assess the prescient exactness of the FFNN prepared to utilize the Learning-Based Artificial Algae Algorithm (FFNN-LBAAA). The outcomes were contrasted and notable ML calculations, to be specific: KNN, NB (Naïve Bayes), SVM (Support Vector Machine), MLP (Multi-layer Perceptron Neural Network), RF (Random Forest) approaches. The recommended approach showed prevalent execution in segregating ordinary and strange semen quality occasions over the other analyzed algorithms [7].

The identification of variables affecting semen features is critical. A few investigations have revealed that masculine age and way of life openings, as opposed to hereditary issues, are principally answerable for strange semen quality. Way of life elements can be effortlessly adjusted without clinical interventions, and explaining the way of life factors influencing semen quality can direct males to go to suitable measures in the preconception time. Nonetheless, as depicted over, the ways of life prompting strange semen quality have not been explained, while the difficulty of this information made related examination troublesome. Mingjuan Zhou et al. (2022) developed a primer way of life and general component-based semen quality expectation model through ML with the XGBoost calculation by utilizing information gathered from 5,109 solid men. Moreover, since the exactness of ML calculations might be disabled due to over fitting or deficient information preparation, appliedLR (Logistic Regression) integrated with cross-validation to check the exactness and the possibility of an ML-based forecastingmodel [8].

Strategies for automatic examination of clinical information are normally focused on a particular methodology and don't utilize all important information accessible. In male reproduction, clinical data and biological information are not used to their fullest potential. Manual assessment of a semen test utilizing a magnifying lens is tedious and requires broad preparation. Moreover, the validity of manual semen examination has been addressed because of restricted reproducibility, and frequently high inter-personnel variation. The earlier computer-aided systems helped sperm analyzer frameworks are not prescribed for routine clinical use because of systemic difficulties brought about by the consistency of the semen test. Consequently, there is a requirement for a better system. Steven A. Hicks et al. (2019) utilize present-day and old-style ML strategies along with a dataset comprising 85 recordings of human semen tests and related member information to foresee sperm motility consequently. Adding member information didn't further develop the execution of the calculation. In all, ML-based programmed examination might turn into an important device in male infertility examination and investigation [10].

Current semen examination still ordinarily relies upon a manual microscopy strategy in clinical research facilities around the world. In any case, a portion of the significant hindrances of this procedure is that it is labor-intensive, emotional, based on laboratory, and time-taking. Even though CAAs (Computer Assisted Semen Analyzers) have empowered halfway computerization of routine semen examination, they need more extensive acknowledgment due to their complex work. Consequently, the improvement of an open, fast and normalized strategy for semen investigation is direly required. Ashok Agarwal et al. (2019) depict the turn of events and clinical testing of a novel, computerized, AIOM (AI Optical Microscopic) based innovation. In outline, our outcomes showed that the new X1 Master semen analyzer is a dependable symptomatic device for repetitive semen examination giving clinically satisfactory outcomes given World Health Organization (WHO) 5th Version instructions [11].

The motility of sperm is a significant file to assess semen quality. CASA (Computer Assisted Sperm Analysis) depends on the sperm picture, through an image-processing concept to recognize the place of the sperm goal and track the following, to pass judgment on the sperm movement. Due to the little and thick sperm focuses in sperm pictures, traditional image-processing algorithms calculations consume more time to recognize sperm focuses, while target-location calculations in light of the DL have a ton of missed identification issues during the time spent on sperm target recognition. To precisely and productively break down sperm action in sperm picture succession, Zhong Chen et al. (2022) propose a sperm action examination technique that depends on the DL approach. In the first place, the sperm position is identified through the DL highlight point identification network in the better SuperPoint, then the multi-sperm target following is brought out through SORT and the sperm movement direction is drawn, and finally, the sperm endurance is decided through the sperm direction to understand the examination of sperm action. The trial results demonstrate the way that this technique can examine sperm action in sperm picture succession. Simultaneously, the typical identification speed of the sperm target discovery technique in the recognition cycle is 65 fps, and the identification location exactness is 92% [12].

Fertility rates have decisively diminished over the most recent twenty years, particularly in men. It is portrayed that ecological variables, and s life propensities, may influence the quality of semen. . AI strategies are presently an arising procedure as DSS (Decision Support System) inhealthcare. In this research paper David Gil et al. (2012) analyze three AI procedures, MLP (Multilayer Perceptron), SVM, and DT tree to assess their exhibition in the prediction of the original quality from the information of the ecological elements and way of life. The authors gather information by a standardized survey from young strong volunteers and afterward, utilize the outcome of a semen examination to detect the exactness of the expectation of the three ML concepts already mentioned. The outcomes show that MLP and SVM show the most noteworthy precision, with expectation exactness upsides of 86% for a portion of the original boundaries. Conversely, DT gives a pictorial and illustrative methodology that can manage the marginally lower exactness got. Finally, all the AI methods are valuable devices to foresee the fundamental profile of a person from the environmental features and habits of life. From the concentrated strategies, MLP and SVM are the most reliable in the expectation. These models along with the visual assistance that DT offers are the recommended techniques to be remembered for the assessment of the infertile individual [13].

3   Proposed Methodology

The reproductive health condition of the male is significantly impacted by smoking and liquor consumption. Smoking has a priceless commitment to the decrease in sperm thickness, amount, and motility. Smoking is profoundly connected with lower semen quality. Sperm cells of more aged males are less motile and are exposed to sperm DNA discontinuity. Furthermore, diet, stress, caffeine, obesity, and habit-forming drugs are likewise among the way of life factors that influence semen quality [7]. The target of this work is to distinguish the way of life and environmental features that influences the quality of semen and fertility rate in man utilizing DL techniques. WOA Procedure applied for choosing significant highlights from a given dataset. DT, RF, SVM, and CNN prescient models are applied for Semen quality investigation. Following Fig. 1 exhibits the cycle stream of the proposed model.

Feature selection is the most common way of diminishing the number of information factors while creating a forecasting model. It is desirable to diminish the number of info factors to both lessen the computational expense of demonstrating and, now and again, to work on the exhibition of the model. SMOTE data balancing strategy was utilized to adjust typical and strange instances. WOA is presented for selecting major elements from the dataset. RF, DT, SVM, and CNN classifiers are presented for seminal predictive examination.

Decision Tree (DT)

DT is a kind of supervised type learning approach that is used in regression and categorization issues. The structure of the DT looks like a tree. Here the nodes indicate the dataset features, twigs denote the rules and every leaf node represents the result. DT

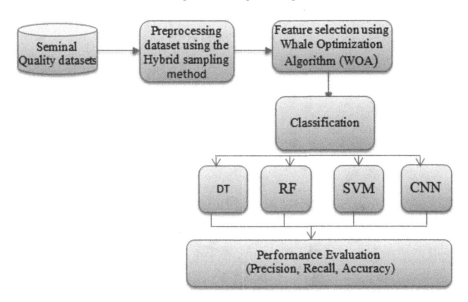

Fig. 1. Process flow of the proposed model

consists of two types of nodes like decision and leaf nodes. Decision nodes are normally used to take any choice and leaf nodes denote the final decision. Leaf nodes do not have any additional branches. Final decisions are taken based on the dataset features. Information Gain(IG) and Gini Index(GI) values can be used to choose the best features from the given dataset.

$$IG = Entrophy(s) - [(wewwghtedavg) * Entrophy(each\ f\ feature) \qquad (1)$$

$$Entrophy(s) = -p(yes) \log 2P(yes) - P(no)\ \log 2P(no) \qquad (2)$$

From the above equations, S denotes the whole quantity of samples, P(yes) denotes the yes probability, and P(no) denotes the no probability.

Random Forest (RF)
RF is a kind of supervised type ML models that is normally applicable in regression and classification-based applications. It develops DTs on various samples and identifies their popular vote for categorization and mean value in regression. The major feature of RF is to manage datasets with continuous attributes in regression-type applications and categorical attributes in categorization problems [14].

Support Vector Machine (SVM)
SVM is a regulated ML model for both regression and categorization. It is gotten from the statistical learning hypothesis by Boser et al. (1992). The most common way of finding out the right hyperplane for order with the assistance of Support vectors, or at least, the places of each class present at the edge is the fundamental guideline of SVMs.

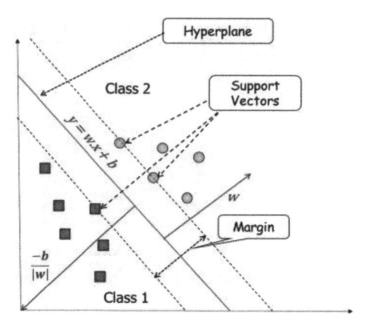

Fig. 2. Elements of SVM

Figure 2 portrays all parts of the SVM. Model At the point when SVM is utilized for regression, then it is commonly called SVR (Support Vector Regression).

Convolutional Neural Network (CNN)
CNN is commonly applied to find common patterns in images and to identify faces, objects, and various scenes. It is also more effective for categorizing non-image type data like time series, signal, and video information. This proposed approach mainly focuses on CNN to classify sperm cells from the given online dataset. Male infertility is analyzed utilizing different clinical intercessions and research facility evaluation of semen. Much of the time, research center investigation is performed on semen tests gathered from donors supplemented with information on givers' way of life. Depending upon the information on the way of life of male donors, DL approaches explicitly CNN, attributable to its high and solid accuracy, and capacity in uncovering the nonlinear connection among input and output attributes can be utilized to estimate the quality of the semen.

4 Result and Discussion

The major target of this work is to plan DL-based predictive models to execute an infertility monitoring system for the successful information of the executives. Furthermore to develop a bunch of value care standards that can be utilized to guarantee the quality of infertility care.

Dataset Description: Semen quality is acquired from the UCI public information source. The information was gathered from 100 sperm donors between the ages of 18 and 36. Out of the aggregate, 88 contributors were distinguished as expected while 12 of them were considered to have unusual or other semen. It has been gathered from https://archive.ics.uci.edu/ml/datasets/Fertility. It contains the accompanying attributes:

semen_analysis_data: The consequences of standard semen investigation.
fatty_acids_spermatozoa: The levels of a few unsaturated fats in the spermatozoa of the members.
fatty_acids_serum: The serum levels of the unsaturated fats of the phospholipids (estimated from the blood of the member).
sex_hormones: The serum levels of sex chemicals estimated in the blood of the members.
participant_related_data: General data about the members, for example, age, restraint time, and BMI (Body Mass Index).

Evaluation Metrics: The outcome of the proposed strategy was assessed by parting the dataset into preparing/testing allotments and k-fold cross-validation schemes. The considered metrics are precision, accuracy, and recall. More often than not, the productivity of supervised algorithms is estimated depending on their accuracy rate, which is the correct rate of categorized instances.

$$Accuracy = \frac{TN + TP}{TN + FN + TP + NP} \tag{3}$$

Accuracy exclusively, be that as it may, neglects to sufficiently measure how accurately occurrences are grouped into their separate classes. Subsequently, recall and precision were utilized to assess the model's performance.

$$Preision = \frac{TP}{TP + FP} \tag{4}$$

$$Recall = \frac{TP}{TP + FP} \tag{5}$$

Accuracy Analysis: Now we are going to apply our proposed CNN+WOA algorithm along with existing algorithms such as DT, RF and SVM over Semen Dataset. The following Table 1 and Fig. 3 represents Accuracy Analysis of proposed CNN+WOA compared over DT, RF and SVM. From the results its proved that proposed CNN+WOA produces Accuracy of about 95% which is higher than DT Accuracy which is 89%, RF Accuracy which is 92% and SVM Accuracy which is 93% respectively.

Precision Analysis: Now we are going to apply our proposed CNN+WOA algorithm along with existing algorithms such as DT, RF and SVM over SemenDataset. The following Table 2 and Fig. 4 represents Precision Analysis of proposed CNN+WOA compared over DT, RF and SVM. From the results its proved that proposed CNN+WOA produces Precision of about 94% which is higher than DT Precision which is 88%, RFPrecision which is 90% and SVM Precision which is 92% respectively.

Table 1. Accuracy comparison of proposed CNN + WOA with other existing algorithms

No of iterations	DT + WOA Accuracy (%)	RF + WOA Accuracy (%)	SVM + WOA Accuracy (%)	CNN + WOA Accuracy (%)
10	88.66	91.94	92.29	94.69
20	88.93	92.12	92.69	94.92
30	89.10	92.46	92.93	95.61
40	89.46	93.23	93.67	95.99
50	89.83	93.69	93.99	96.13

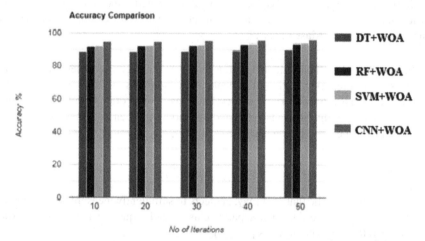

Fig. 3. Accuracy comparison of proposed CNN + WOA with other existing algorithms graph

Table 2. Precision comparison of proposed CNN + WOA with other existing algorithms

No of iterations	DT+WOA Precision (%)	RF+WOA Precision	SVM+WOA Precision (%)	CNN+WOA Precision (%)
10	87.67	87.38	90.50	91.36
20	88.12	88.45	91.12	92.59
30	89.46	89.70	92.10	94.91
40	89.69	90.97	92.53	94.69
50	89.12	90.18	92.64	94.87

Recall Analysis: Now we are going to apply our proposed CNN+WOA algorithm along with existing algorithms such as DT, RF and SVM over SemenDataset. The following Table 3 and Fig. 5 represents Recall Analysis of proposed CNN+WOA compared over DT, RF and SVM. From the results its proved that proposed CNN+WOA produces Recall

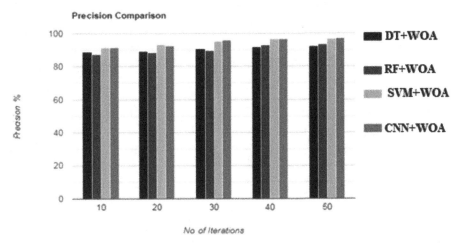

Fig. 4. Precision comparison of proposed CNN + WOA with other existing algorithms graph

of about 89% which is higher than DT Recall which is 84%, RF which is 87% and MLP Recall which is 88% respectively.

Table 3. Recall comparison of proposed CNN + WOA with other existing algorithms

No. of iterations	DT + WOA recall (%)	RF + WOA recall (%)	SVM + WOA recall (%)	CNN + WOA recall (%)
10	81.59	85.97	87.98	88.79
20	82.69	86.93	89.37	88.76
30	83.72	86.97	89.49	89.47
40	83.99	87.97	89.69	89.69
50	84.97	87.79	89.79	89.69

In terms of Accuracy we have evaluated four algorithms with 50 iterations on semen dataset. From the Accuracy Table and graph we can analyze that the average Accuracy of DT+WOA is 89%, RF+WOA is 92%, SVM+WOA is 93% and CNN+WOA is 95%. From the results we can prove that CNN+WOA outperforms other algorithms in terms of Accuracy.

In terms of Precision we have evaluated four algorithms with 50 iterations on semen dataset. From the Precision Table and graph we can analyze that the average Precision of DT+WOA is 0.88, RF+WOA is 0.90, SVM+WOA is 0.92 and CNN+WOA is 0.94. From the results we can prove that CNN+WOA outperforms other algorithms in terms of Precision.

In terms of Recall we have evaluated four algorithms with 50 iterations on semen dataset. From the Recall Table and graph we can analyze that the average Recall of

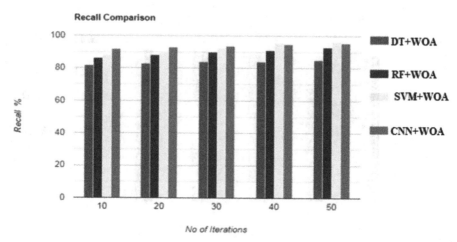

Fig. 5. Recall comparison of proposed CNN + WOA with other existing algorithms graph

DT+WOA is 0.84, RF+WOA is 0.87, SVM+WOA is 0.88 and CNN+WOA is 0.89. From the results we can prove that CNN+WOA outperforms other algorithms in terms of Recall.

5 Conclusion

The quality of the semen is a significant factor in fertility. Recently the quality of semen has reduced, and this is a major concern research area. Because of various reasons like demographic features, genetic disorders, pollution, temperature, radiation, lifestyle, smoking, drinking habits, and ecological features affects the quality of semen. This research study proposes feature selection and classification techniques for the prediction of the quality of the semen donors. The WOA approach contributed to identifying possible attributes in the given dataset. Due to an imbalanced ratio of samples, among usual and changed samples causes the popular class used the familiar SMOTE technique to stabilize the classes by renewing the class minority instances. Here DT, RF, SVM and CNN classifiers are applied to classify the semen dataset. Among these four classifiers, CNN+WOA classifies the dataset with better Accuracy, Precision, And Recall.

References

1. Macaluso, M.,Wright-Schnapp, T.J., Chandra, A., Johnson, R., Satterwhite, C.L., Pulver, A.: A public health focus on infertility prevention, detection, and management. Fertil Steril. **93**(1), 16, pp. 1–10 (2010)
2. Hardee, K., Gay, J., Blanc, A.K.: Maternal morbidity: neglected dimension of safe motherhood in the developing world. Glob. Public Health **7**(6), 603–617 (2012)
3. Direkvand-Moghadam, A., Sayehmiri, K., Delpisheh, A., Direkvand- Moghadam, A.: The global trend of infertility: an original review and meta-analysis. Int. J. Epidemiol.Res. **1**(1), 35–43 (2014)

4. CDC. A national Public Health Action Plan for the Detection, Prevention, and Management of Infertility. Centers for Disease Control and Prevention, Atlanta, GA (2014)
5. Mishra, R.K., Verma, H.P., Singh, N., Singh, S.K.: Male infertility: lifestyle and oriental remedies. J. Sci. Res. **56**, 93–101 (2012)
6. Esteves, S.C., Agarwal, A.: Novel concepts in male infertility. Int. Braz J. Urol. **37**(1), 5–15 (2011)
7. Abdulkerim, M.Y., Koçer, B.: Int. J. Eng. Sci. Technol. **24**(2), 310–318 (2021)
8. Zhou, M., et al.: Preliminary prediction of semen quality based on modifiable lifestyle factors by using the XGBoost algorithm. Front. Med. **9,** 811890 (2022)
9. Santi, D., et al.: Multilevel approach to male fertility by machine learning highlights a hidden link between haematological and spermatogenetic cells. Andrology **8**(5), 1021–1029 (2020)
10. Hicks, S.A., et al.: Machine learning-based analysis of sperm videos and participant data for male fertility prediction. Sci. Rep. **9**, 16770 (2020)
11. Agarwal, A.: Automation of human semen analysis using a novel artificial intelligence optical microscopic technology. Andrologia **51**(11), e13440 (2019)
12. Chen, Z., Yang, J., Luo, C., Zhang, C.: A method for sperm activity analysis based on feature point detection network in deep learning. Front. Comput. Sci. **25** (2022). https://doi.org/10.3389/fcomp.2022.861495
13. Gil, D., Girela, J.L., De Juan, J., Jose Gomez-Torres, M., Johnsson, M.: Predicting seminal quality with artificial intelligence methods, Expert Syst. Appl. **39**, 12564–12573 (2012)
14. https://www.analyticsvidhya.com/blog/2021/06/understanding-random-forest/

An Energy & Cost Efficient Task Consolidation Algorithm for Cloud Computing Systems

Sachin Kumar[1(✉)], Saurabh Pal[1], Satya Singh[2], Raghvendra Pratap Singh[3],
Sanjay Kumar Singh[3], and Priya Jaiswal[1]

[1] Department of Computer Applications, V.B.S.P.U, Jaunpur, U.P., India
jaiswalsachin009@gmail.com
[2] Department of Computer Science and Applications, M.G.K.V.P, Varanasi, U.P., India
[3] Department of Computer Science and Engineering, Kashi Institute of Technology-Varanasi,
Varanasi, U.P., India

Abstract. The power consumption of untapped resources, especially during a cloud background, represents a significant sum of the specific power use. By its nature, a resource allotment approach that takes into account the use of resources would direct to better power efficiency; this, in clouds, expands even additional, and with virtualization techniques often jobs are easily combined. Job consolidation is an effective way to expand the use of resources and sequentially reduce power consumption. Current studies have determined that server power utilization extends linearly with processor resources. This hopeful fact highlights the importance of the involvement of standardization to reduce energy utilization. However, merging tasks can also cause freedom from resources that will remain idle as the attraction continues. There are some remarkable efforts to decrease idle energy draw, usually by putting computer resources into some kind of power-saving/sleep mode. Throughout this article, we represent 2 power-conscious task reinforcement approaches to maximize resource use and explicitly consider both passive and active power consumption. Our inferences map each job to the resource at which the power consumption to perform the job is implicitly or explicitly reduced without degrading the performance of that task. Supporting our investigational outcome, our inference methods reveal the most promising power-saving potential.

Keywords: Load balancing · Cloud computing · Power-aware computing

1 Introduction

Cloud computing is a beneficial model for both providers and consumers. Cloud computing usually contains several applications that may be heterogeneous and distributed. Virtualization technology has made cloud computing more fruitful. The deployments of cloud applications have several advantages like reliability and scalability; on the other hand at its core, the cloud aims to provide more cost-effective solutions for providers as well as consumers. In economic terms, buyers should buy resources as per their requirements while service providers can make good use of underutilized cloud resources. As

© The Author(s), under exclusive license to Springer Nature Switzerland AG 2022
S. Rajagopal et al. (Eds.): ASCIS 2022, CCIS 1759, pp. 446–454, 2022.
https://doi.org/10.1007/978-3-031-23092-9_35

per the service provider's point of view, maximization of profits may be a higher priority. For this purpose, reducing the consumption of energy plays an important role. Alternatively, by increasing the use of resources, service providers can reduce power consumption.

Resource use and energy consumption in cloud computing are extremely correlated. Especially, computing resources use a large amount of power for their low utilization in comparison to the sufficiently used loader. As per the latest review [1–4], task consolidation is an efficient method for increasing the use of resources and reducing power consumption. Task consolidation technology is largely used by cloud technologies that make it easier to run multiple applications on a single cloud platform at the same time.

Recent studies have determined that server power consumption is measured sequentially with resource usage [5–7]. This information also calls for a significant contribution to the standardization of ta sks in reducing energy consumption. However, merging tasks can also free up resources that could exist idling however still pulling force. Our inference sets every task for the cloud resource in which power consumption is reduced to perform the job without any deterioration in performance.

We have calculated results based on the objective function for energy consumption. This means when more than one task was combined for a single resource only then the consumption of energy will be drastically decreased. Our inductive methods show promise in the ability to save energy.

The remainder of the research document is prepared in the following manner. Section 2 explains the cloud applications, energy, and task integration model used in this research article. Section 3 explains relevant work. Inference in MaxUtil and ECTC is described in Sect. 4 followed by outcomes and wrapping up of performance evaluation in Sects. 5 & 6 respectively.

2 Related Works

The paradigms of green and cloud computing are interrelated and growing. Cloud energy efficiency has become one of the major research challenges. Advances in computer hardware equipment [8], like solid-state drives, low power energy-efficient CPUs, and monitors of computers have assisted a lot to alleviate this energy problem to a certain extent. Meanwhile, energy issues are also handled by using several software approaches like allocation of resources [9–15] and standardization of tasks [16–19].

The allocation of resource and scheduling policy is mainly facilitated using the grace period retrieval with the support of a dynamic potentiometer [20] is integrated into many processors. This technology provisionally reduces the supply voltage to re duce the computation speed.

The task consolidation in [16] is handled using a traditional container filling problem with 2 main properties, for example, disk usage and CPU. The algorithm proposed in [16] attempts to standardize performance and power consumption.

In [17], an analytical model has been presented to standardize internet-oriented tasks. The model takes into account the functions required for services such as e-commerce network services or an e-book database. The main objective is to maximize the use of resources to reduce power consumption.

The mechanism for consolidating tasks was developed in [18, 19] to manage power declination through various techniques, such as [18]. Unlike computing job consolidation strategies, the approach used in [18] adopts 2 techniques, memory compression and asked for discrimination.

A virtual power approach is suggested in [19] the integration of tasks in the integration of energy management "Hard" and "Soft" scaling techniques. These 2 techniques belong to energy management utilities equipped with physical processors and virtual machines.

In [21], a supportive Nash bargaining and game model is introduced to deal with the network load balancing issue. The key goal is to reduce power utilization while preserving the limited quality of services, such as time.

In [22], a similar task has been performed as in [21] in that they deal with fixed scheduling situations with independent functions. Additionally, both take advantage of dynamic voltage frequency scaling energy reduction technology.

3   Task Consolidation Algorithm

Job consolidation is an efficient way to manage computing resources, mainly in the long and short term cloud. As for the short-term is concerned, volume flows on arriving jobs can be treated as "power-saving" by decreasing the number of running computing resources, and planting excess computing resources into the energy-saving mode, or by systematically switching off some non working computing resources. For the long period of time, cloud service providers should follow energy saving models; it relieves the excessive load of computing operational rate due to increased provisions. The main orientation of this research article; despite of the result of merging tasks; our method may be used for file estimation.

In this part, we have presented 2 power-conscious job fusing methods, MaxUtil and ECTC. In this maxUtil unifies resourceful decision-making tasks; it is one of the key indicators of power efficiency under our settings.

Description of the Algorithm

MaxUtil and ECTC trail analogous steps with the main difference in their cost functions (Fig. 2). In short for a given job, 2 inferences are validated for each computing resources and select the most power-efficient computing resource for the job. Assessment of the most power efficient computing resource depends on the heuristic used. The real power utilization of the existing job is calculated by cost function of ECTC by subtracting the minimum power (pmin) utilization. No power consumption in the overlapping period of time between those jobs and the present job is taken into account explicitly. The job function tends to distinguish a job that is performed alone. The Fi,j value of a job tj is defined on the computing resource ri attained through the cost function of the ECTC as follows:

$$Fi, j = \{(P\Delta \times Vj + Pmin) \times \tau 0) - ((P\Delta \times Vj + Pmin) + \tau 1 + P\Delta \times Vj \times \tau 2)\} \tag{1}$$

The relation for this cost function is that the power consumption at its lowest use is much larger than that at its idle state.

Input: A set R of r cloud resources and a task tj and
Output: A task-resource match

1. Let $r^* = \emptyset$
2. For $\forall\ r_i \in R$ do
3. Compute the cost function value $f_{i,j}$ of t_j on r_i
4. If $f_{i,j} > f^*j$ then
5. Let $r^* = r_i$
6. Let $f^*j = f_{i,j}$
7. End if
8. End for
9. Assign tj to r^*

Fig. 1. Description of Algorithm

The cost function of MaxUtil is considered with average use during computation time for the existing job-as an essential component of it. This cost function intends to amplify the intensity of uniformity. The 1st benefit is to reduce power utilization. The 2nd benefit is that MaxUtil's cost function implicitly reduces the number of active computing resources because it tends to intensify the use of few computing resources compared to the cost of the ECTC function. The value Fi,j of the task tj on the computing resource ri using cost function of MaxUtil's is given below:

$$Fi,j = \frac{\sum_{\tau=1}^{\tau 0} Ui}{\tau 0} \qquad (2)$$

3.1 Discussion and Analysis of performance

As integrated into our power model, the consumption of power is directly proportional to the use of resources. At a glance, for any 2 task computation resource matches, 1 with higher use can be chosen. On the other hand, determining the correct matching is not completely reliant on the existing job. The decision made by ECTC is based that instead of consuming (the only) energy for that job. In Fig. 3a, job 3 (t3) arrives at 14 s after job zero, job one, job 2 and is assigned to computing resource one (r1) based on power utilization, still the utilization of computing resources uses 0(r0) is more.

4 Experimental Evaluations

In the experimental evaluation section, we have explained the settings and methods including the characteristics of the job and their creation. Then the experimental observation is presented based on the consumption of energy. While computing resource usage may be a better measurement of performance, Average usage rates are not presented on all resources because they are already presented by consumption of energy.

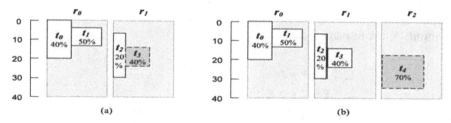

Fig. 2. Consolidation examples for tasks in Table 1 using ECTC

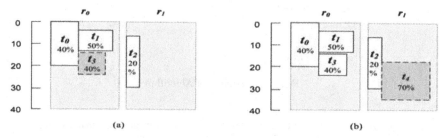

Fig. 3. Consolidation examples for tasks in Table 1 using MaxUtil

Table 1. Task properties

Task	Processing time	Arrival time	Utilization %
Zero	Twenty	Zero	Forty
One	Eight	Three	Fifty
Two	Twenty Three	Seven	Twenty
Three	Ten	Fourteen	Forty
Four	Fifteen	Twenty	Seventy

4.1 Experiments

The performance of MaxUtil and ECTC is calculated thoroughly using a large number of experiments using a variety of tasks. Along with the characteristics of the task, we have used three algorithms i.e. ECTC, MaxUtil, and random. These three algorithms have been with the integration of job migration.

Since (as far as we know) the current task merging algorithms are cannot be directly compared with our inference, comparisons were made between Randomization, MaxUtil, and ECTC. Especially most power -saving technologies are closely related to specific deadlines and/or interrelated tasks; In addition, it does express the relationship between energy consumption and resource utilization i.e. standardization of tasks is not taken into account. This is the current task of introducing unification techniques in the Sect. 3 fundamental differences appear from our inference in scheduling and power models.

As per the early experiments with those 3 experimental methods (MaxUtil, ECTC, and randomized), we noticed that in some conditions the transfer of a few jobs can decrease power consumption. This result encouraged us to implement randomization, ECTC, MaxUtil for task migrations. This transfer is taking into account for every running job at what time the use of resources varies, i.e. get the job done or start the job.

4.2 Results

The outcomes achieved from widespread simulations are explained in Table 2. The outcome of different cloud resources is shown in Fig. 4. Nevertheless, Simulation on cloud platform performed with fifty dissimilar jobs as mentioned in Sect. 5.1.

The savings of power in Table 2 are relative rates of the outcomes attained from the experimentation carried out by means of random algorithms. These results are shown in Table 2. Figure 4 shows the capability of energy saving of Max and ECTC in general. MaxUtil and ECTC Outperform stochastic algorithms – whatever their dependence on immigration – by 18% and 13%, correspondingly.

Saving energy with uncertainty and high resource usage is still in demand. The use of cloud resources is most appropriate for the consolidation of tasks as presented in Fig. 4a. It is basically because the jobs that have been carried over tend to have a short duration remaining to process & these jobs are creating a hindrance for upcoming new jobs. As a result, more power depreciation is there in comparison when immigration is not considered.

Table 2. Relative energy saving

Usage Pattern	MaxUtil Algorithm					
	Low		High		Random	
Energy Saving %	Twenty Five	Twenty Three	Four	Five	Twelve	Eleven
Migration	No	Yes	No	Yes	No	Yes
Average %	Thirteen					
Usage Pattern	ECTC Algorithm					
	Low		High		Random	
Energy Saving %	Twirty Three	Thirty Two	Nine	Nine	Seventeen	Sixteen
Migration	No	Yes	No	Yes	No	Yes
Average %	Eighteen					

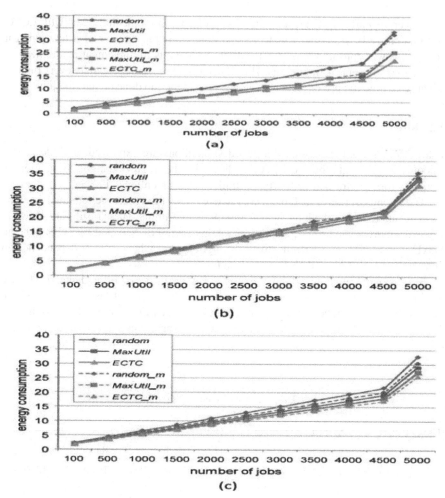

Fig. 4. Consumption of energy using task consolidation approaches: (a) Low Resource Utilization (b) High Resource Utilization (c) Random Resource Utilization

5   Conclusion

TASK consolidation especially in cloud computing is a significant method to develop energy efficiency. As per the fact that e nergy consumption is directly related to resource utilization, we succeeded in modeling their association and developing two energy-aware task inferences. Cost functions are effectively integrated into these inferences Energy-saving capabilities and capacity demonstrated by our experimental evaluation. The outcome of this article will not only reduce the electricity invoices for cloud service providers, but it also involves potential earnings by saving operating charges. It also plays an important role in th e reduction of carbon footprint in cloud computing.

References

1. Singh, P., Prakash, V., Bathla, G., Singh, R.K.: QoS aware task consolidation approach for maintaining SLA violations in cloud computing. Comput. Electr. Eng. **99**, 107789 (2022)
2. Nayak, S.K., Panda, S.K., Das, S., Pande, S.K.: A renewable energy-based task consolidation algorithm for cloud computing. In Control Applications in Modern Power System, pp. 453–463. Springer, Singapore (2021)
3. Pattnayak, P.: Optimizing power saving in cloud computing environments through server consolidation. In: Advances in Micro-Electronics, Embedded Systems and IoT, pp. 325–336. Springer, Singapore (2022)
4. Arshad, U., Aleem, M., Srivastava, G., Lin, J.C.W.: Utilizing power consumption and SLA violations using dynamic VM consolidation in cloud data centers. Renew. Sustain. Energy Rev. **167**, 112782 (2022)
5. Varvello, M., Katevas, K., Plesa, M., Haddadi, H., Bustamante, F., Livshits, B.: BatteryLab: A collaborative platform for power monitoring. In: International Conference on Passive and Active Network Measurement (pp. 97–121). Springer, Cham (2022, March)
6. Bustamante, F., Livshits, B.: BatteryLab: a collaborative platform for power monitoring. In: Passive and Active Measurement: 23rd International Conference, PAM 2022, Virtual Event, March 28–30, 2022: Proceedings (Vol. 13210, p. 97). Springer Nature (2022)
7. Song, M., Lee, Y., Kim, K.: Reward-oriented task offloading under limited edge server power for multiaccess edge computing. IEEE Internet Things J. **8**(17) 13425–13438 (2021)
8. Venkatachalam, V., Franz, M.: Power reduction techniques for microprocessor systems. ACM Computing Surveys (CSUR) **37**(3), 195–237 (2005)
9. Bal, P.K., Mohapatra, S.K., Das, T.K., Srinivasan, K., Hu, Y.C.: A Joint Resource allocation, security with efficient task scheduling in cloud computing using hybrid machine learning techniques. Sensors **22**(3), 1242 (2022)
10. Al-Wesabi, F.N., Obayya, M., Hamza, M.A., Alzahrani, J.S., Gupta, D., Kumar, S.: Energy aware resource optimization using unified metaheuristic optimization algorithm allocation for cloud computing environment. Sustain. Comput.: Inform. Syst. **35**, 100686 (2022)
11. Nanjappan, M., Albert, P.: Hybrid-based novel approach for resource scheduling using MCFCM and PSO in cloud computing environment. Concurr. Comput.: Pract. Exp. **34**(7), e5517 (2022)
12. Kumar, C., Marston, S., Sen, R., Narisetty, A.: Greening the cloud: a load balancing mechanism to optimize cloud computing networks. J. Manag. Inf. Syst. **39**(2), 513–541 (2022)
13. Belgacem, A.: Dynamic resource allocation in cloud computing: analysis and taxonomies. Computing **104**(3), 681–710 (2021). https://doi.org/10.1007/s00607-021-01045-2
14. Peng, K., Huang, H., Zhao, B., Jolfaei, A., Xu, X., Bilal, M.: Intelligent computation offloading and resource allocation in IIoT with end-edge-cloud computing Using NSGA-III. IEEE Trans. Netw. Sci. Eng. (2022)
15. Wadhwa, H., Aron, R.: TRAM: Technique for resource allocation and management in fog computing environment. J. Supercomput. **78**(1), 667–690 (2021). https://doi.org/10.1007/s11227-021-03885-3
16. Srikantaiah, S., Kansal, A., Zhao, F.: Energy aware consolidation for cloud computing (2008)
17. Song, Y., Zhang, Y., Sun, Y., Shi, W.: Utility analysis for internet-oriented server consolidation in VM-based data centers. In: 2009 IEEE International Conference on Cluster Computing and Workshops, pp. 1–10. IEEE (2009, August)
18. Torres, J., Carrera, D., Hogan, K., Gavaldà, R., Beltran, V., Poggi, N.: Reducing wasted resources to help achieve green data centers. In: 2008 IEEE International Symposium on Parallel and Distributed Processing, pp. 1–8. IEEE (2008, April)

19. Nathuji, R., Schwan, K.: Virtualpower: coordinated power management in virtualized enterprise systems. ACM SIGOPS Oper. Syst. Rev. 41 6 265 278 (2007)
20. Kuroda, T., et al.: Variable supply-voltage scheme for low-power high-speed CMOS digital design. IEEE J. Solid-State Circuits **33**(3), 454–462 (1998)
21. Subrata, R., Zomaya, A.Y., Landfeldt, B.: Cooperative power-aware scheduling in grid computing environments. J. Parallel Distrib. Comput. *70*(2), 84–91 (2010)
22. Khan, S.U., Ahmad, I.: A cooperative game theoretical technique for joint optimization of energy consumption and response time in computational grids. IEEE Trans. Parallel Distrib. Syst. 20 3 346 360 (2008)

Author Index

Printed in the United States
by Baker & Taylor Publisher Services